D1083068

The Psychomotor Domain
Movement Behaviors

The Psychomotor Domain
Movement Behaviors

Edited by Robert N. Singer
Florida State University

BF
295
·S52
1972

RITTER LIBRARY
BALDWIN-WALLACE COLLEGE

Lea & Febiger   *Philadelphia • 1972*

Health Education, Physical Education, and Recreation Series

RUTH ABERNATHY, Ph.D.

EDITORIAL ADVISER

Director, School of
Physical and Health Education
University of Washington, Seattle

Copyright © 1972 by Lea & Febiger. Copyright under the International Copyright Union. All rights reserved. This book is protected by copyright. *No part of it may be reproduced in any manner or by any means, without written permission from the publisher.*

ISBN 0-8121-0391-2

Library of Congress Catalog Number 72-79355

Published in Great Britain by Henry Kimpton Publishers, London

Printed in the United States of America

PREFACE

Why this book? Is it useful in any way, and if so, to whom? Why are scholars with apparent dissimilar backgrounds, training, interests, and research bents contributing chapters in a volume containing a title with such broad connotations?

The reasons for this endeavor may not be apparent at first glance. If they were evident, there would be no need to attempt to explain the rationale for this book. Perhaps a logical starting point would be to recognize the psychomotor domain as including a wide variety of movement behaviors. Parents are concerned with the way children learn to control their body, play, and acquire skills. So are developmental psychologists and physical educators. When an individual approaches maturity and, of course, even afterwards, there are many kinds of psychomotor skills he may attempt to acquire, either for enjoyment and recreation, as a vocational necessity, or merely for meeting life's daily demands in a satisfactory way. Thus teachers, instructors, supervisors, leaders, and trainers are involved in assisting a person to fulfill his objectives of obtaining a wide variety of skills. Here is where researchers and educators provide direction for understanding the nature of psychomotor skills and the acquisition process, but usually within a framework restricted to particular areas of concern.

The following examples will help to illustrate this point. The industrial psychologist is interested in such matters as predicting worker proficiency in manual tasks, efficient and effective training procedures, worker motivation and morals, and ideal work-rest schedules for optimal output. In the military and aerospace area, researchers study similar problems but under different conditions and with other goals. With athletic and recreational skills, the same is true. Learning psychologists, primarily laboratory-oriented experimentalists, investigate the process of learning and factors pertinent to it and provide a basis for the formation of learning principles hopefully applicable to all individuals and varied tasks. Classic areas of study in the learning process are acquisition, motivation, retention, and transfer.

Many other researchers, practitioners, and educators are, in one way or another, also involved with types of skilled motor activity patterns and behaviors. Teachers of music, art, and dance attempt to inspire others toward meaningful skillful and expressive movements. Instructors in special education and early education direct their efforts to promote the movement patterns of normal and handicapped youth. Other scholars study lower forms of organisms in order to make analogies with man and his behavior. There are media specialists who have to determine the appropriate usage of equipment and instruments in the instructional process. In a number of instances, man has been compared to a machine in order to develop a more plausible theory of human behavior. As a result, elaborate man-machine systems are formulated, the information processing ability of the individual is determined, and input-output comparisons are made. Those interested in sport psychology examine psychologic parameters such as personality and motivation that contribute to athletic proficiency. Neuropsychologists analyze neurologic mechanisms, pathways, and the chemistry of learning and performing movement patterns. Some psychologists investigate the nature of abilities and how they contribute to achievement while others look at the way individuals vary and differ in the process associated with the acquisition of skill. Finally, there are educators who attempt to organize and synthesize research and authoritative opinion in order to form taxonomies, classifications, and theories.

If so many educators and researchers are involved in behavioral understanding, learning, and modifications in some form in the psychomotor domain, the question must be raised as to the extent each is familiar with the other's work. Unfortunately, probably not enough. Although each sphere of interest develops research and its own peculiar jargon, communication and interaction lag among these scholars. A pooling of information, sharing of ideas, and breakdown of barriers must be beneficial for those who deal with psychomotor behaviors. Not only will educators and researchers expand their own knowledge, but the recipients—students and the lay public—surely will gain individually as well. Thus the main objective of this book is to serve scholar, student, and the individual concerned with the learning of psychomotor skills.

This book contains chapters contributed by authors who have unique qualifications and interests. The intent was to span the spectrum of areas comprising the psychomotor domain to obtain a reasonable representation of it in terms of the content presented here. The authors were asked to participate on the basis of demonstrated expertise in specialized interest areas. To the extent that certain aspects of the psychomotor domain and many outstanding scholars knowledgeable in those aspects were omitted, apologies are offered. Obviously, lines had to be drawn somewhere.

Appreciation is acknowledged to the many specialists and recognized authorities who gave of their time to contribute to this endeavor. Excellent scholars are overworked scholars. They are constantly requested to speak and to contribute articles to other publications while fulfilling personal obligations to research and publishing on their own. It is certainly gratifying that so many recognized scholars participated in this project. Hopefully, the contents of this book will be rewarding to the reader.

Robert N. Singer
Tallahassee, Florida

CONTRIBUTORS

Bryant J. Cratty
Department of Physical Education
University of California
Los Angeles, California

Edwin A. Fleishman
American Institutes for Research
Washington, D. C.

James W. Fleming
Department of Elementary and
   Special Education
Michigan State University
East Lansing, Michigan

Robert S. Hutton
Department of Physiology
School of Medicine
University of California
Los Angeles, California

Marshall B. Jones
Department of Behavioral Science
Milton S. Hershey Medical Center
Pennsylvania State University
University Park, Pennsylvania

M. David Merrill
Department of Instructional
   Research and Development
Brigham Young University
Provo, Utah

Elmo E. Miller
Human Resources Research
   Organization
Division No. 5
Fort Bliss, Texas

William P. Morgan
Department of Physical Education–
   Men
University of Wisconsin
Madison, Wisconsin

Joseph B. Oxendine
Department of Health, Physical
   Education, and Recreation
Temple University
Philadelphia, Pennsylvania

E. C. Poulton
Medical Research Council
Applied Psychology Unit
Cambridge, England

Stanley C. Ratner
Department of Psychology
Michigan State University
East Lansing, Michigan

Richard A. Schmidt
Department of Physical Education
University of Michigan
Ann Arbor, Michigan

Robert N. Singer
Department of Physical Education
Florida State University
Tallahassee, Florida

Karl U. Smith
Department of Psychology
University of Wisconsin
Madison, Wisconsin

CONTENTS

Chapter 1

INTRODUCTION TO THE PSYCHOMOTOR DOMAIN

ROBERT N. SINGER
Florida State University

Man responds passively or actively to environmental situations. He may react covertly or overtly. He learns to think, to rationalize, to conceptualize, to verbalize, and to attach labels to objects, occurrences, and living organisms. Cognitive behaviors such as those just mentioned constitute a large part of man's learning and methods of communicating throughout life. He also develops attitudes and values, and these and other affective learnings will determine his behavior.

Man's interaction with his environment is not solely influenced by cognitive and affective behaviors, however. There is another category of behaviors which includes a vast repertoire of expressions. These are psychomotor, and include activity associated with agricultural duties, industrial, professional, technical, and vocational skills, military tasks, secretarial functions, business operations, home economic responsibilities, driving and piloting demands, music, art, and dance works as well as physical education, sport, and recreation endeavors. These means of expression are often taken for granted. Whereas research attention has generally been focused on the cognitive and affective areas, the psychomotor domain has gone relatively neglected.

We walk, run, throw, and catch; operate complex machinery; and execute skilled movement. Yet, we apparently do not concern ourselves with how these skills and the abilities that underly them are acquired and developed. Obviously, genetic factors and growth and development variables as well as personal experiences contribute to the means of expression and their effectiveness. Yes, the psychomotor sphere includes a vast assortment of

1

behaviors, many of which are performed routinely during our existence. Complex, sophisticated psychomotor responses are not acquired easily, however. Many processes along with much work and training interact to influence skilled performance.

At this point we might pause and ask why three domains are required to categorize behaviors. More important, however, is the question of whether behaviors are really mutually exclusive of each other. For the greater part, probably they are not. It is mostly for the sake of convenience that we attempt to place man's behaviors in any of the categories. Those that are *primarily* movement-oriented and emphasize overt physical responses are the activities which bear the label "psychomotor." Even the layman can realize, though, that typical psychomotor skills are achieved only within the framework of a complex involvement of cognitive, affective, and psychomotor abilities. Thus economically, labels serve to bring order as well as confusion to our understanding of man's behavior.

Basically, this book deals with psychomotor activities. The study of the learning process and the learning-performance variables related to the acquisition of motor skills is of concern to numerous interest groups and a variety of disciplines. Whatever knowledge we have has essentially accrued because of the efforts of scholars in various branches of psychology, e.g., industrial, social, experimental, differential, military, engineering, comparative, and developmental; physical education; special education; neuropsychology; traffic safety; business; and education in general. Although the skills studied and terms used are often unique to each field, common bonds tie these areas of interest together. Perhaps this will become more apparent with the reading of each succeeding chapter.

In any learning situation, three factors must always be considered: (a) the learner, (b) that which is to be learned, and (c) the learning environment. Regardless of the nature of the matter, similar considerations are expressed in the learning process as it involves the learner and the context in which he performs. Indeed, much can be learned about human behavior from observing animal behavior, as is indicated in Stan Ratner's chapter. Sometimes, though, unique factors associated with the learner, the learning matter, and the learning environment arise. This unusual development holds true between the cognitive, affective, and psychomotor areas as well as within each one. Let us first discuss the learner.

THE LEARNER AND PSYCHOMOTOR SKILLS

Because of genetic factors, growth and developmental considerations, and prior environmental experiences, learners come to a learning situation with dissimilar probabilities for success. Although we are typically concerned with the group, or gear instruction for the average individual within the group, there are many reasons why this concern and procedure can be questioned. In support of this approach, we of course assume that principles of learning or laws of behavior generally apply to most individuals. Doubtless, it is practical to instruct in numbers rather than on an individual basis. Thus, if we assume the uniqueness of the skill to be learned and a relative homogeneity of the would-be learners in relevant variables, group education or training can be defended on reasonable grounds. Let us begin by isolating some learner factors, regardless of the matter to be acquired and then turn our attention to those unique to the psychomotor domain.

Genetic Factors

Since there is a moderate correlation between the physical and temperamental characteristics displayed by the child and his parents (McClearn 1964), heredity must influence the probability of success in any endeavor. To the extent that intelligence, abilities (which are genetically and experientially determined), body build, or other factors may differ from person to person as a result of genetics, they must be taken into consideration in any learning situation where their impact on the learners may be suspected. Genetics sets the framework within which the organism can operate. The same instructional procedures, however, do not produce the same outcomes in all learners, and one of the determining variables is differences in learning and performing potential for that task as influenced by heredity.

Early Childhood Experiences

There exists an abundance of research with lower forms of organisms (Scott, 1962; Melzack and Thompson, 1956; Ravizza and Herschberger, 1966; Sluckin and Salzen, 1961; Newton & Levine, 1968) and some with man (McGraw, 1935; Hilgard, 1932; Gesell and Thompson, 1941) that indicates that enrichment, deprivation, or merely the timely introduction of certain behavioral experiences will influence later behaviors. It has been established that early experiences serve as the foundation blocks for learnings and expressions of behavior later in life. They enable the individual to develop the capacities necessary to undertake more complex learnings. Educators generally do not disagree on the importance of early enriched experiences, although they do differ about the appropriate programs and methods to be followed. With the acknowledgment of the relevance of early experiences in life to later accomplishments (Hebb, 1949; Piaget, 1952; Scott, 1968; Bruner, 1963), we must conclude that since a child's potential achievement in learning tasks is linked to his background it is sound practice to enhance the developmental process.

Abilities

Those human traits underlying potential success in a number of endeavors certainly differ in degree from person to person due to genetic and environmental factors. Although they are difficult to define, isolate, and measure, their existence can be determined to some satisfaction from daily observations and experimental research literature. Very few researchers with the exception of Edwin Fleishman (whose chapter includes relevant material on this topic) have extensively studied abilities related to proficiency in psychomotor skills. This is unfortunate, for success in specific acts, tasks, or skills is partially dependent on the developmental state of those abilities important to the endeavor. By being able to identify abilities related to a given skill at various stages in the acquisition process, one of course is more likely to further instructional methodology. The relationship of learning and abilities in the cognitive domain (Duncanson, 1966; Stake, 1961; Allison, 1960) and in the psychomotor domain (Adams, 1957; Fleishman and Hempel, 1954; Fleishman, 1967; Hinrichs, 1970) is becoming better known. An overview of the research on abilities by Roberts (1968–1969) is most helpful for those interested in noting direct applications of our knowledge of human abilities to school endeavors.

Sense Acuity

The senses, as receptors of the stimuli that surround us, provide the information for translation and response to express effective behavior. Viewed as an information-processing model, the organism attempts to match output with input. When errors occur, or mismatches, fault may well rest with the translation machinery or with the response mechanism. Errors may also be due to a faulty input. If the senses are not functionally and operationally sound, the probability of an appropriate response is lessened. Many youthful classroom learners classified as mentally retarded or slow demonstrate remarkable improvement after visual or auditory disorders have been detected and corrected. In motor learning and performance, visual, proprioceptive, and tactile receptors play an important role in assisting the individual toward the achievement of his objectives. The keenness and sharpness of these receptors as they are employed as a means of information gathering can be reflected in the type of behavior that follows. Also related to successful performance is the auditory modality in that verbal commands or comments from the instructor are often provided in the form of directions and cues for performance. Sense acuity thus becomes another individual-difference variable not to be taken lightly.

Perception

Once information is received, it must be processed and translated to determine its relevancy to the activity at hand. A person cannot effectively respond until meaning is made of the surrounding stimuli. One major function of perception is to isolate selectively those stimuli of most consequence in a situation. The "good" learner or highly skilled performer is more capable of selectively attending to relevant cues while disregarding irrelevant ones. Berelson and Steiner (1964) state that this process is dependent upon (a) the type of stimuli present; (b) prior learning or experience as it influences the learner's "set," that is, his expectations; and (c) the motives of the learner in the situation, e.g., his needs and desires. It can be seen that two of the three considerations are individual in kind, and will vary from learner to learner. Although perceptual organization is determined from general laws of behavior, it is also, as Berelson and Steiner (1964) suggest, affected by past experiences and present motives that influence expectations. The same is true with regard to stimulus interpretation and judgment.

Attitudes and Motives

Since the learner's attitude towards the task at hand will help to influence his behavior, it too must be recognized as a source of performance variability. Interest in succeeding, favorable predisposition to master the task, and general intent, eagerness, and motivation to gain proficiency will differ with the learner and the task. Attitudes can be influenced by external stimulation and motivation and/or internal developed tendencies to act in a certain way. The intent to improve reflects a favorable attitude toward the particular activity, whether it is cognitive in nature or a psychomotor skill.

Level of Aspiration

A person's attitude in a learning situation is partially recognized through his level of aspiration. This level can imply the goal minimally satisfied with, hoped for, or expected. Since the goal level is affected by prior successes and failures in the same or similar circumstances, it will be different from learner to learner. Because research indicates the value of setting realistically high levels of aspiration for best results, the implications are clear for instructional settings. A goal level is a personal matter. Similar expectations in performance outcomes for all learners are oftentimes unnecessary, impractical, uncalled for, and unrealistic. However, goal levels and resultant performance measures can be elevated through the proper motivation techniques. For one thing, successes and failures are personally determined by whether goal levels are achieved. If the goal levels are set on an individual basis with the cooperation of instructor and learner and they are high but attainable as determined from prior performance (Locke and Bryan, 1966), success is more probable. After attaining success, goal levels are raised, and when these levels are raised, performance increments usually follow.

Personality

Much of the research in the area of personality testing, state and test anxiety levels, reactions to stress-induced situations, and task nature and complexity reveals the manner in which task type X anxiety level X personality traits X induced stress interact to influence performance. Personality is usually defined as a way of behavior peculiar to the individual. As such, each person may be expected to react in a fairly consistent but unique manner in a particular situation. The complex dimension of the human personality will not be discussed here, but temperament, as represented by emotional reactions and anxiety levels, is one aspect of personality that indicates how individuals differ and how, therefore, corresponding performance results are dissimilar when contrived stress and task distinctions are considered. For instance, studies usually show that in complex tasks, subjects with greater anxiety perform more poorly than those low in anxiety. Also, those who score low on anxiety tests perform more effectively under stress than under normal conditions. Weiner (1959) indicates that this is not the case with high-anxiety people, for they are less effective performers under stress. Other lines of research have attempted to relate activity interests and success to clusters of personality traits or to a novel personality profile. Because of the difficulties and limitations inherent in such work, it is not surprising that findings have not been consistent from study to study. Nevertheless, the strong possibility exists that persons tend to undertake tasks more compatible with their personalities and that proficiency may be partially related to that unique combination of personality traits possessed by the highly skilled.

Age Differences

As in the case of all learning endeavors, the organism is more capable of handling complex tasks as it matures. Obviously, dissimilar performance levels may be expected from different age groups from infancy on through adolescence. The development of motor, perceptual, cognitive, and conceptual abilities allows the individual to achieve in various endeavors. Some achievement will be due simply to the maturation process; the bulk of it will probably occur from the interaction between developmental variables and experiences, instruction, and training. Lehman's data (1953) on the peak years for scientific output and athletic accomplishments are fairly similar; they point to the early thirties. An examination of intellectual achievements (chemistry) and motor performance (billiard shooting) reveals very similar optimal age curves. Most output and best performance were shown at approximately 26 and 27 years of age. Certainly in the motor skills area, there is no doubt that reaction time and movement speed become faster with age for both sexes until at least the late teens (Noble et al., 1965; Hodgkins, 1963). After early adulthood and with advanced age, factors relating to speed, motivation, perception, attention, and the physiology of the organism will tend to dampen performance. Also, with the years the individual is inclined to become more fixed in his response pattern and less likely to show flexibility in alternative responses to specific stimuli. Thus, behavior is very much a function of chronologic and maturational age for the reasons briefly cited and many others.

The preceding variables as well as others illustrate learner considerations without regard to learning matter. In addition, a few factors seem to be more closely associated with behavior unique to the psychomotor domain, thereby requiring special consideration as contrasted to the other behavioral domains.

Body Build

A particular type of build can not be identified for academic success. At best, studies of the genius earlier in this century revealed him to be slightly heavier and larger than persons of average intelligence. By the same token, it is also true that there are numerous psychomotor tasks in which performance will be relatively unaffected by the build of the individual. On the other hand, specific somatotypes (body builds) have been found to be related to excellence in particular athletic events (Carter, 1969). Furthermore, within a sport such as football, Carter (1968) reports that dissimilar somatotypes are associated with the various positions. It is not inconceivable that certain builds are favorable for particular military and industrial tasks. The same holds true in dance. Although it would be unwise to conclude that a specific body type is a necessary condition for success in a given situation, it certainly appears that a person's build increases or decreases his probability of success in learning and performing motor skills.

Physical Measures

Closely allied with body build are such physical characteristics as strength, muscular endurance, cardiovascular endurance, flexibility, speed, balance, and the like. The development of these physical attributes means little in cognitive learning situations. The learning of psychomotor tasks and the maintenance of skills place a physical demand on the organism. Certain physical characteristics must be adequately developed in order that successful execution might be possible; that performance really illustrates what is being learned, that performances are correctly demonstrated, that there is sufficient strength and endurance to practice repeatedly before fatigue necessitates quitting. Obviously, the nature of the task will dictate the type and extent to which physical measures should be developed for adequate returns. Finally, physical disabilities (as will be seen in Bryant Cratty's chapter) impose restrictions that require unique considerations by the special educator and student.

Sex Differences

On many kinds of tests differences in performance are noted between the sexes, perhaps due to sociocultural influences, physiologic and anatomic factors, or all of these. From infancy to later years, normative data have been acquired comparing the sexes in maturational rates, cognitive abilities, academic accomplishments, motor skills, physical characteristics, and much more. There is little doubt that familial encouragement, peer group influence, and cultural demands help to create many of the distinctions noted between males and females in abilities and aptitudes. Nowhere is this point better applied than to athletics and mechanically oriented tasks. When environmental circumstances encourage participation and excellence, it may be difficult to determine other causative factors as well. Biologic, physical, and anatomic distinctions between the sexes apparently favor males in many gross motor activities. Unfortunately, lack of social approval, opportunities, and motivation in the past has severely curtailed the female's involvement and achievement in many psychomotor endeavors. Many of these social taboos are currently being challenged, and with currently shifting mores, females are demonstrating capability in many skills.

Intelligence

At first glance, it would appear that level of intelligence should be related to academic success rather than to psychomotor domain accomplishments. Yet, the abundance of literature published in the last decade reveals that compared to similarly chronologically-aged youth of average intelligence, the mentally retarded tend to lag in motor development. Special considerations must therefore be given to a retarded youngster with regard to motor performance expectations and methods of instruction (see Cratty's chapter). As a result of this observation and theoretic reasoning, perceptual-motor or sensorimotor training programs have become extremely popular today in preschool programs and in the elementary schools. Jim Fleming's chapter will deal with this problem. At any rate, the formulation of these programs is based on the belief of transitional stage of development, from physical to conceptual. Presumably, the stimulation of the senses, the development of body coordination, and the demonstration of skillful motor acts will lead to more advanced academic accomplishments.

Fears

It cannot be denied that a number of the daily situations we face are anxiety-producing, stressful, and unpleasant. As far as psychomotor skills are concerned, learning to swim, dive, drive a car, pilot a plane, operate complex machinery, acquire gynmastic skills, fire weapons, and achieve in many other athletic, vocational, and military tasks contains elements of fear that are quite identifiable. The very nature of elaborate, dangerous equipment induces fear in the beginning learner. Likewise this is true when the person feels his safety threatened with bodily harm. For the beginning swimmer with a fear of water, the relatively easy swimming skills become acquired, if at all, only after long, laborious hours of practice. And this practice primarily involves experience of overcoming the dread of water. Once emotional blocks are removed, many swimming skills are mastered in a reasonable period of time. Anxiety-producing situations, the experiments suggest, are detrimental in the early stages of learning.

ENVIRONMENTAL INFLUENCES ON MOTOR BEHAVIOR

We could discuss at great length those individual-difference factors worthy of consideration when psychomotor behavior is to be modified. Surely, the manner in which individuals become more alike or more dissimilar with practice is worth attention. Fortunately, M. B. Jones treats his topic in theoretic and practical detail in one of the following chapters. Let us therefore turn to an overview of that aspect of the learning process in which environmental manipulations are of prime influence in the way group behavior may be expected to change. Learning psychologists have vigorously applied their talents in this area for the most part during the century. Their aim was to develop learning postulates, theories, principles, and models. Data from learning tasks, primarily cognitive, and controlled means of experimental treatment have usually served as the scientific basis for understanding behavior.

As was the case with learner variables, the studies alluded to above indicate that there are a number of environmental situations which, when they are altered in a certain way, will yield results fairly expected with all types of behavior. Again, however, considerations unique to the psychomotor domain must be recognized. Briefly highlighted, they are as follows.

Input (Stimulus) Variables

Essentially, the learning and performance environment can be dealt with at one of two ends: by modifying stimuli or movement responses. Stimuli may be altered, simplified, or emphasized in order to facilitate the learning process. Responses required of the learner may be altered, simplified, or reinforced for the same purpose. The implications are clear: the learner is not left completely on his own to master a problem. Trial and error learning by itself is an inefficient use of time. Research suggests changes and modifications that can be introduced in the learning situation, from input to output, to hasten and direct skill acquisition.

With regard to stimuli, a particular learning situation typically contains many irrelevant cues, some very pertinent ones, and a number of partially relevant ones. An extremely difficult problem for the learner is to attend selectively to the most important cues while he disregards the others.

In all learning situations, detection of and concentration on the appropriate stimuli enhance the learning process. At advanced levels of proficiency, this ability is characteristically demonstrated. Psychomotor behavior contains many varied examples of situations in which appropriate signal detection is necessary for the correct response. The batter must decide instantly whether the pitch is curving or straight, whether it is ball or strike, and whether he is going to swing or not. With the aid of an instrument panel, the operator of a vehicle or stationary machinery scans the display and makes appropriate adjustments with levers, dials, and other gadgetry. The dancer's movements correspond to signals in the form of musical accompaniment and the layout of the stage.

In these and other performance circumstances, signals are detected, recognized, and responded to. The nature of the stimuli varies between and among domains of behavior. Within the psychomotor domain, however, cues can be generally approached with unique modifications for the benefit of the learner. Where it is important, besides the verbal and written cues which are commonly used in many forms of learning, visual, kinesthetic, or both kinds of cues can be provided, emphasized, isolated, and modified with the aid of the instructor.

Many skilled movements depend on the operation of the appropriate sense modalities at the right time. For this reason, cues are treated with much concern, e.g., emphasis, to call them to the learner's attention. Not only are they enhanced or merely isolated, but the presentation of certain information during and/or after performance helps to direct and reinforce responses. Motivation is also elevated as a result of this procedure. Stimuli that serve in any one or all of these capacities have been termed feedback or knowledge of results. Although it is true that feedback or knowledge of results can be obtained by the learner as a consequence of his own actions, auxiliary information can facilitate the skill acquisition process. Media can be effectively used in the instructional setting.

Output (Response) Variables

Motor performance is often evaluated in terms of response effectiveness. Whether the acts be discrete or continuous, criteria in the form of speed, accuracy, coordination, adaptability, style, and such factors are applied. More complex activities naturally demand more practice on the part of the individual. Flexibility of responses to unexpected stimuli, characterized by the properly timed behavior conditioned to a particular situation, reflects the highest levels of skills. Understandably, the more numerous and varied the stimuli that are introduced with the inevitable increase in the number of possible acceptable responses, the more difficult the learning situation.

Responses can of course be modified, simplified, and "built-up" to more advanced behaviors. Learning, too, can be programmed or "shaped," or trial and error conditions can be present. Where speed and accuracy are of importance in task execution, responses may be practiced with emphasis on one variable to the relative neglect of the other, or with equal emphasis on both. Also transfer situations can be created in which some tasks are first learned to influence positively the acquisition of other tasks.

Movement patterns can be affected through other means, too. Observation, demonstration, and guidance techniques influence the manner in which tasks will be executed. For example, mentally rehearsing an act may prove beneficial in its overt performance. The learning of mechanical or other principles related to the act of concern may positively transfer over to the skill acquisition. As can be seen, motor response learning is thus a function of many cognitive variables as well as attitudinal ones.

The arrangement of practice sessions can also have a bearing on performance. These practice factors are no strangers to the literature of the psychology of learning. We may point to massed or distributed practice trial arrangements, part or whole learning situations, audio and visual aids or their absence in instruction, warm-up, fatigue, and other performance variables, and the use of trainers and simulators or direct practice as practice variables affecting performance output. Within a practice period or a particular trial, modifications may be induced to influence the formation of desirable motor responses and movement patterns. Experimental psychologists have contributed to our knowledge on variables affecting motor learning for a long time, and Richard Schmidt discusses some of more prominent considerations in his chapter.

THE LEARNING PROCESS

When we put it all together, from input to output, the net result is the learning process at work. Psychologists have preferred to describe and explain behavior on the basis of overt activities. They have developed all-encompassing learning theories, systems, and miniature models to cope with the learning situation. Without exception, all of these efforts have been marred by shortcomings and limitations. One of the newer approaches is offered by K. U. Smith in his chapter dealing with cybernetic theory. E. C. Poulton presents some interesting ideas from an information processing point of view in a later chapter.

Can a theory or model, no matter how elaborately drawn, explain all of learning? Are there different kinds of learning, to the extent that special models must be developed for motor learning, verbal learning, concept learning, and others (Melton, 1964)? Certainly it has been convenient to form separate taxonomies in the cognitive domain (Bloom et al., 1956), affective domain (Krathwohl et al., 1964), and the psychomotor domain (Simpson,

1966). M. David Merrill's chapter will provide some direction for thought on these questions.

Another problem which arises during analysis of the learning process is the obvious omission of reference by psychologists to the neurology and chemistry of learning. Changes occur internally as well as externally when learning occurs and behavior is modified. Ideally, the efforts of psychologists, neurophysiologists, and biochemists would be combined to provide a more fruitful model. Findings in neurophysiology and behavior are contained in Hutton's chapter, and they indicate the direction research has taken in this area.

TRAINING AND EDUCATION

Instructional modes vary, depending on the matter to be learned and the stated objectives. In a number of resource books, distinctions are made between training and education, with the usual implications that cognitive matter is primarily the concern of education whereas psychomotor skills are connected with training programs. Both training and education are forms of instruction, with subtle distinctions and commonalities. The objectives of both are to modify behavior. Instruction involves systematic, guided experiences, as do training and education.

However, it is said that education is more concerned with individual differences and with long-range effects which often are not measureable. Training encompasses teaching people similar operations with the expectation of uniform outcomes. As a result less attention is paid to individual changes and outcomes in a training program. There are more short-term goals in training programs, relatively speaking, than in educational programs. When individuals are trained, they come with a certain set of skills to a program. The major objective is to advance most of them to a given level of skill at the end of a specified period of time. For further clarification of the training-education semantic issue as well as research information on training techniques, books by Glaser (1962) and Holding (1965) are recommended.

Current developments tend to refute some of the convenient distinctions presented between education and training programs. For instance, the present wave of enthusiasm for the learning systems approach in educational courses (e.g., Churchman, 1968; DeCecco, 1968; Banathy, 1968) includes the specification of terminal objectives for the students. On the training side, McFann (1969) would innovate techniques in training so that all learners do not proceed through a predetermined sequenced curriculum structure. With regard to military training programs, he calls for variable curricula and variable time schedules to best suit individual differences in abilities.

The psychologist views training as the practical application of that which is known of learning phenomena. The study of processes associated with learning concerns researchers and theorists; the applied aspects of this study can be seen in industry, the military (see Elmo Miller's chapter), the gymnasium (see Joseph Oxendine's chapter), and in sport (William P. Morgan's chapter). It is often hard to separate the trainer and the educator, especially in the educational institution setting. The coach, the industrial technologist, the home economist, and others appear to be both trainer and educator. They work at the level of each individual, but goals are usually short-range and specified. By relative standards, it is probably true that most programs in the psychomotor domain are training-oriented. As in the case of all instructional environments, however, variables are combined, manipulated, and forced to interact in such a way as to produce the desired end products.

PROFICIENCY

The most obvious goal of psychomotor behavior instruction is to develop the highest skill levels possible in the learner in the time allocated. This may be a justifiable end in itself or it may serve as a means for contributing to other objectives. For example, many special educators and clinical and developmental psychologists believe that experience in the development of motor skills increases the probability of success in academic endeavors. In any event, ultimately in order to attain proficiency in a skill, a host of variables must be considered. A number of them have been briefly discussed thus far. They and others will be dealt with in more detail in the forthcoming chapters.

For our purposes, though, figure 1-1 and figure 1-2 will serve nicely to indicate the building blocks leading to task proficiency (Singer, 1970). Figure 1-1 reveals a number of factors contributing to athletic proficiency. Genetics, childhood experiences, personal goals, environmental influences, and other interactions lead to the state of "excellence." Ideally, in order to determine potentials for developing proficiency in any task, genetic factors, familial influences, past experiences, and the individual's personality should be reasonably understood prior to training on a given task in a particular situation. General learning principles and specific considerations with appropriate environmental modifications and instructional techniques could then be utilized. The coach is the ultimate determiner of the athlete's productivity. Figure 1-2 has been drawn to show parallels between the characteristics considered in figure 1-1 for athletic proficiency with those underlying achievement in any vocational task. In this case, it is the teacher, leader, or supervisor who has the final responsiblity of shaping the learning environment for best productivity.

FINAL STATEMENT

Psychomotor behavior, it can be seen, is the result of the complex interaction of many factors. However, numerous psychomotor tasks which possess similar characteristics for consideration have been treated as distinct and separate entities. It should be clear by now that the purpose of this book

Athletic Proficiency

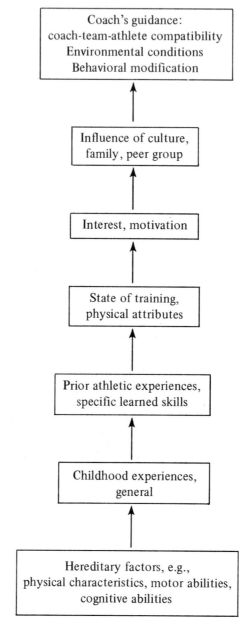

FIG. 1-1 Foundational blocks toward achieving excellence in athletics (*From Singer, 1970*).

Task Proficiency

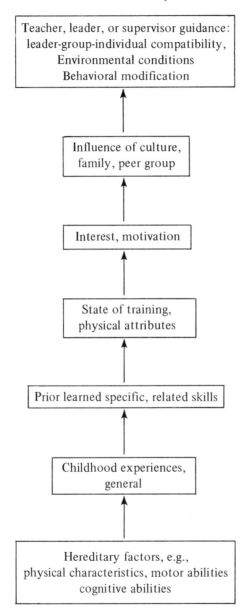

FIG. 1-2. Foundational blocks toward achievement in any psychomotor task (*From Singer, 1970*).

will be essentially twofold: (1) to describe considerations in the shaping of psychomotor skills; and (2) to reveal, if only by implication, similarities in research problems, situations, and tasks from one area of study in the psychomotor domain to another.

The authors of the respective chapters have not made any deliberate attempt to fulfill the second stated purpose. It will therefore be up to the reader to make mental notes while comparing the different fields of interest as described in the chapters. It is hoped that reading the preface and the introductory chapter will help the reader to perceive the relationship of the seemingly unrelated topical areas contained herein. Let us therefore proceed with the material developed expressly for this book and its purposes by the illustrious authors representing their chosen areas of study.

References

Adams, J. A. The relationship between certain measures of ability and the acquisition of a psychomotor criterion response. *Journal of General Psychology,* 1957, 56, 121–134.

Allison, R. B. Learning parameters and human abilities. Office of Naval Research Technical Report. Princeton, N. J.: Educational Testing Service, 1960.

Banathy, B. H. *Instructional systems.* Palo Alto, California: Fearon Publishers, 1968.

Berelson, B., & Steiner, G. A. *Human behavior: An inventory of scientific findings.* New York: Harcourt, Brace & World, Inc., 1964.

Bloom, B. S., Engelhart, M. D., Furst, E., Hill, W. H., & Krathwohl, D. R. *Taxonomy of educational objectives. Handbook I, cognitive domain.* New York: David McKay, 1956.

Bruner, J. S. *The process of education.* Cambridge, Massachusetts: Harvard University Press, 1963.

Carter, J. E. L. Somatotypes of college football players. *Research Quarterly,* 1968, 39, 476–481.

Carter, J. E. L. Somatotype characteristics of champion athletes. Paper presented at the Anthropological Congress, Praha-Humpolec, Czechoslovakia, 1969.

Churchman, C. W. *The systems approach.* New York: Dell Publishing Co., 1968.

DeCecco, J. P. *The psychology of learning and instruction.* Englewood Cliffs, N. J.: Prentice-Hall, Inc., 1968.

Duncanson, J. P. Learning and measured abilities. *Journal of Educational Psychology,* 1966, 57, 220–229.

Fleishman, E. A. Performance assessment based on an empirically derived task taxonomy. *Human Factors,* 1967, 9, 349–366.

Fleishman, E. A., & Hempel, W. E. Changes in factor structure of a complex psychomotor test as a function of practice. *Psychometrika,* 1954, 19, 239–252.

Gesell, A., & Thompson, H. Twins T and C from infancy to adolescence: A biogenetic study of individual differences by the method of co-twin control. *Genetic Psychological Monographs,* 1941, 24, 3–121.

Glaser, R. (ed.). *Training research and education.* New York: John Wiley & Sons, Inc. 1962.

Hebb, D. O. *The organization of behavior.* New York: John Wiley & Sons, Inc., 1949.

Hilgard, J. R. Learning and maturation in preschool children. *Journal of Genetic Psychology,* 1932, 41, 35–56.

Hinrichs, J. R. Ability correlates in learning a psychomotor task. *Journal of Applied Psychology,* 1970, 54, 56–64.

Hodgkins, J. Reaction time and speed of movement in males and females at various ages. *Research Quarterly,* 1963, 34, 335–343.

Holding, D. H. *Principles of training.* New York: Pergamon Press, 1965.

Krathwohl, D. R., Bloom, B. S., & Masia, B. B. *Taxonomy of educational objectives. Handbook II, affective domain.* New York: David McKay, 1964.

Lehman, H. C. *Age and achievement.* Princeton, N. J.: Princeton University Press, 1953.

Locke, E. A., & Bryan, J. F. Cognitive aspects of psychomotor performance: The effects of performance goals on level of performance. *Journal of Applied Psychology,* 1966, 50, 286–291.

McClearn, G. E. Genetics and behavior development. In M. L. Hoffman and L. W. Hoffman (eds.), *Review of child development.* New York: Russell Sage Foundation, pp. 433–474, 1964.

McFann, H. H. Individualization of army training. In *Innovations for training.* HumRRO, George Washington University, Professional Paper 6-69, February, 1969.

McGraw, M. B. *Growth: A study of Johnny and Jimmy.* New York: D. Appleton-Century, 1935.

Melton, A. W. (ed.). *Categories of human learning.* New York: Academic Press, 1964.

Melzack, R., & Thompson, W. R. Effects of early experience on social behaviors. *Canadian Journal of Psychology,* 1956, 10, 82–90.

Newton, G., & Levine, S. (eds.). *Early experience and behavior.* Springfield, Illinois: Charles C Thomas, 1968.

Noble, C. E., Baker, B. L., & Jones, T. A. Age and sex parameters in psychomotor learning. *Perceptual and Motor Skills,* 1964, 19, 935–945.

Piaget, J. *The origins of intelligence in children.* New York: International Universal Press, 1952.

Ravizza, R. J., & Herschberger, A. C. The effect of prolonged motor restriction upon later behavior of the rat. *The Psychological Record,* 1966, 16, 73–80.

Roberts, D. M. Abilities and learning: A brief review and discussion of empirical studies. *Journal of School Psychology,* 1968–1969, 7, 12–21.

Scott, J. P. Critical periods in behavioral development. *Science,* 1962, 138, 949–958.

Scott, J. P. *Early experience and the organization of behavior.* Belmont, California: Brooks/Cole, 1968.

Simpson, E. J. The classification of educational objectives, psychomotor domain. *Illinois Teacher of Home Economics,* 1966, 10, 110–144.

Singer, R. N. The psychomotor domain: General considerations. Paper presented at the National Special Media Institutes Consortium on The Psychomotor Domain, Teaching Research, Monmouth, Oregon (sponsor), at Salishan, Oregon, April, 1970.

Sluckin, W., & Salzen, E. A. Imprinting and perceptual learning. *Quarterly Journal of Experimental Psychology,* 1961, 8, 65–77.

Stake, R. E. Learning parameters, aptitudes, and achievements. *Psychometric Monographs,* 1961, No. 9.

Wiener, G. The interaction among anxiety, stress instructions, and difficulty. *Journal of Consulting Psychology,* 1959, 23, 324–328.

Chapter 2

EXPERIMENTAL PSYCHOLOGY *

RICHARD A. SCHMIDT
The University of Michigan

A discipline or area of investigation is nearly always defined in terms of the phenomena or subject matter of concern, and a discussion of the contributions of experimental psychology to motor behavior and retention must necessarily begin with a definition of the field in these terms. This is not easy to do, as numerous writers in the area fail to agree completely on the boundaries of the field and, to complicate the situation, the area began with a rather limited focus and the subject matter was both increased and redefined over the 100 or so years that it has been recognized. Most writers of the present period agree that the subject matter is *behavior,* but there is considerable disagreement about the types which are to be included. Some writers (e.g., Boring, 1950) would limit the area to the study of the normal human adult, thus eliminating from consideration the behaviors of children, mental patients, and animals. Underwood (1949, p. 1) limits the study of psychology to human responses, while others (Candland, 1968; McGuigan, 1968; Woodworth and Schlosberg, 1954) do not make this distinction, admitting animal behavior as a legitimate topic for experimental psychology.

There is, however, considerable agreement on some topic areas. Perception is and always has been a primary concern of experimental psychology, with the focus on the various senses such as vision, audition, kinesthesis, taste, etc. Learning and memory are almost always included with various subdivisions such as conditioning, concept formation, verbal and motor learning, and

*Appreciation is extended to Jack A. Adams, Irwin L. Goldstein, Joseph R. Higgins, Joan R. Peters, Robert N. Singer, and George C. Stelmach for their helpful comments on an earlier draft of this chapter.

18

transfer. Somewhat less universally accepted topics are social and emotional behavior, attention, motivation, and more recently, work (Underwood, 1949), and human performance (Candland, 1968).

Apart from the type of behavior under investigation, there is one additional point which serves to define experimental psychology. English and English (1966) define experimental psychology as the "investigation of psychological phenomena by *experimental methods*" (p. 194, italics mine), and this distinction is echoed by other writers as well (e.g., Candland, 1968; Postman and Egan, 1949; Underwood, 1949). This makes experimental psychology somewhat unique in that other fields do not, in general, have divisions named for their devotion to the experimental method (e.g., *experimental* chemistry, as opposed to some other type). The distinction probably arose originally (Boring, 1950) out of the need to distinguish the "new" experimental psychology from its predecessors which had emphasized philosophy, introspection, and qualities of the "mind." The adjective "experimental" implies that the methodology was that of the classic scientific method, with an emphasis upon developing hypotheses and theories tested by laboratory techniques stressing use of careful measurement and analysis. The distinguishing feature is the "experiment," which in its simplest form involves the manipulation of an independent variable (with all other variables held constant) and studying its effects on some dependent variable. This methodology leads to the establishment of statements of the type A *causes* B although logically there is some question as to whether *any* operation can lead to such a statement (Lachman, 1956). Causal statements are clearly of a stronger nature than are those such as A *is related* to B, since A *causing* B is only one of the possible reasons for A *being related to* B. The greater logical power provided by the experimental method has made it extremely popular in many fields of study, and it is one recognizable characteristic of all of experimental psychology, regardless of the particular behaviors under investigation. Thus the layman's use of the word "experiment" to mean activity conducted in experimental laboratories, utilizing data collection and analysis, is overgeneral, and the present use of the word "experiment" will be as just defined.

It would, at first glance, seem that all of psychology should fall under the heading of "experimental," but there are a number of areas in the study of behavior which are clearly not experimental in the sense just described (see Cronbach, 1957). For example, the migration patterns of birds and the behavior of large crowds are not usually amenable to experimentation, and studies of such behaviors are almost never experiments in the strict sense. Also, the study of the underlying abilities in motor performance (e.g., Fleishman, 1962) utilizes the concept of individual differences (A *is related to* B) and does not rely upon experiments, although many workers in the abilities area would probably be classed as experimental psychologists, since many use both experimental and differential approaches. Finally, there is a series of somewhat arbitrary divisions within psychology, with but one of the 29 divisions of the American Psychological Association treating experimental psychology. However, experimental psychology as it is defined here is not such a small proportion of the total field as the APA divisions might indicate as many of the divisions are limited by special subject matter (e.g., physiologic aspects, personality and social factors, and such) and others are limited by the types of individuals under study (e.g., the elderly, children in school, the mentally disturbed, etc.). As many of the divisions use experimental methodology, they should be included in a discussion of experimental psychology.

Therefore, experimental psychology should be seen not only as a subject matter area dealing with behavior, broadly defined, but also as a *method* for studying such behavior by using experimental techniques. Using this distinction as a starting point, the present chapter discusses the contributions of experimental psychology with a specific emphasis upon motor behavior. Since motor behavior itself is a very large field, the contributions to motor behavior must be limited, and a discussion of the retention of motor skills, including long- and short-term memory and warm-up decrement, will serve to provide examples of the contributions of experimental psychology to motor performances.

CONTRIBUTIONS TO MOTOR BEHAVIOR

Experimental Psychologists

The most important way in which experimental psychology has con-tributed to the study of motor skills is through the workers in departments of experimental psychology who have had the strongest part of their interest in motor skills. Probably the first of this type was R. S. Woodworth, who in 1899 published a monograph dealing with the accuracy of voluntary movement. This publication was very novel for its day (Boring, 1950) since an interest in motor skills for its own sake was unheard of, the main reason for studying movement being that it provided access to the "mind." There were, of course, a few others who were concerned with movement such as Bryan and Harter (1897) with telegraphy and Swift (1904) with the learning and retention of skills. As there was not a particularly large output of experimental psychology research in the early portion of the twentieth century (by today's standards, at least), there were, not unexpectedly, very few motor skills workers in this period as well. Most of what is known about skills has been established relatively recently. It is beyond the scope of this chapter to provide a thorough historical treatment of the development of research in motor skills. The interested reader should consult Boring's *A History of Experimental Psychology* (1950) and Irion's chapter, A Brief

History of the Research on the Acquisition of Skill, in Bilodeau's *Acquisition of Skill* (1966).

During the period immediately following World War II, and on into the Korean conflict, there was a tremendous growth in research not only in motor skills but also in experimental psychology in general. It was during this time that a number of individuals who had experimental psychology backgrounds emerged and began to apply their knowledge to motor skills research. This trend was undoubtedly motivated by a number of factors, but the most obvious seemed to be the pattern of research priorities established by various funding agencies. During this period, financial support was shifted to problems related to the national defense, and many researchers were forced to work on such problems as gunnery and submarine control or do without financial support. Also, the army, air force, and navy employed a number of experimental psychologists to conduct military research, and a great deal of motor behavior work was completed in the laboratory settings provided by the Department of Defense. A second reason for the increased interest in motor skills was the development of a number of interesting theoretic propositions (most notably that of Hull, 1943) which were easily testable by means of motor tasks. Third, at about this time there was an emergence of engineering psychology (or ergonomics, human factors, human engineering) and with a concern for the design of man-machine systems, a great deal of motor skills work was conducted with this end in mind. Whatever the reason, it is clear (Irion, 1966) that the period immediately following World War II and the Korean conflict was a golden one for motor skills. The volume of research devoted to this area increased many-fold over previous years.

Any of the many review articles dealing with motor skills is laced with the most influential names of this period, e.g., Adams, 1964; Bilodeau and Bilodeau, 1961; Noble, 1965. Very prominent was E. A. Bilodeau who was interested* in problems related to retention of learning, distribution of practice, and, later, with his wife, I. McD. Bilodeau, in performance and learning effects of knowledge of results. Also, E. A. Fleishman, although his individual differences approach is only marginally within the area of *experimental* psychology, contributed a great deal to the understanding of the components of motor abilities by means of the many factor analyses of motor performances conducted by him and his associates during this period. R. B. Ammons was also very active in the area of distribution of practice, warm-up decrement, and reminiscence.

At about the same time in England there were also a number of individuals who seemed to be primarily interested in motor skills problems although the

---

*It is somewhat presumptuous to state the past interests of some other person. This and ensuing discussions of interests and activities of various research workers are based upon examination of the various papers they have published.

problems studied there and in the United States were somewhat different. F. C. Bartlett was recognized as the "father" of motor skills in that country. Slightly later came A. T. Welford with his well-known work on the psychological refractory period and C. B. Gibbs and W. E. Hick, who were primarily known for work in tracking performances. E. C. Poulton, in addition to producing much work concerned with the problems of tracking, was a pioneer in the emerging area of anticipation and timing.

Motor tasks such as the pursuit rotor had a great appeal to workers interested in testing various theories which were prevalent at that time (e.g., Hull's theory, 1943) because of relative ease (as compared to verbal tasks) that performance could be measured and because the pursuit rotor was particularly sensitive to the work-rest phenomena which were predicted by Hull's theory. A number of individuals appeared to concentrate on motor tasks for their tests of theoretic propositions (e.g., Kimble, 1949; Eysenck, 1956). At the same time there was an increased interest in engineering psychology, and a great number of psychologists began studying motor skills in this context. Most notable was P. M. Fitts, who was concerned with problems in movement control and information processing, and after whom "Fitts' Law" was named. Also active were G. E. Briggs in the area of tracking and training, H. P. Bahrick in the area of feedback dynamics of control systems, C. E. Noble in various aspects of learning, and J. A. Adams in flight training and simulation research.

Somewhat later (late 1950's and 1960's) there were several other individuals concerned with motor skills. One of these, K. U. Smith, was involved in the area of cybernetics and feedback control of motor behavior. In Great Britain John Annett was studying the effects of knowledge of results in motor tasks, and in the United States C. E. Noble and D. A. Trumbo were concerned with tracking, and later, with timing in skilled performances. The list of other prominent individuals could continue, but space limitations cause a somewhat arbitrary ending at this point.

Although it may seem that there was a large volume of motor skills work produced by the experimental psychologists of the 1950's and 1960's, it does not seem quite so impressive when viewed in another perspective. There were many individuals working in experimental psychology during this period, and when the size of this group is compared to the small group of motor skills workers, it becomes clear that motor skills was not a particularly popular topic among experimental psychologists. Instead, experimental psychologists seemed to be interested in areas such as verbal learning and retention, brain functions, language, and other "higher" processes which were deemed more important than the "lower" motor processes. In addition to the relatively small number of researchers in motor skills, the types of problems they studied were not maximally suited to bring about an understanding of motor behavior. For example, many of the researchers who studied motor skills only did so because various theoretic notions were most easily investigated with motor tasks. Also, many workers were interested mainly in equipment-design applications, not in the basic nature of motor skills and learning, and most of this work meant more for engineering than it did for motor behavior per se. Finally, a great number of motor skills experiments were directed to the solution of practical problems rather than to the testing of theoretic propositions, and the findings did not have great applicability to situations other than those for which the experiments were designed. Thus, because of the relatively small volume of research done on motor skills compared to other types of behavior, and because much of this research was not directed primarily at an understanding of motor behavior and learning, the conclusion that experimental psychologists have not been particularly interested in motor skills seems to follow.

Experimental Psychologic Methods

It should be emphasized that the conclusions just drawn apply only to the contributions of experimental psychologists—those experimentalists working in departments of psychology—to motor behavior. However, if we impose the distinction made earlier that experimental psychology is a method or approach for studying behavior and not simply that which is practiced in a department of psychology, the contributions of experimental psychology appear very different from those just indicated. Individuals in other fields have borrowed the methodologies developed by experimental psychologists over the past 100 years, and such adoptions by these other fields is clear evidence of one of the most important contributions of experimental psychology. This is particularly true for motor behavior. Thus, even though experimental psychologists in general have not contributed greatly to the specific study of motor behavior per se, they have left behind a solid methodology which is now being used by those individuals interested in motor behavior and, seen in this light, the contributions of experimental psychology seem very large indeed.

Since World War II there has been an increasing interest in motor behavior in a number of related fields, and many of these fields are covered in other chapters in this book (e.g., engineering psychology, physical education, special education, etc.). However, a brief mention of the contributions to motor skills from these fields seems necessary since the methods used are essentially those of experimental psychology. Perhaps the greatest growth has been in the area of physical education. This is understandable since movement and skill are generally regarded as the subject matter of that field. Without doubt, F. M. Henry has to be called the "father" of motor skills in physical education, and it is notable that he was by training an experimental psychologist who later became interested in skills within physical education. He was responsible for making popular an approach to motor behavior which stressed careful laboratory methods, the use of modern statistical techniques, and the employment of novel motor tasks. He criticized experimental psychologists in general for studying motor tasks which were heavily loaded with "cognitive" components (e.g., motor maze learning), and was the designer of many novel gross motor tasks. His message is carried on by his many former graduate students in physical education. Henry's career was closely paralleled by that of A. T. Slater-Hammel, by training an experimental psychologist who also helped to instill a modern approach to the study of motor skills in physical education. Thus, there is a moderate amount of research being done today on motor skills in departments of physical education, and it is in general indistinguishable from that conducted in departments of psychology, concerned as it is with fundamental mechanisms in motor responding.

There continues to be a great deal of motor skills work conducted by engineering psychologists, human engineers, industrial engineers, etc., which is directed to the problems of motor skills in work contexts. Some of this work concerns man-machine interactions and has as its main goal the design of machinery which is compatible with man's capabilities. However, other investigations in this area seek to understand fundamental movement mechanisms in man, and are concerned with problems of fatigue and skills, training and transfer of training, variability in performance, and basic human abilities. The approach used, regardless of the specific goals of the research, is again identical with that used by experimental psychologists, even though the departmental affiliations vary over a wide range.

Experimental psychologic techniques are also seen in areas of recreation in which the concern is with the understanding of play behavior (Wade and Ellis, 1971) and rehabilitation (broadly defined) in which the emphasis is on establishing appropriate movement behaviors in physically and/or mentally handicapped individuals as well as the new areas related to the use of prostheses by amputees.

Very recently, there have been important contributions from fields which use the techniques of experimental psychology but which, at first blush, seem to have little relevance to either experimental psychology or motor behavior. For example, Nottebohm (1970) has reviewed some of the findings concerning the development of bird songs which, if the song is seen as dependent upon complex responses of the vocal musculature, has strong implications concerning the role of feedback, response programming, and motor control in man. Similarly, Wilson's (1961) work on the movements of locusts' wings has implications for the concept of motor programs. Thus, the legacy of experimental research on behavior in laboratory settings has been transmitted to other fields concerned with motor behavior, and the contributions of experimental psychology loom large when seen in this context.

Indirect Contributions

Quite apart from the direct contributions of the workers in, and the legacy produced by, experimental psychologic thought, there are some other important ways that motor behavior has benefitted from experimental psychology. It was mentioned before, but it deserves to be reemphasized, that experimental psychologists conducted a great deal of research using motor skills for the sole purpose of testing theories of learning. The most obvious example is Hull's theory (1943). Adams* has gone so far as to say that Hull's theory was the single most important event which has happened to motor behavior. He did not mean to imply that Hull's theory provided explanations for motor behavior (which, in retrospect, it clearly did not), but that it sent psychologists scurrying to their laboratories to test its predictions with motor tasks. Even though Hull's theory is not relevant today, the data remain, and they have contributed a great deal to the understanding of work-rest phenomena, warm-up decrement, and the distinctions between learning and performance variables. Perhaps what is more important is that these data are now available for others to use in building new theories such as Adams himself has done (see Adams, 1971).

Second, experimental psychology, in addition to providing a basic philosophy concerning the approaches to the understanding of motor behavior, has offered many theories and principles, admittedly designed for behaviors other than motor, which have *potential* applicability to motor performances. Obvious examples are the behavior modification principles worked out in many years of effort by Skinner and his colleagues as well as the interference theory of forgetting and numerous theories of learning. One of the earliest and most important principles was Thorndike's "Law of Effect" which served as the basis for much of the work with knowledge of results in motor performances. Such theoretic propositions have been carefully tested by using various tasks in experimental psychology contexts, and motor behavior is fortunate to have the theories available for possible application. However, although there are many instances where the theories seem directly appropriate, and some have been shown to be, there are other instances where application of well-established theories to motor behavior is being questioned; an example is the "Law of Effect" as discussed by Adams (1971). It should be understood that it is not sufficient merely to "apply" theories designed for other response classes to motor behavior, as it must be shown experimentally that the theory has explanatory power for response classes other than those for which it was designed. But even so, having these theoretic propositions with potential application to motor skills is an asset, and motor behaviorists should take advantage of the thinking of experimental psychologists in this respect.

*Jack A. Adams, personal communication, 1966.

Third, the methodologic sophistication which experimental psychology has produced in 100 years has important implications for motor behavior as well. Psychologists have always felt a need for inferential and differential statistical techniques to handle the highly variable data typical of the behavior laboratory and, although many of these techniques were originally developed for use in agricultural situations, the experimental psychologists have been active in refining them. Such techniques have been adopted by motor behaviorists as well. Also, the design of apparatus and techniques for measurement of various physiologic and psychologic parameters (e.g., arousal, information-processing load, etc.) has been a major contribution, and they are used often by motor behaviorists. There has been a great deal of critical thinking about various ways of treating data to arrive at meaningful conclusions, including the measurement of transfer of learning (Murdock, 1957), the pitfalls in the use of "learning curves" (Bahrick, 1964; Bahrick, Fitts, and Briggs, 1957; Estes, 1956; Sidman, 1952), and the necessity of equating groups at the beginning of the retention interval in studies of retention (Underwood, 1964), all of which have strong implications for procedures in motor skills research. Finally, there are a number of ingenious experimental paradigms which have been used by experimental psychologists to tease out the effects of confounded variables in experiments such as (a) the paradigm for determining whether a variable is a learning variable or a performance variable or both (Adams and Reynolds, 1954); (b) the partitioning of reaction time into premotor and motor components (Botwinick and Thompson, 1966; Schmidt and Stull, 1970); and (c) the measurement of decremental influences on well-learned skills by measuring the decrement in secondary nonmotor tasks (Bahrick and Shelly, 1958). It is obvious that experimental psychologists have contributed a great deal in the way of methodology, and serious students of motor behavior have acquainted themselves with the progress in experimental psychology in order to take advantage of the methodologies which are relevant to the study of motor behavior.

THE RETENTION OF MOTOR SKILLS

The points which have been made concerning the contributions of experimental psychology to motor skills hold very well for a number of subareas within motor skills, and a clear example is the area of retention of skills. Within the study of motor skills retention, examples of all the types of contributions just mentioned can be found, and it is probably true that nearly everything known about motor skills retention is closely associated with either experimental psychologists or other workers using the methodology of experimental psychology. The purpose of the remainder of this chapter is to point out specific examples of the contributions of experimental psychology to motor skills by examining the research completed in motor skills retention.

As the area of motor skills retention is extensive and has a history dating back to the early 1900's, a complete review within the confines of this chapter is not possible. Rather, a treatment which discusses the recent developments in the area, with an emphasis on the mechanisms involved and the evidence for them, will be most appropriate.

An analysis of the retention of motor skills concerns the decrement in performance on a motor task which typically follows a period of no practice. A number of factors are thought to be responsible for the loss in proficiency following rest. For convenience the area of investigation can be divided into a number of subareas, depending largely upon the type of process thought to be responsible for the decrement. The first and historically oldest is the forgetting of well-learned skills which is thought of as a loss in the strength of the stimulus-response bonds which are the product of practice on the task (variously termed "habit" or the "memory trace"), and the area has been termed *long-term memory* (*LTM*). A relatively new area which is concerned with the retention of very poorly learned items began with the finding by Peterson and Peterson (1959) that once-presented verbal items without rehearsal were lost very rapidly from memory. This has led to a concern for a separate system called *short-term memory* (*STM*), and the concern here will be with the motor *STM* system. Finally, other factors can cause decrements in performance which are not obviously related to either *LTM* or *STM,* and the most important of these is *warm-up decrement* (*WUD*), which is thought to be a need for the subject to "warm up" to the task following a layoff. The present chapter includes each of these areas in turn. It gives a brief review of the older issues and presents some of the new thinking and data on each of these problems which contribute to response decrements following periods of no practice.

Long-Term Memory

The improved performance of some task (commonly called "learning") is taken to reflect changes in an internal state which are thought to develop as a result of practice (called "habit," the "memory trace," etc.); thus learning is *not* simply the improvement in performance of some task as measured by the score but *the gains in the strength of habit or of the memory trace* which is inferred from the gain in task score. Memory *is* habit and the position is taken here that *"memory research has as its battlefront habit and the variables which affect it over the retention interval"* (Adams, 1967). This distinction is an important one, as it focuses on the study of the factors which influence the strength of the memory trace over time. Unfortunately, many would assume that because a subject displayed a reduction in proficiency for a task after a period of no practice that he had suffered a memory loss—that is, a loss in the strength of the memory trace. This is one possibility, but it is also possible that memory trace strength is high and temporary factors are preventing the subject from responding. These factors include fatigue, boredom, illness, and others. Thus it is important to remember that *memory is habit,* and just as we study the gains in performance on motor tasks to determine the influences on habit (learning), we study the decrements in performance as possible indicants of the loss of habit (or memory). This loss of habit is what is commonly called "forgetting."

The Interference Theory. There has been considerable interest in memory and forgetting in the realm of verbal learning in psychology, and the understanding of the process of forgetting is quite well advanced in that field. Much of this work has been concerned with the mechanisms of forgetting, and involves tests of the two most important theories for forgetting: (a) the "trace decay theory" and (b) the "interference theory." The trace decay theory states that losses in memory occur spontaneously only as a function of time and that forgetting *must* occur if periods of no-practice are presented. On the other hand, the interference theory states that forgetting occurs through the interaction of other learned habits which "interfere" with the habit for the criterion response. This interference is thought to occur in two ways, either (a) proactively (proactive interference, *PI*), in which responses learned prior to the criterion response interfere with the retention of that response, or (b) retroactively (retroactive interference, *RI*), in which responses acquired subsequent to the learning of the criterion response interfere with it. In either case, the result is usually a decrement in response proficiency on the retention test. However, Adams (1967) reminds us of the logical problem involved in attributing forgetting to interference with an analogy to the famous "all crows are black" syllogism:

A decrement in retention is caused by interference.
Forgetting is a decrement in retention.
Therefore, all forgetting is caused by interference.*

Students of retention of skills too often assume that the decrements in performance caused by "interfering activities" during a retention interval imply that all forgetting is caused by interference, but that conclusion does not necessarily follow. While it is possible that all forgetting might be caused by interference, it is also possible that the interfering activities cause one type of decrement which is unrelated to the decrements which occur as a result of empty periods of no practice. In the paragraphs which follow, evidence will be presented which indicates that "interfering activities" cause decrements in performance, and these facts are given as tentative support of the interference theory. It should be recognized that they do not provide proof of it.

In contrast to the active theory testing and theoretic thinking of the verbal learning researchers (for a thorough review, see Adams, 1967) with the

*Adams, 1967, p. 120.

resultant understanding of the process of verbal forgetting, the motor skills workers have not made nearly the same progress in their research. Much of the motor work has been motivated by practical matters such as providing answers to applied problems in industry or the military. Very little work has been done to determine the causes of forgetting, as, for example, in verbal learning. Further, most of the research in motor performance has been "empiric" rather than "theoretic" in nature (Adams, 1967) and has sought only to determine *if* forgetting occurs as a function of time without being concerned with mechanisms of forgetting. However, there have been a few studies which have dealt with the interference theory, and they deserve to be mentioned here.

Retroactive Interference. In a series of studies from the University of Iowa in the early 1950's, Lewis and his associates sought to determine the extent to which retroactive interference was a cause of motor forgetting as it had been shown to be for verbal skills. In one of the key papers, Lewis, McAllister, and Adams (1951) provided either 10, 30, or 50 original learning (*OL*) trials on a continuous tracking task (Mashburn task), and then gave either 10, 20, 30, or 50 potentially interfering interpolated learning (*IL*) trials in which the control directionalities were reversed. The decrement in performance on subsequent practice on the standard task was taken as the extent of *RI;* this is analogous to the procedures used in many verbal studies of *RI* (e.g., Briggs, 1957). The amount of forgetting (th *RI*) of the standard task was positively related to the amount of *IL* practice, which provided support for the interference theory for motor skills. Very similar findings were provided in other studies by McAllister and Lewis (1951) and by McAllister (1952).

While the Iowa data were clear in providing massive interference in the tasks studied, the role of the interference theory for motor skills remains somewhat tentative. First, all of the Iowa studies used continuous tracking tasks and, since this is the only work investigating *RI* and motor skills, the generalization to other tasks is not necessarily complete. More work is needed to determine if interference is also possible in discrete tasks. Second and more important, however, is the fact that it is not clear what is being interfered with in the Iowa studies. In an attempt to provide designs analogous to the verbal *RI* situations, Lewis and his associates (1951) used interpolated responses which were opposite to the responses to the same stimuli in the original task. It is possible that the interference was caused by a decrement in the "cognitive" components of the task, and that the interference was not "motor" at all in the sense that the motor patterns were impaired. Thus, it could be that the *IL* trials produced confusion as to "what to do" in response to the stimulus patterns, and that the procedures may not have provided a fair test of *motor* interference. Work is needed to determine if this contention is correct, however, and it is sad testimony to the state of affairs in motor retention work that follow-up work to the Iowa studies has not been completed to answer this question.

Proactive Interference. Work in verbal learning in which interfering lists were presented prior to presentation of the criterion list, with retention of the criterion list measured after a retention interval, has indicated that *PI* is a strong determiner of forgetting in such tasks. A paper by Underwood (1957) summarizing much of this work indicated that *PI* may be of even greater importance than *RI* in producing forgetting. However, the parallel work in motor skills has not been as complete, since motor skills workers have not, with but few exceptions, studied this problem. However, Duncan and Underwood (1953) studied *PI* in motor skills with a manual task involving moving a lever to one of six slots according to lights which were presented, and the subject's task was to learn which slot was paired with a given light and to move the lever to the slot when the light came on. Subjects learned two tasks successively, and Duncan and Underwood varied the level of learning on the two tasks as well as their similarity (the number of light-slot pairings which were similar across tasks). The retention of the second task was measured after 24 hours, and thus the effects of the first task on the retention of the second task was the primary consideration (a *PI* design). Duncan and Underwood failed to show *PI* for their two tasks but, as Adams (1967, p. 224) points out, this does not necessarily mean that *PI* does not operate in motor tasks. First, the typical pattern displayed in the verbal studies is for the first of two interfering tasks to display *negative* transfer to the second. In the Duncan-Underwood paper, however, there was strong *positive* transfer, indicating that the basic tasks were probably not interfering and leading to the conclusion that the basic conditions for motor interference were not met. Second, as with Lewis and his associates (1951) and *RI*, it is uncertain whether the interference was motor or cognitive, as there is the possibility that changing the light-slot pairings from the first to the second task would result in a confusion as to "what to do" rather than in the motor patterns. This task seems especially prone to such effects, as the learning of the light-slot pairings rather than the movement patterns themselves appeared to be the subject's major problem.

Schmidt (1968) attempted to eliminate this latter problem by using a *PI* design with a task which seemed to minimize the cognitive components of the performance. The task required a rapid arm movement in which the subject had to remove his finger from a reaction key, knock down three barriers in a left-center-right order, and return to the key as quickly as possible. Four variations of the task were created by varying the locations (but not the order) of the three barriers. Subjects in the *PI* group learned Tasks 1, 2, and 3 prior to learning Task 4, and subjects in a control group learned only Task 4. Retention of Task 4 was tested 48 hours later for both groups. Even though the problem of the cognitive components seemed to be eliminated with these tasks, there was still great positive transfer from Tasks 1, 2, and 3 to Task 4 even after the 48-hour retention interval and there were no differences in retention as a function of the previous tasks. Again, as in the Duncan and Underwood (1953) study, the basic requirements of *PI* seemed not to be met, since the verbal *PI* effects are usually associated with great negative transfer from the first to the second task. These studies were the only two found which tested the interference theory for motor *LTM*, and it seems clear that our understanding of the mechanisms of motor forgetting is very small compared to our understanding of the verbal area. More work is clearly needed to define the nature of interfering tasks, and to determine whether the laws of motor and verbal interference are similar. The lack of work dealing with the laws of motor interference behavior should not convey the impression that motor memory has not been studied; on the contrary, the questions surrounding the forgetting of well-learned skills has been studied extensively, and a number of issues not related to the mechanisms underlying forgetting are defined.

Motor Versus Verbal Forgetting. An early question concerned the supposed superiority of motor skills over verbal skills in terms of the degree to which they were retained over time. The classic example seems to be the excellent retention of continuous sports skills such as bicycle riding, skiing, and ice skating despite many years of no practice. A number of investigations in the 1930's addressed themselves to this question, using, for example, techniques in which motor and verbal mazes were learned and the retention of these habits studied as a function of the retention interval. This basic research is summarized in a review by Naylor and Briggs (1961), but the various findings produce many discrepancies. Many of the studies, because they were conducted early in the history of motor skills, suffered from weak methodology, but there are more serious problems not mentioned by Naylor and Briggs which make this question difficult to answer. These are discussed below.

First, it was stated earlier that the study of forgetting concerns itself with the fate of habit over the retention interval. In a typical study investigating verbal and motor habits, the two types of material are learned to some criterion (e.g., one perfect trial of the mazes), and then the retention interval begins. Following the retention interval, the proportion (typically) of the original learning (that is, the original change in the task performance score) which was lost over the retention interval is taken as the statistic which measures forgetting. This statistic is compared for verbal and motor tasks, with the usual result showing only small differences. Underwood (1964) has pointed out that it is necessary to insure that treatment groups undergoing forgetting begin the retention interval with the same level of habit strength. There is no way of knowing whether the habit strength for the verbal and motor tasks are equivalent even though they were learned to a common criterion, as the performances representing such criteria might represent quite different levels of habit strength. If the amount (or rate) of forgetting is a function of the amount of habit strength, then in the case where the habit was not equated at the end of original learning, an erroneous conclusion would follow.

A second problem concerns the concept of "ceiling effects." This concept has been discussed by Underwood (1964), Bahrick and his associates (1957), and more recently, by Schmidt (1971), and concerns the fact that the performance score for many tasks becomes increasingly insensitive to improvements in habit strength as it approaches the upper limit for the task. An example is in paired associates learning where the performance score is percent correct, which cannot exceed 100 percent. Performance on most tracking tasks is evaluated in terms of time-on-target (*TOT*) scores, and the maximum allowable score for a 30-second trial is 30 seconds. Scores for performance on tasks involving timed measures (movement time, reaction time, etc.) have a corresponding "floor" which is zero seconds. In each case, when the performance of a subject reaches the ceiling or is very close to it, he continues to gain in habit strength with increasing practice trials, but his performance score remains constant, and thus the gains in habit are not reflected by gains in performance score. The same is true for decreasing habit in the case of forgetting. When subjects forget, the measureable changes are the changes in the performance score, and if the score is insensitive to changes in habit, the degree of forgetting (that is, loss of habit) is not estimated correctly. Underwood (1964) and Schmidt (1971) have argued that the degree of forgetting is underestimated in tasks with ceiling effects, and increasingly so as subjects practice for a number of trials when their scores are near the ceiling. If verbal and motor tasks have different degrees of ceiling or floor effects, we have no way of determining whether a decrement of some number of score units in the motor task is representative of the same amount of habit decrease as the comparable decrement in the verbal task. The question seems unresolvable until some method of estimating habit strength independently of the performance score is realized; such a method would be difficult to imagine, as the basic understanding of the learning theorists has always been that the *only* measure of habit was performance. In any case, the question seems seriously complicated by these two methodologic issues.

Whether the basic nature of habit loss is similar or different for verbal and motor tasks is open to question, but there is no question that many verbal tasks show very rapid and complete retention losses (Adams, 1967, especially Chap. 4), and many motor tasks show almost no losses over long retention intervals. For example, Fleishman and Parker (1962), by using a three-dimensional tracking task, Ryan (1962), by using the pursuit rotor, and Meyers (1967), by using the Bachman ladder have all produced evidence showing nearly no forgetting after no-practice periods of as long as two years. Some investigators have found other motor skills which were not retained quite as well (e.g., Ryan, 1965; Martin, 1970; Lersten, 1969), and still other investigators have shown that some motor skills are poorly retained (e.g., Ammons et al., 1958; Adams and Hufford, 1962).

One method of reconciling the differences between the findings for the studies just cited is in terms of the tasks used. A subjective analysis of the tasks indicates that those which are well retained seem not to be dependent upon "cognitive" decisions concerning what to do in a given stimulus situation but rather are concerned with making a well-defined movement correctly or quickly. On the other hand, those tasks which seem to show the most losses over time seem to be dependent upon cognitive learning of sequences of operations, learning to pair switches with lights, etc. Thus, it appears that the tasks which are best retained could be classified as more "motor" than the tasks which are poorly retained, with this classification being based upon the degree to which the subject must make a decision about what to do (cognitive task) rather than how to do it (motor task).

In addition to determining whether the absolute amount of forgetting is different for verbal and motor tasks and using such differences as evidence that verbal and motor forgetting are different processes, another approach is to determine whether the laws which govern the loss of verbal information are the same as those which govern the loss of motor skill. This is a difficult problem because of the scarcity of laws of motor forgetting, but there are a few instances where laws have been fairly well established. These will serve as a basis for a tentative comparison of the two types of materials.

It was mentioned earlier that the laws of interference seem to be similar for motor and verbal tasks. Briggs (1957), by using verbal paired associates, and Lewis and his associates (1951), by using the Mashburn motor task, found that increased interpolated learning with reversed stimulus and response pairings led to an increase in the RI for the criterion task. Thus, motor and verbal tasks appeared to operate in much the same way as a function of the IL trials. However, in both investigations the amount of original learning (OL) prior to the interpolated trials was a variable; in Briggs' study greater OL led to decreased RI, but Lewis and his associates found that greater OL led to *increased RI*—just the opposite result. This finding has indicated to many (Adams, 1967; Williams et al., 1969) that the laws of verbal and motor interference may not be the same and that motor and verbal forgetting may be different processes, as suggested by the differential rates of forgetting of the two types of task mentioned earlier. This conclusion has serious consequences for those who would hope for a unified theory of memory which could explain all forgetting, and leads to the requirement that different theories of verbal and motor retention be created to explain the existing findings.

As it would be more parsimonious to have a unified theory of forgetting for both motor and verbal tasks, Schmidt (1971) reanalyzed the data from the investigations of Briggs (1957) and Lewis and his co-workers (1951) to determine if there were not some artifact or procedural detail which could explain the obtained verbal-motor differences. The first observation was that Briggs used "relative *RI*" as the measure of interference (which was the difference in performance between an experimental group with *IL* practice and a control group without *IL* trials divided by the control group performance level), whereas Lewis and his associates used the mean decrement in performance (the numerator in Briggs' relative *RI*). A reexamination of the Briggs data in terms of mean decrement (as used by Lewis and his co-workers) revealed that the relationship between *OL* and *RI* was now positive, just as had been found in the Lewis study in the motor task, suggesting that a simple scoring difference was responsible for the motor-verbal differences. Data from McAllister (1952), similarly reanalyzed, revealed the same positive trend. However, reanalyzing all data with relative *RI* scores produced differences again, with the McAllister (1952) and Briggs (1957) data showing negative relationships between *OL* and *RI,* and the Lewis data showing a positive relationship.

Further analysis of the pattern of findings led to the conclusions that the tasks which were sensitive to the method of measuring interference (that is, those of Briggs and McAllister) had marked ceiling effects whereas the Mashburn task (Lewis and his associates) had neither ceiling effects nor sensitivity to the methods of measurement of interference. Schmidt (1971) concluded from this analysis (a) that ceiling effects tend to underestimate the habit strength at the end of acquisition; (b) that the decrement in performance as a function of *IL* is also underestimated when ceiling effects are present; (c) that the amount of *OL* tends to push scores further toward the ceiling and thus the amount of interference is increasingly underestimated as *OL* increases; and (d) that the use of the relative *RI* score even further underestimates the loss in habit when the ceiling effects are present. The basic conclusion from the reanalysis was that there was no evidence that motor interference and verbal interference are different processes, and that increasing *OL* (that is, overlearning) tends to *increase* the susceptibility of the task to interference from interfering tasks. This latter finding is somewhat surprising in the light of the generally accepted conclusion that increased overlearning should render the task inaccessible to interference from other sources. What is perhaps contributing to the confusion is that the performance after the retention interval (that is, the absolute retention) is often used interchangeably with the *change* in performance over the retention interval (relative retention). Greater *OL* leads to greater absolute retention (Melnick, 1971) but poorer relative retention (Schmidt, 1971).

Thus, there is reason to believe that the fine work conducted by the researchers concerning the interference theory and verbal skills may have applicability to motor skills as well. In order that we may speak with confidence about motor interference, the generality of the interference theory to motor tasks needs much more work than it has received in the past.

Discrete Versus Continuous Tasks. Upon examining the literature in the area of motor skills retention, it appears that another factor associated with the amount of retention is whether the task is discrete (that is, characterized by a recognizable beginning and end, e.g., throwing a ball) or continuous (without such initial and final limits, e.g., steering a car). When the studies are classified according to the location of the task used on the discrete-continuous dimension, it becomes clear that the best-retained tasks are continuous tracking tasks such as the pursuit rotor (Bell, 1950; Ryan, 1962), various compensatory tracking tasks (Battig et al., 1957; Ammons et al., 1958; Fleishman and Parker, 1962), or other continuous tasks such as the stabilometer (Ryan, 1965) and the Bachman ladder (Meyers, 1967). To the contrary, tasks which are discrete in nature such as those requiring pairing of lights and switches (Neumann and Ammons, 1957) or in which a series of discrete operations is learned in the proper sequence (Adams and Hufford, 1962) are nearly completely forgotten over similar retention intervals. It is a challenge to motor behaviorists to determine the explanation of such obvious differences in retention for these two classes of task.

One explanation is in terms of the observation that the discrete tasks seem to be heavily loaded with cognitive components. For example, the tasks involving pairing of lights and switches seem to have as the subject's greatest problem the learning of the association of lights and switches, and the sequential tasks seem to require the subject to learn the order of operations. In both cases, the primary problems are verbal-cognitive, and once the decisions have been made as to which response to make, the motor responses required have been well learned previously and are nearly trivial. If this is the case, and it is true that verbal responses show poorer retention than motor responses as indicated in the previous section, then one cause for the large forgetting in discrete responses could be the forgetting of the verbal responses upon which they so heavily depend. While it is true that there are a number of discrete tasks where the performance does not seem to be heavily dependent upon such cognitive responses, there has been very little research done concerning the retention of these tasks. One study by Lersten (1969) using the Rho task (a discrete arm movement time task requiring a circular and linear phase) showed only moderate levels of retention, with the circular phase at 79 percent and the linear phase at 29 percent after retention intervals of one year. Similarly, a recent study by Martin (1970), who used a left-hand movement time task involving knocking down a pair of barriers and returning to a stop switch, showed that subjects lost approximately 50 percent of the original amount learned over retention intervals of up to four months. Thus, the use of discrete tasks which are not highly cognitive in nature seems to create somewhat better retention than was present with the highly cognitive tasks of Neumann and Ammons (1957) and Adams and Hufford (1962), but the levels of retention are not nearly as high as in the case with continuous tracking tasks. Clearly, the problem is dependent upon factors other than the amount of verbal component in the task.

A second possibility is that continuous skills are more highly overlearned than are discrete tasks. It is generally held that the gain in habit is most highly dependent upon the number of reinforcements provided for the correct responses. A discrete response with its relatively short duration and finite beginning and end probably receives only a very few reinforcements in a given trial. On the other hand, subjects practicing continuous responses such as the pursuit rotor may produce up to three responses per second (Hick, 1948, 1949; Pew, 1966), and if each of these subresponses is reinforced, this could produce as many as 90 reinforcements in a single 30-second practice trial. If the amount of gain in habit is related to the number of times the correct response is reinforced, then a discrete task would have much less habit strength for a constant number of trials than would a continuous task. Since *absolute* retention is highly dependent upon the habit remaining at the end of the retention interval (Ammons et al., 1958), and subjects with the continuous tasks gain more habit as a result of the increased reinforcements in a trial, this could provide an explanation of the continuous-discrete differences in retention. To date, no attempts have been made to equate the number of reinforcements for the two types of task so that habit strength is equivalent at the end of acquisition. Such research would probably prove helpful in understanding the problem. A further complication, however, is that the continuous tasks (especially those scored with *TOT*) often have serious ceiling effects, and it was shown earlier that ceiling effects lead to underestimations of the amount of habit loss, providing another variable which must be controlled in such research.

A second problem lies in the definition of a "trial," which can refer to anything from one reaction time attempt requiring 0.2 second to an entire afternoon of practice in a driver simulator. Typically, retention is based on the first "trial" after the retention interval, and if such trials vary in terms of the number of subresponses they contain, there could be a serious underestimation of retention loss when temporally lengthy trials are employed. A 30-second pursuit rotor trial with perhaps 90 subresponses is scored in terms of "average" proficiency over all 30 seconds. Since the later responses in the sequence should be more proficient than the earlier ones, this should lead to a score which is insensitive to the level of proficiency on the first response of the trial. Discrete task retention is, on the other hand, only based on the first attempt following the retention interval and does not have this pooling effect. Thus, the performance on the first response of a continuous task could show a nearly complete retention loss of the first subresponse which might never be evidenced when the subresponse is averaged with the later subresponses in the same "trial." Thus, when only the first of the subresponses are considered following the retention interval, discrete and continuous tasks might show no differences in retention. This question seems easily answered by examining progressively smaller and smaller early units of the continuous first trial, but data on this question are not available.

Another possibility, if the interference theory is able to explain forgetting, is that discrete tasks, with their relatively heavy verbal loadings, may be more susceptible to interference from other verbal tasks than are continuous tasks. This is possible in the light of the specificity which is usually shown with motor tasks and the somewhat more generality which is shown for verbal tasks. The continuous tasks, being specific unto themselves, might not be interfered with by other tasks in the environment as are discrete tasks and thus there would be less loss of habit over time. Other possibilities mentioned in the literature are that (a) continuous tasks are retained better because they are more dependent upon proprioceptive (and other) feedback (Adams, 1967) for their control and (b) that continuous tasks are organized so that there is greater "meaningfulness," which should enable the subject to rely upon very well learned principles and relationships (Naylor and Briggs, 1961). Which of these many hypotheses is correct is certainly open to question at present, and a solid research effort must be exerted to understand the retention of well-learned materials.

Short-Term Memory

The topic of short-term memory (*STM*) is quite new in experimental psychology, the initial studies being by Brown (1958) and Peterson and Peterson (1959). The growth of interest in this area since then has been very rapid. Peterson and Peterson showed that when subjects were presented with a single consonant trigram (e.g., LRT), and then began to count backward from a given number by threes to prevent rehearsal, the probability of correctly recalling the trigram decreased rapidly as the retention intervals were increased, with recall as low as 10 percent at 18 seconds. This finding created an entirely new field of research, with workers becoming interested in the mechanisms of the rapid retention loss. A considerable amount of research followed these experiments, but it is beyond the scope of this chapter to review the verbal work here. Instead, the interested reader should consult Adams (1967, Chap. 5) for a review. However, for background information which will be important for the understanding of the rationale for the motor work which followed in *STM*, a few of the more important findings will be outlined here.

Hellyer (1962) studied the effects of the number of reinforcements of the to-be-remembered item by having the subject repeat aloud the item either one, two, four, or eight times prior to the retention interval, with digit naming the activity within the retention interval to prevent rehearsal, and found that the amount of practice markedly decreased the forgetting over 27 seconds. A number of individuals sought to determine the cause of forgetting in *STM,* and provided some tests of the interference theory as it was used with long-term memory (*LTM*). Keppel and Underwood (1962) found that the later trigrams in a series were recalled less accurately than the earlier ones; the implication was that the traces from the early items were interfering proactively with the later ones, which provided support for the interference theory for *STM.* Peterson and Gentile (1965) argued that *PI* should be less strong if more time is allowed for the traces created on a given trial to weaken and become ineffective in producing *PI* for the subsequent trials, and their results supported their predictions. More recently, evidence has been produced to show that the basis of storage in verbal *STM* is acoustic, with items being interfered with because they sound alike (Conrad, 1964; Sperling, 1963; Wickelgren, 1965).

It is not parsimonious to assume that *STM* is a different system than *LTM* simply because items seem to be lost more rapidly from *STM* than from *LTM.* This result, of course, could merely represent the fact that retention is poorer for poorly learned items, and since *STM* experiments typically have presented the item only once, the rapid loss could be explained by a rapid loss from *LTM* of these poorly learned items. However, there are other lines of evidence which contribute to the belief that *LTM* and *STM* are fundamentally different systems. First, depending upon the conditions, the number of items which can be held in *STM* is around eight (Miller, 1956), whereas there seems to be no limit for *LTM.* Second, semantic (that is, meaning) interference produces decrements in *LTM* and acoustic interference produces decrements in *STM.* Third, well-learned items (presumably in *LTM*) do not cause *PI* in *STM* (Scott et al., 1967). In summary, *STM* is thought to be a system, separate from *LTM,* in which a limited number of items can be held in store for only a brief time without rehearsal and in which losses are due to decay and/or interference from other items. Rehearsal is thought to "transfer" the items from *STM* to a more permanent *LTM* store. A popular misconception is that *STM* is distinguished from *LTM* by the length of the retention interval. However, the fundamental distinction is the way in which information is stored and lost. These could be a *STM* experiment with retention intervals of one year, and a *LTM* experiment with retention intervals of 15 seconds.

Motor Short-Term Memory. Those interested in motor skills soon began to ask whether the findings which were present in verbal *STM* could also be shown for motor *STM.* Two important questions were whether (a) there was justification for separate *STM* and *LTM* systems for motor responses and (b) whether the laws governing the loss of information from motor and verbal *STM* were similar. The earliest study conducted in this area was by Adams and Dijkstra (1966) in which the authors attempted to extend the findings of Peterson and Peterson (1959) and Hellyer (1962) to motor responses. Their task was simple linear positioning; the subject moved a slide (hidden from view) until it hit a stop defining the position to be recalled, and then a retention interval of from 5 to 120 seconds began. Following the retention interval, the subject attempted to replace the slide in the defined position without the aid of the stop. This procedure was formally similar to that used for verbal *STM* studies in that the subject received only one presentation of the item, he was not permitted rehearsal (that is, movements of his arm to that position), the retention intervals were short, and he practiced a given item only once to prevent it from being transferred to *LTM*. Adams and Dijkstra found that, as for verbal *STM,* absolute errors were an increasing function of the length of the retention interval. Other conditions in their experiment provided multiple reinforcements of the defined locations (that is, moving to the stop either 1, 6, or 15 times) as an extension of Hellyer's (1962) findings for verbal materials, with the result that increased reinforcements decreased the amount and rate of forgetting. At about the same time, Posner and Konick (1966) showed that there were similar retention losses in other motor tasks and that the losses in absolute accuracy are not a function of the amount of verbal information processed during the retention interval.

Proactive Inhibition. A few experimenters sought to determine whether the interference theory could account for the forgetting found in motor *STM* experiments. Adams and Dijkstra (1966) and Posner and Konick (1966) provided multiple trials (with different positions on each trial) of their present-recall sequences. They thought that if the laws are similar to those for verbal *STM, PI* should result, as in the Keppel and Underwood study (1962) and the Peterson and Gentile study (1965). However, there was no tendency for error to be an increasing function of trials in either experiment, offering negative evidence for *PI* and for the interference theory. One possibility why these studies did not demonstrate *PI* was that the inter-trial intervals were very long (3 minutes in the Adams-Dijkstra study) and may have allowed the traces to weaken (as in the study by Peterson and Gentile, 1965) and become ineffective in producing *PI.* Therefore, Ascoli and Schmidt (1969) and slightly later Stelmach (1969) investigated this question with a design in which either zero, two, or four positions were presented just prior to a criterion movement. Then, following a retention interval, the criterion movement was recalled and followed by the prior movements (if any). This procedure produced large decrements in absolute errors of recall for four prior movements relative to zero or two, with the results of the Ascoli-Schmidt and Stelmach studies agreeing nearly completely. Thus, it was possible that the failure to produce *PI* in the Adams-Dijkstra and Posner-Konick studies was due to long inter-trial intervals, and presenting a number of movements just prior to a criterion movement produced many strong traces which were active in interfering with the criterion. The findings of the Ascoli-Schmidt and Stelmach studies were taken as evidence for the interference theory.

However, if more close temporal spacing of the traces in *STM* could explain the differences between results of the Ascoli-Schmidt and Stelmach studies on the one hand and the Adams-Dijkstra and Posner-Konick studies on the other, then simply reducing the inter-trial intervals in a present-recall-present-recall sequence analogous to Adams-Dijkstra and Peterson-Gentile (1965) should produce *PI*. Recall error should be an increasing function of trials. Schmidt and Ascoli (1970b) tested this prediction by administering 10 trials, each with a different location, to two groups, with 10- or 90-second inter-trial intervals. It was predicted that shortening the interval from 90 to 10 seconds would increase *PI*. Results were negative in that there were no differences between groups as a function of the inter-trial interval, with neither group showing any evidence of *PI* at all. This finding led Schmidt and Ascoli (1970a) to wonder whether the Ascoli-Schmidt and Stelmach findings were not artifacts produced by having the subject attend to the prior information while he was storing or retaining the criterion information. Posner and Konick (1966) found that attention demand during the retention interval was not a factor in motor *STM,* but there still remained the possibility that the decrement in recall was produced by a failure to store the traces efficiently because of attention demand during the storage time. Schmidt and Ascoli (1970a) conducted two experiments in which (a) subjects were to remember either zero, two, or four prior trigrams or (b) they had to count forward by ones or backward by threes during the storage process which is defined as the time during which they were moving to and holding against the stop which determined the criterion locations. Results of the trigram manipulation were negative, but counting backwards by threes created nearly twice the absolute error as counting forward by ones (the latter presumably less attention demanding), and the implication was that attention demand during the storage of traces may have accounted for some of the decrement in the Ascoli-Schmidt (1969) experiment. Williams (1971) has challenged this view, however, as he found that prior positions did not affect recall at a 10-second retention interval, but did as retention intervals increased. This indicated that if Schmidt and Ascoli (1970a) were correct in their idea that attention demand caused inefficient storage, it should have shown up with immediate recall. More work is needed on this issue.

Retroactive Inhibition. Along with the investigations concerned with *PI* in motor *STM* mentioned above, there has been some interest in determining to what extent *RI* was a factor. Some of the earlier studies were concerned with the effects of non-motor information-reduction tasks (e. g., Posner, 1967; Posner and Konick, 1966; Williams et al., 1969) and the general conclusion was that absolute error of motor recall is not influenced by opportunities for rehearsal. Other investigators studied the effects of interpolated motor activities. Schmidt and Stelmach (1968) and others failed to produce evidence of increased absolute errors as a function of their interpolated movements, providing little support for the interference theory. Most of these papers did not report algebraic (that is, constant) error. Pepper and Herman (1970) have reanalyzed some of the earlier work with interpolated activities. They found that algebraic errors are strongly influenced by such activities, and have proposed a model to account for the various findings.

The Pepper-Herman model requires a number of assumptions about the nature of the stored materials and their recall. First, the memory trace is accurately stored but is subject to decay over time, and this decay acts in the dimension of intensity or extent of the original motor act. Empty time during a retention interval weakens the trace, and multiple reinforcements prior to the retention interval tend to strengthen it. Also, the subject has some response set (that is, a tendency either to over- or undershoot the target location which depends upon the task) which remains constant over time. According to the Pepper-Herman model, changing the strength of the stored trace, either by making it weaker as a function of empty time or stronger by multiple reinforcements, will influence the magnitude of the response which is produced in an attempt to match it at recall. This set of assumptions leads to the predictions that (a) empty time will weaken the trace and lead to more negative (shorter or less forceful) responses at recall; (b) reinforcement of the trace prior to the retention interval will lead to more positive responses; (c) interpolated non-motor activities (e.g., number sorting, etc.) will lead to increased general muscular tension and proprioceptive feedback which serves to strengthen the trace and cause a shift toward more positive algebraic errors; and (d) interpolated motor movements will either strengthen or weaken the trace, depending upon their location relative to the criterion trace, with smaller responses leading to decreased algebraic error and larger responses leading to increased algebraic error.

Pepper and Herman (1970) provide a great deal of support for their model both in terms of reanalyses of previous data and with their own data by means of a force estimation task. However, there are a number of papers which bear on their model which they did not cite (some of them done subsequent to their paper), and it would be helpful to determine how these data pertain to their model.

First, with respect to the prediction that empty time leads to a decreased algebraic error because a weaker trace requires a weaker response to match it, the predicted trends are clearly shown in the positioning data by Adams and Dijkstra (1966) and Posner (1967). The Pepper-Herman (1970) data with force estimation tasks show a similar tendency for decreased (that is, more negative) algebraic error over time, and Norrie's data show very similar trends, with a force estimation task when only one practice trial is provided (Norrie,

1968, 1969). However, Ascoli and Schmidt (1969) and Montgomery (1970) revealed only weak trends toward increased undershooting, and Williams (1971) noted the opposite trends, but no differences were significant. Thus the data do not uniformly support the Pepper-Herman weakened trace notion. Their notion is, however, in keeping with recent findings on the mechanisms of kinesthesis. Recent evidence (Marteniuk, 1971; Mountcastle et al., 1963) indicates that the position sense is mediated by a prothetic continuum in which increased extent is represented by increased *intensity* of stimulation. Thus there is some justification for assuming (as Pepper and Herman did) that reinforcement and decay may result in strengthened and weakened traces, respectively, and that biases in movement length are necessary in order to match the stored level of stimulation at recall. The motor *STM* data do not, however, completely support this position.

With respect to the second prediction, Adams and Dijkstra (1966) showed that as the number of reinforcements of the criterion location was increased from 1 to 15, there was a tendency for algebraic errors to become more positive in keeping with the prediction from the Pepper-Herman model. That this tendency was only strong at the shortest retention intervals may indicate that the nature of the stored trace was being biased by the reinforcement procedures and that the decay at longer retention intervals was confounding this effect somewhat. Williams (1971) also showed that increased reinforcements led to more positive directional errors, but the effect was strongest at the long retention intervals, the opposite to the effect found by Adams and Dijkstra. Also, Montgomery (1970) found that more reinforcement, defined in his case by the time the subject remained at the criterion location (either zero or 10 seconds), tended to produce more negative errors, but the differences were not significant. Thus there appeared to be some support for this prediction of the Pepper and Herman hypothesis.

Third, the Pepper-Herman prediction that interpolated activities should increase muscular tension, produce augmentation of the trace, and lead to a positive response bias, was supported in the data they reanalyzed (Posner, 1967; Posner and Konick, 1966; Williams et al., 1969). Montgomery (1970) also showed that either digit classification or holding a weight (both of which should increase the general muscular tension) produced more positive biasing than the resting control conditions, supporting the Pepper-Herman model. However, the trend was opposite to that predicted by the model for very long movements, and this led Montgomery to conclude along with Posner (1967) and Stelmach (1970) that the type of forgetting was a function of the code used to store the information, with shorter positions being coded as movement lengths and longer positions as locations. One possibility is that the task used by Montgomery (1970) and Posner (1967), which was dial-setting, may have been coded verbally by analogy to the face of a clock, whereas the Pepper-Herman task (force estimation) did not permit such verbalization. More work is needed to resolve this difficulty.

The final prediction, that interpolated movement of the limb effecting the response should bias the recall in the direction of the interpolated movements, had received strong support in the Pepper and Herman (1970) data. Additional work published subsequent to this by Stelmach (1970), Patrick (1971), and Milone (1971) shows similar trends, and provides support for the Pepper-Herman model as well as the interference theory. The data support the hypothesis that the movement produced at recall is a "pooling" of the criterion trace and the interpolated traces.

The Pepper-Herman model has provided some structure to the diversity of findings in motor *STM,* and it appears to account for the data fairly well. Whether the exact mechanisms responsible for losses of motor information are those specified by Pepper and Herman will remain to be seen, but there is strong evidence that loss is by some type of interference process, working both retroactively and proactively. This provides some support for the idea that the verbal and motor systems may follow similar laws. Due to a lack of work on laws of motor *STM,* the data do not permit solid conclusions about whether motor *STM* and *LTM* should be considered to be similar or different systems.

Warm-Up Decrement

It was mentioned before that a memory loss is not necessarily the same as a retention loss because other factors could be at play at the retention test and decrease performance (a retention loss), while the habit could be left intact (no memory loss). A number of such factors have been mentioned (e.g., fatigue, boredom, drugs, etc.), but one of the most important is the decrement in performance which nearly always follows a short (e.g., 2-minute) period of no practice. This decrement occurs in nearly every task that has been studied, is found with rest periods as short as 2 minutes (Adams, 1952; Ammons, 1947a, 1947b; Carron, 1967), has been thought of as the need to "warm up" to the task, and has been unwisely termed "warm-up decrement" (*WUD*). Because *WUD* "behaves like" forgetting in either *STM* or *LTM* (it is evidenced by a retention loss over time), it has been referred to as the "second facet of forgetting" (Adams, 1961), and it therefore deserves attention as one of the factors which contribute to the loss in proficiency at the retention test.

WUD was first noticed, according to Adams (1961), in studies of work in the last part of the nineteenth century by Kraepelin and his students (Arai, 1912), who noticed that the first portion of the practice curve following rest was typified by a rapid rise in efficiency. Mosso (1906) gave reports of poets' and writers' need to "warm up" prior to performing and Wells (1908) found *WUD* in tapping tasks. More recently, its characteristics have been studied as a function of a host of variables. For example, *WUD* has been found to appear in both massed and distributed practice schedules (Adams, 1952; Digman, 1959), has been found in both discrete (Nacson and Schmidt, 1971; Schmidt and Nacson, 1971; Schmidt and Wrisberg, 1971) and continuous tasks (Adams, 1952), and decreases as a function of the number of practice trials (Barch, 1954; Welch and Henry, 1971). It is beyond the scope of this chapter to review the large body of literature dealing with *WUD,* but for an excellent review and discussion of the various theoretic positions surrounding it, see Adams (1961). The focus of the present discussion will be on the evidence and ideas presented since the Adams review, with a concentration on the various theories which have been proposed to explain *WUD,* and some of the evidence for them.

WUD as Forgetting. Simply because a number of researchers observed a rapidly disappearing decrement in performance and named it *WUD* for an assumed dependence upon the need to warm up to the task does not mean that such is the cause of *WUD.* Since forgetting (loss of habit) is thought to occur most rapidly immediately following the end of acquisition trials, it is entirely possible that the *WUD* which is typically observed is simply the initial stages of forgetting. The argument that the decrement both appears and is eliminated "too rapidly" in order to be forgetting (e.g., Welch and Henry, 1971, p. 83) does not solve the problem, as it is not known just how rapid the initial stages of long-term forgetting might be. An essential test of the distinction of *WUD* and forgetting is whether they follow different laws. Experimental manipulations which affect them in different ways would provide such evidence. If it cannot be shown that WUD and forgetting are explained by different laws, then it is scientifically most parsimonious to regard them as different aspects of the same phenomenon, forgetting.

Some early evidence was provided by Irion and his associates (Irion, 1948, 1949; Irion and Wham, 1951) that *WUD* and forgetting may be different processes and are therefore deserving of separate status. Irion showed that naming colors on the memory drum immediately prior to recall of verbal paired associates was beneficial to recall (relative to groups without such color naming), and the interpretation was that the color naming on the memory drum reinstated the rhythm of responding which reduced the *WUD* present on the verbal task. Since there is no reason to believe that the color naming created any positive transfer to the habit for the verbal paired associates, the improvement in performance was shown to be due to non-habit mechanisms, and explanation in terms of forgetting would not be possible. However, a number of investigators has failed to replicate Irion's findings (Hovland and Kurtz, 1951; Lazar, 1967; Rockway and Duncan, 1952; Whithey et al., 1949). Even so, recent evidence indicates that non-habit activities prior to the recall of motor tasks reduce the *WUD* (Nacson and Schmidt, 1971; Schmidt and Nacson, 1971; Schmidt and Wrisberg, 1971), and the position that *WUD* is different from forgetting has strong support at present.

Inhibition Hypothesis. The inhibition hypothesis (Eysenck, 1956) was derived from Hull postulates (1943) and stated that *WUD* was a result of the extinction of conditioned inhibition (*sIr*). The theory stated that *sIr* was a habit of not responding created by the reinforcing qualities of the dissipation of fatigue (*Ir*) when the subject rested. Then when the subject resumed practicing after the rest period, *sIr* was strong and produced a decrement in performance. The *sIr* was gradually extinguished (as in classic conditioning) because the habit *for* responding was being reinforced more often than was the habit for *not* responding (that is, *sIr*), and the latter became extinguished, resulting in the rapidly improving performance following rest. The fundamental prediction of this hypothesis was that no *WUD* should occur under distributed practice conditions since no *Ir* (the fatigue state) was available to be reduced when the subject rested, and hence no *sIr* (the cause of *WUD*) would be produced. This fundamental prediction was supported by Eysenck (1956) who found with the pursuit rotor that distributed practice schedules produced no *WUD* following rest while massed schedules produced a great deal of *WUD,* as predicted by the inhibition hypothesis. However, there is ample evidence of *WUD* in distributed practice (e.g., Adams, 1952; Ammons, 1950; Welch and Henry, 1971), and this led Adams to state that "Eysenck's hypothesis cannot be taken seriously" (Adams, 1961, p. 268).

The Activation Hypothesis. This hypothesis states that as the subject practices the task from trial to trial he develops an elevated level of activation (or arousal) which is allowed to dissipate over the rest period. When he returns to the task following rest, he resumes practice with a decrement in activation, and performance is depressed until the practice can reinstate the activation level. The hypothesis predicts that procedures which will increase the arousal level over the retention interval just prior to practice will reduce *WUD.* Evidence (Catalano, 1967; Catalano and Whalen, 1967) has indicated that treatments involving cranking an arm ergometer or squeezing a grip dynamometer (which presumably increase the activation level relative to resting) increased the reminiscence (the increment in performance over rest due to the dissipation of fatigue), and these findings might be taken to indicate that the *WUD* was reduced as a function of these treatments.* However, Wolfe (1970) attempted to measure *WUD* directly as a function of interpolated grip squeezing treatments designed to increase the activation level and failed to support the activation hypothesis. At present, there is no conclusive evidence for the activation hypothesis, and the Catalano findings could be explained by the activity-set hypothesis which will be presented later.

The Set Hypothesis. The hypothesis which has received the greatest attention over the years has been the set hypothesis, which states that the

---

* Since reminiscence is the gain in performance over rest due (usually) to a dissipation of fatigue, any decrease in *WUD* would elevate performance after the rest and be evidenced as increased reminiscence.

decrement in recall of the criterion task after a rest is due to the loss of set, which is defined as an "aggregate of postural and attentive adjustments which are positively related to the goal response" (Adams, 1961, p. 261). In addition, it consists of "various secondary responses [which] are learned, such as the patterns for visual receptors, proper postural attitudes, and muscular tensions" (Adams, 1961, p. 262). Although it is not completely obvious from reading the various definitions of set, Schmidt and Nacson (1971) have argued that the set hypothesis is an "identical elements" hypothesis which posits a non-habit state (the set) which is made up of elements closely related to the criterion task such as the proper stance or movements of the eyes in pursuit rotor performance, and the rhythm of responding in the Irion color-naming experiments. The rapid elimination of *WUD* with practice is thought to be due to the reinstatement of these specific adjustments.

Support for the set hypothesis has been mixed. The verbal experiments of Irion and his associates (Irion, 1948, 1949; Irion and Wham, 1951) have provided support for the set hypothesis with color naming as a neutral activity, but numerous experiments have failed to replicate these findings (Hovland and Kurtz, 1951; Lazar, 1967; Rockway and Duncan, 1952; Whithey et al., 1949). In motor behavior there have been a number of attempts to reinstate the lost set in a manner analogous to the color naming but, in general, neutral tasks which reduce *WUD* have not been found (Ammons, 1951; Hamilton and Mola, 1953; Walker et al., 1957). However, Adams (1955) and Rosenquist (1965, 1969) have shown that subjects who watched a partner perform on the pursuit rotor during a rest period and pressed a button when the partner was judged to be "off target" showed less *WUD* on subsequent pursuit rotor practice than did subjects who simply rested, and the implication was that the watching of the performance decreased the *WUD* in the visual following response. Also, Barch (1963) showed that transfer from left- to right-hand pursuit rotor performance resulted in less *WUD* on the right-hand task when the transfer was immediate than when 24 hours elapsed, with the implication that the set which was reinstated by the left-hand task was lost again when subjects waited 24 hours to transfer. However, Spatz and Irion (1969) have failed to replicate Barch's findings. Thus, it appears that while there is some support for the set hypothesis, there are a number of instances of contradiction as well. Although it is possible that the experiments which have tested the set hypothesis have not provided fair tests of that view, another possibility is that the assumptions underlying set, with its rather task-specific nature, were wrong. A hypothesis in terms of a more generalized set which underlies the criterion response might provide a better alternative. Thus, Nacson and Schmidt (1971) proposed an alternative to the set hypothesis which they termed the activity-set hypothesis.

The Activity-Set Hypothesis. The activity-set hypothesis is somewhat similar to the set hypothesis. It proposes a non-habit internal state (the activity set) which is lost over the retention interval, but the activity set is seen as a *generalized* readiness to respond which is appropriate for any one of a given class of responses rather than the specific readiness defined by the set. This activity set is thought to consist of an aggregate of adjustments which are created by practice on the criterion task. For example, activation must stabilize at some optimum level according to the type of task performed, since Martens and Landers (1970) have shown that both too much and too little activation can be detrimental to performance. Also, it is well known that subjects adjust their speed-accuracy trade-off to a value which is compatible with instructions and nature of the task (Fitts, 1966). Further, the subject must adjust his expectancy for upcoming events in the practice sequence, and such expectancy effects are easily shown in reaction-time situations (e.g., Gottsdanker, 1970). Also he must adjust his attention to appropriate sources of feedback, with some tasks requiring attention to visual feedback (e.g., choice reaction time) and other tasks requiring attention to proprioceptive feedback (e.g., blindfolded positioning). There are undoubtedly other mechanisms, but the basic point is that all of these mechanisms come into adjustment so that they support the type of task being performed, with this internal, multidimensional state defining the activity set. This activity set is appropriate for *any* member of a narrow class of activities having the same response requirements, and it is assumed that the activity set for blindfolded positioning is appropriate for *any* other blindfolded positioning task. However, when the requirements of the task change, such as by adding vision or force to the response, the underlying activity set changes also, and it is subjectively easy to see that the activity set for threading a needle is different from that for producing maximum grip force.

The activity-set hypothesis states that as the subject practices the task he brings all of the component mechanisms into adjustment, so that he is prepared to respond well to the task at hand. When he rests, the various mechanisms go "out of adjustment" and the activity set is lost, either by a process of "decay" in which the levels of the mechanisms spontaneously drift to other values, or by a process of replacement (interference) in which the activity set is replaced by the activity set of another activity, possibly that for efficient resting. Returning to the criterion task following rest quickly reinstates the lost activity set, but not before the subject has performed poorly on a number of trials, and the result is the rapidly diminishing *WUD* seen in most motor tasks.

Schmidt and his associates (Nacson and Schmidt, 1971; Schmidt and Barnett, 1971; Schmidt and Nacson, 1971; Schmidt and Wrisberg, 1971) have provided strong support for this hypothesis. In the first of these experiments, Nacson and Schmidt (1971) used a right-hand non-visual force estimation task. All groups were given a 10-minute rest after 20 trials, and then had 10 additional trials. The activity during the rest period was the variable of chief interest. Group REST simply rested and read magazines for the entire 10 minutes. Another group (EXP) practiced a left-hand, non-visual force estimation task. This task was designed to use the same activity set as the right-hand task since it was a member of the same class (e.g., blindfolded force estimation), but did not provide habit strength for the right-hand task since a different apparatus, criterion tension, and musculature were used. The activity-set hypothesis would predict that the left-hand task would instate the activity set required for that class of tasks, and would eliminate *WUD* relative to the group which simply rested. A third group (ACT) was controlled for the effects of activation produced by the left-hand activities, and this group performed left-hand force estimation trials, but they had the use of vision and no particular tension was learned. This task was seen as a member of a different class than the criterion task and it should not reduce *WUD* on the criterion task since it provided an inappropriate activity set.

The results of this experiment are presented in figure 2-1. Following the rest period, Group REST showed considerable *WUD*, a result which is typical of other studies using tasks such as this. However, Group EXP, which had the activity set reinstated by the left-hand task, showed nearly no *WUD*, and considerably less error than Group REST. The activation control group

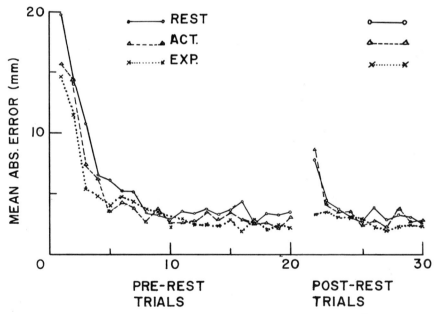

Fig. 2-1. A comparison of the effect of activities during rest on retention (*From Nacson and Schmidt, 1971*).

(ACT) showed slightly more *WUD* than Group REST and considerably more than Group EXP, and the statistical analysis indicated that Group EXP differed significantly from both Groups REST and ACT, the latter two not differing from each other. The interpretation is that the left-hand force estimation task reinstated the lost activity set, reducing the *WUD* on subsequent right-hand practice, and that the activating effects of this task, *per se*, were not responsible. This experiment was repeated with a linear positioning task with similar results, and a third experiment ruled out the effects of motivation from the *KR* provided in the EXP treatment as an explanation (Nacson and Schmidt, 1971).

Subsequent work with the activity-set hypothesis (Schmidt and Nacson, 1971) has indicated that the reinstated activity set is completely lost in approximately 25 to 40 seconds, and can be disrupted completely by activities which are of a different class than the criterion task. Schmidt and Wrisberg (1971) also showed that the activity set could be reinstated in tasks requiring rapid speed of limb movement, adding to the generality of the earlier findings.

In addition to supporting the predictions for the activity-set hypothesis, the findings just presented have important consequences for a number of other hypotheses for *WUD*. First, they invalidate the hypothesis that *WUD* is another aspect of forgetting (that is, loss of habit strength for the task) since the performance on the criterion task was improved using techniques which had nothing to do with the habit strength for the task, using different musculature, apparatus, side of body, criterion forces and locations, etc. If *WUD* was simply the loss of habit, then the techniques used should have been ineffective in reducing the errors on the criterion task. Second, the findings invalidated the activation hypothesis since the activation task (Group ACT) did not reduce the *WUD* relative to resting in one experiment (Fig. 2-1) and actually produced *increased WUD* relative to resting in a positioning experiment (Nacson and Schmidt, 1971, Exp. II). Although the rejection of this hypothesis is not as strong as it might be since the activation activities during the retention interval were relatively "mild" so that they would be comparable to the treatment used with Group EXP, they nonetheless provide no support for the activation hypothesis. Third, and most important, the findings invalidate the set hypothesis, which states that the set is specific to the task, being composed of postural adjustments, eye movements, etc., which are components of the task. It states that practicing tasks without these common components would not reduce *WUD*. However, the activities of Group EXP, which had no components in common with the criterion task, eliminated *WUD* for the criterion task, and the set hypothesis cannot explain these findings. Thus, there is strong evidence for the activity set notion of *WUD*, in which the *WUD* is the loss over rest of essential adjustments of the central mechanisms underlying the response.

SUMMARY AND CONCLUSIONS

Experimental psychologists in departments of psychology have provided an enormous contribution to the field of motor behavior, and the donations have been of many types. There has been a large number of individuals who have contributed their talents to the understanding of motor behavior as a primary research interest. Also, another large group of scientists, although probably not primarily interested in motor behavior for its own sake, has contributed a great deal of research dealing with man-machine systems, industrial psychology, and vehicle control, which is of relevance for an understanding of motor behavior. In addition, workers in experimental psychology have contributed numerous important theories for other types of performances, notably verbal learning and forgetting, and these theories are of potential use to those interested in motor skills. Important methodologies including designs for teasing out effects of confounded variables and the very important statistical techniques used in motor behavior research have been developed for the most part by experimental psychologists. Also, in testing a number of theoretic propositions (e.g., Hull's theory), experimental psychologists have developed a great deal of data on motor skills which is of use to motor behaviorists in developing newer and more powerful theories about motor skills. Finally, the methodology which has evolved over the last 100 years has left a legacy for those interested in motor behavior, perhaps as their greatest contribution. Each of the various contributions just mentioned occurs in any discussion of the research in motor skills, and the preceding discussion of the recent developments in the area of the retention of motor skills shows all of these contributions to be present in the motor retention field. Irion's statement (1966) to the effect that "the history of motor skills research *is*, in large measure, a history of experimental psychology" (1966, p. 2) could be strengthened according to the arguments presented here to state that the field of motor skills *is* the field of experimental psychology, regardless of where that research might be conducted.

References

Adams, J. A. Warm-up decrement in performance on the pursuit rotor. *American Journal of Psychology,* 1952, 65, 404–414.

Adams, J. A. A source of decrement in psychomotor performance. *Journal of Experimental Psychology,* 1955, 49, 390–394.

Adams, J. A. The second facet of forgetting: A review of warm-up decrement. *Psychological Bulletin,* 1961, 58, 257–273.

Adams, J. A. Motor skills. *Annual Review of Psychology,* 1964, 15, 181–202.

Adams, J. A. *Human memory.* New York: McGraw Hill, 1967.

Adams, J. A. A closed-loop theory of motor learning. *Journal of Motor Behavior,* Vol. 3, 1971.

Adams, J. A., & Dijkstra, S. Short-term memory for motor responses. *Journal of Experimental Psychology,* 1966, 71, 314–318.

Adams, J. A., & Hufford, L. E. Contributions of a part-task trainer to the learning and relearning of a time-shared flight maneuver. *Human Factors,* 1962, 4, 159–170.

Adams, J. A., & Reynolds, B. Effects of shift in distribution of practice conditions following interpolated rest. *Journal of Experimental Psychology,* 47, 1954, 26–32.

Ammons, R. B. Acquisitions of motor skill: I. Quantitative analysis and theoretical formulation. *Psychological Review,* 1947, 54, 263–281. (a)

Ammons, R. B. Acquisition of motor skill: II. Rotary pursuit performance with continuous practice before and after a single rest. *Journal of Experimental Psychology,* 1947, 37, 393–411. (b)

Ammons, R. B. Acquisition of motor skill: III. Effects of initially distributed practice on rotary pursuit performance. *Journal of Experimental Psychology,* 1950, 40, 777–787.

Ammons, R. B. Effects of pre-practice activities on rotary pursuit performance. *Journal of Experimental Psychology,* 1951, 41, 187–191.

Ammons, R. B., Farr, R. G., Bloch, E., Neumann, E., Dey, M., Marion, R., & Ammons, C. H. Long-term retention of perceptual motor skills. *Journal of Experimental Psychology,* 1958, 55, 318–328.

Arai, T. Mental fatigue. *Teachers College Contributions to Education,* 1912, No. 54

Ascoli, K. M., & Schmidt, R. A. Proactive interference in short-term motor retention. *Journal of Motor Behavior,* 1969, 1, 29-36.

Bahrick. H. P. Retention curves: Facts or artifacts? *Psychological Bulletin,* 1964, 61, 188–194.

Bahrick, H. P., Fitts, P. M., & Briggs, G. E. Learning curves–facts or artifacts? *Psychological Bulletin,* 1957, 54, 256–268.

Bahrick, H. P., & Shelley, C. H. Time-sharing as an index of automatization. *Journal of Experimental Psychology,* 1958, 56, 288–293.

Barch, A. M. Warm-up in massed and distributed pursuit rotor performance. *Journal of Experimental Psychology,* 1954, 47, 357–361.

Barch, A. M. Bilateral transfer of warm-up in rotary pursuit. *Perceptual and Motor Skills,* 1963, 17, 723–726.

Battig, W. F., Nagel, E. H., Voss, J. F., & Brogden, W. F. Transfer and retention of bidimensional compensatory tracking after extended practice. *American Journal of Psychology,* 1957, 70, 75–80.

Bell, H. M. Retention of pursuit rotor skill after one year. *Journal of Experimental Psychology,* 1950, 40, 648–649.

Bilodeau, E. A., & Bilodeau, I. McD. Motor skills learning. *Annual Review of Psychology,* 1961, 12, 243–280.

Boring, E. G. *A. history of experimental psychology.* New York: Appleton-Century-Crofts, 1950.

Botwinick, J., & Thompson, L. W. Premotor and motor components of reaction time. *Journal of Experimental Psychology,* 1966, 71, 9–15.

Briggs, G. E. Retroactive inhibition as a function of the degree of original and interpolated learning. *Journal of Experimental Psychology,* 1957, 53, 60–67.

Brown, J. Some tests of the decay theory of immediate memory. *Quarterly Journal of Experimental Psychology,* 1958, 10, 12–21.

Bryan, W. L., & Harter, N. Studies on the telegraphic language: The acquisition of a hierarchy of habits. *Psychological Review,* 1897, 6, 345–375.

Candland, D. K. *Psychology: The experimental approach.* New York: McGraw-Hill, 1968.

Carron, A. V. Performance and learning in a discrete motor task under massed versus distributed practice. Unpublished Ed.D. dissertation, University of California, Berkeley, 1967.

Catalano, J. F. Arousal as a factor in reminiscence. *Perceptual and Motor Skills,* 1967, 74, 1171–1180.

Catalano, J. F., & Whalen, P. M. Factors in recovery from performance decrement: activation, inhibition, and warm-up. *Perceptual and Motor Skills,* 1967, 24, 1223–1231.

Conrad, R. Acoustic confusions in immediate memory. *British Journal of Psychology,* 1964, 65, 75–84.

Cronbach, L. J. The two disciplines of scientific psychology. *American Psychologist,* 1957, 12, 671–684.

Digman, J. M. Growth of motor skill as a function of distribution of practice. *Journal of Experimental Psychology,* 1959, 57, 310–316.

Duncan, C. P., & Underwood, B. J. Retention of transfer in motor learning after 24 hours and after 14 months. *Journal of Experimental Psychology,* 1953, 46, 445–452.

English, H. B., & English, A. C. *A comprehensive dictionary of psychological and psychoanalytical terms.* New York: David McKay, 1966.

Estes, W. K. The problem of interference from curves based upon group data. *Psychological Bulletin,* 1956, 53, 134–140.

Eysenck, H. J. Warmup in pursuit rotor learning as a function of conditioned inhibition. *Acta Psychologica,* 1956, 12, 349–370.

Fitts, P. M. Cognitive aspects of information processing: III. Set for speed versus accuracy. *Journal of Experimental Psychology,* 1966, 71, 849–957.

Fleishman, E. A. The description and prediction of perceptual-motor skill learning. In R. Glaser (ed.) *Training research and education.* Pittsburgh: University of Pittsburgh Press, 1962.

Fleishman, E. A., & Parker, J. F. Factors in the retention and relearning of perceptual-motor skill. *Journal of Experimental Psychology,* 1962, 64, 215–226.

Gottsdanker, R. Uncertainty, timekeeping, and simple reaction time. *Journal of Motor Behavior,* 1970, 2, 245–260.

Hamilton, C. E., & Mola, W. R. Warm-up effect in human maze learning. *Journal of Experimental Psychology,* 1953, 45, 437–441.

Hellyer, S. Supplementary report: Frequency of stimulus presentation and short-term decrement in recall. *Journal of Experimental Psychology,* 1962, 64, 650.

Hick, W. E. Discontinuous functioning of the human operator in pursuit tasks. *Quarterly Journal of Experimental Psychology,* 1948, 1, 36–57.

Hick, W. E. Reaction time for the amendment of a response. *Quarterly Journal of Experimental Psychology,* 1949, 1, 175–179.

Hovland, C. I., & Kurtz, K. H. Experimental studies in rote learning theory: IX. Influence of work-decrement factors on verbal learning. *Journal of Experimental Psychology,* 1951, 42, 265–272.

Hull, C. L. *Principles of behavior: An introduction to behavior theory.* New York: Appleton-Century-Crofts, 1943.

Irion, A. L. The relation of "set" to retention. *Psychological Review,* 1948, 55, 336–341.

Irion, A. L. Retention and warming-up effects in paired associates learning. *Journal of Experimental Psychology,* 1949, 39, 669–675.

Irion, A. L. A brief history of research on the acquisition of skill. In E. A. Bilodeau (ed.) *Acquisition of skill.* New York: Academic Press, 1966.

Irion, A. L., & Wham, D. S. Recovery from retention loss as a function of amount of pre-recall warming up. *Journal of Experimental Psychology,* 1951, 41, 242–246.

Keppel, G., & Underwood, B. J. Proactive inhibition in short-term retention of single items. *Journal of Verbal Learning and Verbal Behavior,* 1962, 1, 153–161.

Kimble, G. A. An experimental test of a two-factor theory of inhibition. *Journal of Experimental Psychology,* 1949, 39, 15–23.

Lachman, S. J. *The foundations of science.* Detroit: Hamilton Press, 1956.

Lazar, G. Warm-up before recall of paired adjectives. *Journal of Verbal Learning and Verbal Behavior,* 1967, 6, 321–327.

Lersten, K. C. Retention of skill on the Rho apparatus after one year. *Research Quarterly,* 1969, 40, 418–419.

Lewis, D., McAllister, D. E., & Adams, J. A. Facilitation and interference in performance of the modified Mashburn apparatus: I. The effects of varying the amount of original learning. *Journal of Experimental Psychology,* 1951, 41, 247–260.

Marteniuk, R. G. An informational analysis of active kinesthesis as measured by amplitude of movement. *Journal of Motor Behavior,* 1971, 3, 69–77.

Martens, R., & Landers, D. M. Motor performance under stress: A test of the inverted-U hypothesis. *Journal of Personality and Social Psychology,* 1970, 16, 29–37.

Martin, H. A. Long-term retention of a discrete motor task. Unpublished Masters thesis, University of Maryland, 1970.

McAllister, D. E. Retroactive facilitation and interference as a function of the level of learning. *American Journal of Psychology,* 1952, 65, 218–232.

McAllister, D. E., & Lewis, D. Facilitation and interference in performance on the modified Mashburn apparatus: II. The effects of varying the amount of interpolated learning. *Journal of Experimental Psychology,* 1951, 41, 356–363.

McGuigan, F. J. *Experimental psychology: A methodological approach.* Englewood Cliffs, N.J.: Prentice-Hall, 1968.

Melnick, M. J. Effects of overlearning on the retention of a gross motor skill. *Research Quarterly,* 1971, 42, 60–69.

Meyers, J. Retention of balance coordination learning as influenced by extended lay-offs. *Research Quarterly,* 1967, 38, 72–78.

Miller, G. A. The magical number seven, plus or minus two: Some limits on our capacity for processing information. *Psychological Review,* 1956, 63, 81–97.

Milone, F. Interference in motor short-term memory. Unpublished Masters thesis, Penn State University, 1971.

Montgomery, J. M. Interaction of movement length and interpolated activity in short-term motor memory. Paper presented at the Second Canadian Psycho Motor Learning and Sports Psychology Symposium. University of Windsor, October, 1970.

Mosso, A. *Fatigue.* (Translation by M. Drummond). New York: Putnam, 1906.

Mountcastle, V. B., Poggio, G. R., & Warner, G. The relation of thalamic cell response to peripheral stimuli varied over an intensive continuum. *Journal of Neurophysiology,* 1963, 26, 807–834.

Murdock, B. B. Transfer designs and formulas. *Psychological Bulletin,* 1957, 54, 313–326.

Nacson, J., & Schmidt, R. A. The activity-set hypothesis for warm-up decrement. *Journal of Motor Behavior,* 1971, 3, 1–16.

Naylor, J. C., & Briggs, G. E. Long-term retention of learned skill. A review of the literature. *U.S.A.F. WADD Technical Report,* 1961, No. 61–390.

Neumann, E., & Ammons, R. B. Acquisition and long-term retention of a simple serial perceptual-motor task. *Journal of Experimental Psychology,* 1957, 53, 159–161.

Noble, C. E. The learning of psychomotor skills. *Annual Review of Psychology,* 1965, 19, 203–250.

Norrie, M. L. Short-term memory trace decay in kinesthetically monitored force production. *Research Quarterly,* 1968, 39, 640–646.

Norrie, M. L. Number of reinforcements and memory trace for kinesthetically monitored force reproduction. *Research Quarterly,* 1969, 40, 338–342.

Nottebohm, F. The ontogeny of bird song. *Science,* 1970, 161, 950–956.

Patrick, J. The effect of interpolated motor activities in short-term motor memory. *Journal of Motor Behavior,* 1971, 3, 39–48.

Pepper, R. L., & Herman, L. M. Decay and interference effects in the short-term retention of a discrete motor act. *Journal of Experimental Psychology,* 1970, 83, (Monograph Supplement 2).

Peterson, L. R., & Gentile, A. Proactive interference as a function of time between tests. *Journal of Experimental Psychology,* 1965, 70, 473–478.

Peterson, L. R., & Peterson, M. J. Short-term retention of individual verbal items. *Journal of Experimental Psychology,* 1959, 58, 193–198.

Pew, R. W. Acquisition of hierarchical control over the temporal organization of a skill. *Journal of Experimental Psychology,* 1966, 71, 764–771.

Posner, M. I. Short-term memory systems in human information processing. *Acta Psychologica,* 1967, 27, 267–284.

Posner, M. I., & Konick, A. F. Short-term retention of visual and kinesthetic information. *Organizational Behavior and Human Performance,* 1966, 1, 71–86.

Postman, L., & Egan, J. P. *Experimental psychology: An introduction.* New York: Harper, 1949.

Rockway, M. R., & Duncan, C. P. Pre-recall warming-up in verbal retentions. *Journal of Experimental Psychology,* 1952, 43, 305–312.

Rosenquist, H. S. The visual response component of rotary pursuit tracking. *Perceptual and Motor Skills,* 1965, 21, 555–560.

Rosenquist, H. S. Rotary pursuit performance as a function of watching demonstrations at slower speeds. *Psychonomic Science,* 1969, 14, 157–159.

Ryan, E. D. Retention of stabilometer and pursuit rotor skills. *Research Quarterly,* 1962, 33, 593–599.

Ryan, E. D. Retention of stabilometer performance over extended periods of time. *Research Quarterly,* 1965, 36, 46–54.

Schmidt, R. A. Proactive inhibition in retention of discrete motor skill. Proceedings of the International Society of Sports Psychology, Washington, D.C., October, 1968.

Schmidt, R. A. Retroactive interference and amount of original learning in verbal and motor tasks. *Research Quarterly,* 1971, 42, 314–326.

Schmidt, R. A., & Ascoli, K. M. Attention demand during storage of traces in motor short-term memory. *Acta Psychologica,* 1970, 34, 497–504. (a)

Schmidt, R. A., & Ascoli, K. M. Intertrial intervals and motor short-term memory. *Research Quarterly,* 1970, 41, 432–438. (b)

Schmidt, R. A., & Barnett, M. Unpublished manuscript, 1971.

Schmidt, R. A., & Nacson, J. Further tests of the activity-set hypothesis for warm-up decrement. *Journal of Experimental Psychology,* 1971, 90, 56–64.

Schmidt, R. A., & Stelmach, G. E. Postural set as a factor in short-term motor retention. *Psychonomic Science,* 1968, 13, 223–224.

Schmidt, R. A., & Stull, G. A. Premotor and motor reaction time as a function of preliminary muscular tension. *Journal of Motor Behavior,* 1970, 2, 96–110.

Schmidt, R. A., & Wrisberg, C. A. The activity-set hypothesis and warm-up decrement in a task requiring rapid speed of movement. *Journal of Motor Behavior,* 1971, 3, 318-325.

Scott, K. G., Whimbey, A. E., & Dunning, C. Separate LTM and STM systems? *Psychonomic Science,* 1967, 7, 55–56.

Sidman, M. A note on functional relations obtained from group data. *Psychological Bulletin,* 1952, 49, 263–269.

Spatz, K. C., Jr., & Irion, A. L. Note on the transfer of bilateral warm-up pursuit rotor performance. *Journal of Experimental Psychology,* 1969, 81, 607–608.

Sperling, G. A model for visual memory tasks. *Human Factors,* 1963, 5, 19–31.

Stelmach, G. E. Prior positioning responses as a factor in short-term retention of a simple motor task. *Journal of Experimental Psychology,* 1969, 81, 523–526.

Swift, E. J. The acquisition of skill in type-writing: A contribution to the psychology of learning. *Psychological Bulletin,* 1904, 1, 295–305.

Underwood, B. J. *Experimental psychology.* New York: Appleton-Century-Croft, 1949.

Underwood, B. J. Interference and forgetting. *Psychological Review,* 1957, 64, 49–60.

Underwood, B. J. Degree of learning and the measurement of retention. *Journal of Verbal Learning and Verbal Behavior,* 1964, 3, 112–129.

Wade, M. G., & Ellis, M. J. Measurement of free range activity in children as modified by social and environmental complexity. *American Journal of Clinical Nutrition,* 1971, in press.

Walker, L. C., DeSoto, C. B., & Shelly, M. W. Rest and warm-up in bilateral transfer on a pursuit rotor task. *Journal of Experimental Psychology,* 1957, 53, 394–404.

Welch, M., & Henry, F. M. Individual differences in various parameters of motor learning. *Journal of Motor Behavior,* 1971, 3, 78–95.

Wells, F. L. Normal performance on the tapping test before and during practice with special reference to fatigue phenomenon. *American Journal of Psychology,* 1908, 19, 437–483.

Whithey, S., Buxton, C. E., & Elkin, A. Control of rest interval activities in serial verbal learning. *Journal of Experimental Psychology,* 1949, 39, 173–176.

Wickelgren, W. Acoustic similarity and retroactive interference in short-term memory. *Journal of Verbal Learning and Verbal Behavior,* 1965, 4, 53–61.

Williams, H. L., Beaver, W. S., Spence, M. T., & Rundell, O. H. Digital and kinesthetic memory with interpolated information processing. *Journal of Experimental Psychology,* 1969, 80, 530–536.

Williams, I. D. The effects of practice trials and prior learning on motor memory. *Journal of Motor Behavior,* 1971, 3, 289–300.

Wilson, D. M. The central nervous control of flight in a locust. *Journal of Experimental Biology,* 1961, 38, 471–490.

Wolfe, K. F., Jr. Activation as a factor in warm-up decrement. Unpublished Masters thesis, University of Maryland, 1970.

Woodworth, R. S., & Schlosberg, H. *Experimental psychology.* New York: Holt, 1954.

Chapter 3

COMPARATIVE PSYCHOLOGY

STANLEY C. RATNER
Michigan State University

This chapter is organized around three objectives. The first is to review various approaches to comparative psychology that have preceded the present view, that comparative psychology involves the application of the comparative method. The second objective is to present the major elements of the comparative method, and the third is to relate the comparative method to a problem in the psychomotor domain.

The position that comparative psychology involves a method leads to our working definition of the topic. *We define comparative psychology as the application of the comparative method to the study of behavior or organisms including man* (Denny and Ratner, 1970). While this definition says nothing about comparisons per se, the reader will see that one of the stages of the comparative method involves comparison. However, one of the central themes of the present approach to comparative psychology is that making comparisons in the context of the comparative method is a rigorous and advanced activity that requires prior work at a number of preliminary stages. In other words, making comparisons is an almost ubiquitous human activity that can be either trivial or powerful, depending on the thoroughness of the preliminary work and the rigor of the comparison.

The behavior process that we will use to illustrate the application of comparative psychology to the psychomotor domain is the process of *habituation.* Groves and Thompson (1970, p. 49) say that "habituation defined simply as decreased response to repeated stimulation, is perhaps the most elementary and ubiquitous form of behavioral plasticity." This definition is congruent with the majority of descriptive definitions of

56

habituation (Ratner, 1970) and suggests the relations between habituation and psychomotor processes. That is, response decrements are conspicuous aspects of the psychomotor domain which occur for a variety of behaviors and a variety of species. In addition, research on habituation is sufficiently advanced to permit the application of a number of stages of the comparative method.

THE CHANGING FOCUS OF COMPARATIVE PSYCHOLOGY

The topic of comparative studies concerns investigators in all but a few areas of scholarship. So, for example, an extensive comparative literature exists in such diverse areas as follows: religion, embryology, geography, sociology, economics, psychology, physiology, education, political science, and literature. When we review writings in these and other comparative areas, we find several important themes. One theme relates to the question of the circumstances in which an area develops comparative study. A second theme relates to the identification of some common elements in the development of the various areas of comparative study. The third theme, more obscure than the others, relates to the idea that *comparative study refers to a method of analysis* rather than a particular content or subject matter. Thus, in the present section we will consider each of the three themes in broad outline, and in the next section of the chapter we will specify, characterize, and illustrate the comparative method as it applies to the analysis of habituation.

When Is An Investigation Comparative?

The answer to the question of the circumstances in which an investigator uses comparative analysis is remarkably simple. He uses the technique whenever he becomes aware of diversity among the things he studies. So, for example, the early students of biology noted the diversity of biologic forms, structures, and processes. Aristotle (Ross, 1942) wrote in detail of this diversity in animal form and so by definition and probably by intention Aristotle provided some of the early documents in comparative biology and psychology. Among these documents are his books entitled *Parva Naturalia,* and *De Anima* (Ross, 1942). Aristotle displays his appreciation of diversity of animal form and behavior in the following selection (Ross, 1942, *De Anima,* Section 414a,b):

> Of the psychic powers above enumerated some kinds of living things, as we have said, possess all, some less than all, others one only. Those we have mentioned are the nutritive, the appetitive, the sensory, the locomotive, and the power of thinking. Plants have none but the first, the nutritive, while another order of living things has this *plus* the sensory. If any order of living things has the sensory, it must also have the appetitive; for appetite is the genus of which desire, passion, and wish are the species; now all animals have one sense at least, viz. touch, and whatever has the capacity for pleasure and pain and therefore has the pleasant and the painful present to it, and wherever these are present, there is

desire for desire is just appetition of what is pleasant. Further, all animals have the sense for food (for touch is the sense for food); the food of all living things consists of what is dry, moist, hot, cold, and these are the qualities apprehended by touch; all other sensible qualities are apprehended by touch only indirectly. Sounds, colours, and odours contribute nothing to nutriment; flavours fall within the field of tangible qualities. Hunger and thirst are forms of desire, hunger a desire for what is dry and hot, thirst a desire for what is cold and moist; flavour is a sort of seasoning added to both. We must later clear up these points, but at present it may be enough to say that all animals that possess the sense of touch have also appetition. The case of imagination is obscure; we must examine it later. Certain kinds of animals possess in addition the power of locomotion, and still another order of animate beings, i.e. man and possibly any other order of being like man or superior to him, the power of thinking, i.e. mind.

Since the primary focus of this chapter is comparative analysis in psychology, it is necessary to agree that the events of psychology have diversity. For present purposes, we will do this by example. Psychology deals with behaviors or activities of organisms. While students of psychology do not yet have a unified or generally accepted language to describe diversity of behaviors, it is clear that behavior includes such activity as eyeblink, feeding, sexual activities, hysterical paralysis, learning, memory, etc.

The question may be raised as to why the observation of diversity of events moves the investigator towards comparative analysis. Once again, the answer is relatively simple and direct. If the investigator feels that a number of different events belong in his domain for his study, he must somehow *organize* and *relate* these different things to each other. These tasks of establishing the organization and relations among diverse events are the basis of comparative analysis. The superficial simplicity of the tasks must be viewed in terms of the fact that biology required several millenia to develop an adequate approximation of understanding their events in order to organize the observation of diverse species and then to understand the relations of the species to each other (Darwin's theory of evolution).

It seems clear that students of psychology will require some reasonable amount of time to achieve the success similar to that of students of biology. However, it is also clear that the early stages of comparative analysis have been underway in psychology for at least several hundred years. In addition, a number of approaches to comparative analysis has been tried in social science, including psychology. Thus, we are not starting anew, and perhaps we can profit from the success of other areas of comparative study. To date, in the social sciences this has been most effectively done by anthropologists. However, it is of importance to review and consider some of the familiar approaches to comparative analysis in order to understand how prior investigators have dealt with diversity of events and in order to identify some difficulties of these approaches.

Early Approaches to Comparative Analysis and Problems with Them

Comparative analysis has taken a number of different forms that have been influenced by the development in general ideas about the nature of science, the nature of social science, and particularly, the success of biology in comparative analysis. The success of biology in comparative analysis was conspicuously associated with Charles Darwin's postulations in *The Origin of Species* (1863). His great and provocative insights prompted the forward rush of comparative analysis in other areas also, including psychology. This forward rush involved adopting aspects of the theory of evolution although the adoptions were typically uncritical, unfounded, and inaccurate, as we will describe in later sections. Other approaches to comparative analysis that preceded and followed the Darwinian period are early functionalism, structural or capricious comparison, problem or process comparison, and the evolutionary approach.

Early Functionalism. Aristotle devised a classification of behavior and biologic process in terms of their broad functions. This approach allowed a general description of all living organisms in terms of behavior functions that the organisms shared. Among these behavior functions are discrimination, nutrition, and locomotion. Aristotle's treatise is presented in *De Anima* and *Parva Naturalia* (Ross, 1942) and a sample of it is presented on the preceding pages. Another characteristic of the early functional approach is the amazing amount of background information that was collected and used for its development. The functional approach to comparative analysis disappeared from the social sciences, but it remained in biology to a large extent.

Structural or Capricious Comparison. This approach to comparative analysis has appeared in virtually every area of study. It involves selecting two different things or activities and measuring them in order to describe the features of similarity and features of difference. While comparison is clearly explicit in this approach, the conclusions that can be drawn from such comparisons are typically uninteresting and trivial. As Oscar Lewis (1956, p. 259) points out, "Comparison is a generic aspect of human thought rather than a specific method of anthropology or any other discipline." In this case, Lewis is reminding us that comparison, in a simple sense, is a relatively trivial activity. Thus, in the absence of useful concepts, valid reasons for comparison, and some theory, we can consider comparison *per se* to be a weak process for analysis. This is particularly true when comparisons are made between *formal* or *structural* properties of events.

Many examples of formal or structural comparisons exist in psychology. These are called *capricious comparison* (Denny and Ratner, 1970) because the investigator could have used any pair or trio of events for comparison. In one type of such comparisons, the investigator puts individual animals of two or more species through some apparatus such as a maze. He then calculates the scores of each species and states that the score for one species is greater or lesser than that of the other. Positive benefits of structural or capricious comparison do exist. One such benefit is that information is collected and deposited in archives for use as background information, although this poses the usual problems of retrieving items of information that are not classified in a functional way. Thus, the general positive consequence of capricious comparison is *not* inherent in the comparison, but in the facts that are collected about the things that are capriciously compared.

Problem or Process Comparison. In this approach to comparative study the investigator selects some problem or process such as learning, and examines the process as it occurs in a variety of forms. So, for example, Bitterman (1960) and Dethier and Stellar (1964) are concerned with the comparative study of learning, by which they mean the study of learning across a variety of species and types of learning situations. Dethier and Stellar (1964, p. 81) first characterize learning as follows: "Of all of the behavioral characteristics of living organisms, perhaps none is as striking as the ability to learn." Then they examine the process in terms of the ideas of increasing neural complexity of animals and the increasing complexity of learning from habituation at one extreme to trial-and-error learning at the other.

This approach represents an advance over the approach of capricious comparison and occurs in comparative study for a number of different areas. For example, Bereday (1964), a comparative investigator in education, and Macridis and Brown (1964, p. 7), comparative political scientists, give detailed analyses of the logic and the procedures required for problems or process comparison. In the context of the present chapter, this approach is seen as an essential aspect of comparative analysis and one that moves comparative study to its final goals, but by itself it is incomplete.

The Evolutionary Approach. The success of comparative analysis was so great in biology that the *general theory of evolution* that resulted from the application of the comparative method strongly affected all other areas of comparative study. So, the evolutionary approach, meaning the application of aspects of the theory of evolution, appeared in such areas as anthropology, religion, economics, and psychology within a short time after the theory was available.

The evolutionary approach has taken a number of different forms in the social sciences, but all of them share the general idea that the structures or processes have undergone gradual changes along some dimension or dimensions, typically from primitive to advanced. In psychology, the evolutionary approach is usually keyed to evolutions of species and behavior. Thus, many psychologists assume that higher evolutionary forms have greater complexity of behavior.

While the evolutionary approach is very powerful under some conditions, it is deceptive under others. Specifically, it requires a full and subtle comprehension of evolution, either in the biologic sense or as an analog of the biologic process. However, inappropriate analogies are very easy to create when the thing used for the analog is not well understood. The errors of oversimplification of evolution and uncritical acceptance of it whenever diversity is observed have weakened the evolutionary approach in psychology. Hodos and Campbell (1969, p. 337) argue the point as follows:

The concept that all living animals can be arranged along a continuous "phylogenetic scale" with man at the top is inconsistent with contemporary views of animal evolution. Nevertheless, this arbitrary hierarchy continues to influence researchers in the field of animal behavior who seek to make inferences about the evolutionary development of a particular type of behavior. Comparative psychologists have failed to distinguish between data obtained from living representatives of a common evolutionary lineage and data from animals which represent divergent lineages. Only the former can provide a foundation for inferences about phylogenetic development of behavior patterns. The latter can provide information only about general mechanisms of adaptation and survival, which are not necessarily relevant to any specific evolutionary lineage. The widespread failure of comparative psychologists to take into account the zoological model of animal evolution when selecting animals for study and when interpreting behavioral similarities and differences has greatly hampered the development of generalizations with any predictive value.

COMPARATIVE METHOD: THE STAGES APPROACH

According to our definitions in the first section, comparative psychology is *not* a subject matter, but rather involves the application of the comparative method to the subject matter of psychology. The reader may then wonder why comparative psychology so often deals with lower animals. The answer to this question seems to lie in two characteristics of contemporary psychology. One is that some psychologists believe that comparative psychology is exclusively the study of lower animals. (I reject this idea.) The other characteristic is that aspects of each of the various approaches to comparative psychology involve the study of many species of animals. Thus, the coincidence of comparative psychology and study of animals is accurate but not exclusive.

The Analogy of Comparative and Quantitative Methods

The problem of the present treatise is to identify and describe the general characteristics of the comparative method as it is properly applied in psychology. I believe that the comparative method has been extraordinarily successful in biology and, like the quantitative method, the comparative method can be *stated* and adroitly *applied* in psychology. As in the quantitative method, the clear statement and adroit application of this method must be emphasized. Application of the axioms of geometry uncritically to a social process that achieves nothing does not mean that quantitative methods are defective. Rather, the investigator may not have understood the principles of the method or he may have applied them inappropriately.

It is clear that the development of the comparative method is less mature than that of the quantitative method. Thus, the comparative psychologist has the double problem of developing an immature method and at the same time advancing his area of study. This double problem is not unique to comparative study or to psychology, however. The students of physics frequently participate in the development of quantitative methods to advance their analyses of physical processes.

Another characteristic of the quantitative method is the degree of complexity and rigor that is now associated with it. Is this true of the comparative method? The answer is equivocal because the comparative method is still immature, so that the details of the stages and their applications are tentative. While we acknowledge the immaturity of the comparative method, its complexity can be illustrated by examining one of the stages that has received explicit attention from biologists. This is the stage of *classification* (taxonomy). Through the time of Linnaeus, the techniques of classification of biologic events involved an elaboration of principles used by Aristotle. Such classification used one characteristic of an animal group to show relations or differences in terms of other groups. Sokal and Sneath (1963) argue strongly against the principle of *monotypic classification* and refer to other biologists who are aware of the dilemmas associated with such simple procedures. They then bring together the intuitions of the critics of Aristotelian classification and refine the ideas into a technique of classification that they describe as *polytypic classification* and call *numerical taxonomy*. This technique uses a number of characteristics of animal groups and assesses similarities and differences between groups by numerical methods. So we see that this stage of comparative analysis can be characterized in terms of complexity and even rigor, much like some aspects of the quantitative method.

A third characteristic of the quantitative method is that it can be applied to any subject matter. We will show through the remaining sections that the comparative method can also be applied to a variety of subject matters if the assumptions necessary for comparative analysis can be met.

The Premise of the Stages Approach

The premise of the present work is that the comparative method consists of a number of interlocking and mutually supporting stages of research and theoretic activities. Support for this premise comes from a number of sources. These sources are the writings of comparative analysts in a variety of areas of social science and deductions from the examination of the history of comparative biology. While the validity of the stages approach cannot be established by citing writers who allude to it or by relating it verbally to the great success of biology, we will note several social scientists whose works have supported us and then we will proceed directly to an outline of the stages approach to comparative analysis.

A first approximation to the present stages approach was proposed by Ratner and Denny (1964, p. 4), who described comparative psychology as follows: "Five related objectives of comparative analysis can be identified: (1) to identify, characterize, and classify behavior processes of animals; (2) to understand the characteristics of behaviors sufficiently well to identify the animal form that shows the behavior most clearly or to its best advantage; (3) to establish and conceptualize relations between behaviors of similar species and different species; (4) to identify the origins of behavior processes and trace their developments both within and between species; and (5) to develop general theories that summarize, relate, and predict specific facts and relationships."

The objectives of comparative analysis identified by Ratner and Denny were only incompletely used in their review of comparative psychology, but they were used systematically by Ratner (1967) in a study of a complex reaction of animals that is commonly called "animal hypnosis." Between the time of the initial formulation of the objectives of comparative analysis and the formulation of the stages approach, support for the stages approach was found in the writings of Bereday (1964), Eggan (1954), and others.

The relations among the aspects of the stages approach and comparative biology are so intricate and important at each stage of the approach that we cannot treat them in detail. In general, we will focus on the importance of the long history of biology and the stages of development in this history that *preceded* the postulation of the general theory of evolution. Thus, we emphasize the activities of biology that were *precursors* to the development of the theory of evolution. We see the theory of evolution as the eventual and natural outcome of the interlocking and mutually supporting stages of comparative method. Clearly, no area of social science, including psychology, has developed far enough through the stages of comparative analysis to be at the brink of the general theory. However, the acceleration of research and theory of this century suggests that the absolute time for development of comparative analysis in areas such as psychology will be less than the absolute time that was necessary in biology. The present view of comparative analysis leads to the unusual conclusion that *chemistry is another area in which the comparative method evolved and was used in an effective way.*

An Outline of the Stages Approach to Comparative Analysis

The comparative method has at least six stages that require *sequential development.* The stages that comprise the comparative method are listed in table 3-1.

Three points about the relations among the stages of comparative analysis require emphasis. (1) The early development of each stage involves incomplete information and approximate formulations, but this state of affairs gradually changes as data and theory accumulate. (2) The development of each stage is influenced by the development of other stages, so that interdependence among the stages is typical and necessary. (3) The development within higher stages, especially V (origins and comparisons) and VI (general theory) is dependent on advances in the lower stages, especially

TABLE 3-1

The Stages Approach to Comparative Analysis*

Order	Stage	Major activity
I	Background information	Search for informal and formal information sources
II	Taxonomy	Develop functional classification system
III	Research preparations	Specify valid and reliable examples of each class
IV	Variables	Identify variables that affect classes
V	Origins and comparisons	Trace origins of classes and compare classes
VI	General theory	Identify general mechanisms that relate all classes

*Adapted from Denny and Ratner (1970).

stages II and III. Thus, we assume that an adequate general theory only appears after adequate classification and identification of the variables have occurred. In the early stage of chemistry, for example, general theories were proposed, but they were proposed without benefit of adequate classification of elements or adequate understanding of variables that affect chemical process. From a contemporary perspective, these theories are remarkable in the extent to which they reflect the prejudices of their times and the ingenuity of the theorist. The understanding of fire and its action provides a good example. The key concept was that of "phlogiston," a property of some objects such as wood. According to Asimov, (1965, p. 46), the German chemist G. E. Stahl (1660–1734) advanced the name phlogiston for the principle of inflammability. "Combustible objects, Stahl held, were rich in phlogiston, and the process of burning involved the loss of phlogiston to the air. What was left behind after combustion was without phlogiston and therefore could no longer burn. Thus, wood possessed phlogiston, but ash did not. . . . Air itself was considered by Stahl to be only indirectly useful to combustion, for it served only as a carrier, holding the phlogiston as it left the wood or metal and passing it on to something else (if something else were available). . . . the phlogiston theory gained popularity throughout the eighteenth century. By 1780 it was almost universally accepted by chemists, since it seemed to explain so much so neatly."

The stages approach to comparative analysis is itself viewed as an approximation of the comparative method that will have to be modified and elaborated as our understanding of comparative method is advanced. However, the explicit statement of the method and analysis of techniques for its application in psychology are judged to be essential at this time for the development of mature comparative studies. Biologists, for example, continue to work at the first and second stages of comparative analysis although their field has progressed through all stages of comparative analysis.

In summary then, comparative psychology involves the application of the comparative method to the domain of psychology, namely, the behavior of organisms. Thus, we get background information, propose classifications and the like for behavior. This idea is simple, but unusual in a number of respects. Several of the approaches to comparative psychology, especially capricious comparison and evolutionary approaches, dominate the scene and lead investigators away from a full focus on the behavior of organisms and analysis of them by means of the comparative method.

COMPARATIVE ANALYSIS OF HABITUATION

This section is organized to illustrate how the comparative method can be used in psychology for the analysis and understanding of the behavior process that is presently under investigation by an increasing number of psychologists. Specifically, this section deals with the comparative analysis of habituation. For present purposes, that is, prior to the conclusions that will be drawn from the comparative analysis, we will consider habituation in terms of the general observation that when an individual encounters a stimulus repeatedly, his response to that stimulus weakens and may disappear. In other words, responses show decrements with repeated stimulation.

Stage I. Background Information

The main function of this stage is to gain perspective about the behavior process that is under investigation. This includes getting ideas about its diversity, its form, and its function, and establishing guides for the later stages of analysis. As suggested in table 3-1, two sources of information can contribute to this stage of analysis—*formal sources* that include the books and journals of professional investigators, and *informal sources* that include the observations of informed amateurs who often have subtle understanding if not the "official vocabulary."

When the investigator approaches habituation, which is viewed in a general way as response decrements, in terms of Stage I, several things become evident. A large formal literature exists that deals with decrements in response. This literature occurs in the areas of zoology, physiology, and psychology, and it is classified under a variety of labels that may or may not refer to the same thing. (One of the functions of the later stages of comparative analysis is to determine the answer to this question.) The term *habituation* is used in major reviews by both zoologists (Thorpe, 1963) and psychologists (Harris, 1943; Ratner, 1970). The term *satiation* is used by psychologists (Glanzer, 1953), while the terms *inhibition* and *adaptation* are used both by psychologists such as C. L. Hull and by physiologists, especially sensory physiologists (Mueller, 1965). In addition, the term fatigue is used with a particular theoretic slant, like the others, but also refers to the decrements in responses associated with repeated stimulation.

The second characteristic of habituation that emerges from a review of formal sources is the wide variety of species and biologic systems for which habituation-like decrements are reported. As we will review in Stage III, laboratory studies reveal such processes for species ranging from single-cell organisms to man. Thirdly, such processes are reported for systems ranging from intact adult humans to receptor cells and muscle-nerve preparations. And finally, as Konrad Lorenz (1965) the ethologist, points out: habituation is clearly an adaptive behavior from the point of view of effective functioning of an animal. It keeps the animal from repeated responses to irrelevant stimuli and therefore has probably been selected for as one of the characteristics that fits an animal to its environment.

Review of formal sources of background information also indicates that habituation is regarded as a form of learning (Thorpe, 1963; Thompson and Spencer, 1966). It appears to involve a relatively permanent change in behavior and the extent of the change appears to be influenced by a number of conditions that operate in other learning situations.

A review of informal sources of background information such as magazine articles written by people who are concerned with training man and other animals supports the idea that habituation-like processes are general across species. For example, a number of articles deals with training adults to shoot guns and the changes in "flinching" in response to the loud report of the gun. These articles call our attention to the fact that the response does not disappear in a simple way; rather it changes its form by going from a multiple component response to a minimal component response with eyeblink as the last component to habituate. Articles that deal with taming animals or training them with regard to some specific stimulus such as a saddle verify the change in form of response as a function of repeated stimulation. Like the discussions of flinching, these articles also suggest that habituation is not totally permanent and if the stimulus is withheld for a period of time the habituation procedures for taming or reducing flinching must be repeated.

In summary then, habituation-like processes are important to many investigators. The process or processes are general across species and response systems. They share properties with learning and fit into the picture of the evolution of species as adaptive behavioral processes. Habituation also appears to involve a change in the form of responses, from large to minimal, but the change may be "forgotten" by the individual.

Stage II. Classification

The importance and general characteristics of this stage of comparative analysis are described in the preceding section that gives an overview of comparative method. At this point we want to apply the general ideas to the problem of habituation. One of the points on which the comparative method is especially demanding is that the investigator identify clearly and effectively what he is talking about. In other words, we have to decide what we want to talk about both in terms of a classification of decrements in behavior and in terms of the classification of behavior in general. This means more than the investigator's providing operational definition of his concepts; it means that he attempts to use background information to establish valid and useful categories. Among other things, processes are separated from each other unless they clearly belong together, since a later stage of the comparative method, Stage V, provides the opportunity to show relations among categories. Thus, the principles of classification emphasize functional classification, in which function means behavioral function, valid classification, and a separation of classes until analyses at later stages suggest putting them together if appropriate. An example of the use of several of these criteria that also uses some of the other stages of comparative analysis is seen in the work of Hilgard and Marquis (1940) and then Kimble (1961), who all deal with the question of the classification of learning.

Classification of Response Decrements. Which of the many response decrements associated with repeated stimulation will be included by the concept of habituation? The *criterion of behavioral function* means that we first identify the function of the behavior and then proceed to include or exclude processes or examples in terms of this definition. The behavioral function of habituation is a change in behavior that reduces or eliminates responses to stimuli when other responses to other stimuli are of equal or greater strength, that is, of equal or greater importance to the animal. Several conclusions follow from this description of the function. One is that changes in the receptors or muscle-nerve locations are at least temporarily excluded from consideration, the other is that we concentrate on behavior changes of intact animals and only later ask about the relations between habituation and the processes of sensory adaptation, and neural and muscular inhibition. Another criterion for classification involves *the validity of the class,* in this case, habituation. Validity refers to the question of whether the class reflects behavior that actually occurs for behaving organisms and is distinct from other behavioral processes. While systematic research is required to establish these points in rigorous detail, even the first approximations in classifications should be constrained by this criterion. An example of a class with questionable validity is that of extrasensory perception. In this case, the class is questionable primarily because it does not seem to be distinct from other behavior processes that may include it. In addition, it seems to depend primarily on the use of a very complex operational definition and, perhaps, even special attitudes of the investigator.

Classification of Behavior of Organisms. In order to talk most effectively about decrements in behavior, it is necessary to provide a language for the description of behavior, that is, a classification of behavior. This is particularly important in relation to the discussion of habituation because, as we will see in Stage IV, different types of behaviors habituate differentially, and this habituation is differentially remembered.

Denny and Ratner (1970) give a full description and discussion of the classification of behavior that is presented in table 3-2. For present purposes the principal ideas are as follows:

(1) Behavior consists of repetitions of sequences of three-component activities.

(2) The activities involve behaviors that are vital to the organism such as feeding, drinking, sleeping.

(3) Three components of each activity are the orienting component, the consummatory component, and the post-consummatory component.

(4) The components are differential from each other in terms of the degree of genetic fixedness of the eliciting stimuli and associated responses, and the degree of modifiability of the stimuli and responses through learning.

Table 3-2 presents the eleven classes of activity that characterize the behavior of organisms. Each class involves appropriate orienting, con-

TABLE 3-2

Taxonomy of Consummatory Behaviors and Related Biological Processes
Arranged in Order of Behavioral Development in Higher Vertebrates*

Behavior class	Biological system	Example
Resting	Recuperative	Sleeping
Contacting	Arousal	Visual following
Eliminating	Eliminative	Urinating
Drinking	Ingestive	Sucking
Feeding	Ingestive	Pecking
Care of body surface	Skin sensitivity	Grooming
Predator defenses	Defensive	Freezing
Fighting	Defensive	Biting
Sexual behavior	Reproductive	Ejaculating
Nesting	Reproductive	Fur pulling
Care of the young	Reproductive	Retrieving

* Adapted from Denny and Ratner (1970).

summatory, and post-consummatory components, but the label for the class implies the consummatory component. So, for example, activities associated with sexual behavior involve an orienting component, typically called courting, a consummatory component that progresses gradually from the courting component, and a post-consummatory component that for some species such as rodents involves licking the genitals. According to this taxonomy, all behaviors can be described in these terms, although as we acknowledged obliquely in the general description of the comparative method, some individuals in some test situations show these behaviors more clearly than others. We assume that this idea is true for all behaviors or behavior processes; therefore, the next stage of comparative analysis involves determining exactly what individuals and test situations reveal the behaviors or processes most clearly.

Stage III. Research Preparations

This stage of comparative analysis follows from both of the preceding stages. The first stage, called background information, gives us perspective about the behavior processes, and the second sharpens our view of what we are going to talk about, but it also sets limits on the research preparations that we can use to study the process. That is, the preparation must reflect the behavior class that has been identified. Another consequence of the first stage of analysis is that it gives us some general ideas about what organisms and what test situations, either laboratory-derived or field-derived, may profitably reflect the behavior processes that are under investigation. In other words, we get leads about good research preparations from the coordination of background information with the classification of behavior.

A research preparation for study of behavior involves the specification of three ingredients: (1) the organism, (2) the history that the organism should bring to the test situation, (3) the details of the test situation and testing procedure. Thus, statements about research preparations involve statements about these three ingredients.

As noted above, however, some preparations may be better than others for the study of a behavior process. That is, preparations can be evaluated along several dimensions. The first dimension is the extent to which the behavior shows itself in an *unconfounded and clear way.* For example, a poor preparation for the study of classic conditioning would be one in which the organism makes responses like the conditioned response with a high base rate so that the investigator cannot discriminate the conditioned response from an unconditioned response. This problem arises to some extent in eyelid conditioning and is of special importance in the conditioning of certain invertebrates such as planaria. Another example that illustrates the lack of clearness of the preparation is one involving behavior that is so fragile and susceptible to change that the presence of the experimenter or a cage, for instance, eliminates the behavior. So, for example, the study of courting and sexual behavior of gorillas in a zoo constitutes a poor preparation for the study of these components of sexual behavior. The second dimension for evaluating a research preparation involves the *reliability of the preparation,* in which case we mean the reliability of the measurement of the behavior with a specific preparation. Curiously, in spite of the many studies of learning and the many preparations used for such study, the number of observations on the reliability of the preparations are few and often incomplete. However, the importance of this dimension will be considered as self-evident. For example, the great controversy about learning by flatworms and planarians resides in part in the questionable reliability of the measurement of learning by these animals (Ratner, 1968).

The third dimension involved in evaluation of a research preparation is its *economy and convenience.* The significance of a positive evaluation of a preparation along this dimension relates to the availability of the preparation and the extent to which it will be used. That is, the greater the extent to which it will be used, the more information investigators get about the preparation and the behavior process the preparation reflects.

At this point, we are concerned with the preparations that are available for the study of habituation. Table 3-3 presents a summary of preparations that investigators have used to study habituation as we defined it in the previous section.

Table 3-3 shows clearly the generality of species and response systems that investigators have used to study habituation. The various preparations for the

TABLE 3-3

Some Research Preparations for the Study of Habituation*

Animal	Response	Investigators
Hydra	contraction	Rushforth, 1967
Planaria	contraction	VanDeventer & Ratner, 1964
Polychaete (worm)	contraction	Clark, 1964
Lumbricus (worm)	contraction to light	Ratner, 1967a
	contraction to vibration	Gardner, 1968
Turtle	alarm reaction	Hayes & Saiff, 1967
Frog	wiping response	Kimble & Ray, 1965
Fish	startle (alarm)	Russell, 1967
Bird	mobbing response	Hinde, 1960
	immobility display	Ratner, 1967b
Rat	startle and heart rate	Korn & Moyer, 1966
	headshake	Askew, et al., 1969
	exploration	Denny & Leckart, 1965
Dog	rotational nystagmus	Collins & Updegraff, 1966
Cat	rotational nystagmus	Collins & Updegraff, 1966
Primate	exploration	Butler & Harlow, 1954
Infant	heart rate	Clifton, et al., 1968
	startle	Engen, et al., 1963

* Adapted from Ratner (1970).

study of habituation can be further described in terms of the classification of the behavior into orienting, consummatory and post-consummatory components, although no studies are known in which post-consummatory components have been investigated. Ratner describes the relations between preparations and behavior components in the following way (Ratner, 1970, pp. 61–62):

> The dimension from early orienting components to late consummatory components relates: (1) to the ease of eliciting a response and (2) the retention of habituation of the response. Specifically, the later the response in the appetitive to consummatory sequence, the more limited the stimuli that can elicit the response and the more rapid the forgetting of habituation. The data to support these generalizations about the characteristics of a research preparation are discussed in part by Denny and Ratner (1970, Chap. 10) and will be examined later. In the present section these points are important as general guides concerning the preparation in the study of habituation. That is, if a late consummatory response is to be studied, only a limited number of stimuli can be used to elicit this response. Conversely, if an early orienting response is to be studied, then many stimuli can be used. So, for example, the study of habituation of head shake response with the rat (Askew, et al., 1969) involves a late component in the consummatory activities associated with care of the body surfaces. Only direct stimulation of the ear, for example, by an insect or insect substitute, elicits this response. On the other hand, approaching an object as an exploratory behavior is typically an early response in the orienting sequence and can be elicited by many stimuli.

Since several processes can confound interpretations of the results of studies of habituation, research preparations used to study habituation should limit the confounding. One of these, noted above, is the *base rate of responding* that involves responses independent of the presentations of the specific eliciting stimuli. A good research preparation is one in which the base rate is known and is known to be low. In the absence of this information the experimenter cannot evaluate occurrences of the responses or the point at which habituation has occurred. Other processes that can confound interpretations of habituation are those of *sensory adaptation* and muscle fatigue, that is, the concept of habituation implies that a decrement in response reflects more than a decrement from adaptation and fatigue. If it were based simply on these processes, then the special class of decrement identified as habituation is redundant and confusing. Thus, a good research preparation for the study of habituation is one in which recovery from habituation can be assessed and, when assessed, is found to involve a greater time duration than recovery from adaptation or fatigue. In addition, a good preparation should permit immediate evaluation of the effects of adaptation and fatigue. So, for example, in studies of habituation of earthworms, Gardner (1968) used two techniques to establish that the response decrements that he found were not due to these confounding processes. Specifically, he presented different stimuli that elicit the same response that had been habituated and he got the response with the different stimuli. He also presented different values of the original stimulus to which the response had been habituated and again, got the response.

While evaluations of reliability of good preparations of the study of habituation are almost as infrequent as such evaluations for other learning preparations, work in our laboratory with three preparations has evaluated this dimension. The reliability of preparations that use planarians and their responses to tactile stimulation (VanDeventer, 1967) and to light (Van-Deventer and Ratner, 1964) have been evaluated in two ways. The investigators calculated reliability coefficients using the split-half technique for the animal's responses during habituation and they calculated them for responses to original habituation and rehabituation. In both cases correlations beyond .85 were obtained. Gardner used similar procedures with the preparation that involves responses of earthworms to vibration and got similar high positive correlations. Askew and his associates (1969) and Leibrecht (1969) assessed the reliability of their preparation that involved elicitation by air puff of the head-shake response of rats. They also report high positive correlations of greater than .85 using split-half and test-retest techniques. Thus, several of the preparations that investigators have used for the study of habituation have been tested for reliability and found to be adequate in this respect. Other preparations require such evaluation.

As Ratner describes (1970), investigators have measured a number of aspects of responses of organisms to repeated stimulation in order to provide indexes of habituation. Among these are frequency of response, amplitude of response, and latency of response. They have also used indexes that use rates of changes of these individual measures. In general, these indexes are very similar to indexes used in a number of other learning situations.

The third aspect of research preparations that requires evaluation is that of *economy and convenience.* None of the preparations that are listed in table 3-3 involves extremely exotic or expensive organisms or test situations. However, in terms of the typical laboratory that is concerned with the study of behavior of organisms, it seems likely that the chaffinch and human infant are the least convenient organisms listed.

Stage IV. Identification of Variables

Once the investigator has good research preparations available for the study of a process, he can determine the variables that affect the process. As is evident from our discussion of Stage III, investigators have a number of preparations available for the study of habituation. Thus, the reviews of variables by Thompson and Spencer (1966) and Ratner (1970) provide both an extensive list of variables that affect habituation and the experiments that report such effects. Table 3-4 presents a summary of some of the variables that affect the course of the habituation function. As shown in table 3-4, the variables are evaluated in terms of their effects on one or more aspects of the typical graph of habituation. As indicated in table 3-4, at least three aspects of this graph can show the effects of a variable. These are the initial level of responding to the stimulus; the slope of the graph which reflects the rate of

TABLE 3-4

Variables that Affect Habituation Where the Effect of Each Is
Indicated in Terms of the Aspect of the Habituation Curve
That Is Changed by the Variable

Variable	Aspect of Habituation Function That Changes		
	Initial Response Level	Rate	Asymptote
Number of stimulus presentations	—	X	X
Stimulus intensity	X	—	X
Stimulus duration	(like stimulus intensity when effective)		
Fading—in a stimulus	X	—	—
Inter-stimulus interval	—	X	X
Compatible concurrent stimulus	—	X	X
Incompatible concurrent stimulus	—	X	X

habituation; and the asymptote, the place at which the graph shows a slope of
zero.

While a number of the variables noted in table 3-4 is familiar, the ways in
which several of them are used in studies of habituation may be unclear. The
variable of *fading-in a stimulus* is studied by comparing habituation to a
constant and high-intensity stimulus with habituation to a stimulus that has
different and increasing intensity from trial to trial. Davis and Wagner (1968)
report that the level of response to the high-intensity stimulus following
fading-in is significantly less than the level of response for the group that
received the high-intensity stimulus only.

The variables associated with *concurrent stimulation* refer to secondary
stimulus conditions that affect an animal before, during, or after the time the
primary eliciting stimulus is presented. For example, if a high-intensity
thermal stimulus affects an animal while habituation trials are conducted with
light as the primary eliciting stimulus, then the thermal stimulus is a
concurrent one. It is the effects of such a stimulus that we are evaluating. If
the concurrent stimulus elicits a response that is like or compatible with the
primary stimulus, then habituation to the primary stimulus is affected. As
noted in table 3-4, it is affected in two respects. The rate of habituation is
decreased and the asymptote of the habituation curve is elevated. In a study
of habituation of the responses of planarians to light with a concurrent
thermal stimulus, the effect of the concurrent stimulus was so great that the
habituation curve was reversed in direction and successive presentations of
light were associated with increasing the frequencies of response to the light
(VanDeventer and Ratner, 1964). If the concurrent stimulus elicits responses
that are incompatible with the response elicited by the primary stimulus, the

rate of habituation to the primary stimulus is increased and the asymptote of the habituation function is lowered. That is, the incompatible concurrent stimulus leads to faster habituation and a greater amount of habituation.

This analysis of the effects of concurrent stimulation suggests that the effect of the variable depends on the specific relations between the response to the primary eliciting stimulus and response to the concurrent stimulus. In addition, it predicts the effect of occasionally presented concurrent stimuli such as are used in studies of dishabituation. While Sokolov (1963), Thompson and Spencer (1966), and Leibrecht (1969) discuss dishabituation, data to support the theories they presented are still incomplete as are data to support other interpretations of dishabituation. However, in general, a dishabituating stimulus affects habituation as predicted from the type of response it elicits.

Stage V. Relations Among Classes

Comparative analysis at Stage V can also be called the first theoretic stage of analysis. That is, at this stage, the investigator *compares and relates classes of behavior*. In the context of the analysis of habituation using the comparative method we will consider briefly two types of relations: those between habituation and the component classification of behavior, and those between habituation and several other types of response decrements.

Relations Between Habituation and Components of Behavior

The main thesis of this section is derived from a close analysis of the effect of variables on habituation, especially the variable of intensity of the eliciting stimulus. In general, intensity of the eliciting stimulus refers to the strength of the association between the eliciting stimulus and its response. The greater the intensity of the stimulus, the stronger the associations between the stimulus and the response. The classification of behavior into orienting, consummatory, and post-consummatory components also refers to the strengths of the associations between eliciting stimuli and appropriate responses. So, for example, as we have indicated above, a small moving object may elicit an approach response for a rat, but this stimulus is less strongly associated with the response of approach than the stimulus of a piece of food is associated with chewing.

Thus, we are assuming that both the intensity of a stimulus and its function in an orienting versus a consummatory component relate to the strength of the association between the stimulus and response. From Stage IV, we see that initial level of response and asymptote of habituation or rate of habituation are affected by the strength of the association. For example, Askew (1969) found that stronger elicitors lead to a higher initial level of responding and a higher asymptote than weaker elicitors. A somewhat surprising relationship exists between the *strength of an association prior* to habituation and the *retention of habituation* of the response to the stimulus.

As mentioned above, data from several studies support this converse relation between the strength of the association and the amount of retention of habituation. Specifically, the stronger the association between a stimulus and a response, the less well habituation with this stimulus and response are retained. So, for example, habituation of an animal's response to a weak elicitor is well remembered and he may not respond to this stimulus for a number of days, whereas habituation of an animal's response to a strong elicitor, a stimulus in the consummatory component, is typically remembered less than one day (Ratner, 1970, pp. 78–81).

Relations Between Habituation and Other Response Decrements

A number of behavioral processes are characterized by response decrements. Among them are extinction of learned responses, forgetting, sensory adaptation, and fatigue. While close analysis of all of them in relation to habituation would be interesting, we will examine adaptation and fatigue only because of the apparent close relations among habituation, adaptation, and fatigue, and because of the theoretic use we will make of these relations.

Specifically, we hypothesize that the processes differ from each other in ways that have been noted in preceding sections, but they are related in the following way. Sensory adaptation and fatigue are assumed to occur each time a stimulus is presented to an animal and the animal responds. Thus, each habituation trial leads to some adaptation and fatigue, and the animal is at least slightly less responsive to the stimulus on the next trial. At the same time, if the concurrent sources of stimulation are eliciting some competing responses, these competing responses now have a greater chance of occurring. So, habituation is described as the result of occurrences of competing responses that can occur when decrements arise from adaptation and fatigue. While the decrements may have a relatively short life, they permit concurrent sources of stimulation to elicit competing responses. On the other hand, if the concurrent sources of stimulation elicit compatible responses, habituation is retarded since adaptation and fatigue to both primary and concurrent stimuli are now required. In addition, this view of habituation is consistent with the findings about the powerful effects of inter-stimulus interval on habituation. If the interval between trials is increased, decremental effects of adaptation and fatigue dissipate between trials, and the response to the primary stimulus habituates very slowly. Thus, we suggest that habituation, sensory adaptation, and fatigue are different processes, but decrements in response from habituation depend on adaptation and fatigue.

SUMMARY

Comparative psychology has a long history during which it has been approached in a variety of ways. Among these are functional analysis, capricious comparison, evolutionary analysis, and problem comparison. Each approach implies a method of analysis that is considered to be comparative. This method, used effectively in both zoology and chemistry, consists of six interlocking stages. The method is required whenever the events to be studied have diversity. Thus, psychology that focuses on the diverse behaviors of organisms requires the comparative method. The stages of the comparative method are described and applied in detail to the analysis of habituation as one of a number of forms of response decrements.

References

Asimov, I. *A short history of chemistry.* New York: Doubleday, 1965.

Askew, H. R. Effects of intertrial interval and stimulus intensity on habituation of the head-shake response in rats. Unpublished doctoral dissertation, Michigan State University, 1969.

Askew, H. R., Leibrecht, B. C., & Ratner, S. C. Effects of stimulus duration and repeated sessions of habituation of a head-shake response in the rat. *Journal of Comparative and Physiological Psychology,* 1969, 67, 497–503.

Bereday, G. Z. F. *Comparative method in education.* 2nd ed. New York: Holt, Rinehart & Winston, 1964.

Bitterman, M. E. Toward a comparative psychology of learning. *American Psychologist,* 1960, 15, 704–712.

Clifton, R. K., Graham, F. K., & Hatton, H. M. Newborn heart-rate response and response habituation as a function of stimulus duration. *Journal of Experimental Child Psychology,* 1968, 6, 265–278.

Collins, W. E., & Updegraff, B. P. A comparison of nystagmus habituation in the cat and dog. *Acta Otolaryngology,* 1966, 62, 19–26.

Davis, M., & Wagner, A. R. Startle responsiveness after habituation to different intensities of tone. *Psychonomic Science,* 1968, 12, 337–338.

Denny, M. R., & Leckart, B. T. Alternation behavior: Learning and extinction one trial per day. *Journal of Comparative Physiological Psychology,* 1965, 60, 229–232.

Denny, M. R., & Ratner, S. C. *Comparative psychology* (Rev. ed.) Homewood, Illinois: Dorsey, 1970.

Dethier, V. G., & Stellar, E. *Animal behavior.* (Rev. ed.) Englewood Cliffs, New Jersey: Prentice-Hall, 1964.

Eggan, F. Social anthropology and the method of controlled comparison. *American Anthropologist,* 1954, 56, 743–763.

Engen, T., Lipsitt, L. P., & Kaye, H. Olfactory responses and adaptation in the human neonate. *Journal of Comparative Physiological Psychology,* 1963, 56, 73–77.

Gardner, L. E. Retention and overhabituation of a dual-component response in *Lumbricus terrestris. Journal of Comparative Physiological Psychology,* 1968, 66, 315–318.

Glanzer, M. Stimulus satiation: An explanation of spontaneous alteration and related phenomena. *Psychological Review,* 1953, 60, 257–268.

Groves, P. M., & Thompson, R. F. Habituation: A dual-process theory. *Psychological Review,* 1970, 77, 419–450.

Harris, J. D. Habituatory response decrement in the intact organism. *Psychological Bulletin,* 1943, 40, 385–423.

Hayes, W. N., & Saiff, E. I. Visual alarm reactions in turtles. *Animal Behaviour,* 1967, 15, 102–106.

Hilgard, E. R., & Marquis, D. G. *Conditioning and learning.* New York: Appleton-Century, 1940.

Hinde, R. A. Factors governing the changes in the strength of a partially inborn response, as shown by the mobbing behavior of the chaffinch. III. *Proceedings of the Royal Society B,* 1960, 153, 398–420.

Hodos, W., & Campbell, G. B. G. *Scala Naturae:* Why there is no theory in comparative psychology. *Psychological Review,* 1969, 76, 337–350.

Kimble, D. P., & Ray, R. S. Reflex habituation and potentiation in *Rana pipiens*. *Animal Behaviour*, 1965, 13, 530–533.

Kimble, G. A. *Hilgard and Marquis' conditioning and learning*. New York: Appleton-Century-Crofts, 1961.

Korn, J. H., & Moyer, K. E. Habituation of the startle response and of heart rate in the rat. *Canadian Journal of Psychology*, 1966, 20, 183–190.

Leibrecht, B. Dishabituation of the head-shake response in the rat. Unpublished doctoral dissertation, Michigan State University, 1969.

Lewis, O. Comparisons in cultural anthropology. In W. L. Thomas, Jr. (ed.), *Current anthropology: A supplement to anthropology today*. Chicago, Ill.: University of Chicago Press, 1956. Pp. 259–292.

Lorenz, K. *Evolution and modification of behavior*. Chicago: University of Chicago Press, 1965.

Macridis, R. C., & Brown, B. E. *Comparative politics: Notes and readings*. Homewood, Illinois: Dorsey, 1964.

Mueller, C. G. *Sensory psychology*. Englewood Cliffs, New Jersey: Prentice-Hall, 1965.

Ratner, S. C. Annelid learning: A critical review. In W. C. Corning and S. C. Ratner (eds.), *Chemistry of learning*. New York: Plenum Press, 1967. Pp. 391–406. (a)

Ratner, S. C. Comparative aspects of hypnosis. In J. Gordon (ed.), *Handbook of clinical and experimental hypnosis*. New York: Macmillan, 1967. Pp. 550–587. (b)

Ratner, S. C. Reliability of indexes of worm learning. *Psychological Reports*, 1968, 22, 130.

Ratner, S. C. Habituation: Research and theory. In J. H. Reynierse (ed.), *Current issues in animal learning*. Lincoln, Nebraska: University of Nebraska Press, 1970. Pp. 55–84.

Ratner, S. C., & Denny, M. R. *Comparative psychology*. Homewood, Illinois: Dorsey, 1964.

Ross, W. D. (ed.) *The student's oxford aristotle, Vol. III. psychology*. Oxford, England: Oxford University Press, 1942.

Rushforth, N. B. Chemical and physical factors affecting behavior in hydra: Interactions among factors affecting behavior in hydra. In W. C. Corning & S. C. Ratner (eds.), *Chemistry of learning*. New York: Plenum Press, 1967, Pp. 369–390.

Russell, E. M. Changes in the behaviour of *Leibistes reticulatus* upon a repeated shadow stimulus. *Animal Behaviour*, 1967, 15, 574–585.

Sokal, R. R., & Sneath, P. H. A. *Principles of numerical taxonomy*. San Francisco: Freeman, 1963.

Sokolov, Y. N. *Perception and the conditioned reflex*. New York: Macmillan, 1963.

Thompson, R. F., & Spencer, W. A. Habituation: A model phenomenon for the study of neuronal substrates of behavior. *Psychological Review*, 1966, 73, 16–43.

Thorpe, W. T. *Learning and instinct in animals*. London: Methuen, 1963.

VanDeventer, J. M. Responses to repeated tactile stimulation in the planarian, *Dugesia tigrina*. Unpublished doctoral dissertation, Michigan State University, 1967.

VanDeventer, J. M., & Ratner, S. C. Variables affecting frequencies of responses of planaria to light. *Journal of Comparative Physiological Psychology*, 1964, 57, 407–411.

Chapter 4

STRUCTURE AND MEASUREMENT OF PSYCHOMOTOR ABILITIES *

Edwin A. Fleishman
American Institutes for Research
Washington, D.C.

The contribution I feel best able to make to this book is a description of our research on psychomotor skills over the past 18 years. Specifically, I will deal with several interrelated areas. The primary program to be discussed concerns the identification of psychomotor abilities accounting for individual differences in performance of a wide variety of psychomotor tasks. Within this program I will deal with a variety of ability areas ranging from fine manipulative performance to areas of gross physical proficiency. A second program area in our work deals with relationships between these abilities and the learning of more complex psychomotor skills. Within this second area we have dealt with a number of learning variables including amount of practice, transfer, and retention.

In describing our research it may be of particular interest to stress the definitions of the psychomotor abilities which have been derived from this research; to specify the kinds of tests and task materials utilized in these studies and to describe those found to best measure these abilities.

The specifications of these abilities, measures, and materials have particular relevance to curriculum development in that they: (a) help specify the range of activities that need to be covered in order to be comprehensive in this area; (b) specify measures for possible use in assigning or selecting students for particular training efforts or for evaluating progress and proficiency in various areas of psychomotor performance; and (c) provide

*Taken from The Contribution of Behavioral Science to Instructional Technology. Volume III, The Psychomotor Domain of Learning, Floyd Urbach (ed.). National Special Media Institutes, Washington, D.C.: Gryphan House, 1972.

suggestions for materials and apparatus development for inclusion in particular psychomotor development and training activity.

CONCEPTUAL AND METHODOLOGIC FRAMEWORK

First I would like to define some concepts which have been developed. I find it useful to distinguish between the concepts of "ability" and "skill." As we use the term, *ability* refers to a general trait of the individual which has been inferred from the correlations obtained among performances of individuals on certain kinds of tasks. Some abilities (e.g., color vision) depend more on genetic than learning factors, but most abilities depend on both to some degree. In any case, at a given stage in life, they represent traits or organismic factors which the individual brings with him when he begins to learn a new task. These abilities are related to performance in a variety of human tasks. For example, the fact that spatial visualization has been found to be related to performance on such diverse tasks as aerial navigation, blue print reading, and dentistry makes this ability somewhat basic.

The term *skill* refers to the level of proficiency on a specific task or limited group of tasks. As we use the term, it is task-oriented. When we talk about proficiency in flying an airplane, in operating a turret lathe, or in playing basketball, we are talking about a specific skill. Thus, when we speak of acquiring the skill of operating a turret lathe, we mean that this person has acquired the sequence of responses required by this specific task. The assumption is that the skills involved in complex activities can be described in terms of the more basic abilities. For example, the level of performance a man can attain on a turret lathe may depend on his basic abilities of manual dexterity and motor coordination. However, these same basic abilities may be important to proficiency in other skills as well. Thus, manual dexterity is needed in assembling electrical components, and motor coordination is needed to fly an airplane.

Implicit in the previous analysis is the important relation between abilities and learning. Thus, individuals with high manual dexterity may more readily learn the specific skill of lathe operation. The mechanism of transfer of training probably operates here. Some abilities may transfer to the learning of a greater variety of specific tasks than others. In our culture, *verbal* abilities are more important in a greater variety of tasks than are some other types of abilities. The individual who has a great many highly developed basic abilities can become proficient at a great variety of specific tasks.

Elsewhere (Fleishman, 1964a; Gagné and Fleishman, 1959) we have elaborated our analysis of the development of basic abilities. This included a discussion of their physiologic bases, the role of learning, environmental and cultural factors, and evidence of the rate of ability development during the life span. With this much conceptualization in mind, we can say that in much of our previous work one objective has been to describe certain skills in terms of these more general ability requirements.

Perhaps a not too extreme statement is that most of the categorization of human skills, which is empirically based, comes from correlational and factor-analytic studies. Many of these studies in the literature are ill-designed or not designed at all. This does not rule out the fact that properly designed, systematic, programmatic, correlational research can yield highly useful data about general skill dimensions. We can think of such categories as representing empirically derived patterns of *response consistencies* to task requirements varied in systematic ways. In a sense this approach described tasks in terms of the common abilities required to perform them. As an example, let us take the term "tracking," a frequent psychomotor behavioral category employed by laboratory and systems psychologists alike. We can all think of a wide variety of different tasks in which some kinds of tracking are involved. Can we assume that the behavioral category of tracking is useful in helping us generalize results from one such situation to another? Is there a general tracking ability? Are individuals who are good at compensatory tracking also the ones who are good at pursuit tracking? Do people who are good at positional tracking do well with velocity or acceleration controls? What happens to the correlations between performances as a function of such variations? It is to these kinds of questions that our program was directed.

PART I—IDENTIFICATION OF PSYCHOMOTOR ABILITY FACTORS

In previous years we conducted a whole series of interlocking, experimental, factor-analytic studies in an attempt to isolate and identify the common variance in a wide range of psychomotor performances. Essentially this is laboratory research in which tasks are specifically designed or selected to test certain hypotheses about the organization of abilities in a certain range of tasks (e.g., Fleishman, 1954). Subsequent studies tend to introduce task variations aimed at sharpening or limiting our ability-factor definitions. The purpose is to define the fewest independent ability categories which might be most useful and meaningful in describing performance in the widest variety of tasks.

Our studies generally start with some gross area of human performance. Thus, we have conducted studies of fine manipulative performances (Fleishman and Ellison, 1962; Fleishman and Hempel, 1954a), gross physical proficiency (Fleishman, 1963, 1964a; Hempel and Fleishman, 1955), positioning movements and static reactions (Fleishman, 1958a), and movement reactions (Fleishman, 1958b; Fleishman and Hempel, 1956).

Thus far, we have investigated more than 200 different tasks administered to thousands of subjects in a series of interlocking studies. From the patterns of correlations obtained, we have been able to account for performance on this wide range of tasks of a relatively small number of abilities. In subsequent studies our definitions of these abilities and their distinctions from one another have become more clearly delineated. Furthermore, it is now possible to specify the tasks which should provide the best measure of each of the abilities identified.

There are about 11 psychomotor abilities and 9 abilities in the area of physical proficiency which consistently appear to account for the common variance in psychomotor tasks. Before turning to the physical proficiency area let me list some of these psychomotor abilities and describe some of the tasks which best measure each ability.

Control Precision. This ability is common to tasks which require fine, highly controlled, but not over-controlled, muscular adjustments, primarily where larger muscle groups are involved (Fleishman, 1953b; Fleishman and Hempel, 1956; Parker and Fleishman, 1960). This ability extends to arm-hand as well as to leg movements. It is most critical where such adjustments must be rapid, but precise. Tasks which best measure this ability include the Rotary Pursuit and the Controls Adjustment Tasks (Fig. 4-1, Fig. 4-2).

Multilimb Coordination. This is the ability to coordinate the movements of a number of limbs simultaneously, and is best measured by devices involving multiple controls (Fleishman, 1958b; Fleishman and Hempel, 1956; Parker and Fleishman, 1960). The ability has been found general to tasks requiring coordination of the two feet (Fig. 4-3, the Rudder Control Test), two hands (the Two-hand Pursuit and Two-hand Coordination Tests (Fig. 4-4, Fig. 4-5, respectively) and hand and feet (the Complex Coordination and Plane Control Tests, Fig. 4-6, Fig. 4-7, respectively).

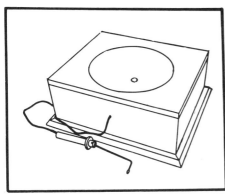

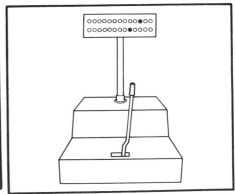

FIG. 4-1. Rotary Pursuit.*   FIG. 4-2. Controls Adjustment.

*Figs. 4-1 through 4-5, Figs. 4-8 through 4-10, Figs. 4-12 through 4-14, and Figs. 4-20 and 4-23 are from Fleishman, E. A. Dimensional analysis of movement reactions. *J. Exper. Psychol.*, 55, 1958, 438-453. Copyright (1958) by the American Psychological Association, and reproduced by permission.*

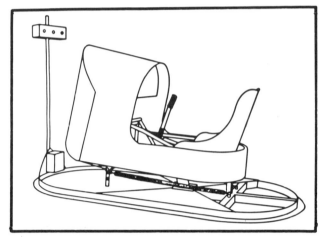

FIG. 4-3. Rudder Control.

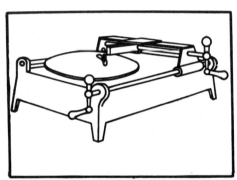

FIG. 4-4. Two-hand Pursuit.

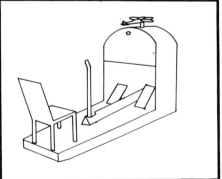

FIG. 4-5. Two-hand Coordination.

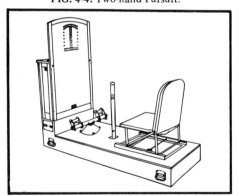

FIG. 4-6. Complex Coordination.*

FIG. 4-7. Plane Control.

*Figs. 4-6 and 4-7 are from Fleishman, E. A. A comparative study of aptitude patterns in unskilled and skilled psychomotor performances. *J. Appl. Psychol., 41, 1957, 263-272. Copyright (1957) by the American Psychological Association, and reproduced by permission.*

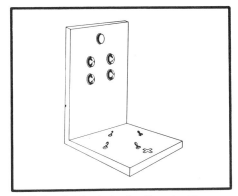

FIG. 4-8. Discrimination Reaction Time.

Response Orientation. This ability has been found general to visual discrimination reaction psychomotor tasks involving rapid directional discrimination and orientation of movement patterns (Fleishman, 1957a,b, 1958b; Fleishman and Hempel, 1956, Parker and Fleishman, 1960). It appears to involve the ability to select the correct movement in relation to the correct stimulus, especially under highly speeded conditions. Figure 4-8 illustrates the Discrimination Reaction Task and figure 4-9 shows the Multidimensional Pursuit Task found to measure this ability.

Reaction Time. This represents simply the speed with which the individual is able to respond to a stimulus when it appears (Fleishman, 1954, 1958b, Fleishman and Hempel, 1955; Parker and Fleishman, 1960). There are

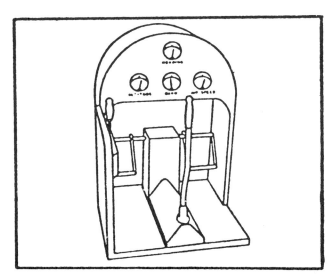

FIG. 4-9. Multidimensional Pursuit.

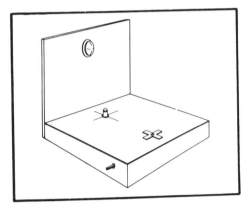

FIG. 4-10. Reaction Time.

consistent indications that individual differences in this ability are independent of whether the stimulus is auditory or visual and are also independent of the type of response which is required. However, once the stimulus situation or the response situation is complicated by involving alternate choices, reaction time is not the primary ability that is measured. Figure 4-10 illustrates the basic reaction time device.

Speed of Arm Movement. This represents simply the speed with which an individual can make a gross, discrete arm movement where accuracy is not the requirement (Fleishman, 1958b; Fleishman and Hempel, 1954b, 1955; Parker and Fleishman, 1960). There is ample evidence that this ability is independent of the reaction-time ability. Tasks such as two-plate tapping (Fig. 4-11), in which the plates are separated at least 12 inches, best measure this ability.

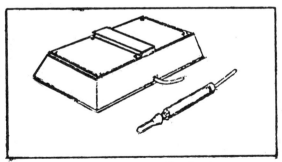

FIG. 4-11. Two-plate Tapping.*

*Fig. 4-11 and Figs. 4-15 through 4-19 are from Fleishman, E. A. Dimensional analysis of psychomotor abilities. *J. Exper. Psychol., 48, 1954, 437-454. Copyright (1954) by the American Psychological Association, and reproduced by permission.*

Rate Control. This ability involves the making of continuous anticipatory motor adjustments relative to changes in speed and direction of a continuously moving target or object (Fleishman, 1958b; Fleishman and Hempel, 1955, 1956). This ability is general to tasks involving compensatory as well as following pursuit, and extends to tasks involving responses to changes in rate. Our research has shown that adequate measurement of this ability required an actual response in relation to the changing direction and speed of the stimulus object, and not simply a judgment of the rate of the stimulus movement. Figures 4-12, 4-13, and 4-14 respectively illustrate the tasks, Rate Control, Single-dimensional Pursuit, and Motor Judgment Tasks, which measure this ability.

Manual Dexterity. This ability involves skillful, well-directed arm-hand movements in manipulating fairly large objects under speeded conditions (Fleishman, 1953b, 1954; Fleishman and Hempel, 1954b; Fleishman and Ellison, 1962; Parker and Fleishman, 1960; Hempel and Fleishman, 1955). The best generally available measures include the Minnesota Rate of

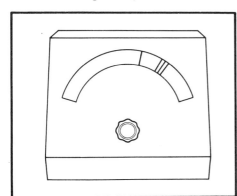

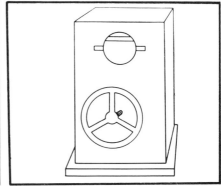

FIG. 4-12. Rate Control.   **FIG. 4-13.** Single-dimensional Pursuit.

FIG. 4-14. Motor Judgment.

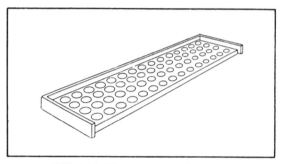

FIG. 4-15. Minnesota Rate of Manipulation.

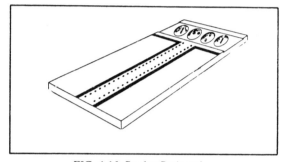

FIG. 4-16. Purdue Pegboard.

Manipulation Tests (Fig. 4-15), but there are newer experimental tasks which
provide better measures.

Finger Dexterity. This is the ability to make still-controlled manipulations
of tiny objects involving, primarily, the fingers (Fleishman, 1953b, 1954;
Fleishman and Hempel, 1954a; Parker and Fleishman, 1960; Hempel and
Fleishman, 1955; Fleishman and Ellison, 1962). Tests such as the Purdue
Pegboard and O'Connor Finger Dexterity (see Fig. 4-16 and Fig. 4-17) provide
good measures.

Arm-hand Steadiness. This is the ability to make precise arm-hand
positioning movements where strength and speed are minimized; the critical
feature, as the name implies, is the steadiness with which such movements can
be made (Fleishman, 1953b, 1954, 1958a, b; Fleishman and Hempel, 1955;
Hempel and Fleishman, 1955; Parker and Fleishman, 1960). The ability
extends to tasks requiring steady movements or holding steady limb positions
(see Fig. 4-18, Fig. 4-19, and Fig. 4-20).

Wrist-finger Speed. This ability is of limited generality and is best
measured by printed tests requiring rapid tapping of the pencil in relatively
large areas (Fleishman, 1954; Fleishman and Hempel, 1954a; Fleishman and
Ellison, 1962). Pendular and/or rotary wrist movements may be involved.
Figure 4-21 shows typical page sections of tests used to measure this ability.

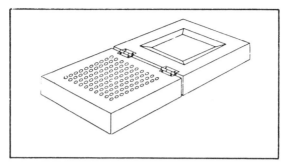

FIG. 4-17. O'Connor Finger Dexterity.

Aiming. This ability appears to be measured by printed tests requiring the rapid placing of dots in very small circles under highly speeded conditions (Fleishman, 1953b, 1954; Hempel and Fleishman, 1955; Fleishman and Ellison, 1962) (see Fig. 4-22).

Of course, there are detailed descriptions of the operations involved in each ability category; some of them are more general in scope than others, but it is important to know, for example, that it is not useful to talk about strength as a single dimension. Rather, it is more useful to talk in terms of what psychomotor tasks the same people can do well in terms of at least four general strength categories which may be differentially involved in a variety of physical tasks.

Perhaps it might be useful to provide some examples of how the generality of an ability category is determined and how its limits are defined. The definition of the rate control ability may provide an example. In early studies it was found that this ability was common to tracking tests requiring one to follow a moving target (following pursuit tasks) as well as to tasks requiring one to keep a target points centered (compensatory pursuit tasks). To test the generality of this ability, tasks to emphasize rate control ability were developed which were *not* conventional tracking tasks (e.g., controlling a ball rolling through a series of alleyways). The ability was found to extend to such tasks. Later studies attempted to discover if emphasis on this ability is in judging the rate of the stimulus as distinguished from ability to respond at the appropriate rate. A task involving only button pressing in response to judgments of moving stimuli was developed (see Fig. 4-23). Performance on this task did *not* correlate with other rate control tasks. Finally, several motion picture tasks were adapted in which the individual was required to extrapolate the course of a plane moving across a screen. The only response required was on an IBM answer sheet. These tasks did not relate to the core of tasks previously found to measure "rate control." Thus, our definition of this ability was expanded to include measures beyond conventional "pursuit" tasks, but restricted to tasks requiring the *timing of a muscular adjustment* to the stimulus change.

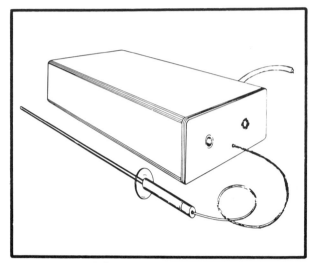

FIG. 4-18. Steadiness Precision.

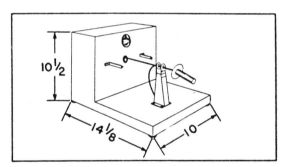

FIG. 4-19. Steadiness Aiming.

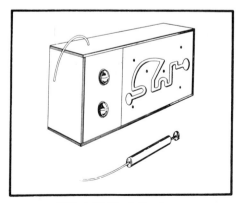

FIG. 4-20. Track Tracing.

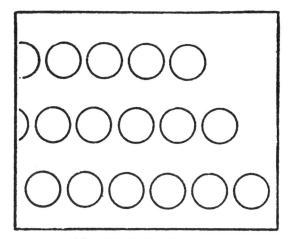

FIG. 4-21A. Medium Tapping.

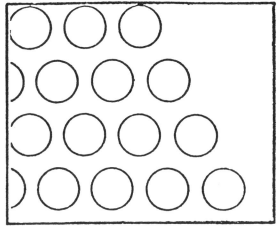

FIG. 4-21B. Large Tapping.

A similar history can be sketched for each ability variable identified. Thus, we know that an individual must have a feedback indicator of how well he is coordinating before the multilimb coordination ability is measured; we know that by complicating a simple *reaction-time* apparatus, by providing additional choice reactions, we measure not operation time but a separate ability (response orientation); however, varying the stimulus modality in a simple reaction-time device results in the measurement of the same ability of reaction time and does not result in measurement of a separate ability.

*Figs. 4-21A,B and 4-22A,B are from Fleishman, E. A., & Ellison, G. D. A factor analysis of fine manipulative performance. *J. Appl. Psychol., 46, 1962, 96-105.* Copyright (1962) by the American Psychological Association, and reproduced by permission.

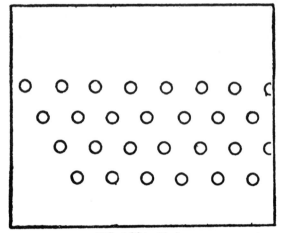

FIG. 4-22A. Aiming.

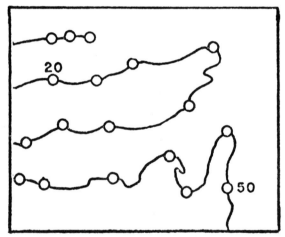

FIG. 4-22B. Pursuit Aiming.

Some later studies using experimental-correlational approaches provide encouraging results which indicate that it is possible to build up a body of principles through systematic studies of ability-task interaction in the laboratory (Fleishman, 1956). The approach is to develop tasks which can be varied along specified physical dimensions; to administer these tasks, systematically varied along these dimensions, to groups of subjects who also receive a series of "reference" tasks known to sample certain more generalized abilities (e.g., spatial orientation, control precision, and certain cognitive abilities). Correlations between these reference tasks and scores on variations of the criterion task specify the ability requirements (and changes

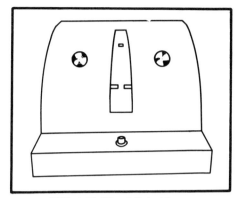

FIG. 4-23. Visual Coincidence.

in these requirements) as a function of task variations. Thus far we have studied tasks varied along the following dimensions: (a) degree of rotation of display panels relative to response panels, (b) the predictability or unpredictability of target course or response requirements, (c) the extent to which the task allows the individual to assess the degree of coordination of multilimb responses, (d) the degree of stimulus-response compatibility in display-control relationships, (e) whether there is a constant "set" or changing "set" from one stimulus presentation to the next, (f) whether certain kinds of additional response requirements are imposed in a visual discrimination reaction task, and (g) whether certain kinds of feedback are provided. Hopefully, once such principles are established, it should be possible to look at new tasks, operational or otherwise, and specify the ability requirements.

PART II–RESEARCH ON PHYSICAL FITNESS
DIMENSIONS AND MEASUREMENT

We turn now to a more intensive look at our research on a special class of motor performance, that of physical proficiency. We will describe this area of our motor ability work in more detail because physical fitness programs are already an integral part of school curricula.

Literature Integration. As the first phase in this line of work, we conducted a comprehensive review of the literature on previous and currently used physical fitness tests. The literature in this area is replete with terms such as "velocity," "speed," "explosive and static strength," "muscular endurance," "stamina," etc. Are these useful categories? Which categories of performance represent essentially different abilities and tests to measure them? The primary objective of this review was to examine the correlations found among such tests and to describe the factors they are presumed to measure. Special emphasis was placed on reviewing previous factor analytic studies of physical fitness tests in order to compile a comprehensive catalog of tests according to the abilities they seemed to measure (Fleishman, 1964a). It was possible to integrate these abilities into a meaningful schema. The main conclusion was that commonly used test batteries do not cover the range of possible fitness abilities and many of the tests which are used overlap with one another in the ability measured. Fourteen possible abilities were described and questions were raised about other possible abilities.

The Experimental Studies. Considerable pre-testing of more than 100 tests was carried out with the objective of providing better measures of the abilities hypothesized from the literature review and other sources. The more reliable tests of these pre-tests were included with more familiar tests in two large-scale studies with United States Navy recruits. The design of these studies allowed for the confirmation or redefinition of the hypothesized abilities as well as for the isolation of new abilities. Testing teams, under the supervision of the Yale University project, were established at the Great Lakes Naval Training Center in Illinois and at the San Diego Naval Training Center in California. At Great Lakes, 30 tests designed to measure different abilities in the areas of strength and endurance were administered; at San Diego, 30 tests in the areas of flexibility, balance, speed, and coordination were administered. At each center all the tests were administered to more than 200 navy recruits. Correlations among all these tests and background variables were obtained and subjected to factor analytic studies. Where previous factor analytic studies had focused on relatively small test batteries, here it was possible to combine alternative measures of practically *all* previously identified abilities within these two large-scale studies. Both of these studies provided both better definitions of the abilities that need to be assessed for a more comprehensive evaluation of physical proficiency and recommendations for tests most diagnostic of these different abilities. In all, it was possible to explain the correlations among these 60 different tests in terms of 11 primary abilities. A few of these abilities were quite specific (e.g., those confined to balancing weights) and were not considered further, but the more general ones were retained for further study.

To illustrate the research strategy let us examine more closely the design of the study to identify ability factors in the area of strength. Tests were chosen so that some emphasized flexor and other extensor muscles, some emphasized leg and others arm or trunk strength, some emphasized short and others long runs. Some emphasized continuous, repeated, or minimal strain, others were timed or untimed. The design made it possible to examine the correlations among tests given to the same subjects to answer questions such as the following: Do we get two abilities separating flexor or extensor muscles? Is there a general strength ability common to all these tasks? Does prolonged strain on muscles (pull-ups, push-ups) introduce a new ability (e.g., endurance) compared with tasks using the same muscles in a shorter but speeded period (Do as many push-ups as possible in 20 seconds)? Are there abilities common to muscle groups (arms versus legs) as distinguished from abilities dependent on the pattern of activity? What is the role of strength in running tasks? Table 4-1 shows the possible ability factors that could have been obtained when we examined the actual relations among performances.

A similar design was followed in the areas of speed, flexibility, coordination, and balance. The intercorrelations may be seen elsewhere (Fleishman, 1964a). For the present we will merely summarize the abilities that emerged from these studies and the tests which had the highest factor loading (correlations with that ability). By examining the tests which grouped together on the same ability it was possible to define the abilities. The abilities identified and the test found to best measure each ability are as follows:

1. *Extent Flexibility.* Ability to flex or stretch the trunk and back muscles *as far as possible* in either a forward, lateral, or backward direction.

a. *Extent Flexibility Test*: (Originally called Twist and Touch). The subject stands with his left side toward the wall, and an arm's length away from the wall. With feet together and in place, he twists back around as far as he can, touching the wall with his right hand at shoulder height.

2. *Dynamic Flexibility.* The ability to make repeated, *rapid,* flexing movements in which the resiliency of the muscles in *recovery* from strain or distortion is critical.

a. *Dynamic Flexibility Test*: (Originally called Bend, Twist, and Touch). With his back to the wall and hands together, the subject bends forward, touches an "X" between his feet, straightens, twists to the left and touches an "X" behind him on the wall. He repeats the cycle, alternately twisting to the right and to the left, doing as many as possible in the time limit.

3. *Explosive Strength.* The ability to expend a maximum of energy in one or a series of explosive acts. This factor is distinguished from other strength factors in requiring mobilization of *energy* for a burst of effort, rather than continuous strain, stress, or repeated exertion of muscles. The two tests chosen to represent this factor emphasize different specific activities.

a. *Shuttle-Run Test*: Twenty-yard distance, covered 5 times for 100-yard total.

b. *Softball Throw Test*: The subject throws a 12-inch softball as far as possible without moving his feet.

4. *Static Strength.* The maximum *force* which a subject can exert, for a brief period, where the force is exerted continuously up to this maximum. In contrast to other strength factors, this force can be exerted against external objects (e.g., lifting heavy weights, pulling against a dynamometer) rather than in supporting or propelling the body's own weight.

a. *Hand-grip Test*: The subject squeezes a Narragansett Company grip dynamometer as hard as possible.

5. *Dynamic Strength.* The ability to exert muscular force *repeatedly* or continuously over time. It represents muscular endurance and emphasizes the

resistance of the muscles to fatigue. The common emphasis of tests measuring this factor is on the *power* of the muscles to propel, support, or move the body repeatedly or to support it for prolonged periods.

a. *Pull-ups Test*: The subject hangs from bar with palm facing his body, and does as many pull-ups as possible.

6. *Trunk Strength.* This is a second, more limited, dynamic strength factor specific to the trunk muscles, particularly the abdominal muscle.

a. *Leg-lifts Test:* While flat on his back, the subject raises his legs to a vertical position and lowers them to the floor as many times as possible in the time limit.

7. *Gross Body Coordination.* Ability to coordinate the simultaneous actions of different parts of the body while making gross body movements.

a. *Cable Jump Test*: With both hands, the subject holds, in front of him, a short rope. He attempts to jump through this rope without tripping, falling, or releasing the rope.

8. *Gross Body Equilibrium.* The ability of an individual to maintain his equilibrium despite forces pulling him off balance, while he has to depend mainly on nonvisual (e.g., vestibular and kinesthetic) cues.

a. *Balance A Test*: Using his preferred foot, and keeping his hands on his hips, the subject balances for as long as possible on a ¾-inch wide rail.

9. *Stamina.* The capacity to continue maximum effort, requiring prolonged exertion over time. This factor has the alternate name of "cardiovascular endurance."

a. *600-yard Run-Walk Test*: The student attempts to cover a 600-yard distance in as short a time as possible.

The National Study. The next step in this program was to establish *standards* for evaluating the performance of *individual* boys and girls on the separate tests. Tests found to be most reliable and diagnostic of the different ability factors were assembled into "batteries" and administered to high school students throughout the country.

In all, 14 tests found to cover 9 basic abilities were administered to more than 20,000 boys and girls between the ages of 12 and 18 in 45 cities throughout the United States. (The list of cities and description of the cross sections achieved is presented in Fleishman 1964a). This phase produced the norms (percentile tables) for these tests as well as developmental curves showing changes with age on the different physical fitness components for the 14 tests. Finally, 10 tests were recommended as the most efficient and reliable for measuring the 9 basic abilities. These tests have been called the *Basic Fitness Tests.*

Norms and developmental curves for these tests may be found elsewhere (Fleishman, 1964a,b). Additionally, a record keeping system, called the Performance Record (Fleishman, 1964c) was developed to provide fitness profiles, conversions of raw scores to percentiles, a "fitness index," and the plotting of progress as a function of conditioning programs.

Summary of Findings and Implications

The fruits of this research program are of several sorts. First, we have a better understanding of the structure of the physical fitness areas—the dimensions which best describe the variety of performance called for by the plethora of available physical fitness tests. It is seen that a relatively small number of such dimensions (or abilities) account for these diverse performances. In this sense the program was scientifically useful in bringing additional order to this field and in simplifying our descriptions of what needs to be measured in this area.

1. These results confirm that "physical proficiency" is not a single general ability; rather physical proficiency can best be described in terms of a number of broad, relatively independent abilities. The same individuals may be high on some abilities and low on others. In these terms, the more abilities an individual scores high on, the more "physically fit" he can be said to be. The results also allow more precise definition of each ability than was possible before.

2. A second category or result includes the many specific facts discovered about the nature of physical proficiencies and their interrelationships. For example, we now better understand the role of muscular endurance in strength tests, the relations between capacities of flexor and extensor muscles, and the primary abilities that account for running speed. Also confirmed is the distinction between two primary flexibility abilities and the generality of static strength across different muscle groups.

The "developmental curves" derived from the research are additional results in this second category. These curves show the rate of "growth" of the different physical proficiencies from age to age (Fleishman, 1964a). It was found that the curves for girls differed in form from those for boys in showing more marked developmental stages. For the boys the shapes of most curves were similar, but there were different critical ages at which the curves leveled out, depending on the ability measured.

Especially illuminating were the detailed analyses of strength tasks. Any characterization of individual strength which ignores one or more of the four strength abilities identified is incomplete.

Since several abilities were found to extend across different muscle groups (e.g., limbs and trunk), this points up the importance of "central" factors in physical fitness in addition to those reflected in the specific muscle apparatus. Such central factors include central nervous system involvement, responses to kinesthetic feedback mechanisms, heart and circulatory system development, general energy level, etc.

TABLE 4-1

Possible Strength Factors Hypothesized in The Experimental Strength Tests

	Dynamic Strength Arms		Dynamic Strength		Endurance			Explosive Strength		Possible General Factors				
	Flex.	Ext.	Legs	Trunk	Dynamic	Static	Runs	Arms	Legs	Dynamic Strength	Static Strength	Explosive Strength	Arm Strength	Leg Strength
1. Leg Lifts			x							x				
2. Push-ups (in 15 sec.)		x								x			x	
3. Reverse Sit-ups				x						x				
4. Deep Kneebends			x							x				x
5. Sit-ups				x						x				
6. Squat Thrusts	x		x							x				
7. Pull Weights										x	x		x	
8. Hand Grip											x		x	

	Push Weights-Arms	Arm Pull-Dyna.	Push Weights-Feet	Trunk Pull-Dyna.	Rope Climb	Dips (in 10 sec.)	Vertical Jump	Dips (to limit)	Standing Broad Jump	Leg Raiser	Ten-Yard Dash	Bent Arm Hang	Fifty-yard Dash	Chins (to limit)	Shuttle Run	Chins (in 20 sec.)	Medic. Ball Put (stand.)	Hold Half Sit-up	Medic. Ball Put (sit.)	Hold Half Push-up	Softball Throw	Push-ups (to limit)

9. Push Weights-Arms
10. Arm Pull-Dyna.
11. Push Weights-Feet
12. Trunk Pull-Dyna.
13. Rope Climb
14. Dips (in 10 sec.)
15. Vertical Jump
16. Dips (to limit)
17. Standing Broad Jump
18. Leg Raiser
19. Ten-Yard Dash
20. Bent Arm Hang
21. Fifty-yard Dash
22. Chins (to limit)
23. Shuttle Run
24. Chins (in 20 sec.)
25. Medic. Ball Put (stand.)
26. Hold Half Sit-up
27. Medic. Ball Put (sit.)
28. Hold Half Push-up
29. Softball Throw
30. Push-ups (to limit)

3. A third category of results of this research relates to specific fitness measurement principles discovered. We now know that variations in test procedures produce given variations in the fitness factors measured and in the reliability of the measure. For example, (a) speeded administration (timed) of a dynamic strength test reduces its "purity" and brings in a second ability factor (explosive strength); (b) longer shuttle run tests are more reliable than shorter ones in use; (c) simple dynamometer tests are preferred (over weightlifting tests) as measures of static strength; (d) a gross body equilibrium ability factor is best measured by one-foot, rail standing tests with the eyes closed; (e) a leg lifts test is more valid and reliable than sit-ups for measuring trunk strength.

4. A fourth major kind of outcome was the specification of the most efficient, practical, and reliable tests for measuring each ability and their assembly into a battery of *Basic Fitness Tests* (Fleishman, 1964b). This battery, which will undoubtedly be further improved by additional research, is based on our present state of research knowledge. A major phase of this work was the development of normative standards for the tests on a much larger national sample than has been possible heretofore. Simplified interpretative tables were provided for ages 12 through 18. Improved methods of evaluating and interpreting individual performances were developed using modern measurement principles. These included forms of profile analysis, computation of a simplified Fitness Index, and evaluation of the rate of progress.

5. There are, of course, still many unanswered questions. Some of the most intriguing ones concern the nature of "coordination" and "agility." A concerted effort needs to be made to see if these are usefully considered "separate" abilities or if we can account for such performances in terms of the abilities already identified. Additional studies would involve a greater variety of "coordinated" performances than it has been possible to include so far. The use of our battery of tests, in the same study with these complex tests, should allow us to specify how much of the variance in such performances we still need to explain. At present, a multilimb coordination ability appears distinct from any gross body coordination. The former is involved in perceptual-motor tasks involving simultaneous use of multiple controls (feet-hand, two-hand, two-feet), where the subject is typically seated. The latter appears to require movement of the entire body.

There is a need to use these tests to predict more complex skilled performances. This would tell us what portion of such performances are specific to the individual skills and how much can be related to the physical fitness factors identified in our present program. There is also the practical question of how valid our tests are in predicting performance in complex jobs involving physical skills.

6. We also need to know more about the trainability of these component abilities and the degree of transfer of training across tasks representing the

same abilities. We would expect high transfer between tasks on the same ability and low transfer between abilities. A more interesting question is the amount of transfer of training from these ability components to more complex skilled performances.

PART III—STUDIES OF SKILL LEARNING

Effects of Practice

For a number of years, we have been interested in the relations between reference ability measures developed around our perceptual-motor taxonomy and a variety of learning phenomena (Fleishman and Hempel, 1954b; Fleishman and Hempel, 1955; Fleishman, 1957a; Fleishman, 1960; Fleishman and Rich, 1963). Our results have allowed us to show the differential role of these abilities at different stages of learning more complex tasks. These studies have as an additional goal the specification of abilities predictive of advanced levels of learning.

One of our early studies was confined to the analyses of inter-trial correlations of two similar tasks practiced in different orders (Fleishman, 1953a); but subsequent studies have always included "reference measures," external to the practice task. In a typical study, 200 to 300 subjects received a battery of reference tests known to sample certain abilities and then received practice on a criterion practice task. Through the use of factor-analytic techniques of the correlation patterns obtained, we could examine the loadings of successive trial scores on the criterion task on the abilities defined by the reference tasks.

In general, these studies, dealing with a great variety of practice tasks, show that: (a) as practice continues, changes occur in the particular combinations of abilities contributing to performance; (b) these changes are progressive and systematic and eventually become stabilized; (c) the contribution of "nonmotor" abilities (e.g., verbal, spatial), which may play a role early in learning, decreases systematically with practice relative to "motor abilities"; and (d) there is also an increase in a factor specific to the task itself.

Figure 4-24 illustrates a typical result obtained using a visual discrimination reaction task. Figure 4-25 shows that certain abilities discriminate individuals high and low in proficiency early in the learning of a complex task, but not later in learning, while other abilities discriminate mainly at advanced levels of learning.

The repeated finding of an increase in specificity of the tasks learned indicates that performance in perceptual-motor tasks becomes increasingly a function of habits and skills acquired in the task itself. But pre-task abilities play a role, too, and their interactions with learning phenomena are important sources of variance to be studied. Furthermore, it appears desirable

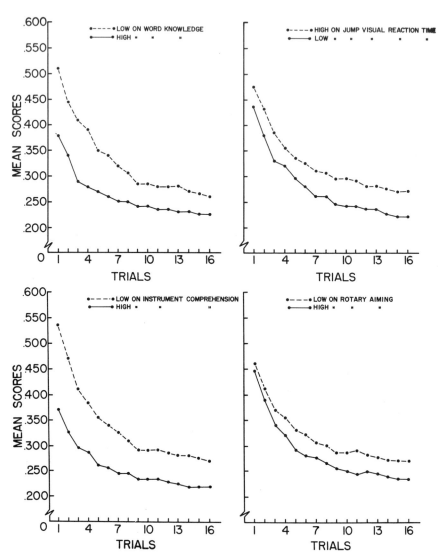

FIG. 4-24. Comparison of learning curves on a discrimination reaction time task for groups stratified on different test variables.*

*Figs. 4-24 and 4-25 are from Fleishman, E. A., & Hempel, W. E., Jr. The relation between abilities and improvement with practice in a visual discrimination reaction task. *J. Exper. Psychol., 49, 1955, 301-312. Copyright (1955) by the American Psychological Association, and reproduced by permission.*

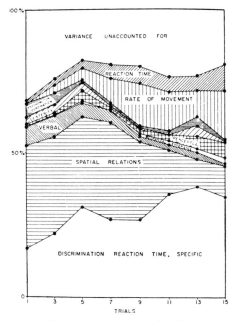

FIG. 4-25. Percentage of variance represented by loadings on each ability factor at different stages of practice on the discrimination reaction time task (percentage of variance is represented by the size of the shaded areas for each factor).

to define better the variance now termed specific to individual tasks. I am optimistic that some of this variance is not really "specified"; rather, we may need to be more ingenious at teasing it out.

Much of our later work has been concerned with the pursuit of this variance now defined as specific to late stages of learning tasks. Hypotheses we have explored are as follows: (a) late-stage measures of different tasks have abilities in common not found in early stages of the same tasks (Fleishman, 1957a); (b) the ability to *integrate* component abilities represents a separate individual difference variable not found in early-stage learning; (c) kinesthetic ability factors play an increasing role in psychomotor learning relative to spatial-visual abilities. Confirmation of this hypothesis(c) was found in a recent study (Fleishman and Rich, 1963). In this study, we first had to develop a measure of "kinesthetic sensitivity" on which subjects differ reliably. Performance in this measure was a good indicator of late learning in a two-hand coordination task, but not of early learning.

Use of the Paradigm in Training Settings. Lately our findings and methods have been extended to more complex tasks studied over lengthy periods of time. In one study (Parker and Fleishman, 1960), we developed a simulation of an air intercept mission on which subjects learned a highly complex tracking task over a seven-week period. The same 203 subjects received one of the most extensive batteries of perceptual-motor and cognitive tests ever assembled. The design allowed for the identification of 15 ability factors and the specification of their contribution to tracking performance at different stages of learning over this lengthy period.

In a later study (Parker and Fleishman, 1961) we attempted to make sure of our analytic information about the ability requirements of this task in designing a skill training program. In terms of our integrated error measure of performance during the last three training sessions, the experimental group showed a 39 percent increase in proficiency over the second best training condition investigated.

We have also studied the relation of ability variables to learning in a real training environment (Fleishman and Fruchter, 1960). In this latter case, we were able to show the abilities underlying the acquisition of skill at different stages of Morse code learning in an air force radio telegraphy school. Specifically, early learning depended on two auditory-perceptual abilities while later learning was more a function of an ability named "speed of closure." This latter represented the ability to unify or organize an apparently disparate field into meaningful units. This study extends our findings on learning and individual differences to perceptual learning.

Individual Differences and Component-total Task Relationships. A recent study (Fleishman, 1965) investigated the relations between individual differences in performance on task components and subsequent performance on a total task. Two hundred and four subjects practiced the components of a complex multidimensional compensatory pursuit task singly and in combination. These components involved discrete display-control relationships. The total task, which was practiced last, required an integration of these components; that is, the subjects had to operate the multiple controls in order to minimize error indications on all displays simultaneously. The problems investigated were as follows: (a) the extent to which performance on task components, individually practiced, is predictive of subsequent total task performance; (b) the extent to which practice on combinations of components is predictive of total task performance; (c) the inter-relationships among component performances; and (d) the relative contribution of various component performances to total and subtask performances. The analysis provides some tentative principles of part-whole task relationships relevant to the understanding of skilled performance.

Prediction of Retention. I would not like to leave the topic of individual differences and skill learning without mentioning our studies on retention (Fleishman and Parker, 1962). Very little is known about individual differences in retention. We were able to give people extended (seven weeks) practice on a highly complex perceptual-motor skill and obtain matched groups of subjects back after periods of no practice of 1, 4, 9, 14, and 24 months. Thus, we varied retention intervals as well as type of initial guidance and level of original learning. The main points of interest here are that there was virtually no loss in skill regardless of the length of the retention interval, and that the most powerful variable operating was individual differences in the level of original learning. The prediction of retention from original learning was independent of the length of the retention interval. Thus, for all intervals, even up to two years, individual differences at the end of learning correlated in the .80's and .90's with subsequent performance after periods of no practice. Our design also allowed us to say that this prediction was not accounted for by the subject's pre-task abilities, but rather, was explainable in terms of individual differences among subjects in the specific habits acquired in practicing the original task.

Individual Differences and Other Motor Learning Phenomena

A variety of other learning phenomena have been studied in relation to motor skill (see Bilodeau, 1966). These include transfer of training, habit interference, reminiscence, performance during massed versus distributed practice, etc. Little study has been made of abilities and other individual differences which predict performance under such conditions. A recent study has provided encouragement that a subject's previously developed abilities can help us make such predictions (Fleishman and Ellison, 1969). Subjects were given practice on a complex perceptual-motor task and later the display control relationships on the task were changed. Subjects were later shifted back to the original task. During initial learning subjects performed on massed as well as distributed trials. The same subjects received a series of motor, spatial ability tests and personality measures.

The study showed that certain ability measures predicted which subjects would show the most transfer or interference at the shift points, but there was no "general susceptibility to interference" trait identified. Personality tests of "rigidity-flexibility," anxiety, etc., did not predict habit interference effects. Performance during massed practice was just as predictable from ability measures as performance during distributed practice. A major finding was the sharp *decrease* in prediction by ability tests of the trial following the massed practice (the reminiscence trial). There was also an increase in the predictions by the personality tests during this trial. Thus individual differences in recovery from "fatigue like" states (occasioned by massed practice) would seem to depend on different abilities than do other learning phenomena.

CONCLUDING REMARKS

Before closing, we may mention that little systematic work has been done in school settings with regard to motor skills development, prediction, and evaluation. There are several additional issues here. One is the problem of using indices of motor abilities as diagnostic tools in predicting subsequent academic achievement and adjustments. Some educators feel this is a significant area, but this still needs to be demonstrated.

Another general issue is that of developing motor and other noncognitive abilities and skills by some systematic educational program in the schools. It is probably safe to say that our educational system, while providing certain specific skills (e.g., spelling) is also aimed at developing certain general abilities capable of transfer to a variety of substantive areas and skills. The general abilities which tend to be developed are cognitive abilities, e.g., verbal, numerical, conceptual abilities. Relatively little is done in the way of systematic, sequenced curriculum development to promote abilities such as spatial visualization, manual dexterity, or perceptual speed. Many of these abilities are more likely to be critical to non-academic fields or to areas of vocational or special education. Yet, early in a child's schooling it is impossible to know if the development of such abilities will eventually be relevant to his subsequent occupational choice.

Often overlooked is the relevance of such non-cognitive abilities to highly complex academic professions. For example, many potential engineers are lost, or make slower progress, not for lack of conceptual or mathematic abilities, but because of poor spatial orientation; many students have difficulties in dental school because of poor manual-dexterity or spatial visualization. The point is that there is ample justification and need for systematic programs for developing non-cognitive skills, in their own right, within the framework of our school system. With respect to the area of motor skill this underlines the need for techniques to assess base-line levels and progress through whatever program is developed.

The same need applies to the problems utilizing motor ability assessment techniques in predicting subsequent achievements in early school grades. There are many hypotheses, but little actual data, on the relevance of motor difficulties to later problems in learning academic skills. Many techniques used by teachers are too subjective (for example, noting how a pupil holds his pencil) and subject to error. It is difficult to have much confidence in such assessments. What is needed is a set of standardized motor skill tests, with sufficient normative data and predictive validity.

What do we know at present and what can we do? We know from a vast body of research, much of which has been cited above, that there is no such unitary thing as motor skill. Although most of the research has been with older children and young adults, it is very clear that there are several dimensions of motor abilities which need to be assessed. Measures of each of these dimensions (or factors) correlate poorly with each other and have different predictive abilities and lead to different programs of training for their development. A conclusion drawn from a measure of manual dexterity, for example, may be quite different from one drawn from a test of multilimb coordination.

The specification of the motor ability factors identified provides the idealized coverage for a comprehensive battery of motor ability tests. If it is not feasible to cover each factor, they at least provide a basis for selecting measures of particular abilities. The factors specified also provide the basis for materials development for use in training particular motor abilities.

References

Bilodeau, E. (ed.) *Acquisition of skill.* New York: Academic Press, 1966.

Fitts, P. M. Engineering psychology. In S. S. Stevens (ed.) *Handbook of experimental psychology.* New York: John Wiley & Sons, Inc., 1951.

Fleishman, E. A. A factor analysis of intra-task performance on two psychomotor tests. *Psychometrika,* 1953, 18, No. 1. (a)

Fleishman, E. A. Testing for psychomotor abilities by means of apparatus tests. *Psychological Bulletin,* 1953, 50, 241–262. (b)

Fleishman, E. A. Dimensional analysis of psychomotor abilities. *Journal of Experimental Psychology,* 1954, 48, 437–454.

Fleishman, E. A. Psychomotor selection tests: Research and application in the U. S. Air Force. *Personnel Psychology,* 1956, 9, 449–467.

Fleishman, E. A. A comparative study of aptitude patterns in unskilled and skilled psychomotor performances. *Journal of Applied Psychology.* 1957, 41, 263–272. (a)

Fleishman, E. A. Factor structure in relation to task difficulty in psychomotor performance. *Educational and Psychological Measurement,* 1957, 17, 522–532. (b)

Fleishman, E. A. An analysis of positioning movements and static reactions. *Journal of Experimental Psychology,* 1958, 55, 13–24. (a)

Fleishman, E. A. Dimensional analysis of movement reactions. *Journal of Experimental Psychology,* 1958, 55, 438–453. (b)

Fleishman, E. A. Abilities at different stages of practice in rotary pursuit performance. *Journal of Experimental Psychology,* 1960, 60, 162–171.

Fleishman, E. A. Factor analyses of physical fitness tests. *Educational and Psychological Measurement,* 1963, 23, 647–661.

Fleishman, E. A. *The structure and measurement of physical fitness.* Englewood Cliffs, N.J.: Prentice-Hall, 1964. (a)

Fleishman, E. A. *Examiner's Manual for the Basic Fitness Tests.* Englewood Cliffs, N.J.: Prentice-Hall, 1964. (b)

Fleishman, E. A. *Performance Record for the Basic Fitness Tests.* Englewood Cliffs, N.J.: Prentice-Hall, 1964. (c)

Fleishman, E. A. The prediction of total task performance from prior practice on task components. *Human Factors,* 1965, 7, 18–27.

Fleishman, E. A. Performance assessment based on an empirically derived task taxonomy. *Human Factors,* 1967, 9, 349–366.

Fleishman, E. A., & Ellison, G. D. A factor analysis of fine manipulative performance. *Journal of Applied Psychology,* 1962, 46, 96-105.

Fleishman, E. A., & Ellison, G. D. Prediction of transfer and other learning phenomena from ability and personality measures. *Journal of Educational Psychology,* 1969, 60, 300–314.

Fleishman, E. A., & Fruchter, B. Factor structure and predictability of successive stages of learning morse code. *Journal of Applied Psychology,* 1960, 44, 97–101.

Fleishman, E. A., & Fruchter, B. Component and total task relations at different stages of learning a complex tracking task. *Perceptual and Motor Skills,* 1965, 20, 1305–1311.

Fleishman, E. A., & Hempel, W. E., Jr. A factor analysis of dexterity tests. *Personnel Psychology,* 1954, 7, 15–32. (a)

Fleishman, E. A., & Hempel, W. E., Jr. Changes in factor structure of a complex psychomotor test as a function of practice. *Psychometrika,* 1954, 18, 239–252. (b)

Fleishman, E. A., & Hempel, W. E., Jr. The relation between abilities and improvement with practice in a visual discrimination reaction task. *Journal of Experimental Psychology,* 1955, 49, 301–312.

Fleishman, E. A., & Hempel, W. E., Jr. Factorial analysis of complex psychomotor performance and related skills. *Journal of Applied Psychology,* 1956, 40, 96–104.

Fleishman, E. A., & Parker, J. F. Factors in the retention and relearning of perceptual-motor skill. *Journal of Experimental Psychology,* 1962, 64, 215–226.

Fleishman, E. A., & Rich, S. Role of kinesthetic and spatial-visual abilities in perceptual-rotor learning. *Journal of Experimental Psychology,* 1963, 66, 6–11.

Gagné, R. M., & Fleishman, E. A. *Psychology and human performance: An introduction to psychology.* New York: Henry Holt, 1959.

Hempel, W. E., Jr., & Fleishman, E. A. A factor analysis of physical proficiency and manipulative skill. *Journal of Applied Psychology,* 1955, 39, 12–16.

Parker, J. F., & Fleishman, E. A. Ability factor analysis of physical proficiency and manipulative skill. *Journal of Applied Psychology,* 1953, 39, 12–16.

Parker, J. F., & Fleishman, E. A. Ability factors and component performance measures as predictors of complex tracking behavior. *Psychological Monographs,* 1960, 74, No. 16 (Whole No. 503).

Parker, J. F., & Fleishman, E. A. Use of analytical information concerning task requirements to increase the effectiveness of skill training. *Journal of Applied Psychology,* 1961, 45, 295–302.

Chapter 5

INDIVIDUAL DIFFERENCES

MARSHALL B. JONES

The Pennsylvania State University

Except for a persistent but distinctly minoritarian tradition originating in the work of Herbert Woodrow in the 30's and hardened in the Air Force Personnel and Training Research Command following World War II, the study of skills and skill acquisition has been and is an experimental area. Psychologists have manipulated task or procedural variations—for example, distribution of practice, knowledge of results, or task equipment—and studied the effects on group performance. Individual differences have figured into this enterprise in two ways. To the experimentalist they are "within-group error," background variation against which experimental effects are evaluated. To the differential psychologist they are motor or psychomotor tests.

The study of individual differences in motor skills and learning has always been understood as a branch of psychologic testing—and properly so, because a skill is not acquired except as the occasion for its acquisition is arranged; skills are not found "in nature." Whenever we teach people skills, we inevitably test them at the same time because some people reach higher levels of performance or reach them more quickly than others. People sort themselves out in the process of learning or training. Hence, from a differential point of view the task or the process of mastering it becomes a test.

Psychomotor tests have been important in applied psychology, principally as predictors of success or failure in pilot training. Many of the most familiar tasks in motor-skills research were developed to predict the air force pilot-training criterion, a differential purpose. However, no sooner were these tests developed than they were "taken over" by experimental psychologists, who quickly converted them into standard instruments for the study of human learning in the general or experimental sense. The differential study of these same tasks, their study as tests, if you like, continued but always under the lowering shadow of its experimental big brother.

Meanwhile, no one seemed fully to appreciate that individual differences in motor skills are sharply demarcated from other areas of psychologic testing. This demarcation takes place along two clear frontiers. First, motor skills involve a "continuous interaction of response processes with input and feedback processes" (Fitts, 1962, p. 177). Tracking or two-hand coordination, learning to play tennis or billiards, typewriting—these skills all involve an integrated, continuing, and active process. They may be done badly but they must be done in a more or less unitary fashion or not at all. In the rest of psychology a test consists of *items,* each one of which is separate and distinct from the others. When psychologists build tests of intelligence, ability or personality, they select and weight items. Psychomotor tests, however, cannot be constructed in this fashion because they are not made of items. In constructing a psychomotor test we build or modify equipment, design or redesign testing requirements or procedures. In short, we do the same things experimentalists do; and when we evaluate the tests, we perform experiments. We study the standard and revised versions of the Mashburn Apparatus, for example, and see which best suits our purposes.

The second difference has to do with learning. In the rest of psychology a test is administered; it is given once, and each subject provides a single score for the test as a whole. This total score may have parts, for example, verbal and numerical subtotals in an intelligence test; and sometimes a test is given twice, usually to determine test-retest reliability. The test itself, however, is a one-shot, one-time affair. Skill testing, on the other hand, usually involves learning. The test is not administered but practiced, and instead of one total score for each subject we have as many overall scores as there are trials of practice. If there are 16 trials, we have 16 overall scores of performance. This complication might be no more than a nuisance were it not that differential composition varies systematically from trial to trial, that different abilities are involved at different stages of practice (Fleishman, 1967). Hence, from a differential point of view we can no longer speak of "the" test, because each trial is somewhat different and taps a somewhat different mix of abilities. What then should we do? Should we accept the last trial of practice as "the" test? Should we average the trials? Or should we, perhaps, simply admit to having k distinct tests?

It is always possible to make a decision on purely formal grounds, by means of some kind of statistical argument, and psychologists take advantage of this possibility more than most people—more than they should, because good decisions are not made this way. Individual differences in practice form themselves into a highly organized process; and before we can decide how to "score" or analyze this process, we must first determine its critical dimensions. The problem we face can only be solved by finding out how the differential process that accompanies learning breaks down as a matter of fact. Once this much is understood, a decision as to how skill acquisition should be analyzed is automatic.

The next step, once the question of analysis has been settled, is to review the process of building psychomotor tests so they have desirable properties. Many people treat tests as if they were natural phenomena, as if there were some point in trying to find out "what they measure." These tests, we need to remember, are instruments of our own devising. Sometimes they have properties we did not intend them to have and all of them lack properties we wish they had; but in no case can they be adequately understood except as a human product, as something artificial. Hence, once the terrain has been scouted out, the construction of psychomotor tests becomes the next order of business. The chapter concludes with a discussion of factor isolation in the context of ability and motor testing.

ANALYSIS

Superdiagonal Form

The differential process that accompanies learning is partly expressed in the trial variances. Do they increase, decrease, or remain the same with practice? The question was asked early in the differential study of learning and has cropped up sporadically ever since. The most general answer is that trial variance tends to follow the mean. If performance is measured by number of errors or some other score that decreases with practice, trial variance tends also to decrease with practice. If performance is measured by time-on-target or some score that increases with practice, then trial variance increases with practice. Though it has exceptions, for example, rotary pursuit (Fleishman, 1960, p. 163), this generality holds widely enough. Nevertheless, it lacks interest because of its technical character. Mean and variance are positively associated in all sorts of data, almost certainly as a scaling phenomenon. When the mean increases or decreases, the scale or unit of measurement changes and, with it, the variance.

Individual differences in skill acquisition are also expressed in the inter-trial correlations, and this time a substantive or nontechnical regularity is observed. Correlations among trials of practice always show *superdiagonal form* (M. B. Jones, 1962). First, all correlations are positive. Second, the closer together two trials come in the practice series, the more positive the correlation between them is. The strongest correlations are between neighboring trials, while the weakest correlation appears in the upper, right-hand corner of the matrix, between the first and last trials.

The differences among the three idealized correlation patterns in table 5-1

TABLE 5-1

Increasing, Level, and Decreasing Superdiagonal Forms (Hypothetic)

Trial	1	2	3	4	5	6
1	—	.70	.66	.60	.60	.60
2		—	.80	.73	.73	.73
3			—	.82	.82	.82
4	INCREASING			—	.92	.92
5					—	.92
6						—
1	—	.81	.72	.69	.63	.60
2		—	.80	.77	.70	.67
3			—	.82	.75	.72
4	LEVEL			—	.79	.76
5					—	.81
6						—
1	—	.70	.41	.19	.07	−.02
2		—	.47	.22	.08	.01
3			—	.29	.11	.00
4	DECREASING			—	.14	−.03
5					—	.04
6						—

are as significant as their all being superdiagonal forms. In the increasing pattern the superdiagonal correlations, $r_{i,i+1}$, get larger and larger with practice—in this example, increasing from .70 for the first two trials to .92 for the last two. At the same time, the correlations decrease regularly going up any column or across any row to the right. As practice proceeds, the trials correlate less and less with the first trial and more and more with the last.

In the middle pattern, marked "level," the superdiagonal correlations remain stationary around .80. Nevertheless, the same regularities hold here as in the increasing pattern. If $i \rightarrow j \rightarrow k$ where "$\rightarrow$" means "precedes," then

$$r_{i,j} \geqslant r_{i,k}$$

and

$$r_{i,k} \leqslant r_{j,k},$$

as in all superdiagonal forms. These same inequalities also hold in the decreasing pattern. The only difference is that here the superdiagonal correlations weaken with practice and finally vanish.

Of course, in empiric cases the patterns are not as regular as in these hypothetic examples. Nevertheless, one or another of these patterns is always recognizably present. The superdiagonal character of inter-trial matrices is universal.

Stabilization

The increasing pattern in table 5-1 also serves to illustrate what is meant by "stabilization." The last three trials subtend three correlations, all equal to .92. Also, each one of the first three trials relates identically to the last three trials. Trial 2, for example, correlates .73 with trials 4, 5, and 6. Wherever stabilization is reached, the trials of practice are divided into two groups: those that precede a critical trial x_o —trial 4 in this example—and those that follow x_o plus x_o itself. The two groups consist of *learning* and *terminal* trials respectively. Formally, stabilization occurs whenever there exists a critical trial x_o such that

$$r_{x_i x_j} = r_{x_k x_l} \ (o \to i, j, k, l)$$

and

$$r_{x_i x_j} = r_{x_j x_k} \ (i \to o \to j, k).$$

In practice, of course, we do not insist on identity. It is sufficient if after some point the correlations neither increase nor decrease going along the rows to the right; they may bob around a bit as long as there is no tendency for systematic change. Similarly, the correlations among trials following the critical point are all essentially equal.

The great majority of motor tasks shows increasing superdiagonal form with stabilization. A few tasks, about which we will talk more in a moment, show decreasing superdiagonal form with stabilization (M. B. Jones, 1969). Technically, the decreasing form in table 5-1 cannot be said to stabilize because we do not know that subsequent trials would show zero-order correlations with all preceding trials. However, if trials of this description did exist, we would have stabilization under the formal definition just given. It is not uncommon in the increasing patterns for the defining conditions of stabilization to be met with no deviations exceeding .01 or .02. In decreasing patterns, however, correlations often vary widely around zero, both positively and negatively. The reason for this difference is technical, viz., the sampling error for correlations near zero is much greater than for correlations near unity.

The level pattern in table 5-1 indicates what happens when stabilization does not occur. The rows are the most telling feature. As long as the correlations keep falling along the rows to the right as more and more trials are taken, stabilization is not reached.

Of course, the stabilization we are talking about is *differential* stabilization. It is the differential analog of a plateau in the study of mean changes with practice. Indeed, it may be a plateau in the sense that the differential process, after stabilizing for awhile, starts changing again. For this reason it might be better, technically, to define stabilization in terms of three or four trials without change instead of "no further change." But there is no real problem here; wherever any confusion might arise, we can always make the change. It is more important to note that stabilization need not occur at all, just as it need not occur in the means. It may be that differential change continues indefinitely; in fact, where the mean continues to improve indefinitely, as in the examples cited by Fitts (1962), we would expect the differential process also to continue indefinitely without stabilization.

If and when stabilization does occur, all terminal trials become differentially equivalent. Formally,

$$x_0 \quad = t + s_0$$
$$x_{0+1} = t + s_{0+1}$$
$$\dots\dots\dots\dots\dots$$
$$x_m \quad = t \mid s_m$$

and

$$\sigma^2_{s_i} = \sigma^2_{s_{j'}}$$

where t is an errorless measure of terminal proficiency common to all terminal trials and the s_i are specific factors. In short, the terminal trials constitute a Spearman unit hierarchy with equal loadings on the one common factor t.

Simple and Complex Tasks

All psychomotor tests, except very simple ones, show level or increasing superdiagonal form, almost always with stabilization. Table 5-2 contains data for a representative case: eight one-minute trials on the two-hand coordination test in a sample of 152 basic airmen. The results are more regular and stabilize at a higher level than is generally the case but the exaggeration is not great in either respect. The measure of performance is the number of brass contacts over which the pin passes per trial. This number increases with practice as the subjects learn to keep the pin on the track, and the variance follows the mean. Stabilization is reached at the sixth trial. The correlations among trials 6, 7, and 8 do not differ by more than .01 from .93; and the correlations with the last three trials are stable along the rows within equally narrow limits.

Table 5-3 contains data for 16 trials on micrometer adjustment, and this time the results are unusual. In addition to micrometer adjustment, decreasing superdiagonal form has been reported for only two other tasks, also very simple—line drawing and level positioning (M. B. Jones, 1969). In

TABLE 5-2

Means, Standard Deviations, and Inter-trial Correlations
for the Two-Hand Coordination Test*

Trial	1	2	3	4	5	6	7	8	$\overline{X}$	SD
1	—	.79	.77	.74	.73	.71	.71	.70	34.9	11.8
2		—	.87	.87	.84	.82	.82	.82	42.9	14.9
3			—	.91	.89	.87	.85	.86	46.1	15.8
4				—	.91	.88	.86	.88	50.4	16.2
5					—	.89	.90	.90	54.7	18.9
6						—	.93	.93	58.1	18.1
7							—	.94	61.0	18.6
8								—	63.3	18.7

* From Jones (1962, p. 274). *Copyright by the American Psychological Association, and used by permission.*

micrometer adjustment the subject turns the knob of a micrometer. For each turn he is credited with 25 points. Since target is 200 points, the subject must learn to make exactly eight turns. After each trial he is told how many units "long" or "short" he was from target. On the first trial the subject is told to turn the knob around once and given feedback—on the average, 178 units short. Thereafter, the subject is instructed to approximate target as closely as he can. Performance is scored in absolute deviations from 200 units.

After the first trial the mean falls quickly; by the eighth trial it is still dropping, but very gently. Differences between subjects are low on the first trial, jump dramatically on the second trial, and follow the mean thereafter. Meanwhile, the inter-trial correlations are being systematically degraded. For the first seven trials a superdiagonal pattern is plainly present, though the rows dip very low by the seventh trial, in two instances becoming negative. After the seventh trial the correlation pattern becomes disorganized. The correlations among trials 8 through 16 show no evidence of superdiagonal form except a small tendency for the correlations to be positive and two substantial correlations in the superdiagonal. The correlations between the first seven and the last nine trials are devoid of pattern except, again, for some tendency toward positivity. In this task, therefore, we see a decreasing superdiagonal form stabilizing at the eighth trial with correlations near zero.

Micrometer adjustment is not a challenging task. After 16 trials the subjects deviate on the average by less than half a turn from target and, as already noted, there is very little consistency in these deviations after trial 7. Those subjects who overshoot on one terminal trial are no more likely than other subjects to overshoot on the trial just before or after it. However, if a trial does not correlate with its immediate neighbors in the practice series, it seems fairly certain that it will not correlate with anything else either; to put it differently, the true scores for all terminal trials approximate zero for all

TABLE 5-3

Means, Standard Deviations, and Inter-trial Correlations in Micrometer Adjustment*

Trials	1	2	3	4	5	6	7	8	9	10	11	12	13	14	15	16	$\bar{X}$	SD
1	—	.30	.33	.29	.12	.14	-.16	.07	.05	.10	-.00	.04	.03	-.16	-.06	.05	178	7
2		—	.72	.56	.43	.20	-.10	.34	.11	.15	.22	.08	.01	-.02	.13	.06	73	54
3			—	.72	.66	.47	.15	.34	.17	.31	.20	.03	-.08	.06	.03	.18	41	42
4				—	.57	.57	.26	.08	.06	.29	.20	.10	.13	.13	-.05	.20	32	44
5					—	.77	.44	.14	.23	.48	.09	-.10	-.04	-.05	.00	-.04	26	32
6						—	.65	.15	.30	.62	-.01	.11	.01	.02	-.09	.14	23	30
7							—	.19	.36	.60	-.08	.22	.17	.13	.09	.23	18	17
8								—	.19	.09	-.04	.28	.33	.27	.27	.42	20	18
9									—	.47	.14	-.08	.20	.04	.12	.05	13	11
10										—	.08	-.00	.19	.20	.27	.20	15	15
11											—	-.16	.17	.09	.19	-.03	14	9
12												—	.09	.38	.20	.41	11	9
13													—	.09	.06	.12	13	12
14														—	.52	.31	14	11
15															—	.22	12	9
16																—	11	9

* From Jones (1970a, p. 226).

subjects. Except for error, everybody terminates at the same level of near perfection; hence in this task subjects differ only with respect to the rates, routes, or paths they follow in arriving at a common termination.

Correlations or components of correlations generated exclusively by differences in the ways subjects approach terminal proficiency constitute a *rate process.* And all matrices of inter-trial correlations involve a rate process because subjects never go to terminal levels in exactly the same way; but in tasks more complex than line drawing, lever positioning, or micrometer adjustment there are reliable terminal differences too. In the two-hand coordination test, for example, subjects are spread out in a highly reliable fashion over a great range of terminal proficiencies, but note that these proficiencies lie in a single dimension, t. Hence, the correlational expression of terminal proficiency, the terminal process, is a Spearman unit hierarchy. In complex tasks there are at least two processes at work. One derives from differences in terminal proficiency and expresses itself correlationally as a Spearman unit hierarchy, while the other reflects differences in the paths or routes people follow in arriving at terminal proficiency and expresses itself correlationally as a superdiagonal form that wastes away and vanishes with practice.

Intuitively, it seems that terminal and rate processes should exhaust the total matrix. What else is there, after all, except where you are going and how you get there? Nor do our intuitions mislead us in this instance. All matrices of inter-trial correlations break down into rate and terminal processes with no residuum other than sampling error. Since this proposition is central to the differential analysis of skill acquisition, I hasten to give it a more formal treatment.

Decomposition

Wherever practice continues long enough for individual differences to stabilize, it is possible to determine the correlation of each trial with terminal proficiency. Since terminal trials and terminal proficiency, t, differ only by an error score, finding the correlation between t and the terminal trials is a simple matter of correcting for attenuation. Finding the correlations between t and learning trials is only a short step further.

For example, suppose we wanted to find the correlations of all trials with t, the terminal loadings as we will call them, in the data for the two-hand coordination test. The information we need consists of all empiric correlations involving the terminal trials in this instance, trials, 6, 7, and 8. Table 5-4 presents this information in the first three columns. Theoretically, the correlations for any one learning trial should be the same. Since they are not, because error is involved, we enter their average as the single value theory requires, rounded to the second place. Hence trial 1 is put down as having a theoretic correlation of .71 with each of the terminal trials. The correlations

TABLE 5-4

Terminal Loadings in the Two-Hand Coordination Test,
with Data and Preliminary Calculations

Trial	*Empiric Correlations*			*Theoretic Correlation*			*Correlation with* t
	6	7	8	6	7	8	
1	.71	.71	.70	.71	.71	.71	.736
2	.82	.82	.82	.82	.82	.82	.851
3	.87	.85	.86	.86	.86	.86	.892
4	.88	.86	.88	.87	.87	.87	.902
5	.89	.90	.90	.90	.90	.90	.923
6	—	.93	.93	—	.93	.93	.964
7		—	.94		—	.93	.964
8			—			—	.964

among the terminal trials should be equal. Again, error disturbs things; and again we put down the average, rounded to the second place, for the one theoretic value.

Now, the loading of the terminal trials with t is simply the square root of their common intercorrelation. Thus, the terminal loadings for trials 6, 7, and 8 in table 5-4 all equal the square root of .93 or .964. The terminal loadings for the learning trials are obtained from the relation.

$$\lambda_i = \frac{\rho_{it}}{\lambda} ,$$

where λ is the loading for the terminal trials, λ_i the loading for the *ith* learning trial, and ρ_{it} the theoretic or average correlation between the *ith* learning trial and the terminal trials. For example, the loading for trial 2 is

$$\lambda_2 = \frac{.82}{.964} = .851.$$

These loadings define the terminal process. The matrix of covariance components,

$$t_{ij} = \lambda_i \lambda_j ,$$

tells us what the correlations between trials would be if they were determined exclusively by terminal proficiency.

If the total matrix is a stabilized superdiagonal form, the residuals,

$$\mu_{ij} = r_{ij} - t_{ij},$$

will also be a superdiagonal form, decreasing and finally vanishing with practice. Formal proof of this proposition requires some restatement and more technical material than is appropriate here (see M. B. Jones, 1970b). For the present, let us see how the decomposition works in practice.

Table 5-5 presents the decomposition for the two-hand coordination data. The correlations in the upper, right half of the matrix constitute the terminal process and were generated from the terminal loadings in table 5-4. The correlations in the lower, left half of the matrix are residuals, inclusive of sampling variations. Even so, the decreasing superdiagonal character of the residual matrix is plain.

In table 5-3, of course, there is nothing to decompose since the terminal process vanishes anyway. The total correlations are already residual as they stand, that is, rate process plus sampling error.

Rate and Terminal Processes

We can now answer the questions we asked at the beginning as to how we should "score" or analyze the differential process that accompanies motor learning. This analysis should center in terminal proficiency. We do not average the trials, nor do we regard each trial as separate and distinct from every other. A subject's score on a stabilized psychomotor test is best understood as his terminal proficiency. In practice, this means averaging a subject's scores on all *terminal* trials. Since t is errorless, we cannot measure it directly. However, we can approximate it with a high degree of precision. Each terminal trial involves t plus an error component. Hence, as we take more and more terminal trials—and, in principle, we can take as many as we like—the averages approach closer and closer to t. If t does not stabilize, no trial is free from all elements of the rate process. The last trial has fewer of these elements than any other. Hence, we use it—but not without a certain reluctance.

When we speak of typewriting, two-hand coordination, or rotary pursuit

TABLE 5-5

Rate and Terminal Processes in the Two-Hand Coordination Test

Trial	1	2	3	4	5	6	7	8
1	—	.63	.66	.66	.68	.71	.71	.71
2	.16	—	.76	.77	.79	.82	.82	.82
3	.11	.11	—	.80	.82	.86	.86	.86
4	.08	.10	.11	—	.83	.87	.87	.87
5	.05	.05	.07	.08	—	.89	.89	.89
6	.00	.00	.01	.01	.00	—	.93	.93
7	.00	.00	−.01	−.01	.01	00	—	.93
8	−.01	.00	.00	.01	.01	.00	.01	—

we mean the finished or accomplished skill. We refer to terminal proficiency to the exclusion of the rate process. An ability we use in learning a task is not so much part of the task as preparatory to it—related, yes, but in a preliminary way. It happens that terminal proficiency is also more specific to the task than abilities which pass off before stabilization is reached (Fleishman, 1967). Early in practice subjects are often differentiated on the basis of variations having widespread implications. Initial performance, for example, is often heavily weighted with general intelligence because the ability to read or listen to instructions and get them straight is the kind of thing intelligence tests measure. As practice proceeds, people sort themselves out along lines that have more and more to do with specific task requirements; and it becomes harder and harder to predict performance from pre-practice measures. Hence, terminal proficiency is not only what we mean by the task in a differential sense, it also characterizes or reflects the task with a fidelity no learning trial does.

The rate process is usually small, accounting for only a fraction of the total covariance, and the factors in it are transient. The most likely factor structure for the rate process is a simplex (Guttman, 1954). The first trial is most complex, the second less so, the third still less, and so on. With each trial the factor structure simplifies, as some factor or set of factors drops out, not to return. Formally, the structure requires that

$$
\begin{aligned}
x_1 &= f_1 + f_2 + \ldots + f_{m-2} + s_1 \\
x_2 &= f_1 + f_2 + \ldots + f_{m-2} + s_2 \\
x_3 &= f_2 + \ldots + f_{m-2} + s_3 \\
&\cdots\cdots\cdots\cdots\cdots\cdots\cdots\cdots\cdots\cdots \\
x_{m-1} &= f_{m-2} + s_{m-1} \\
x_m &= f_{m-1} + s_m
\end{aligned}
$$

where f and s are common and specific factors respectively. Simplexes of this sort, that is, simplifying with no factor common to all trials, easily generate superdiagonal forms that waste away and vanish with practice. In 1962 M. B. Jones suggested the simplex as a structure for the total matrix. However, in the light of subsequent findings and developments, particularly the decomposition of the total matrix into terminal and rate processes, it now seems that this notion applies only to the rate process. The rest of the matrix and, generally, much the larger part of it is governed by terminal proficiency.

The rate process is heterogeneous in its contents and these contents vary from one task to another. The last point has particular interest. It used to be common for psychologists to define intelligence as "the ability to learn," but before this definition can be entertained it must first be established that such an ability exists. Do the same people who learn well or quickly on one task also learn well or quickly on others? The question was first tackled by Herbert Woodrow more than 20 years ago. Woodrow (1946) used improvement scores in a variety of laboratory and classroom tasks, defining improvement as the difference between first and last trials. So defined, "improvement," though it is closely related, is not entirely due to rate processes. If the definition were modified to read "the difference between initial score and initial score as estimated from final score," then improvement would be pure rate process. However, even as it is, with improvement defined as the raw difference, Woodrow's results are important for us. He found positive but generally low and often zero-order correlations among improvement scores from different tasks and no general factor. So Woodrow concluded there is no "ability to learn."

More recent investigators (Duncanson, 1964; Stake, 1961) have reached different conclusions. For example, Stake (1961, p. 44) says that "unlike the majority of previous studies, there is support here for defining intelligence as the ability to learn." Nevertheless, Stake's findings were essentially the same as Woodrow's, if anything, they were even less supportive of an "ability to learn." Stake administered 12 tasks—for example, memory for words, maze learning, and word matching—to 240 children. Individual performance data were fit with Thurstone's hyperbolic learning curve, using three parameters: total errors or asymptotic performance, "curvature" or resistance to change, and a goodness of fit parameter. The parameter that concerns us is "curvature," which Stake took as his measure of improvement or ability to learn. The same subjects were also given the Otis intelligence test as well as other reference tests.

The average correlation among the 12 curvature measures was +.099, and the average correlation between them and the Otis I.Q. score was +.236. Stake subjected his results to elaborate factor analyses. Nevertheless, it is hard to see how even factor analysis could discover in these findings support for either an "ability to learn" or a relation to intelligence. Moreover, even these results are deceptively favorable. Stake's subjects included both white and Negro children and race was related to both the curvature measures and the I.Q. score. When the effects of race are partialled out, the average correlation among curvature measures drops to +.067 and the average correlation with I.Q. score drops to +.140. Within race the curvature measures have no appreciable relationship to each other or to I.Q. score.

In hindsight, Stake's results and Woodrow's before him make good sense in terms of what we now know about the differential process in acquisition. "Ability to learn" is either identical with or closely related to the rate process. And the rate process is usually unreliable and always heterogeneous. It is small wonder, therefore, that it shows no appreciable consistency as a trait or much relationship to measured intelligence.

Task Definition

Task definition is the analog in skill acquisition of internal consistency in other areas of psychology. More formally, it means the loading of a terminal trial or an average of terminal trials on terminal proficiency.* In the rest of psychologic testing, reliability is a purely structural idea. The test is administered, and internal consistency tells us how closely its parts hang together. However, task definition is an end product of a dynamic process. It tells us how closely the parts of a test *come* together, how strongly they converge with practice. Since the abilities involved in performance become more specific with practice, task definition also involves the idea of focusing. It is not just a quantitative matter; there are qualitative changes too as practice proceeds and performance converges on terminal proficiency.

Where tests are composed of items, internal consistency may be increased by lengthening the test or writing new items. The first principle is also involved in skill acquisition. If we take more terminal trials, their average will correlate more strongly with t and, therefore, will have higher definition. In skill testing, however, we cannot write new items. The essence of an item is that each one is separable and independent of all others. The new items we write have no effect on the old ones since there is no interaction between them. In skill testing we do not have this option. Any change we make in the equipment or conditions of testing is likely to interact with everything else. We cannot select materials and put them together on structural principles. We can only modify equipment or test procedures and try out the modifications to see how they work.

A study by Bilodeau (1952) involving alternate forms of the two-hand coordination test illustrates the point. In one of the two forms the pathway was flush with the plate while in the other it was recessed .25 inches into the plate. There were 152 subjects, all basic airmen, in each group. Table 5-5 contains the results for the "track" or recessed unit. Table 5-6 contains the correlations between the first seven trials of practice and the last on both units. Task definition is decidedly better on the track than on the flush unit. Correlations with the last trial are significantly higher for the track unit at all stages of practice. Nor is there any tendency for the difference to be greater earlier than later on; in fact, it is just the reverse. As practice proceeds, the gap between the track and flush units widens. By the end of practice the differential process on the track unit has stabilized around .93, while on the flush unit the stabilization level is .78. Note, however, that stabilization is achieved at the fourth trial on the flush unit, two trials earlier than on the track unit. For some purposes, this difference could take precedence over task definition and give the advantage to the flush unit.

---

* In a previous review of individual differences in motor learning (Jones, 1969), I used the phrase "task definition" in a related but different sense. The older idea should be understood as transitional to the current usage, which supersedes it.

TABLE 5-6

Correlations Between the First Seven Trials of Practice and
the Last (Eighth) on the Track and Flush Units of the
Two-Hand Coordination Test*

Trial	Track	Flush	Significance
1	.70	.48	2.97
2	.82	.63	3.59
3	.86	.70	3.68
4	.88	.78	2.86
5	.90	.78	3.69
6	.93	.78	5.29
7	.94	.79	5.76

*Critical ratios for the differences between corresponding correlations on the two units are given in the right-most column.

Here, then, is a relatively simple modification of an apparatus task that makes an emphatic difference in the level of reliability after extended practice. In all probability other tasks can be engineered to increase reliability late in practice, though, of course, we can have no *a priori* guarantees. It is likely, too, that there are rules as to what kinds of modifications affect task definition. Unfortunately, we do not know what they are, largely because we have not looked for them.

CRITERIA OF CONSTRUCTION

If a test property is desirable or undesirable under some set of circumstances or for some purpose, it deserves consideration as a criterion of construction—provided the property is subject to manipulation in some degree. Since these conditions eliminate nothing, the construction of psychologic tests is coterminous with their study. The difference is a matter of approach, whether we are building tests or studying them. Note, too, that a "criterion" does not have to be something we want to maximize. We may want a test to be free from certain kinds of response bias. In some instances we may want a test to correlate in a particular *range* with some external variable, neither much more nor much less. Normal distribution may be a criterion of construction, or equality between the genders. Any property we think a test should have qualifies as a criterion. My purpose in this section is to touch briefly on the most important criteria and, in so doing, locate them in the context of construction.

Pragmatic Criteria

The amount of time or number of trials it takes for a test to stabilize is a pragmatic criterion. So are ease of administration, scoring, and, where apparatus is involved, maintaining the equipment. Anything that can be done mechanically should be, because electric or electronic gear is notoriously difficult to keep in operating condition. A feature like portability, whether or not the test equipment can be moved, may be a decisive factor. The complex coordination test and related apparatus tests are the best predictors of success or failure in pilot training ever developed. Nevertheless, the navy has never used them for selection in naval air training because the tests are not portable. The air force used to bring potential recruits to a few selection centers scattered around the country for testing, but the navy has always insisted that a flight surgeon be able to evaluate a man for naval air training wherever the two of them might be, even aboard ship. In consequence, the navy has limited itself to paper-and-pencil tests, setting aside the universally accepted technical criterion for a selection instrument in favor of a pragmatic consideration. The case is by no manner of means unique and should discourage an overly theoretic view of test construction or, for that matter, of the tests themselves.

In psychologic testing, most pragmatic problems are more serious in the motor area than elsewhere, with one critically important exception. All tests of ability have face validity, particularly motor tests. In other areas of testing, subjects wonder why they should answer questions about their feelings, ideas, traits, and attitudes; they wonder too about how much stock can be placed in their answers, since they know they will hedge even as they scan the test booklet. Subject motivation and attitude are not major problems in motor tests. First, a motor test generally samples a recognizably relevant universe of behaviors; the test has *content validity,* and the subject can see that it does. Second, the subject has no problems knowing what the instructions mean. He has been "doing the best he can" in test-taking and other situations most of his life. The testing of motor skills and abilities is strong where it matters most. It has solid, pragmatic foundations in content validity, an understood test-taking attitude, and secure subject motivation.

Task Difficulty

Test construction takes place in a field of restraints. A test constructor contends constantly with limitations in his materials or, implicitly, in his subjects. Many things are not possible, particularly in combination. The problem for the test constructor is how to get as many of the test properties he wants into the test in maximal degree. This effort is constantly subverted by interactions between one test-aspect and another.

For example, a test should be built so that most people in the study population, with whom the test will be used, perform well within the test limits in both directions. If the test is too easy or too difficult, individual differences will be small and the test will discriminate only among the very able or the most inept. It happens, however, that the differential composition of a task and, therefore, its relations with external variables cannot be assumed to remain constant when task difficulty is changed (Fleishman, 1957). Rotating a display panel, for example, may increase task difficulty but alter the differential composition of the task at the same time. Nor can we exclude the possibility that what we want by way of external relations may be most difficult to attain at the levels of difficulty we want the test to have.

Predictive Validity

The "field of restraints" that confronts anyone who sets out to build a test is nowhere more obvious than in personnel selection. If it could be arranged, psychologists would like to predict perfectly how well people will do in school, on the job, or in military training programs. They fall far short of this ambition. Predictive validities of .60 or higher are occasionally reported for scholastic criteria, considerably higher than in other areas. With the aid of apparatus tests the air force obtained some predictive coefficients greater than .50 for the pilot training criterion. In naval air training predictive validity never exceeds .40. In many programs any coefficient over .30 is considered a success.

Predictive validity is often treated uncritically, as if the relation between test and criterion were an unchanging fact of nature. Suppose a test is constructed in 1961 and cross-validated in 1962 with a validity coefficient of .43. It does not follow that the test will still correlate .43 with the criterion a year later, in 1963. As a matter of fact, in many situations we can be sure it will not. Predictive validity is a function of time. Sometimes it stays the same as time passes; generally it gets worse. It never improves. In applied situations these differences can be fully as important as initial validity, that is, at cross-validation. Many selection instruments have to be updated every year or two or they become useless as predictors. It would be a major advance if we could classify test materials according to how well they "hold validity" but, unfortunately, we cannot—because the question has never been systematically studied. It would be necessary to build homogeneous tests out of different kinds of materials—attitudinal items, personality items, biographical data, ability materials—all against the same criterion, cross-validate them, and then check validity coefficients over a period of several years. The lore of personnel psychology has it that the attitudinal items would do worst with time and the ability tests best. If so, it is an important argument in favor of ability testing. Questionnaires are easy to build, but this advantage wears pretty thin if a test has to be rebuilt every year because it starts losing validity in a matter of months.

Stability

Stability over time is the most underrated criterion in psychologic testing. E. A. Fleishman is one of few workers who give the property its due weight. A test that does not correlate with itself after a year or more does not qualify for Fleishman's attention; in his terminology, it does not measure an ability. And it is hard to argue with him. Whatever else we may mean by abilities or personality traits we certainly mean to suggest that they last for more than a little while. A transient variation may reflect a state or mood, a phase, or even a period in a man's life but it can hardly be called basic to personality, temperament, character, or abilities.

Nevertheless, no one has ever built a test with stability over time as a criterion. The closest anyone comes is *test-retest reliability,* a completely different idea. All notions of reliability involve estimates of true variance and all of them, including test-retest reliability, are located in a momentary theoretic framework. At the moment the test is given part of the test's variance is attributable to reliable variance and part to error. It is the function of a reliability coefficient to tell us how large these two parts are in relation to each other. Unfortunately, this function can be carried out precisely only under counterfactual circumstances—when both administrations are given to the same subjects *for the first time.* Theoretically time has nothing to do with it and, in practice, the interval between administrations in test-retest reliability is as short as conditions permit, generally 24 hours, sometimes as long as a week, rarely any longer.

Stability is not even a related idea. In the first place, it is not intended to partition test variance into true and error components. Second, time is essential to it. Third, there is no one stability coefficient. There is stability after a month or six months, after a year, five years, or ten years.

Stability is a difficult criterion to use because few investigators want to wait for two or three years while they are in the process of building or evaluating a test. The consequence is that information on stability is sparse. We do know that attitudinal materials decay rapidly with time. Personality inventories and self-ratings so somewhat better. Vocational interests and values do better yet, but even these materials are far from good. Test-retest correlations for the Allport-Vernon Scale of Values average less than .70 after one year and less than .45 after 20 years. Intelligence tests stand up much better over time, correlating close to .80 over periods as long as 30 years (Kelly, 1955).

Surprisingly enough, the stability of motor tests is not well established. Motor learning is well retained over long periods of time (Ammons et al., 1958; Battig et al., 1957; Bell, 1950; Jahnke, 1958; Jones and Bilodeau, 1953; Leavitt and Schlosberg, 1944; Mengelkoch et al., 1958; Reynolds and Bilodeau, 1952). However, these studies report means only; they tell us nothing about individual differences. The only study that does we owe to Fleishman and Parker (1962), who studied retention of a complex tracking skill in male college students over periods as long as two years. The correlations they obtained between first and second testings ranged upwards from .80 throughout this period. This study is encouraging; but how typical its findings are for motor skills generally, we just do not know.

Heritability

Though heritability has been often and widely debated as a test property, no one has suggested until recently (M. B. Jones, 1970c) that it be made an explicit criterion in the construction of psychologic tests. Nevertheless, the argument for doing so is strong. Many psychologists, for example, Burt (1958), make heritability essential to what they mean by "intelligence." That being the case, why not administer preliminary materials to identical and fraternal twins and include in the final test only those items that show good heritability? If someone else understands "intelligence" differently, let him build a test that meets the criteria implicit in his understanding. In any case, there is no point arguing about it. Since no one can measure "intelligence" apart from the tests and we make the tests, the question of heritability is foreshadowed in the process of construction. It is a matter of fact, independent of human decision, only to the extent that we are unable to build tests that have or lack heritability and also meet other criteria we expect in a test of intelligence. The odds are, however, that we have considerable latitude in this regard.

Motor testing has not been thoroughly investigated from a genetic point of view, though we do have a few studies. As long ago as 1933 McNemar compared the performances of 46 pairs of fraternal and 47 pairs of identical twins on five motor tests: pursuit rotor, steadiness, speed drill, card sorting, and spool packing. He found Holzinger heritability coefficients of .90, .80, .69, .46, and .25 in that order. The range could hardly be more extreme. He also found a slight tendency for heritability to decrease with practice.

Table 5-7 contains Holzinger heritability coefficients for the Differential Aptitude Tests broken down by gender. The data were collected by Bock and Vandenberg in 106 pairs of monozygotic and 81 pairs of like-sexed dizygotic twins. The heritability coefficients for males (or females) were obtained by

TABLE 5-7

Holzinger Heritability Coefficients for the Seven Scales of
the Differential Aptitude Tests, by Gender*

	Heritability	
	Male	*Female*
Spatial	.753	.324
Numerical	.244	.266
Abstract	.236	.060
Verbal	.462	.627
Mechanical	.000	.541
Clerical	.673	.709
Language Usage	.551	.706

* From Bock and Vandenberg (1968, pp. 251–252), in S. G. Vandenberg (ed.) *Progress in human behavior genetics.* Baltimore: The Johns Hopkins Press.

comparing within-pair differences for monozygotic and dizygotic male (or female) twins. Of the tests in the battery, spatial and clerical have the heaviest motor components; and both of them show relatively strong heritabilities. Only language usage is as strong, both genders considered.

The table brings out another point, viz., that the heritability of a test is not necessarily the same among males as females. Environment may contribute more heavily to differences among boys than girls; or genetic variation may be more damped in one sex than another, mainly through sex limitation. Nor do these differences in heritability bear any necessary relation to mean differences. What matters in the present context is that, with heritability as a criterion, optimal test composition may be different for the two genders.

The possibility is not restricted to heritability. A test composite that is stable among men may not be among women. A predictive relation may hold in one gender but not in the other. A test developed among women may lose definition when given to men. The point is quite general. It holds for all criteria, and groupings other than gender. We cannot assume *a priori* that a test's properties will be the same in different social classes or different age groups. "Test properties" are always joint functions of the test and the people who take it.

Concurrent Validity

"Concurrent validity" refers to the relation between a test and a concurrent criterion. Maximizing this relation is sometimes the only objective in construction, for example, in tests designed to detect organic brain damage. The logic here is the same as in predictive validity except the criterion is hidden some other place than in the future. More commonly, however, concurrent validity follows another logic.

When a psychologic test is used for investigative purposes, "to measure something," the number of criteria relevant to its construction may be myriad. In order to pass muster as "a measure of spatial ability," a test must distinguish between groups, associate with other variations, show mean changes when test conditions are varied, predict applied criteria—all in determinate ways. No test is ever constructed against all these criteria at once, partly because it is not feasible but also because there is an easier way. Instead of trying to satisfy these many criteria directly, the test is built against another variation that already has most of the properties we want the test to have. We want a standardized test that relates strongly to school grades. We want a test like the California F Scale but without the response bias (acquiescence) so pronounced in the original inventory. We want to modify Fleishman and Parker's complex tracking device so that it shows better task definition. The hope is that the test or its modification will offer advantages not present in the criterion against which it is built, while retaining many of the criterion's desirable properties. Test construction becomes a process of progressive modifications, hopefully, of improvements.

In addition to building tests, psychologists also think and theorize about them. How is the test to be understood in terms of general ideas like intelligence, anxiety, authoritarianism, spatial ability? How are abilities developed? How are tests to be classified? Important as these questions are, they cause confusion if their relation to the process of construction is misunderstood. The function of theory and hypothetic ideas in psychologic testing is to help us decide on criteria of construction, the properties we want tests to have. Their role is prior to construction and, then again, after the test is built. They have no role in construction itself, because a test can only be built against determinate criteria, not hypothetic constructs.

The importance of this point has to do with the idea of validity. Test validity is best understood as the general relation between a test and its criteria of construction. A test is valid according to whether it meets the specifications laid down for it, according to whether it has whatever properties a test of its description should have. Tests of motor abilities should satisfy pragmatic requirements; they should be stable and have good definition; they should relate to other variations, both predictive and concurrent; in some instances, they should be heritable. Validity is the degree to which these criteria are met. Interpretation in terms of theoretic constructs, even when it asks whether new or additional criteria should be imposed, is another matter.

FACTOR ISOLATION

One of the first generalities psychologists reached was that abilities are positively correlated. Correlations between abilities in unselected populations are never negative. The fact was noted by Spearman (1904) and provided much of the impetus for his two-factor theory of intelligence. It still sustains the British school of factor analysis in its insistence on one general factor in tests of ability. No matter how it is analyzed, the general positivity among tests of ability is an empirical regularity of major importance. It means that nature is not equalitarian; there is no law of compensation in individual talents. Bright people are no poorer athletes than the next person; in fact, they are generally somewhat better in sports. By the same token, good athletes tend to be brighter than average, not duller. On the average, people who are good at numbers are also good with words. If one man sings better than another, the odds are that he can do anything else at least as well. As far as abilities are concerned, all good things go together—at least, in an unselected population.

The qualification is important because this "going together," this positivity, refers to the *total* correlation. It does not mean there are no negative components in the covariance among tested abilities. Let me digress.

A factor is *bipolar* with reference to a class of variations if some of the variations load positively and others negatively on the factor. A bipolar ability factor would be one on which some abilities load positively and others negatively. Such a factor would generate negative covariance between abilities with differently signed loadings. Nevertheless, the total correlation might still be positive—because other factors, with positive loadings only, contributed heavier components to the total correlation.

If we administer tests of ability to unselected subjects who have not been subjected to special treatment, for example, drugs, we get positive correlations. It does not follow that in specially selected or specially prepared samples, a bipolar factor might not be brought out.

Up to now, however, no negative component in the covariance among tested abilities—no bipolar factor—has ever been established. The problem is that bipolar factors are so hard to separate from general-ability factors producing positive covariance. Of course, with factor analysis it is always possible to hypothesize bipolar factors; but theoretic decomposition will not do because the factors in which it results are only hypothetic and, with a positive manifold, other rotations involving positive loadings only are always possible. What is needed is an empiric showing. The bipolar factor must be empirically isolated from obscuring general-ability factors—or concentrated sufficiently so that its bipolar character becomes unmistakably apparent. In my opinion, factor isolation is the most needed undertaking in present-day differential psychology, including most definitely motor skills and abilities. So far only one major effort (Broverman and Klaiber, 1969) has been made in this direction, but it is a good first step and fully merits detailed consideration.

Broverman and Klaiber begin by calling attention to a pair of well-known sex differences. Women have long been known to do better than men at fine motor skills such as naming colors, crossing out letters, and coding as quickly as possible. They show this advantage as children and hold it throughout life. Women are also superior to men in speech and reading from early in life through adulthood. It is probable, morever, that these two areas are related. Whatever else they may be, speech and reading are also fine motor skills, requiring the precise coordination of tongue, larynx, diaphragm, and eyes in small movements of large importance. Men, on the other hand, seem to have the advantage in tasks requiring the subjects to restructure a geometric field. The Thurstone-Gottschaldt Hidden Figures are characteristic; related tests include the Kohs Block Design and Witkin's Embedded Figures.

Broverman and Klaiber cite the results in table 5-8, originally from

TABLE 5-8

Simple Perceptual-Motor and Perceptual-Restructuring Tasks*

		Mean	
Test	*Score*	*Boys*	*Girls*
Color naming	Seconds	71.5	64.5
Crossing-out	Number correct	33.2	37.8
Thurstone Gottschaldt	Number correct	44.3	38.6
Kohs Blocks	Weighted score	94.3	76.7
		N=80	N=138

* From Broverman and Klaiber (1969, p. 9).

Thurstone, Thurstone, and Strandskov (1955), as illustrating the point. All differences between boys and girls, ages 14 to 17, are significant at the .01 level or beyond. The boys take longer to name colors and cross out fewer letters in a fixed interval of time. However, they do better on the Thurstone-Gottschaldt Hidden Figures and the Kohs Block Design tests. With respect to sex, therefore, these two pairs of tasks are inversely related. The boys do better on one pair and the girls on the other.

The question then arises: Does this inversion hold within genders? Do boys who easily restructure a geometric field do poorly on fine motor tests while boys who are quick and accurate on the fine motor tests do poorly at restructuring? The answer is no. Within gender all correlations are positive. Nevertheless, it could still be that *some* of the variance in these two pairs of tests is negatively related; and these negative components could be specific to the tests in ways the positive covariance is not. Overall the correlations are positive because the general-ability factors outweigh the more specific, bipolar factors. Nevertheless, the bipolar factors could be decisive in comparisons between genders. If they are essentially related to sex while the general-ability factors are evenly distributed, then only the bipolar factors will make for sex differences; the general-ability factors will balance out.

It remains to be indicated in what ways the bipolar factors might be "essentially related to sex." Figure 5-1 presents schematically the rationale used by Broverman and Klaiber. They cite evidence that "increased stimulation of the adrenergic portion of the CNS tends to increase immediate responsivity to stimuli as required by simple perceptual-motor tasks. At the same time, adrenergic activation should diminish the cholinergic ability to inhibit or delay immediate responses to obvious stimulus attributes in favor of less obvious stimulus relationships as required by perceptual-restructuring tasks." The two authors then mount an argument that leads backwards from adrenergy-cholinergy to androgenicity. The argument takes place in three steps: (a) "the activity of the adrenergic nervous system is, in part, a function

FIG. 5-1. Schematic presentation of the rationale used by Broverman and Klaiber to concentrate negative components in the relations between fine-motor and perceptual-restructuring tasks.

of the level of the neurotransmitter norepinephrine in the neural tissues," (b) "neural norepinephrine, however, is regulated, in part, by the enzyme monoamine oxidase (MAO)," and (c) "MAO activity in brain tissues, in turn, is inhibited by the gonadal 'sex' hormones, estrogens and androgens." The estrogens are more potent MAO inhibitors than the androgens.

Altogether, then, women do better at simple perceptual-motor tasks because estrogens strongly inhibit MAO, leading to high norepinephrine levels, hence, adrenergic predominance. In men, whose androgens inhibit MAO less strongly, the norepinephrine levels are lower and cholinergic activity predominates.

Broverman and Klaiber then focus on indices of androgenicity among men. One hundred and fifteen male college students, ages 21 to 24, were assessed on four androgen indicators:

 —excretion of 17-ketosteroids
 —ratings of pubic hair development
 —the circumference of the chest
 —the circumference of the biceps

The 115 men were then arranged in order of androgenicity and broken down into sixths. The most androgenized sixth and the least were pooled to form a group with "maximal variance in androgenicity"; the second and the fifth sixths were pooled to form a group with "moderate variance in andro-genicity," while the two middle sixths were pooled to form a "minimal variance group."

All subjects were administered two fine motor tasks—color and object naming—and two perceptual-restructuring tasks—Witkin's Embedded Figures and the WAIS Blocks Test. The two workers then calculated correlations among the four tests in each of the variance groups. According to the rationale pursued by Broverman and Klaiber, the general-ability factors should hold sway in the minimal variance group because the extremes of androgenicity and, hence, of adrenergic or cholinergic tendency are missing. In the maximal variance group adrenergy-cholinergy should be most strongly concentrated. True, the general-ability factors are still present, but their field

TABLE 5-9

Correlations of Fine-Motor with Perceptual-Restructuring Tasks in
Groups Differing in Androgenicity Variance*

Group	N	Color Naming vs. EPF	Color Naming vs. WAIS Blocks	Object Naming vs. EFT	Object Naming vs. WAIS Blocks
I (Maximal Variance)	38	−.23	−.10	−.42	−.17
II (Moderate Variance)	39	+.12	+.05	−.16	−.07
III (Minimal Variance)	38	+.40	+.10	+.22	+.06
All Subjects	115	+.12	+.03	−.10	−.05

*From Broverman and Klaiber (1969, p. 14).

of action relative to the bipolar factor has been reduced by the elimination of the middle two-thirds on the androgenicity scale. We would expect, therefore, to find positive correlations among the four tests in the minimal variance group, mixed correlations in the moderate variance group, and negative correlations in the maximal variance group. As can be seen in table 5-9, the two investigators did in fact obtain something like these results.

The Broverman-Klaiber study is not without shortcomings. The biochemical argument is somewhat tenuous; and the results themselves, while supporting the *existence* of a bipolar factor, fall far short of defining it. Nevertheless, in recognizing the need for factor isolation and in moving to meet this need, Broverman and Klaiber have taken us a distinct step forward.

References

Ammons, R. B., Farr, R. G., Bloch, E., Neumann, E., Dey, M., Marion, R., & Ammons, C. H. Long-term retention of perceptual-motor skills. *Journal of Experimental Psychology,* 1958, 55, 318–328.

Battig, W. F., Nagel, E. H., Voss, J. F., & Brogden, W. J. Transfer and retention of bidimensional compensatory tracking after extended practice. *American Journal of Psychology,* 1957, 70, 75–80.

Bell, H. M. Retention of pursuit motor skill after one year. *Journal of Experimental Psychology,* 1950, 40, 648-649.

Bilodeau, E. A. Transfer of training between tasks differing in degree of physical restriction of imprecise responses. *USAF Human Resources Research Center Research Bulletin,* 1952, No. 52–54.

Bock, P. D., & Vandenberg, S. G. Components of heritable variation in mental test scales. In S. G. Vandenberg (ed.), *Progress in human behavior genetics.* Baltimore: The Johns Hopkins Press, 1968, pp. 233–260.

Broverman, D. M., & Klaiber, E. L. Negative relationships between abilities. *Psychometrika,* 1969, 34, 5–19.

Burt, C. The inheritance of mental ability. *American Psychologist,* 1958, 13, 1–15.

Duncanson, J. P. *Intelligence and the ability to learn.* Princeton, N. J.: Educational Testing Service, 1964.

Fitts, P. M. Factors in complex skill training. In R. Glaser (ed.), *Training research and education.* Pittsburgh: University of Pittsburgh Press, 1962, pp. 177–197.

Fleishman, E. A. Factor structure in relation to task difficulty in psychomotor performance. *Educational and Psychological Measurement,* 1957, 17, 522–532.

Fleishman, E. A. Abilities at different stages of practice in rotary pursuit performance. *Journal of Experimental Psychology,* 1960, 60, 162–171.

Fleishman, E. A. Individual differences and motor learning. In R. M. Gagné (ed.) *Learning and individual differences.* Columbus: Charles E. Merrill, 1967, pp. 58–65.

Fleishman, E. A., & Parker, J. F., Jr. Factors in the retention and relearning of perceptual-motor skills. *Journal of Experimental Psychology,* 1962, 64, 215–226.

Guttman, L. A new approach to factor analysis: the radex. In P. F. Lazarsfeld (ed.) *Mathematical thinking in the social sciences.* Glencoe, Illinois: Free Press, 1954, pp. 258–348.

Jahnke, J. C. Retention in motor learning as a function of amount of practice and rest. *Journal of Experimental Psychology,* 1958, 55, 270–273.

Jones, E. I., & Bilodeau, E. A. Retention and relearning of a complex perceptual-motor skill after ten months of no practice. *USAF Human Resources Research Center Research Bulletin,* 1953, No. 5, 3–12.

Jones, M. B. Practice as a process of simplification. *Psychological Review,* 1962, 69, 274–294.

Jones, M. B. Differential processes in acquisition. In E. A. Bilodeau (ed.) *Principles of skill acquisition.* New York: Academic Press, 1969, pp. 109–146.

Jones, M. B. Rate and terminal processes in skill acquisition. *American Journal of Psychology,* 1970, 83, 222–236. (a)

Jones, M. B. A two-process theory of individual differences in motor learning. *Psychological Review,* 1970, 77, 353–360. (b)

Jones, M. B. Heritability as a criterion in the construction of psychological tests. *Psychological Bulletin,* 1970, 75, 92–96.

Kelly, E. L. Consistency of the adult personality. *American Psychologist,* 1955, 10, 659–681.

Leavitt, H. J., & Schlosberg, H. The retention of verbal and motor skills. *Journal of Experimental Psychology,* 1944, 23, 404–417.

McNemar, Q. Twin resemblances in motor skills, and the effect of practice thereon. *Journal of Genetic Psychology,* 1933, 42, 70–97.

Mengelkoch, R. F., Adams, J. A., & Gainer, C. A. The forgetting of instrument flying skills as a function of the lack of initial proficiency. *USN Training and Development Center Technical Report,* 1958, No. 71–16–18.

Reynolds, B., & Bilodeau, I. McD. Acquisition and retention of three psychomotor tests as a function of distribution of practice during acquisition. *Journal of Experimental Psychology,* 1952, 44, 19–26.

Spearman, C. General intelligence, objectively determined and measured. *American Journal of Psychology,* 1904, 15, 201–293.

Stake, R. F. Learning parameters, aptitudes, and achievements. *Psychometric Monographs,* 1961, No. 9.

Thurstone, T. W., Thurstone, L. L., & Strandskov, H. H. A psychological study of twins: 2. Scores of one hundred and twenty-five pairs of twins on fifty-nine tests. The Psychometric Laboratory, University of North Carolina, Chapel Hill, N. C., 1955, No. 12.

Woodrow, H. A. The ability to learn. *Psychological Review,* 1946, 53, 147–158.

Chapter 6

MILITARY PSYCHOLOGY AND TRAINING

Elmo E. Miller
Human Resources Research Organization

Since World War II, military agencies have been involved in scientific studies of psychomotor skills, and since then a large proportion of the support for such studies has been provided by the department of defense. The army, navy, and air force have established their psychologic research laboratories, which employ civilian and military scientists to study psychomotor as well as cognitive skills. Various defense agencies have also funded psychomotor studies in academic laboratories and in industry.

The main concern of this chapter is training of psychomotor skills, with less emphasis on other contributions to psychomotor research such as personnel selection or equipment design. Training is concerned with the effective management of the learning environment to produce performance on specifiable criteria, and it turns out to be distinctly different from the traditional psychologic field of learning. The psychomotor domain of training is here construed rather broadly to include any practice conditions which involve the musculature in some nontrivial sense. Hence, procedural learning generally will be considered as part of the psychomotor domain, because it appears that involvement of the musculature is important for learning most procedures. Other procedures which involve only minimal movement (e.g., adding numbers) will not concern us here, although there are many borderline procedures which involve both mental and muscular processes in important respects.

Military research on psychomotor performance has been characterized by two strong influences which are sometimes conflicting, sometimes complementary: (a) the highly analytic tradition of experimental psychologists, and

(b) the practical concern with particular jobs. From the interplay of these two influences came the technology of *task analysis,* which is a unique contribution of military psychologists to our knowledge of effective training. The business of task analysis for training is the intensive study of the component activities of a task, the inter-relations among these activities, and the effective sequencing of corresponding practice activities in a training program.

This chapter will begin with a very brief sketch of some events in military psychology which were critical for training of psychomotor skills, and then it will consider substantive contributions to training technology. The main purpose will be to aid those readers who might design training programs or conduct training research. The discussion of training techniques will be organized according to kinds of the subtasks which result from a process of task analysis.

EARLY MILITARY DEVELOPMENTS

World War II

Professional psychology had made substantial contributions to the military effort in World War I, but these involved the development of mental tests on the Binet model, not the study of psychomotor skills. Between the wars, military psychology was dormant. In 1939, personnel classification testing for the armed services began to be organized. As part of the pilot selection program, plans were made in 1941 to include several apparatus tests in the battery. Use of the apparatus tests for pilot selection began in 1942 (Melton, 1947, p. 4).

Psychologists also were thrust into a role requiring decisions about the conduct of training, and their background in learning gave them scant basis for these decisions. In conjunction with the testing and training activities, some directly related research was conducted. Research on psychomotor skills involved primarily selection of pilots, and to a lesser extent, flexible gunnery training and selection of air crew personnel. The work on flexible gunnery training yielded discouraging results. No really good training method was developed, and although gradual adaptation to the task seemed to occur, the final performance could hardly be called satisfactory (Melton, 1947, p. 943).

The standard classification battery at first included four apparatus tests, some of which were later modified. Later a fifth test was added. In addition, several experimental apparatus tests were administered to samples of flight applicants. The standard apparatus tests were somewhat effective for predicting success in pilot training, with biserial validity coefficients of the various tests generally ranging from the .20's to the low .40's. Melton (1947, p. 938) states that compared with other tests, "there were indications that the battery of apparatus tests were roughly equal to the battery of printed tests in the efficiency of prediction of the criterion, and that both together gave a predictive efficiency which was greater than either alone, both in terms of statistical significance and practical importance."

However, none of the pilot selection tests, whether it was printed or an apparatus tests, would be considered a very good predictor according to general standards of psychometric practice. Apparatus tests continued to be in use by the air force until 1956.

The pattern of correlations indicates that the apparatus tests generally predict to the degree that they resemble the flight situation. The face validity fortunately led military psychologists to generally appropriate choices of the initial standard test battery. The best predictor was the complex coordination test, which is a simplified representation of the flight control situation. Standard tests further removed from the flight task, such as rudder control or rotary pursuit, did not predict elimination from training as well. Simple tests such as simple reaction time evidenced no appreciable validity. Also, the tests tend to predict early performance in flight training better than later performance. The correlations indicate a high degree of specificity of factors in psychomotor performance.

Other Correlation Research

Fleishman and his colleagues have conducted extensive factor analyses in an attempt to identify the multiplicity of factors in psychomotor skills (reviewed by Fleishman, 1966; Noble, 1968). Generally, the factorial structure of a complex task changes as the task is learned, with an increasing proportion of the variance accounted for by the specific task being learned. In view of low validity of tests for predicting psychomotor skills, especially at advanced skill levels, Jones (1966, p. 132) has taken the "minority" view that it is not useful to speak of psychomotor abilities or factors. Instead, he has developed "simplicial analysis," a process of analyzing the patterns of correlations among stages of practice of various skills in order to posit underlying processes (Jones, 1962). One of the practical implications of his model is that stages of training which correlate most highly should be together in the sequence of training. He has used such analysis to help determine the desirable sequence of stages for navy flight training (Jones, 1959).

The specificity of pilot skills has led Berkshire and his associates (Berkshire and Lyon, 1959; Schoenberger, Wherry, and Berkshire, 1963) to develop the techniques of secondary selection for the navy flight training program. Unlike conventional selection, secondary selection takes into account empirically established validities of early training grades in eliminating men from later stages of the program. Substantial savings are thus achieved because of the high cost of flight training, especially in the later stages.

Trends in Psychomotor Research

After World War II, most of the psychologists who had been involved with the apparatus tests for air crew selection returned to academic life, but their interest in psychomotor performance continued. They constituted a large part of the academic community interested in skills research. The continued interest of military agencies in psychomotor research led to funding a large proportion of such research at academic laboratories. Also, psychomotor research was conducted at many newly established military laboratories.

The psychomotor research tended increasingly to avoid particular practical skills, and instead focused upon learning of special laboratory tasks to such a degree that the learning of practical skills seemed to be hardly considered a part of motor skills. In the 1961 *Annual Review of Motor Skills Learning,* Bilodeau and Bilodeau document the move away from the use of the apparatus tests of World War II during the 1950's and the gradual adoption of more finely specifiable laboratory devices. They find scarcely any reason to mention studies of practical tasks.

The selection of tasks for "rcscarchablcncss" is apt to introduce marked bias in the kinds of tasks considered, and consequently, a bias in the kinds of relationships discovered. For example, who would want a laboratory task which the subject can learn at the first trial? So, based on laboratory tasks, we may conclude that people learn all tasks gradually. The laboratory tasks chosen frequently are similar to certain aspects of real jobs, but one of the most critical issues is how the component performances are interrelated.

Not all academic researchers avoid gross, practical tasks by any means. A distinguished example is the late Paul Fitts, who was not only a leader in laboratory studies, but also had a lively interest in relating his thinking to such everyday concerns as problems of athletic coaches (Fitts, 1962).

Task Analysis

Meanwhile during the 50's, psychologists in the military laboratories were developing a training technology which was to affect our outlook on training of both cognitive and psychomotor skills. Those psychologists who took seriously the challenge of trying to improve training programs found scant guidance in the psychologic literature on learning. On this point, there is a strong consensus of psychologists who have confronted military training problems which is especially striking in view of their heavy investment of time and effort in the traditional research methodology and findings.

The consensus on the marginal value of traditional learning research for design of training was presented most cogently by Gagné (1962). He noted that experimental psychologists as well as laymen generally make a very basic assumption which is seldom stated explicitly, that "the best way to learn a performance is to practice that performance." He contended that the assumption is misleading and often false. In applying his craft, the learning psychologist usually supplements the assumption with various *principles* based upon laboratory findings such as reinforcement, distribution of practice, meaningfulness, and so on. Gagné asks, "How does one fare if he seriously attempts to use this basic assumption and these principles to design effective training situations? *Not particularly well.*" (Italic are his.) Gagné does not contend that psychologists have not made useful contributions to training; quite to the contrary. Rather, he questions the applicability of the particular principles from learning laboratories, and the appropriateness of the assumption. As alternatives Gagné (p. 88) suggested three most useful psychologic principles for training:

1. Any human task may be analyzed into a set of component tasks which are quite distinct from each other in terms of the experimental operations needed to produce them.

2. These task components are mediators of the final task performance; that is, their presence insures positive transfer to a final performance, and their absence reduces such transfer to near zero.

3. The basic principles of training design consist of: (a) identifying the component tasks of a final performance; (b) insuring that each of these component tasks is fully achieved; and (c) arranging the total learning situation in a sequence which will insure optimal mediational effects from one component to another.

Robert Miller (1953a,b, 1954, 1956a,b, 1962a,b, 1965) has authored the best-known work on task analysis, but almost any publication by professional psychologists on training development in the last two decades can be considered a part of the literature on task analysis. The methods of task analysis are made increasingly powerful through use of systems concepts (Crawford, 1962). When a man's performance is conceived as part of a system, then defining the system enables derivation of the man's required contribution to the system's effectiveness, and thus establishment of a criterion of relevance for training activities. The business of task analysis is not so much an empiric study of what people actually do on the job, as might be supposed, but rather, an orderly consideration of the functions the man *must* accomplish for the system as a whole to be effective. (A good example is the analysis of the automobile driver's task by McKnight and Adams, 1970a,b.)

Recently other educational developments akin to task analysis have appeared, including specification of behavioral objectives and criterion-references tests (as contrasted with norm-referenced tests, Glaser and Klaus, 1962). No sharp delineation of the role of military psychology is possible, but its strong involvement continues.

In the process of task analysis and development of training, seven basic steps may be distinguished (Crawford, 1968):

(1) Develop human factors systems analysis model

(2) Develop job model

(3) Specify knowledges and skills
(4) Determine instructional objectives
(5) Construct training program
(6) Develop proficiency test
(7) Evaluate training program

Although these steps may appear obvious, their application has led to several divergences from the way learning research is customarily conducted by psychologists from academic laboratories (MacCaslin and Cogan, 1968). (a) Training programs are most usefully evaluated by an absolute standard of adequate job performance rather than in comparison with alternative programs (sometimes called "conventional" instruction). (b) The design of a training device generally has an implicit assumption of a corresponding training method, so it does not make sense to compare the various possible combinations of training methods and training devices. (c) A task-analytic description is conducted for particular purposes, so a task description which is conducted for equipment design is not likely to be very useful for design of training; therefore, task analysis is not a completely "objective" or "neutral" activity. (d) Finally, "few tasks in today's man-machine systems contain discriminations or motor coordinations that pose more than moderate difficulties for the trainees in those systems." People often learn simple tasks in one or two trials if the required behavior is formulated clearly and communicated effectively. Consequently, training research in the military has tended to emphasize the structure of tasks and the communication of task requirements to the trainee rather than the absolute difficulty of any of the particular task elements (e.g., Whitmore, 1967).

The efforts in recent years toward a taxonomy of human performance (Melton, 1964; Bloom, 1956) are a direct attempt to advance the techniques of task analysis. The following discussion is oriented around one such taxonomy (E. E. Miller, 1969), designed specifically to aid in the development of training for psychomotor skills.

KINDS OF TASKS

The tasks are distinguished on the basis of the kinds of feedback loop involved in the response process, which generally has a very direct relation to the kind of training which is likely to be effective. The major categories to be considered are (a) tracking, (b) keyboard skills, (c) procedural skills, and (d) a catch-all category, skilled performance. Tracking and skilled performance tasks involve "closed-loop" feedback—that is, the feedback from previous responses defines what should be done next. In steering a car, for example, the "correct" response depends on whether the car at present is to the left or to the right of the desired path, and how far. With procedural or keyboard skills, the feedback from previous responses is irrelevant to what should be done next. In typewriting, for example, if one incorrectly strikes a key, there is nothing he can do about it on the next stroke. Tracking and keyboard skills tend to be homogeneous over time and do not entail control of an evolving process, so they tend to be simpler to perform.

Tracking

In tracking, a person operates a control continuously to adjust some stimulus dimension to be as close as he can to some "optimal" condition. For example, an auto driver uses the steering wheel to hold his car as close as possible to the center of his lane. Implicit in the definition of tracking is some disturbing force (the "track") which tends to move the stimulus dimensions from the optimal state. Generally, the stimulus dimension(s) are spatial, although auditory (pitch) tracking has been attempted.

As a general rule, training in tracking tasks may best be accomplished by providing for ample practice in the "real task" situation or a reasonably faithful simulation of it. The "real task" consists not only of the operational hardware but also of the control dynamics, and simulation may turn out to be the easiest way to achieve such dynamics. Although there may be many other tasks which have some positive transfer, rarely are there systematic alterations of the task which result in better learning than practice on the task itself.

There may be great benefit, however, for some cognitive learning early in tracking training. Fitts (1962, pp. 186–188) distinguishes three phases of learning a psychomotor skill: (a) cognition, (b) fixation, and (c) automation. (These phases are useful in thinking about all kinds of skill learning.) For the two latter phases of tracking skill development, and much of the first, direct practice of the task is the best policy.

What to provide in early cognitive learning must be answered by analysis of the particular task rather than general principles applicable to all tracking. Poulton, in an excellent review of tracking research (1966, p. 398), has distinguished four engineering variables which relate to what the man must learn in tracking: (a) the track or tracks, and interrelations, (b) the display or displays, and interrelations, (c) the fuel of the control(s), and how the direction of control movement relates to the direction of display movement, and (d) the dynamics of the control system(s). It is the qualitative aspects of the variables which tend to be most aided by cognitive learning, especially learning the control-display relationships (part of variable c). For example, in flight training, the student must learn to operate the rudder pedals to keep the aircraft in balanced flight, and to do this, he has an instrument with a ball (which employs the same principle as a carpenter's level) which he is to keep centered. When the ball is to the right, he steps on the right pedal, and when the left, the left pedal, which is somewhat unnatural (contrary to population stereotype). Flight instructors have found an effective mediator for this relationship: they tell the student to think of the ball as a grape which he is squeezing between his feet. Besides the analogy, considerable practice is needed before the rudder pedal movements become automatic and smooth, of course.

The engineering variables are experienced by the man in the system in various ways. The track may be highly predictable (coherent) as with the circular path of the pursuit rotor. Similarly, the path may be predictable because it is visible ahead, e.g., steering a car down a road. On the basis of the display, compensatory tracking is commonly distinguished from pursuit tracking. In compensatory tracking, a single moving element is affected both by the track (a disturbing force) and by the man's corrective movements. In pursuit tracking, one element (the target) is moved by the disturbing force (the track) while the man tries to move the other element (reticle or sight pattern) to the target. The mechanical display may be related to bodily motion, as in steering a vehicle, and the bodily sensations make an appreciable difference in task difficulty (Ruocco, Vitale, and Benfari, 1965). The feel of the control includes such properties as inertia, various kinds of friction, and spring loading.

The control dynamics are generally described in mathematic terms. Difficult control dynamics began to be a problem in World War II, when many power-assisted tracking systems were higher-order systems. A zero-order (position) system is one in which the person directly moves the indicator, as when tracing a line with a pencil. In a first-order (rate) system, the position of the control determines the rate of movement of an indicator, as when a joystick position determines the rate at which a pip moves across a cathode ray tube (CRT). Second-order (acceleration) systems are fairly common, and submarine controls may even be third-order ("jerk") systems. In the higher-order systems the full effect of a control movement is not perceived immediately, so operating such systems is somewhat like operating a system with a simple time lag (difficult). High-order systems tend to be more difficult to control than position systems, although the optimal system will depend somewhat upon the track being followed, and whether any rapid slewing is required in acquiring the target initially. If the "correct" control dynamics cannot be provided in training, it is better to train on a simpler, lower-order system; generally there is positive transfer of training from lower-order tracking systems to higher-order systems, but negative transfer in the other direction (Poulton, 1966, p. 191).

Certain developments in control dynamics warrant special mention because they make the task so much easier and also because they have been tried as training methods. A quickened (or predictor) display indicates a position which will be achieved at some time in the future (assuming control input is continued), rather than present position. Another way to simplify the task is "aided" tracking, in which zero-order, first-order, and second-order effects are mixed in a supposedly optimal combination for a particular kind of track. For example, if a target generally moves at an almost constant rate, it may be helpful for a control to have some general rate effect (to help match the general movement of the target) along with a position (to correct small deviations quickly). The efficacy of aided tracking is somewhat more dubious than that of quickening.

Quickening or aided tracking may be used early in training to simplify the task early in training commensurate with a person's ability at that stage. Such simplification early in training does not generally appear to be an advantage over practice of the more difficult task from the start (Briggs, 1961, Exp. 1), although one schedule of aided tracking was found to be best by a small but reliable margin. Various other methods of simplifying a tracking task early in training were attempted (Briggs and Naylor, 1962) but continuous practice on the difficult task, toward which all groups were progressing, was the most efficient.

Although it may seem only sensible in training to follow a policy of gradually increasing difficulty, and although such a policy definitely seems advantageous for verbal learning, it appears not to be generally effective for tracking skill. The critical difference may lie in the continua which underlie tracking skill, particularly the control dynamics. The feedback is a quantity on the continuum, a quantity which informs the man not only of the error of his response, but also what would have been the best response. The trainee's first approximation in tracking, however crude according to task standards, is still essentially the same performance, with the same kind of feedback information. By way of contrast, in a verbal task, a wrong guess is just wrong; and when a math problem is demonstrated, if the student loses the "train of thought," he is effectively out of the problem.

In some kinds of tracking (or similar skills with feedback continua) too difficult conditions in the beginning may effectively remove the person from the learning conditions. In water skiing, for example, if the learner cannot manage to get up out of the water, he gets very little practice on each "trial." Similarly, in learning to ride a bicycle, little is learned until the person can balance well enough to experience the task dynamics. Although such tasks would not be likely candidates for study in a motor skills laboratory because of the erratic learning curve which would be generated, yet such skills are common indeed in athletics.

Tracking skills are extremely resistant to forgetting, as are motor skills generally. Procedural skills are a notable exception. Retention of skill has been reviewed by Bilodeau (1966) and by Bilodeau and Bilodeau (1961).

For practical tasks involving tracking, cognitive learning is likely to extend throughout training. Tracking tasks almost never exist in pure form except in the laboratory, and new kinds of task demands are generally added as practice proceeds, requiring new cognitive learning. Sometimes the task demands may increase quite suddenly, as when a highly experienced driver from a warm climate first experiences ice and snow on the road. Cognitive learning is especially likely to be critical when, under a special set of circumstances, the control-display relationships are sharply modified or reversed.

Tracking skills, in their natural task context, tend to be only a part of the task, and sometimes a small part. Driving skill, in essence, is not simply being able to hold a car in the center of the lane, although such tracking is certainly an essential part of the task. Skill in aiming a rifle is not merely pointing it, but holding the direction as the trigger is squeezed. The critical process, for design of effective training, is task analysis.

Keyboard Skills

Keyboard skills (typewriting or operating a key punch) are those in which the operator must strike one of several locations (the keys) in response to a series of conventional symbols in his environment. For purposes of this discussion, if the person must generate his own series of symbols (e.g., composing while typewriting), the composing will be considered a separate task.

A skilled keyboard operator performs too fast to use the kind of closed-loop feedback so important for tracking skill; that is, feedback which defines the next appropriate response in a series of responses. The keyboard operator tries to strike the keys with "ballistic" motions which are so quick that reaction time simply does not allow modification of a response on that particular occasion once the response is initiated. The keyboard skills thus do not provide useful "action" feedback, although "learning" feedback is provided (as these kinds of feedback have been distinguished by R. B. Miller, 1953b; Annett and Kay, 1957). Also, there is no continuum underlying the cues and responses of keyboard skills as there is in tracking tasks. The difference in feedback mechanism seems to be the basis of the classic distinction between "continuous" and "discrete" skills (although the terms have usually been somewhat vague).

The most widely used keyboard skill is typewriting, and it will serve as the prime example. Certainly more United States military man-hours are spent operating a typewriter than operating a rifle. Much of the military training in typewriting is heavily influenced by the ideas of Dr. Leonard West (now of CUNY) who spent part of his early career as an air force scientist. His work is particularly applicable to classroom practice because he summarizes the research in a series of practical and comprehensible rules. His early air force review of typewriting research and recommendations (West, 1957a,b) have recently been extended in a comprehensive text for teachers of typewriting (West, 1969).

For developing general rules of psychomotor skill training, perhaps it would be useful to have a general principle of typewriting training. Although

West does not state an overall principle underlying his rules, a general metarule may be formulated: Practice typing realistic materials under realistic conditions in an attempt to approximate the performance of expert typists as closely and as rapidly as possible. The essence of expert performance is typing at speed. A corollary may also be stated: Avoid the many artifices which have been developed in the colorful mythology of teaching typewriting. In view of the widespread misconceptions about learning typewriting, it would seem that much better teaching could be achieved. For example, West (1969, p. 15) reports the results of a test administered to about 200 students at the beginning of their courses on methods of teaching typing. The answer to each of the 25 true-false propositions has been well documented by research, yet the students scored only a little better than chance. Presumably, such misconceptions frequently have led to bad teaching. One of the intriguing things about typewriting research is the great number of a person's acquaintances who have been taught typewriting by instructors who used virtually all the wrong methods known to typewriting science.

Consideration of some of West's revolutionary techniques may suggest some basic properties of psychomotor skills, and of keyboard skills in particular. At first, the student should watch his fingers as he strikes the keys. Capped (blank) keys should not be used. In fact, the student should be encouraged to watch his fingers and keyboard, and it is even desirable to provide text in some form that allows him to watch his performance (e.g., via tape recorder), because vision is the only way to get immediate and accurate feedback. There is but one spatial sense, and that, for man, is primarily visual. There is no sound basis for the fear that students who watch their fingers at first may be unable to break the habit. Such "sight typing" generally will drop out naturally as the student gains speed, and if sight typing should persist unduly, speed forcing will eliminate it.

West also deemphasizes accuracy. He points out that speed is the reliable index of typing skill, not accuracy. In fact, if one wishes to predict either speed or accuracy later in the course, speed is the best predictor. West endorses the general motto, "Technique first, speed second, accuracy last." For technique he recommends some very brief stroking exercises in early training before the keyboard is taught, to ensure sharp "ballistic" motions, but then rapid transition to realistic materials while continuing to require crisp stroking motions. Very soon, the emphasis upon speed induces proper stroking technique. Similarly, the keyboard should be introduced rapidly (dispensing with the old "vertical" or "horizontal" approaches) by using common prose for material. The prose may be somewhat restricted for a while so that new letters are added somewhat gradually, allowing rapid responding throughout practice. Nonsense syllables are to be avoided. A variety of materials should be practiced rather than repetition of one passage. Practice should not be restricted to the commonest words. Rhythm drills (e.g., typing to music) are bad, since they are based upon the assumption that expert typists use even strokes (they do not).

Generally speed and accuracy cannot be developed at the same time. When developing speed, a modest increase (three to five words per minute) should be the goal, and a rather sharp increase in errors is acceptable. When developing accuracy, speed should not drop sharply, but rather remain about constant. It appears that typing is a somewhat different skill at different speeds.

Errors are random, so there is little point in prescribing different kinds of remedial exercise for various kinds of errors. "Technique" charts and "error analysis" charts are a waste of time and effort. Another irony is that capable, experienced typists are unaware of many of their errors, in spite of their belief to the contrary. It may be also somewhat surprising that straight copy speed has only a modest correlation with speed at normal work activities, so the "words per minute" of a typical employment test is not a very good indicator of job performance.

Various devices to teach typing have been developed, but there has been no clear demonstration that they produce faster learning. One difficulty is that they often entail features which run counter to some aspect of effective teaching practice. For example, the Saki (Lewis and Pask, 1965) has a keyboard replica panel on the wall in front of the student, and each key position on the panel lights up as the student is to type that character. Watching the replica display prevents the student from watching his hands (which is known to be important early in training). Also, translating a cue from a replica position to a real keyboard position takes some attention, and is thus likely to attenuate any advantage derived from the prompting. Another disadvantage of some of the typing trainers is that they use one display for a whole class, and thus they are committed to group-paced practice.

A training device should be derived as a constituent of a training technique. Task analysis is as basic to the training device as it is to the training method.

West's rules indicate the importance of being specific in describing the task to be practiced. They also illustrate the importance of speed, timing, and vision in psychomotor skill learning. The work of West should encourage training researchers. It demonstrates how research can be relevant to training, and by no means trivial.

Procedural Learning

Procedural learning is learning what steps to perform, and the sequence in which to perform them. Procedural learning is learning the qualitative aspects of a performance. Procedural learning is not a matter of skill of performing the individual steps; either the individual has the skill to perform the individual steps at the start so that he can be prompted through the performance, or he perfects (shapes) them after he learns the general procedure. In either case procedural learning comes first.

Procedural learning often is not even considered under psychomotor skills, especially if the discussion is restricted to laboratory tasks. Yet procedural learning is a very important part of our daily activity, and not likely to be considered under cognitive learning. Also, procedural learning is generally the first step in learning the more refined movements of *skilled performance* tasks.

Sometimes the prompts are kept on the job as job aids. The Maintenance Laboratory of the Air Force Personnel and Training Research Center investigated job aids in a pioneering program for proceduralizing job performance (summarized by Hoehn and Lumsdaine, 1958). The effort stressed the methodology of task analysis and carefully designed prompting media. A prominent industrial application is Videosonics, developed by Hughes Aircraft to guide electronics production workers. The Videosonic projects a 35 mm. slide, accompanied by audio directions for each step in the process, and the worker uses a foot switch to pace the presentation as he performs his job. Striking improvements in production have been reported (Harker, 1961; Hill and Tamsen, 1961). Chalupsky and Kopf (1967) have reviewed the state of the art of job aids, many of which can be adapted to training techniques.

General Guidelines. The general rule for procedural learning is as follows: place the learner in a realistic work environment (the simulation may be rather crude) and prompt him through repeated practice of the criterion behavior until he can perform without prompts. When each prompt covers a task segment which is short enough so that the learner may be expected to perform correctly without further aid, this is "guided learning." Note that such practice conditions differ markedly from conditions for learning tracking or keyboard skills, primarily in the addition of prompts which are withdrawn in the criterion test situation. (Keyboard skills do have prompts in the form of textual material, but the prompts are not withdrawn for the test situation.) The reason for prompts is that the sequence of procedural steps have a somewhat arbitrary character, at least from the learner's point of view, so they are not readily derived or discovered by trial and error. For procedural tasks, the performance criteria are qualitative, and if the learner does the wrong thing, there is little informative feedback intrinsic to the task situation so there is little chance to improve. The adage "practice makes perfect" may be more or less true of other psychomotor tasks, but it certainly is not true of procedural tasks, unless prompting or at least confirmation is provided.

Procedural learning resembles verbal learning in its qualitative character and in the apparent arbitrariness of the steps. There is some overlap in research on verbal and procedural learning. With verbal learning, several experiments have shown the superiority of prompting over the confirmation (trial and error, or guessing) procedure (Cook, 1958; Cook and Kendler, 1956; Hillix and Marx, 1960; Irion and Briggs, 1957; Kaess and Zeaman, 1960; Lau, 1966; McCrystal and Jacobs, 1966; Sidowski, Kopstein, and Shillestad, 1961) especially during early trials when the person is especially prone to err (Hawker, 1964, 1965a,b; Kopstein and Roshal, 1961; Peterson and Brewer, 1963). Cook and Spitzer (1960) found that forcing a student to guess actually interferes with learning; apparently incorrect guesses lead to incorrect associations. Yet there may be some advantage in responding without prompts. Angell and Lumsdaine (1960) found that prompting three-fourths of the responses was superior to continuous prompting. However, Cook and Miller (1963) made several comparisons of pure prompting with several combinations of prompting and confirmation, and in no case was the combination procedure better than pure prompting. Aiken and Lau (1967), in reviewing studies of prompting versus confirmation, concluded that "a variety of prompting procedures are equal to or superior to a variety of confirmation procedures in the learning of verbal paired-associates" (p. 33). Prompting is to be preferred over confirmation, especially when the consequences of error are severe, as in dangerous tasks; Annett and his associates (Annett and Clarkson, 1964; Annett and Paterson, 1966, 1967) have noted a relatively bold response tendency in their unprompted subjects during discrimination learning. However, either prompting or confirmation is far preferable to practice with neither prompting nor confirmation (Irion and Briggs, 1957).

A common mistake in procedures training is to withhold both prompts and confirmation, letting the learner fumble for extended periods. Most commonly, in fact, the procedure is nowhere stated explicitly. Instead, the trainee is seated in a classroom and assailed with lectures and literature containing diverse "facts" about the hardware, few of which are relevant to his performance, and he is supposed to derive the procedure for himself. Even when the procedures are explicit, they usually can be made much more efficient for accomplishing the task or for ease of recall. In no other area of skill training could one expect more striking improvements.

Fidelity of Simulation. The environment in which a procedure is practiced may be rather crudely simulated, in engineering terms. Studies with flight training (Dougherty et al., 1957; E. E. Miller, 1958; Prophet and Boyd, 1970) as well as with other procedural learning (Cox et al., 1965; Denenberg, 1954; Fox et al., 1969; Grimsley, 1969a, b, c) have found effective training with only gross appearance fidelity (by such means as dummy instruments, or photographs glued to plywood, or even mere line drawings). Crawford (1966) has designated such appearance fidelity as "open loop" simulation because the controls are not effective in modifying the stimulus inputs to the man.

Dougherty, Houston, and Nicklas (1957), in a classic study of low-cost simulation, compared the effectiveness of various training environments:

(1) The SNJ aircraft itself.
(2) A fully operational flight trainer, with all instruments working normally and with cyclorama providing simulation of cues from outside the cockpit.
(3) The operational flight trainer locked in the straps with the flight systems disconnected, but with engine electric and hydraulic systems operating normally (called a "procedures trainer").
(4) The operational flight trainer configured like the procedures trainer, but with the addition of a tracking task (holding pitch constant). This condition tested the importance of requiring division of attention during training.
(5) A simple photographic cockpit mock-up, life-size, with all front and side panels represented.

After five training sessions in the varied devices, all groups received another five training sessions, but in the aircraft. On the transfer trials (sessions six to ten) there were no significant differences on procedural items. Even the simple photographic mock-ups produced about 80 percent as much improvement on procedural items as actual flight experience, although on other flight items the mock-up group showed only about 28 percent as much improvement. It appears that procedures can be taught separately with very crude simulation, and without adverse effects on other aspects of performance. Training on the operational flight trainer (group 2) or on the "procedures" trainer (group 3) did not differ significantly from the same amount of training on the aircraft itself, even on the flight items. There was no indication that the division of attention for group 4 was of any advantage.

Since the rather crude simulation of cockpit mock-ups seems sufficient for learning procedures, one might wonder whether the training methods alone, without any simulation, might be effective. The importance of the cockpit mock-up was demonstrated in an experiment by E. E. Miller (1958). He compared three conditions of procedural training for groups of navy pre-solo flight students: (a) condensed procedural material used in cockpit mock-ups, (b) the same condensed procedural material used in ordinary chairs, and (c) control conditions involving no special training. The condensed procedural material for all pre-solo procedures consisted of brief phrases for each cue (e.g., at "100 knots") and subsequent action (e.g., "full throttle"). Thus, the regular climb description, 577 words long, was condensed to 35 words (see Table 6-1). After a brief demonstration of how to use the material, the students in the experimental groups would drill and test each other until they could correctly recite each procedure without prompting. After pre-solo training, the flight grading sheets for all students were examined, and procedural criticisms by flight instructors were tallied (e.g., "forgot to lower wheels" or "forgot to make his 90° check report"). The students who used the condensed material in cockpit mock-ups made only half as many procedural errors in the air as the control group, but the group practicing

TABLE 6-1

Condensed Procedural Materials for the Climb Maneuver in the T-34B*

CUE	ACTION
	Raise nose
	Advance prop to full
100 knots	Full throttle
	Retrim
	"S" turns
At desired altitude	Lower nose
	Start retrimming
120 knots	Throttle back, 19 inches manifold pressure
	RPM, 2000
	Trim, and adjust power

*From E. E. Miller (1958).

with the same condensed material in ordinary chairs had no apparent advantage over the control group. (The differences were significant statistically at the .01 level.) It can be concluded that the special environment of the mock-ups was critical to the effectiveness of the special procedural training. The importance of the mock-ups for learning is one of the reasons for considering procedural learning something more than simply verbal learning.

It is conceivable, but not plausible, that the cockpit mock-ups alone might account for the effectiveness of the first experimental procedure, without use of the condensed procedural descriptions. Without the experimental procedural material there is no guide for inducing practice, and all students had access to the cockpit mock-ups. It seems likely that the students practicing in the mock-ups performed the procedures in much greater detail (e.g., actually glancing at the manifold pressure gauge when the printed guide says "throttle back, 19″ manifold pressure") than did the other experimental group. The special printed procedures may also constitute a more efficient "coding" or "grouping" in hierarchic form (another practical example is given and analyzed by Whitmore, 1963).

Somewhat more refined simulation may be beneficial as the man develops skilled performance. Rudimentary simulation is sufficient for the early cognitive phase of skill learning during which procedural items predominate. Later, during the fixation and automation phases (as distinguished by Fitts, 1962) the quantitative aspects of the skill become prominent, and the person is able to respond to more subtle features of his environment. In flight training, carrier landing practice is one of the most demanding performances; the importance of simulating motion cues in such practice was investigated by Ruocco, Vitale, and Benfari (1965). A sophisticated aircraft simulator was used under two conditions: kinetic (with motion system on) and static. Extra-cockpit cues were provided all subjects by a video display which was appropriately responsive to the control movements. Kinetic cueing significantly improved performance in terms of percentage of successful landings, altitude error, time outside the flight path, and variability of pilot inputs. The group trained without motion showed a decrement in performance which persisted on the criterion flights (on which all subjects received kinetic cues). The results of the experiment by Ruocco and his associates (1965) contrast markedly with the experiments on procedural learning. They illustrate the relation between early procedural learning and the subsequent refinements of skilled performance (to be discussed further later in this chapter).

Forms of Prompting. The prompts needed for efficient procedural learning may be in the form of a series of phrases describing the sequence of steps, as illustrated by the flight procedure given in table 6-1. The phrases are apt to be somewhat cryptic for the complete novice, since they are designed to approximate the covert verbalizing of the pilot in the flight situation. For instance, it is assumed that the initial state is normal cruise (120 knots) and that the pilot has decided to climb. It is also assumed that the phrase "S turns" is meaningful to the student, suggesting the weaving path that the aircraft makes to ensure that no other aircraft is approaching from below on a collision course. Some introductory explanation or demonstration may be needed. However, the typical procedural description can be condensed and simplified to a degree that is almost unbelievable.

The prompts may be in the form of a demonstration, either "live" or pictorial. The live demonstration is the classic method of prompting, but it has severe limitations. A live demonstration can be viewed effectively by only a few students, and it is difficult to give the subjective (over-the-shoulder) viewpoint, which is superior (Roshal, 1949). Also, a pictorial demonstration can be validated through tryouts with students and subsequent revisions. Empiric validation has been shown to make pictorial communication more reliable (Jaspen, 1950; van der Meer et al., 1965; Gropper and Lumsdaine, 1961a, b, c; Gropper et al., 1961; E. E. Miller, 1971). With procedural skills the validation process is especially sensitive to program shortcomings because overt responses are so prominent, and hesitations can indicate difficulties well below the threshold of overt errors.

There were three early programs of intensive research involving demonstration films (Lumsdaine, 1962, p. 252): (1) the Yale University Program, 1946 to 1949, reported by May and Lumsdaine (1958), (2) the Pennsylvania State University program, 1947 to 1955, under the direction of C. R. Carpenter, under the sponsorship of the Office of Naval Research, and (3) the U.S. Air Force program under A. A. Lumsdaine, 1950 to 1953, and continuing somewhat thereafter in the context of more general training research. (Another early analytic program on instructional films (Hovland, Lumsdaine and Sheffield, 1949) tended more to emphasize attitudinal and cognitive factors.) Many of the studies from the programs are reported in the landmark

volume *Student Response in Programmed Instruction: A Symposium.*
(Lumsdaine, 1961).

A demonstration movie should allow time for responding (Jaspen, 1950;
Lau, 1966; McGuire, 1961). It may be effective to direct the student's
attention to the relevant task cues by testing (Levine, 1953; Lumsdaine et al.,
1958; Maccoby et al., 1961; Michael and Maccoby, 1953, 1961) or by
animation (arrows, etc., Lumsdaine and Sulzer, 1951) while avoiding
embellishments which are irrelevant (Lumsdaine and Gladstone, 1958).
Instructional narrative can aid instruction (Jaspen, 1950; May, 1946, 1958;
Wulff, 1955) as can motion (Roshal, 1949) and slow motion (Sheffield and
Maccoby, 1961). There is evidence that the hands of the demonstrator may
sometimes obscure critical cues (Roshal, 1949). Vividness may increase a
film's effectiveness (Sheffield and Maccoby, 1961). Repeating a demonstration may also increase its effectiveness (Kurtz et al., 1950; McTavish, 1949;
E. E. Miller, 1971; Rimland, 1955; Sulzer et al., 1962). Twyford and
Carpenter (1956) have formulated several guidelines for film makers based
upon 70 of the earlier experimental studies.

Another form of prompting is the pictorial programmed book, or
"picture-guide." Baker and his HumRRO associates at Div. 2 (Armor)
developed earlier versions of picture-guides for Armor Crewmen (HumRRO,
1957, 1958a, b). Ware, Miller, and Constantinides (1968) have described
more recent versions and techniques. Compared with demonstration movies,
the picture-guides can teach assembly and disassembly of a weapon in about
the same training time (Miller, 1971). Compared with an audiovisual
presentation for aircraft maintenance, a picture-guide was as effective for
learning and was actually preferred by the men in training (PIMO, 1969).

While a movie may offer greater photographic realism, a picture-guide has
several other advantages. In printed copy it is relatively easy to closely
integrate directions and pictures by putting the words on the picture directly,
or by using call-out lines or arrows. Also, the intrinsic task cues may more
easily be emphasized by such techniques as rubbing chalk on machinery at
critical edges, ridges, or textures. When verbal prompts are used, the
vocabulary often must be learned first, but when pictorial prompts are used,
the technical terms may be introduced succinctly as titles. Perhaps the
greatest advantage of the printed picture-guides is their flexibility in use: the
student can readily scan ahead or go back and view again, and booklets are
easily carried and filed.

Audio prompting is another significant form, as when a student is "talked
through" his task. Some activities such as square dancing or marching have
audio prompts as part of the job. Dance choreographers and directors can use
audio prompts profitably, and tape recorders can provide synchronized music
and prompting. One should remember that audio prompts generally entail
two parts: first, the specification of what is to be done, and then a timing (or
execution) cue (for instance, in marching, "about, face").

Size of Behavioral Unit Prompted. Generally, demonstrating the whole performance to students before they begin practice has been found less efficient than prompting (by demonstrating) somewhat smaller segments (Kimble and Wulff, 1961; Maccoby and Sheffield, 1958, 1961; Sheffield, 1961). Demonstrations of whole tasks, or of segments too long to be remembered, are apt to lead to the same kinds of inefficiencies as trial and error learning, but to a somewhat lesser degree (to the degree that some parts are remembered). One might expect that the most effective demonstration segment would be the longest one the student could remember, which Sheffield and his associates call the demonstration-apprehension (D-A) span (Sheffield, 1961). Of course, the D-A span varies with individuals; Margolius and Sheffield (1961) found that better learners, as indicated by final test scores, chose longer demonstration segments before practice; similarly, Gropper (1968) found a significant interaction between I.Q. and optimal length of demonstration unit. Tasks are not infinitely divisible, but have natural units, the finest division being smaller than the D-A span. Also, Margolius, Sheffield and Maccoby (1961) found it more effective to have students practice each unit *twice* before going on to practice the next unit rather than practicing the complete performance in sequence twice.

Practically, however, the optimal length of a demonstration segment is apt to depend upon a variety of classroom variables which might be termed *logistic* (e.g., student-instructor ratio). E. E. Miller (1971) found that division into small demonstration-practice units reduced the need for further assistance from the instructor, although the total time necessary to learn was comparable. With a minimum of instructors it is probably better to overprompt than to underprompt, since failure to give a needed prompt is apt to leave a student at a loss until an instructor is available, while giving too many prompts will reduce efficiency of practice only slightly.

The issue of the ideal size of prompt is likely to be answered practically by finding some means of giving the student a high degree of control over his own prompts. The picture-guide books are one highly flexible prompting medium which is student-controlled.

Task Variables. With some kinds of procedural tasks such as assembly and disassembly operations, the student discovers a great deal about the task by performing it, even when the performance is prompted. The feedback from task performance not only confirms the correctness of the actions, but makes the actions more meaningful and better remembered. With other tasks, such as aircraft flight procedures, the feedback may be meager or ambiguous, and thus the procedure may continue to seem somewhat arbitrary. Therefore, considerable repetitious practice may be required.

A related task variable is the degree of understanding which is helpful in the performance of a task. It seems pointless to make sharp distinctions between cognitive and psychomotor tasks because tasks tend to involve various degrees of cognition and different people tend to use different levels of "understanding" for any particular task. However, when a total procedure is oriented around developing a concept, then step-by-step guidance may be ineffective. For instance, Weiss, Maccoby and Sheffield (1961) were surprised to find that a step-by-step demonstration movie was ineffective for guiding the learning of a geometric construction task even though performance during training (with the prompts) was satisfactory. More typically in procedures learning, understanding may aid in acquisition or retention of some segments of the performance, but it may not be essential to guiding the overall performance. Sometimes the critical insight may be instilled as the man is guided through the task, and this is one of the main reasons for using carefully programmed pictorial prompts.

Often the cognitive or imagery skills are analyzed as a sub-task and trained first, sometimes by using visual training aids. In a beautifully designed and executed study, Silverman (1958) investigated the importance of *dynamic* imagery in operating man-portable weapons. The training employed transparent plastic models of the mechanism inside the weapons, showed by means of an overhead projector for the whole class to see. The plastic parts moved realistically so that the whole projection was "animated." Under one condition the "animated transparencies" were employed with accompanying text, as designed by the Navy Training Devices Center (who financed the study). Under the control condition essentially the same text and devices were used, but with the parts fixed in place. Another dimension of the experiment was weapon complexity, represented by four different weapons. On a multiple-choice criterion test oriented toward action items, no differences were apparent, but on a performance criterion test there was a substantial and significant difference favoring those who had seen the animated version of the presentations. Weapon complexity seemed to make no significant difference, but a *post hoc* analysis indicated that the effectiveness of animation was correlated with number of simultaneously moving parts; in other words, animation of the images seems especially important when there is a whole chain of parts moving. Silverman's results also provide a lesson in methodology for researchers in motor skills; important effects may not be apparent on paper-and-pencil tests, even if the tests are carefully designed.

The realism required in training aids or other forms of prompting is likely to depend upon the amount of experience of the person being trained. Swanson (1954), using highly experienced maintenance technicians as subjects, found no difference in value of training aids with various levels of realism. Not surprisingly, well-trained prople can perform effectively from general verbal directions or abstract symbols, as they have been trained to do. In a follow-up experiment, Swanson, Lumsdaine and Aukes (1956) used inexperienced airmen as subjects. Three groups all heard the same tape-recorded lecture, but for one group the lecture was supplemented by an elaborate visual mock-up; for a second group the lecture was supplemented by a schematic diagram, and the control group received only the lecture. Three criterion tests were administered. The mock-up group was superior on a parts-recognition test, the diagram group was superior on a test of functional inter-connections, and there were no significant differences on the test of verbal knowledge. The conclusion was that the effectiveness of each training aid depends upon the specific instructional objectives.

Another important task characteristic is "branching" (i.e., alternative modes of performance, depending upon the circumstances). Many training people would readily accept the methods of task guidance and low-fidelity simulation for routine (linear) tasks, yet they might be dubious of their effectiveness if the training methods were applied to branching tasks. Currently under HumRRO's Work Unit Interface, I am exploring the effectiveness of guided learning for branching procedures, with special attention to electronics maintenance. The project differs from most previous work in electronics maintenance primarily in its emphasis upon physical environment (mock-up or equipment) coordinated with task guidance during practice. One promising technique is to put the prompts in the form of a flow-chart, and have the trainee follow different branches on repetitions of practice on simulated equipment.

Integration of Training. After desirable features of a training program have been identified, there remains the problem of putting the program all together. This is especially true of procedures training because it tends to be the most complex kind of psychomotor performance. A useful strategy of organization is "functional context" training, in which a sequence of job performance is the organizing concept, and basic skills and ideas are introduced, explained, or practiced as they are needed for job performance.

One persistent problem is relating the task requirements (printed or spoken directions) to a particular location or action taking place. In audiovisual presentations, the directions are usually on the audio channel, and correspondence can be indicated by having the directions consistently lead the action by about a second, as if the actor is "following directions." In pictorial instruction books, correspondence can be established by having the directions (words like "turn" or "push") printed right over the picture, and graphic conventions such as arrows can also be used effectively. Traditional texts require a person to go through many tenuous steps in establishing the relation of pictures to the action required.

Quality Control and Program Validation. The "systems" approach to training would require that the learner demonstrate the criterion performance without prompts before proceeding with other activities. Such testing is the "quality control" which should be built into training situations. Another facet of quality control is the validation of the prompting medium (tryout with novices and revisions) until errors are virtually eliminated if prompting is provided. Yet even with a validated program it is risky to omit direct testing of each trainee in each critical performance. If the instructor does not have time to check each student on each sub-task, the students may be able to check each other and perhaps the instructor can recheck occasionally. If a performance is likely to be forgotten, a proficiency test may have to be administered periodically to ensure continued adequate performance.

With psychomotor tasks, the validation process is extremely sensitive to program shortcomings because of the readily observable overt responses involved. The validation process is also a rich source of principles of programming. There is usually a rationale for making each change, and the ideas underlying the successful changes may be organized into a coherent set of principles of programming. Through such a process E. E. Miller (1971) developed a preliminary set of principles of pictorial demonstrations.

Although the "evidence" from program validation is somewhat suspect from a statistical viewpoint, there are other advantages. Each generalization is likely to be based upon a variety of instances. The principles cover problems which actually have arisen. The principles are interrelated with each other and with the other research findings, and the resulting guidelines seem to be conservative and almost common sense (however often one sees these principles violated). Also, the goal of formulating such principles is to develop an effective "language" system of pictorial communication, given our population stereotypes; there should be no implication that it is the most efficient possible language of pictures. Empirically validated pictorial programs seem likely to become increasingly common when the costs of their development are amortized over a larger market for instructional programs.

Skilled Performance

"Skilled performance" tasks require control of an evolving process (that is, a process that develops through different phases on any particular instance of task performance) with procedural aspects, by definition, excluded. The characteristic training method is to extract, through task analysis, the procedural aspects, and first to train the procedural aspects by the methods discussed previously. This strategy is generally effective; the procedural (qualitative) aspects should be performed correctly from the start because feedback from task cues are uninformative, whereas the task cues are highly relevant for shaping the quantitative skill aspects of the task. Sometimes the procedural aspects cover only brief episodes, as when a coach will tell a man what kind of grip or stance to use. Experienced coaches and instructors often become very clever at extracting the procedural aspects and communicating them. In fact, such cleverness may be one of the defining characteristics of good coaching.

There are tasks which border between "tracking" and "skilled performance," but such ambiguities are not likely to be troublesome practically because in such cases the same training strategies are likely to apply to both categories. Both categories involve closed-loop feedback processes (such as displacement from an ideal position) which are critical to learning the task. The difference is that "skilled performance" tasks also entail control of an evolving process.

Craftsmanship. "Craftsmanship" tasks are those skilled performances which have as their primary criterion the quality of some resulting product. (The emphasis upon criteria is typical of skilled performances.) A military example is soldering technique in electronic maintenance. The focus on product makes it potentially profitable to try to promote understanding of the materials, tools, and processes of forming the product. Often it is necessary for a craftsman to discriminate between a well-made product and one resulting from various kinds of inadequate methods. Often such a variety of products, or a rather good simulation thereof, is needed in training because random job experience may not provide the instructive comparisons. Discriminations are formed more readily when the objects are seen together (simultaneous comparison) than when they are viewed successively (Gavurin, 1965). Studies of concept identification also have indicated the advantages of simultaneous presentation (Cahill and Hovland, 1960; Hovland and Weiss, 1953), especially with more complex problems, and with greater numbers of simultaneously available instances (Bourne, Goldstein and Link, 1964; Kates and Yudin, 1964). Craftsmanship almost always involves first learning procedural sub-tasks and the procedural learning may be nearly adequate with most learners for beginning skill on the job.

In certain kinds of craftsmanship, understanding the process is particularly important because the kind of feedback, although quantitative, is apt to be misinterpreted. For example, when using a hacksaw to cut thick mild steel (as in a hinge or strap-iron) the person must not hurry the work or the heat of sawing will temper the iron, thus slowing the cut and perhaps breaking saw teeth.

Athletics. "Athletics," as the term is used here, involves the rest of skilled performance; that is, control of an evolving process *not* associated with development of a product. The criteria, therefore, involve such standards as strength, accuracy, coordination, speed, and perhaps gracefulness. Military examples include quick firing of a rifle or a pistol. The exclusion of product formation tends to reduce emphasis upon understanding of the process in abstract terms. It is legendary that knowing the equations of trajectories has little or no transfer value when trying to catch a ball. Another kind of understanding, however, may be critical; that is, knowing of some improvement of technique. Often a coach will either direct a change in movement patterns or muscular tension or the set to respond. The coach presumably diagnoses weaknesses in the performance and direct verbal commands are usually sufficient to change performance. Such diagnostic processes, as training strategies, have been discussed and classified elsewhere (E. E. Miller, 1969).

The performance criteria of games (e.g., football) generally involve interactive competition (that is, a skillful response takes into account what the opponent has done). Learning games may therefore involve learning a strategy of misleading opponents. Other sports (e.g., a 100-yard dash) may be judged on an absolute performance basis. Other athletics (e.g., dancing) involve subjective, perhaps esthetic, standards. One of the delights of competitive athletics is that the winner is determined by objective criteria, not by the opinions of sportscasters or other experts (in contrast to so much of vocational competition).

The performance criteria of various sports bear obvious relationships to factors of strength, stamina, speed, accuracy, or coordination. These factors have been refined considerably by Fleishman and his associates by using the statistical technique of factor analysis. In early work (Hempel and Fleishman, 1955) four clusters of factors were identified: (a) strength (of trunk and of limbs), (b) suppleness, (c) "explosive" strength, such as needed for putting a shot, and (d) balance factors. Fleishman's later (1964) extensive factor analyses of athletic skills in 12-to-18-year-old boys produced eleven major factors: (a) control precision, (b) multilimb coordination, (c) response orientation, (d) reaction time, (e) speed of arm movement, (f) rate control, (g) manual dexterity, (h) finger dexterity, (i) arm-hand steadiness, (j) wrist-finger speed, and (k) aiming.

In order to formulate the various aspects of skill learning, Fitts (1962) analyzed interview reports from two sources: (a) 40 athletic coaches and instructors and (b) the air force flight instructors of 1000 flight students who were eliminated from training. Four aspects were mentioned frequently: (a) cognitive aspects, (b) perceptual aspects, (c) coordination, and (d) tension-relaxation (with moderate tension being desirable).

When an athletic kind of performance occurs as part of a military system, often the greatest training improvements result from establishing precisely the conditions and criteria of "good" performance. In analyzing ability with a rifle, for example, it was found that the most common battle requirement was to get several shots off into a moving target at rather close range (McFann, Hammes, and Taylor, 1955). The then-current training emphasized firing at clear, fixed targets at known distances (far). Dramatic improvement resulted from using the "pop-up" targets along with associated training procedures which were developed in cooperation with the instruction staff which eventually administered the training. Currently, the small-arms training methods are being updated and improved under HumRRO's Work Unit MARKSMAN (Dees, Magner, and McCluskey, 1971).

A militarily important subclass of "athletic" skills (as defined here) is vehicular control, especially flying an aircraft. Flying involves tracking as an important sub-task; but the judgment of ideal path, compared with present status (speed, heading, and position) introduces important additional considerations. Later stages of flight training involve increasingly demanding judgments of speed, path, and position, as in landing on a carrier, long after simple tracking (holding to altitude or attitude) has apparently reached an asymptote.

An excellent example of research on skilled performance is the work of Williams and his associates at the University of Illinois Aviation Psychology Laboratory (Williams and Flexman, 1949; Flexman, Matheny and Brown, 1950). They used a variety of motivational, cognitive and procedural techniques to reduce pre-solo flight time to three or four hours, which is roughly a third of typical flight training time before solo.

SUMMARY

Beginning in World War II, the Department of Defense through its various agencies became a primary source of support and encouragement for scientific studies of motor skills. Experimental psychologists who confronted military training problems and issues were impelled both by their concern for the practical and by their highly analytic discipline. They found little application for any of the specific conclusions from the learning laboratory, yet when their analytic outlook and methods were focused on practical problems, they generated an effective technology of task analysis, a unique contribution of military psychology to instructional practice. Task analysis focuses less upon what people actually do on a job, and more upon what a person must do to be effective in the context of a system.

Different kinds of psychomotor tasks require different kinds of training, depending upon the kind of feedback involved. Learning a tracking task requires direct practice under conditions of rather faithful representation of the critical closed-loop feedback. Systematic alterations of the task environment during tracking practice are either of little or no advantage, or sometimes a marked disadvantage, although some cognitive instruction may be helpful early in training, especially for learning the control-display relationships. Keyboard skills, e.g., typewriting, benefit from forcing the pace, from realistic practice materials and conditions, from a rather tolerant attitude about errors, and from watching one's fingers in the beginning (even though the ultimate goal is to type without watching the fingers). Efficient training of procedural tasks requires first a clear, succinct, and well-ordered statement of the procedure, then practice of the procedure with the statement handy for prompting or confirmation. The procedural statement is critical because there is little feedback intrinsic to the task (hence, the apparent arbitrariness of the task). Procedural learning has much in common with purely verbal learning, but in addition the task environment is critical for effective practice (although the simulation of environment may be rather crude in engineering terms). Learning skilled performance (such as in craftsmanship or athletics) involves closed-loop feedback like tracking, but in addition control of an evolving process (which should be a focus of attention during training) must be learned. A common and effective training strategy is to first treat it as a procedural task in order to elicit a reasonable approximation of the desired skilled performance.

The discipline of task analysis is being extended into civilian practice through such related developments as programmed instruction, behavioral objectives, modular instruction, and systems analysis. We can expect increasing benefits from such intensive, analytic study of particular instruction programs as our technologic society finds wider instruction markets for amortizing investment in research and development activities.

References

Aiken, E. G., & Lau, A. W. Response prompting and response confirmation: A review of recent literature. *Psychological Bulletin,* 1967, 68, 330–341.

Angell, D., & Lumsdaine, A. A. *Prompted plus unprompted trials versus prompted trials alone in paired-associate learning.* Pittsburgh: American Institutes for Research, 1960.

Annett, J., & Clarkson, J. K. *The use of cuing in training tasks.* Technical Report 3143-1, U.S. Naval Training Device Center, Orlando, Florida, 1964.

Annett, J., & Kay, H. Knowledge of results and skilled performance. *Occupational Psychology,* 1957, 31, 69–79.

Annett, J., & Paterson, L. *The use of cuing in training tasks: Phase II.* Technical Report 4119-1, U.S. Naval Training Device Center, Orlando, Florida, 1966.

Annett, J., & Paterson, L. *The use of cuing in training tasks: Phase III.* NAVTRA-DEVCEN 4717-1, U.S. Naval Training Device Center, Orlando, Florida, 1967.

Berkshire, J. R., & Lyon, V. W. Human quality control in naval air training. *American Psychologist,* 1959, 14, 153–155.

Bilodeau, E. A. Retention. In E. A. Bilodeau (ed.) *Acquisition of skill.* New York: Academic Press, 1966, pp. 315–350.

Bilodeau, E. A., & Bilodeau, I. McD. Motor-skills learning. *Annual Review of Psychology,* 1961, 12, 243–280.

Bloom, B. S. (ed.) *Taxonomy of educational objectives, Handbook I, cognitive domain.* New York: David McKay, 1956.

Bourne, L. E., Jr., Goldstein, S., & Link, W. E. Concept learning as a function of availability of previously presented information. *Journal of Experimental Psychology,* 1964, 67, 439–448.

Briggs, G. E. *On the scheduling of training conditions for the acquisition and transfer of perceptual-motor skills.* NAVTRADEVCEN Technical Report 836-1, U.S. Naval Training Device Center, Orlando, Florida, 1961.

Briggs, G. E., & Naylor, J. C. The relative efficiency of several training methods as a function of transfer task complexity. *Journal of Experimental Psychology,* 1962, 64, 505–512.

Cahill, H. E., & Hovland, E. I. The role of memory in the acquisition of concepts. *Journal of Experimental Psychology,* 1960, 59, 137–144.

Chalupsky, A. B., & Kopf, T. J. *Job performance aids and their impact on manpower utilization.* WDL-TR3276, Philco-Ford Corporation, Palo Alto, California, May, 1967.

Cook, J. O. Supplementary report: Processes underlying learning a single paired-associate item. *Journal of Experimental Psychology,* 1958, 56, 455.

Cook, J. O., & Kendler, T. S. A theoretical model to explain some paired-associate learning data. In G. Finch & F. Cameron (eds.) *Symposium on air force human engineering, personnel, and training research.* Washington, D.C.: National Academy of Sciences National Research Council, 1956.

Cook, J. O., & Miller, H. G. *Studies in guided learning.* Cooperative Research Project No. 1242, University of North Carolina, 1963.

Cook, J. O., & Spitzer, M. E. Supplementary report: Prompting versus confirmation in paired-associate learning. *Journal of Experimental Psychology,* 1960, 59, 275–276.

Cox, J. A., Wood, R. O., Jr., Boren, L. M., & Thorne, H. W. *Functional and appearance fidelity of training devices for fixed-procedures tasks.* Technical Report 65-4, Human Resources Research Organization, Alexandria, Virginia, June, 1965.

Crawford, M. P. Concepts of training. In Robert M. Gagné (ed.) *Psychological principles in system development.* New York: Holt, Rinehart and Winston, 1962, pp. 301–341.

Crawford, M. P. Dimensions of simulation. *American Psychologist,* 1966, 21, 788–796.

Crawford, M. P. A new approach to training programs. *Science Publication News,* December, 1968.

Dees, J. W., Magner, G. J., & McCluskey, M. R. *An experimental review of basic combat rifle marksmanship: MARKSMAN, Phase I.* Technical Report 71-4, Human Resources Research Organization, Alexandria, Virginia, March 1971.

Denenberg, V. H. *The training effectiveness of a tank hull trainer.* Technical Report 3, Human Resources Research Organization, Alexandria, Virginia, February, 1954.

Dougherty, D. J., Houston, R. C., & Nicklas, D. R. *Transfer of training in flight procedures from selected ground training devices to the aircraft.* Technical Report NAVTRADEVCEN 71-16-16, U.S. Naval Training Device Center, Port Washington, New York, September, 1957.

Fitts, P. M. Factors in complex skill training. In R. Glaser (ed.) *Training research and education.* Pittsburgh: University of Pittsburgh Press, 1962, pp. 177–198.

Fleishman, E. A. *The structure and measurement of physical fitness.* Englewood Cliffs, N.J.: Prentice-Hall, 1964.

Fleishman, E. A. Comments on Professor Jones' Paper. In E. A. Bilodeau (ed.) *Acquisition of skill.* New York: Academic Press, 1966, pp. 147–168.

Flexman, R. E., Matheny, W. G., & Brown, E. L. Evaluation of the school link and special methods of instruction. *University of Illinois Bulletin,* July, 1950, 47(80).

Fox, W. L., Taylor, J. E., & Caylor, J. S. *Aptitude level and the acquisition of skills and knowledges in a variety of military training tasks.* Technical Report 69-6, Human Resources Research Organization, Alexandria, Virginia, May, 1969.

Gagné, R. M. Military training and principles of learning. *American Psychologist,* 1962, 17, 83–91.

Gavurin, E. I. *An evaluation of various tachistoscopic and WEFT techniques in aircraft recognition.* Technical Report NAVTRADEVCEN IH-40, U.S. Naval Training Devices Center, Port Washington, N.Y., 1965.

Glaser, R., & Klaus, D. J. Proficiency measurement: Assessing human performance. In R. Gagné (ed.) *Psychological principles in system development.* New York: Holt, Rinehart and Winston, 1962, pp. 419–476.

Grimsley, D. L. *Acquisition, retention, and retraining of skills: Effects of high and low fidelity in training devices.* Technical Report 69-1, Human Resources Research Organization, Alexandria, Virginia, February, 1969. (a)

Grimsley, D. L. *Acquisition, retention, and retraining: Group studies on using low fidelity training devices.* Technical Report 69-4, Human Resources Research Organization, Alexandria, Virginia, March, 1969. (b)

Grimsley, D. L. *Acquisition, retention, and retraining: Training Category IV personnel with low fidelity devices.* Technical Report 69-12, Human Resources Research Organization, Alexandria, Virginia, June, 1969. (c)

Gropper, G. L. Programming visual presentations for procedural learning. *AV Communication Review,* 1968, 16(1), 33–56.

Gropper, G. L., & Lumsdaine, A. A. *Issues in programing instructional materials for televised presentation, report no. 5. Studies in televised instruction: The use of student response to improve televised instruction.* Pittsburgh: American Institutes for Research, March, 1961. (a)

Gropper, G. L., & Lumsdaine, A. A. *An overview, report no. 7. Studies in televised instruction: The use of student response to improve televised instruction.* Pittsburgh: American Institutes for Research, March, 1961. (b)

Gropper, G. L., & Lumsdaine, A. A. *Requiring active student response, report no. 2. Studies in televised instruction: The use of student response to improve televised instruction.* Pittsburgh: American Institutes for Research, March, 1961. (c)

Gropper, G. L., Lumsdaine, A. A., & Shipman, V. *Improvement of televised instruction based on student responses to achievement tests, report no. 1. Studies in televised instruction: The use of student response to improve televised instruction.* Pittsburgh: American Institutes for Research, March, 1961.

Harker, W. A. Audio-visual learning–it's more than hear-say! *Electronic Industries,* August, 1961, 103–105.

Hawker, J. R. The influence of training procedure and other task variables in paired associate learning. *Journal of Verbal Learning and Verbal Behavior,* 1964, 3, 70–76.

Hawker, J. R. The effects of training procedure response availability, and response meaningfulness in multiple-choice paired-associate learning. *Psychonomic Science,* 1965, 3, 329–330. (a)

Hawker, J. R. The effects of training procedure, response similarity, and number of response alternatives in multiple-choice paired-associate learning. *Psychonomic Science,* 1965, 3, 331–332. (b)

Hempel, W. E., & Fleishman, E. A. Factor analysis of physical proficiency and manipulative skill. *Journal of Applied Psychology,* 1955, 39, 12–16.

Hill, D. A., & Tamsen, J. J. Videosonic system instructions raise quality standards. *Industrial Quality Control,* July, 1961, 15–20.

Hillix, W. A., & Marx, M. H. Response strengthening by information and effect in human learning. *Journal of Experimental Psychology,* 1960, 60, 97–102.

Hoehn, A. J., & Lumsdaine, A. A. *Design and use of job aids for communicating technical information.* Technical Report AFPTRC-TR-58-7, Air Force Personnel and Training Research Center, Lackland AFB, Texas, January, 1958.

Hovland, C. I., Lumsdaine, A. A., & Sheffield, F. D. Experiments on mass communication. Princeton: Princeton University Press, 1949.

Hovland, C. I., & Weiss, W. Transmission of information concerning concepts through positive and negative instances. *Journal of Experimental Psychology,* 1953, 45, 175–182.

Human Resources Research Organization. *The tank gunner's guide (M48A1 tank).* Alexandria, Virginia: HumRRO, October, 1957.

Human Resources Research Organization. *The tank driver's guide (M48A1 tank).* Alexandria, Virginia: HumRRO, May, 1958. (a)

Human Resources Research Organization. *The tank loader's guide (M48A1 tank).* Alexandria, Virginia: HumRRO, May, 1958. (b)

Irion, A. L., & Briggs, L. J. *Learning task and mode of operation variables in use of the subject-matter training.* Technical Report AFPTRC-TR-57-8, Air Force Personnel and Training Research Center, Lackland AFB, Texas, October, 1957.

Jaspen, N. *Effects on training of experimental film variables: Study II: Verbalization, "how-it-works," nomenclature, audience participation, and succinct treatment.* Technical Report No. SDC 269-7-11, U.S. Naval Training Device Center, Port Washington, New York, March, 1950.

Jones, M. B. *Simplex theory.* Monograph 3, U.S. Naval School of Aviation Medicine, Pensacola, Florida, 1959.

Jones, M. B. Practice as a process of simplification. *Psychological Review,* 1962, 69, 274–294.

Jones, M. B. Individual differences. In E. A. Bilodeau (ed.) *Acquisition of skill.* New York: Academic Press, 1966. pp. 109–146.

Kaess, W., & Zeaman, D. Positive and negative knowledge of results on a Pressey-type punchboard. *Journal of Experimental Psychology,* 1960, 60, 12–17.

Kates, S. L., & Yudin, L. Concept attainment and memory. *Journal of Educational Psychology,* 1964, 55, 103–109.

Kimble, G. A., & Wulff, J. J. "Response guidance" as a factor in the value of student participation in film instruction. In A. A. Lumsdaine (ed.) *Student response in programed instruction: a symposium.* Washington, D.C.: National Academy of Sciences–National Research Council, 1961.

Kopstein, F. F., & Roshal, S. M. Verbal learning efficiency as influenced by the manipulation of representational response processes. In A. A. Lumsdaine (ed.) *Student response in programed instruction: a symposium.* Washington, D.C.: National Academy of Sciences–National Research Council, 1961.

Kurtz, A. K., Walter, J. S., & Brenner, H. R. *The effects of inserted questions and statements on film learning (rapid mass learning).* Technical Report No. SDC 269-7-16, U.S. Naval Training Device Center, Port Washington, New York, September, 1950.

Lau, A. W. *A comparison of prompting versus feedback in verbal and perceptual learning.* Technical Bulletin STB 67-8, U.S. Naval Personnel Research Activity, San Diego, October, 1966.

Levine, S. The role of motivation in the effects of 'active review' on learning from a factual film. *American Psychologist,* 1953, 8, 388–389.

Lewis, B. N., & Pask, G. The theory and practice of adaptive teaching systems. In R. Glaser (ed.) *Teaching machines and programed learning.* Washington, D.C.: National Education Association, 1965, pp. 213–266.

Lumsdaine, A. A. (ed.) *Student response in programed instruction: a symposium.* Washington, D.C.: National Academy of Sciences–National Research Council, 1961.

Lumsdaine, A. A. Instructional materials and devices. In R. Glaser (ed.) *Training research and education.* Pittsburgh: University of Pittsburgh Press, 1962, pp. 247–294.

Lumsdaine, A. A., & Gladstone, A. Overt practice and audio-visual embellishments. In M. A. May & A. A. Lumsdaine (eds.) *Learning from films.* New Haven: Yale University Press, 1958, pp. 58–71.

Lumsdaine, A. A., May, M. A., & Hadsell, R. S. Questions spliced into a film for motivation and pupil participation. In M. A. May & A. A. Lumsdaine (eds.) *Learning from films.* New Haven: Yale University Press, 1958, pp. 72–83.

Lumsdaine, A. A., & Sulzer, R. L. *The influence of simple animation techniques on the value of a training film.* HRRL Report No. 24, USAF Human Factors Research Laboratory, Washington, D.C., 1951.

MacCaslin, E. F., & Cogan, E. A. *Learning theory and research paradigms applied to training research: Some dissonances.* Professional Paper 13-68, Human Resources Research Organization, Alexandria, Virginia, May, 1968.

Maccoby, N., Michael, D. N., & Levine, S. Further studies of student participation procedures in film instruction. In A. A. Lumsdaine (ed.) *Student response in programed instruction: a symposium.* Washington, D.C.: National Academy of Sciences–National Research Council, 1961.

Maccoby, N., & Sheffield, F. D. Theory and experimental research on the teaching of complex sequential procedures by alternate demonstration and practice. In G. Finch & F. Cameron (eds.) *Symposium on air force human engineering, personnel, and training research.* (Publication 516.) Washington, D.C.: National Academy of Sciences–National Research Council, 1958.

Maccoby, N., & Sheffield, F. D. Combining practice with filmed demonstration in teaching complex response sequences. Summary and interpretation. In A. A. Lumsdaine (ed.) *Student response in programed instruction: a symposium.* Washington, D.C.: National Academy of Sciences–National Research Council, 1961.

Margolius, G. J., & Sheffield, F. D. Optimum methods of combining practice with filmed demonstration in teaching complex response sequences: Serial learning of a mechanical-assembly task. In A. A. Lumsdaine (ed.) *Student response in programed instruction: a symposium.* Washington, D.C.: National Academy of Sciences–National Research Council, 1961.

Margolius, G., Sheffield, F. D., & Maccoby, N. Repetitive versus consecutive demonstration and practice in the learning of a serial mechanical-assembly task. In A. A. Lumsdaine (ed.) *Student response in programed instruction: a symposium.* Washington, D.C.: National Academy of Sciences–National Research Council, 1961.

May, M. A. The psychology of learning from demonstration films. *Journal of*

Educational Psychology, 1946, 37, 1–12. May, M. A. Verbal responses to demonstrational films. In M. A. May & A. A. Lumsdaine (eds.) *Learning from films.* New Haven: Yale University Press, 1958.

May, M. A., & Lumsdaine, A. A. (eds.) *Learning from films.* New Haven: Yale University Press, 1958.

McCrystal, T. J., & Jacobs, T. O. *The effect of programed instruction response conditions on acquisition and retention.* Technical Report 66-20, Human Resources Research Organization, Alexandria, Virginia, December, 1966.

McFann, H. H., Hammes, J. A., & Taylor, J. E. TRAINFIRE I: *A new course in basic rifle marksmanship.* Technical Report 22, Human Resources Research Organization, Alexandria, Virginia, October, 1955.

McGuire, W. J. Some factors influencing the effectiveness of demonstrational films. In A. A. Lumsdaine (ed.) *Student response in programed instruction: a symposium.* Washington, D.C.: National Academy of Sciences–National Research Council, 1961.

McKnight, A. J., & Adams, B. B. *Driver education task analysis: Volume I. Task descriptions.* Interim Report, Human Resources Research Organization, Alexandria, Virginia, 1970. (a)

McKnight, A. J., & Adams, B. B. *Driver education task analysis: Volume II. Task analysis methods.* HumRRO IR-D1-70-1, Human Resources Research Organization, Alexandria, Virginia, November, 1970. (b)

McTavish, C. L. *Effect of repetitive film showings on learning.* Technical Report No. SDC 269-7-12, U.S. Naval Training Device Center, Port Washington, New York, November, 1949.

Melton, A. W. (ed.) *Apparatus tests.* Washington, D.C.: U.S. Government Printing Office, 1947. AAF Aviation Psychology Program Research Report No. 4.

Melton, A. W. (ed.) *Categories of human learning.* New York: Academic Press, 1964.

Michael, D. N., & Maccoby, N. Factors influencing verbal learning from films under conditions of audience participation. *Journal of Experimental Psychology,* 1953, 46, 411–418.

Michael, D. N., & Maccoby, N. Factors influencing the effects of student participation on verbal learning from films. In A. A. Lumsdaine (ed.) *Student response is programed instruction: a symposium.* Washington, D.C.: National Academy of Sciences–National Research Council, 1961.

Miller, E. E. *Transfer effects of special training upon pre-solo flight training.* Research Report NM 16 01 11 (Subtask 13, Report No. 1), U.S. Naval School of Aviation Medicine, Pensacola, Florida, September, 1958.

Miller, E. E. *A taxonomy of response processes.* Technical Report 69-16, Human Resources Research Organization, Alexandria, Virginia, September, 1969.

Miller, E. E. *Comparison of pictorial techniques for guiding performance during training.* Technical Report 71–12, Human Resources Research Organization, Alexandria, Virginia, June, 1971.

Miller, R. B. *A method for man-machine task analysis.* WADC Technical Report 53-137, Wright Air Development Center, Wright-Patterson AFB, Ohio, 1953. (a)

Miller, R. B. *Handbook on training and training equipment design,* WADC Technical Report 53-136, Wright Air Development Center, Wright-Patterson AFB, Ohio, 1953. (b)

Miller, R. B. *Psychological considerations in the design of training equipment.* WADC Technical Report 54-563, Wright Air Development Center, Wright-Patterson AFB, Ohio, December, 1954.

Miller, R. B. *A suggested guide to position-task description.* Technical Memorandum ASPRO-TM-56-6, Armament System Personnel Research Laboratory, Air Force Personnel and Training Research Center, Lowry AFB, Colorado, April, 1956. (a)

Miller, R. B. *A suggested guide to functional characteristics of training and training equipment.* Technical Memorandum ML-TM-56-14, Air Force Personnel and Training Research Center, Lackland AFB, Texas, 1956. (b)

Miller, R. B. Analysis and specification of behavior for training. In R. Glaser (ed.) *Training research and education.* Pittsburgh: University of Pittsburgh Press, 1962, pp. 31-62. (a)

Miller, R. B. Task description and analysis. In R. M. Gagné (ed.) *Psychological principles in system development.* New York: Holt, Rinehart and Winston, 1962, pp. 187–230. (b)

Miller, R. B. Task analysis and task taxonomy: inventive approach. Paper for symposium at American Psychological Association convention, Chicago, September, 1965.

Noble, C. E. The learning of psychomotor skills. *Annual Review of Psychology,* 1968, 19, 203–250.

Peterson, L. R., & Brewer, C. L. Confirmation, correction, and contiguity. *Journal of Verbal Learning and Verbal Behavior,* 1963, 1, 365–371.

PIMO Final Report Summary, AFHRL-TR-69-155 Volume I. Chatsworth, California, Serendipity, Inc., May, 1969.

Poulton, E. C. Tracking behavior. In E. A. Bilodeau (ed.) *Acquisition of skill.* New York: Academic Press, 1966, pp. 361–410.

Prophet, W. W., & Boyd, H. A. *Device-task fidelity and transfer of training: Aircraft cockpit procedures trainong.* Technical Report 70-10, Human Resources Research Organization, Alexandria, Virginia, July, 1970.

Rimland, B. *Effectiveness of several methods of repetition of films,* Technical Report No. SDC 269-7-45, U.S. Naval Training Device Center, Port Washington, New York, May, 1955.

Roshal, S. M. *Effects of learner representation in film-mediated perceptual-motor learning.* Technical Report No. SDC 269-7-5, U.S. Naval Training Device Center, Port Washington, New York, 1949.

Ruocco, J. N., Vitale, P. A., & Benfari, R. C. *Kinetic cueing in simulated carrier approaches.* NAVTRADEVCEN 1432-1, Grumman Aircraft Engineering Corp., Bethpage, N. Y., April, 1965.

Schoenberger, R. W., Wherry, R. J., Jr., & Berkshire, J. R. *Predicting success in aviation training.* Research Report 7, U.S. Naval School of Aviation Medicine, Pensacola, Florida, 1963.

Sheffield, F. D. Theoretical considerations in the learning of complex sequential tasks from demonstration and practice. In A. A. Lumsdaine (ed.) *Student response in programed instruction: a symposium.* Washington, D.C.: National Academy of Sciences–National Research Council, 1961.

Sheffield, F. D., & Maccoby, N. Summary and interpretation of research on organizational principles in constructing filmed demonstrations. In A. A. Lumsdaine (ed.) *Student response in programed instruction: a symposium.* Washington, D.C.: National Academy of Sciences–National Research Council, 1961.

Sidowski, J. B., Kopstein, F. F., & Shillestad, I. J. Prompting and confirmation variables in verbal learning. *Psychological Reports,* 1961, 8, 401–406.

Silverman, R. E. *The comparative effectiveness of animated and static transparencies.* Orlando, Florida: U.S. Naval Training Device Center, 1958.

Sulzer, R. L., Lumsdaine, A. A., & Kopstein, F. F. *The value of using multiple examples in training film instruction.* HRRL Report No. 25, USAF Human Resources Research Laboratory, Washington, D.C., May, 1962.

Swanson, R. A. *The relative effectiveness of training aids designed for use in mobile training detachments.* AFPTRC-TR-54-1, Air Force Personnel Training Research Center, Lackland AFB, Texas, March, 1954.

Swanson, R. A., Lumsdaine, A. A., & Aukes, L. E. Two studies in evaluation of maintenance training devices. In G. Finch & F. Cameron (eds.) *Symposium on air force human engineering, personnel, and training research.* Washington, D.C.: National Academy of Sciences–National Research Council, 1956.

Twyford, L. C., & Carpenter, C. R. (eds.) *Instructional film research reports–Volume II.* Orlando, Florida: U.S. Naval Training Device Center, 1956.

van der Meer, A. W., Morrison, J., & Smith, P. *An investigation of educational motion pictures and a derivation of principles relating to the effectiveness of these media.* University Park, Pennsylvania: Pennsylvania State University Press, 1965.

Ware, J. R., Miller, E. E., & Constantinides, J. L. *Pictorial methods of instruction for the M-73 machine gun and the caliber .45 automatic pistol.* Alexandria, Virginia: Human Resources Research Organization, December, 1968.

Weiss, W., Maccoby, N., & Sheffield, F. D. Combining practice with demonstration in teaching complex sequences: Serial learning of a geometric-construction task. In A. A. Lumsdaine (ed.) *Student response in programed instruction: a symposium.* Washington, D.C.: National Academy of Science–National Research Council, 1961.

West, L. J. *Review of research in typewriting learning with recommendations for training.* AFPTRC-TN-57-69, Air Force Personnel & Training Research Center, Lackland AFB, Texas, June, 1957. (a)

West, L. J. *Recommendations for typewriting training,* AFPTRC-TN-57-68, Air Force Personnel & Training Research Center, Lackland, AFB, Texas, June, 1957. (b)

West, L. J. *Acquisition of typewriting skills.* New York: Pitman Publishing Corporation, 1969.

Whitmore, P. G. *Studies of fixed procedures training: A preliminary test of a self-instructional method.* Research Memorandum, Human Resources Research Organization, Alexandria, Virginia, July, 1963.

Whitmore, P. G. *A suggested general SOP for the preparation of equipment serviceability criteria.* Technical Report 67-10, Human Resources Research Organization, Alexandria, Virginia, June, 1967.

Williams, A. C., & Flexman, R. E. Evaluation of the school link as an aid in primary flight instruction. *University of Illinois Bulletin,* June, 1949, 46(71).

Wulff, J. J. *The teaching effectiveness of a filmed mechanical assembly demonstration with supplementary nomenclature training.* TARL-LN-58-8, Training Aids Research Laboratory, Air Force Personnel and Training Research Center, Lackland AFB, Texas, 1955.

Chapter 7

PHYSICAL EDUCATION

Joseph B. Oxendine

Temple University

In order to deal effectively with the psychomotor domain of physical education those motor skills or categories of skills as well as the psychologic factors that are most closely related to the field of physical education must first be identified. In either case, whether it is determination of the motor skills or the psychologic factors, the decision is rather arbitrary. Although it could be argued that all movement behavior is a part of physical education and that most psychologic factors have some implications for this field, certain limitations will be established for the purpose of focusing attention on the generally accepted concept of physical education.

This discussion will be centered primarily on those movement activities which are customarily included in physical education programs at the elementary and secondary school levels. These include activities such as sports, gymnastics, acquatics, and leisure skills as well as basic movement patterns which underlie the development of such specialized skills. Limiting discussion to these skills and movement patterns excludes a great variety of motor behaviors that are of importance to man. Excluded, for example, are occupational skills varying from gross body movements such as construction work or farming tasks to the finer responses involved in the use of office machines or the manipulation of precision tools. In addition, survival skills more prevalent in earlier times included fighting proficiency necessary for defense as well as hunting and fishing competency essential for the procurement of food or protection against wild beasts. Thus, in this discussion of physical education skills for the school, the author does not presume to deal with the total gamut of motor skills.

Similarly, in the discussion of psychologic factors a significant limitation has been imposed. In this discussion, primary attention will be devoted to those matters over which the teacher can exercise some influence and which closely relate to the learning and performance of motor skills. Consequently, such topics as the learning process, feedback, motivation, and practice variables in motor learning will be dealt with in some detail. This orientation means that extensive attention will not be devoted to such important psychologic variables as personality development, heredity, counseling, and the senses.

This chapter is divided into four sections: first, the interrelationship of mental and physical components involved in the learning and performance of gross motor skills is investigated; secondly, the role of information feedback is discussed; the third section includes an analysis of motivation as a factor in skill performance; and, lastly, a discussion of practice conditions for efficient learning of skills is included.

MENTAL AND PHYSICAL PROCESSES IN THE DEVELOPMENT OF SKILLS

The learning of motor skills is an active, thoughtful process requiring complete physical and intellectual involvement on the part of the participant for greatest efficiency. Traditional assumptions of a dichotomy in learning processes (mental versus motor) are misleading. The successful physical education teacher addresses himself to both physical and mental processes. The elimination of all intellectual involvement during the practice of a skill would result in blind trial-and-error activity that would prove both frustrating and ineffective.

Cognitive processes are particularly important in the early phases of skill development. In a description of three phases of skill learning, Fitts (1962) identified the "cognitive" phase as coming first and being followed by "fixation" and "automatic" periods. The cognitive phase encompasses the reception of input from various stimuli and is the period in which the learner gains an understanding of the task and the appropriate responses. This dependence of skill acquisition on early mental involvement can be illustrated in many typical sports activities. For example, the student who wishes to do a one and one-half gainer in diving must first conceptualize the task on the basis of observing a performance, viewing a film, listening to a description, or in some other way gaining an understanding of what the task involves. After conceptualizing the dive and making some effort to internalize this understanding the learner attempts to perform it successfully. During the performance he receives some proprioceptive feedback concerning the correctness or incorrectness of his responses. Following the dive, he may also receive comments or coaching cues from a teacher or from other observers. Thus, he gains some understanding of the relationship between the sensation of his movement behavior and the efficiency of the performance. He attempts to coordinate the internal and external information and then tries the task again, varying his response on the basis of this feedback. If he is to be most successful, subsequent trials (practices) involve the process of self-analysis, internalizing coaching tips, and thinking through the performance. Whereas Fitts describes the cognitive, fixation, and automatic phases of skill learning as following in sequential order, a careful analysis of most skills indicates that cognition does not cease at the time "fixation," or practice, begins. Refinement of skills or improvement in proficiency requires continued mental involvement. However, there is little reason to believe that any appreciable cognition is involved during the "automatic" phase of familiar skills.

Efficient learners are able to grasp quickly the concept of the task, to understand and follow directions, to sustain concentration, and to see the relationship of the skill to previously learned movement patterns. Inefficiency in skill development results when the individual makes no attempt to think through the activity or does not make use of internal and external cues. In addition, if the individual is unable to conceptualize the task he is at a distinct disadvantage. These factors are more important in facilitating rapid acquisition of the skill than in determining the ultimate level of performance. Eventual proficiency in motor skill is primarily dependent upon innate physical components rather than the speed of initial learning.

Intelligence and Skill Learning

It is assumed by a great many people that learning and performance in motor skills are closely related to one's general intelligence. This is based on casual observations, traditional assumptions, and the opinions of some authors rather than on convincing research evidence. Davis (1935) has stated: "In the complex skills intellectual control and training are necessary. Complex skills, therefore, become an index to intelligence" (p. 139). Other authors, including Vince (1953) and Nason (1965) have expressed similar views relative to the dependency of skill development on intelligence.

While it is clear that groups of retarded children do not perform as well in motor skills as do those in the normal intelligence range, research evidence does not indicate a high intelligence-motor ability relationship for persons within the normal or above-normal range. However, Garfiel (1923), Kulcinski (1945), and Thompson (1952) showed low positive correlations between intelligence scores and performance in gross motor skills for normal children of various ages. Ellis (1938), Brace (1946), and Fitzhugh and Fitzhugh (1965) worked with feeble-minded and brain-damaged children and found positive relationships between measured intelligence and performance in a variety of motor skills. Most of the correlations, though significant, were small.

Conversely, other studies fail to support a relationship between intelligence and motor behavior. Start (1962) showed that grammar school boys who were grouped according to intelligence did not exhibit differences in rugby or football performance. In addition, studies by Ryan (1962), Westendarp (1923), Hertzberg (1929), DiGiovanna (1937), and Johnson (1942) failed to show substantial relationships between intelligence and performance in gross motor skills.

The whole matter of intelligence and motor abilities has been confused by the use of a variety of research designs and procedures. Whereas some studies have compared physical fitness scores to measured intelligence, others have related athletic skills to intelligence, fitness to school achievement, general motor abilities to school achievement, extent of athletic participation to intelligence or school grades, and speed of skill acquisition to intelligence. This diversity of studies reveals many findings in the general area of mental and physical traits, but they do not provide conclusive evidence to support a relationship between intelligence and the learning or performance of motor skills, especially for persons in the normal and above-average intelligence range. However, persons in the feeble-minded range do appear to be similarly handicapped in motor skills. Problems arising with "slow learners" are frequently in terms of time, not ability. Consequently, instruction should be individualized to provide more time when it is needed for thorough comprehension by the learner.

Overall, it must be assumed that motor abilities and general intelligence (as measured by current intelligence tests) are distinct and largely unrelated factors. The ability to learn complex motor skills (such as driving a car or performing a complex gymnastic stunt) is *different* from the ability to remember word definitions or to solve mathematics problems. The latter two traits are rather arbitrarily described as intelligence measures while the performance of motor skills is usually not so designated. Therefore, if the term intelligence is limited to "that which intelligence tests measure" little connection can be shown between this trait and general motor ability. On the other hand, when intelligence is viewed as "the aggregate or global capacity of the individual to act purposefully, to think rationally, and to deal effectively with his environment" (Wechsler, 1944, p. 3), "the ability to adjust adequately to new and different situations" (Cruze, 1951, p. 241), and by others as "the ability to learn rapidly" or "the ability to solve problems," perhaps motor learning proficiency *is* an indication of one's "intelligence."

Precisely which components do enable a person to learn and perform gross motor skills effectively have not been fully identified and accepted. Many physical and personality traits are assumed to be strategic in motor performance. These components are discussed extensively in other sources and therefore will not be dealt with here except in reference to some of them. Several factor analysis studies, including those by Cumbee (1954), Fleishman (1964), and Guilford (1958), have identified certain physical factors as particularly important. These include strength, endurance, speed, size, agility, balance, and various types of coordination and precision movements. Psychologic and personality traits assumed to be important in relation to motor performance include perseverance, interest in the activity, concentration span, freedom from inhibitions, and competitive spirit. Cratty (1966) has developed a three-level theory of perceptual-motor behavior which identifies general supports of behavior, perceptual motor ability traits, and task specifics. This model perhaps more than any other identifies and discusses the interrelatedness of the psychologic and physical components as well as the environmental conditions which are influential in skill learning.

INFORMATION FEEDBACK

The single most important factor contributing to skill acquisition is feedback. Therefore, efficiency in the use of feedback is essential for physical education teachers as it is for all other teachers. The term feedback is often used interchangeably with reinforcement, knowledge of results, rewards, and motivation as well as certain other terms. On occasion, feedback may be identical to any of these but it is important to distinguish it as a separate entity. Sometimes modifiers are used to indicate the role of feedback in specific situations. Thus, information feedback, reinforcing feedback, regulating feedback, and psychologic feedback are used by different authors from time to time. In this discussion, primary attention is devoted to the role of *information* as a means of promoting skill development.

Bourne (1966) states that "information feedback is a term which refers to some signal occurring after or at the time of response, providing an indication of the correctness, accuracy, or adequacy of that response" (p. 299). This precise emphasis on information about the response is not usually associated with other terms related to performance improvement. For example, *knowledge of results* most often refers to externally provided information which follows the completion of a given response. *Reinforcement* is a more generalized term and is used in reference to any occurrence which increases the probability of a response. This does not necessarily mean that any information about the accuracy of the response is provided. Similarly, *reward* does not imply making any knowledge about performance available to the learner. The term *motivation* makes broad reference to a general state of excitement or interest in a given situation, with no information about the particular response necessarily taking place.

Importance of Information Feedback

The critical importance of information feedback in the development of skills can be illustrated by research results or by observations of students engaged in the practice of common physical education skills. Research generally indicates that little if any improvement takes place during practice sessions in which no feedback is made available to the learner. Thorndike (1931), in a classic study involving blindfolded subjects in a line drawing experiment, showed that without any information no improvement in ability to draw four-inch lines occurred even after 3,000 trials. Kingsley (1946) showed similar results when blindfolded students made 400 attempts to draw four-inch lines. Not until the students were *told* how they performed in relation to a standard four-inch line or *saw* their drawing compared to the standard line was improvement exhibited. Even greater improvement was exhibited when students saw the line in comparison to their own performance. Kingsley concluded that the greater specificity of this information made it more valuable to the learner than the less impressive information provided by a second person.

Research and casual observations of regular physical education activities also reveal that no improvement is shown when the learner is unaware of the results of his previous performance. Several studies in marksmanship show that when the rifleman is unable to determine where the bullet hits on the target or indeed whether or not it hits the target he has no basis for altering his performance for improvement. Most physical education teachers or coaches have observed young performers who, in diving, gymnastics, dance, or other activities, repeat the same error over and over when no one provides them any coaching cues or if they are unable to comprehend the information that is given.

Types of Feedback

Robb (1966) states that information feedback may be categorized according to (1) the source of information (intrinsic versus augmented), (2) the timing of the information (concurrent versus terminal), and (3) the mode of receiving the information (internal versus external). *Intrinsic* feedback refers to information which is inherent in the task itself; that is, it is usually an unavoidable consequence of responding in activities such as bowling, darts, archery, horseshoes, or piano playing in which the performer himself senses the results of his responses.

Augmented feedback is that information which is provided by an external source in activities in which it is not obvious to the performer. This feedback is not usually a direct and necessary consequence of the response. In many sports activities it is essential that this type information be provided if the performer is to make any improvement whatsoever. Augmented feedback may be provided by a teacher, a coach, a "program," or equipment such as instant-replay television or films. Although augmented feedback is usually helpful in most physical education activities, it is especially beneficial for the performer in gymnastics, karate, diving, modern dance, or other activities in which the individual may not be immediately aware of the accuracy of his movement responses. Novice performers in these activities are particularly inept at determining the nature of their own performance.

Timing factors in feedback may be discussed in terms of concurrent and terminal feedback. *Concurrent* feedback refers to information that is provided simultaneously with the performance. *Terminal* feedback is received at the conclusion of the response. In either case (concurrent or terminal) the feedback may be intrinsic, that is, a consequence of the response, or it may be augmented by an outside source. Feedback which is received from the kinesthetic or proprioceptive sense is referred to by Robb as *internal* feedback. Conversely, information received from those senses which are stimulated by external stimuli such as vision, hearing, touch, etc., is termed *external* feedback.

Techniques in Promoting Information Feedback

The superior physical education teacher makes every effort to identify and intensify information feedback for the student. In order to do this effectively, the instructor must first analyze the task to determine those responses most strategic for success. After becoming thoroughly familiar with the given activity there are several techniques by which the instructor may communicate vital information to the learner.

Augmenting Information Feedback Through Verbal Cues. Probably the most widely used and certainly one of the most effective means for providing feedback to the learner is an explanation of the reason for his success or failure. When learners fail to comprehend the reason for a performance problem the teacher can explain and perhaps demonstrate the specific source of the problem, that is, "this is what you did" (demonstrate), "and this is how you should do it" (demonstrate), and "do you understand the difference?"

Several difficulties arise in the provision of information feedback to students. Very frequently too much information is provided so that it confuses the learner. At other times, the feedback is so generalized and vague that it fails to communicate the specific information. Sometimes the information is delayed so that it has little meaning at the time it is provided. This writer recalls his early efforts to learn to play golf when he experienced extreme frustration from the provision of too much information. The instructor, assuming far too much comprehension on the part of this learner, advised in one sentence, "Make sure you keep your head down and your eye on the ball, and this time take a slower back swing, move the club from the inside out, and shift your weight to the front foot as you follow through, and by the way remember to. . . ." This feedback, though accurate, specific, and well intended, caused confusion and resulted in regression in performance.

The good teacher should try to have the student concentrate on one response at a time. Learners do not very effectively concentrate on several responses simultaneously. However, cues can be given for two responses that occur at different points in the performance. For example, the student can be reminded to take a slow back swing and to take an inside out swing because these responses do not have to be dealt with at the same time during the performance.

Research evidence and empiric observation conclusively indicate that the more immediate the feedback the more valuable it is likely to be. Thus, the teacher in physical education should make every effort to provide verbal feedback as soon after the response as possible. This means that he should not wait until the final result of the activity is apparent to the performer. For example, the three- or four-second period that it takes for the bowling ball to roll down the alley is sufficient delay for the bowler to forget the kinesthetic feel of his delivery or perhaps that his follow through was across his body rather than in a vertical plane. The problem is not only a matter of the short-term interval but the fact that there is a great deal of input from other sources around him before the ball actually strikes the pins. Teachers who wait until the bowler returns to the bench to provide feedback about the delivery greatly reduce the value of that information. It is too often assumed that such delays are unavoidable in many activities. Where errors or problems have been detected the teacher or coach must actually "catch the student in the act" in order to communicate to him clearly the nature of the problem. The instructor should place himself in close proximity to the student and provide forceful, concise information at the instant the inappropriate response is initiated. The young baseball batter, when informed after a delay that he took his eye off the ball during a particular swing, will often have serious doubts about the accuracy of that information. Likewise, the novice basketball player, when told after a ten-second delay that he jumped off the wrong foot, will often question the honesty or at least visual ability of the coach who provides this information, particularly if the goal happened to be successful. Therefore, it is most helpful if the teacher can be on the spot and provide immediate information to the learner so that he is forced to realize that he did indeed perform in the manner described.

Some Novel Ideas to Promote Feedback. In an effort to provide more immediate feedback to the learner during the early stages, gimmicks and other novel techniques can be built in as an integral part of the act itself. The extent to which such techniques can be used is limited only by the ingenuity of the teacher. It should be kept in mind that such techniques are for the purpose of emphasizing or exaggerating feedback during the initial learning stages and should not be a long-term device upon which the learner becomes dependent.

One such technique is to paint stripes (or use colored tape) on a basketball, volleyball, or baseball for the purpose of more clearly illustrating the direction of ball rotation. Very frequently the coach attempts to get the young basketball player to shoot a free throw or a jump shot so that the ball rolls off the end of the fingers with some backspin on the ball. (Backspin on the basketball is preferable to overspin or lateral rotation in that the ball is more likely to fall into the basket if it happens to bounce around the rim. A nonrotating or "knuckle ball" is also undesirable since it is likely to travel in an unpredictable manner toward the basket.) Once the teacher illustrates the relationship between the proper release (including wrist roll and releasing the ball off the ends of the fingers) and the resultant backspin on the ball, the player will be able to test or measure his success more easily if there are brightly colored stripes or lines on the ball. Likewise, the use of the multicolored basketball used by the American Basketball Association will also provide vivid feedback regarding rotation.

A problem is often encountered in soccer, where beginners experience difficulty in consistently kicking the ball with the instep or top of the foot. Early success in the soccer kick could be enhanced if the young player were made vividly aware of the relationship between proper foot placement on the ball and resultant rotation. Too prominent use of the toe on the lower portion of the ball usually results in a weak kick with a rapid backspin. Evidence of this improper kick (rapid backspin on the ball) is sometimes difficult for the young player to determine when an all-white soccer ball is used. A checkered soccer ball such as is used in standard professional play or a striped ball makes the rotation more evident, thus providing an indication of foot placement.

The use of stripes to indicate ball rotation has also been used in work with young pitchers in baseball. Proper rotation of the ball is the critical factor in causing the ball to curve in the desired direction. Sometimes players are unable to observe clearly the rotation of the regulation baseball; therefore, the painting of vivid stripes facilitates this observation and enables the player to make the association between release and ball rotation. Such stripes, therefore, not only provide faster feedback to the learner from the time the ball is released, but also more accurate feedback in terms of the speed of rotation and the exact direction of curve. In addition, outfielders and infielders who always desire to throw a straight ball sometimes have difficulty in that the ball curves. The cause for this problem can be more easily detected when they use a striped ball which will indicate more clearly the direction of ball rotation.

Litwhiler has discussed the use of a Yo-Yo as a means of aiding young pitchers to identify proper wrist action when learning to throw a curve ball. In attempting to develop an effective curve ball beginners often have difficulty in getting the "feel" of the proper wrist action. Litwhiler's suggested use of the Yo-Yo is based on the fact that the wrist snap essential for throwing a curve ball is similar to that for delivering a Yo-Yo successfully. Informing the young pitcher of the similarity of wrist action and having him practice with this understanding may prove helpful on the basis of the transfer of skill. However, Litwhiler (1966, p. 201) suggests actually having the pitcher assume the windup position with the Yo-Yo in hand.

He takes his wind-up and follows through slowly with his delivery. As he comes through with his arm and hand, they follow the same path taken when throwing a ball. When the hand gets about at his head, he bends and shortens his arm. His palm is facing his face, and the yo-yo is held by the thumb, middle, and index fingers, so that it will roll off the side of the index finger, down toward his feet.

The smooth spinning Yo-Yo and its successful return to the hand provide "feedback" that the delivery has been proper. As most children already know, an improperly delivered Yo-Yo does not return to the hand.

Establishing the Habit of Self-analysis. One important way of emphasizing feedback and making it more useful for the learner is to promote the *habit* of regularly evaluating one's own performance. Emphasis should be placed on an early awareness of the relationship of a given response to the desired result. For example, basketball players can be encouraged to "call" their shots as soon as the ball leaves the hand. This requires the learner to establish a clear understanding between the release and the initial flight of the ball and the likelihood of its going into the goal. This *immediate* self-analysis has great potential for improving the mechanics of most motor activities.

Performers in track and field events should be encouraged to estimate their times or distances following the performance but before they receive any external information. The runner who estimates his times in this manner is required to evaluate his performance constantly and relate it to his previous times. Likewise, shot putters, discus throwers, high jumpers, and others can be taught to be more sensitive to feedback so that they can make an accurate estimation of their performance. The value of such a practice is that it requires self-analysis and an understanding of the relationship between motor responses and outstanding performance.

Awareness of or sensitivity to feedback can be promoted in some activities by having learners perform while they are blindfolded. Such practice encourages the individual to get the "feel" of the activity and consequently learn it more thoroughly. Gripping a golf club or swinging a baseball bat while blindfolded or with the eyes closed enables the performer to analyze the task without interference from visual stimuli. This places greater emphasis on kinesthetic cues and may enable the learner to make the performance a more "automatic" part of his behavior.

Another technique for emphasizing feedback is that of noting progress or improvement in the performance of any activity. The benefits of this technique are primarily motivational but they tend to heighten a person's awareness of his performance level at any stage of his development. In this practice, learners are encouraged to keep a detailed record of performances in various activities. This tends to accentuate improvement in performance even though it may be slight. Number of putts in a round of golf, number of strikes and balls thrown by the pitcher, scores in archery, bowling, gymnastics, and even physical conditioning scores provide the learner with immediate and forceful information as to how he is doing in relation to previous performance. Frequent tests or trials in which the scores are gathered are valuable for this reason. It is usually a good idea to maximize the number of opportunities the individual has to establish a score or evaluate himself. This may be done by a buddy-system, partners who judge each other, or by some sort of program in which there is a built-in scoring system.

Although it is usually a good idea to maximize feedback for the benefit of the learner, it should be noted that additional information is not always helpful. Bell (1968) concluded that where sufficient knowledge is inherent in the task, the use of additional information from an external source does not further aid the acquisition of a skill. In a study of the badminton serve, she had students hit the shuttlecock into marked off areas which were within easy viewing range. She reported that additional visual or precise measurement information regarding the landing of the shuttlecock did not prove helpful, apparently because no additional information was actually provided.

In most physical education activities, carefully selected feedback does prove helpful, especially during the early phases of the learning process. The teacher may facilitate skill development by making the feedback self-evident in the activity and by using various methods of speeding the information to the learner.

MOTIVATION IN PHYSICAL EDUCATION

Motivation is a condition which has profound significance for both learning and performance in physical education activities. Certainly one of the most widely accepted concepts of education is that individuals must be "motivated" in order to learn effectively. Similarly, teachers in physical education and athletic coaches agree that the motivated individual usually performs better in sports skills. These assumptions are substantiated by research evidence as well as by casual observations of children in classrooms, gymnasia, and playing fields.

Needs and Drives

Motivation refers to an internal state in which the existence of needs arouse the individual to seek ways of satisfying those needs. The term *need* refers to a deprived state: a condition in which some physical, psychologic, or social element is missing. They may be created by factors within or outside the individual. Needs, and related drives, are the basis of motivation and are related to the concept of homeostasis which, in the simplest terms, refers to the tendency of the body to take compensatory action for the purpose of maintaining a balance. Evidence of homeostasis in the physiologic realm is shown in the self-regulating control of body temperature and body chemistry. The psychologic counterpart to this takes place when social or personal goals of the individual cause him to subdue physiologic or self-protection needs.

In order for any teacher to attain success in motivating children, he must first understand the relationship between needs and behavior. Unfulfilled needs, whether physiologic or psychologic, lead to drives, psychologic phenomenona. The relationship of needs to drives can be illustrated quite vividly with the phenomenon of hunger. When the body becomes depleted of its food supply a condition of hunger emerges. The physiologic need for food results in general bodily tensions, contractions of the stomach, and eventually an awareness of this state and a craving for food. The resulting desire to overcome this deprivation, that is, obtain food, is referred to as a drive. The intensity of the drive varies according to the degree of food deprivation. In like manner, other needs, both physical and psychologic, can be illustrated in relation to accompanying drives.

Individuals are "motivated" by the creation of needs from within which activate them to seek particular goals to satisfy those needs. Therefore, the teacher who is most effective in motivating students is the one who can most skillfully establish and nurture student needs. However, not being magicians, teachers often have difficulty in creating and manipulating student needs in exactly the desired manner. More realistically, the teacher must determine what the student needs are and then in some way work in accordance with them rather than to the contrary.

In today's school setting, children's physiologic needs are usually cared for quite adequately. Only occasionally are there physical inconveniences such as uncomfortable temperatures, inappropriate furniture, painful or fatiguing chores, accidents, or sicknesses. For most teachers, therefore, motivational techniques are restricted to the areas of personal and social concerns. However, the physical education teacher and athletic coach more than anyone else do have an opportunity to deal with the physical, affective, and intellectual domains of the student. For example, the student in physical education or athletics is often motivated to withstand some pain, fatigue, or fear of physical danger. The tendency to surrender to the needs for comfort and safety are countered by our (psychologic) needs such as achievement, self-image, recognition, and belonging.

Many situations in physical education and sports can be illustrated in which the student subdues a physiologic or self-protection need in order to satisfy another need. For example, when facing a "wild" pitcher the batter in baseball usually has a strong tendency to position himself a great distance away from home plate. Such a position reduces his likelihood of getting hit by the baseball but at the same time it reduces his chances of getting a base hit. The need for achieving success, therefore, runs counter to the need for self-preservation. In football, the 150-pound defensive halfback, when confronted with a hard-charging 200-pound fullback, usually has a strong desire to disappear or at least get taken out of the play by a blocker. The need for self-preservation urges that he avoid a physical confrontation, whereas the need for accomplishment demands that he stop the runner at all costs.

The physical education teacher or the athletic coach is in a unique position to aid in the psychologic and physical development of children. In sports activities the student is encouraged to delay the gratification of certain physical (and sometimes psychologic) needs in order to achieve a desired goal in the activity. Personal needs to achieve success or to excel in the presence of one's peers cause the young person to practice long and hard for excellence. He will continue an all-out effort in a wrestling match or in a race long after fatigue has appeared. The physical educator and coach, therefore, have opportunity to aid in the maturation of students by guiding and encouraging them in the establishment of meaningful personal and social goals.

Emotional Arousal and Performance

A high level of emotional arousal may result from intense motivation to attain some goal. In addition, such conditions as fear, anger, joy, embarrassment, and a multitude of other emotion-producing situations may also lead to an aroused state. Despite the fact that arousal or excitement may result from widely varying stimuli, the physiologic and psychologic responses of the individual are usually quite similar. These include conditions such as accelerated heart rate, increased blood pressure, greater muscular tension, more rapid breathing, alterations in the galvanic skin response, and many other measurable changes in bodily functions.

Level of arousal or motivation may be placed on a continuum from high to low activation as follows: excited, alert, and attentive; relaxed, drowsy, light sleep, deep sleep, and coma. Different levels along the continuum are reflected in physiologic changes which are controlled by the automatic nervous system. Various arousal states along with accompanying physiologic changes have important implications for performance in motor activities.

Cratty (1968) and Husman (1969) have pointed out that the optimum level of arousal varies with the particular motor activity, that is, different tasks require different levels of excitement for most effective performance. A point of reference for this concept was established more than a half century ago by the Yerkes-Dodson Law. According to this law, complex tasks are performed better when an individual's level of drive is low while simple tasks are performed better when the drive is high. Therefore, drive which is either too great or too low for a particular task may result in impaired performance. Although helpful as a point of reference, this law does not answer many of the specific questions that the physical education teacher and the athletic coach have. For example, the task of classifying the great variety of physical education activities into "complex" or "simple" categories is an uncertain exercise. Furthermore, the determination of "high drive" and "low drive" is not a simple matter. Consequently, there appears to be a need for a more definitive statement of the relationship between arousal level and perform-ance in various motor activities.

After reviewing the research evidence and literature on the relationship between arousal and performance, Oxendine (1970, p. 25) offered the following generalizations:

1. A high level of arousal is essential for optimal performance in gross motor activities involving strength, endurance, and speed.
2. A high level of arousal interferes with performances involving complex skills, fine muscle movements, coordination, steadiness, and general concentration.
3. A slightly-above-average level of arousal is preferable to a normal or subnormal arousal state for all motor tasks.

Newspaper stories as well as the personal experiences of most readers can be used to cite situations in which individuals have exhibited extraordinary feats of strength, endurance, and speed while under great emotional stress. Cannon (1929) discusses physiologic evidence and cites incidents of strength and endurance advantages. Conversely, both children and adults have been shown to lose coordination, concentration, precision of movement, and generally become "all thumbs" when they are in a highly aroused state. Such examples can be found both in and out of sports activities.

After analyzing many popular sports activities in terms of the essential requirements for strength, endurance, and speed versus the degree of complexity, fine muscle movement, coordination, steadiness, and concentra-tion, this author prepared table 7-1 to indicate suggested optimal arousal levels for the typical participant in a variety of motor activities.

Techniques in Motivation

Speculating about the optimal level of arousal for given motor activities can be done with a minimum of risk, though with an uncertain degree of confidence. However, *controlling* the arousal level or manipulating it to a desired point for oneself or for others is a more troublesome matter. In some situations, a student or a group of athletes may need to be "motivated" or brought up to a higher level of arousal for optimal performance. On other occasions, they may need to be "calmed down" in order to demonstrate their greatest proficiency. An analysis of some of the practical techniques of motivating individuals will be made.

One of the most frequently used and perhaps most effective techniques for stimulating people to greater effort or to a higher level of emotional arousal is that of *competition*. Competition comes in many forms and is easy to arrange and manage in most school situations. In addition, it is usually a socially accepted practice. Students may be organized to compete against other individuals or as team members against other teams. Team competition may vary from the very highly organized competitive sports to intramural, class, or informal pick-up games. Individual activities also have a wide range of

TABLE 7-1

Optimum Arousal Level for Some Typical Sports Skills

Level of Arousal	Sports Skills
#5 (extremely excited)	football blocking and tackling performance on the Rogers' PFI test running (220 yards to 440 yards) sit up, push up, or bent arm hang test weight lifting
#4	running long jump running very short and long races shot putt swimming races wrestling and judo
#3	basketball skills boxing high jumping most gymnastic skills soccer skills
#2	baseball pitchers and batters fancy dives fencing football quarterback tennis
#1 (slight arousal)	archery and bowling basketball free throw field goal kicking golf putting and short irons skating figure 8's
0 (normal state)	

*From Oxendine (1970).

competitive levels. In a research study with sixth-grade boys and girls Strong (1963) found that best performances took place when subjects were organized as members of competing teams. Individual competition against classmates was also found to be more effective than no such competition. Strong reported that competition was a more effective technique of motivation with boys than with girls.

In a study of motor fitness items involving speed, strength, accuracy, and sports skills, Gerdes (1958) had students compete as members of teams as well as against their own previous scores in these items. He reported improved scores in all performance items and observed that physical fitness test results in school are highly dependent upon the particular motivation technique used. Martin (1961) found that the mere presence of classmates resulted in better achievement than when individuals were performing alone. She also reported that information about one's performance level was effective in increasing scores on subsequent performances.

The technique of using competition to stimulate one to greater effort is common in sports. As a rule, athletes try to avoid providing the necessary spark that will intensify the competitive drive of the opposition. This is particularly true of a favored team which usually adheres to the policy of "letting sleeping dogs lie." However, on occasion teams or individuals, particularly underdogs, boast of their prowess either to boost their own level of confidence or to try to intimidate the opposition. Boxing promotors and sports writers often try to encourage brash statements and a general air of bravado in order to stimulate interest in the upcoming event. Such behavior is less frequently initiated by the performers themselves.

This author is reminded of an incident a few years ago which happened at his own institution. An upcoming wrestling meet with a rival school was scheduled to match two unbeaten wrestlers. The coach of the local school believed that his wrestler could benefit from an increased amount of desire or enthusiasm regarding the match. The day before the meet the young man in question received a letter from his "opponent" which was highly derogatory toward his institution, his heritage, his courage, his manhood, and raised serious questions about his wrestling abilities and thus his right to be on the same mat with his opponent. The letter did have the effect of stirring the wrestler to an intense level of arousal and determination. During the wrestling match the recipient of the letter won the event overwhelmingly. His ferocity and general unfriendliness surprised his opponent. It was later revealed that the letter was "planted" by the coach. In this case, the effort to intensify the feeling of competition did have the desired effect. There are hazards, however, to such techniques, not the least of which is the possibility of the athlete's questioning the honsety or the sincerity of his coach. Nevertheless, there can be little doubt that competition is one of the most effective means of stimulating individuals to greater effort.

Perhaps the most frequently used technique for motivating school children to greater interest and effort is that of *reward* in some form. Rewards may be (1) symbolic, such as praise, athletic letters or certificates, gold stars, school grades, or other types of recognition; (2) materialistic, such as ahtletic prizes, money, scholarships, or other types of remuneration; or (3) psychologic, such as an internal feeling of accomplishment, acceptance, or improvement. Symbolic and material rewards are usually referred to as external while psychologic rewards are viewed as internal. Educators generally consider internal rewards or motivation of the highest order and the type to be emphasized. However, external rewards are still widely used in schools, especially in the lower grades.

As with most other motivation techniques there are advantages and problems associated with the use of rewards. The primary advantages seem to be that they do tend to create a pleasurable association with the desired response, develop enthusiasm, and generally enhance the ego of the performer. However, when used too frequently there is the tendency for the individual to develop a dependency on extrinsic rather than intrinsic stimuli. Another problem is that a few "good" children seem to excel in most activities and therefore receive most of the rewards. The non-winners, frequently with a greater need for recognition, rarely receive rewards.

Another motivation technique frequently used both in and out of schools is that of *punishment.* Over the past half century the use of punishment as a means of getting children to behave in a certain way has generally been discouraged by educators. However, in some situations it continues to be used frequently as a means for encouraging behavior in a particular direction. The primary advantage in the use of punishment is that it is effective with many children. Some children respond well to both reward and punishment; however, the results of punishment are more unpredictable. Most teachers or coaches have observed individuals who sulk for long periods after being punished. This generally results in a detrimental effect on subsequent learning and performance. Other persons seem to behave in the desired manner after punishment. For example, after receiving a severe tongue lashing from the coach some football players go out and "take it out" on the opponents.

Though seemingly necessary from time to time with most children, punishment does have certain negative side effects. Very frequently this technique tends to destroy the rapport between the teacher and the student. In some situations punishment and resultant fear of punishment may reinforce the undersired behavior by establishing a high level of anxiety on the part of the participant. When used very frequently, punishment tends to lose its effectiveness. Furthermore, when inappropriate techniques are used, punishment may be humiliating and destructive to the self-image of the student.

Just as with rewards, it is impossible to equalize the punishment for all children. Even though given fairly by the teacher, different types of punishment, be it scolding, outside homework or spanking, seem to cause children different levels of pain. This is similar to two adults being fined $500 or having their driver's license suspended for 30 days. For one person this sentence may be trivial while for the other it may be a great sacrifice. Therefore, in order to use either reward or punishment effectively the teacher should have an understanding of the personality and the needs of the students.

Another long-standing practice for promoting athletes to greater effort has been the use of the *pep talk* immediately prior to the commencement of a sports event. Depending on the personality of the coach, or the nature of the situation, these pep talks have varied from tense, stirring, loud, and generally emotional appeals to a more logical, quiet, and instructional approach. The former type, popularized by famous football coaches, has perhaps been the more frequently used technique for team sports in past years. Even recordings of such speeches are sometimes presented for the same purpose prior to an athletic event. Films with emotional overtones are occasionally shown before athletic contests and even during war time to evoke a certain arousal on the part of the participants. Pep talks may be used to intensify the competitive tendency on the part of participants or on other occasions to provide punishment or reward that the coach believes might be helpful. There can be little doubt that skillful pep talks are effective in arousing the emotions and energy level of athletes.

In recent years the use of *music* as a technique of motivating students has increased. Though very little research has been conducted to establish its effectiveness there is a growing belief that certain types of music tend to stimulate a person to a higher energy level. This is consistent with the observation that "rock" music and marching music tend to elicit movement on the part of many listeners. Consequently, the practice of using music in a locker room prior to an athletic contest has become widespread. More recently music is being used during practice and during pre-contest warm-up for both team and individual sports. Obviously, the selection of music is important in this situation. For promoting a more alert state, a stirring, rhythmic piece with ample volume would be preferable to soft chamber music.

Sometimes music is used during the performance of an activity in order to increase the tempo or the level of output. "Exercise" records are being widely used in schools as a means of stimulating students to keep up with the pace and perhaps perform a maximum of activity with a minimum of conscious pain. Band music has traditionally been used with marching armies not only to regulate uniformity and order in the movement of a group but also to provide psychologic stimulation for soldiers to keep up with the beat. The use of carefully selected music to increase the output in such activities as rope skipping, general exercise routines, and dance movements appears to be based on sound motivation principles.

An analysis of table 7-1 along with an understanding of the realities of some high-pressure sports situations leads one to assume that it is desirable on occasion to calm down or "demotivate" certain individuals. Performances involving precision, steadiness, and complex muscle movements demand a relatively relaxed state for optimum performance. In these situations efforts should often be made to reduce the tension level of the performers. This is frequently true with gymnasts, young pitchers in baseball, and basketball players in specific situations such as shooting a free throw in a very critical moment of a game.

Many of the same techniques used for motivating performers may be used in reverse for reducing motivation or tension. For example, talking with individuals or groups prior to a contest in a calm, relaxed, and reassuring manner will have the opposite effect of the traditional pep talk. Similarly, minimizing the importance of the competitive situation or the contest may be helpful in situations where young performers are unable to control their emotions effectively or to focus them in the appropriate direction. Obviously, soft, flowing music tends to have a relaxing and oftimes sleep-inducing effect. Many coaches have encouraged practice in deep breathing and progressive relaxation on the part of their athletes. Some athletes have even used techniques of self-hypnosis with varying degrees of success for the purpose of either motivating or relaxing themselves.

It is generally accepted by athletic coaches that skill in the use of psychologic techniques, particularly in motivating athletes, is of critical importance to the success of the coach, perhaps second only to recruiting effectiveness. Understanding of and skill in motivation are no less important to the teacher who wishes to promote maximum learning and performance on the part of his students.

ARRANGING AND CONDUCTING PRACTICES IN PHYSICAL EDUCATION

Since the scheduling and conduct of practice sessions constitute an extremely influential role both for learning and performance in motor skills, it is important that the teacher and coach devote most serious attention to this matter. Practice variables include among other matters, timing of work sessions, size of the learning units, and stimulation of related mental processes in the development of skills. These practice variables are intimately related to the efficiency with which skills are acquired. This efficiency not only saves time but promotes more positive attitudes and enthusiasm for the activities that are learned rapidly and easily. Conversely, one is likely to avoid those activities which have proven frustrating in early attempts.

Distribution of Work Sessions During Practice

It has long been established that individuals do not learn simply because they engage in practice. Yet there is still a general assumption among many teachers and coaches that the amount of learning is directly proportional to the time spent in practice. There is abundant research evidence involving verbal and novel motor tasks to indicate that practice sessions which are distributed and relatively short are more efficient for learning and perform-ance than practices which are more concentrated and which last for long periods of time. Observations of practices with athletic teams during recent years seem to provide a similar conclusion. However, some difficulty, or at least some uncertainty, exists when teachers attempt to implement this generalization in the arrangement of schedules for specific activities.

Within a class period or within a practice session most effective use of time can be made if work sessions are kept relatively short. The insertion of frequent "rest periods" during the practice session is one way of accomplishing this. These rest periods or breaks do not necessitate that the individual remain idle; rather he may be fully involved in alternative activities. The primary deterrent to skill acquisition or to performance improvement during long practice sessions is not fatigue but rather inhibition as described by Hull (1943). Hull's reactive inhibition theory suggests that the individual becomes increasingly reluctant to repeat responses after they have been performed several times. The continuation of this practice therefore results in a diminution in learning and performance effectiveness of one task while practice at a different task is performed with near optimal effectiveness. Inhibition is therefore clearly distinguishable from fatigue, which would render the individual incapable of effectively practicing anything.

With the emergence of inhibition, a change in tasks rather than complete rest is a practical way of keeping the individual involved in useful learning activity. Most activities commonly included in physical education programs or in varsity schedules have several sub-tasks which might be practiced to allow variety within a work session. Use of short practices during a class session may be illustrated with reference to a unit of soccer. The instructor may wish to include kicking (various types, right and left foot), dribbling, trapping, heading, passing, volleying, tackling, and many other fundamentals of individual and team play. The traditional way of teaching such a unit is to have the teacher introduce one or two of these skills during each of the early class periods and attempt to develop thoroughly these specific fundamentals during that session. As a result, relatively long practices for the few skills usually result. The teacher who wishes to make effective use of short, distributed practice in soccer might introduce the students to dribbling, have them spend a short period of time in practice, then introduce kicking for a short practice, then trapping, and so on for several different skills. This would mean that the student would have only a few trials on a particular task in a class period during the early part of the unit. Over a period of time, however, the same amount of practice would be devoted to each skill, with the advantage that the trials would have greater distribution.

Rather than have the basketball player take 25 free throws consecutively, it is preferable to have him alternate with another player and take five rounds of five shots each. Thus, effective use of short and distributed practices can be implemented by rotating through a circuit of skills more than one time or having the learner engage in a greater number of tasks during a particular class period. An example of the use of short work sessions in varsity athletics may be illustrated with reference to a practice period in baseball. One skill which needs a great deal of practice for improvement as well as the maintenance of a high level of proficiency is that of batting. In a typical practice session, each player may be allocated a total of 15 swings in batting practice. This is usually accomplished by having the player take all of his batting practice at one time. However, this does not appear to make the most effective use of the distribution principle. It is probable that the player who takes 15 swings consecutively will not gain as much from the last five swings as he did from the first five swings. Both inhibition and muscular fatigue factors became evident. Therefore, it seems preferable to separate each player's swings into two rounds of eight and seven, or perhaps three rounds of five swings. Since there is some evidence that progressively decreasing work schedules are most effective, a schedule of seven, five, and three swings might be used. Assuming that speed and precision are established in the rotation of players to different areas, this technique seems effective in minimizing the level of inhibition.

It is probable that practice periods for most athletic teams are too long. Even if the inhibition theory is disregarded, it is generally accepted by teachers and athletic coaches that whenever the individual becomes fatigued both learning and performance are diminished. One very real hazard is that during a fatigued state performances may deteriorate with the development of faults or bad habits. Such faults, if repeated several times, may become firmly established and this become a part of the individual's habitual behavior in subsequent performances. In addition, players who are fatigued or are aware of the fact that improvement is not taking place often lose some enthusiasm for the activity. A decline in the performance is both obvious and frustrating.

It is conceivable that even after the individual has ceased improving, additional physical conditioning may still be necessary. In such cases, the student or athlete might take part in conditioning activities which are unrelated to the task at hand. In this way, the development of negative attitudes and erroneous movement patterns can be avoided.

Mental Practice

There is growing evidence that the learning and performance of motor skills can be greatly enhanced through the use of mental practice, particularly when such practice is used in conjunction with physical or overt practice. In fact, research has shown that time spent in a combination of conceptualization and regular practice can result in as much improvement as if the total amount of time were spent in overt practice.

Mental practice refers to the imaginary experience which mentally duplicates overt performance of a particular task. Other terms frequently used interchangeably with mental practice are conceptualization, introspection, implicit trial-and-error, ideational functioning, and mental rehearsal. However, in view of the neural and muscular responses which are evoked, it is probably more accurate to refer to the process as sedentary practice than to imply that it is restricted to "mental" activity.

There are many reasons why mental practice should be encouraged to a greater extent in regular physical education classes. This technique can, in effect, add to the practice session by providing more "trials" within a particular work period. A great deal of time is often wasted while the student waits his turn. At other times the learner does not have access to the necessary facilities or equipment. Use of appropriate mental practice during these between-trial periods not only provides for additional learning but should also enable individuals to *comprehend* the task more thoroughly both from a cognitive and kinesthetic viewpoint. The traditional emphasis upon physical practice with a neglect of the associated mental processes does not seem to take full advantage of man's intellectual ability. Too frequently learners seem to go through the motions rather mechanically, without much thought or kinesthetic awareness of the essential movement responses.

No doubt the process of mental practice in relation to the performance of motor skills dates back to the beginning of man. However, not much attention seems to have been devoted to this topic until the early part of the twentieth century when Köhler (1925) conducted research to identify and analyze the matter of *insight* and its relationship to learning as reflected in Gestalt psychology. In addition, Tolman (1934), another learning theorist, investigated the relationship of "implicit" trial-and-error to learning and expressed the belief that mental practice is an important ingredient in all types of learning.

Corbin (1965), Egstrom (1964), and Trussel (1958) have suggested, on the basis of their research, that for mental practice to be most effective it must be used in combination with overt practice. Thus, it is to be expected that attempts to have the individual learn a complex gymnastic maneuver or to develop a fancy dive to a high level of proficiency solely through mental practice would prove largely ineffective. On the other hand, if the individual had become fully oriented to the task and in addition had made some attempts to execute it he would be most ready to benefit from such mental rehearsal.

There appears to be no basis for the assumption that the technique of mental practice should be reserved for those children with extraordinary powers of conceptualization. On the contrary, there is evidence that this technique can be used effectively with students of widely varying intellectual abilities. Start (1960) showed that within the range of ability normally found in the public school, intelligence does not make a difference in a child's capacity to benefit from such rehearsal.

Techniques for Promoting Mental Practice. A great variety of techniques have been used for eliciting appropriate conceptualization from the learner. Unfortunately, no particular techniques have been established as universally superior. Some mental practice methods used thus far include having the subject read a description of the task, memorize descriptions and "think them through" at regular intervals, view a demonstration or film of the proper execution, have the teacher read a description to the students, and many others. Although none of these has proven best for all situations there are some indications that attempts to control too rigidly the individual's thought processes will inhibit his ability to conceptualize. For example, asking the learner to think along as the instructor reads the description appears not to permit him to slow down and deliberate or concentrate on particular aspects of the performance. Thus, some freedom for the learner to think at his own rate seems to have some merit.

Clark (1960) encouraged subjects to "feel" their way through the performance during the mental practice session. This is in contrast to some other experimenters who ask subjects either to "picture" themselves or "see" themselves performing the task. Clark's suggestion seems especially helpful in that it tends to emphasize an awareness of the kinesthetic sensation related to the movement. On the other hand, seeing oneself as a third person does not appear to personalize the response to the same extent.

In a recent study (1969) involving seventh grade boys learning to shoot a jump shot in basketball, this author, after having the boys take part in overt practice, gave them the following verbal instructions to elicit the desired mental rehearsal:

> Now that you know how to do the jump shot, I'm going to have you take part in a special kind of practice. Today you will again take twelve shots. Some of the shots will be just as you did yesterday. Then at other times I will have you *imagine* shooting a jump shot in the same way. During this imaginery shot you will stand in the starting box, look at the basket, and concentrate on shooting the ball properly. When you do this, however, you will not have the ball and you will not be allowed to move.
>
> Your first shot today will be an imaginery shot. To do this I want you to think your way through the shot, that is, imagine what it feels like to shoot the ball properly. Remember that you place your right hand behind the ball and the left hand out to the side. Then you jump into the air and at the same time bring the ball up just over the eyes. When you reach the top of your jump you push the ball with the right hand so that the ball rolls off the end of the fingers. Keep your eyes on the closest part of the rim and try to push the ball just hard enough so that it goes over the rim and into the basket. Try to actually *feel* yourself doing this without moving your body. Do you get the idea?
>
> Okay, now move into the starting box and go through the imaginery practice. As soon as you have completed it, let me know.

On each subsequent day the following reminder was given to all mental practice groups:

> Today's practice will be exactly like yesterday's. Your first try will be an imaginery shot. Remember that you are to concentrate on jumping, watching the rim, and pushing the ball off the end of the fingers so that it goes just over the rim and into the basket. Try to *feel* yourself going through a perfect shot. Step into the starting box and go through with the imaginery shot. When you have completed it, let me know.

In this study the boys overwhelmingly expressed the belief that mental practices helped them learn the jump shot. They made comments such as "it was fun" or "it was like a game." Others indicated that it was particularly helpful in the beginning stages of practice and that it made the jump shot easier after the mental practice sessions. Many children reported that they could not help rehearsing the activity in a similar manner at times when they were away from the testing situation. Still others reported dreaming about the jump shot. Despite the unusual nature of this activity for most teachers and class situations, it is probable that children would respond positively to suggestions of mental practice.

Use of Mental Practice in Physical Education. In the learning and performance of motor skills, mental practice may take several forms. These include (1) preview or review which immediately precedes, follows, or coincides with performance; (2) formal or informal rehearsal which takes place between work sessions; and (3) conceptualization related to the planning of alternative responses in the given activity. The review technique is most apparent when the gymnast, the diver, the bowler, or the high jumper pauses briefly prior to the beginning of his performance to "think through" the execution of the task. This is done so that during the actual performance which follows, the sequence of responses will be most vivid in his mind. The individual who rushes into the performance without such deliberation often gets confused or repeats common errors.

After the technique of mental practice has been established as a habit, there is every reason to assume that it could be used effectively between daily practice sessions. Already this practice is used rather casually, either consciously or subconsciously, by most persons involved in skill learning. The assignment of a prescribed schedule of mental practice is appropriate homework for students in physical education, or for varsity athletes. Obviously, such practice is likely to be performed most diligently, and thus is likely to be most effective if motivation regarding the particular activity is high.

Pre-planning for situational decision-making is used informally by persons in most competitive sports. Athletes are often encouraged to plan ahead for any eventuality that may occur in the activity. For example, baseball players are asked to assume that every ball will be hit to them and they should be ready to respond "automatically," that is, without further thought. Other players often do likewise to "outsmart" their opponents with unexpected behavior based on plans conceived during quiet moments. More frequent and more formalized use of this type of conceptualization would undoubtedly reduce the "mental errors" and contribute to more alert performance.

Whole and Part Learning

Another important practice variable under the control of the teacher is the size of the learning unit which is presented to the individual. The unit size appears to be intimately related to both speed of acquisition and retention of the material. During recent years, discussion has centered around this topic of "whole and part" learning.

The overall question on unit size is whether the individual should be presented with the total concept of the activity of material, or a major portion thereof, and practice the "whole" task from the beginning or whether he should learn small portions separately until the total task has been learned. The former approach is referred to as the whole method and may be illustrated by the practice of reading a poem from beginning to end until it has been learned completely, or perhaps by engaging in practice or games of soccer as a complete activity until all-around skill has been developed. The part approach is illustrated when the poem is practiced by concentrating on each line or sentence until it has been learned prior to going to the next part. Similarly, in learning the game of soccer by the part method, separate skills such as dribbling, heading, trapping, and kicking are practiced individually and separately until all aspects of the game of soccer have been acquired.

Research has been overwhelmingly supportive of the concept of whole learning in motor skills. A primary advantage seems to be that when an activity is learned as a total unit, an understanding of the relationship between all parts is insured. On the other hand, when learned by the part method, the total activity may be viewed as a series of disjointed or unrelated parts. Consequently, additional practice time is required for the purpose of tying together or blending the parts in the mind, and behavior, of the learner.

In using the whole method it is essential that the size of the unit or material be such that it can be comprehended by the learner. When the unit is too large or beyond the ability level of the learner, he may be confused by the enormousness of the task. More mature and bright individuals are able to comprehend larger units than are less mature or less intelligent persons. Therefore, to take advantage of the whole method of teaching it is essential that the teacher keep the size of the unit within the comprehension of the learner.

Use of the whole approach in teaching does not necessarily mean that the learner engages in the total activity continuously. He may switch from the whole unit to various parts from time to time as they need specific attention. In addition, smaller "wholes" within the activity should be identified and practiced where this is appropriate. Within any major sport or motor activity there are combinations of individual responses with meaningful relationships between them which make them important to be practiced as a unit. The advantage in grouping smaller units exists primarily where the parts are performed in sequence to each other without interruption.

A major problem with part learning is that when skills are practiced in isolation teachers tend to spend too long on items with little meaning or interest to the learner. There are certainly times when practice on isolated responses is essential but such practice is usually more fruitful if the learner has first become fully acquainted with the total activity. After this has occurred he can return to the various parts with a full understanding of their relevance to the total activity.

Using Whole Units in Physical Education. Effective use of large units or variations of the whole method requires careful analysis of the activity. Emphasis on the whole method does not mean that the teacher in field hockey or soccer tosses out a ball to novices and says "Go to it." Teachers who have tried this technique at the junior high school level realize that the students do not gain an understanding of what the whole game is really like under these circumstances. More frequently, mass chaos results. The teacher must keep in mind that in order for the benefits of the whole technique to be realized, children must become oriented to the major concepts involved in the activity. Therefore, from the beginning students should engage in such activities as watching a game, films, and observing chalk board illustrations and discussions of overall purposes, strategies, and rules. Then a modified game could be initiated which would require the participants to move at a slower than normal speed. This approach would familiarize the student with the total activity and the essential elements. Thereafter, practice may involve the full game or the parts that are now understood to be primary ingredients.

In physical education activities or sports, it is frequently desirable to group two or more fundamental skills into a "smaller whole," that is, a combination of responses that does not make up the total activity. For example, the shortstop in baseball may practice fielding ground balls in combination with positioning his body and making a quick delivery in the direction of first base. This grouping of skills in practice has distinct advantages over practicing fielding at one time and throwing to first base at another time. In like manner, the outfielders should not restrict their practice to catching fly balls but should, rather, catch the balls while making preparatory body adjustments and then immediately delivering a throw to the infield, The batter, when practicing drag bunting, should not remain stationary in the batter's box to bunt the ball but should be making preparatory movements to run to first base as he makes contact with the ball. In football, the punter should receive the snap from the center each time he punts in order to establish the relationship between receiving the ball, positioning it in his hands, dropping it, and punting it. The gymnast should practice routines or combinations of skills rather than restrict his practice to isolated tricks. The same is true with modern dance techniques. Such combination practices are illustrations of a "whole" approach and tend to make for a smoother overall performance when the particular responses are called for in a practice situation.

Lead-up games are also appropriate and interesting ways to make use of the whole concept, that is, to combine several parts into a meaningful whole. These games tend to bridge the gap between skill drills and the total game. In addition to the advantage of combining activities that are performed in relation to each other, they have a built-in interest factor based on competition.

References

Bell, V. L. Augmented knowledge of results and its effect upon acquisition and retention of a gross motor skill. *Research Quarterly,* 1968, 39, 25–30.

Bourne, L. E. Information feedback: Comments on Professor I. McD. Bilodeau's paper. In E. A. Bilodeau (ed.) *Acquisition of skill.* New York: Academic Press, 1966, pp. 273–313.

Brace, D. K. Studies in motor learning of gross motor skill. *Research Quarterly,* 1946, 17, 242–254.

Cannon, W. B. *Bodily changes in pain, hunger, fear and rage.* (2nd ed.) New York: Appleton-Century-Crofts, 1929.

Clark, L. V. The effect of mental practice on the development of a certain motor skill. *Research Quarterly,* 1960, 31, 560–569.

Corbin, C. The effects of mental practice on the development of a unique motor skill. *Proceedings of the National College Physical Education Association for Men,* 1966, 69, 100–102.

Cratty, B. J. A three-level theory of perceptual-motor behavior. 1966, *Quest, Monograph VI,* 3–10.

Cratty, B. J. *Psychology and physical activity.* Englewood Cliffs, N.J.: Prentice-Hall, 1968.

Cruze, W. W. *General psychology for college students.* Englewood Cliffs, N.J.: Prentice-Hall, 1951.

Cumbee, F. Z. A factor analysis of motor-coordination. *Research Quarterly,* 1954, 25, 412–428.

Davis, R. A. *Psychology of learning.* New York: McGraw-Hill, 1935.

DiGiovanna, V. G. A comparison of the intelligence and athletic ability of college men. *Research Quarterly,* 1937, 8, 96–106.

Egstrom, G. H. Effects of an emphasis on conceptualizing techniques during early learning of a gross motor skill. *Research Quarterly,* 1964, 35, 472–481.

Ellis, W. D. *A source book of gestalt psychology.* New York: Harcourt, Brace and World, 1938.

Fitts, P. M. Skill training. In R. Glaser (ed.) *Training research and education.* Pittsburgh: University of Pittsburgh Press, 1962, pp. 117–197.

Fitzhugh, K. B., & Fitzhugh, L. C. Effects of early and later onset of cerebral dysfunction upon psychological test performance. *Perceptual and Motor Skills,* 1965, 20, 1099–1100.

Fleishman, E. A. *The structure and measurement of physical fitness.* Englewood Cliffs, N.J.: Prentice-Hall, 1964.

Garfiel, E. The measurement of motor ability. *Archives of Psychology,* 1923, 9, 1–47.

Gerdes, G. R. The effects of various motivational techniques upon performance in selected physical tests. Unpublished doctoral dissertation, Indiana University, 1958.

Guilford, J. B. A system of psychomotor abilities. *American Journal of Psychology,* 1958, 71, 164–174.

Hertzberg, O. E. Relationship of motor ability to the intelligence of kindergarten children. *Journal of Educational Psychology,* 1929, 20, 507–519.

Hull, C. L. *Principles of behavior.* New York: Appleton-Century-Crofts, 1943.

Husman, B. F. Sport and personality dynamics. *Proceedings of the National College Physical Education Association for Men,* 1969, 72, 56–69.

Johnson, G. B. A study of the relationship that exists between skill as measured and general intelligence of college students. *Research Quarterly,* 1942, 13, 57–59.

Kingsley, H. L. *The nature and conditions of learning.* Englewood Cliffs, N.J.: Prentice-Hall, 1946.

Köhler, W. *The mentality of apes.* Translated by E. Winter. New York: Harcourt, Brace and World, 1925.

Kulcinski, L. E. The relation of intelligence to the learning of fundamental muscular skills. *Research Quarterly,* 1945, 16, 266–276.

Litwhiler, D. *Baseball coach's guide to drills and skills.* Englewood Cliffs, N.J.: Prentice-Hall, 1963.

Martin, M. M. A study to determine the effects of motivational techniques on performance of the jump and reach test of college women. Unpublished master's thesis, University of Wisconsin, 1961.

Nason, L. J. Physical coordination helps improve grades. *Nason on education. The Evening Bulletin,* 1965.

Oxendine, J. B. *Psychology of motor learning.* New York: Appleton-Century-Crofts, 1968.

Oxendine, J. B. Effect of mental and physical practice on the learning of three motor skills. *Research Quarterly,* 1969, 40, 755–763.

Oxendine, J. B. Emotional arousal and motor performance. 1970, *Quest, Monograph XIII,* 23–32.

Robb, M. Feedback, 1966, *Quest, Monograph VI,* 38–43.

Ryan, E. D. Retention of stabilometer and pursuit rotor skills. *Research Quarterly,* 1962, 33, 593–598.

Start, K. B. The relationship between intelligence and the effect of mental practice on the performance of a motor skill. *Research Quarterly,* 1960, 31, 644–649.

Start, K. B. The influence of subjectively assessed games ability on gain in motor performance after mental practice. *Journal of Genetic Psychology,* 1962, 67, 169–173.

Strong, C. H. Motivation related to performance of physical fitness test. *Research Quarterly,* 1963, 34, 497–507.

Thompson, M. E. A study of reliabilities of selected gross muscular coordination test items. *Human Resources Research Center Research Bulletin,* 1952, 52–59.

Thorndike, E. L. *Human learning.* New York: Appleton-Century-Crofts, 1931.

Tolman, E. C. Theories of learning. In F. A. Moss (ed.) *Comparative psychology.* Englewood Cliffs, N.J.: Prentice-Hall, 1934, pp. 367–408.

Trussel, E. M. Mental practice as a factor in learning a complex motor skill. Unpublished doctoral dissertation, University of California, Berkeley, 1958.

Vince, M. A. The part played by intellectual processes in a sensori-motor performance. *Quarterly Journal of Experimental Psychology,* 1953, 5, 75–86.

Wechsler, D. *Measurement of adult intelligence.* (3rd ed.) Baltimore: Williams and Wilkins, 1944.

Westendarp, D. Mental capacity and its relation to physical efficiency. *American Physical Education Review,* 1923, 28, 216–219.

Chapter 8

SPORT PSYCHOLOGY

WILLIAM P. MORGAN
University of Wisconsin

OVERVIEW

Sport psychology is a specialized area of concentration which in the broadest sense can be defined as *the study of the psychologic foundations of physical activity*. Investigators in this specialized area represent various fields such as anthropology, history, physical education, psychology, psychiatry, and sociology. However, most of the workers in sport psychology at present are physical educators. At any rate, sport psychology in the United States is not a specialized sub-field of psychology, but rather, it represents an emerging multidisciplinary area of specialization.

Sport psychology in Europe differs in several respects from this description. First of all, most of the European sport psychologists have been trained in either psychology or psychiatry. Furthermore, sport psychology is regarded as a specialized facet of psychology in countries such as Russia (Rudik, 1967) and Czechoslovakia (Vanek and Cratty, 1970). Indeed, chairs of sport psychology exist at various universities in Europe (Vanek and Cratty, 1970). A second distinction is that European sport psychologists seem to use the term sport as a synonym for athletics, and this is usually done within the context of high-level competitive athletics. On the other hand, United States workers tend to view sport in a multidimensional context to include physical activities ranging from noncompetitive recreational pursuits through high-level competitive athletics (Kenyon, 1970; Morgan, 1970e). At the same time, it is of interest to note that a psychologist, Coleman R. Griffith, is regarded as "America's first sports psychologist," and furthermore, Professor Griffith was commissioned "to study problems in the physiology and psychology of athletic activities" (Kroll and Lewis, 1970, p. 1).

The history of sport psychology in Europe and the United States has been presented by Vanek and Cratty (1970). Also, Hammer (1970) has discussed the status of sport psychology in Western Europe and the Far East. Therefore, a comprehensive discussion of the field's history does not seem necessary. However, a cursory commentary follows in order to make the general discussion more meaningful.

In 1965, Ferrucio Antonelli invited thirty-five physical educators to Rome for the purpose of participating in the First International Congress of Sport Psychology (Vanek and Cratty, 1970), and the proceedings of this gathering were published the same year (Antonelli, 1965). Preliminary plans were made during this congress to form a North American Society, and this objective was realized the following year. The North American Society for the Psychology of Sport and Physical Activity (NASPSPA) was organized in 1966 on the eve of the annual convention of the American Association for Health, Physical Education and Recreation (AAHPER) in Chicago. Since that time, annual meetings of the NASPSPA have been held on the day preceding the AAHPER meetings in Las Vegas, St. Louis, Boston, Seattle, and Detroit in 1967, 1968, 1969, 1970, and 1971, respectively. These gatherings have typically involved an invited address, presentation of original papers, and a business meeting.

In addition to these annual meetings, the NASPSPA hosted the Second International Congress of Sport Psychology, which was held in Washington, D.C. during the fall of 1968. The proceedings of the congress were edited by Professor Gerald S. Kenyon and published in 1970 (Kenyon, 1970). The contents of this volume clearly indicate that workers in this field represent various disciplines, and their investigations cover the many specialized facets of psychology. The variety of interests and disciplines involved in this area is further evidenced by *Contemporary Readings in Sport Psychology* (Morgan, 1970e). On the other hand, the publication of *Psychology and the Superior Athlete* by Vanek and Cratty during the same year reflects the specialized interests of given sport psychologists.

Books by Arnold (1968), Beisser (1967), Cratty (1967, 1968), Griffith (1928), Layman (1955), Millar (1968), Moore (1966), Ogilvie and Tutko (1966), Singer (1968), and Vanek and Cratty (1970); edited volumes by Loy and Kenyon (1969), Morgan (1970e), Sage (1970), Slovenko and Knight (1967) and Smith (1970b); edited congress proceedings by Antonelli (1965) and Kenyon (1970); and a monograph edited by Mordy and Locke (1970) dealing with the psychologic foundations of sport and physical activity have been published. The vast majority of these published works have appeared within the past five years. Also, the International Society now publishes the *International Journal of Sport Psychology* and the North American Society publishes the *Sport Psychology Bulletin*.

While there is objective evidence which attests to the reality of sport psychology, the embryonic nature of this specialized area prohibits the prediction of this field's ultimate direction. On the other hand, the history of sport psychology thus far resembles the growth and development of other multidisciplinary fields such as (a) bioengineering, (b) human factors, (c) psychophysiology, and (d) sports medicine. Each of these fields has national and international organizations which meet periodically, each publishes national and international journals, and several universities have established separate multidisciplinary departments for these specialized areas.

While it would be premature to specify the composition and boundaries of sport psychology, two discussions follow for the purpose of reflecting the nature of inquiry in this field at present. The scope of this chapter prohibits an in-depth examination of all possible topics. Therefore, in the first section, a topical summary of research activities in contemporary sport psychology is presented. The purpose of this section is simply to serve as an overview of the various types of investigations being conducted by contemporary workers. Comprehensive coverage of these topics will be found in Kenyon (1970), Mordy and Locke (1970), Morgan (1970e), and Smith (1970b). Also, this overview does not consider topics such as motor learning, skilled performance, physical education, special education, and perceptual-motor training since these areas have been covered in other chapters. It should be understood, however, that such topics might well be relevant in any discussion on sport psychology.

Research concerning the personality dynamics of various athletic subgroups has been the most frequently investigated topic in the field of sport psychology. For this reason, a comprehensive review of this area is presented in the second section. In other words, the first review is topical and intended as an overview, whereas the second review represents an in-depth examination of a selected topic (i.e., personality dynamics).

CONTEMPORARY SPORT PSYCHOLOGY

Various sub-fields of study have traditionally been listed under the rubric psychology. These sub-fields are (a) comparative and physiologic psychology, (b) engineering psychology, (c) learning, (d) measurement, (e) mental health, (f) motivation, (g) perception, (h) personality theory, (i) psychophysiology, and (j) social psychology. While these are not arbitrary categories, it is obvious that certain of the topics might be combined or other topical areas added. For example, separate categories such as sensory, child, educational, or applied psychology might be included. Also, depending upon an individual's orientation, perceptual and motivational phenomena might be listed under learning. At any rate, the category system chosen for this discussion seems to lend itself well to the consideration of sport psychology phenomena. Again, the scope of the present chapter does not permit a discussion of each study, and therefore, this section is simply intended to serve as a categorical review of representative research.

Comparative and Physiologic Psychology

Workers in sport psychology have seldom utilized comparative research models. On the other hand, several investigators have conducted animal research in their attempts to understand the psychologic foundations of sport and physical activity. For example, Scott (1970) has investigated hostility and aggression in various species of animals and Dodwell and Bessant (1960) have conducted learning research on rats in water mazes; Welker (1956) has evaluated the determinants of play and exploration in chimpanzees; Montgomery (1953) has assessed the effect of activity deprivation upon the exploratory behavior of rats; and Weber and Lee (1968) have assessed the effect of prepuberty exercise on the postpuberty emotionality of rats. Also, Dawson and Horvath (1970) have presented a thorough discussion of swimming in small laboratory animals. Individuals contemplating the development of comparative models will find these papers to be of interest.

Engineering Psychology

The interface of the man-machine system has been covered in other chapters of this volume. Typical examples of this research from a physical educator's point of view are information feedback studies of the type conducted by Malina (1969), Pierson and Rasch (1964), and Robb (1968).

Learning

Workers in the field of sport psychology have been concerned primarily with the psychomotor domain. Theoretic formulations advanced by educational and learning psychologists have frequently been employed in an attempt to understand psychomotor behavior. In recent years there have been two psychomotor-oriented theories advanced which complement existing cognitive theories. Henry (1960) has developed a "memory drum" theory of neuromotor reaction, and Cratty (1966) has advanced a three-level theory of perceptual-motor behavior.

As pointed out in other chapters of the current volume, various learning phenomena have been studied by investigators concerned with the psychologic foundations of motor performance. Comprehensive reviews of this research will be found in the present volume as well as in Cratty (1967, 1968), Kenyon (1970), Morgan (1970e), Singer (1968), and Smith (1970b).

Measurement

Test construction has represented an important activity for psychologists, but sport psychologists have seldom engaged in this enterprise. The usual procedure has been to employ available psychometric devices. This approach has been satisfactory in most instances, but such instrumentation has sometimes failed to tap the apparent construct being investigated (Morgan, 1970b, 1971e). Various problems associated with sport psychometry have been discussed elsewhere (Kroll, 1970; Morgan, 1968a, 1970b).

Kenyon's (1968) work represents an exception to the above generalization. He has developed a series of scales for use in assessing attitude toward physical activity. Investigators interested in developing instruments for use in assessment of a given hypothetic construct will find his paper to be extremely useful.

Mental Health

The role of sport and physical activity in the development and maintenance of mental health has been pursued by a number of investigators. Reviews of this topic have been presented by Arnold (1968), La Cava (1967), Layman (1955), Martin (1969), Menninger (1948), Moore (1966), and Morgan (1968a, b). Also, the relationship of recreation to mental health has been described by Cavanaugh (1942), Gordon, Rosenberg, and Morris (1966), and Martin (1969). Factors influencing participation in sport and physical activity have been examined by Brunner (1969), Flanagan (1951), Ibrahim (1969), Kenyon (1968), Lentz (1943), Slovenko and Knight (1967), and Sutton-Smith, Roberts, and Kozelka (1963).

The psychologic correlates of physical fitness and physique have been described by Cattell (1960), Eysenck (1947), Franks and Jetté (1969), Howell and Alderman (1967), Kane (1964), Morgan (1968b, 1969b, 1970d,f), Morgan, Roberts, Brand, and Feinerman (1970) and Tillman (1965). In addition, the mental health of athletes and nonathletes has been compared by Carmen, Zerman, and Blaine (1968), Little (1969), and Pierce (1969).

The effect of *acute* physical activity on psychologic states has been evaluated by Cooper and Caston (1970), Handlon, Byrd, and Gaines (1963), Harmon and Johnson (1952), Husman (1955), Johnson (1949), Johnson and Hutton (1955), Martin and Seymour (1969), Morgan (1970b), Morgan, Roberts, and Feinerman (1971), Morgan and Hammer (1971), and Pitts and McClure (1967). Also, the psychologic effect of *chronic* physical activity has been examined by Cureton (1963), Husman (1955), Kellermann, Wintner, and Kariv (1969), Lukehart and Morgan (1969), McPherson and his associates (1967), Milverton (1943), Morgan and his colleagues (1970), Naughton, Bruhn, and Lategola (1968), and Pyecha (1970).

Motivation

The topic of motivation has been of central concern to human performance investigators. This is understandable considering that several tenths of a second often represent the degree of improvement necessary for a world record in sport. Various motivational phenomena such as information feedback, mental practice, music, hypnosis, physical warm-up, and social facilitation have been employed in attempts to improve muscular performance. These topics are pursued in detail in a recently edited volume entitled *Ergogenic Aids and Muscular Performance* (Morgan, 1971).

Perception

The topic of perception in general and perceptual-motor learning specifically has been covered in other chapters of the present volume. Therefore, this discussion will be limited to selected investigations which have important implications for sport *per se.*

Borg (1962), Borg and Linderholm (1970), Docktor and Sharkey (1971), Frankenhaeuser and her associates (1969), and Skinner, Borg, and Buskirk (1969) have studied the relationship between man's perceived exertion, in a psychophysical sense, and various physiologic parameters. More recently, Morgan, Raven, Drinkwater, and Horvath (1971) have manipulated perceived exertion by means of hypnotic suggestion. Also, Morgan, Needle, and Coyne (1966) have evaluated the influence of perceptual distortion on the maximal performance of highly trained men.

Ryan and Kovacic (1966) have studied pain tolerance and athletic participation, and Ryan and Foster (1967) have examined the interaction of athletic participation and perceptual augmentation and reduction. Also, Drowatzky (1967) has evaluated the relationship of size constancy to selected measures of motor ability.

Personality Dynamics

As mentioned earlier, investigations dealing with the personality dynamics of various athletic sub-groups have represented the most frequently examined topic in the field of sport psychology. Therefore, a comprehensive review of this subject is presented in another section of this chapter.

Psychophysiology

The autonomic nervous system activity of trained and untrained individuals has been compared by Hahner and Rochele (1968). Also, the emotional reactions of athletes have been studied by Harmon and Johnson (1952), Imhof and his colleagues (1969), Johnson (1949, 1951), and Skubic (1955). Lakie (1967) examined the relationship of GSR (galvanic skin response) to task difficulty, personality, and motivation. In addition, Ryan (1962, 1963) has studied the relationship between motor performance and arousal.

Ulrich (1957) evaluated the effect of competition on stress in college females. Eosinophil count, pulse rate, and respiration were used to measure stress. The responses of sportsmanlike and unsportsmanlike football players to a problem-solving task have been assessed by Slusher (1966b). Comparisons were made between overt and covert (GSR) responses.

Social Psychology

Workers in sport psychology have been concerned with the influence of social facilitation on motor performance. Examples of this research are studies by Martens (1969), Martens and Landers (1969), Roberts and Martens (1970), and Singer (1965, 1970). An equal amount of interest has related to the factors associated with selection of various sports and physical activities by participants. Representative of this area of inquiry are studies by Brunner (1969), Flanagan (1951), Ibrahim (1969), Kenyon (1968), Klausner (1967), Lentz (1943), Lukehart and Morgan (1969), and Sutton-Smith, Roberts, and Kozelka (1963).

PERSONALITY DYNAMICS AND SPORT

Overview

As one observes sport and physical activity, whether as an athlete, coach, trainer, team physician, or spectator, it becomes quite obvious that participants from various athletic sub-groups differ in a number of respects. Indeed, there is a wealth of research literature attesting to the differences in physiologic and somatotype differences of athletes from various sub-groups. While observers of sport seem to be equally confident that such differences have psychologic correlates, there is actually little agreement as to the psychologic ways in which these same athletic sub-groups differ from each other or from nonathletes. The purpose of this section shall be to (1) review the existing literature concerning the athlete's personality, (2) attempt to explain the lack of agreement which seems to exist on this topic, and (3) offer suggestions for research strategies to be employed in the future.

Interpretation of the literature dealing with athletes' personalities might be approached from a number of perspectives. However, the author feels that it is efficacious first to examine this literature from the standpoint of the independent and dependent variables which have been used historically.

Independent Variables. First of all, numerous independent variables have been employed, and furthermore, various operational definitions have been used for the same variable by different investigators. For example, research designs have included comparisons of (1) athletes from various sub-groups, (2) athletes and nonathletes, (3) team and individual sport athletes, (4) combative and non-combative sport groups, (5) the same athletic sub-groups from different types of educational institutions, and (6) athletes of differing ability levels. Also, investigators such as Golas (1971) have compared athletes from team and individual sports and then reassigned the athletes into combative and non-combative sport groups for comparative purposes.

Most of the investigations dealing with personality and the athlete have failed to control the factor of multiple-sport participants; that is, a wrestler tested during wrestling season might be classified as representing an *individual* or *combative sport,* but this same athlete might participate in a *non-combative team sport* such as baseball during the following season. Anyone familiar with high school and college athletics can readily recognize the likelihood of numerous such possibilities. This particular methodologic contaminant has not been adequately controlled for by most investigators. In short, does the multiple-sport participant differ from the athlete who participates in only one sport?

Another general problem has been that investigators have failed to employ universally acceptable definitions of group affiliation. The general practice has simply consisted of testing intact athletic sub-groups, with no attempt to differentiate between ability levels. The athlete who "rides the bench" throughout his athletic career might differ in a number of ways from the "starter." In other words, while athletes from one sub-group may not differ from those in another, it is quite possible that the "successful" and "unsuccessful" members of such groups would differ both within and between sports.

In view of the fact that investigators have failed to employ adequate operational definitions of the independent variables used in this area of inquiry, it is not surprising that general confusion seems to exist. It is clear, of course, that subsequent investigations must include rigorous operational definitions of the independent variable.

Dependent Variables. The assessment of personality can be pursued with either direct or indirect methods. The majority of investigators in the field of sport psychology have elected to employ direct methods which consist of self-reports such as the Edwards Personal Preference Schedule (EPPS), Eysenck Personality Inventory (EPI), Minnesota Multiphasic Personality Inventory (MMPI), and the Sixteen Personality Factor Questionnaire (16PF). Several investigators have employed indirect procedures which are un-structured. Examples of these projective techniques are the Rorschach Test, Figure-Drawing Test, Thematic Apperception Test (TAT), House-Tree-Person (H-T-P) Test, Sentence Completion Test (SCT), and the Rosenzweig Picture-Frustration Study.

The use of direct methods of personality assessment as compared to indirect techniques as well as the efficacy of employing a battery of both direct and indirect procedures in sport psychology have been discussed previously (Morgan, 1968c). In view of the nosologic problems associated with projective methods, it would seem that sport psychologists have chosen the correct approach; that is, direct techniques facilitate within and between laboratory replication.

Unfortunately, investigators have employed various personality inventories such as the EPI, EPPS, MMPI, and 16-PF, and then attempted to make direct comparisons with one another's work. The traits measured by these inventories are essentially psychologic constructs that have been derived from factor analytic work. The output of such analyses is dependent in large part upon the input. Also, were factor analysts to begin with the same input, subsequent rotation and labeling might differ markedly. On the other hand, independently constructed inventories such as Cattell's 16-PF, Guilford's personality inventory, and the Eysencks' EPI measure the dimensions of extroversion-introversion and neuroticism-stability "with almost complete agreement" (Eysenck et al., 1970, p. 13). At the same time, while the MMPI contains a measure of extroversion-introversion (E) it was not designed for the measurement of E in "normal groups and it is not well adapted for this purpose" (Eysenck, 1967, p. 111). Also, fractionation of the MMPI is hazardous and the specific scales should be examined in light of scores on other dimensions of the MMPI. At any rate, while it is difficult to make direct comparisons of investigations which have used different inventories, this is certainly possible if the investigator has an understanding of the various instruments and the recommended procedures for their administration and interpretation.

Methodologic Problems. Rather than simply review investigations which have dealt with the psychologic characteristics of the athlete, the author has elected first to comment on the methodologic problems which have historically plagued this area of inquiry. One of the more obvious problems has been the general inadequacy of operational definitions of the independent variables used in these investigations. Also, while more acceptable operational definitions have been employed for the dependent variables, the variety of instruments employed does not make for ready comparisons. These points should be kept in mind when attempting to interpret the literature in this area.

Several additional methodologic problems have characterized research in this area. First, the method of sampling has generally been questionable. The usual approach has consisted of simply administering paper-pencil tests to available intact groups; that is, acceptable principles of sampling have usually been ignored. Also, "informed consent" policies have seldom been employed (Morgan, 1970b), suggesting coercion (intentional or unintentional) of subjects to participate in the majority of these investigations, which not only violates ethical considerations, but coupled with the absence of reference to the use of lie scales, brings into question the validity of such studies.

Another shortcoming, and perhaps the most serious of all, has been the general failure of investigators to pursue the study of personality and sport within a theoretic framework. This particular point will be pursued in more detail following a review of personality research and the athlete.

PERSONALITY CHARACTERISTICS OF ATHLETIC GROUPS

The present review deals with investigations which have been directed toward an understanding of the personality characteristics of various athletic sub-groups. Studies have been conducted on participants in baseball, basketball, cross-country, football, golf, karate, marathon running, parachuting, swimming, scuba diving, tennis, track, weightlifting, and wrestling. Also, psychoanalytic observations of sport have been made by Adatto (1963), Beisser (1961, 1967), Deutsch (1926), Harlow (1951), and Whitman (1969).

In addition to evaluating athletes from different sub-groups, investigators have also compared athletes and nonathletes, athletes from different types of educational institutions, and athletes of differing skill levels. Also, numerous psychometric tools have been employed in these studies. Therefore, any categorization of this research for discussion purposes must obviously be arbitrary. In most instances there has not been sufficient research on specific sports to justify a review. It does seem, however, that several common research strategies have been adopted by investigators, and these have been used in developing a topical outline for this review.

Sampling

Most investigators have tested readily available, intact groups of athletes. The assumption has been that participants in a given sport in one educational institution or geographic locale are similar to those athletes in the same sports in other schools and areas. There is evidence which suggests that athletes from different sports have different somatotypes (Morehouse and Rasch, 1963). Also, a gymnast or diver at one school would not be expected to be a football tackle or heavyweight wrestler at another institution. Therefore, if Sheldon's theory of personality (Hall and Lindzey, 1970) were adopted, this sampling technique might not be as dangerous as it seems. At any rate, there is evidence which suggests that sampling is a very important consideration in attempting to explain the athlete's personality.

This point is well illustrated in an investigation by Lakie (1962), who administered five scales of the Omnibus Personality Inventory to 230 athletes from two state colleges, a state university, and a private university. The athletes consisted of participants in basketball, football, tennis, golf, track, and wrestling. The athletes from the four schools were grouped according to sport and a comparison made irrespective of type of institution. This analysis revealed that the athletes from the various sports did not differ from each other. However, significant differences between sports were observed when within-school analyses were conducted. Furthermore, in certain instances, athletic groups not only differed from other teams at their respective schools, they also differed significantly from the same sport groups at other institutions. These observations led Lakie (1962) to suggest that "it may be that unique groups found in this study and other studies may be persons of similar characteristics being attracted to, or recruited for, specific athletic programs" (p. 572).

A similar methodologic problem was encountered by Morgan (1968c), who administered the Eysenck Personality Inventory to English-speaking wrestlers participating in the 1966 world championships. The group consisted of the Canadian, South African, and United States teams. When viewed collectively, this sample was stable, but somewhat more extroverted than normal. However, when the teams were evaluated independently the United States team was found to score significantly lower on the neuroticism-stability dimension than the South African team. In short, a somewhat typical profile was observed at the collective level which actually clouded the rather unique characteristics of these two sub-groups. These findings are illustrated in figure 8-1.

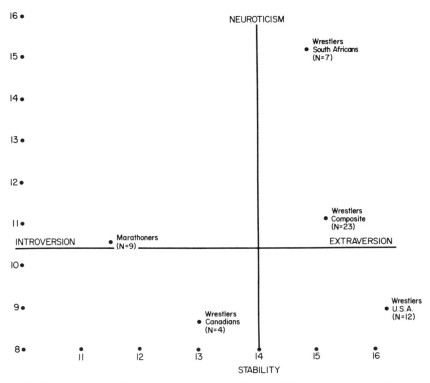

FIG. 8-1. Extraversion-introversion and neuroticism-stability in wrestlers and marathoners (*Reprinted in part from the Journal of Sports Medicine & Physical Fitness, 1968, 8, 212–216*).

Furthermore, experimental investigations have been carried out on college wrestlers in Missouri (Morgan, 1970c) and California (Morgan and Hammer 1971), and it has been observed that the wrestlers from these two states differed significantly on anxiety as measured by the IPAT Anxiety Scale. The testing was carried out under normal "base-line" conditions in both cases. These examples emphasize the necessity of multiple analyses in exploratory research. Until there is extensive normative data available, it is recommended that sport psychologists not assume that athletes in the same sport from different institutions are similar.

Ability Levels

In addition to comparing athletic sub-groups, several investigators have directed their attention toward an understanding of the relationship between personality and level of performance. For example, in one of the earliest investigations Johnson, Hutton, and Johnson (1954) administered the Rorschach and House-Tree-Person Test to 12 athletes from contact and noncontact sports who were either of All-America or national champion caliber. These outstanding athletes were found to possess several distinguishing characteristics. These characteristics included "extreme aggressiveness, a freedom from great emotional inhibition, high and generalized anxiety, high level of intellectual aspiration, and feelings of exceptional self-assurance" (p. 547).

Another investigation of outstanding athletes was conducted by La Place (1954), who administered the MMPI to 49 major league players who served as his "successful" group and 64 minor league players who represented his "unsuccessful" group. The major league players scored significantly lower than the minor league players on the Schizophrenia and Psychopathic Deviate Scales. Both groups, however, scored within one standard deviation of the mean for the general population, and therefore, it would appear that neither group differed appreciably from the normal. This investigation revealed that the major league players were better adjusted than the minor league players. Whether these differences existed prior to each group's entrance into professional baseball and hence played a role in determining success, or whether these differences were a consequence of achievement levels cannot be inferred.

A related investigation was conducted by Singer (1969), who administered the Edwards Personal Preference Schedule (EPPS) to 69 athletes at Ohio State University. The athletes consisted of 26 varsity baseball players, 33 freshman baseball players, and 10 varsity tennis players. The ability level of each athlete was ranked by his coach. Comparisons were made between the baseball players, tennis players, and the EPPS norms. Also, comparisons were made between the highest- and lowest-ranked athletes in both sports and the EPPS norms. The baseball team scored significantly higher than the other two groups on the Abasement factor, significantly lower than the other two groups on the Intraception variable, lower than the tennis group on the Achievement variable, lower than the norm group on Autonomy, and lower than the tennis group on Dominance. Both the baseball and tennis groups scored significantly higher than the norm group on the Aggression factor. No differences were noted between high- and low-rated baseball players, and the high- and low-rated tennis players only differed on one of the 15 measures.

This investigation would be difficult to replicate since ability was not assessed with a universally recognized tool. Also, one would expect differences on numerous variables to be greater between major and minor league players (La Place, 1954) than between high- and low-rated athletic groups from the same university team. Similarly, high- and low-rated baseball and tennis groups from the Big Ten Conference might differ on a number of the EPPS scales, but such differences might not necessarily exist within any given conference school. It is recommended that sport psychologists employ clear distinctions of ability in testing high- and low-performance groups.

The MMPI was administered to freshman and upper-class athletes and nonathletes by Booth (1958). Comparisons were made between (1) athletes rated as poor or good competitors, (2) athletes who participated in team, individual, or team-individual sports, and (3) freshman and upper-class athletes and nonathletes. The results revealed that the athletes and non-athletes and the athletes from the various sport groups differed significantly on several of the MMPI scales.[1] Also, an analysis of the 550 MMPI questions revealed that 22 of the items discriminated between poor and good competitors.

Rasch and Hunt (1960) administered the Berdie scale, which measures masculinity-feminity, to 14 candidates from the 1960 United States Olympic team. These athletes were found to be quite similar to norms which had previously been established for college males. Hence, these wrestlers of Olympic caliber were not characterized by a unique profile.

In a later investigation, Rasch (1962) administered the Maudsley Personality Inventory (MPI) to 85 wrestlers from five different colleges. Their mean scores on the introversion-extroversion and neuroticism-stability scales were 22.0 and 27.6 respectively, which did not differ from the means of 20.19 and 28.40 for these same variables on the norm sample. Rasch intended to compare the winners of conference championships with less successful wrestlers, but only four of the 85 wrestlers won conference championships. For some reason, he elected not to compare the high- and low-rated wrestlers. While the wrestlers did not collectively differ from the mean values of the norm group, it is quite possible that certain of the teams may have differed

---

[1] It is of interest to note that the varsity athletes in the individual sports were significantly more depressed than those from the team and team-individual groups. A later report by Carmen, Zerman, and Blaine (1968) revealed that the highest incidence of depression in Harvard athletes occurred among swimmers (an individual sport).

from the average on one or both of the dimensions examined. At any rate, this investigation suggests that college wrestlers do not differ from the norm sample.

In a related investigation Kroll (1967) administered the 16 PF to 94 amateur and collegiate wrestlers consisting of 28 superior athletes who had been on the United States Olympic team or had been NCAA or NAIA champions or place winners, 33 college wrestlers who were rated as excellent by their coaches and had won at least 60 percent of their matches that year, and a group of 33 wrestlers from the same teams who were rated as average or below average. Discriminant function analyses failed to demonstrate differences for the criterion groups. Also, the wrestlers differed significantly from established norms only on the tough-mindedness factor.

On the other hand, Morgan (1968c) administered the Eysenck Personality Inventory (EPI) to English-speaking wrestlers who participated in the 1966 world tournament, and he reported that performance in the tournament was significantly correlated with the extroversion dimension. Success, however, was not related to neuroticism.

More recently, Morgan and Costill (1971) administered the EPI, the IPAT Anxiety Scale, and the Depression Adjective Check List to a group of experienced marathoners. Correlations were computed between performance in the marathon, the maximal oxygen intake of these subjects, and the psychologic variables. Marathon performance was not significantly correlated with any of the variables. This is somewhat surprising since most observers of the marathon readily agree that these runners represent a "special breed." They are, of course, quite unique from an anatomic and physiologic standpoint. This uniqueness, at least in part, explains the lack of significant correlations between the variables cited; that is, they are so similar that their homogeneity suppresses the likelihood of significant correlations. This group of marathoners scored much lower on the anxiety and extroversion variables than the average population; that is, they were characterized by introversion and low anxiety.

Kroll and Petersen (1965) administered the 16 PF to 139 football players from five colleges who had winning or losing teams. The data were analyzed by discriminant function analyses which revealed significant discrimination between the five teams. The highest contributors to the discriminant function were factors B (intelligence), H (shy versus bold), O (confident versus worrying), and Q^3 (casual versus controlled). Since the teams were from university, state, and private church colleges, it is difficult to determine if the observed discriminant function reflects winning versus losing teams or type of school. This point was reviewed earlier in the present chapter in connection with Lakie's report (1962).

The 16 PF was administered to 246 football players from four colleges by Straub and Davis (1971). The teams were from a small private college, an Ivy

League university, a Big Ten university, and a small state college. It is interesting to note that the purpose of this investigation "was to determine if there were significant differences in team personality profiles" (p. 39), since this particular question seemed to be answered by Lakie (1962) and Kroll and Petersen (1965). At any rate, subsequent analysis revealed that the Big Ten team differed significantly from the other three teams. Whether this difference reflects primarily (1) recruitment, (2) gravitation, (3) mortality, (4) cause and effect, or (5) an interaction effect remains to be demonstrated.

Kroll and Carlson (1967) administered the 16 PF to 71 karate participants. They evaluated the profiles of advanced, intermediate, and novice participants by means of multiple discriminant analysis. No significant profile differences were observed between the three groups. Also, the subjects did not differ from the normal population.

Parsons (1963) administered the 16 PF to champion swimmers and found that they differed from the average population on 15 of the 16 factors. However, those swimmers in this champion group who were selected to participate on the 1962 Canadian team did not differ from those swimmers who were not selected. This might simply reflect the homogeneity of the group. Also, it should not be assumed that members of any country's team are necessarily the best athletes available. Indeed, it is rather clear that numerous economic, political, sociologic, and personal factors influence the composition of national teams.

The Thurstone temperament schedule was administered to 21 high school swimmers by Newman (1968). The subjects were ranked in swimming ability as measured by actual mean competitive times in dual meets. Correlations were then computed between ranks on performance and the seven Thurstone traits. Three of the correlations were statistically significant, but since approximately two would be expected due to chance alone, this suggests that there was no relationship between personality and swimming performance in the sample studied. However, as mentioned earlier in this chapter, testing such hypotheses in isolated, intact, readily available samples does not lend itself to demonstration of significant relationships. The primary reason for not observing significant correlations relates to the homogeneity of variance which often characterizes such samples.

More recently, the 16 PF was administered to 338 swimmers from two Olympic Development Swim Clinics; swim clubs from California, Indiana, and New Jersey; and five college and university teams by Rushall (1970). The swimmers were pooled from the respective teams in order to form performance and maturational categories. The data were evaluated by means of stepwise multiple discriminant function analyses. Rushall concluded that "personality appeared to have no relation to success in swimming" (p. 103).

While not bearing directly on the question of competitive ability and personality, a report by Whiting and Stembridge (1965) is relevant to the general question of swimming ability and personality. These investigators administered the Maudsley Personality Inventory (MPI) and the Junior Maudsley Personality Inventory (JMPI) to college-age and 11- and 12-year-old male students respectively. Comparisons were made between those subjects who had received previous swimming instruction but were still unable to swim (persistent nonswimmers), and those subjects who had never received previous instruction. The *persistent* nonswimmers in the college sample were significantly more introverted than the other nonswimmers, but they did not differ on the neuroticism dimension. The 11- and 12-year-old subjects who were classified as *persistent* nonswimmers were found to be significantly more introverted and neurotic than the other nonswimmers. This investigation has implications for the swimming instructor, since it suggests that the personality of the persistent nonswimmer be taken into account in the teaching process. Furthermore, while certain personality types may well gravitate toward certain sports, this investigation suggests that other types may also avoid certain sports. At any rate, this study tends to support the selection hypothesis for explaining personality differences in sport, and it also serves to demonstrate the efficacy of Eysenckian theory for sport psychology.

The findings of Whiting and Stembridge (1965) were supported by the later report of Behrman (1967); that is, the persistent nonswimmers (nonlearners)[2] were more introverted and neurotic. Therefore, it seems quite clear that learning in swimming is dependent in part on the learner's personality. Had Whiting and Stembridge and Behrman included measures of body density, percent body fat, and somatotype, it is likely that the constitutional basis of this problem would have been more evident.

Several years ago, Kane (1964) reviewed the literature pertaining to personality and physical ability and came to the conclusion that a positive relationship exists between "athletic ability and (1) Stability as opposed to Anxiety, and (2) Extraversion as opposed to Introversion" (p. 89). On the basis of the present review, it would be hazardous to advance any generalizations regarding the interaction of personality and physical performance. The results of investigations conducted since Kane's review (1964) have been equivocal. The equivocal nature of this research can be explained in a number of ways.

First of all, one of the most serious shortcomings of investigations in this field has been the unitary nature of inquiry; that is, attempts to understand physical performance have been limited to the personality domain. This is rather interesting since considerable evidence is available which suggests that success in sport is dependent upon certain physical capacities. In other words, sport psychologists have attempted to discriminate between high- and low-performance groups on the basis of their scores on various personality inventories. There has been a general failure to consider biologic and

---

[2] Behrman classified the persistent nonswimmers as nonlearners.

sociologic factors as well as additional psychologic phenomena which might contribute to high-level performance.

An exception to the preceding generalization has been the research strategy of Kane (1964), who has examined the relationships between various physical abilities, personality factors, physique, and sociometric status. His factor analytic work prompted the advancement of the following hypotheses (1964, p. 94):

> (1) that a high level of physical ability favours extravert development; (2) that among those of high physical ability only those achieve high standards in competitive conditions who rate highly in Extraversion, and (3) that size supports stability.[3]

Confusion regarding the relationship of personality and physical ability will persist until different research strategies are used. It is recommended that investigators concerned with this problem (1) organize multidisciplinary teams, (2) adopt theoretic models, (3) employ precise operational definitions of dependent and independent variables, and (4) use meaningful sampling procedures.

Psychologic Effects of Sport

While physical education texts contain countless statements regarding the positive influence of athletics on personality, there is very little objective evidence which supports this view. The few investigations which have been conducted can be classified as either acute or chronic in that adopted research strategies have consisted of testing athletes before and after a given competitive contest (acute) or prior to and following a competitive season (chronic). In one instance athletes and nonathletes were tested at the beginning and conclusion of their college careers (Werner and Gottheil, 1966). Research dealing with the psychologic effect of acute and chronic participation in sport will be reviewed in this section.

A number of investigators (Cofer and Johnson, 1960; Kroll, 1970; Lakie, 1962; Singer, 1967; Smith, 1970a) have raised the question of whether athletes from various sub-groups differ because of their participation in the respective sports or because they were different first and gravitated toward various sports because of inherent differences. The answer to this question awaits rigorously controlled longitudinal study. In the meantime the author proposes that a gravitation model be tentatively adopted. This suggestion is made on the basis of theoretic views and experimental findings generated from Eysenckian theory. This particular point will be elaborated later in the present chapter. First, however, research pertaining to the psychologic effects of sport will be reviewed.

Johnson and Hutton (1955) administered the House-Tree-Person Test to

---

[3] Stability refers to lack of neurotic signs in this sentence.

college wrestlers (1) prior to the season, (2) five hours prior to the most important match of the season, and (3) the day after this same match. In the pre-match setting the wrestlers were characterized by a decrease in functioning intelligence, increased anxiety, and a prominence of neurotic signs. However, neurotic tendencies were no longer evident and functioning intelligence was normal the following day.

Alternate forms of the IPAT 8-Parallel-Form Anxiety Battery were administered to college wrestlers by Morgan (1970c) at pre-season and one hour prior to easy and difficult matches. A significant *reduction* in anxiety was reported for both pre-match settings, which does not confirm the report of Johnson and Hutton (1955). However, their observations were supported in a more recent investigation by Morgan and Hammer (1971), who administered alternate forms of the IPAT 8-Parallel-Form Anxiety Battery to wrestlers from four California colleges in (1) early season, (2) following their weigh-in at a state tournament (that is, four hours prior to the first match), (3) one hour before the first match, and (4) 15 to 30 minutes following the tournament. The findings are illustrated in figure 8-2. Statistical analysis revealed that the four teams did not differ at any point in time, but collectively there was a significant *increase* in anxiety in the pre-match setting which was followed by a significant *decrease* in anxiety in the post-match

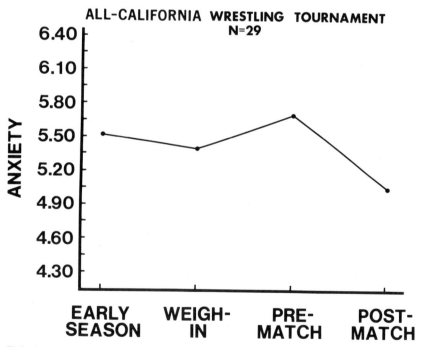

FIG. 8-2. Psychologic effect of wrestling competition.

period. It should also be emphasized that the post-match anxiety level was significantly lower than the "base-line" measure obtained in early season.

It will also be noted in figure 8-2 that anxiety levels did not change during the three-month interval between the early-season (base-line) and weigh-in periods. On the other hand, had the wrestlers scored high on anxiety during the early season it is possible that a decrease might have been observed. In a related investigation, Morgan and his collegues (1970) reported that depressed adult males experienced a significant reduction in depression following six weeks of physical training. These investigations have involved measures of psychologic states known to fluctuate under various conditions such as drug administration, hypnotic suggestion, and stress. Of major importance to the present discussion is the observation that the same psychologic states increase and decrease in physical activity settings.

In contrast to psychologic *states* such as anxiety and depression which are regarded as transitory and situationally determined are psychologic *traits*. These are regarded as being enduring and stable features of an individual's personality. Therefore, it is appropriate to distinguish between measures of *state* and *trait* anxiety. Psychologic characteristics such as anxiety, depression, aggression, neuroticism, and hostility should be viewed as either state or trait components of a personality structure. On the other hand, it should be emphasized that stable, enduring traits such as extroversion and neuroticism, as measured by the EPI (Eysenck and Eysenck, 1962), can be altered by powerful drugs; that is, the preceding generalization is subject to certain reservations.

It is surprising to note that investigators have employed *trait* measures which are thought to be relatively enduring components of a personality to assess the effect of athletic participation. Why should an investigator think that psychologic *traits* fixed by heredity might change following participation in athletics for one or more years? The 16 PF actually contains state and trait factors and yet sport psychologists have typically treated all 16 factors as if they were measures of *states*.

For example, the 16 PF was administered to entering cadets at the United States Military Academy by Werner (1960). He then compared the personality profiles of those cadets who had won varsity letters in high school and those classified as nonathletes. The entering freshmen who had won letters in high school athletics differed from the nonathlete group on 8 of the 16 factors $(A, E, F, H, I, N, Q_1, Q_2)$. Werner commented that this difference could be due either to individuals with different personality structures electing to participate in sport or the actual participation might have been responsible for the differences. This is surprising since certain of these factors are regarded as trait measures. At any rate, this same suggestion, it will be recalled, has been advanced by other investigators.

The study by Werner (1960) was replicated and amplified by Werner and

Gottheil (1966). In this later investigation the 16 PF was administered to 340 freshmen cadets who had participated in high school athletics. At the time of entrance to the United States Military Academy the athletes were found to differ significantly from the nonathletes on seven of the 16 factors (A, F, H, Q_1, Q_2, Q_4), supporting Werner's earlier report (1960). This group, like the former, differed on factors A and H which Cattell and Eber (1962) feel are largely determined by heredity.[4] This tends to suggest a gravitation explanation for differences in athletes and nonathletes. Werner and Gottheil (1966) tested these same subjects at the time of graduation, when the original "nonathletes" had participated in athletics for a period of four years. The two groups were still different at this point, indicating that participation in athletics did not alter the personality of former nonathletes or athletes. Also, participation in sport did not cause the former nonathletes to become more like the athletes.

The observations of Werner (1960) and Werner and Gottheil (1966) tend to suggest that athletes and nonathletes differ from the outset, and participation in athletics does not influence personality. This, of course, is precisely the prediction one would advance if Eysenckian theory were employed to explain differences between athletes and nonathletes. Lukehart and Morgan (1969) conducted a pilot investigation on junior high school males who had never participated in organized sports in an attempt to evaluate whether athletes and nonathletes differ on personality dimensions from the outset. They administered the Junior Eysenck Personality Inventory (JEPI) to 33 males. Twenty-one of these subjects subsequently elected to participate in football and 11 did not. Those subjects electing to participate in football were significantly more extroverted from the outset than the nonparticipants, but the two groups did not differ on the neuroticism dimension. The groups were retested at the conclusion of the season and were still found to differ on the extroversion dimension. As expected, neither group experienced a change in personality over the three-month period. While these pilot observations do not permit generalizations of any sort, it should be pointed out that they are in complete agreement with predictions derived from Eysenckian theory.

The findings relative to the psychologic effects of sport and physical activity are easily interpreted, and for the most part they are in agreement with predictions from theoretic psychology. As could be expected, personality traits remain largely unaffected as a result of athletic participation. Furthermore, it seems reasonable to propose that differences which have been observed between athletic sub-groups as well as differences between athletes and nonathletes are probably attributable to constitutional factors. Such is

---

[4] Pyecha (1970) reported that students in a 16-week judo class experienced a significant change in factor A. This is difficult to explain since the test authors regard this factor as being determined largely by heredity.

the prediction derived from Eysenckian theory, and experimental evidence to date supports this postulate. In addition, actual increases and decreases in *state* measures have been associated with acute, but generally not chronic, athletic participation. This too, on the basis of sport's obvious psychodynamic nature, is in keeping with expectations.

Athletes and Nonathletes

The previous section dealt primarily with the question of psychologic effects of sport. However, certain of these investigations also involved comparisons of athletes with nonathletes, and this research supported the view that athletes differ from nonathletes on certain personality traits. Investigations which have been concerned specifically with comparisons of athletes and nonathletes will be reviewed in this section.

Henry (1941) administered a questionnaire consisting of items from the Thurstone neurotic inventory and questions pertaining to ascendence-submission to student pilots, members of a college track team, physical education major students, and a group of students enrolled in weightlifting. The track athletes and pilots were found to be quite similar and these groups were significantly less hypochondriacal and introverted than the weightlifters. Also, they were significantly more neurasthenic than the physical education majors.

Thune (1949) constructed an inventory which he describes in his paper, and he administered it to 100 YMCA weightlifters and 100 YMCA athletes who did not engage in weightlifting. The weightlifters appeared to be "more shy, lacking in self-confidence, and more concerned with body build" (p. 305). Furthermore, the weightlifters exhibited a desire "to be strong, healthy, and dominant, to be more like other men" (p. 305).

Twenty weightlifters and a matched control group of 20 subjects who were comparable to the weightlifters in various ways with the exception that they did not lift weights were administered a Sentence Completion Test (SCT) and six cards from the Thematic Apperception Test (TAT) by Harlow (1951). These groups were then compared on the basis of 18 variables derived from psychoanalytic theory. The weightlifters differed from the nonweightlifters on 13 of the 18 variables. One of the major differences was that the weight men were found to have "significantly greater feelings of masculine inadequacy" (p. 322). The title of Harlow's paper, "Masculine Inadequacy and Compensatory Development of Physique," summarizes his findings and discussion rather well.

Slusher (1964) administered the MMPI to high school athletes who had won letters in baseball, basketball, football, swimming, and wrestling, and to nonathletes from the same population. The athletes and nonathletes differed on all of the MMPI scales except the M (hypomania) and K (validity). These MMPI scales are known to fluctuate with various treatments. For example, scores on the depression scale decrease following the administration of antidepressants and numerous other therapies. At any rate, since the MMPI is not comprised of *trait* measures *per se*, it cannot be inferred that the athlete and nonathlete groups differed prior to the athletes electing to participate in sport.

Schendel (1965) administered the California Psychological Inventory (CPI) to ninth-grade, twelfth-grade, and college athletes and nonparticipants in athletics. The ninth-grade athletes differed from the nonathletes on eight of the CPI scales, differences existed on 4 scales for the twelfth-grade sample, and nine differences were observed for the college *S*s. This investigation supports the view that athletes and nonathletes differ in personality structure, and while cross-sectional studies have obvious limitations, it also suggests that athletes and nonathletes differ from the outset since both the younger and older groups differed.

The Gordon Personal Profile was administered to 22 Negro and 35 white athletes and 19 Negro and 35 white nonathletes by Hunt (1969). He reported that Negro and white varsity athletes had similar personality profiles as did the Negro and white nonathletes. Also, the athletes, regardless of ethnic background, tended to differ from the nonathletes.

The Edwards Personal Preference Schedule (EPPS) was administered to 950 male freshmen by Fletcher and Dowell (1970). These subjects were further divided into groups who had participated in high school athletics and those who had not. The two groups were found to differ on the Dominance, Aggression, and Order scales of the EPPS.

College wrestlers and experienced marathoners have been found to score significantly lower than the population average on anxiety (Morgan and Hammer, 1971; Morgan and Costill, 1971). Also, American world-class wrestlers were found to be more extroverted than the normal population and marathoners (see figure 8-1), who in turn were more introverted than the normal population and most other athletic sub-groups (Morgan, 1968c; Morgan, 1968d; Morgan and Costill, 1971). These investigations as well as the majority of the studies reviewed in this section suggest that athletes represent a unique population. Perhaps it is inappropriate to make comparisons between athletic sub-groups and published norms for the "normal" or "average" population if, in fact, athletes represent another population; that is, extensive norming on athletes might be appropriate.

The California Psychological Inventory (CPI) was administered to 39 freshmen and 4 sophomore college football players, 44 freshmen and 5 sophomores who had played high school football, and 44 freshmen and 5 sophomores who had never participated in athletics by Berger and Littlefield (1969). Also, the Scholastic Aptitude Test (SAT) was administered to these subjects. Hence, there were three groups consisting of 43 athletes, 49 former athletes, and 49 nonathletes. The groups differed significantly on the SAT and the composite CPI. The authors do not explain why they used a composite CPI score. The groups were then equated on the basis of SAT scores and reduced to a number of 30 each. The authors do not present a rationale for equating the subjects on SAT scores. At any rate, they report that "none of the 18 items of the CPI was able to discriminate significantly between groups at the .01 level" (p. 665). It is surprising that an alpha level of .01 was employed in the absence of any reference to statistical power. While this investigation suggests that athletes and nonathletes do not differ, the findings should be viewed with caution because of the design and statistical procedures employed.

The Eysenck Personality Inventory was administered to 46 team sport and 36 individual sport athletes as well as 40 nonathletes by Golas (1971). The 82 athletes were also classified as representing either a combative ($N = 41$) or noncombative ($N = 41$) sport. Regardless of classification procedure, the athletes were found to be significantly more extroverted than the non-athletes. The sport groups did not differ on the E dimension, however. Also, none of the groups differed on the neuroticism-stability dimension.

One consistent finding throughout the sport psychology literature has been the observation that athletes tend to be normal on the neuroticism-stability dimension of personality. Indeed, American wrestlers were noted to be extremely stable even when tested 24 to 48 hours before competition in a world tournament (Morgan, 1968c). It may well be that stability is a prerequisite for high-level competition. A report by Yanada and Hirata (1970) suggests that this observation may reflect selective mortality. They reported that those students who dropped out and those who continued in their athletic clubs scored within the abnormal and normal ranges respectively on the Tokyo University Personality Inventory (TUPI). Those students who continued in their sport clubs were less neurotic, less depressive, and more hypomanic than those who dropped out.

A different interpretation, however, might follow from the work of Carmen, Zerman, and Blaine (1968), who compared the use of the Harvard Psychiatric Service by athletes and nonathletes. Athletes used the service less frequently, but those athletes who requested treatment tended to have more problems than did the nonathletes. Also, Pierce (1969) reported that athletes are less likely to make use of campus psychiatric facilities than are other students. Of further interest was his observation that differences between athletes and nonathletes were "related to ability to take the role of patient than to actual degree of pathology, and the suggestion is made that ways of helping these less verbal, less intellectually oriented students be developed and used" (p. 249).

More recently, Little (1969) compared athletic and nonathletic neurotics. There had been an absence of neurotic markers in the life histories of the athletes, whereas neurotic markers were quite common in the nonathletic group. Also, the athletic group was highly extroverted and sociable while the nonathletic group was characterized by introversion and a lack of sociability. Despite histories of good mental health, "the prognosis under treatment for the athletic group was, in general, less favourable" (p. 194). Neurotic breakdowns were associated with a threat to physical well-being (that is, illness or injury) in 73 percent of the cases for the athletic group, while the percentage was only 11 for the nonathletic group. The implication here for directors of athletic programs is that psychologic first aid is just as important as physical treatment for the injured athlete. Little's findings are essentially in agreement with those of Carmen, Zerman, and Blaine (1968), and Pierce (1969); that is, athletes display fewer neurotic symptoms than nonathletes, but prognosis for the athlete is not favorable once he is referred to a psychiatric service.

On the basis of this review as well as the material contained in the previous section, it seems reasonable to conclude that athletes have consistently been found to differ from nonathletes on a number of personality traits. The athlete tends to be stable and extroverted, with the exception of cross country runners and marathoners who are characterized by introversion. There is some evidence which suggests that even though they might be in need of such attention, athletes are less likely to seek psychiatric service than nonathletes. Once the athlete arrives at a psychiatric service, however, it appears that his prognosis is less favorable than that of the nonathlete.

The Female Athlete

There have been very few investigations directed toward an understanding of the female athlete's personality. Most of the research in this area has taken place within the past four years. However, with increased emphasis on age group competition for the female athlete as well as national tournaments for the college-age female, it is quite likely that personality studies will become more frequent.

The 16 PF was administered to 38 female athletes who participated on the 1964 United States Olympic teams by Peterson, Weber, and Trousdale (1967). This sample consisted of individual sports participants in swimming, diving, riding, fencing, canoeing, gymnastics, and track and field. These subjects were compared to 59 team sport athletes who participated on either the 1964 Olympic Volleyball Team or one of the top ten AAU basketball teams for 1964. The two groups were found to differ on 7 of the 16 factors. The athletes from the individual sports were significantly more dominant and aggressive, adventurous, sensitive, imaginative, radical, self-sufficient, re-sourceful, and less sophisticated than the team sports group. The athletes from the individual sports were more introverted than the team sport athletes, and both groups were characterized by emotional stability. These female athletes were found to be more intelligent, conscientious, persevering, and aggressive than female nonathletes of similar age and educational background.

The findings of Peterson, Weber, and Trousdale (1967) were corroborated by Ogilvie (1968) in part. He compared their results with the 16 PF profiles of female swimmers from San Jose State College who were found to have profiles similar to the individual sport athletes in their study.

A related investigation was conducted by Malumphy (1968), who administered the 16 PF and a personal information questionnaire to 77 female athletes and 43 randomly selected nonathletes from five state universities. Comparisons were made between athletes in team sports, individual sports, team-individual sports, subjectively judged sports, and the nonathletes. The four groups of female athletes differed from the nonathletes on various factors, a result which is in agreement with the report of Peterson, Weber, and Trousdale (1967). Also, the participants in the various sports groups differed on a number of factors. Of major interest was the observation that athletes from individual sports were more extroverted than those athletes from team and team-individual groups. This seems to be in disagreement with the findings of Peterson, Weber, and Trousdale (1967). However, they tested high-level competitors whereas Malumphy's sample only included one Olympic athlete. This might easily explain the apparent contradiction. Malumphy also found that the team sport group was less extroverted than the nonathlete. If this in fact is the case, it would represent a major distinction between the personality of male and female athletes; that is, with the exception of distance runners, male athletes tend to be extroverted.

More recently, Williams and her associates (1970) administered the 16 PF and the EPPS to 30 female fencers who participated in the 1968 national championships. Comparisons were made between high- and low-level achievers, and they were found to differ only on the measure of dominance. Since they did not differ on any of the other 38 variables, this one variation was probably due to chance. However, this group of female athletes was found to differ from national norms on a number of 16 PF factors and EPPS measures. The authors concluded that a definite fencer's personality emerged from their analysis, and this profile was different from that of participants in other sports. In this respect it was reported that "the 'sport type' to which their profile was the most related was the male and female competitive race car driver" (p. 452). In general, these athletes tended to be reserved, self-sufficient, autonomous, assertive, and aggressive, and they scored below average on affiliation and nurturance.

It has previously been demonstrated that participants in psychologic investigations differ from both nonvolunteers and pseudovolunteers (Morgan, 1971). In the study by Williams and her associates (1970), 45 of the 60 participants in the tournament volunteered to complete the tests. Subsequently, 15 of the subjects failed to return the tests. Hence, there were 30 volunteers, 15 pseudovolunteers, and 15 nonvolunteers. It is quite likely that these three groups differed on certain features of the 16 PF and EPPS. Therefore, it is suggested that the "fencer's profile" identified by Williams and her associates be viewed with caution.

The female athlete, like the male athlete, tends to differ from the nonathlete on a number of personality factors. Also, female athletes from different sub-groups tend to differ on various dimensions of personality. On the other hand, we know much less about the personality of the female athlete than the male athlete. Hopefully, investigators concerned with the study of the female athlete will not commit the same methodologic errors which have characterized research with the male athlete. Specifically, it is recommended that investigations be conducted on the personality of the female athlete with the following points in mind: (1) such investigations should be pursued within the framework of a theoretic model, (2) from the very outset an attempt should be made to gather extensive normative data, (3) appropriate sampling procedures and statistical techniques should be employed, (4) rigorous definitions of the dependent and independent variables should be adopted, and (5) a longitudinal model would seem to be necessary.

THEORETIC MODELS

Sport psychologists might elect to employ psychoanalytic, social psychologic, organismic, constitutional, or factor theories in attempting to understand the psychologic foundations of sport and physical activity. Unfortunately, most of the investigations reviewed in this chapter do not appear to have been pursued within the framework of a theoretic model. Those investigators who have elected to employ theoretic models have opted for factor theories such as the Cattellian or Eysenckian as opposed to the Freudian, Lewinian, or Aderian theories. On the other hand, one of the most fruitful and widely cited investigations in this field employed derivations from Freudian theory (Harlow, 1951). Of course, the decision to rely upon factor theory has been a pragmatic one, and in the author's opinion, the preferred choice.

Simply constructing a theoretic model is not sufficient, however. Berger has been one of the few investigators who attempted to understand the athlete's personality within the framework of a theoretic model. In her paper, Berger acknowledged that various athletic sub-groups have been demonstrated to differ in personality measures. She also stated that "little information concerning the possible influences of such differences is available" (Berger, 1971, p. 1). Such a view completely ignores the contributions of Sheldon's constitutional psychology to the understanding of sport (Hall and Lindzey, 1970) since it has been recognized for some time that athletes from various sub-groups are characterized by different somatotypes (Morehouse and

Rasch, 1963). Furthermore, the holistic model used by Kane (1964) which includes Cattellian theory as well as physique and sociometric dimensions demonstrates the efficacy of somatotypic considerations.

As mentioned earlier, several authors have addressed themselves to the question of whether athletes with particular personality types gravitate toward certain sports or whether sport modifies the personality of participants. Following such a review, Singer (1967) concluded that this question could best be answered by longitudinal research. This, of course, would represent the ultimate approach to answering the gravitation versus modification question. However, this would not be the most economic approach. For example, predictions from Eysenckian theory would support the gravitation view. It would seem wise to test out such predictions before engaging in the arduous enterprise of longitudinal inquiry.

More recently, Smith (1970a) has directed his attention toward this same problem, and he has come up with essentially the same conclusions as Singer (1967) and Kroll (1970). Both Smith and Kroll, however, fail to emphasize the necessity of viewing psychologic characteristics as being either states (transitory) or traits (enduring). The major dimensions of personality measured by the EPI are extroversion-introversion (E) and neuroticism-stability (N), which are regarded as traits. Hence, an investigator would not expect athletes to experience shifts in E or N following a season or career in a given sport. Selective mortality occurring between "little league" or "age group" athletics and world-class competition might easily mislead the cross-sectional investigator unless he employed a trait model.

Even though psychologic traits are regarded as stable dimensions of a personality, physical educators have persisted in claiming that sport and physical activity evoke desirable changes in personality. It is not surprising that attempts to support this view have been unsuccessful. Actually, if changes were observed they would tend to serve as an indictment of the psychometric tool rather than reflect the value of sport. On the other hand, shifts in psychologic states have been demonstrated to occur following participation in sport and physical activity (Handlon et al., 1963; Johnson and Hutton, 1955; McPherson et al., 1967; Milverton, 1943; Morgan et al., 1970; Morgan and Hammer, 1971; Morgan et al., 1971).

In contrast to the EPI, the 16 PF contains measures of psychologic characteristics which are thought to be affected by environmental influences as well as factors that are regarded as being fixed by heredity. For this reason, the 16 PF would seem to lend itself to the testing of hypotheses from both a cross-sectional and longitudinal standpoint. It is interesting to note, however, that numerous sport psychologists have demonstrated that significant differences exist between athletic sub-groups and/or nonathletes on various 16 PF factors, and they have then concluded that the evidence did not permit speculation as to whether nature or nurture were involved. Such a practice simply fails to take full advantage of Cattelian theory.

The author and his associates have employed Eysenckian theory in an attempt to understand the relationship between personality and physical performance (Morgan and Coyne, 1965; Morgan et al., 1966; Morgan et al., 1967; Morgan, 1968c; Morgan, 1968d; Lukehart and Morgan, 1969; Morgan and Costill, 1971). Thus far, this approach has seemed to be fruitful in that the EPI and JEPI have been sufficiently sensitive to detect differences between athletes and nonathletes as well as between selected sport groups on the dimensions of extroversion-introversion (E) and neuroticism-stability (N).

A plea is not being made here for adoption of Eysenckian theory in sport psychology, but rather, for investigators to employ meaningful theoretic models in an attempt to understand the psychodynamics of sport. The scope of this chapter does not permit a comprehensive discussion of Eysenckian theory or the reasons the author has adopted this particular theoretic framework. Also, recent publications by Eysenck (1967), Eysenck, Easting, and Eysenck (1971), Eysenck and Eysenck (1970), and Gray (1970) make this task unnecessary. However, it does seem appropriate to present a brief summary of why this model has been employed.

First of all, Eysenckian theory emphasizes the biologic basis of personality (Eysenck, 1967), which lends itself to the study of sport. For example, Eysenck and his followers have postualted and demonstrated relationships between extroverison and variables such as pain tolerance, constancy phenomena, vigilance, conditioning, level of aspiration, and, to a lesser extent, somatotype. Also, the neuroticism factor has been postulated and found to be related to the inherited degree of lability of the autonomic nervous sytem. Further, the extroversion factor has been found to be related to the degree of excitation and inhibition prevalent in the CNS. There is also convincing evidence which suggests that these functions are largely inherited. For this reason, the author has speculated that differences between athletic sub-groups are due to gravitation of certain types rather than the consequence of sport participation.

The Eysencks have pursued the development of the EPI and the JEPI with the most rigorous of psychometric principles serving as guides. Of equal importance has been the attempt of Eysenck and his followers to link up personality with the main body of experimental and theoretic psychology.

SUMMARY

The intention of this chapter has been threefold in that an attempt has been made to (1) state the nature of inquiry in contemporary sport psychology, (2) review the literature dealing with the personality of the athlete, and (3) make recommendations for the improvement of research strategies in this field. A review of contemporary sport psychology reveals that this embryonic, multidisciplinary field has been concerned with the many specialized facets of psychology. Investigations in this field have been concerned with comparative and physiologic psychology, human engineering, motor learning, motivation, perception, personality dynamics, psycho-physiology, mental health, and social psychology. The present chapter emphasized only one of these specialized areas, personality dynamics.

This review of literature indicates that athletes differ from nonathletes in various psychologic characteristics. Also, most investigators in this area have reported that athletes from different athletic sub-groups tend to differ on a variety of personality traits. On the other hand, the results of attempts to elucidate the psychologic differences between athletes of differing perform-ance levels have tended to be equivocal. This is probably due to the homogeneity of variance in the groups examined as well as less than rigorous operational definitions of ability levels. There is evidence, however, which suggests that high-level competitors are quite stable. Indeed, it seems reasonable to state that the lack of neuroticism is probably a prerequisite for high-level performance. While athletes tend to be extroverted, there is evidence which suggests that certain athletic sub-groups are introverted. Although there is considerably less information available on female athletes these same generalizations seem to apply to their behavior in sport.

Numerous methodologic problems have characterized investigations in this area. First and foremost has been the scarcity of theoretic models. A fruitful model derived from Eysenckian theory was briefly reviewed and it was recommended that investigators consider the adoption of factor theories such as those developed by Eysenck and Cattell. Also, while Cattell's 16 PF has been employed extensively, there has been a failure to discuss findings within the context of Cattellian theory. Furthermore, there has been a consistent lack of reference to state and trait theory in attempts to explain differences between athletic sub-groups as well as differences between athletes and nonathletes.

A second methodologic problem has been related to the use of inappropriate sampling techniques. The usual procedure has involved the administration of personality inventories to readily available, intact groups. Unfortunately, there has been an absence of informed consent procedures, and authors have frequently commented that they had "obtained permission from the coach to test the athletes." Such a practice is not only unethical, but it also raises the question of validity since lie, fake, and random response scores have seldom been employed in this research. Furthermore, when actual volunteers (noncoerced subjects) have been employed, there has been no concern for the problems associated with volunteerism in psychologic research.

Most of the studies reviewed in this section have attempted to explain the psychologic foundations of sport in a rather narrow sense; that is, the majority of investigators have limited their inquiry to the responsivity of subjects to standardized tests of personality. It has been recognized for some time that numerous anatomic and physiologic characteristics play an important role in activity selection as well as success in sport. Furthermore, there is also evidence which suggests that sport selection and success are dependent on certain sociologic factors. It is recommended that multi-disciplinary models be developed for the study of sport selection and success in sport. Such models should not only consist of personality theory; they should also be holistic and include sociologic and biologic parameters in their theoretic frameworks.

References

Adatto, C. On play and the psychopathology of golf. Paper presented at the meeting of the New Orleans Psychoanalytic Society, New Orleans, January, 1963.

Alderman, R. B. A sociopsychological assessment of attitude toward physical activity in champion athletes. *Research Quarterly,* 1970, 41, 1–9.

Antonelli, F. (ed.) *Proceedings of the first international congress of sport psychology,* Rome, 1965.

Arnold, P. *Education, physical education and personality development.* New York: Atherton Press, 1968.

Behrman, R. M. Personality differences between nonswimmers and swimmers. *Research Quarterly,* 1967, 38, 163–171.

Beisser, A. R. Psychodynamic observations of a sport. *Psychoanalytic Review,* 1961, 48, 69–76.

Beisser, A. R. *The madness in sports.* New York: Appleton-Century-Crofts, 1967.

Berger, B. G. Effect of temporal-spatial uncertainty, probability of physical harm, and nature of competition upon selected personality characteristics of athletes. Paper presented at the meeting of the North American Society for the Psychology of Sport and Physical Activity, Detroit, April, 1971.

Berger, R. A., & Littlefield, D. H. Comparison between football athletes and nonathletes on personality. *Research Quarterly,* 1969, 40, 663–665.

Blonstein, L. Some psychological observations on amateur boxers. *Journal of Sports Medicine & Physical Fittness,* 1964, 4, 247.

Booth, E. G., Jr. Personality traits of athletes as measured by the MMPI. *Research Quarterly,* 1958, 29, 127–138.

Borg, G. A. V. Physical performance and perceived exertion. *Lund Studies in Psychology and Education,* 1962, No. 11.

Borg, G., & Linderholm, H. Exercise performance and perceived exertion in patients with coronary insufficiency, arterial hypertension and vasoregulatory asthenia. *Acta Medica Scandinavica,* 1970, 187, 17–26.

Brunner, B. C. Personality and motivating factors influencing adult participation in vigorous physical activity. *Research Quarterly,* 1969, 40, 464–469.

Carmen, L. R., Zerman, J. L., & Blaine, G. B., Jr. Use of the Harvard psychiatric service by athletes and nonathletes, *Mental Hygiene,* 1968, 52, 134–137.

Cattell, R. B. Some psychological correlates of physical fitness and physique. In *Exercise and Fitness.* Chicago: Athletic Institute, 1960, pp. 138–151.

Cattell, R. B., & Eber, H. W. *Manual for the sixteen personality factor questionnaire.* San Diego, Educational and Industrial Testing Service, 1962.

Cavanaugh, J. O. Relation of recreation to personality adjustment. *Journal of Social Psychology,* 1942, 15, 63–74.

Cofer, C. N., & Johnson, W. R. Personality dynamics in relation to exercise and sports. In W. R. Johnson (ed.), *Science & Medicine of Exercise & Sports.* New York: Harper, 1960, pp. 525–529.

Cooper, L. Athletics, activity, and personality: a review of the literature, *Research Quarterly,* 1969, 40, 17–22.

Cooper, L., & Caston, J. Physical activity and increases in *M* response. *Journal of Projective Techniques & Personality Assessment,* 1970, 34, 295–301.

Cratty, B. J. A three-level theory of perceptual-motor behavior. *Quest,* 1966, Monograph VI. 3–10.

Cratty, B. J. *Movement behavior and motor learning.* (2nd ed.) Philadelphia: Lea & Febiger, 1967.

Cratty, B. J. *Psychology and physical activity.* Englewood Cliffs, N.J.: Prentice-Hall, 1968.

Cureton, T. K. Improvement of psychological states by means of exercise-fitness programs. *Journal Association of Physical & Mental Rehabilitation,* 1963, 17, 14–25.

Dawson, C. A., & Horvath, S. M. Swimming in small laboratory animals. *Medicine & Science in Sports,* 1970, 2, 51-78.

Deutsch, H. A contribution to the psychology of sport. *International Journal of Psychoanalysis,* 1926, 7, 223–227.

Docktor, R., & Sharkey, B. J. Note on some physiological and subjective reactions to exercise and training. *Perceptual & Motor Skills,* 1971, 32, 233–234.

Dodwell, P. C., & Bessant, D. E. Learning without swimming in a water maze. *Journal of Comparative and Physiological Psychology,* 1960, 53, 422–425.

Drowatzky, J. N. Relationship of size constancy to selected measures of motor ability. *Research Quarterly,* 1967, 38, 375–379.

Eysenck, H. J. *Dimensions of personality.* (1st ed.) London: Kegan Paul, 1947.

Eysenck, H. J. *The biological basis of personality.* Springfield, Ill.: Charles C Thomas, 1967.

Eysenck, H. J., & Eysenck, S. B. G. *Manual for the Eysenck personality inventory.* Educational & Industrial Testing Service: San Diego, 1962.

Eysenck, S. B. G., & Eysenck, H. J. A factor-analytic study of the lie scale of the junior Eysenck personality inventory. *Personality,* 1970, 1, 3–10.

Eysenck, H. J., Easting, G., & Eysenck, S. B. G. Personality measurement in children: A dimensional approach. *Journal of Special Education,* 1971, 4, 261–268.

Fine, B. J. Introversion-extraversion and motor vehicle driver behavior. *Perceptual & Motor Skills,* 1963, 12, 95–100.

Flanagan, L. A study of some personality traits of different physical activity groups. *Research Quarterly,* 1951, 22, 312–323.

Fletcher, R., & Dowell, L. Selected personality characteristics of high school athletes and nonathletes. *Journal of Psychology,* 1971, 77, 39–41.

Franks, B. D., & Jetté, M. Manifest anxiety and physical fitness. *Proceedings of the National College Physical Education Association for Men,* 1969, 73, 48–57.

Frankenhaeuser, M., Post, B., Nordheden, B., & Sjoeberg, H. Physiological and subjective reactions to different physical work loads. *Perceptual & Motor Skills,* 1969, 28, 343–349.

Golas, R. W. A comparative study of two personality dimensions in athletes and non-participants. Paper presented at the meeting of the Eastern District Association for Health, Physical Education, and Recreation, Philadelphia, April, 1971.

Gordon, H. L., Rosenberg, D., & Morris, W. E. Leisure activities of schizophrenic patients after return to the community. *Mental Hygiene,* 1966, 50, 452–459.

Gray, J. A. The psychophysiological basis of introversion-extrovation. *Behavior Research & Therapy,* 1970, 8, 249–266.

Griffith, C. R. *Psychology of coaching.* New York: Charles Scribner's Sons, 1928.

Hahner, R. H., & Rochelle, R. H. A comparison of autonomic nervous system activity between physically trained and untrained individuals. *Research Quarterly,* 1968, 39, 975–982.

Hall, C. S., & Lindzey, G. *Theories of personality.* (1st ed.) New York: John Wiley & Sons, Inc., 1970.

Hammer, W. M. Status of sport psychology in Western Europe and the Far East. *Journal of Sports Medicine & Physical Fitness,* 1970, 10, 114–121.

Handlon, J. H., Byrd, O. E., & Gaines, J. D. Psychometric measurement of the relief of tension by moderate exercise. *Journal California Physical Education Association,* 1963, 26, 4–7.

Harlow, R. G. Masculine inadequacy and compensatory development of physique. *Journal of Personality,* 1951, 19, 312–323.

Harmon, J. M., & Johnson, W. R. The emotional reactions of college athletes. *Research Quarterly*, 1952, 23, 391–397.

Henry, F. M. Personality differences in athletes, physical education, and aviation students. *Psychological Bulletin*, 1941, 38, 745.

Henry, F. M. Increased response latency for complicated movements and a "memory drum" theory of neuromotor reaction. *Research Quarterly*, 1960, 31, 448–458.

Howell, M. L., & Alderman, R. B. Psychological determinants of fitness. *Canadian Medical Association Journal*, 1967, 96, 721–726.

Hunt, D. H. A cross racial comparison of personality traits between athletes and nonathletes. *Research Quarterly*, 1969, 40, 704–707.

Husman, B. F. Aggression in boxers and wrestlers as measured by projective techniques. *Research Quarterly*, 1955, 26, 421–425.

Ibrahim, H. Comparison of temperament traits among intercollegiate athletes and physical education majors. *Research Quarterly*, 1967, 38, 615–622.

Ibrahim, H. Recreational preference and personality. *Research Quarterly*, 1969, 40, 76–82.

Imhof, P. R., Blatter, K., Fuccella, L. M., & Turri, M. Beta-blockade and emotional tachycardia: Radiotelemetric investigations in ski jumpers. *Journal of Applied Physiology*, 1969, 27, 366–369.

Johnson, W. R. A study of emotion revealed in two types of athletic sports contests. *Research Quarterly*, 1949, 20, 72–79.

Johnson, W. R. Psychogalvanic and word association studies in athletes. *Research Quarterly*, 1951, 22, 427–433.

Johnson, W. R., & Hutton, D. C. Effects of a combative sport upon personality dynamics as measured by a projective test. *Research Quarterly*, 1955, 26, 49–53.

Johnson, W. R., Hutton, D. C., & Johnson, G. B. Personality traits of some champion athletes as measured by two projective tests: The Rorschach and H-T-P. *Research Quarterly*, 1954, 25, 484–485.

Kane, J. E. Psychological correlates of physique and physical abilities. In E. Jokl & E. Simon (eds.), *International Research in Sport and Physical Education*, Springfield, Ill.: Charles C Thomas, 1964, pp. 85–94.

Kellermann, J. J., Wintner, I., & Kariv, I. Effect of physical training on neurocirculatory asthenia. *Israel Journal of Medicine*, 1969, 5, 947–949.

Kenyon, G. S. Six scales for assessing attitude toward physical activity. *Research Quarterly*, 1968, 39, 566–574.

Kenyon, G. S. (ed.) *Contemporary psychology of sport: Proceedings of the second international congress.* Chicago: Athletic Institute, 1970.

Keogh, J. Relationship of motor ability and athletic participation in certain standardized personality measures. *Research Quarterly*, 1959, 30, 438–445.

Klausner, S. Z. Sport parachuting. In R. Slovenko & J. A. Knight (eds.), *Motivation in play, games and sports.* Springfield, Ill.: Charles C Thomas, 1967, pp. 670–694.

Kroll, W. Sixteen personality factor profiles of collegiate wrestlers. *Research Quarterly*, 1967, 38, 49–57.

Kroll, W. Personality assessments of athletes. In L. E. Smith (ed.), *Psychology of motor learning.* Chicago: Athletic Institute, 1970, pp. 349–367.

Kroll, W., & Carlson, R. B. Discriminant function and hierarchial grouping analysis of karate participants' personality profiles. *Research Quarterly*, 1967, 38, 405–411.

Kroll, W., & Lewis, G. M. America's first sports psychologist. *Quest, Monograph XIII*, 1–4, 1970.

Kroll, W., & Petersen, K. H. Personality factor profiles of collegiate football teams. *Research Quarterly*, 1965, 36, 433–440.

La Cava, G. The role of sport in therapy. *Journal of Sports Medicine & Physical Fitness*, 1967, 7, 57–60.

Lakie, W. L. Personality characteristics of certain groups of intercollegiate athletes. *Research Quarterly*, 1962, 33, 566–573.

Lakie, W. L. Relationship of galvanic skin response to task difficulty, personality traits, and motivations. *Research Quarterly*, 1967, 38, 58–63.

La Place, J. P. Personality and its relationship to success in professional baseball. *Research Quarterly,* 1954, 25, 313–319.

Layman, E. M. *Mental health through physical education and recreation.* Minneapolis: Burgess, 1955.

Lentz, T. F. Evidence for a science of recreational guidance. *Research Quarterly,* 1943, 14, 310–320.

Little, J. C. The athlete's neurosis—a deprivation crisis. *Acta Psychiatrica Scandinavica,* 1969, 45, 187–197.

Loy, J. W., Jr., & Kenyon, G. S. *Sport, culture, and society.* New York: Macmillan, 1969.

Lukehart, R., & Morgan, W. P. The effect of a season of interscholastic football on the personality of junior high school males. Paper presented at the meeting of the American Association for Health, Physical Education, & Recreation, Boston, April, 1969.

Malina, R. M. Effects of varied information feedback practice conditions on throwing speed and accuracy. *Research Quarterly,* 1969, 40, 134–145.

Malumphy, T. M. Personality of women athletes in intercollegiate competition. *Research Quarterly,* 1968, 39, 610–620.

Martens, R. Effect on performance of learning a complex motor task in the presence of spectators. *Research Quarterly,* 1969, 40, 317–323.

Martens, R., & Landers, D. M. Coaction effects of a muscular endurance task. *Research Quarterly,* 1969, 40, 733–737.

Martin, A. R. Idle hands and giddy minds: Our psychological and emotional unpreparedness for free time. *American Journal of Psychoanalysis,* 1969, 29, 147–156.

Martin, L. A., & Seymour, E. W. Effects of competition upon the aggressive responses of college athletes. APA Experimental Publication System, 1969, No. 073C.

McPherson, B. D., Paivio, A., Yuhasz, M. S., Rechnitzer, P. A., Pickard, H. A., & Lefcoe, N. M. Psychological effects of an exercise program for post-infarct and normal adult men. *Journal of Sports Medicine & Physical Fitness,* 1967, 7, 95–102.

Menninger, W. Recreation and mental health. *Recreation,* 1948, 42, 340–346.

Millar, S. *The psychology of play.* Baltimore: Penguin, 1968.

Milverton, E. J. An experimental investigation into the effects of physical training on personality. *British Journal of Educational Psychology,* 1943, 13, 30–38.

Mongillo, B. B. Psychological aspects in sports and psychosomatic problems in the athlete. *Rhode Island Medical Journal,* 1968, 51, 339–343.

Montgomery, K. C. The effect of activity deprivation upon exploratory behavior. *Journal of Comparative & Physiological Psychology,* 1953, 46, 438–441.

Moore, R. A. *Sports and mental health.* Springfield, Ill.: Charles C Thomas, 1966.

Mordy, M. A., & Locke, L. F. (eds.) *Psychology of sport. Quest, Monograph XIII,* 1970.

Morehouse, L. E., & Rasch, P. J. *Sports medicine for trainers.* Philadelphia: Saunders, 1963.

Morgan, W. P. Psychological considerations. *Journal of Health, Physical Education and Recreation,* 1968, 39, 26–28. (a)

Morgan, W. P. Selected physiological and psychomotor correlates of depression in psychiatric patients. *Research Quarterly,* 1968, 39, 1037–1043. (b)

Morgan, W. P. Personality characteristics of wrestlers participating in the world championships. *Journal of Sports Medicine & Physical Fitness,* 1968, 8, 212–216. (c)

Morgan, W. P. Extraversion-neuroticism and athletic performance. Symposium presented at the meeting of the American College of Sports Medicine, State College, Pennsylvania, May, 1968. (d)

Morgan, W. P. Physical fitness and emotional health: A review. *American Corrective Therapy Journal,* 1969, 23, 124–127. (a)

Morgan, W. P. A pilot investigation of physical working capacity in depressed and non-depressed psychiatric males. *Research Quarterly,* 1969, 40, 859–861. (b)

Morgan, W. P. Selected psychometric considerations. 1970, *Quest, Monograph XIII,* 5–11. (a)

Morgan, W. P. Pre-match anxiety in a group of college wrestlers. *International Journal of Sport Psychology,* 1970, 1, 7–13. (b)

Morgan, W. P. Psychological effect of weight reduction in the college wrestler. *Medicine and Science in Sports,* 1970, 2, 24–27. (c)

Morgan, W. P. Physical working capacity in depressed and non-depressed psychiatric females: A preliminary study. *American Corrective Therapy Journal,* 1970, 24, 14–16. (d)

Morgan, W. P. (ed.). *Contemporary readings in sport psychology.* Springfield, Ill.: Charles C Thomas, 1970. (e)

Morgan, W. P. Physical fitness correlates of psychiatric hospitalization. In G. S. Kenyon (ed.), *Contemporary psychology of sport.* Chicago: Athletic Institute, 1970, pp. 297–300. (f)

Morgan, W. P. (ed.). *Ergogenic aids and muscular performance.* New York: Academic Press, 1972.

Morgan, W. P., & Costill, D. L. Psychological characteristics of the marathon runner. *Journal of Sports Medicine & Physical Fitness,* 1972, in press.

Morgan, W. P., & Coyne, L. L. The effect of stereotyped suggestion on the expression of muscular strength and endurance. Paper presented at the meeting of the American Congress of Physical Medicine and Rehabilitation, Philadelphia, August, 1965.

Morgan, W. P., & Hammer, W. M. Psychological effect of competitive wrestling. Paper presented at the meeting of the American Association for Health, Physical Education, & Recreation, Detroit, April, 1971.

Morgan, W. P., Cooper, J. K., & Goeckerman, R. W. Personality, muscular performance, and placebo reaction: A double-blind study. Paper presented at the meeting of the American College of Sports Medicine, Las Vegas, March, 1967.

Morgan, W. P., Needle, R. H., & Coyne, L. L. Psychophysical phenomena and muscular performance. Paper presented at the meeting of the American Association for Health, Physical Education, & Recreation, Chicago, April, 1966.

Morgan, W. P., Roberts, J. A., Brand, F. R., & Feinerman, A. D. Psychological effect of chronic physical activity. *Medicine and Science in Sports,* 1970, 2, 213–217.

Morgan, W. P., Raven, P. B., Drinkwater, B. L., & Horvath, S. M. Perceptual and metabolic responsivity to standard bicycle ergometry following various hypnotic suggestions.

Morgan, W. P., Roberts, J. A., & Feinerman, A. D. Psychological effect of acute physical activity. *Archives of Physical Medicine and Rehabilitation,* 1972.

Naughton, J., Bruhn, J. G., & Lategola, M. T. Effects of physical training on physiologic and behavioral characteristics of cardiac patients. *Archives of Physical Medicine and Rehabilitation,* 1968, 49, 131–137.

Newman, E. N. Personality traits of faster and slower competitive swimmers. *Research Quarterly,* 1968, 39, 1049–1053.

Ogilvie, B. C. Psychological consistencies within the personality of high-level competitors. *Journal of the American Medical Association,* 1968, 205, 156–162.

Ogilvie, B. C., & Tutko, T. A. *Problem athletes and how to handle them.* London: Pelham, 1966.

Parsons, D. R. Personality traits of national representative swimmers–Canada, 1962. Unpublished master's thesis, University of British Columbia, 1963.

Peterson, S. L., Weber, J. C., & Trousdale, W. W. Personality traits of women in team sports vs. women in individual sports. *Research Quarterly,* 1967, 38, 686–690.

Pierce, R. A. Athletes in psychotherapy: How many, how come? *Journal of American College Health Association.* 1969, 17, 244–249.

Pierson, W. R., & Rasch, P. J. Effect of knowledge of results on isometric strength scores. *Research Quarterly,* 1964, 35, 313–315.

Pitts, F. N., Jr., & McClure, J. N., Jr. Lactate metabolism in anxiety neurosis. *New England Journal of Medicine,* 1967, 277, 1329–1336.

Pyecha, J. Comparative effects of judo and selected physical education activities on male university freshman personality traits. *Research Quarterly,* 1970, 41, 425–431.

Rasch, P. J. Neuroticism and extraversion in United States intercollegiate wrestlers.

Journal of the Association of Physical and Mental Rehabilitation, 1962, 16, 153–154.

Rasch, P. J., & Hunt, M. B. Some personality attributes of champion amateur wrestlers. *Journal of the Association of Physical and Mental Rehabilitation,* 1960, 14, 163–164.

Robb, M. Feedback and skill learning. *Research Quarterly,* 1968, 39, 175–184.

Roberts, G. C., & Martens, R. Social reinforcement and complex motor performance. *Research Quarterly,* 1970, 41, 175–181.

Rudik, P. A. Fifty years of psychology of sport in the USSR. *Soviet Psychology,* 1967, 13, 59–74.

Rushall, B. S. An investigation of the relationship between personality variables and performance categories in swimmers. *International Journal of Sport Psychology,* 1970, 1, 93–104.

Ryan, E. D. Relationship between motor performance and arousal. *Research Quarterly,* 1962, 33, 279–287.

Ryan, E. D. The relationship of galvanic skin conductance to ring-peg performance. *Research Quarterly,* 1963, 34, 526–528.

Ryan, E. D., & Foster, R. L. Athletic participation and perceptual augmentation and reduction. *Journal of Personality & Social Psychology,* 1967, 6, 472–476.

Ryan, E. D., & Kovacic, C. R. Pain tolerance and athletic participation. *Perceptual & Motor Skills,* 1966, 22, 383–390.

Sage, G. H. (ed.). *Sport and American society: Selected readings.* Reading: Addison-Wesley, 1970.

Schendel, J. Psychological differences between athletes and non-participants in athletics at three educational levels. *Research Quarterly,* 1965, 36, 52–67.

Scott, J. P. Sport and aggression. In G. S. Kenyon, (ed.) *Contemporary psychology of sport.* Chicago: Athletic Institute, 1970, pp. 11–24.

Seymour, E. W. Comparative study of certain behavior characteristics of participant and non-participant boys in Little League baseball. *Research Quarterly,* 1956, 27, 338–346.

Singer, R. N. Effect of spectators on athletes and non-athletes performing a gross motor task. *Research Quarterly,* 1965, 36, 473–483.

Singer, R. N. Athletic participation: Cause or result of certain personality factors. *Physical Educator,* 1967, 24, 169–171.

Singer, R. N. *Motor learning and human performance.* New York: Macmillan, 1968.

Singer, R. N. Personality differences between and within baseball and tennis players. *Research Quarterly,* 1969, 40, 582–588.

Singer, R. N. Effect of an audience on performance of a motor task. *Journal of Motor Behavior,* 1970, 2, 88–95.

Skinner, J. S., Borg, G. A. V., & Buskirk, E. R. Physiological and perceptual reactions to exertion of young men differing in activity and body size. In B. D. Franks (ed.) *Exercise and fitness.* Chicago: Athletic Institute, 1969, pp. 53–66.

Skubic, E. Emotional responses of boys to Little League and Middle League competitive baseball. *Research Quarterly,* 1955, 26, 342–352.

Slovenko, R., & Knight, J. A. (eds.) *Motivations in play, games and sports.* Springfield, Ill.: Charles C Thomas, 1967.

Slusher, H. S. Personality and intelligence characteristics of selected high school athletes and non-athletes. *Research Quarterly,* 1964, 35, 539–545.

Slusher, H. S. Perceptual differences of selected football players, dancers, and non-performers to a given stimulus. *Research Quarterly,* 1966, 37, 424–428. (a)

Slusher, H. S. Overt and covert reactions of selected athletes to normative situations as indicated by an electronic psychometer. *Research Quarterly,* 1966, 37, 540–552. (b)

Smith, L. E. Personality and performance research—new theories and directions required. 1970, *Quest, Monograph XIII,* 74–83. (a)

Smith, L. E. (ed.) *Psychology of motor learning.* Chicago: Athletic Institute, 1970. (b)

Straub, W. F., & Davis, S. W. Personality traits of college football players who participated at different levels of competition. *Medicine and Science in Sports,* 1971, 3, 39–43.

Sutton-Smith, B., Roberts, J. M., & Kozelka, R. M. Game involvement in adults. *Journal of Social Psychology*, 1963, 60, 15–30.

Thune, A. R. Personality of weight lifters. *Research Quarterly*, 1949, 20, 296–306.

Tillman, K. Relationship between physical fitness and selected personality traits. *Research Quarterly*, 1965, 36, 483–489.

Uhrbrock, R. S. Laterality of champion athletes. *Journal of Motor Behavior*, 1970, 2, 285–291.

Ulrich, C. Measurement of stress evidenced by college women in situations involving competition. *Research Quarterly*, 1957, 28, 160–172.

Vanek, M., & Cratty, B. J. *Psychology and the superior athlete.* New York: Macmillan, 1970.

Weber, J. C., & Lee, R. A. Effects of differing prepuberty exercise programs on the emotionality of male albino rats. *Research Quarterly*, 1968, 39, 748–751.

Welker, W. I. Some determinants of play and exploration in chimpanzees. *Journal of Comparative and Physiological Psychology*, 1956, 49, 84–89.

Weltman, G., & Egstrom, G. H. Personal autonomy of scuba diver trainees. *Research Quarterly*, 1969, 40, 613–618.

Werner, A. C. Physical education and the development of leadership characteristics of cadets at the United States Military Academy. Unpublished doctoral dissertation, Springfield College, Springfield, Mass., 1960.

Werner, A. C., & Gottheil, E. Personality development and participation in college athletics. *Research Quarterly*, 1966, 37, 126–131.

Whiting, H. T. A., & Stembridge, D. E. Personality and the persistent non-swimmer. *Research Quarterly*, 1965, 36, 348–356.

Whitman, R. M. Psychoanalytic speculations about play: Tennis–the duel. *Psychoanalytic Review*, 1969, 56, 197–214.

Williams, J. M., Hoepner, B. J., Moody, D. L., & Ogilvie, B. C. Personality traits of champion level female fencers. *Research Quarterly*, 1970, 41, 446–453.

Yanada, H., & Hirata, H. Personality traits of students who dropped out of their athletic clubs. *Proceedings of the College of Physical Education*, University of Tokyo, 1970, No. 5.

Chapter 9

SPECIAL EDUCATION

BRYANT J. CRATTY

University of California, Los Angeles

INTRODUCTION

Special education is that branch of education dealing with atypical children. These children may evidence orthopaedic problems, learning deficiencies of several kinds, emotional disturbances, sensory abnormalities including hearing or visual impairment, and/or some kind of neurologic impairments manifested in varying degrees of perceptual-motor malfunction.

There are several common fallacies prevalent concerning children within programs of special education. A first is that most atypical children only evidence a single type of problem and thus their placement in a given program is rendered easy. In truth, more often than not, a child will have several concomitant deficiencies in his makeup, and the one which seems most critical in stunting his development is the one which determines the type of program to which he is exposed. Thus a blind child may, for example, evidence degrees of emotional disturbance and/or neurologic impairment manifest in motor problems; the severely retarded child usually evidences parallel motor problems; while the orthopaedically handicapped child is sometimes beset with problems of personal adjustment. Thus the program of remedial education in which a given atypical child finds himself is dependent upon a subjective decision, which in turn is based upon the most obvious and dramatic deficiency which he seems to evidence.

A second misconception by some whose knowledge about special education may only be superficial is that children may be neatly categorized as either neurologically impaired or normal, as emotionally disturbed or well-adjusted and the like. In truth, I believe it is more accurate to consider

229

children and the abilities they manifest or the problems they present on various continuums. For example, there is a good percentage of normal children who may be considered well functioning motorically in every way; however, about 15 to 20 percent of a population of normal children may have minimal neurologic problems. Many children have moderate emotional problems which do not preclude their participation in normal classrooms while some children with slight to moderate degrees of visual impairment are found within most elementary school classrooms. A reasonably substantial percent of all elementary school classroom populations evidences some kind of learning problem in one or two areas of the curriculum. However, to be classified as retarded a child must usually score below about 80 on one of the standardized I.Q. tests.

Programs in special education are found within various administrative arrangements in both public and private schools. Some are conducted in separate residential schools in which the children reside most of the time.

Others are held in private or public day schools containing only children with some kind of impairment(s). Other classes in special education are found within regular elementary or secondary schools. A blind child in this latter context may, for example, spend an hour or more a day learning braille, while during the remainder of his day he is in regular classes with sighted companions.

MOTOR ACTIVITY IN SPECIAL EDUCATION

Within the past two centuries, the rise of an enlightened naturalistic philosophy within education and in society in general spawned by the new outlook of Renaissance Europe began to encourage interest in just how some of the abnormal posturings of the physically handicapped, the emotional problems of the disturbed, and the intellectual handicaps of the retarded might be changed. These early beginnings of concern were seen during the first decades of the nineteenth century when some educators began to explore programs incorporating movement experiences for the mentally impaired and the physically subnormal.

The role of exercise and games of various kinds permeates the medical specialties of physical medicine, neurology, and the like, and the paramedical professions of physical therapist, occupational therapist, and recreational therapist. At the same time, however, movement activities have been for years incorporated into programs for the retarded and for children evidencing various sensory handicaps. For example, within the past century, Itard (1932) and Seguin (1846) began to advocate various motor experiences for atypical children while shortly after the turn of the century Maria Montessori, working with retarded children in the slums of Rome, began to explore the manner in which activities, including manipulative tasks, contributed to perceptual and intellectual unfolding (Montessori, 1914).

Following World War II, there was a renewed interest in the manner in which movement experience might aid the capacities of children other than those evidencing obvious movement deficiencies. The manner in which the psychologic health of the perceptually confused and often hyperactive child with minimal neurologic impairment might be improved with various coordination tasks was dealt with in a 1947 text by Strauss and Lehtinen while in the 1950's other monographs and books (Getman, 1952; Oliver, 1958) spurred the educators' interest in the role of motor activities in the education of the normal as well as the atypical child. Within the 1960's this interest reached even greater heights due to the publication of various research studies dealing with motor activity and sensory, learning, and emotional handicaps. Impetus was also given to further explorations of the role of physical education, recreation, and various structured programs of motor activity for atypical children funded by private foundations as well as by federal agencies.

In the paragraphs which follow the interactions of movement experiences, motor ability traits, and various other facets of the personalities of atypical children will be illuminated. Studies of children diagnosed as physically and/or orthopaedically handicapped will not be given extensive treatment for, by definition, these children are primarily identifiable by means of the existence of movement problems. Those etiologic, corrective, and subtle and obvious nuances deserve more discussion than is available within the pages of this chapter.[1]

Emphasis will be placed upon a review and interpretation of the literature pairing psychomotor activities and various problems evidenced by children and youth labeled mentally retarded, those possessing various sensory handicaps including the deaf and the blind as well as those diagnosed as evidencing minimal neurologic impairments. Two primary types of investigations will be surveyed: (a) those which in some way describe the various attributes of the children and youth under consideration, with primary emphasis upon data emanating from correlational and factorial studies; and (b) to survey evidence which may illuminate the manner in which several kinds of motor activity programs may aid these children to somehow change not only their movement behaviors but other facets of their personalities.

The concluding section of the chapter contains a summary of the information presented, and implications which the presently available data may hold for physical educators and special educators as they work with children. Researchers who may possibly be interested in further expanding their knowledge about the general topic area scrutinized may also locate guideposts in the final part of this section of the book.

---

[1] A review of work on the physically handicapped may be found in Licht's survey reference (Licht, 1965).

THE RETARDED

Introduction

The two previously cited references produced in the last century dealing with the education of the retarded are the first of which I am aware containing descriptions of various programs which utilized psychomotor behavior as a teaching modality (Juurmaa, 1965; Seguin, 1846). The writings of Montessori (1914) and others after the turn of the century similarly contained descriptions of methods rather than the more penetrating and scientific exploration of the movement capacities of retarded children and adults which have appeared in recent years.

Not until the 1950's, however, were definitive investigations available whose data has been treated with a reasonable degree of sophistication and precision and which dealt with various motor attributes of the retarded.[2]

Studies of retarded children's motor abilities may be classified within several categories. Although some of these subdivisions contain little viable evidence, they include children or youth classified as follows: 1) profoundly retarded, 2) severely retarded, 3) trainable, or 4) educable retardate. Within each of these four categories are those who can be classified as retarded from causes termed either exogenous or endogenous (that is, retardation due to external cultural factors or to genetically based, inherent factors).

Furthermore, studies of the ability of retarded children or youth to learn motor skills may be reviewed. Investigations (either correlational studies or factor analyses) may be surveyed which describe ability-trait structure, and interrelationships of performance scores elicited from the retarded. Another type of study that is appearing with increased frequency in the literature is that which explores possible causal effects of some program of physical education or motor education applied over a time span upon other abilities of retarded children and youth. These studies may be perhaps better understood by studying figure 9-1.

The review which follows is meant to be a survey rather than a penetrating consideration of all the available literature on the subject. For a more thorough coverage, the reader might consult the various texts listed in the bibliography (e.g., Cratty, 1966; Malpass, 1963).

Motor Abilities of the Retarded

In general, most groups of retarded children and youth perform the skills of many simple and complex motor ability tests at levels beneath those achieved by normal groups of the same age and sex. In studies by Francis and Rarick (1960), for example, the mean grip strength of retarded boys and girls

---

[2] A review of the studies from 1945 to 1961 may be found in Malpass's chapter in Ellis' *Handbook of Mental Deficiency* (Malpass, 1963).

THREE DIMENSIONS OF STUDIES DEALING WITH
THE PSYCHOMOTOR ABILITIES OF RETARDED CHILDREN

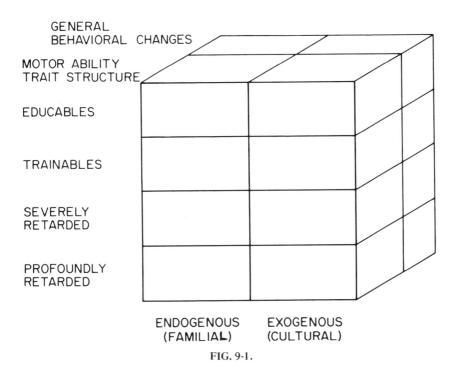

FIG. 9-1.

was inferior to the scores in these same tests achieved by normal children of the same ages (eight to twelve years). Other measures utilized by these scholars included running speed, jumping and throwing for distance, agility (squat thrusts), and balance beam walking. Although both the retarded and normal groups improved as a function of age in the various tests, differences between the two groups increased as they grew older. This difference in scores of the older retarded and normal children was most marked in the more complex skills (standing broad jump, distance throw and the squat thrust measures).

There is more likely to be more marked motor impairment in groups of the retarded children and youth successively lower on the mental scale. For example, in a study I found that groups of trainables were significantly poorer than educables in each test of a six-category battery including measures of balance, agility, locomotor ability, ball throwing and catching, and body part identification (Cratty, 1966).

These differences are due to several factors. More children whose mental retardation is due to endogenous factors accompanied by neurologic impairment of a moderate or pronounced degree reflected in coordination problems are likely to be found within the trainable category than in the more capable educable category.

In an investigation carried out a few years ago by the Joseph P. Kennedy, Jr. Foundation, the expected hypothesis, that a lack of good physical education programs can exert a significant influence upon the motor abilities of retarded children, was substantiated. In this study higher motor ability test scores were obtained from children who had been exposed to more extended periods of physical education during the school year than from children who had little or no formal programs of physical education interposed into their school day (Rarick, Widdop, and Broadhead, 1967).

Several trends are seen in the ability-trait patterns obtained when various ability scores of retarded children are subjected to various kinds of correlational and factor analyses. For example, it is usual to find that there will be a higher correlation between I.Q. and motor ability when the test of the latter quality is reasonably complex. Most studies, including those by Rabin (1957), Distefano and his associates (1958), and Malpass (1963), have produced data which indicate low to moderate positive correlations between measures of motor ability (the Lincoln-Oseretsky has been a favored instrument), and tests of I.Q. as measured by the Stanford-Binet and the Wechsler Intelligence Scale for Children.

A second trend seen in the more recent literature, and particularly in the ambitious research program reported by Clausen, is that the ability-trait structure (including motor ability test scores) becomes more diffuse and complex as the I.Q. increases (Clausen, 1966).

Overall, Clausen suggests, upon reference to his data, that the proliferation and diffusion of discrete ability traits in retarded children normally reach the degree of diffusion seen in normal children who are ten years old and then terminates. Whereas the ability-trait structure of normal children continues to become more complex after the age of ten, the groups of retardates Clausen tested did evidence this same increase in complexity, even in adolescence (Clausen, 1966).

I obtained similar results in a study carried out in 1966. The common variance obtained between the motor ability scores in a six-category test on the part of trainables was about 25 percent (based upon an average r, using the z score conversion method, of .55). On the other hand, when the scores of educables on the same test battery were contrasted the average inter-correlation obtained was .32 (a common variance of about 10 percent) (Cratty, 1966).

The increased tendency of retardates to evidence general and not highly diffused abilities is also seen in another part of Clausen's data. He found that when the scores of retarded children were subjected to a factor analysis, a general factor emerged which was contributed to by as many as 29 tests (about half of which involved some component of motor ability), whereas in the normal populations a general factor was obtained which was contributed to by only 10 tests (loading .30 or above).

Differentiation of abilities is thought to be a process whereby various psychologic functions change from homogeneity to relative heterogeneity. Hebb (1949), Lewin (1946), and Werner have suggested that through maturation, a continuous process of both differentiation and integration takes place within normal individuals.

Retardation, the cited data suggest, results in a blunting of these two processes. More than that, however, the findings of these and other studies point out that the ability-trait structures of retarded children and youth may also be qualitatively different from that of a normal individual.

Another interesting finding was uncovered by both Cratty and Clausen. Motor ability test scores by various groups of retardates during late childhood and adolescence were often significantly lower than scores in the same tests obtained from groups of younger retarded children (Cratty, 1966; Clausen, 1966)! Again, in opposition to the trend usually obtained when groups of normal children are exposed to tests of motor ability, this phenomenon has been explained by these authors as perhaps reflecting a kind of "failure

THE MANNER IN WHICH ABILITY TRAITS DIFFUSE
IN VARIOUS GROUPS OF RETARDATES

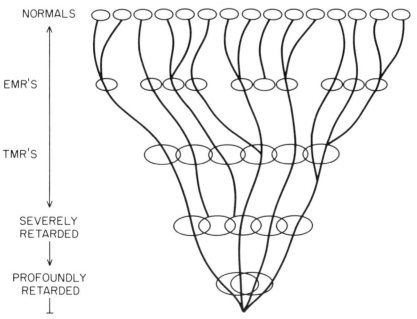

FIG. 9-2.

syndrome" caused by the fact that older retardates do not seem to be highly motivated to perform due to a lifetime of little success. They may have reduced motor capacities also because of a chain reaction between perceived failure, a lack of inclination to participate in vigorous gross motor activities, and a reluctance to engage in the more complex and difficult fine motor skills.

Indeed, in a previous factor analysis by McKinney in which he used rather subjective daily observations of behavior exhibited by 48 severely retarded boys, a quality named "purposefulness" emerged (McKinney, 1962). Most investigators including Clausen have emphasized the extent to which effort, initiative, and the ability of the retarded child to adjust his level of arousal commensurate with the task, markedly influence the level of performance scores obtained (Clausen, p. 126).[3]

Very seldom, however, do investigators attempt to describe adequately the populations of the retarded children with whom they are dealing. Clausen, for example, is one of the few researchers to differentiate between his total populations the sub-groups diagnosable as retarded due to endogenous (familial) versus exogenous factors. Since 1947, Strauss and Lehtinen have distinguished between these groups, and it is to be expected that marked motor ability differences will be obtained when children and youth within these two categories are compared.

Various other sub-groups have not been thoroughly surveyed to ascertain the characteristics of their motor ability traits. Except for the studies by Cratty (1966) and Share (1970), for example, little work has been done to survey adequately the movement characteristics of mongoloid children in a comprehensive group of tasks. Cratty used a six-category motor ability battery while Share employed the Gesell scale to describe the nature of the development lag in infants evidencing Down's syndrome as contrasted to normal infants. Even within the mongoloid category (Down's syndrome), however, investigators have yet to explore various movement differences evidenced by the three subcategories: the mozaic, trisomy, and transloca-tion types. Also absent are studies in which some kind of motor education program has been applied to children with Down's syndrome.

Further study needs also to be carried out concerning the influence of environmental factors upon motor ability traits in retarded children. In addition to the apparent blunting of ability traits previously alluded to and seen in the measures obtained from older retardates, it is possible that performance in tasks usually practiced between parent and child will indeed improve as a child ages (that is, throwing and catching balls), while other

---

[3] This review no more than scratches the surface of the extensive amount of data collected by Clausen, who administered 33 tests to 388 subjects, 75 percent of whom were retarded. It is suggested that those who wish a deeper understanding of the abilities of retarded children and youth consult the text by this researcher (Clausen, 1966).

more basic abilities usually not considered by parents (that is, measures of balance), may not change as a retarded child grows older (Cratty, 1966). However, appropriate longitudinal studies which would clarify this hypothesis are absent from the literature.

Motor Learning in Retarded Children

Although the suggestion that the retarded can somehow learn motor skills as quickly and efficiently as can normal children occurs with some frequency in the literature there is an increased amount of data which suggest that there are many obvious and subtle variables which may inhibit the motor skill learning of retarded children and youth.

As might be expected, when reasonably complex tasks are presented to retarded children their rate of learning is not equal to that of normal children. Both normal children and adults usually begin to give themselves appropriate subvocal directions when they are confronted with performing motor skills. It is likely that most retarded people will not engage in initial self-instruction in a capable manner. There are some data suggesting that retarded persons have a particularly difficult time learning manual skills.

A study recently completed at the University of Illinois which used both retarded and normal subjects points out the subtle relationships between the intellectual strategy adopted when beginning to learn a motor skill and the ultimate performance level attained. Both groups performed equally well; however, in an attempt to equate the intellectual differences each group brought to the task under study, the retardate group was afforded an extensive amount of verbal pre-training the normal subjects did not receive (Ellis, 1969).

Other factors probably influence the motor learning of retarded children and youth. For example, studies by Hirsch and others point out that when teaching retarded children reasonably complex manual skills a part method of teaching is likely to elicit quicker learning to higher performance levels than the whole method of teaching (Hebb, 1949; Hirsch, 1965).

Moreover, the spacing of practice trials in time should probably be different for a retarded group engaging in motor skills practice than for practice in the same task by normal subjects. It is probable that not so much boredom (response inhibition) occurs for retardates engaged in the continuous practice of relatively simple tasks when practice is massed in time than for normal subjects performing the same tasks when little time for rest is permitted between trials.

In general, the research literature dealing with characteristics of motor skill learning using retarded subjects is scarce indeed. Additional work is needed to identify precisely the manner in which various subcategories within retardate populations learn skills as well as the cues most appropriate for retarded children when they are exposed to skills novel to them.

Causal Studies, in Which Movement Has Been Employed
as a Critical Variable

Since the 1950's, there has been a proliferation of investigations exploring the manner in which both unstructured and structured programs of movement activities purportedly affect not only motor abilities but intellectual, social, and academic competencies. At the same time, however, a substantial percent of these studies has been poorly conceived and executed, and has often lacked proper controls or contained inappropriate statistical treatments of the data.

At times it has been suspected that their findings may be distorted by the well-known Hawthorne Effect, the influence of the personal attention accorded the subjects upon the results obtained. At other times the findings have been probably influenced by the emotional commitment of the investigator, with a resulting "placebo" effect.

The following brief review may be supplemented by the more enterprising reader through consultation of some of the references listed at the end of the chapter (e.g., Malpass, 1963; Cratty, 1969).

In 1958, James Oliver reported a study carried out with 40 subnormal boys ages 13 and 15 (20 experimentals and 20 controls) from a residential training school in England. Following a 10-week program of physical conditioning (taking place three hours a day and replacing several school subjects), the experimental subjects posted significantly higher scores than did the controls not only in tests of physical performance, but also in the Terman Merrill I.Q. test and in the Goodenough Draw-a-Person test of intelligence. Although in two other measures of mental ability no significant differences were obtained, the findings attracted others to explore the interesting possibilities which were raised by these findings (Oliver, 1958).[4]

Later, for example, Corder (1965) found similar gains in I.Q. scores following a program of physical education exercises. He also explained his findings by reference to the Hawthorne Effect noted by Oliver, and by "success experiences" and "improved pride" as well as to the improvement in "coordination, agility balance and stamina" noted in his 24 subjects.

It is of course desirable to know just what is contributing to the change in retarded children when they are afforded a special program of physical activities; therefore, subsequent research efforts began to include control groups to whom special attention of various kinds was afforded unaccompanied by a physical education program. In 1966, for example, Solomon and Prangle, using proper controls, concluded that a program of physical education and fitness improved only the qualities trained for in the program. They found no concomitant improvement in scores on tests of

---

[4] The I.Q. changes were attributed by Oliver to "the effect of achievement and success, improved adjustment, improved physical condition, and the effect of feeling important."

intelligence also administered to their subjects (EMR's) (educable mentally retarded).

More recent studies by Rarick and Broadhead (1968), Widdop and his colleagues (1969), and Cratty and Martin (1970), which used both trainable and educable subjects have begun to insert other variables within the movement education programs whose effects they have studied. Rarick and Broadhead, for example, studied the influences of a highly individualized program of physical education upon the development of educable children. A program administered in this manner did indeed result in a significant gain in the I.Q. score of the subjects involved. Following the 20-week program which used 275 EMR's, special treatment, whether in physical education or in a special art program included as a control group, resulted in greater changes in the motor, intellectual, and emotional behavior of retarded children than as a result of the usual instructional program which groups experience.

Rarick and Broadhead also found that more positive changes were seen in the boys than in the girls. The art program played a larger role in the modification of emotional behavior. Finally, the physical education program, individually-oriented, was more successful in eliciting intellectual, emotional, and motor changes than the group-oriented program.

In a study carried out in 1969, Widdop and his colleagues also evidenced a creative approach to the study of whether a motor education program would elicit positive changes in the personalities of trainables. They used the English approach to movement education by encouraging the children to explore various modifications of performance in a number of motor tasks. This resulted in significant gains in the experimental group in the I.Q. test administered at the end of the program (Widdop et al., 1969).

A program conducted by Cratty and Martin also inserted, in obvious and direct ways, various academic operations into the movement program utilized. They used Negro and Mexican-American children from the central city of Los Angeles who had severe learning problems. They concluded that games encouraging letter and pattern recognition, self-control, spelling, and serial memory ability did elicit a significant change in the behavior of the experimental group in contrast to the terminal improvement and performance of the various control groups (classroom tutoring, physical education games, and no special attention). In this latter study, however, when the final performance of the experimental group was contrasted to the final performance of the other groups in the same measure of intelligence, no significant change in I.Q. score (Peabody Picture Vocabulary Test) was evident on the part of the experimental group.

A number of studies have been undertaken to explore the effects of visual-motor training, perceptual-motor training, and patterning techniques upon the academic, perceptual, and intellectual achievement of retarded children. The quality of some of these investigations has been questioned by several reviewers (Rarick et al., 1967; Widdop et al., 1969).

In general the influence of these programs upon qualities other than those directly inserted into their content is questionable. Typical of the findings are those from a report by Fisher describing a study which he carried out in 1969.[5] Following Kephart's principles, Fisher employed 102 educable mentally retarded children as subjects who were considered deficient in perceptual-motor abilities. They were given training twice each week for four and one-half months with a pupil-teacher ratio of 2 to 1. At the completion of the training no significant changes were elicited either in several I.Q. tests or in perceptual-motor ability. Fisher concluded that such short-term training does not "affect the intellectual functioning or the school achievement of such children." Cawley (1968) and his colleagues have also executed factoral analyses which indicate the independent nature of reading scores, academic scores, and psychomotor abilities in retarded children.

Similar negative findings have been obtained by three doctoral students as a result of the application of the Delacato method, which purports to enhance neurologic organization of children and adults with intellectual and/or movement problems (Anderson, 1965; Robbins, 1968; Yarborough, 1964). The efficiency of this latter method of motor therapy has been questioned also by several national organizations in the United States and Canada.[6]

A number of studies in which profoundly and/or severely retarded children have been exposed to a variety of sensory and motor techniques involving a number of types of sensory (visual, auditory, tactual) and motor experiences has been published recently (Fisher, 1969).

Dr. Clara Lee Edgar in California and Dr. Ruth Webb in Glenwood, Iowa have reported significant changes in the motor and adaptive behavior as well as in the degree of responsiveness evidenced by severely and profoundly retarded children exposed to programs of sensory-motor stimulation extending over most of the day and for as long as a year at a time (Edgar et al., 1969; Webb, 1969).

Summary

It is believed that a survey of the available literature prompts the following tentative conclusions:

[5] They are similar to the findings of 12 other studies reviewed by Cratty in *Perceptual and Motor Development in Infants and Children,* New York: The MacMillan Company, 1970, Chap. 9.

[6] The American Academy for Cerebral Palsy, American Academy of Physical Medicine, American Congress of Rehabilitation Medicine, Canadian Association for Children with Learning Disabilities, Canadian Association for Retarded Children, Canadian Rehabilitation Council for the Disabled, National Association for Retarded Children. Official Statement: "The Doman-Delacato Treatment of Neurologically Handicapped Children," *Archives of Physical Medicine and Rehabilitation,* 1968, 49, 185–186.

1. Movement attributes in retarded persons are both qualitatively and quantitatively different from those same trait patterns in normal persons.

2. Groups of individuals successively lower on the intelligence scale tend to evidence more pronounced motor problems as well as simpler, less diffused patterns of motor ability and perceptual and intellectual ability traits.

3. Scores in tests of academic and intellectual ability may be modified in trainable and educable persons. Improvement in academic competencies is likely to be elicited through motor activity only if thought and the classroom abilities desired are inserted directly into the movement training programs engaged in, or if a significant change in self-concept occurs which prompts the child to be more highly motivated when he is taking an I.Q. test at the termination of the physical education program.

4. There is a significant change in the developmental level of severely and profoundly retarded children only if an extensive and comprehensive program of sensory and motor stimulation is afforded these individuals over a prolonged period of time.

MINIMAL NEUROLOGIC IMPAIRMENT

A large group of elementary and secondary school children labeled minimally neurologically impaired have, during the past twenty years, attracted the attention of neurologists, pediatricians, psychologists, and educators. From the best estimates we have, this group of children constitutes from 15 percent to 18 percent of the total population of children in regular schools for normal children. They usually evidence motor problems, and various subtle and obvious perceptual, educational, and emotional deficiencies.

Depending upon which state a retarded child resides in, he may be labeled either neurologically impaired, minimally brain-damaged, or educationally handicapped.[7] In an analysis employing 150 such children to whom a battery of 35 tasks was administered, six factors in their total makeup were identified. These included: (a) body-image deficit, which was reflected in tasks involving the ability to duplicate accurately various bodily and hand movements presented by the experimenter, tasks requiring the accurate awareness of the fingers and in other tests of tactual perception. The factor loadings suggested that the body image and hand-finger perception were related attributes in these children; (b) perceptual-dysfunction, which was a lack of awareness of form and position in two-dimensional space seen in scores from tests evaluating perception of form using both visual and tactual kinesthetic cues without vision; (c) hyperactivity-distractibility, which was

---

[7] The label "educationally handicapped," however, is a much more global term which may be applied to children with academic difficulties and normal I.Q.'s, but who may or may not evidence motor problems attributable to structural-organic abnormalities.

identified by scores from tasks indicating that the child was attempting to escape the testing situation with both verbal and motor behaviors (that is, "Are the tests through now?"); (d) integration of the two sides of the body, which was represented by scores from tests of rhythm and the proficiency with which a child could cross his body or attempted to avoid doing so; (e) figure-ground discrimination, which was seen in tests evaluating the ability to select superimposed figures out of visually complex backgrounds "loaded" in this factor; and (f) balance, which was determined by tests of static (standing) balance with eyes open and closed.

As can be seen upon consulting this list, these children suffer from both perceptual and motor deficiencies. However, there is not extensive evidence to suggest that improvement of their motor abilities will be accompanied by comcomitant improvement in perceptual functioning. Indeed, some of the studies indicate that improving the motor abilities of such children is often a difficult undertaking.[8]

In the previously cited study by Rarick and Broadhead, a group of 206 children identified as minimally brain-injured were included. The findings suggested that the positive changes elicited in motor, emotional, and social functioning were even more marked within the group of children labeled minimally neurologically impaired who were exposed to an individualized program of motor education than in the educable mentally retarded group.

In another study Bednarova (1968) found that programs of relaxation training could significantly reduce the hyperactivity of children purportedly neurologically impaired. This improvement was accompanied by parallel improvement in academic performance. In a study by Cratty and Martin, measures of self-control underwent significant improvement in children whose I.Q.'s were as low as 40. These self-control measures were also accompanied by positive changes in various academic skills including letter recognition, spelling, pattern recognition, and serial memory ability of auditory and visual stimuli (Cratty and Martin, 1970).

At the same time the findings emanating from most studies of these kinds of children are often hard to interpret. The subject populations are rarely well defined, and often the well-meaning investigators lack the research skills needed to produce valid results. Improvement in motor functioning, sometimes elicited in groups of children within this category, often is not accompanied by improvement in perceptual and academic functioning, or in measures of self-concept (Cratty and Martin, 1970; Fisher, 1969; La Pray and Ross, 1966). Indeed, Abercrombie and his associates have found no differences in scores reflecting perceptual ability between normal children and those evidencing rather severe motor problems (Abercrombie et al., 1964).

---

[8] It is virtually impossible to determine, for example, whether improvement in motor measures is caused by an increase in basic neurologic efficiency or by the adoption of better strategies of how one performs motor tasks (that is, learning how to learn).

At the same time, children within this category characteristically exhibit I.Q. scores, based upon verbal and cognitive abilities, which are significantly superior to I.Q. scores based upon their perceptual-motor attributes. Thus, it is to be expected that their awareness of the extent to which they are measuring up to the performance levels expected by their peers can elicit feelings of social rejection. These feelings of censure might be engendered by the observations and pronouncements of their peers. Indeed, this is the case (Cratty and Martin, 1970). In a study we completed recently in our laboratory we found that neurologically impaired children with average or above average I.Q. scores were more likely to report that their friends "made fun" of them, that they were "the last to be chosen in games," and that "boys did not like" them. These pronouncements indicated social problems that were apparently real and significant to them (Cratty and Martin, 1970). In another investigation with a group of these children a "topping off" of motor ability scores was seen by late childhood that had been previously documented in a group of retarded children. In this study adolescents within this category performed at levels below those exhibited by children in middle childhood, indicating the probable operation of the "failure syndrome" previously alluded to (Cratty, 1966).

Further problems are likely to beset boys with minimal neurologic impairments who cannot keep up with their more capable male peers. In a study completed by several of my postdoctoral students, for example, they found that the game choices of boys with minimal neurologic problems to a large degree paralleled those of normal girls of the same age.

While data indicate that the motor ability scores in this group can be changed positively, particularly in younger children, there needs to be further study concerning the extent to which such improvement is accompanied by concomitant changes in self-concept, emotional adjustment, academic performance, social adjustment, intelligence, and similar traits.

The available findings indicate that motor ineptitude is one symptom of a larger syndrome of perceptual and motor malfunction due to a variety of possible subtle neurologic deficits. The hypothesis that motor ability change is inevitably accompanied by change in other traits is not supported by the presently available evidence. There are indications, however, that if started early enough and contained in a highly individualized program, movement activities of a developmental nature do offer promise in the general remediation of the developmental lag so often seen in children bearing the vague label of neurologically impaired.

BLIND CHILDREN AND YOUTH

Motor Attributes

Obtaining an accurate picture of the motor abilities of the blind is beset with problems. For example, there is usually a large percentage of children with visual impairments who evidence parallel motor problems of various magnitudes. When testing blind children, making clear the exact nature of the task to be executed is often difficult, and a lack of understanding can of course significantly affect the score obtained. Some motor tasks require a great deal of visual accompaniment, for instance, those evaluating balance. Others (measures of simple applications of strength) require significantly less visual involvement. Thus, it has been found that the blind indeed perform less capably than those with vision in some tasks and score about the same as those with vision in others.

Lack of vision restricts opportunities of children and youth to move vigorously, and thus is likely to blunt their motor ability scores. In such tasks as running, the blind must, by necessity, perform differently. The totally blind run by holding on to a rope, thus restricting normal arm movement and resulting in decreases in running speed.

In general, the totally blind perform less well in physical tests than do the partially sighted. Children and youth who are totally blind, in turn, perform less capably than do those with sight. The extent of motor ineptitude has been traced in some studies to the amount of freedom permitted the maturing blind child. Those children whose parents report that they apply an inordinate number of physical restrictions upon them perform less capably than those whose parents say that they give them more freedom.

One study found that blind children may be expected to perform as capably as the sighted youngster (the standing broadjump). Similarly another investigation reveals that groups of blind children who have been exposed to vigorous programs of physical activities evidenced reasonably good fitness scores (Buell, 1966).

Similar to the findings previously outlined concerning the ability-trait structure of the retarded, the loss of vision seems to result in an aptitude pattern in the blind which is in basic ways different from the ability-trait mosaic testable in those with sight.

Interesting relationships uncovered in factor analyses have been discovered between measures of tactual perception of spatial relationships and the ability of the blind to orient themselves in space employing locomotive behavior. This same relationship was not seen when a similar group of sighted subjects was exposed to the same extensive test battery by Finnish researchers (Juurmaa, 1965).

Although a recent text advocates the use of a variety of movement activities which purport to improve the blind infant's body image development and the older child's spatial orientation and awareness, there are few studies in which some of these assumptions have been investigated (Cratty, 1971). An exception is the study carried out at the Ohio School for the Blind by Mills and Adamshick (Meyers and Dingman, 1964). Highly useful results were obtained by using a structured program of "sensory-motor experiences" including training to elicit better right-left discrimination as well as a traditional physical education and exercise program. The experimental group exposed to this program later evidenced, in a program of mobility training, performance which was significantly superior to that seen in the controls. A similar program using mentally retarded blind children in another residential school resulted in findings which were similar in nature (Cratty, 1971).

Summary

Motor ability test scores elicited from the blind are in most cases inferior to those seen in those with vision. These differences are the result of a number of possible complexities of variables including the difference in movement experiences between the two groups and the incidence of neurologic impairments among the blind as well as the inability of the blind at times to understand the manner in which a motor task is to be performed. Some observers, for example, have stated that they have never seen a blind child throw a ball with the proper arm-leg coordination and weight shift. This could have arisen from the fact that perceiving how to throw a ball correctly would involve the extremely difficult undertaking of "tactually brailling" the throwing movements by the blind child as a sighted companion performs such a task.

THE DEAF AND DEAF-BLIND

A group of totally deaf children and youth will ordinarily contain an inordinate number of individuals evidencing various movement problems. More severe problems and more numerous ones will be seen in groups of the totally deaf and the deaf-blind. Also present, and compounding the problems of education for the deaf and deaf-blind are rather severe emotional problems due to the frustrations of attempting to communicate in the absence of hearing ability.

To my knowledge there are no definitive studies describing the motor ability patterns within a substantial number of deaf children. At the same time several important questions should be answered prior to instituting programs of movement education into schools for the deaf. Most important among these concerns the amount of time such training might subtract from the time needed to enlarge the important communication skills lacking in this group of children and youth.

The techniques outlined previously, which seem appropriate for the profoundly and severely retarded, might also be considered by those attempting to work with the deaf-blind. This type of child is appearing with more frequency in the schools in both the western and eastern coasts of the United States due to the rubella epidemics of the middle sixties in these locations. I am not aware of definitive studies which offer more than vague guidelines for the improvement, through movement experiences, of these types of unfortunate infants and children.

THE MULTIPLY-HANDICAPPED

An often difficult undertaking is to ascertain the intellectual potential of children who are born with more than one type of impairment. The bright versus dull infants afflicted with cerebral palsy, for example, are often not easily separable although some inroads are being made relative to scales through which categorization may be accomplished. The multiply-handicapped child cannot be placed into any kind of global classification; each exhibits a unique set of problems and compensations. While various kinds of movement experiences may aid some of these children, these experiences must be incorporated into comprehensive programs which also include tasks designed to improve intellectual, social, and perceptual abilities.

Summary

To an increased degree educators and behavioral scientists have begun to examine the manner in which psychomotor activities may be incorporated in helpful ways into programs of special education. Although at this point this interest has sometimes become a kind of fad, data appear almost daily from which practical guidelines may be formulated.

Motor abilities are incorporated into the personalities of atypical children and youth in ways different than they are manifested in the trait patterns of normal children. In virtually all classifications, atypical children and youth perform significantly more poorly in tests of motor ability than do children free from defects.

At the same time the reasons for these differences are not often easily discernible. They may be due to a lack of opportunity on the part of the atypical individual to adjust to differences in the manner in which the handicapped child and the normal child attend to testing procedures and to various neurologic and/or emotional problems which often accompany the more obvious physical or psychologic problems.

Opportunities for further research on some of the topics only briefly scanned within the previous pages are virtually limitless. From a theoretic standpoint, there is increased emphasis upon studies dealing with the identification of a motor ability-trait structure within various subpopulations of atypical children. Other studies of this nature should attempt to describe the manner in which motor ability traits appear in atypical children and youth of various mental and chronologic ages.

Potentials for exploration of problems of a practical nature also present themselves. In many areas, for example, there are no studies evaluating the way programs of sensory as well as motor stimulation may influence the development of the children involved. Studies of this nature using profoundly retarded children are scarce; investigations of the manner in which similar programs may aid the deaf-blind are, to my knowledge, absent.

Most imperative, when carrying out "program" studies of this nature, would seem to be the identification of those components of a given program which really seem to be changing the behavior of those whose upgrading is desired. Designing studies with a number of sub-groups, each exposed to a different combination of training components, could serve the needs of the children without subjecting them to an oppressive one-variable (e.g., balance training) program for a prolonged period of time. At the same time, the results of this kind of study would reveal which combination of items is most likely to elicit the desired change (or conversely, which component should not be omitted when designing a program of this nature).

To be avoided in future studies is the previously seen fallacy of attempting to improve some attribute high on the developmental scale, such as reading, by inserting a program composed of items developmentally lower and far removed from the behavior it is designed to change (e.g., balance). Most helpful will be studies which indicate how various training ploys transfer to some kind of behavior change which is desired and also demonstrate how the child's cognitive abilities may be incorporated into programs in which various motor abilities are exercised.

References

Abercrombie, J. J., Gardiner, P. A., Hanson, E., Jockheere, J., Lindon, R. L., Solomon, G., & Tyson, M. C. Visual, perceptual and visual-motor impairment in physically handicapped children. *Perceptual and Motor Skills,* 1964, 18 (Monogr. Suppl. 3).

Anderson, R. W. *Effects of neuro-psychological techniques on reading achievement.* Doctoral dissertation, Greeley State College, Greeley, Colorado, 1965.

Ayres, J. Patterns of perceptual-motor dysfunction in children: A factor analytic study. *Perceptual and Motor Skills,* 1965, 20 (Monogr. Suppl. 1).

Bednarova, V. An investigation concerning the influence of psychotonic exercise upon indices of concentration of attentiveness. *Teo Prax Teles Vychow,* 1968, 16 (7), 437–442.

Buell, C. *Recreation for the blind.* New York: American Foundation for the Blind, 1951.

Buell, C. *Physical education for blind children.* Springfield, Ill.: Charles C Thomas, 1966.

Cawley, J. F., Goodstein, H. A., and Burrow, W. H. *Reading and psychomotor disability among mentally retarded and average children.* Storrs, Connecticut: University of Connecticut, School of Education, 1968.

Clausen, J. *Ability structure and subgroups in mental retardation.* Washington D. C.: Spartan Books, London: Macmillan and Co., Ltd., 1966.

Corder, W. D. Effects of physical education on the intellectual, physical and social development of educable mentally retarded boys. Unpublished special project, George Peabody College, Nashville, Tennessee, 1965.

Cratty, B. J. *Perceptual and motor attributes of mentally retarded children and youth.* Los Angeles: Mental Retardation Services Board, 1966.

Cratty, B. J. *Motor activity and the education of retardates.* Philadelphia: Lea & Febiger, 1969.

Cratty, B. J. *Perceptual and motor development in infants and children.* New York: The Macmillan Co., 1970.

Cratty, B. J. *Some educational implications of movement experiences.* Seattle, Washington: Special Child Publications, 1970.

Cratty, B. J. *Active learning.* Englewood Cliffs, N. J.: Prentice-Hall, 1971.

Cratty, B. J. *Movement and spatial awareness in blind children and youth.* Springfield, Ill.: Charles C Thomas, 1971.

Cratty, B. J., & Martin, Sister Margaret Mary. *Perceptual-motor efficiency in children.* Philadelphia: Lea & Febiger, 1969.

Cratty, B. J., & Martin, Sister Margaret Mary. *The effects of a program of learning games upon selected academic abilities in children with learning difficulties.* Washington, D. C.: U. S. Office of Education, Bureau of Handicapped Children, 1970.

Cratty, B. J., Martin, Sister Margaret Mary, Ikeda, N., Morris, M., & Jennett, C. *Movement activities, motor ability and the education of children.* Springfield, Ill.: Charles C Thomas, 1970.

Delacato, C. H. *Neurological organization and reading.* Springfield, Ill.: Charles C Thomas, 1966.

Distefano, M. K. Jr., Ellis, N. R., & Sloan, W. Motor proficiency in mental defectives. *Perceptual and Motor Skills,* 1958, 8, 231–234.

Edgar, C. L., Ball, T. S., McIntyre, R. B. T., & Shotwell, A. M. Effects of sensory-motor training on adaptive behavior. *American Journal of Mental Deficiency,* 1969, 5, 73.

Ellis, M. J., & Craig, T. T. On the inferiority of retardates' motor performance. *1968–1969 Annual Report of Motor Performance and Play Research Laboratory,* Children's Reserach Center, University of Illinois, Monograph.

Fisher, Kirk L. Effects of a structured program of perceptual-motor training on the development and school achievement of educable mentally retarded children. Pennsylvania State University. Research sponsored in Washington, D. C.: U. S. Office of Education, Department of Health, Education, and Welfare, Bureau of Research, 1969.

Francis, R. J., & Rarick, G. L. *Motor characteristics of mentally retarded.* Washington, D. C.: U. S. Office of Education, Cooperative Research program #1, 1960.

Getman, G. N. *How to develop your child's intelligence: A research publication.* Luverne, Minn.: Getman, 1952.

Glass, G. V., & Robbins, M. P. The Doman-Delacato rationale: A critical analysis. *Educational Therapy,* Seattle, Washington: Special Child Publications, 1969, 1, 321–378.

Hebb, D. O. *Organization of behavior.* New York: John Wiley & Sons, Inc., 1949.

Hirsch, W. *Motor skill transfer by trainable mentally retarded and normal children.* Doctoral dissertation, UCLA, 1965.

Howe, C. A comparison of motor skills of mentally retarded and normal children. *Exceptional Child,* 1959, 23, 352–354.

Itard, J. M. G. *The wild boy of aveyron.* Translated by G. & M. Humphrey, New York: Century Co., 1932.

Juurmaa, J. An analysis of the components of orientation ability and mental manipulation of spatial relationships. Helsinki, Finland: Institute of Occupational Health, 1965, 28.

La Pray, M., & Ross, R. Auditory and visual perceptual training. *Vistas in Reading.* J. Allen Figurel (ed.), International Association Conference Proceedings, 1966, IX, 530–532.

Lewin, K. Behavior and development as a function of the total situation. In L. Carmichael (ed.), *Manual of child psychology.* New York: John Wiley & Sons, Inc. 1946, pp. 791–844.

Licht, S. *Therapeutic exercise.* (2nd ed.) New Haven, Connecticut: Licht Publishers, 1965.

Malpass, L. F. Motor skills in mental deficiency. In N. R. Ellis (ed.), *Handbook of mental deficiency.* New York: McGraw-Hill Co., 1963, pp. 602–631.

Meyers, C. E., & Dingman, J. F. Factor analysis and structure of intellect: Models in the study of mental retardation. Paper presented at the Conference on Cognitive Models and Development in Mental Retardation. Haddonfield, New Jersey, November, 1964.

McKinney, J. P. A multidimensional study of the behavior of severely retarded boys. *Child Development,* 1962, 33, 932–938.

Mills, R. J., & Adamshick, D. R. The effectiveness of structured sensory training experiences prior to formal orientation and mobility instruction. Monograph sponsored by the Ohio State Bureau of Services for the Blind, in cooperation with the Department of Special Education and Rehabilitation of Boston College, 1968.

Montessori, M. *Dr. Montessori's own handbook.* New York: Frederick A. Stocks, 1914.

Myler, P. A study of the motor ability of the blind, Master's thesis, University of Texas, 1936.

Oliver, J. The effect of physical conditioning exercises and activities on the mental characteristics of educationally sub-normal boys. *British Journal of Education Psychology,* 1958, 28, 155–165.

Rabin, H. M. The relationship of age, intelligence and sex to motor proficiency in mental defectives. *American Journal on Mental Deficiency,* 1957, 62, 507–516.

Rarick, G. L., & Broadhead, G. *The effects of individualized versus group oriented physical education programs on selected parameters on the development of educable mentally retarded and minimally brain injured children.* Madison, Wisconsin, Sponsored by U. S. Office of Education and Joseph P. Kennedy, Jr. Foundation, 1968.

Rarick, G. L., & Widdop, J. H., & Broadhead, G. D. *Environmental factors associated with the motor performance and physical fitness of educable mentally retarded children.* Madison, Wisconsin: Department of Physical Education, University of Wisconsin, 1967.

Robbins, M. The Delacato interpretation of neurological organization. *Exceptional Child,* 1966, 32, 517–523.

Robbins, M., & Glass, G. V. The Doman-Delacato rationale: A critical analysis. *Educational Therapy,* J. Hellmuth (ed.), Seattle, Washington: Special Child Publications, 2, 1968.

Seguin, E., *Traitment morale, hygiene et education des idiots,* 2 Vols., Paris, 1846.

Share, J. Differences between the early development of infants with Down's syndrome versus normal infants. La Verne, California: Paper presented at the First Annual Symposium on Movement Education, La Verne College, 1970.

Solomon, A. H., & Prangle, R. The effects of a structured physical education program on physical, intellectual and self-concept development of educable retarded boys. *Behavioral Science Monograph,* 1966, 4.

Strauss, A. A., & Lehtinen, L. E. *Psychopathology and education of the brain-injured child.* New York: Grune and Stratton, 1947.

Webb, R. Sensory-motor training of the profoundly retarded. *American Journal of Mental Deficiency,* 1969, 74, 283–295.

Werner, H., & Strauss, A. A. Causal factors in low performance. *American Journal of Mental Deficiency,* 1940, 45, 213–218.

Widdop, J., Barton, P., Cleary, B., Proyer, V., & Wall, A. The effects of two programmes of physical education upon the behavioural and psychological traits of trainable retarded children. Sponsored by Quebec Institute of Research in Education, Montreal: McGill University, 1969.

Whitsell, L. J. Delacato's neurological organization: A medical appraisal. *California School Health.* 1967, 3, 1–13.

Yarborough, B. H. *A study of the effectiveness of the Leavell language-development service in improving the silent reading ability and other language skills of persons with mixed dominance.* Doctoral dissertation, University of Virginia, 1964.

Chapter 10

PERCEPTUAL-MOTOR PROGRAMS

JAMES W. FLEMING
Michigan State University

A review of present educational literature finds the terms perceptual-motor and sensory-motor ever increasing in the texts, journals, and publications dealing primarily with special education programs, techniques, and research. Historically, the prominence of perceptual-motor programs was established in public schools in the 1950's and 1960's; however, their conception and development began much earlier. The early forms of Greek and Roman civilizations, with their emphasis on dance and physical fitness, were aware of many parts of today's programs. It was not until the works of Delacato (1959), Kephart (1960), and Barsch (1965) that we find educators actively exploring the role of perceptual-motor programs in public schools. Earlier investigations by Seguin, Montessori, and Strauss have influenced all the theoretic models proposed (McCarthy and McCarthy, 1969; Magdol, 1968).

Perceptual-motor training programs are being explored by numerous educators. Although many proponents worked in this area earlier, the popular acceptance of these programs came in the 1960's. The strongest theorists and developers of specific programs are Barsch, Frostig, Kephart, Getman, and Delacato. There are others with varying degrees of similarity in approach to those just mentioned such as McLeod (1967) and Robins (1968). Criticism of the programs is strong and perhaps justifiable (see Cratty, 1970). This author plays the devil's advocate in his review of these programs.

DEFINITIONS AND DESCRIPTIONS

Perceptual-motor (P-M) programs are more individualized than many group-oriented physical education programs. Teaching basic physical move-

250

ments in a P-M program involves breaking down activities into component parts, developing awareness of the sensory skills involved, and working at the developmental level at which the child is functioning. Perceptual-motor programs are also defined as a means of teaching the child use of the body mechanisms which serve to monitor and control body positions and movements and enable him to derive meaning from sensory experiences.

The perceptual-motor program developed by Barsch (1965) is referred to as a "movigenics" curriculum. He (Barsch, 1967, p. 33) defines this as "the study of the origin and development of patterns of movement in man and the relationship of those movements to his learning efficiency." Kephart (1960, p. 63) notes that "we cannot think of perceptual activities and motor activities as two different items, we must think of the hyphenated term 'perceptual-motor.'" Many times, however, we find some educators limiting the perceptual-motor programs to visual and/or motor processes, for example, in the work of Frostig and Getman. Frostig (1970) has recently expanded her writing from visual perception programs to a more global approach in her text, *Movement Education.*

Theory and Practice

Reviewing the major contributions by Barsch, Delacato, Frostig, Getman, and Kephart provides us with some clues as to a definition of perceptual-motor programs. Semantics, as well as one's own personal biases, do play a part in defining the term. Sensory-motor is still another term which is used interchangeably with perceptual-motor. Valett differentiates between these two terms in his texts (1968, 1969).

"Perceptual-motor" is viewed as a more global term that deals with sensory perceptions coupled with movement or exploration in the learning process. A second element involves the incorporation of the P-M program within the present-day curriculum. All proponents of P-M programs do advocate a change in curriculum to develop learning efficiency. Barsch's (1965) "A Movigenic Curriculum" is perhaps the most extensive; but M. Frostig (1970) is still another advocate of the curriculum change idea.

Many fields of study are drawn upon in developing the framework and procedures for P-M programs. Psychology and medicine are frequently used for the theoretic basis; from physical education and physical therapy various methods and procedures are utilized for forming the programs. The special educator's role might be viewed as providing the academic setting and using P-M programs as remedial and/or preventive measures.

The common variables found in all of the proposed perceptual-motor programs appear to be:

(a) the use of gross motor activities or physical exercises incorporating awareness of the necessary body movements
(b) the use of structured activities organized in planned programmed procedures

(c) training to improve basic sensory skills (visual, auditory, and tactile) as well as motor skills

(d) the relative importance and emphasis that is placed on P-M programs in relation to academic learning and/or gains.

Differences within the various P-M programs appear to stem from:

(a) the theoretic models from which Delacato (1959, 1963), Kephart (1960), and Barsch (1965) base their programs
(b) the areas of major emphasis in remediation
(c) the claims linked to the specific programs and procedures

The works of Getman (1964), Strauss and Lehtinen (1947), Cruickshank (1961), and a host of others have points of commonality that many educators are incorporating into their own P-M programs. This is perhaps due to the newfound focus on the area of "learning disabilities" in education. The child with learning disorders, learning disabilities, minimal brain dysfunction, or brain damage is the center of much controversy in education today. Many of the remedial programs for this child are indeed P-M programs.

Perceptual-motor programs today are considered by many educators as "remedial" or "habilitation" training programs. This narrow approach excludes the normal child from a good sound developmental P-M program such as the kind proposed by Cratty (1970) and Frostig (1970).

The advantages and disadvantages of establishing any specific P-M program in a school curriculum, either as a "developmental" or "remedial" program must be examined.

Advantages:

(1) will provide structured activities to assist the teacher in helping the child to learn
(2) will provide a motivation element (which is strongly dependent on the teacher)
(3) will provide structured physical education activities which are many times lacking in the elementary grades
(4) will serve to organize and reinforce learning activities with the classroom teacher and physical educator
(5) will provide a less expensive model (excluding training, resources, and reference materials)
(6) will provide learning experiences for the special and normal child

Disadvantages:

(1) educators may tend to teach "splinter skills" and not incorporate them into the learning or academic realm

(2) emphasis might be placed more on P-M programs as a remedial "panacea" than as a developmental program

(3) unless extended review and research are incorporated into the P-M program, it will fail to develop or expand in a positive manner

(4) limited or few educators are available at the present time to assist schools in developing a P-M program within their curriculum

By examining a few of the leading P-M programs, the particular advantages and disadvantages for the given model can be ascertained. Some of the more popular (and controversial) perceptual-motor programs will be discussed in this chapter. The theoretic suppositions, the highlights, and an evaluation of the respective programs follows. Specifically, the works of Ray Barsch, Glenn Doman and Carl Delacato, Gerald Getman, and Newell C. Kephart will be reviewed.

Ray Barsch: A "Movigenic" Curriculum

This theory views the child as a "terranaut" moving within a self-perceived space world (Barsch, 1967). Barsch implements his program with a perceptual-motor curriculum based on 12 dimensions of learning. Evaluation of these 12 dimensions allows for a placement of the child into one of four groupings on a functional organization scale.

These four groupings are:

(1) integrated function—child performs adequately under stress

(2) organized function—otherwise organized performance breaks down under stress

(3) organized immature function—child's behavior is quantitatively inadequate (8-year-old child functionings as a 5-year-old child)

(4) disorganized or unorganized—level of performance is so inadequate it prohibits learning, checks skill acquisition, and keeps him a poor adaptor

Key factors or considerations in this theoretic model are: (a) world of space; (b) movement; (c) efficiency; and (d) programmed success. The first four dimensions fall under the heading of Postural-Transport Orientation (Barsch's definitions, 1965):

(1) muscular strength—"the capacity of the individual to maintain an adequate state of muscle tonus, power and stamina to meet daily demands appropriate to his body size and chronological age" (p. 15)

(2) dynamic balance—"the capacity of the organism to activate anti-gravity muscles in proper relationship to one another against the force of gravitational pull to maintain alignment, sustain his transport pattern and aid in recovery" (p. 16)

    (3) spatial awareness—"the capacity of the organism to identify his own position in space relative to his surround with constant orientation to surface, elevation, periphery, back and front" (p. 18)

    (4) body awareness—"the capacity of the organism to achieve a conscious appreciation of the relationship of all body segments to movement, to be able to label body parts and to appreciate the functional properties of various body parts" (p. 19)

The next four dimensions are referred to as the Percepto-Cognitive Modes. These are the four primary functional channels of reception and expression. They include:

    (5) visual dynamics—"the capacity of the organism to fixate accurately on a target at near, far, and mid points in space, to scan . . . , to converge and accommodate, to equalize the use of both visual circuits . . . , and to steer the body in proper alignment for movements through space" (p. 20)

    (6) auditory dynamics—"the capacity of the organism to process information on a receiving and a sending basis from the world of sound and to attach appropriate relationships to the world of sound" (p. 22)

    (7) kinesthesia—"the capacity of the organism to maintain an awareness of position in space and to recall patterns of movement from previous experience for utility in resolving continuing demands" (p. 23)

    (8) tactual dynamics—"the capacity of the organism to gain information from the cutaneous contact of active or passing touching" (p. 25)

The last four dimensions represent, as stated by Barsch (1965, p. 27), "those factors which enlarge, enrich, expand, and explicate the performance efficiency of all others." These are classified as Degrees of Freedom:

    (9) bilaterality—"the capacity of the organism to reciprocally interweave two sides in a balanced relationship of thrusting and counter thrusting patterns around the three coordinates of vertical, horizontal and depth in proper alignment from initiation to completion of a task" (p. 27)

    (10) rhythm—"the capacity of the organism to synchronize patterns of movements according to situational demands, thus achieving harmony, grace, and use of movement" (p. 28)

    (11) flexibility—"the capacity of the organism to modify or shift patterns of movement appropriate to the situational demand" (p. 28)

    (12) motor planning—"the capacity of the organism to plan a movement pattern prior to execution in order to meet the demands of the task" (p. 29)

It should be noted, however, that Barsch in his text *Achieving Perceptual-Motor Efficiency* (Vol. I, pp. 78–83, 1967), denotes 15 components for the composite entity labeled "Movement Efficiency." These 15 components are listed in an order that Barsch points out is chronologic in development. The three additional components are "temporal awareness," and the "gustatory" and "olfactory modes" of reception. Temporal awareness is defined as "the composite behavior of the performer as it relates to his awareness of time" (p. 150). This dimension is the fifth of the Postural-Transport Orientations which "are fundamental to movement and set the foundation for all future movement" (p. 78).

The gustatory and olfactory modes of reception are the first two Percepto-Cognitive Modes. These two components are pointed out as those for which more exploration and research are needed of their role in learning. All of the Percepto-Cognitive Modes "provide the channels from which the traveler derives information to organize his movements, direct his actions, control his behavior and attribute meaning to his surround" (Barsch, 1967, p. 78). They are "designed to implement the organization of the Postural-Transport Orientations by adding meaning to movement" (p. 78). The Degrees of Freedom are "designed to enhance and enrich the learner's performance and enable him to achieve range, amplitude and broadness within his behavior.... provide him with alternatives.... permit him to adapt" (Barsch, 1967, p. 82). Suggested remediation activities were established for these 12 dimensions from the experimental program conducted by Barsch in Madison, Wisconsin. The basis for which he establishes his theoretic model is dealt with in his first volume, *Achieving Perceptual-Motor Efficiency* (1967), while his second volume, *Enriching Perception and Cognition* (1968) and a booklet entitled *A Movigenic Curriculum* (1965) deal with remediation procedures and specific suggestions.

Any limitations attached to this program are perhaps the result of limited expansion and not attaching the activities directly to the academic world of the child. This program is viewed as one dimension of the whole curriculum and meets many of the needs in a regular or special education curriculum.

NEWELL C. KEPHART: SLOW LEARNER PROGRAM

The basic premise of the Slow Learner Program is that sensorimotor skills are the foundation on which all learning exists. Kephart (1960) stated that "most of the tasks which we set for the child are complex activities combining many basic sensory-motor skills" (p. 33). Still later it was pointed out, "He places considerable emphasis on early motor learning and on the development patterns, rather than on specific skills" (Roach and Kephart, 1960, p. 2).

Gross motor activities followed by more precise fine motor activity is viewed as necessary to avoid the development of "splinter skills" (Kephart,

1971). A "splinter skill" develops when training remains specific and the child's attention is directed towards performance rather than the goal of the movement. Motor movement patterns must become generalized in order to establish directionality, laterality, and perceptual-motor match skills (Roach and Kephart, 1966).

Kephart's theory is based on stages of development through which the child moves about in his learning environment. These stages are as follows (Kephart, 1967, pp. 20–32):

1. motor stage
2. motor-perceptual stage
3. perceptual-motor stage
4. perceptual stage
5. perceptual-conceptual stage
6. conceptual stage
7. conceptual-perceptual stage

"The essence of the perceptual-motor theory is a sequence of learning stages through which the child progresses. Later complex learnings are built upon initial learning in a hierarchial fashion" (Roach and Kephart, 1966, p. 3).

A great deal of emphasis is placed on the levels of generalization through which the child is taught. These levels are indicated by Kephart as the concept level, the percept level, and the motor level (Kephart, 1967). He stresses the importance of generalizations learned on all three levels. "The school should give major attention to such teaching on all levels of development if it is to promote the maximum achievement of each child according to his potential" (Kephart, 1967, p. 77).

Success in learning or remediation of such activities as reading, writing, or spelling occurs when they are broken down into basic skills and teaching is directed toward them. Rather than using traditional methods to teach a child who is having difficulty with reading, Kephart suggests procedures based on remediating the basic skills involved in the reading process.

Among the various basic skills that Kephart deals with are laterality, directionality, ability to stop eye movements, and dexterity. These skills are assessed with others in the *Purdue Perceptual-Motor Survey* developed by Roach and Kephart (1966). There are eleven subtests used to measure and develop procedures for treatment. This scale measures the following specific perceptual-motor activities:

1. walking board
2. jumping
3. identification of body parts
4. imitation of movements

5. obstacle course
6. Kraus-Weber tasks
7. angels-in-th-snow
8. chalkboard
9. rhythmic writing
10. ocular pursuit
11. visual achievement forms

The tasks are performed by the child, with the examiner giving commands and recording the responses. Each item is assigned a rating from 1 to 4. A four indicates no difficulty and a one indicates a child was unable to perform the task adequately. The survey may be administered by a classroom teacher and is scored subjectively. Normative data were developed for children between six and ten years of age. Areas of difficulty are determined by reviewing the ratings and various training activities are then to be instituted into the child's educational program.

Kephart's training activities are divided into four major sections:

(1) chalkboard training
(2) sensory-motor training
(3) training for ocular control
(4) training in form perception

The remediation activities are aimed at teaching certain generalized skills and abilities. Kephart (1960) points out that "attention must always be focused upon the generalization, and frequent variations of the specific task which will promote generalization should be introduced" (p. 159).

Since writing his text, *The Slow Learner in the Classroom* (1960), which was recently revised (1971), Kephart has published a series on remediation procedures with various authors with the Charles E. Merrill Publishing Company. Dr. Kephart is presently the director of the Glen Haven Achievement Center For Children located in Fort Collins, Colorado.

GLENN DOMAN AND CARL DELACATO: NEUROLOGIC ORGANIZATION

Doman and Delacato rely on the theories of D. O. Hebb and Temple Fay in developing their theory and remediation procedures. They work with children diagnosed as brain-injured at their Institutes for the Achievement of Human Potential in the Philadelphia, Pennsylvania area and various other centers throughout the United States. Their program is based upon the theoretic principle known as neurologic organization. This theory stems from the biogenetic postulate that "ontogeny recapitulates phylogeny" (Delacato, 1959, 1963). Translated this means that individual human development repeats the pattern of man's evolutionary development. Children having difficulty with mobility, communication, and/or learning are said to have *not* neurologically developed in a sequential continuum.

A detailed case history of the child's development is taken along with a clinical examination (Delacato, 1963). This information is recorded on The Doman-Delacato Developmental Profile. The child's performance is evaluated in six basic areas which include: mobility, language, manual competence, visual competence, auditory competence, and tactile competence. The potential for performance is estimated from this information and various standardized tests such as the Wechsler Intelligence Scale for Children, and tests dealing with language, reading, and arithmetic.

The theories upon which the Institutes base treatment of children are these:

(1) A child's central nervous system (brain, spinal cord, and nerve pathways) develops in a definite pattern from conception to about the age of eight.

(2) Progress of this development can be measured on a scale of neurologic organization in six areas:

—movement of body (from birth movements of arms and legs up to skilled walking);

—speech (from crying at birth up to a complete vocabulary and proper sentence structure);

—manual skills (from grasp reflex to writing with dominant hand);

—visual skills (from light reflex at birth to reading);

—tactile skills (from birth reflexes to identification of objects by touch).

(3) The speed at which this development takes place varies widely among individual children.

(4) Neurologic growth can be slowed down slightly by some methods of rearing children. It can be slowed down considerably by depriving a child of necessary stimulation in his environment. It can be stopped completely by brain damage.

(5) An immature child or a slow learner is the result of delay in neurologic development. A youngster with reading problems in school despite good instruction suffers from a disorganization of neurologic growth.

(6) In terms of neurologic development, all children can be included in a range that stretches from the severely brain-damaged child in a coma just one breath away from death to the youngster who is very superior mentally and physically.

(7) By stimulating the development of the central nervous system, it is possible to push children considerably up the ladder of neurologic

development—in other words, to help brain-injured children perform at normal and sometimes better-than-normal levels.

(8) Not only can a child's neurologic development be slowed down by injury to the brain or by deprivations in the environment, it can also be speeded up by simple, nonsurgical methods.

(9) By the same methods, the neurologic development of normal children can be stimulated—in other words, their mental abilities can be increased.

These procedures are based on the premise that certain brain levels, that is, pons, midbrain, and cortex, have *separate, consecutive* responsibilities in terms of mobility.

Treatment begins at the level of neurologic development at which the child fails. The levels considered are medulla, pons, midbrain, and cortex, in which various perceptual-motor activities are linked. Pre-remedial and remedial procedures are said to be treatment of the brain rather than the results of the brain injury. Delacato (Myers and Hammill, 1969) defines this as "treating a central problem where it exists, in the central nervous system, not in the peripheral areas" (p. 277).

Children undergoing treatment are given a specific prescriptive program based on the profile findings. A child must master each successive level before he advances to the next one. One specific technique developed at the Institutes is called "patterning." This is the manipulation of arms, legs, and head by three adults in a rhythmic fashion. These movements are imposed on the child's limbs and head for specific periods of time every day. A great deal of emphasis is placed on the environment as the source of sensory stimuli to which the child reacts with a motor response. This training in turn is said to elicit responses from functionally noninvolved areas of the brain.

Patterning is only one part of the total treatment program. A planned program of sensory (auditory, visual, thermal, and tactile) stimuli is instituted into the treatment program. Respiration exercises are used to enhance the blood supply to the brain. The diet is restricted to reduce fluid intake and thereby reduce intracranial pressure. A program of reading is instituted as early as two years of age to enhance other cortical functions to some degree. A program to establish complete cortical hemispheric dominance is also instituted.

This program requires personnel with specific training and understanding of the complete remedial procedures. Isolated parts of the program and procedures should not be used unless under the auspices of trained personnel acquainted with the program and/or medical personnel such as physical therapists. This does not, however, constitute the total Doman-Delacato program and should not be evaluated as such. The program does not lend itself to a public school use because of the number of personnel and time involved. It is perhaps better suited for clinical or private home settings.

GERALD N. GETMAN: "PHYSIOLOGY OF READINESS"

Getman and Kane (1964) advance the theory that a child's growth, intellectual achievement, and behavior are directly related to a basic sequence with visual development. Statements by Getman reflect (1962 through 1964) his strong emphasis on the visual process: "80% of everything we learn is learned visually" (Getman and Kane, 1964, p. III), and "vision is intelligence" (Getman, 1962, p. 20).

Getman's program is based on the sequence and development associated with the first five years of life. He has organized this sequence into six interrelated stages which are as follows:

(1) general motor patterns—the child learns when he moves
(2) special movement patterns—synchronized use of body parts, such as eye-hand coordination
(3) eye movement patterns—efficient visual patterns free the hands for more economic use
(4) visual language patterns—effective communication patterns assist in verifying visual discriminations
(5) visualization patterns—visual memory skills that substitute for action, speech, and/or time
(6) visual perceptual organizations—ability to interchange sensory stimuli memories with the original stimuli and to interrelate it with the environment.

The basic four premises of the Getman training program are found in his revised text coauthored with Elmer Kane in 1964. They are as follows:

(1) Academic performance in today's schools depends heavily upon form and symbol recognition and interpretation.
(2) There are perceptual skills which can be developed and trained.
(3) The development of perceptual skills is related to the levels of coordination of the body system, that is, the better the coordinations of the body parts and body systems, the better the prospects are for developing perception of forms and symbols.
(4) The child whose perceptual skills have been developed and extended is the one who is free to profit from instruction and to learn independently.

All of Getman's work has a strong visual emphasis; this is perhaps due to his own training and background as a doctor of optometry and of ocular science. His training procedures and techniques do lack scientific verification by controlled research. A great deal of his work and theory, however, when used at the appropriate age or developmental level, is very sound and practical. Again, much of his work would also seem applicable to improving visual efficiency in children exhibiting visual learning problems not attributed to physiologic defects of the eye.

IMPLICATIONS AND FINDINGS:

It is interesting to note that two of the theorists (Kephart and Barsch) whose programs have just been discussed worked together in their earlier years (Wayne County Training School, Michigan) before going to their university positions. Kephart has extended his theoretic work into a clinic in Colorado (Glen Haven Achievement Center For Children, Fort Collins) and has developed a series of texts, the *Slow Learner Series.* Somewhat slower in publishing is Ray Barsch, although he does have two volumes written concerning his theory and program procedures. Delacato has numerous volumes dealing with his theory and program, while Frostig and Maslow (1970) have only recently entered the "movement to learn" publications, not counting Frostig's work in visual perception by herself.

Getman (1962, 1968) appears to stand alone, but his program has similarities to the others. No one program appears on the horizon as the panacea, but too many times they are adopted as such. The claims of these theorists are that basic movement proficiency is necessary for learning to take place more effectively or efficiently. This does not appear to be supported by research, as Cratty (1970) and others have indicated. However, education does have a need for the perceptual-motor programs.

Today more than ever we are finding more "experts" in perceptual-motor programs. These range from teachers, psychologists, optometrists, opthalmologists, physicians to private citizens. Their training, experience, and techniques all vary in their claim to what P-M programs will or can do for the child. The "bandwagon" for many schools is an experimental program with an experimental and a control group followed by a host of tests. In many instances they are preceded by testing programs, and even daily activities as a part of the program.

True, many elementary school programs are lacking in a good substantial physical education program. In most instances, it is due to the lack of trained personnel. Physical education teachers are generally found in the junior and senior high school levels, or they are permitted to have the elementary child for a 45-minute period once a week. The blame cannot be placed here alone; many teacher-training instutions do not include courses in physical education for the elementary school age child in their programs.

We can see measurable success in P-M programs, but it cannot be directly related to the world of academe. A good P-M program may be one basic way of providing elementary schools with an organized physical education program. P-M programs can and should provide the elementary child with:

(a) an eagerness to learn
(b) a highly successful atmosphere
(c) new avenues to explore and reinforcement of classroom learning
(d) an awareness of the basic skills in learning

Measurable gains of P-M programs will perhaps not be measured by I.Q. score gains. The effectiveness should not be directly related to academic achievement alone. If educators were to look at the elements of the classroom atmosphere, for example, self-image, relationships with others, and the classroom teacher's own self-confidence, as factors to investigate as an indication of a good P-M program, then we might be on the right track to seeing relationships.

Eclectic is a word that seems to fit the present P-M programs. However, few proponents would agree to this term. Another way to look at the P-M programs is to see where and with whom they belong in relation to the developmental timeline of the child. In using this model we are not encouraging acceptance of any or all of the theories in total, but perhaps they all can help us in some way in dealing with the child more effectively.

Where does the P-M model fit in today's schools? One might adopt it as the backbone or foundation of a complete physical education program in the elementary school. It may serve as a preventive measure and a way in which to identify children with "learning difficulties" earlier. What is being said dates back to Sequin, Montessori, and others, but now it is said in terms of a curriculum model.

We need to ask about the nature of the P-M programs, and who is involved in regard to change or acceptance of them. All educators are involved, from the university to the one-room school which still exists in many areas. We need to train all teachers in physical education and sensory-motor programs so that they might carry out the proposal effectively, either separately or integratively. Cost is far less in establishing and operating these programs than perhaps starting a "new" reading program or establishing more "special" classes.

The P-M programs reviewed here are not the final answer for learning failures in schools. However, if we examine each of the programs, we will find that they might be applicable for a specific type of child and/or a specific period of time as an aid to normal development. The majority of these programs or methods are found to be appropriate only during the preschool or elementary school years. They are generally remedial in nature, but they could be incorporated into the regular elementary curriculum if selected appropriately. This is to say that consideration should be given to developmental age and grade levels of the children. Care should be taken not to place too much emphasis on any one program or specific perceptual-motor activity, for example, balance board activities.

One way to view where the respective P-M programs might fit into the early years of the child is shown in table 10-1.

The Doman and Delacato program is perhaps more applicable for trainable retarded and multiply-handicapped children and is to be used by parents. Barsch's program appears to be more appropriate for all children if the curriculum suggestions are placed appropriately within the developmental and grade levels. Kephart's program might best be used as a remedial program. Getman and Frostig's programs are seen as applicable only during the preschool or earlier elementary school years. There are numerous other programs such as those of Valett (1968), McLeod (1967), and Frostig and Maslow (1970) that involve programmed materials for the classroom teacher to use with elementary-age school children having difficulties with per-ceptual-motor activities.

The adolescent is in reality too far removed from many of the suggested activities for any of them to be effective. A host of variables are responsible for this conclusion, among these being (1) motivation, (2) interest, and (3) a history of failure. However, one recent theory proposed by Von Hilsheimer (1970) does have many elements of a P-M program. This program's effectiveness has yet to be explored by research or commented upon in the journals. Few if any positive statements are being made, as was the case in the earlier days of the Doman and Delacato program. Acceptance is coming very slowly and this is good for any of the programs. Widespread or wholesale use of any of the programs would only tend to sour too many administrators, educators, and parents who did not see a positive, direct gain as a result of a specific P-M program. Many of us experienced this with Frostig's visual perception program when it was first introduced.

Cratty once stated: "Many experimental findings may have no immediate

TABLE 10-1

The Child

Birth	1 yr.	2	3	4	5	6	7	8	9	10	11	12
	Doman and Delacato					Barsch's Movigenics Curriculum						
				Getman								
					Kephart Program							
					Frostig's Movement to Learn Program							

use, while some teaching practices do not require 'scientific' verification. They may just 'make sense' " (1970, p. 18). These comments are taken out of context but a great deal of worth can be gained from an analysis of them. First of all, we are perhaps trying too hard to find a program or gadget to fit an experimental design; and second, we do not necessarily have to validate all teaching practices. Many just make good sense. Care must be taken in instituting any special program or methods for a sound perceptual-motor program. Expected outcomes should be carefully established, with fewer global claims linked to a specific P-M program. A child may not read better or his I.Q. score may or may not be raised significantly as a result of a P-M program, but these factors alone do not justify abandoning the program.

Balow refers to perceptual-motor activities as "non-specific additions to the curriculum which will probably help teach children important general behavioral skills necessary for success in school, but clearly not replacements for the careful diagnosis and direct teaching of basic school skills" (1971, p. 524). Six reasons for including P-M programs as general additions to the elementary curriculum as listed by Balow (1971, pp. 523–524) are:

1. The enjoyment and developmental appropriateness of motor activity, particularly for primary age school boys for whom sitting still is so inappropriate.
2. The personal recognition of success that can attend motor-perceptual activities, particularly for pupils long used to failure in school.
3. The accompanying positive attention from significant adults; usually the classroom teacher, but often others as well.
4. The fact of teaching, in direct drill form, a set of visual and motor skills that may be weak, or absent, and which relate to school demands but ordinarily are left to develop incidentally.
5. Teaching, by means of such visual and motor activities, habits and skills of attention without which it is most difficult to succeed in school.
6. Teaching, by means of such visual and motor activities, habits and skills of following directions without which it is most difficult to succeed in school.

Research for any or all of the programs is sparse. A review of the literature for the past ten years yields little or no conclusive evidence that any P-M program has been significantly successful (Cratty, 1970; Myers and Hammill, 1969). The writer has found that a great deal of the criticism is because of the manner in which the data have been statistically surveyed or because of a lack of control variables. Yet for every negative report, a positive report can also be found on any of the proposed P-M programs.

Lack of positive gains in learning as a direct result of P-M programs is no doubt the strongest factor that prevents P-M programs from being accepted by today's educators. It will perhaps be the research conducted in the 1970's that will prove or disprove this claim. However, until educators, theorists, and researchers prove otherwise, P-M programs do have a part to play on today's educational stage. Extreme care must be taken with orientation and training programs in the colleges, universities, and the public schools. A careful review of all programs and the literature is essential constantly to adapt, incorporate, or change the programs being presented.

P-M programs have given us a new way to look at the learning process. We can no longer dismiss failures by the child as "he doesn't have it" or "he can't." We are now perhaps closer to a more organized and systematic procedure for examining the learner, the learning process, the environment, the teacher, the method, and the materials used.

References

Balow, B. Perceptual-motor activities in the treatment of severe reading disability. *The Reading Teacher,* 1971, 24, 513–525, 542.

Barsch, R. H. *A movigenic curriculum.* Madison, Wisconsin: State Department of Public Instruction, 1965.

Barsch, R. H. *Achieving perceptual-motor efficiency.* Vol. 1. Seattle, Washington: Special Child Publications, 1967.

Barsch, R. H. *Enriching perception and cognition.* Vol. II. Seattle, Washington: Special Child Publications, 1968.

Cratty, B. J. *Movement behavior and motor learning.* (2nd ed.) Philadelphia: Lea & Febiger, 1967.

Cratty, B. J. *Some educational implications of movements.* Seattle, Washington: Special Child Publications, 1970.

Cratty, B. J., & Martin, Sister M. M. *Perceptual-motor efficiency in children.* Philadelphia: Lea & Febiger, 1969.

Cruickshank, W. A. *A teaching method for brain-injured and hyperactive children.* Syracuse, New York: Syracuse University Press, 1961.

Delacato, C. *The treatment and prevention of reading problems.* Springfield, Ill.: Charles C Thomas, 1959.

Delacato, C. *The diagnosis and treatment of speech and reading problems.* Springfield, Ill.: Charles C Thomas, 1963.

Frostig, M., & Maslow, P. *Movement education: theory and practice.* Chicago: Follett Educational Corporation, 1970.

Getman, G. N. *How to develop your child's intelligence.* Luverne, Minn.: Getman, 1962.

Getman, G. N., & Kane, E. R. *The physiology of readiness: an action program for the development of perception for children.* Minneapolis, Minn.: Programs to Accelerate School Success, 1964. Revised and retitled: Getman, G. N., Kane, E. R., Halgren, M. R., & McKee, G. W. *Developing learning readiness.* Manchester, Missouri: Webster Division, McGraw-Hill, 1968.

Ismail, A. H., & Gruber, J. J. *Motor aptitude and intellectual performance.* Columbus: Charles E. Merrill, 1968.

Kephart, N. C. *The slow learner in the classroom.* Columbus: Charles E. Merrill, 1960.

Kephart, N. C. *Learning disability: an educational adventure.* Danville: The Interstate Printers and Publishers, Inc., 1968.

Magdol, M. S. An historical perspective to physiological education. *Academic Therapy Quarterly,* 1968, 3, No. 3.

McCarthy, J. J., & McCarthy, J. F. *Learning disabilities.* Boston: Allyn and Bacon, 1969.

McLeod, P. *Readiness for learning.* Philadelphia: J. B. Lippincott, 1967.

Mordock, J. B., & DeHaven, G. E. Movement skills of children with minimal cerebral dysfunction. *Rehabilitation Literature,* 1969, 30, 2–8.

Myers, P. I., & Hammill, D. D. *Methods for learning disorders.* New York: John Wiley & Sons, Inc., 1969.

O'Donnell, P. A. *Motor and haptic learning.* San Rafael: Dimensions Publishing Co., 1969.

Roach, E. G., & Kephart, N. C. Purdue perceptual-motor survey. Columbus: Charles E. Merrill, 1966.

Robins, F., & Robins, J. *Educational Rhythmics for Mentally and Physically Handicapped Children.* New York, Association Press, 1968.

Strauss, A. A., & Lehtinen, L. *Psychopathology and education of the brain-injured child.* New York: Grune & Stratton, 1947.

Valett, R. *The remediation of learning disabilities.* Palo Alto, California: Fearon Publishers, 1968.

Valett, R. *Programming learning disabilities.* Palo Alto, California: Fearon Publishers, 1969.

Von Hilsheimer, G. *How to live with your special child.* Washington D.C.: Acropolis Books, 1970.

Chapter 11

SKILLED PERFORMANCE

E. C. POULTON

Medical Reseach Council
Cambridge, England

Kinds of Skilled Performance

The most demanding skills require movements in the correct direction, of the correct size, and made at the correct time. Examples are reaching for or hitting a moving ball. Skills like running around a sports track do not require quite such precise movements. The positioning of the runner's foot on the track does not have to be as exact as the positioning of the hand in catching a ball. The runner is free to decide how quickly to run. His foot does not have to be in a particular position at a particular time, as does the hand in catching a ball. Skills can be ordered from the most demanding skills such as catching a moving ball to less demanding skills such as running.

Fast ball games and athletics have not been studied very extensively. This is partly because they are difficult to bring into the experimental laboratory, and partly because the experimental variables are difficult to control. Tracking is a demanding skill which has been studied extensively in the laboratory. Like catching a ball, it requires precise, accurately-timed movements.

Typing comes at the other end of the range of skills which have been studied in the laboratory. In typing, the movements do not have to be very precise or accurately timed. The exact positioning of a typist's finger on the key does not matter. A touch typist positions her fingers adequately without looking. The exact pressure of the finger on the key also does not matter. Pressure must simply be great enough to type the letter, but not great enough to perforate the paper. Typing is self-paced. The typist goes as quickly as she can without making errors. She does not have to hit a key at a particular instant.

In this chapter we shall be concerned mainly with the more demanding laboratory skills such as tracking. Simpler skills are brought in only to illustrate points which are difficult to illustrate using the more demanding ones.

Short-term Memory Store

In thinking about a skilled performance, it is useful to have a simple model of what a man's brain does as is illustrated in figure 11-1. The inputs on the

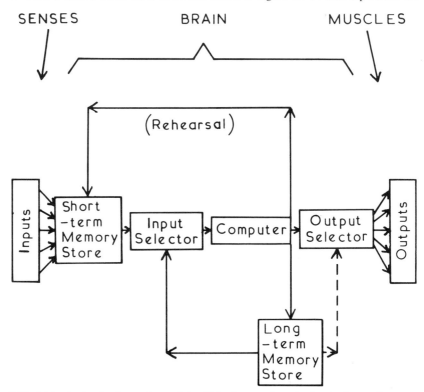

FIG. 11-1. A simple theoretic model which shows what the brain does. The input selector can accept only one message at a time. The computer takes at least .15 second to deal with a message. If the message is complex or difficult, it takes longer. During this time other messages have to wait in the short-term memory store. If they are kept waiting for more than a few seconds, they fade beyond recall. Information which has passed through the computer is fed back to the short-term memory store along the loop labeled rehearsal. It also passes to the long-term memory store, but several repetitions are necessary before it can become well established there. Once information has become established in the long-term memory store, it can be fed by the input selector to the computer. The computer can pass messages to the output selector and produce movements. A well-practiced skill has to be initiated by the computer, but it can then run automatically, leaving the computer free for another activity. This is illustrated by the broken arrow connecting the long-term memory store directly to the output selector (*Modified from Broadbent, 1958*).

left of the figure are from the eyes and ears, and from the sense organs scattered throughout the body. A number of arrows are shown leading from the box labeled inputs to the short-term memory store. This is because the eyes can take in a complete scene at a glance. The ears can receive a number of signals simultaneously, as in listening to orchestral music. There may be inputs from a number of other sense organs. The man may be controlling a light aircraft. The vestibular sense organs in his head will signal changes in tilt, and the accelerations of the aircraft. The man's pressure sense organs will signal changes in the direction and amount of pressure of the seat against his body. The man will also feel the pressure and movements of his hands on the controls.

Information which has entered the short-term memory store fades beyond recall in a few seconds unless it is rehearsed. Figure 11-2 illustrates the layout

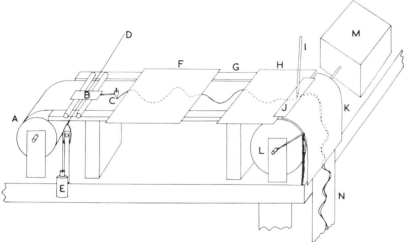

FIG. 11-2. The layout of an experiment to investigate the fading of memory in tracking. Paper tape from roll A on the left moved to the right at a fixed speed of 2.5 centimeters per second. It was pulled by the drum L on the right, which was rotated at a constant speed by the electric motor M. A movable carriage B held a pen C which drew a wavy line on the paper tape as it passed by. The string D was pulled to and fro irregularly by three rotating arms, which are not shown. The freely suspended weight E ensured that the carriage B followed the movement of the string. There were three frequencies of the wavy track. The average number of reversals per second made with each frequency is indicated in the inset to figure 11-3. The left side of the apparatus was screened from the man. He saw only the wavy track after it emerged from beneath the horizontal screen F into the gap G. The track then disappeared for good beneath the screen H. In different trials the size of the screen H was varied from 0 to 20 centimeters, to make the man delay his responses between 0 and 8 seconds. The required delays had ratios of 4:2:1:0 for each frequency of the wavy line. When the frequency was doubled, the required delays were halved. Thus the amounts of wavy line to be remembered were the same at every frequency. When the required delay was zero, the mask J was removed from the ball point pen. The man could then see the tip of his pen and the track he was supposed to hold it on, as in ordinary tracking with preview (*From Poulton, Ergonomics, p. 119, 1963*).

of an experiment which demonstrates how rapidly the memory of a wavy line can fade while a person is tracking it. The paper tape which carried the wavy track moved at a fixed speed. The man held the ballpoint pen I. It could be moved in the slit which lay across the paper tape. The man could see the wavy track for a period of 2.5 seconds some time before it reached his pen. It then disappeared from view beneath the horizontal screen H. The man had to try to keep the invisible tip of the pen on the invisible line as it passed.

The 12 men who served in the experiment did not delay their responses for as long as they should have done. The actual average delays are given on the abscissa in figure 11-3, by means of a logarithmic scale. The ordinate

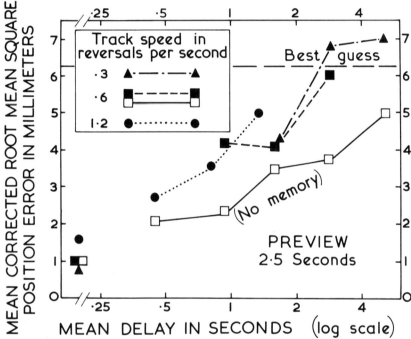

FIG. 11-3. The average accuracy with which 12 men reproduced from memory the positions of the reversals of an irregular wavy line while tracking without rehearsal. Three different track frequencies are represented by the filled triangles, squares, and circles. The corrected root mean square error given on the ordinate represents the standard deviation of the error. Each individual error was corrected for the average extent to which all the man's responses during the trial were too far to the right or left. This was done because constant errors in positioning are more likely to be due to errors in perception than to failures of memory. The unfilled squares represent the performance of a separate group of 12 men. They were instructed to keep the ballpoint pen I of figure 11-2 in line with the wavy line of intermediate frequency as it disappeared beneath the screen H. No memory was required. The width of the screen H between the visible part of the track and the man's pen was the same as in the corresponding memory condition. The horizontal broken line labeled best guess shows the average error if the man had consistently moved his pen from side to side at the average amplitude of the wavy line without noting the positions of the reversals (*Results from Poulton, 1963*).

shows the average variability in the remembered positions of the reversals. It represents the amount of uncertainty which the man had about the remembered positions.

The filled circles, squares, and triangles represent three different frequencies, or rates of wobble of the wavy line. For each duration of delay there is more wobble to remember when the frequency of the wobble is greater. The filled points all lie more or less on a straight line which slopes up to the right. This indicates that memory for the positions of the reversals fades more when the delay is longer. The frequency of the wobble, and the corresponding amount of wobble to remember, make little difference. If more wobble were a disadvantage, the circles would always be the highest points in each column. The triangles would always be the lowest points. This is not so. The relationships are just as often the reverse.

The filled points on the extreme left of the figure represent copying directly without memory. So do all the unfilled squares, which are from a separate group of 12 men. Each man attempted to keep the ballpoint pen I of figure 11-2 in line with the nearest end of the wavy track as it disappeared from the gap G under the screen H. In figure 11-3 the line joining the unfilled squares slopes up to the right. This is because the screen H was wider for the conditions represented by the unfilled squares on the right. Copying at a greater distance produces greater error, but reproducing from memory produces still more error. The slope of the line fitted to the filled squares is reliably steeper than the slope of the line fitted to the corresponding unfilled squares.

Copying behind with a delay of up to about .45 second can be done without difficulty. The filled circle for an average delay of .45 second lies a little above the corresponding unfilled square for copying at the same distance without memory, but the filled circle on the extreme left for no memory lies a similar distance above the corresponding unfilled square on the extreme left. Thus a memory span of .45 second does not matter. In the conditions represented by the four unfilled squares most to the right, the man copied by choice with an average delay of about .45 second.

An appreciable amount of forgetting has occurred by the time the delay has reached an average of .93 second. At this delay the filled square lies reliably above the corresponding unfilled square. The full difference in height between the filled and unfilled squares represents forgetting, for on the extreme left of the figure the filled and unfilled squares are at the same height. With a delay of three seconds or longer, memory of the wavy line has disappeared almost completely. Performance has reached the level of chance. This is illustrated at the top of the figure on the right by the broken horizontal line labeled "best guess."

Figure 11-3 shows that a person can reproduce a wavy line with a delay of .45 second without ill effect. Increasing the delay to .9 second reliably increases the error in the reproduction unless the person rehearses. Memory reaches the level of chance when the delay is increased to about three seconds. Information in the short-term memory store fades at a fairly similar rate when it is presented to the ears and is not rehearsed (Poulton, 1970, Chap. 1).

Rehearsal and the Span of Memory

The fading of memory in the short-term memory store can be delayed by rehearsal. Rehearsal involves selecting information in the short-term memory store, passing it through the computer, and back again to the store along the feedback loop shown in figure 11-1. Rehearsal takes time. In copying behind while rehearsing, memory is more accurate when the information is presented slowly. There may be a longer delay in the short-term memory store, but rehearsal reduces the rate of fading of the information in the store.

If a person rehearses, his memory is more accurate when there are fewer items of information to rehearse. The maximum number of items of information which can be held in the short-term memory store by rehearsal is called the memory span. The memory span is limited by the rate of rehearsal. With too many items, the last items are forgotten before they can be rehearsed.

Figure 11-4 illustrates the effect of rehearsal. The lowest point on each function represents a memory load of one reversal of the wavy track. The highest point represents a memory load of three reversals. Increasing the memory load increases the error in the reproduction.

The error in the reproduction is also larger when the rate of responding is faster. The function represented by circles is for a fast response rate. It lies above the function represented by triangles, which is for a slow response rate. Increasing the response rate increases the error in the reproduction. As a result, shorter delays give, if anything, larger errors at recall, whereas figure 11-3 shows that without rehearsal, shorter delays give smaller errors at recall.

The task of figure 11-4 was rather different from the task of figure 11-3. For the task represented in figure 11-4, the wavy line in figure 11-2 could be seen in a slit just in front of the mask J. The subject was instructed to note only the positions of the reversals. These were the positions at which the small section of wavy line seen through the slit stopped as it moved back and forth. In different trials the subject had to move his pen so that a pointer which it carried lined up with the position of the present reversal, the previous reversal, or the reversals two or three previously. When copying one or more reversals behind, the subject had to time his response movements to synchronize more or less with the times of the reversals which he could see.

The task in figure 11-3 involved memorizing only the positions of the reversals. The position of a reversal comprises only one item of information. Several positions can be rehearsed successfully. Whereas the task of figure 11-3 involved memorizing the whole of the wavy line. The shape of a wavy line com-

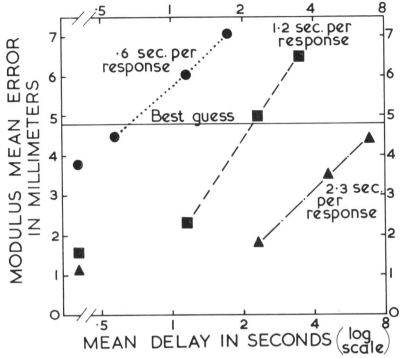

FIG. 11-4. The accuracy with which each of 12 men reproduced from memory the positions of the reversals of an irregular wavy line while rehearsing. The man could see a small section of a wavy line in a slit. He had to note the positions at which the wavy line stopped as it reversed direction. In the conditions represented by the points on the extreme left of the figure, he had to copy these positions with a ballpoint pen as they occurred. In other conditions he had to indicate the last position, the one from last position, or the two from last position. Three rates of responding are represented by the circles, squares, and triangles. The horizontal line labeled best guess shows the average error if the man had consistently moved his pen from side to side at the average amplitude of the wavy line without noting the positions of the reversals. The circle and triangle which lie just below this line are not reliably lower (*Results from Poulton, 1954*).

prises a large number of items of information, one item for every point on the line. The number of items is too large to be rehearsed successfully. Thus, figure 11-3 shows no evidence of rehearsal, while figure 11-4 illustrates the effect of rehearsal.

When copying three reversals behind, the subject needed to rehearse and store three positions, two positions on one side of the slit and one position on the other side. The triangle on the extreme right of figure 11-4 shows that, on the average, this was too much when only 2.3 seconds were available between responses. Some men subjects could manage it reasonably well. Other men tended to confuse the two positions on one side. They would reproduce the position of the last reversal instead of the position of the previous reversal on the same side.

Copying behind while rehearsing is not easy even when unlimited time is available. The computer illustrated in figure 11-1 has to be switched between noting the display, deciding on a response, and rehearsing. Also, order information has to be retained. The oldest item in the running memory span determines the next response, while the item currently displayed has to be tacked on at the other end of the running memory span beside the newest item. The maximum running memory span with rehearsal is only about four items (Poulton, 1970, Chap. 8).

Computer of Limited Capacity

The box labeled computer in figure 11-1 is not like a modern high-speed digital computer. It works relatively slowly. If a task is difficult, the computer takes a long time to carry it out. The difficulty of a task can be increased by increasing the number of alternative responses which may be required. When a man knows what response to make, and is ready waiting for the signal, he can respond in about .2 second. But when there are 10 possible signals, each of which calls for a different response, the man is likely to need .6 second, three times as long (Woodworth, 1938, p. 333). The difference between .2 and .6 second is the average time it takes the computer to decide which of the 10 possible responses should be made, after it has received one of the 10 possible signals.

The values of .2 and .6 second are for signals and responses which are reasonably well matched or compatible. If the responses are allocated to the signals at random, the reaction times are longer. Practice reduces the reaction times, but it would take a great deal of practice before random pairings of signals and responses gave reaction times as short as compatible pairings (Fitts and Seeger, 1953).

The most compatible pairing so far discovered is between a touch on a finger tip and a movement of the finger. Movements of the fingers and touch have been paired frequently throughout life. The computer has simply to select this pairing. The task is so easy that after practice the reaction time with eight alternatives is as short as the reaction time with only two alternatives (Leonard, 1959).

A difficult problem produces a long reaction time. There may be a large number of possible answers. The computer in figure 11-1 may have to carry out complex computations in order to arrive at the correct answer. The computer's task is made more difficult if signals are difficult to discriminate from each other. Reaction time increases as a result.

Precision of Response

The difficulty of a task can be increased by increasing the precision with which a movement has to be made. In the usual experiment on reaction times, the man has simply to press a key. It does not matter how hard he presses, provided he presses hard enough to make an electrical contact. However, movements often have to be made both quickly and accurately. A movement of a specified size takes an average of .03 second longer to get started than a movement of unspecified size (Poulton, 1950, Figure 2). The increase in reaction time is a good deal less than the increase of about .1 second when the number of alternative responses is increased from 1 to 2, for the man knows in advance what response to make. Before starting to move he has simply to ensure that the movement ends in the correct place. When the movement has to be very exact, the average reaction time is slightly longer than when the movement does not have to be quite so exact (Fitts and Peterson, 1964).

The time taken to make a movement behaves rather like the time taken to react. A hand movement of a fixed size takes longer to make when it has to end within a small target area than when the target area is larger. This is illustrated in figure 11-5 (Fitts, 1954). Two target plates were placed a fixed distance apart. Each of 16 men had to tap them alternately as quickly as he could. The ratio of the width of the targets to the size of the separation is given on the abscissa. The figure shows that the average time taken by a movement depended upon this ratio. Halving the width of the targets had the same effect upon the average time taken as doubling the size of the movement. Within the range of 2 to 16 inches, it made little difference how large the movement was, provided the size of the target was adjusted proportionally.

When the ratio of the width of the target to the size of the separation was one, the two target plates were placed side by side. The man could tap them in turn almost as fast as he could tap on the same plate. The maximum rate of tapping varies between about 6 and 8 taps per second. The bottom right hand point in the figure shows that the man could tap the target plates in turn at an average rate of almost six taps per second.

Fitts' ratio rule applies also to the movement times of single responses. Here the times are not quite so long. If the man does not know the direction of the movement in advance, all the movement times are slightly but reliably longer (Fitts and Peterson, 1964).

In these experiments the proportion of errors increases as the target width decreases. The size of the movement makes very little difference to the proportion of errors. For the experiment illustrated in figure 11-5, the average proportion of errors increased from .4 percent with the 2-inch target to 3.3 percent with the .25-inch target. The students did not slow down their movements with the narrower targets quite so much as they should have done to maintain the high level of accuracy which they achieved with the wide targets. If they had done so, the vertical separation of the points for each ratio in figure 11-5 might have been larger. Flexor movements of the wrist and elbow were always made more accurately on the average than extensor movements.

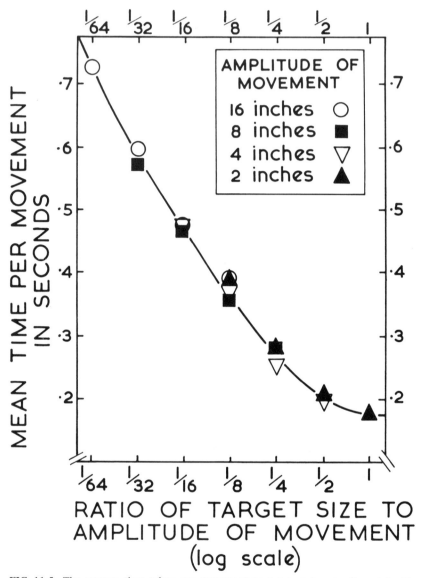

FIG. 11-5. The average time taken per movement to tap two targets alternately. The targets were rectangular with a height of 6 inches. Their widths were 2, 1, .5 or .25 inches. Two targets of the same width were mounted side by side like a Roman II. The separation between their centers was 16, 8, 4 or 2 inches. The ratio of the width of the targets to the distance between them is given on the abscissa. Each of the 16 men was instructed to concentrate on accuracy rather than speed (*Results from Fitts, 1954*).

The limited capacity of the computer in figure 11-1 is responsible both for the time taken to start a movement and for the time taken to make the movement. Provided a signal clearly specifies what movement is required, reaction time is determined principally by the number of choices of movement. The precision of the movement has only a relatively small effect upon reaction time. Movement time is determined principally by the precision of the movement (Fig. 11-5). The number of choices has only a relatively small effect upon movement time.

Single Channel Input Selector and Intermittent Responding

In figure 11-1 there are a number of arrows leading from the box labeled inputs to the short-term memory store, but only one arrow connects the short-term memory store to the input selector. There is a single arrow connecting the input selector to the computer. This is to indicate that only one message at a time can be selected and fed into the computer. While the input selector is set to select one message, other messages have to wait. This is illustrated in figure 11-6.

The man held a small lever. When he heard a first signal, he had to move the lever a fraction of an inch upward or downward to make an electrical contact with a metal stop. When he heard a second signal, he had to move the lever the same distance in the opposite direction. The two auditory signals were presented 12 times during a trial with the same fixed interval between them. There were occasional catch trials to prevent the man from starting to respond before he heard a signal.

In the condition represented by the circles and unbroken lines in the middle of the figure, the man knew that a second signal would almost always follow the first. He also knew when it would arrive. He was told to make his response to the second signal as quick as possible. This is indicated by the underlining of RT2. The average reaction times to the second signal are represented by the filled circles. The reaction times did not increase very much until the interval between the first and second signals had been reduced to .2 second. At this interval RT2 was reliably greater than RT1, which is represented by the unfilled circles. When the interval between signals was reduced to .1 second, the average RT2 increased by an additional .07 second. The extra delay was not caused simply by having to make a second response with the same hand. A similar increase was found by Davis (1957) when the two responses were made with different hands. To prevent the subject from starting to respond before he received the second signal, Davis varied the time interval between the two signals irregularly instead of using catch trials.

The results of this condition agree with a number of subsequent experiments which have been reviewed by Smith (1967) and by Welford (1967). The results suggest that even when a man is expecting to have to respond to a second signal, the computer in figure 11-1 cannot accept the

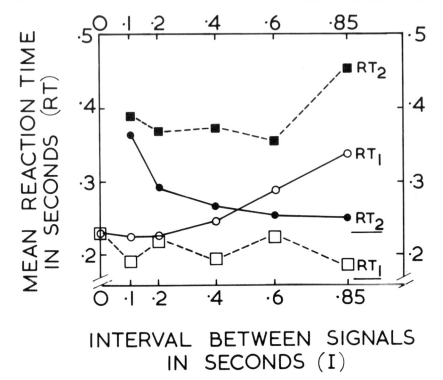

**INTERVAL BETWEEN SIGNALS
IN SECONDS (I)**

FIG. 11-6. The average reaction times to pairs of auditory signals. The second signal
followed the first after a short fixed interval of time. Each of the eight men had to
respond in one direction to the first signal, and in the opposite direction to the second
signal. Except for occasional catch trials, the man knew the order in which the two
responses had to be made. The unfilled points represent the mean reaction times to first
signal (RT1). The filled points represent the mean reaction times to the second signal
(RT2). The interval between signals is shown on the abscissa. The circles and unbroken
lines represent the condition in which the man was told to keep RT2 short. RT1 and
RT2 are reliably different with intervals of .1, .2, and .85 second between signals. The
squares and broken lines represent the condition in which the man was told to keep RT1
short. The second signal followed the first on only one third of the trials. RT1 and RT2
are reliably different at all intervals between signals. The unfilled points on the ordinate
are for a number of simple responses to the first signal only (*Results from Poulton, 1950*).

second signal while it is dealing with the previous signal. The signal has to
wait until the end of RT1.

A second experimental condition is represented by the squares and broken
lines at the top and bottom of the figure. Here a second signal followed the
first on only one third of the trials. The subject did not know which trials
they would be. He was told to make his response to the first signal as quickly
as possible. He was to think about the second signal only when it arrived. This
is indicated by the underlining of RT1. The figure shows that this condition
always produced the shortest average reaction times to the first signal, and

the longest average reaction times to the second signal. At all intervals between the two signals, the average reaction time to the second signal was reliably longer than the average reaction time to the first signal.

In the condition represented by the circles and unbroken lines, the input selector in figure 11-1 was set to select the second signal as soon as it occurred. The only delay was in clearing the computer ready for the next decision. There was no additional delay caused by having to switch the input selector. In the condition represented by the squares and broken lines, the subject was not always expecting the second signal. The input selector was not always set ready. Instead it may have been set to select the kinesthetic feedback from the man's responding hand, or the input selector may have been set to accept the visual or auditory feedback due to arrive when the first response had been completed. There was, therefore, the additional delay while the second signal was capturing the input selector. When an auditory signal is quite unexpected, the average delay may last as long as one second (Poulton, 1950, Experiment 1).

Figure 11-6 shows that when two signals follow each other in close succession, the delay in the second response can consist of two components. First, there is a component which does not usually exceed the reaction time to the first signal. It is caused by the computer in figure 11-1, which cannot deal with the second signal until it has dealt with the first signal. Secondly, there is a component which is more variable, and which can be very much longer. It is due to the input selector, which may be set to select a sensory input indicating how successful the first response has been. The second signal has to capture the input selector before it can be dealt with by the computer.

Long-term Memory Store

When the computer processes material from the short-term memory store, the material starts to become established in the long-term memory store, which is illustrated at the bottom of figure 11-1. Once material has become established in the long-term memory store, it remains available or partly available for hours or days. The long duration of the storage contrasts with the duration of only a few seconds in the short-term memory store.

In talking and in carrying out other practiced movements, the input selector draws upon material in the long-term memory store. The material is passed through the computer to the output selector. It also passes along the rehearsal loop to the short-term memory store. This mechanism supplies the person with a running memory of what he is doing. The person's input selector and computer can use the information when he wants to know where he has got to in his speaking or in his movements. If a person is speaking, he also receives feedback into his short-term memory store through his ears. If he is moving, he obtains feedback from the moving parts of his body. He can also look and see what he is doing. Thus, in speaking and in carrying out practiced movements, the input selector and computer use in turn information from the long-term and short-term memory stores.

Once a person has learned a motor skill, he retains his skill for months or years. In experiments on memory for motor skills, the training time is rarely more than a few hours. The time after which retention is tested is often a number of months. In an experiment by Ammons and his colleagues (1958) on groups of over 40 college students, the learning during one hour of practice had not been forgotten completely after two years. There may be some interference if another rather similar motor skill is learned in the meantime, but a person who has learned a number of difficult and rather different motor skills usually learns and relearns rapidly. An experienced pilot is an example.

It used to be thought that motor skills are remembered considerably better than other tasks. This is not necessarily so. An exact comparison cannot be made between a motor skill and a procedural or verbal task, because it is not possible to equate them for difficulty. Also it is not possible to tell how much learning of one task corresponds to a fixed degree of learning of the other task. Ammons and his colleagues (1958) used a simple three-dimensional tracking task, the Airplane Control Test. Other groups of about 40 college students were given a procedural task to learn instead. A vertical panel had 17 controls mounted on it. The students had to learn to operate 15 of them in the correct order. If anything, the motor skill was remembered better than the procedural task, but both tasks were remembered pretty well.

Mengelkoch, Adams, and Gainer (1971) used a simulated flying task. In addition to learning to fly the simulated aircraft, the 26 students from the Reserve Officers Training Corps had to learn the operating procedures. In the test four months later, the experimenters found a reliable amount of forgetting of all classes of procedures. All six statistical tests showed reliable decrements, whereas on the measures of tracking proficiency, only five of the 10 statistical tests showed reliable decrements. Thus, the acquired tracking skill was, if anything, retained better than was memory of the operating procedures. But as Mengelkoch and his colleagues point out, this could be because the students spent more time flying the simulator than they spent on the operating procedures. Clearly some memory of motor skills, of procedural tasks, and of verbal tasks can be shown to survive for months, probably for years. It is not possible to conclude that motor skills are remembered the best.

Automation of Skill

When a skill has become highly practiced, it needs less computer time. Something like a template has been constructed in the long-term memory store. The input selector has only to select the template, and to pass the information through the computer to the output selector. The highly practiced skill can then be carried out without involving the input selector and computer. This is indicated in figure 11-1 by the broken arrow connecting the boxes labeled long-term memory store and output selector. The input selector and computer are required only when it is necessary to check on how the skill is being carried out, or to change templates. In the meantime, they are available for some other activity. Motor skills such as walking and holding familiar objects have become highly automated in this way. People are used to listening and talking while doing these things.

Gradual automation of skill can be observed in teaching someone to drive an automobile. In the very early stages, practically the whole of the learner's attention is occupied by his control movements. A signal for action, perhaps from the road ahead, is fed by the input selector in figure 11-1 into the computer. The appropriate rudimentary template has then to be found in the long-term memory store. Information from this is fed by the input selector through the computer to the output selector. It leads to a control movement.

The learning driver has then to check that he has done the right thing. He needs sensory information fed back by means of the input selector to the computer from his hands and feet as to what movements were made, to check whether they were correct or not. Later he needs sensory information from his eyes about the behavior of the automobile. Errors are corrected by the input selector choosing a somewhat different template from the long-term memory store. Information from this is then fed by means of the computer to the output selector.

While the learning driver is doing all this, he may have little or no idea of what is happening in the road ahead. His computer capacity is fully occupied in attempting to control the automobile. At this early stage driving instructors report that they have to keep a lookout on the road ahead to see that the automobile does not hit anything.

At a later stage of practice the learning driver does not need to monitor every aspect of his control movements so carefully. Appropriate templates have still to be found in the long-term memory store. The information from them has to be fed by means of the input selector and computer to the output selector. Once this has been done, however, the long-term memory store and output selector can communicate directly along the broken arrow in figure 11-1. The man does not need to keep a close check upon his control movements. This leaves his input selector and computer free to deal with other aspects of driving, such as what is happening in the road ahead.

At a still later stage the driver may have computer time in reserve whenever the amount of relevant information coming from the road ahead is not too great. The surplus computer time can be measured. The man is given questions to listen to and to answer orally when he can. His score on the questions reflects the amount of unused computer time (Brown and Poulton, 1961). Scores have been found to increase with the number of days of training on the road (Brown, 1966). The reserve computer time is needed whenever there is an increase in the amount of relevant information which has to be processed. Signals from the road ahead may fully occupy the computer. When this happens, the man has no spare computer time available for listening and talking.

Performing Two Tasks Simultaneously

A man may be able to perform two tasks simultaneously. To be able to do so, he must have practiced one of the tasks until it has become pretty automatic. The computer of figure 11-1 cannot make two decisions simultaneously, but it can make decisions about one task, while decisions made previously about the other task are being executed using the path represented by the broken arrow in figure 11-1. This is illustrated by an experiment of Brown, Tickner, and Simmonds (1969).

Each of 24 drivers had to answer questions over a radiotelephone while deciding whether or not a gap ahead between two obstacles was just wide enough to drive the automobile through. Brown and his colleagues found that the driver made reliably more wrong decisions while driving and answering questions than while driving in a control condition without questions. The driver also answered the questions reliably less correctly, and took reliably longer to do so when he answered the questions while driving than in a control condition with questions while the automobile was stationary.

The computer in figure 11-1 could not make a decision about the width of the gap in the road ahead while it was occupied with answering a question. The decision about the width of the gap was a difficult one. It probably took several seconds to arrive at the best answer. Answering a question received over the radiotelephone during this period interfered with the decision. If the driver delayed his decision for too long, he had to drive through the gap whether he wanted to or not, because he was not allowed to stop or swerve sharply. If the driver delayed dealing with the question until after he had decided whether or not to accept the gap, there was a chance that he had partly forgotten the question. If so, his answer could be wrong as well as late.

Once the driver had decided to accept a narrow gap, his skill in steering the automobile through it was not reliably degraded by having to answer questions at the same time. This is because steering the automobile had become pretty automatic. The computer in figure 11-1 had simply to decide on the size of the corrective movement which was needed. While the steering correction was being carried out, the input selector could switch the computer back onto the task of answering the questions. Quick checks could be made from time to time, perhaps between questions. The checks would ensure that an error in steering was not developing. The checks would be all that was necessary most of the time.

Two visual tasks which both require direct vision cannot be combined so easily as a visual and a non-visual task. This is because the eyes cannot look directly in two different places at once. While the eyes are fixating one task, visual signals from the other task are less able to capture the input selector. This is the reason for the deterioration in tracking found by Garvey (1960) and by Fuchs (1962) when a subject was given an additional visual task to perform at the same time.

Fuchs (1962) used a second tracking task with a visual display for his additional task. Garvey (1960) used two additional visual tasks, one of which he (Garvey and Taylor 1959) had found previously to interfere markedly with visual tracking. Garvey also used the listening and speaking additional task which he had found previously to interfere very little with visual tracking. Garvey pooled the results from the three tasks. The marked change in tracking performance by the three additional tasks represents very largely the effect of the two additional visual tasks.

With the addition of the simultaneous visual tasks of the kind used by Garvey and by Fuchs, the subject cannot see the displays properly without looking directly at them. While he is looking at the additional-task display, he cannot be looking at the tracking display. Future sources of error in the tracking display can capture the subject's attention if his eyes are directed at the tracking display, but they will not capture his attention if his eyes are directed at the additional-task display. Having to perform the additional visual task makes the practiced man track rather like an unpracticed person. He spends his time correcting errors which have already appeared. He does not prevent errors from appearing, as he does when he can look at the tracking display all the time.

References

Ammons, R. B., Farr, R. G., Bloch, E., Neumann, E., Dey, M., Marion, R., & Ammons, C. H. Long-term retention of perceptual-motor skills. *Journal of Experimental Psychology*, 1958, 55, 318–328.

Broadbent, D. E. *Perception and communication.* Oxford: Pergamon Press, 1958.

Brown, I. D. Subjective and objective comparisons of successful and unsuccessful trainee drivers. *Ergonomics,* 1966, 9, 49–56.

Brown, I. D., & Poulton, E. C. Measuring the spare "mental capacity" of car drivers by a subsidiary task. *Ergonomics,* 1961, 4, 34–40.

Brown, I. D., Tickner, A. H., & Simmonds, D. C. V. Interference between concurrent tasks of driving and telephoning. *Journal of Applied Psychology,* 1969, 53, 419–424.

Davis, R. The human operator as a single channel information system. *Quarterly Journal of Experimental Psychology,* 1957, 9, 119–129.

Fitts, P. M. The information capacity of the human motor system in controlling the amplitude of movement. *Journal of Experimental Psychology,* 1954, 47, 381–391.

Fitts, P. M., & Peterson, J. R. Information capacity of discrete motor responses. *Journal of Experimental Psychology,* 1964, 67, 103–112.

Fitts, P. M., & Seeger, C. M. S-R compatibility: Spatial characteristics of stimulus and response codes. *Journal of Experimental Psychology,* 1953, 46, 199–210.

Fuchs, A. H. The progression-regression hypothesis in perceptual-motor skill learning. *Journal of Experimental Psychology,* 1962, 63, 177–182.

Garvey, W. D. A comparison of the effects of training and secondary tasks on tracking behavior. *Journal of Applied Psychology,* 1960, 44, 370–375.

Garvey, W. D., & Taylor, F. V. Interactions among operator variables, system dynamics, and task-induced stress. *Journal of Applied Psychology,* 1959, 43, 79–85.

Leonard, J. A. Tactual choice reactions: 1. *Quarterly Journal of Experimental Psychology,* 1959, 11, 76–83.

Mengelkoch, R. F., Adams, J. A., & Gainer, C. A. The forgetting of instrument flying skills. *Human Factors,* 1971, 13, 397–405.

Poulton, E. C. Perceptual anticipation and reaction time. *Quarterly Journal of Experimental Psychology,* 1950, 2, 99–112.

Poulton, E. C. Eye-hand span in simple serial tasks. *Journal of Experimental Psychology,* 1954, 47, 403–410.

Poulton, E. C. Sequential short-term memory: Some tracking experiments. *Ergonomics,* 1963, 6, 117–132.

Poulton, E. C. *Environment and human efficiency.* Springfield, Illinois: Thomas, 1970.

Smith, M. C. Theories of the psychological refractory period. *Psychological Bulletin,* 1967, 67, 202–213.

Welford, A. T. Single-channel operation in the brain. *Acta Psychologica,* 1967, 27, 5–22.

Woodworth, R. S. *Experimental psychology.* New York: Holt, 1938.

Chapter 12

CYBERNETIC PSYCHOLOGY *

K. U. Smith
The University of Wisconsin

FEEDBACK PRINCIPLES OF LEARNING AND MOTOR BEHAVIOR

In the last two decades, the traditional field of study of psychomotor activity has undergone major theoretic and experimental changes in which motions of the body, including specific movement patterns, posture, social behavior, tool-using and behavioral-physiologic interactions, have been investigated experimentally as dynamic feedback processes. The field of study concerned with the theory, experimental design, systems analysis, and applied work related to such feedback research is called *behavioral cybernetics*—that is, the understanding of motorsensory mechanisms as dynamic control systems. Behavioral cybernetics is concerned with systems theory and analysis of living activity in which response is conceived of as the dynamic reaction sector of closed-loop control mechanisms that govern and integrate the stimulus environment, sensory input, perception, neural activity, and physiologic function by feedback control (Fig. 12-1). This systems approach thus differs radically from traditional stimulus-response or reflex doctrines of behavior and learning which try to deal with motor activity as an end product determined by the linear, one-way influences of environmental stimuli and internal physiologic states.

*The research described in this chapter has been supported by the National Science Foundation for projects on feedback studies of human motion and vision and by the Biological Training Section of the National Institute of Mental Health in a research training program on psychophysiologic cybernetics. Some limited parts of the research were also supported by the Social and Rehabilitation Service for a project on real-time computer analysis of body motions.

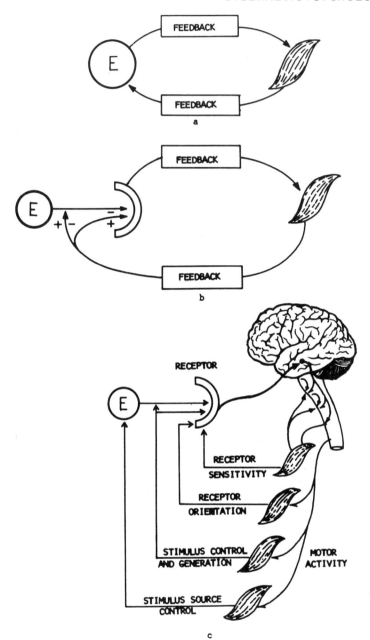

FIG. 12-1. The meaning of feedback control in behavioral systems: (a) feedback as reciprocal interaction between motor and sensory processes; (b) motorsensory feedback involving generation and control of stimuli through positive and negative modes of closed-loop regulation, and (c) the levels of motorsensory feedback control of the skeletal motor system.

Behavioral systems research complements past stimulus-response study in providing information about variable feedback control in perception, learning, motivation, and behavioral-physiologic interactions. Advances in this field have been based on development of experimental feedback techniques of controlling the spatial, temporal, force, multivariate, and integrative feedback relationships between response and receptor input mechanisms (Fig. 12-2). Optical, electronic, electromechanic, television, audiotape, videotape, and computer systems have been developed which can be interposed between response and receptor or neural operations, and thus used to control the feedback variables linking motorsensory systems. In all such experimental methods, the subject, operator, or medical patient regulates his own sensory input and stimulus selection while particular cybernetic laboratory methods are used to make controlled variation in the feedback factors of the self-governed, closed-loop operations.

ORIGINS OF BEHAVIORAL CYBERNETICS

The origins of experimental behavioral cybernetics lie in studies of visual-manual tracking, inversion of the retinal image, optical tracking, and delayed auditory feedback of speech. Stratton's early studies (1896, 1897, 1899) of optical inversion of the retinal image represented the first systematic efforts to produce controlled variations in the dynamic interactions between sensory input and response (Fig. 12-2a,b). The significance of feedback research in these early perception studies was recognized fully for the first time in research on tracking systems in World War II, in which it was observed that learning and performance were primarily governed by space and time compliances between the motor and sensory systems of the human operator, as determined by the design of machines. When military machines produced marked space displacements or time lags between response and sensory factors, they were found to be useless as training and military devices. Lee's studies (1950, 1951) of delayed feedback of speech (Fig. 12-2d) extended experimental cybernetic methods to the scientific investigation of unaided behavior of speech and hearing.

Behavioral cybernetics establishes the study of perception and motion as a unified science of experimental behavioral systems research (Fig. 12-3). Behavior and its underlying physiologic processes are specified as involving at least seven levels of feedback control of (1) metabolic regulation, (2) neural activation and integration, (3) receptor sensitivity, (4) receptor guidance, (5) self-stimulation, (6) environmental stimulus selection, (7) stimulus modulation, and (8) stimulus source control. Postural mechanisms serve to activate neural mechanisms and to effect sensory input by receptor-efferent neural connections. Tremor and other specialized responses maintain sensitivity of the receptors. Transport movements and receptor-motor mechanisms govern sense-organ orientation, stimulus intensity at the receptor surface, stimulus

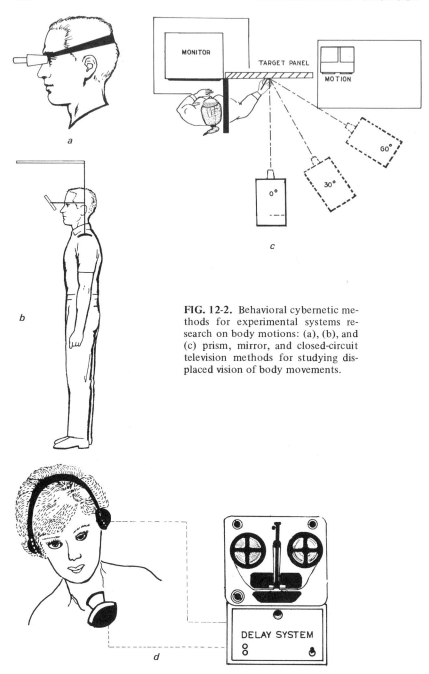

FIG. 12-2. Behavioral cybernetic methods for experimental systems research on body motions: (a), (b), and (c) prism, mirror, and closed-circuit television methods for studying displaced vision of body movements.

(d) Lee's (1951) technique of studying delayed auditory feedback of speech.

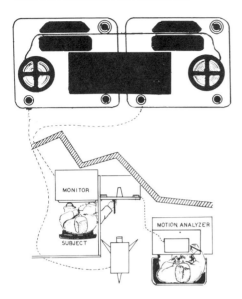

(e) Videotape method for producing delayed auditory feedback.

(f) Electronic behavior sensing technique for controlling feedback stimuli.

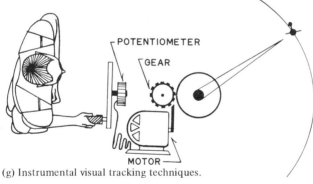

(g) Instrumental visual tracking techniques.

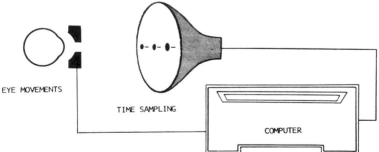

(h) Real-time computer system for controlling the feedback parameters of eye movement-retinal interactions.

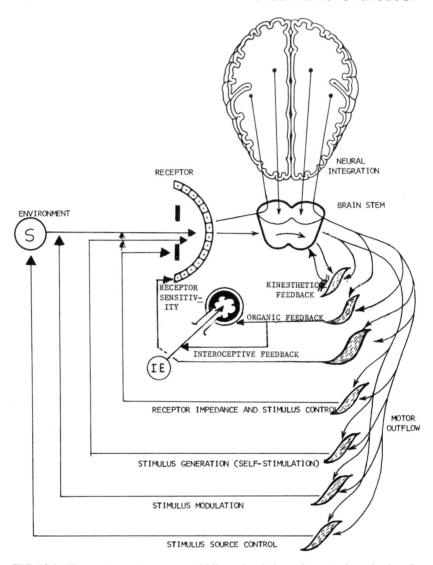

FIG. 12-3. The motor system as a multidimensional dynamic control mechanism for regulation of the environmental, stimulus, sensory, receptor, and neural parameters of perception.

pattern formation, stimulus modulation, and other aspects of stimulus selection. Overt motor response, sometimes transformed by tools, machines, and symbolic language, acts to control object and energy sources of environmental stimulation.

PSYCHOMOTOR FEEDBACK

The motion systems of the body do not consist of collections or chains of discrete reflexes or responses, but are organized in terms of multidimensional feedback circuits for integrated regulation of posture, dynamic transport action, and articulated movements of the limbs and head receptors. Motion systems such as posture, locomotion, hand motion, head movements, and eye movements are studied as feedback-control systems using the experimental cybernetic methods described in figure 12-2.

Cybernetic Analysis of Posture

In using hybrid-computer methods to study posture, the subject stands on a coordinate force platform which registers separately the right-left and front-back movements of the body in maintaining balance (Fig. 12-4). Electric analogs of these two types of movements, as obtained from strain-gauge transducers on the force platform, are amplified and sampled at 200 samples per second by a hybrid-computer system. Dynamic computer programming is used to vary the space relations between the coordinate dimensions of postural motion and directions of action of the feedback indicator which the subject views. Feedback delays and temporal interruptions also can be introduced into one or another of the dimensions of postural motion. After experimental programming, the postural signals are

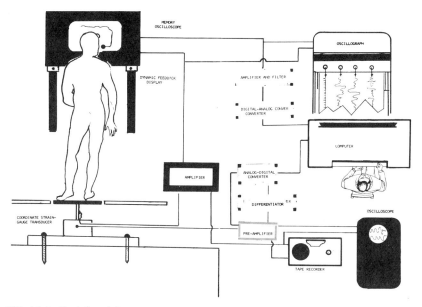

FIG. 12-4. Real-time laboratory computer system and coordinate force platform for the measurement of postural tracking and the feedback factors in postural control and integration.

deconverted to continuous form and amplified. The amplified signal thereafter is used to drive a target spot on a memory oscilloscope in right-left and up-down dimensions.

Two types of posture-controlled, visual-feedback research may be investigated by the computerized force platform—that is, self-generated production of postural drawings or postural writing of letters and designs, and tracking of visual targets displayed on the oscilloscope screen by the coordinate postural movements.

The computerized force platform may be used in conjunction with techniques of varying the visual, labyrinthine, kinesthetic, and tactual modes of regulation of posture. Results of such research have indicated that posture and its sensory channels are regulated as feedback-control mechanisms. Postural balance in dynamic action involves generalized and articulated levels of control of the head and upper limbs and torso and of the lower limbs (Fig. 12-5). These two levels of regulated posture act in direct and compensatory ways to govern the body's center of gravity. In the upper regions of the body, the motor mechanisms guiding the kinesthetic and labyrinthine mechanisms establish rough general levels of postural balance which can be refined by visual control. The inferior levels of postural regulation involve basometric representation of all movements of limbs in the action of the sole of the feet. The tactual factors involved in such basometric representation refine more general kinesthetic factors of the joints of the limbs and pelvis in compensating shifts in posture, which are produced by locomotion and action of the upper sectors of the body. The cybernetic factors in postural control have been checked by observations with a massive anthropomorphous walking machine in which the concept of multivariate feedback regulation of the center of gravity was mechanized and found to be operationally accurate.

The most significant concepts coming out of the experimental analysis of posture are those of yoked body tracking and bilateral neurogeometric detection of body tracking. A central feature of postural reactions is that different parts of the body such as the head and neck, neck and torso, and torso and limbs seem to reciprocally respond to and follow changes in body motion with near zero reaction time. This tracking or following of changes in one part of the body by another is called body tracking. Similar tracking may occur when a limb or response system on one part of the body tracks or coordinates with movements on the other side of the body in bilateral motion.

Bilateral movements of different levels or sectors of the body in controlling visual, vestibular, kinesthetic, and tactual receptor inputs in high-speed body tracking are known to operate in terms of bilateral neurogeometric detection, wherein single neurons lying in the brain stem and spinal cord detect differences in stimulation from matched receptors located on symmetrical, mirrored loci in receptor systems of the two sides of the

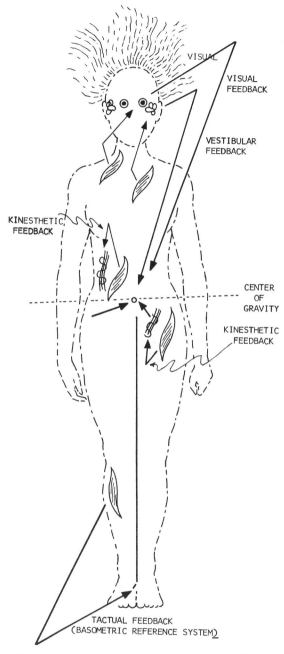

FIG. 12-5. The postural system as a series of cascaded levels of feedback-controlled body tracking which integrate torso, head, and limb movements during motions of the body and in relation to gravity.

body (Fig. 12-6). In such bilateral detection, differences in stimulation at matched, mirrored points in the two vestibular nuclei, on the skin, in the kinesthetic system, and in the two eyes are detected by the central ganglion cells which actuate both motor output and receptor-efferent activity to regulate postural response. These high-speed, bilateral feedback detectors and actuator cells also regulate body tracking in posture. Asymmetries of movement in one sector of the body produce differences in bilateral control in other parts leading to either positive or negative body tracking to compensate or enhance the bilaterally detected sensory variations. The interaction of different sectors of movement of the body through such bilateral neurogeometric control serves to govern the balance and center of gravity of the body as a whole.

Behavior Mechanisms of Locomotion

Locomotion may be conceived and investigated as a series of feedback-controlled mechanisms. The forms of dynamic gait such as walking, running, hopping, skipping, and dancing are based on integrated closed-loop regulation of posture, transport, and articulated movements which guide and regulate their own specific channels of kinesthetic, tactual, visual, and labyrinthine sensory inputs. The actions of locomotion are yoked together and integrated with posture through basometric action of the foot on the substrate. Driving action of the large toe and ball of the foot lifts the body and starts the leg in the stride. As this striding action is going on, the body's center of gravity is shifted to control the foot resting on the substrate, which tracks imbalance by lateral action of the ball and the fifth metatarsal joint and by front and back action of the foot. During the stride, movements of the lower leg generate reactions and track kinesthetic variations in the swing of the leg to determine the locking of the knee for landing. As the striding foot lands, preparatory actions of the massive muscles of the pelvis and buttocks cushion the landing. During the period when both feet are on the substrate, the differences in stimulation on bilaterally symmetrical points of the feet serve to control postural balance in a precise articulated way and to prepare for takeoff in the next striding motion. During the course of these actions, visual tracking mechanisms guide locomotion at long distance on smooth terrain and at short distance on uneven terrain. At the same time, labyrinthine kinesthetic control mechanisms of the upper parts of the body compensate general shifts in postural balance produced by the striding actions of the leg. Evidence for such dynamic, closed-loop mechanisms in locomotion has been obtained through feedback research on locomotion and by systematic studies of the requirements of design of feedback mechanisms of anthropomorphous walking and exoskeleton machines.

Experimental feedback research on locomotion has been concerned with study of the control mechanisms of guidance, timing, and integration of the

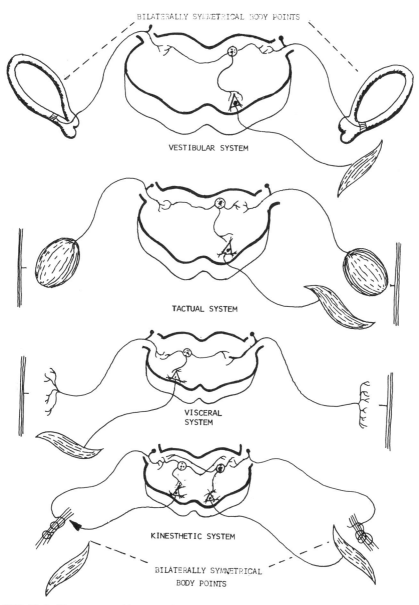

FIG. 12-6. Movement guidance and coordination on the two sides of the body as a bilateral neurogeometric mechanism in which single central neurons act as feature detectors for sensing differences in stimuli between bilaterally symmetrical receptor points.

main motor components of gait—that is, basal action of the foot, stride movements and postural reactions during walking. Studies have been done also on coordination of pedal and manual tracking motions. Figure 12-7 illustrates the methods used in studies of space-displaced visual feedback on guidance of locomotor movements. A special pair of goggles fitted with dove prisms which could be rotated around their longitudinal axis was used to alter the visual feedback which a person got from a marked path during locomotion. Tests were made of the relative effect of inversion, reversal and combined inversion and reversal of visual feedback on accuracy in remaining on the marked path during normal walking. Results showed that of the three displacement conditions, inversion had the most marked effect on performance, that individuals showed the greatest amount of learning with this condition, but that repeated practice over several days failed to produce an accuracy of walking with displaced vision that was as accurate as walking with normal vision. Records of the timing and accuracy of the gait movements confirmed the description of guidance of locomotion just described by showing that any alteration of the normal visual feedback pattern of locomotion leads to a special form of locomotor tracking in which the individual watches every step as he moves and slows the rate and length of striding movements to control such tracking.

Locomotion cannot be reduced to a pattern of bipedal tilting or pendulum movements of the body as Borelli (1681—1682) tried to say three centuries ago and as informational engineers are trying to prove today. The crux of human locomotion in both common forms of gait and in more refined locomotor skills of dancing and athletics is refinement and power control of the basal articulated actions of the foot in controlling both striding action and postural control during coordination with other body movements. The delicate structure of the foot and its elaborate modes of action reflect the role of the basal action of the sole in operationally refining higher level motorsensory components of locomotor function of the legs and their timing and coordination with torso, head, and arm movements. Posture is not only feedback guided; its striding, postural, and articulated components are feedback organized on a systems basis that relates the body to the substrate environment and thereby controls this environment.

Psychomotor Regulation of Hand Motion

Control concepts like those specified for posture and locomotion have been defined and experimentally tested for hand motion. Results of experimental systems research have suggested that the hand and arm act as a feedback-control mechanism which interrelates postural, dynamic-transport, and manipulative hand movement and their critical sensory channels for guidance of both unaided and instrumental motion. In addition to the three postural, transport, and articulated movements and their related control of

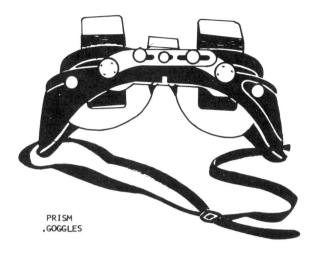

PRISM
.GOGGLES

WALKING WITH INVERTED
VISION

FIG. 12-7. Prism goggles and marked path for study of locomotion with space-displaced visual feedback of locomotor movements.

sensory inputs, the hand-arm system has been evolved to perform specialized apposed motions of the thumb and fingers as well as apposed movements of the fingers and of the two hands in coordination. The hand-arm system thus acts as a multiloop control circuit in which the hand can be focally guided as a unit or as a flexible unimanual or bimanual manipulative mechanism.

In unaided hand motion (Fig. 12-8), hand-arm action generates reactive feedback from movements of different levels of motion, guidance, and operational feedback from holding, grasping, turning, pulling, cutting,

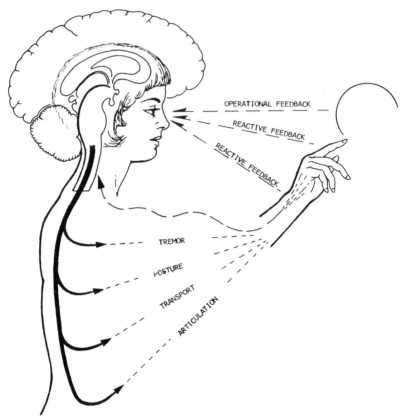

FIG. 12-8. The component movements of hand-arm motions and the modes of visual and tactual-kinesthetic feedback generated by such motion.

smashing, piercing, shaping, pushing, and lifting activities in relation to objects and materials in the environment. Reactive feedback combines tactual, visual, auditory, and kinesthetic sensory inputs. Operational feedback—that is, the environmental effect produced and left by motions—is related most significantly to exteroceptive channels of sensory input. The division of labor between the two hands and between multiloop levels of hand-arm control is the basis of the nearly unlimited flexibility of the hand-arm system in performing compensatory, complementary, apposing, and opposing movements of the two hands and arms, the thumbs and fingers, and the different fingers in the operational functions of grasping, holding, turning, etc.

The guidance of the hand in activities such as cutting, drawing, tracing, writing, forming, shaping, etc., depends primarily on the relative space displacement between movement-generated patterns of sensory input (Fig.

12-9). In dynamic movement, the eye and other receptor organs sense displacement of stimulus effects of movement in different directions. Direction-specific internuncial neurons of the retina and brain detect these displacements and guide further motions.

The relative space displacement between active response and sensory input can be altered by changing postures of the head and body or by devices which vary the relative geometric orientation of the motor and sensory systems. The simplest example of such displacement is the use of optical devices to invert, reverse, or angularly displace the visual pattern of seen movements (Fig. 12-10). The sensory or perceptual effects of such displacements, which occur in all body motions and in use of tools and machines, produce spatial

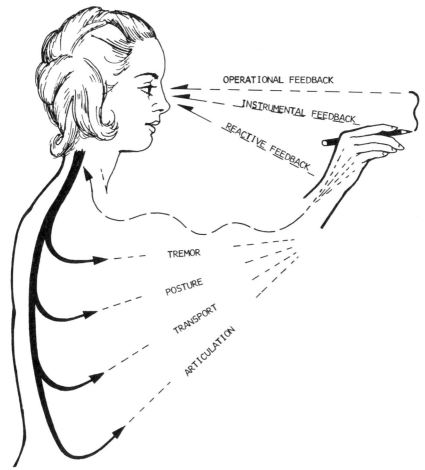

FIG. 12-9. The effect of hand tools in altering the feedback of hand-arm motions by changing the space, time, force, and signal compliances of unaided, reactive, and operational feedback and by introducing an instrumental feedback parameter.

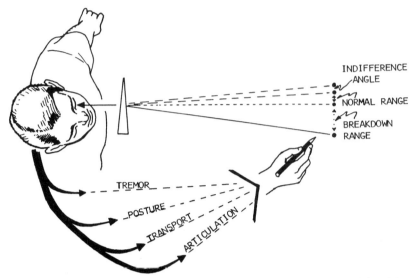

FIG. 12-10. Guidance of hand-arm motion by indifference, normal, and breakdown ranges of angularly displaced visual feedback of movement.

discrepancies between tactual-kinesthetic and exteroceptive sensory inputs of the same movements or of interrelated component movements in the same motion.

The control of hand-arm behavior follows principles of spatial compliance between motion and sensory input (Fig. 12-10). Several ranges of geometric compliance have been defined. In any given motion system such as the eye, there is a small angle of displacement or aberration which the system cannot sense at all. Above this indifference threshold, there is a normal range of relative displacement which can be detected, but which the response mechanism can compensate for with little or no error. For example, the two eyes can be deviated by small angular ranges without overtly impairing the normal binocular alignment for single vision. Beyond this normal range, a breakdown range of binocular angular displacement occurs in which discoordination of movements occurs. In this range, the extent of degradation of movement control varies as a function of the magnitude of displacement. Also, the amount of learning needed to compensate in some degree for the breakdown displacement varies as a function of the magnitude of the angular displacement.

Particular motion systems of the body display specialized spatial compliances in movement-controlled feedback. For example, the variable thresholds of breakdown and recovery of single vision which have been determined for different directions of ocular movement in optometric testing are related to relative geometric compliances in guidance of motion. Compared with the space compliances between the eyes which are needed for single vision, less precise spatial compliance is characteristic of the indifferent, normal, and breakdown ranges of displacements which are involved in guidance of hand motion. The cybernetic theory of specialization of the many thousands of hand-arm motions in development and learning is that each of these motions depends on particular conditions of geometric compliance between movement components of a given direction and their related sensory inputs.

PERCEPTION CYBERNETICS

Experimental receptor cybernetics has analyzed the feedback motor-control factors and mechanisms which determine the closed-loop operations of particular receptor organs. Histologic and microelectrode studies of nerve pathways have disclosed the existence of a widespread receptor-efferent nervous system which is composed of neurons that feed back from the central nervous system over afferent pathways to reflect the state of brain nuclei and ganglia and to influence receptor function (Fig. 12-11). In the case of the kinesthetic system, the receptor-efferent mechanism is the gamma-efferent nerves which innervate muscle spindle receptors to aid in the measurement of the rate of contraction and to determine the sensitivity level of kinesthetic sensory pathways.

Investigation of the mechanisms controlling sensitivity of the retina has disclosed that dynamic, motor-activated feedback circuits govern the state of the visual system by preventing its adaptation to continuous stimulation by light (Fig. 12-12). In such research, the movements of the eye are yoked to retinal stimulation by means of a small mirror mounted on a corneal contact lens. The image of the light target reflected from this lens is directed outward to a mirror surface and then back into the observer's eye. The effect of this arrangement is to yoke the visual image of the light to eye movement in a compensatory way so that with eye movement, the image does not move on the retina. This condition of negating the effect of eye motion on stimulus movement is referred to as stabilized vision. The effect of stabilizing the retinal image is to cause continuously viewed visual targets to disappear for a few seconds and then to reappear. The mechanism normally preventing the adaptation effect is the closed feedback circuits of the flick movements of the eye.

Research on controlling the spatial factors in feedback control of vision has indicated that such closed-loop control underlies both vision and organization of eye movements in optical tracking. One type of study (Fig. 12-13) has inverted, reversed, or displaced the retinal feedback effects of eye movements by means of a small prism mounted in a cylinder located on a contact lens. A lens system of this sort changes the motorsensory feedback displacements between eye motion and the direction of stimulation of retinal cells. Normally, pursuit movements of the eyes require a positive relationship

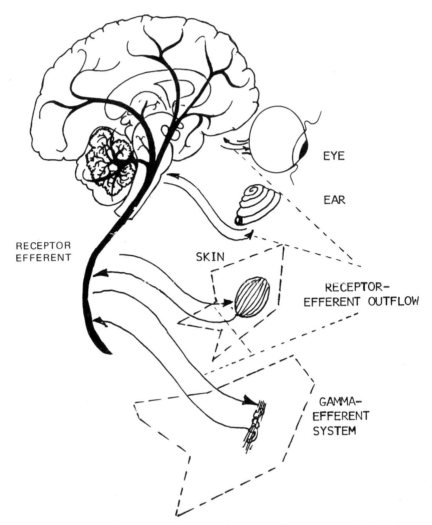

FIG. 12-11. Levels of the gamma-efferent and receptor-efferent systems of the body.

between eye movement and action of visual targets so that a movement of the eye will keep a moving stimulus on the fovea. When an inverting contact lens is worn, the motorsensory directional relations between pursuit movements and retinal stimulation are reversed. The effect of wearing such an inverting prism is to cause skittered vision: the eye skips back and forth trying to bring observed images on the retina, which it cannot do. Similar effects have been found by using a hybrid-computer system to yoke visual targets to eye movement and to invert the directional relations between the ocular motion and retinal stimulation. The findings indicate that pursuit movements of the

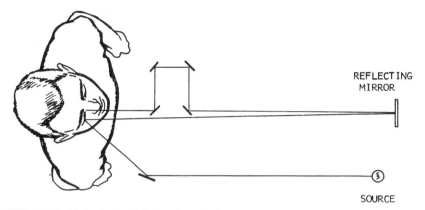

FIG. 12-12. Method of stabilizing the retinal image for studies of eye movement-retinal feedback factors in visual perception (*Based on Riggs et al., 1953*).

eyes operate as positive feedback mechanisms which require specific directional control of input stimulation. If this control is displaced in any marked way, there is little or no effective adaptation through learning to the altered feedback interactions.

Receptor cybernetic research has been extended to analysis of the feedback relations between receptor input control and the brain. Investigations have been conducted on the relations between the alpha rhythm of brain waves and the appearance and disappearance of vision under conditions of stabilized vision (Fig. 12-14). Retinal input is stabilized as described above and a hybrid analog-digital-analog computer system used to automate detection of alpha rhythms of the recorded brain waves of the subject. The

FIG. 12-13. Contact-lens, dove-prism technique used to invert and reverse the retinal feedback of eye movements.

electroencephalogram of the subject is transduced by electrodes placed on the occipital region of the skull. The brain-wave signals are amplified and sampled at 1000 samples per second by means of an analog-to-digital converter. These sampled signals are selected by a high-speed digital computer which is programmed to detect wave variations in the electroencephalogram between 4 and 10 cycles per second. When two successive variations of this type are detected the computer outputs a signal which after deconversion to dc form can be used to activate light, sound, or other stimuli related to the reported appearance or disappearance of vision under conditions of stabilized viewing.

In the experiment illustrated in figure 12-14, the subject views a light target which has been stabilized by a contact-lens mirror and an optical reflecting system, and is given a hand key which he presses when vision of the target appears or disappears. The disappearance and reappearance are recorded along with the indications of alpha rhythm by the computer system. In addition, the computer system is used to simulate in normal vision the timing of appearance and disappearance of the light as seen in stabilized viewing conditions. Using this simulated stimulation with normal viewing, the occurrence of computer-detected alpha rhythms is also correlated with presence and absence of vision. The findings have been that occurrence and absence of alpha rhythm are associated closely with appearance and

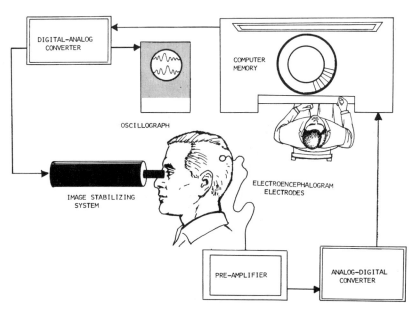

FIG. 12-14. Methods of Keesey and Nichols (1965) for stabilizing the retinal image and using real-time computer methods for analyzing the time relations between the appearance and disappearance of vision under stabilization and characteristics of the alpha rhythm of the brain.

disappearance of vision *only* under the conditions of yoked, stabilized vision. In this case the *disappearance* of alpha rhythm *precedes* the appearance of vision by 0.4 to 0.7 second, and the *appearance* of alpha rhythm *precedes* the absence of vision by about 0.4 second. The findings contradict conventional beliefs that external vision controls the alpha rhythm. Rather, vision is a part of a larger motorsensory-neural feedback circuit which involves control of the alpha rhythm.

Receptor cybernetic research has led to dynamic psychophysical measurement of threshold and discriminative functions in hearing, vision, and the other senses. Bekesy audiometry, which utilizes patient adjustment of the action of a sound stimulus, has established a successful new foundation for threshold testing of hearing in deaf persons. Auditory impedance measurement is based on direct assessment of the reactive control of sound input of the ear mechanism and can be used to analyze the stiffness compliance, mass or reactance, and resistance or friction of different parts of the middle and inner ear mechanism to sounds of different frequency and intensity under a great variety of bodily conditions. In the case of vision, dynamic, observer-controlled psychophysical measurement is based on tracking methodology in which the observer must follow or compensate controlled variations in stimulus sources. In brightness tracking (Fig. 12-15), the observer uses a hand dial to control the rotation of a neutral filter that changes the brightness of a three-degree test spot in a larger field of constant brightness. A hybrid analog-digital-analog computer system is programmed to produce continuous variations in the same filter, causing the brightness of the test spot to change. The observer must continuously compensate these computer-produced variations in test brightness by moving his hand dial. The computer system is programmed also to establish a calibration between the movement and zero position of the observer's hand control and variations in the brightness of the test spot from the surrounding field, and to measure the observer's error in maintaining a match between the spot and the field. Research with such dynamic psychophysical brightness tracking has indicated that brightness perception is governed by real-time, motor-control factors that determine brightness sensitivity in relation to the rates of change in light intensity. Similar methods of automating visual flicker, visual field, and visual-acuity measurement are being developed for optometric and ophthalmologic measurement of vision.

PSYCHOPHYSIOLOGIC CYBERNETICS OF RESPONSE, MOTIVATION, AND LEARNING

One of the most significant research forefronts in behavioral cybernetics is the study of behavioral-physiologic interactions in energy production, emotion, motivation, fatigue, exercise, work, and psychophysiologic disorders. The classic views of behavioral-physiologic interaction are that motor

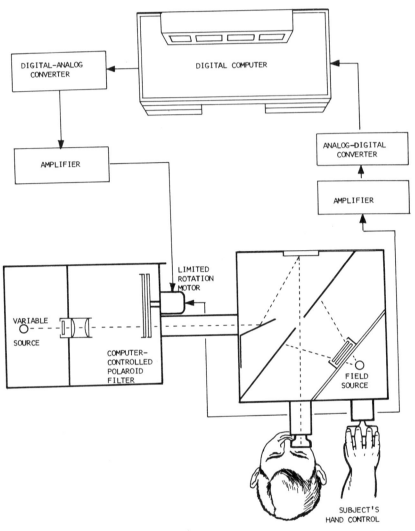

FIG. 12-15. Psychophysical tracking methods used for study of brightness discrimination.

response is an end product of internal physiologic or homeostatic states and does not materially influence these internal states. Another view of psychophysiologic interaction—that is, the general doctrine and dogma of psychosomatic response and disease—is that the "mind" influences physiologic states. This view dismisses external skeletal-motor processes as critical influences in behavioral-organic interactions. Reinforcement learning theorists in psychology (Miller, 1969) attribute so-called psychosomatic effects to visceral conditioning or operant conditioned changes in internal organic processes.

In the past decade, feedback research on the energy-production and energy-control mechanisms of muscular contraction and the motor system has revolutionized the theory, methods of study, and general knowledge of behavioral-physiologic interactions. The crux of the results from this research is that, instead of being an end product of organic functions, motor response regulates by feedback control every level of cellular, physiologic, and organic metabolism including the production of energy for muscular response itself. These findings not only discredit all of the loosely defined concepts of psychosomatic response and disorder, but bring new levels of detailed understanding of the feedback effects of motor response in determining learning, motivation, emotion, and cognitive processes.

Figure 12-16 illustrates some of the main facts which are now known about dynamic control of energy production and regulation by muscular contraction and motor response. This diagram indicates that motor response governs the production of adenosine triphosphate—the energy molecule of cellular metabolism in muscle contraction—as a feedback process and, in addition, feedback regulates every level of physiologic and organic metabolism involved in conversion, distribution, and mobilization of the metabolic precursors of ATP production. The meaning of the diagram is very concrete. Energy production for response as well as for motivation, emotion, and learning involves several specific modes of molecular, cellular, neuro-hormonal, kinesthetic, organic, metabolic, and mechanical modes of feedback control, each of which performs some specific metabolic function in conversion, mobilization, and distribution of biochemical materials for energy production in the processes of muscular contraction for motor response.

In the process of utilization of ATP, muscular contraction manufactures this molecule from adenosine diphosphate and adenosine monophosphate by negative feedback control. The level of ATP and its precursors also feedback control glycolysis in aerobic metabolism and conversion of fat of anaerobic metabolism. ATP levels also feedback regulate epinephrine levels during response which in turn control peripheral circulation and the distribution of blood. The skeletal-motor system is a part of the circulatory system and feedback regulates venous circulation and the distribution of blood by muscular activity. Kinesthetic sensory signals, as produced in muscle spindles by motor response, act as a reciprocal sensory feedback source of movement for neural activation, neurohormonal activation, and synchronization of movements in relation to circulatory and respiratory activities.

The basic theory of energy production in muscle—the adenylate control hypothesis (Atkinson, 1965, 1966; Huxley, 1969)—explains the differential role of muscle fiber contraction in ATP production in terms of the following three main experimentally substantiated assumptions: (1) rate of ATP

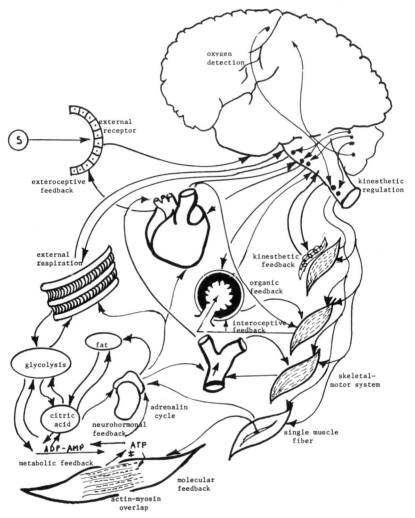

FIG. 12-16. Levels of physiologic feedback in control of bioenergy production, conversion, mobilization, and distribution by muscular contraction and the skeletal-motor system.

production is feedback regulated by rate of ATP expenditure during contraction; (2) the capability of the muscle cell to produce ATP from substrate resources within the cell varies in proportion to the extent of overlap of the actin and myocin contractile fibrils within the cell, which may be varied by the degree to which the cell may be stretched during contraction; (3) the motor system can self-determine the efficiency of energy production during exercise in regulating fatigue and related conditions of aerobic and anaerobic metabolism by adjusting the extent of stretch of muscles during contraction, and hence, the efficiency of related processes of ATP production.

Research on the feedback-control mechanisms of muscular contraction and the motor system in determining energy production and conditions of metabolism requires and involves experimental systems studies of the interdependent, closed-loop mechanism diagrammed in figure 12-16. Experimental studies of interaction and synchronism between respiration and skeletal motor activity are of value in analyzing the feedback relations between energy control by muscle activity and metabolism. Studies of this sort (Smith, 1967; Smith, Luetke, and Smith, 1970) have indicated that the respiratory system acts as a high-precision, motorsensory tracking mechanism to follow and synchronize with various motor systems of the body, including those of limb movements, speech, and head motion. Thus, respiration is not simply a mechanism for oxygen intake; it is a combined skeletal-motor and internal organic mechanism that can be synchronized with and adjusted to other psychomotor mechanisms for different aspects of energy regulation.

With the development of real-time computer systems, it is now possible to conduct many different types of researches on systems interaction between an integration of organic and external skeletal motorsensory mechanisms. Studies of sensory entraining and self-regulated feedback control of brain rhythms (Smith and Ansell, 1965), cardiac rhythms (Ansell, Waisbrot, and Smith, 1967), and other physiologic functions suggest that the adjustment of the motor system is involved in processes of voluntary and learned regulation of organic functions.

The most important application of experimental facts regarding behavioral-physiologic feedback interactions is in understanding the energy control mechanisms of motivation and exercise and the organic and physiologic feedback determinants of learning. Traditional learning theorists have made the sustained effort to explain learning in terms of the most unlikely of all the after-effects of response—that is, delayed extraneous associated or contingent rewards which have no critical sensory relationships with the response to be learned. In trying to justify and substantiate this wholly artificial set of ideas, reinforcement learning theorists (Hull, 1943; Mowrer, 1960; Miller, 1969; Skinner, 1938, 1953, 1955) have overlooked the critical, immediate physiologic feedback effects of response which occur in advance of and irrespective of the delayed reinforcements which may or may not occur after a response is made. Moreover, these molecular, cellular, kinesthetic, organic, neurohormonal, and metabolic feedback effects of particular responses to be learned are integrated with immediate exteroceptive and interoceptive feedback effects of these responses to govern both the neural and overall physiologic effects of the reactions. In the systems or feedback doctrine, these immediate sensory and internal metabolic and energy-production feedback effects not only determine the capability for subsequent response but the changes in the energy-regulating (ATP) levels of brain functions underlying neural learning changes. We believe that of all of the feedback effects of behavior that traditional learning theorists used to explain processes of acquisition and memory, delayed reinforcements and contingent rewards and goal responses are obviously the least likely to have the capability of influencing the subsequent physiologic status of a response to be learned. In contrast, the physiologic feedback events of response are the most likely of all consequences of activity to be critical in inducing the neural and neurohormonal changes underlying learning.

Feedback Mechanisms of Physical Conditioning

The theory and facts of behavioral cybernetic regulation of energy production have given rise to a systems feedback doctrine of cortical-cerebellar integration for the control of physiologic motivation and metabolism of response. Cortical sensory-detection systems not only function as feature detectors for exteroceptive stimulus inputs and as the space-organized outflow of both the pyramidal and extrapyramidal motor system, they also contain cells that are highly sensitive to oxygen level of the blood from particular parts of the body. This localized oxygen detection system is integrated with the more generalized kinesthetic feature-detection systems of the cerebellum which detect velocities, rates, and patterns of motor activities in particular parts of the body and control temporal integration of tremor, postural, and transport movements. Both mechanisms can regulate respiration and heart rate during exercise and emergency states through the activation mechanisms of reticular formation. The interaction between the two can influence the utilization of states of aerobic and anaerobic metabolism and may be affected by training and experience in feedback control of these metabolic states. Thus, the organized pattern of energy regulation and physiologic motivation of response is not determined by interoceptive stimulation or organic homeostatic states. Rather, it is governed at the neural and neurohormonal levels by a reciprocal feedback relationship between the localized oxygen-detecting mechanisms of the cortex and the generalized energy-integrating processes of the cerebellum. This duplicity feedback theory of physiologic motivation is substantiated not only by many anatomic and physiologic facts of the effects of exercise: it also represents a logically coherent account of most of the specific facts of behavioral-metabolic interactions during fatigue, recovery from fatigue, transfer of fatigue, and effects of practice and physical conditioning of metabolic and organic mechanisms.

The duplicity feedback doctrine of behavioral-physiologic interaction is an important theoretic advance in comprehending the mechanisms of physical conditioning in exercise and work. According to this approach, physical conditioning through exercise and physical therapy is more than muscle building: rather, it is both a local and generalized effect of exercise that involves change in the efficiency of cortical-cerebellar integration of the different levels of kinesthetic, neurohormonal, metabolic and organic feedback of motor activity. Specifically, it represents a type of learning in which altered neural organization is linked to the specialized conditions of aerobic and anaerobic metabolic feedback mechanisms of both localized and generalized activity. Therefore, through physical conditioning, the motor system can be specialized to perform particular tasks while it also becomes integrated psychophysiologically in skilled performance. Physical conditioning involves change in body organization at every level of molecular, metabolic, organic, neurohormonal and neural levels of feedback control of muscular contraction. It is both psychologic and physiologic and its course and progress have reciprocal feedback effects on motor behavior which are the most decisive of all the many determinants of skill learning. In fact, it is the overall psychophysiologic feedback framework of skill learning as well as motivational learning.

The obverse processes of positive physical conditioning consist of deterioration of the multilevel energy-production mechanisms of the motor system in disease, inactivity, old age, behavior disorder, or drug addiction. All such mechanisms involve physical disintegration of the behavioral-physiologic mechanisms related to energy production and cortical-cerebellar integration for metabolic organization in exercise. Just as positive physical conditioning probably affects all levels of motor-controlled feedback of energy regulation, so the different negative modes of physical conditioning also very likely entail breakdown of both specific control mechanisms and overall temporal organization of the closed-loop subsystems of psychophysiologic regulation. In these breakdown processes, feedback central time or reaction time is the first to be affected.

LEARNING CYBERNETICS AND MOTOR HABITS

Experimental research on the feedback determination of learning is the most significant current trend in the theoretic and practical study of educational and training design. In a feedback interpretation, the course of human learning is determined primarily by the direct sensory feedback generated by or controlled by movements. It is influenced only secondarily by so-called reinforcing (rewarding) effects which may occur subsequent to the closed-loop sensory-feedback processes that are a part of the systems control mechanisms of the response to be learned.

A feedback or systems theory of learning is a natural extension and refinement of past learning doctrine. Helmholtz (1856–1866) launched the scientific study of learning by formulating his empiric statement that space perception is determined by visual-tactual association. Thorndike (1913) and

Pavlov (1927) extended this point of view by applying associationism to experiments on animal learning and physiologic conditioning. Watson (1924) extended Pavlovian conditioning theory to an explanation of human behavior, including speech and thought. Hull (1943) tried unsuccessfully to systematize these ideas by incorporating conditioning concepts and Thorndike's *Law of Effect* in a drive-reduction theory of learning in which reinforcement by associated stimuli and reduced physiologic drives were assumed to be essential to the learning process. Skinner (1938) provided a simple model of reinforcement learning by inventing the "Skinner box"—a situation in which rats press a lever to obtain rewards such as food and water. Many psychologists have adopted this *operant conditioning* model as the prototype of all animal and human learning.

A fundamental revision of learning theory originated in World War II in research on guidance of response and tracking with systems (Smith, 1945). In this research, it was found that the direct sensory effects of continuously guided movements could determine learning irrespective of rewards, punishments, or other after-effects that fit the reinforcement interpretation. After the war, many psychologists attempted to incorporate the data on sensory-feedback control of behavior and learning into conventional learning theory. In some cases the direct feedback effects of movements were identified as the learning factor called *knowledge of results* (Fitts, 1951). More frequently, dynamic movement feedback was held to be a form of reinforcement along with such after-effects as rewards and punishments (Skinner, 1953, 1955). This confusion of dynamic movement feedback with reinforcement and reward processes strengthened the then prevailing view that all significant learning involves processes of operant conditioning controlled by reinforcers. Although the reinforcement model of human learning has become popular in clinical psychology, it has proved eminently unsatisfactory in that and other areas of human education and training in which the significant design factors cannot be specified in terms of rewards, punishments, or reinforcers (Smith and Smith, 1966). Of these effects, dynamic movement feedback is of primary importance, for behavior cannot be controlled effectively unless the individual can sense the effects of his own movements. Dynamic movement feedback also may provide adequate knowledge of results—that is, knowledge of the accuracy or appropriateness of response. If such knowledge is not provided by dynamic movement feedback, it may be supplied, but usually ineffectively, by some supplemental display or information. Rewarding or punishing after-effects function to some extent in capturing the attention or in encouraging sustained performance, but they do not directly define the course or the final level of complex human learning. It is almost impossible to demonstrate any effects of incentives on adult human learning or performance level (Bilodeau, 1966). Thus the experimental evidence belies the hopes of *S-R* theorists that the operant conditioning doctrine can be made into a control theory of behavior.

Figure 12-17 contrasts the sensory-feedback interpretation of learning with conventional reinforcement theory. The feedback interpretation of learning differs from reinforcement theory principally in holding that learning is determined by self-governed, movement-related stimuli and metabolic processes rather than by environmental after-effects; and that the course and extent of learning are functions of the space, time, and force feedback compliances between movement and sensory input rather than the reinforcing characteristics of after-effects. In the feedback interpretation, learning is

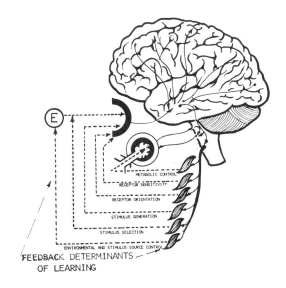

FEEDBACK DETERMINANTS
OF LEARNING

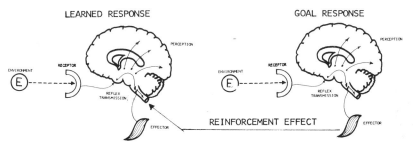

FIG. 12-17. The behavioral cybernetic or feedback doctrine (*top*) and the operant reinforcement or instrumental conditioning theory (*bottom*) of the determination of learning.

determined at the neural level by the effects of response in activating the nervous system, initiating neurohormonal changes, governing metabolic and organic processes and material and gas intake, and regulating sensitivity of receptors and input sensory pathways to the brain. The main effect of these neurophysiologic feedback effects of response is to cause change in the feature-detection properties of central neurons that determine the directional guidance of response.

External Sensory Feedback Factors in Learning

Dynamic sensory feedback from self-generated movements acts primarily to guide, time, and regulate the force of both continuous and discrete motions, and thereby determines the learning of the direction, timing, and force characteristics of motions. Many experiments have shown that such immediate guidance and control factors are the learning determinants which must be considered in designing educational and training situations. The experiment illustrated in figure 12-18, for example, demonstrated that

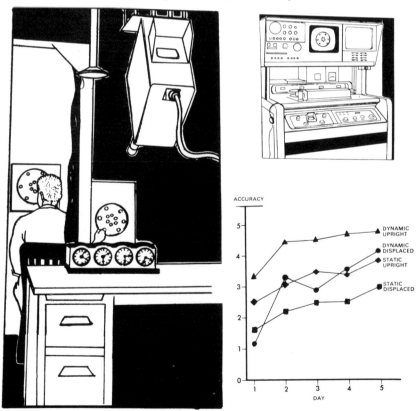

FIG. 12-18. Curves showing the differences between the effects of delayed dynamic and static operational feedback in determining learning (*From Smith and Smith, 1962*).

dynamic sensory effects of response were more effective in aiding learning than static after-effects. A video-tape recorder was used to present a delayed visual feedback display of a target-location task. Subjects saw either a dynamic picture of their performance in the task or a static picture of performance after-effects which indicated their overall accuracy and errors. The learning curves show that learning was more efficient when the subjects saw a dynamic feedback display of their own movements.

Another experiment compared learning of two different tasks under conditions of displaced visual feedback (Gould and Smith, 1962). A closed-circuit television set-up was used to present visual feedback of the experimental tasks and to displace the display angularly 0°, 20°, 40°, or 60°. One group of subjects traced a paper and pencil maze and thus received continual guidance from the feedback display because they could see their own errors. Another group drew freehand circles and thus did not receive continual guidance, that is, their visual feedback did not provide knowledge of accuracy. The learning curves in figure 12-19 show that the circle-drawing group receiving no guidance feedback learned nothing during any of the

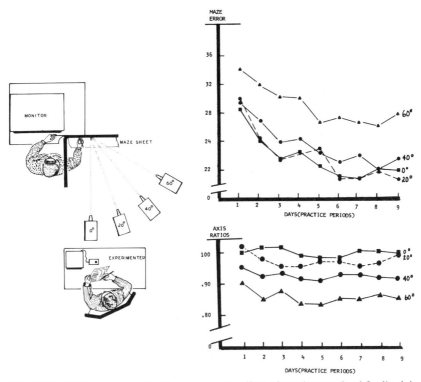

FIG. 12-19. Method and results of measuring the effect of continuous visual feedback in maze tracing (*top right*) and deprivation of critical guidance feedback in circle drawing upon learning (*From Smith and Gould, 1963*).

displacement conditions whereas the maze-tracing group receiving guidance feedback improved progressively under all displacement conditions.

Figure 12-20 illustrates the method and results of a study in which learning of a target-location task was plotted under three conditions of

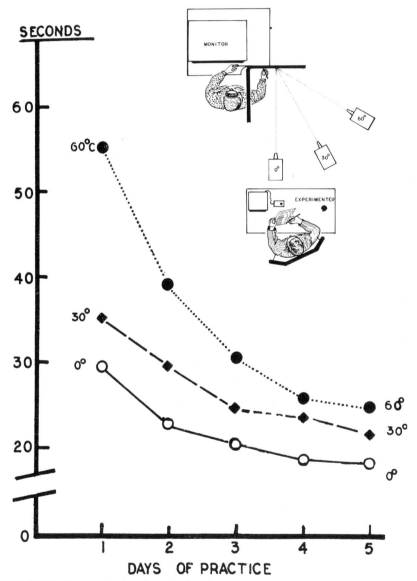

FIG. 12-20. Curves showing the variation in amount and rate of learning at different magnitudes of angular displacement of visual feedback in target location performance (*From Smith and Smith, 1962*).

displaced visual feedback. It can be seen that the course of learning and level of final performance varied with the angle of feedback displacement. These results are in keeping with the assumption that learning varies with the degree of spatial compliance between movement and visual feedback of movement.

Whereas conventional learning theory always has assumed that change in performance is controlled by appropriately timed extrinsic stimuli and after-effects, feedback theory recognizes that self-regulation of both stimulus and response variables in a learning situation tends to enhance learning. The relative advantage of learner control of critical stimuli is illustrated in figure 12-21. These curves compare learning of a visuomanual tracking task when the target was controlled extrinsically and when it was generated by the learner's own breathing movements. It is clear that more learning occurred when the tracking target was self-generated.

The studies described here and many others demonstrate that learning varies systematically with variations in the pattern of sensory feedback which the learner uses to control his movements. Thus the emphasis in educational planning is shifting from reward, incentive, or payoff strategies to human-

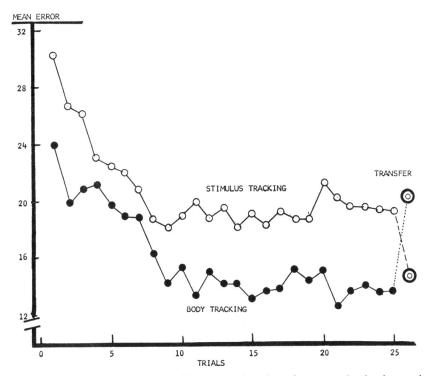

FIG. 12-21. Curves showing the differences in learning of accuracy in visual-manual tracking with self-generated targets (*closed circles*) and with environmentally generated targets (*open circles*).

factors design of the tools, procedures, instructional content, and dynamic feedback relationships in the learning situation.

Feedback Factors in Motor Habits

More than forty years ago, James (1891) formulated some rules of habit formation which have been stated and restated down to the present time as principles of learning and unlearning of all types of behavior. Notwithstanding a half century of learning research, James' principles—the need for active practice, the necessity of maintaining a rigid schedule of performance of the act to be learned, the necessity for making a clean break with the past in breaking old habits—have not been changed materially except to convert them into assumptions regarding stimulus-response learning. In his discussion, James did not bother to go into the scientific meaning of habits: he just took it for granted that everyone knows what habits are and that most people have one or two hanging around which they would like to trim up or get rid of.

Beginning in the 1930's, learning theorists started distorting James' rules of habit making and breaking as principles of associative and conditioned stimulus learning and in that process dismissed the most important substance of his ideas—that is, his emphasis on individual self-regulation of learning. James' ideas have a very modern tone, since he conceived of the learner as a self-controlled person who had critical influence over the stimulus environment and his own learning activity. Actually, a systems analysis of James' principles suggests that they were of two types—that is, general principles of self-governing of learning and specific principles of practice. James gave equal weight to both the general and specific factors.

Systems Feedback Principles of Habit Formation

Using systems feedback theory and facts, we can set forth a much more definitive formulation of the principles of habit formation and change than that given in James' rules and the learning concepts derived from them.

Individual Organization of Habit. Inasmuch as the individual behaves and learns as a self-regulated system, the essence of habit formation and change consists of self-governing of one's own learning processes as well as self-control of the physical and social environment. The potential for making and breaking of habits is directly proportional to the freedom and capabilities which an individual has for self-determination of behavior. Individuals with limited capability and opportunity to govern their own behavior have limited resources for habit control. In contrast, persons with diverse social and environmental resources for self-control and with training in using these resources have much more potential in governing their habit patterns and their own makeup. The first step in changing habits is in developing the resources of the individual for self-control and in expanding opportunities for self-determination in performance. Highly skilled persons not only excel in performance, but this skill gives them the basis for the greatest flexibility in varying their motor, perceptual, and motivational habits as well as their physiologic makeup.

Response Selection in Habit Organization. Habit is the ontogenetic developmental extension of evolutionary selection that affects component responses and physiologic functions in individual adaptation. It consists of processes of response selection in determining perception, motivation, physical conditioning, and skill in self-guided learning. The basic principles of habit formation and habit breaking are rules and techniques of selecting reactions to guide the successive course of future motion in learning. Effective habit making and breaking cannot be separated from knowledge and from the ability to anticipate the implications of future action. Primitive people achieved effective habit control by rigidity of regulation of a limited environment and by ultraconservative methods of social and cultural control. In more complex societies, such rigidity and conservatism may be major barriers in effective adaptive behavior through habit formation. As the biosocial framework of culture has expanded, the necessity for a wide variety of adaptive habits has become essential.

Levels and Modes of Habit Formation. Habits are never specific stimulus-released responses, as past *S-R* and reinforcement theories have stated, but rather, different levels of organized integration of external response, physiologic regulation, and control of self-stimulation and the environment. Most habits such as smoking or masturbation involve special forms of self-stimulation, not guiding effects from the environment. Moreover, many habits are formed and maintained because of sensory and activity restriction in individual behavior. Habit, like behavior itself, involves broad categories of adjustment and organization of behavior—that is, general modes of controlling one's own motivational makeup, learning, perception, thought, and physiologic regulation—and specialized control activities such as skills, talents, manner of speaking, posture, etc. In addition, both general and specialized habits may be classified into various categories related to the types of feedback involved in their guidance and control. Motivational habits related to food, drinking, sex, use of tobacco and drugs attract the most attention because they are strongly related to commercialized products and standards of social behavior. Habits related to skilled performance are the subject of much interest in athletics, music, and work. Activity and emotional habits are closely allied with motivational habits in determining both health status and social interactions. Systematic effort to modify established habits necessarily entails some change in the overall organization in self-regulation of motivation, perception, and learning. The best way to start changing habits is to alter the pattern of living and learn to accommodate the changes to be made.

Habit as Feedforward Anticipation and Projection of Response. Habit is biosocially an established mode of controlling one's self and the environment so as to anticipate and predict future courses of action. Effective habit formation involves and establishes such feedforward control of response and physiologic function on a more or less automatic basis which requires little or no judgment and thought. Thus, in one sense habit is a trap established by a person's past activity to control future response without concentrated judgment. Good habits entail some modulation of the trap of experience to achieve variable ways of behaving in controlling one's self and the surrounding environment with some provision for control of unusual and unexpected events. Thought, planning, and judgment are essential parts of forming habits because they are essential for feedforward and predictive guidance of behavior.

Feedback Determination of Habits. Habits are not determined primarily by environmental stimuli or by artificial and contingent rewards and punishments but by the primary feedback factors determining organization of behavior. The primary properties of feedback regulation of response—that is, continuity of closed-loop control of reaction and physiologic operations, reciprocal, closed-loop integration of multidimensional levels of reaction, self-generation of stimuli in the control of the environment, feedforward control of guidance of movement, and self-determination of the behavioral-physiologic interaction—provide the main guides as to how habits can be acquired and changed. Self-discipline in response selection is not a fuzzy, philosophic principle of habit formation; it is the beginning and core of individual organization of a person's own resources in motivation, skill, and ability to determine the conditions under which learning changes will occur. James' principle of regular practice is an original statement that habits involve nearly continuous and daily regulation of behavior and of response patterns, and if not incorporated into this daily schedule of control, they cannot be changed. Furthermore, to change one's individual habits it is not enough simply to practice: the overall pattern of self-determined integration of different movement systems must be varied. Finally, habits cannot be changed simply by talking about them: activity is essential to alter their basic properties of dynamic regulation and integration. Habits are modes of active existential living and must be formed as processes of natural adjustment.

Activity and Metabolic Factors in Habit. The dynamic factors in habit and learning are not limited to neural processes but involve energy production for response and feedback regulation of all the levels of organic metabolic substrates of production of ATP. All habits, even minor emotional tics and gestures, probably have a deeply ingrained base in behavioral-physiologic feedback control of energy production and physical conditioning. To change habits requires variation in the overall activity pattern in the central motivational life interests—that is, social behavior, work, recreation, sexual activity, etc. The emotional tenseness of most people which leads to formation of compensating habits arises primarily from assumed or real inadequacies of self-control which are typically experienced as guilt or socially unwanted forms of behavior. Effective habit formation presumes the development of a relaxed self-confidence in one's own requirements as an individual.

The Instrumental Factors in Habit. Most skilled habits are organized around instrumental responses and behavior, and their effectiveness depends just as much on the design and effectiveness of these devices as it does on the individual. Work habits, athletic skills such as golf, swimming, etc., may be changed by altering the design of tools and machines for performance. Many limitations of skill can be improved by adjusting the design of tools to fit a person's own makeup. Safety habits can be acquired only when tools and environmental situations make possible and promote anticipatory and predictive guidance of responses which can induce emergency action. In buying tools and machines, a person should remember he is organizing his own behavior and physiology by their use and select accordingly.

The Social Framework of Habit Change. Inasmuch as the social relationships of a person typically determine all phases of his daily activity pattern, the social factors in habit formation are predominant. Furthermore, most habits, including use of alcohol, tobacco, and drugs, are developed in a social context which acts at many psychophysiologic levels to induce and support such habitual behavior. Even more importantly, it is probably impossible for most adult persons to learn relaxation except in the context of association with other people. For example, it is likely that the great majority of men and women never relax unless they frequently are in close association and body contact with a sex partner. The learning principles behind these facts are that coercion and custodial institutionalization of people never develop habits of value for society. Effective habits of every level can be learned only in a framework of social interaction in which the individual can find a positive and meaningful sexual and group role. Unwanted habits can be altered most effectively in such a positive social context. A main function that people can serve in interpersonal interaction is in aiding and contributing to the habit development of others.

Movement Integration in Habit Formation. Skill habits, as in musical instrumentation, athletic skills such as golf, and social interactions involve critical coordination between different movement systems, and especially between breathing and the movement pattern. Often, more effective performance can be achieved by attending carefully to breath control, the proper posture for breath control, and the critical movements which must be carried out. Most skilled performances require that breathing be regulated in a smooth uninterrupted way in coordination with a critical movement such as pulling a trigger on a gun, putting or hitting a golf ball, or shooting a basketball. One of the critical elements of emotional training in skill involves the development of self-control essential to regulate breathing and posture. The learning of such habits probably is also fundamental in achieving satisfaction in sexual activities.

Feedback Control of Perceptual Habits. Perceptual habits such as modes of reading, attention, tracking objects and people, and listening are like skill and activity habits except that control of specific visual, auditory, and tactual stimuli is more prominent in these sensory performances. A main principle is that listening, reading, and observational behavior may be changed mainly by altering modes of self-generation and control of environmental stimuli and thereby reorganizing the activity basis of perception. Reading improvement courses are probably effective in developing self-control over different reading tasks, in socially enhancing reading motivation, and in improving organization of visual coordination and timing. Listening behavior can be improved by similar methods in which persons are trained to actively shadow sounds of music, speech, or other auditory events. Perceptual habits in machine performance depend on effective design of sensory aids and devices such as visors, windshields, and the operational display mechanisms of machines. In such machines, the sensory display, such as a car windshield, must provide distant panoramic vision so that an operator can observe forthcoming stimuli and anticipate their effects before they actually occur. Specialized habits of artistic appreciation, criminal investigation, code analysis, and scientific observation depend on acquisition of the specialized knowledge and activity skills underlying these fields which serve to give a foundation for the specialized visual and auditory behavior.

Time Factors in Habit Regulation. As parts of general activity patterns, many habits of eating, use of tobacco and drugs, sleep, and skilled performance are critically dependent on time schedules of behavior in the day-night cycle and other longer cycles of activity. Well-established habits may be disturbed by changes in daily cycles of performance. To make or break ingrained habits, it may be necessary to change established cycles of eating and working selectively in order to provide a new time base for the new learning. Disabilities of perception may be due in part to habitual modes of seeing and hearing that are organized around developmental disturbances in aural and visual feedback timing.

Developmental Feedback and Habit Formation. In the systems view, learning and habit are processes of articulating and refining behavioral maturation to control self and the environment on an integrated basis. Thus both good and bad habits reflect strengths and weaknesses in opportunities provided for development. Habits may either complement or compensate trends in social, sexual, skill, emotional, and physiologic development. It is likely that the physiologic basis of disturbed emotional, social, and motivational habits are laid down in the early years of childhood and once formed are as difficult to change as other aspects of development. It is likely that ingrained habits of fear and motivation based on developmental trends are never broken: one can simply enhance control over them by expanding related areas of control of behavior. Thus many individuals may be able to reduce the public display of unwanted fears, sexual inadequacies, use of alcohol and drugs, and thus hold their effects in check. Active social help and support are essential for most persons to control motivational and emotional habits. Most persons probably never relax and thus achieve the capability of self-control of habits except in close associations of friends or family associates.

MOTORSENSORY FEEDBACK IN INSTRUMENTAL BEHAVIOR

Instruments and machines both displace and transform the geometric compliances between motion and sensory input by adding special dimensions of dynamic feedback to the motorsensory circuits of the body (Fig. 12-22). In addition to the dimensions of reactive and operational feedback defined for the hand-arm system, the tool user or machine operator generates and senses different *instrumental* sources of feedback from dynamic action of the tool or machine. Thus all forms of implemental behavior are guided and specialized by *instrumental feedback* factors as well as by *reactive* and *operational* feedback observed in unaided motion.

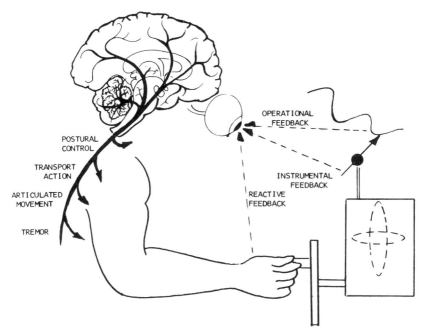

FIG. 12-22. The motor components of manually controlled machines and the general modes of visual feedback of such instrumental behavior.

The sensory feedback effects generated by tools and machines arise from different levels of instrumental action. All implements, from simple hand tools to complex machines, possess three major components—that is, *master, actuator-control,* and *slave* components (Fig. 12-23). The master part of an implement is attached to the motor system of the operator. The slave component is the operational part of a device and must be compliant with the receptor systems of the operator. The actuator-control sector of a tool transmits and transforms the action between the master and control components and can feed back instrumental force effects to the operator. In simple tools such as knives or hammers, the master parts of the devices are represented by the handles, the actuator parts by the lever action between the knife edge or hammer head, and the slave parts by cutting edges or smashing heads. In complex machines such as computers, the master controls may be simple push buttons, the actuator-control sector a complex electronic control

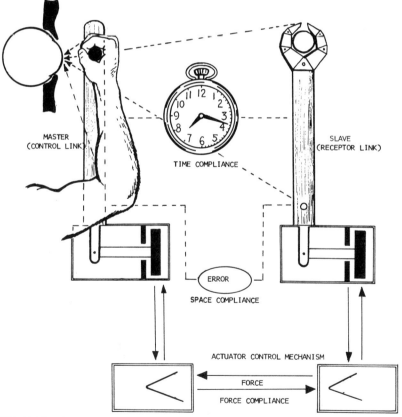

FIG. 12-23. The sectors of machine design—master control, actuator, and slave sectors—and the factors of space, time, and force compliance involved in feedback control of machine behavior.

of memory system, and the slave component an output device such as an electric typewriter or printer. The classification and specification of levels of technology and its evolution may be given in terms of variable features of design of the master, actuator, and slave (operational) features of simple tools and complex machines.

Spatial Compliance of Reactive, Instrumental, and Operational Feedback

Analysis of the feedback factors in the use of tools and machines has suggested that both unaided and instrumental behavior is determined by space, time, and force compliance between motor activity, instrumental factors, and receptor input. Temporal compliance encompasses delay, intermittency, time-spanning, time-sequencing, and other time dimensions of feedback regulation. The optimal condition of tool-using behavior is nondelay, continuity of sensory input, and the broadest possible time-spanning of behavior. With both hand tools and machines, exact force feedback compliance is needed to perceive action of an implement as a dynamic extension of limb movement and to use tactual and kinesthetic feedback in guidance of machines. In almost all modern machines and vehicles, force feedback that is compliant with behavior has been eliminated.

Significant investigations of implemental and machine cybernetics have been based on feedback studies of spatial and temporal compliances in instrumental behavior and by developmental research on the design of feedback factors in anthropomorphous machines. An anthropomorphous machine is one that possesses exact force, time, and space feedback compliance with particular body motions and their sensory inputs.

Isolation of The Critical Feedback Dimensions of Instrumental Behavior

In studies of spatial feedback compliances of instrumental behavior, laboratory optical and television methods have been used to isolate particular reactive, instrumental, and operational feedback dimensions of tool-using activity. In the television techniques illustrated in figure 12-24, the subject does not see his hand and the action of a marking tool directly, but must view his motions in a television monitor. Special illumination and camera techniques are used to display at a given time only one dimension of motion-controlled feedback from a marking tool. In one condition, the subject's vision is limited to seeing only the action of his hand. In another condition, he sees only the movement of the marking pen and does not see his hand or the tracings that are made in tracing a visual maze. In a third condition, he sees only the tracing as it is made and does not see his hand or the action of the marking pen. The successful isolation and measurement of the effects of variable compliances of the different dimensions of tool-using

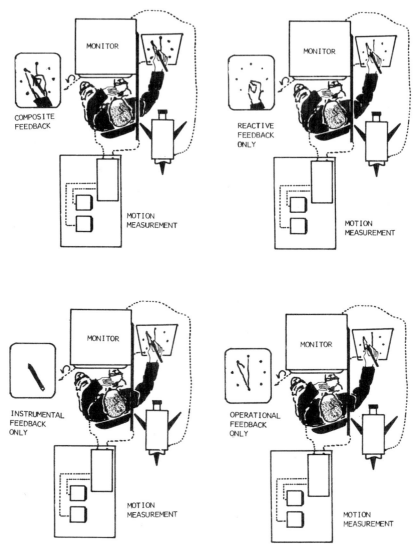

FIG. 12-24. Experimental systems designs for study of the relative role of instrumental and operational feedback factors in tool-using behavior.

feedback have provided direct evidence for the theory of multidimensional cybernetic regulation of instrumental behavior. In using marking tools, the spatial compliance between the action of the marking point and the operation of forming letters or other forms is particularly significant for legibility in writing and accuracy in drawing and tracing.

Temporal Feedback Compliances in Design
and Operation of Tools and Machines

Temporal compliances in unaided and tool-using behavior have been investigated by using the audio tape, video tape, and electronic hybrid-computer laboratory devices illustrated in figure 12-2 to delay the feedback effects of tool-using motions. In applying these methods, the operator does not observe the sensory effects of his motions directly but must hear or see them after they have been delayed by one of the special laboratory procedures. Of the different laboratory techniques for controlling time factors in motion, the laboratory hybrid-computer system is the most significant because it can be used in diverse ways as a universal laboratory time machine to control both feedback delay and other dimensions of intermittency, time-spanning, and time synchronism of feedback.

Laboratory hybrid-computer techniques have been used to study feedback delay and other aspects of temporal compliance in visual-manual tracking and steering, as used for example in automobile driving (Fig. 12-25). In such techniques, the hand motions of the subject are transduced and their electric analog sampled and converted to digital form. The digital signal is selected by the digital computer which is programmed to store input motion information for predetermined periods of time before it is deconverted and amplified for feedback display to the subject. In the experiment concerned, an oscillograph cursor is used as a feedback display. The subject's task is to regulate his hand motions to keep the cursor in constant zero position. The effect of feedback delays on instrumental motions is to impair the learning of hand control and other types of movements (Fig. 12-26). The extent of this effect depends on the type of motion and the instrumental actions involved. However, the learning of all forms of instrumental behavior, such as musical instrumental activities, tracing, drawing, handwriting, speech, visual-manual tracking, postural control, keyboard activities, and work motions are affected by such delays.

Delayed feedback and other dimensions of temporal feedback compliance are critical in design and operation of both common machines and advanced technologic systems. Marked feedback delays occur in and impair learning of operation of heavy machines and vehicles such as heavy aircraft, cranes, diggers, hoists, ships, artificial lungs, and computer-controlled tracking devices. The main accident-producing factor in operation of automobiles is the variable feedback delays which are produced in turning and stopping the vehicle at different speeds. These delays result mainly from the effects of the momentum and inertia of the vehicle at particular speeds on the feedback effects of steering and breaking movements. Feedback delay also is a critical factor in accuracy of earth control of space satellites and lunar vehicles. In guidance of lunar vehicles, there is a feedback delay of 2.38 and 2.71 seconds between earth-operator action and any televised feedback signals that he can

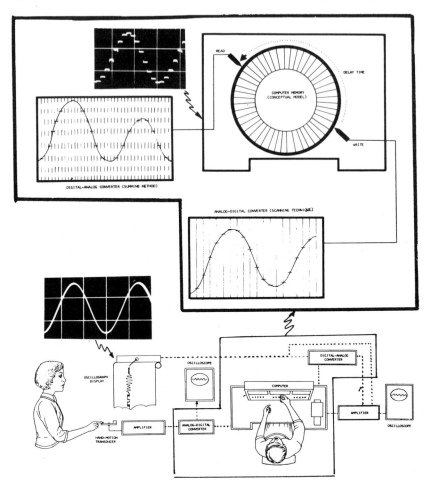

FIG. 12-25. Real-time computer methods used in the study of the transmission lags and other feedback variables in visual-manual tracking.

get from the moon vehicle of the effects of his control movements. Thus, lunar delayed-feedback time is variable in relation to the distance of the moon from the earth in its different phases. Delayed feedback also is a very critical factor in training astronauts in guidance and control of space vehicles.

The relative effects of feedback delay on control and operation of operating systems depend on the magnitude of the delay (Fig. 12-27). For most motion systems except the eye movements, feedback delays of less than 0.1 second have only transient effects on motion and skill with tools and machines. As the magnitude of the delay is increased, the disturbing effects are proportionately increased up to 3 to 5 seconds, at which levels complete

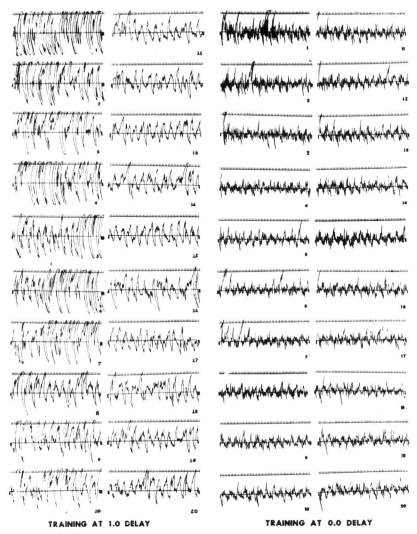

TRAINING AT 1.0 DELAY   **TRAINING AT 0.0 DELAY**

FIG. 12-26. The effects of feedback delay of 1.0 second (*left*) upon learning of breath-control visual tracking compared with learning over twenty-five trials with normal feedback delay. Each record shown in the two displays represents a separate trial of one minute duration. If performance in tracking had been perfect, each trace would appear as a straight line (*From Smith, 1966*).

breakdown of motorsensory coordination can occur. Speech is affected maximally by auditory feedback delays of about 0.2 seconds, at which value stuttering and blocking of speech can occur in a majority of people. Different magnitudes of delay affect the velocity components of movement somewhat differently from the actual movement patterns. Generally, as the magnitude

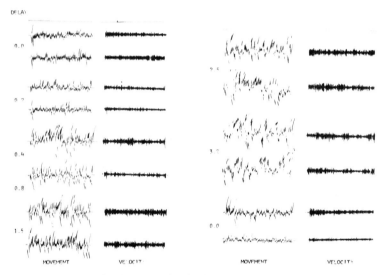

FIG. 12-27. Variation in the error level of manual-visual tracking performance at different magnitudes of feedback delay. The darker traces represent the velocity of tracking movements. The velocity level of the tracking movements also varied with the magnitudes of feedback delay.

of the feedback delay is increased above 0.1 second, the dominant wavelength of the pattern of a given motion is increased, thus reducing the rapidity with which the operator can correct errors of control. It is this factor of slowed speed of corrective response which defines the critical role of feedback delay in causation of vehicular accidents.

Temporal Integration of Feedback in Machine Operations

Some movement systems of the body such as the eye perform movements of different form and velocity. The tracking or pursuit movements of the eye are relatively slow and vary in velocity in relation to moving objects which are exploited by the ocular tracking. Successive fixation or saccadic movements are very fast in shifting the eye from one fixation point to the other. If we attempt to build a machine operated by eye movements (rather than by hand movements), we must take these time factors into account and design the actuator-control component of the machine so that it can govern and guide instrumental action in relation to both types of eye motion.

Eye-movement anthropomorphous machines can be designed and constructed with a hybrid-computer system as the actuator-control mechanism (Fig. 12-28). In such an optokinetic machine, the eye movements of an operator are transduced by photoresistor elements mounted in viewing goggles. These photoresistors record eye movements by sensing the amount of red light reflected from the cornea and transduce this variation to an electric

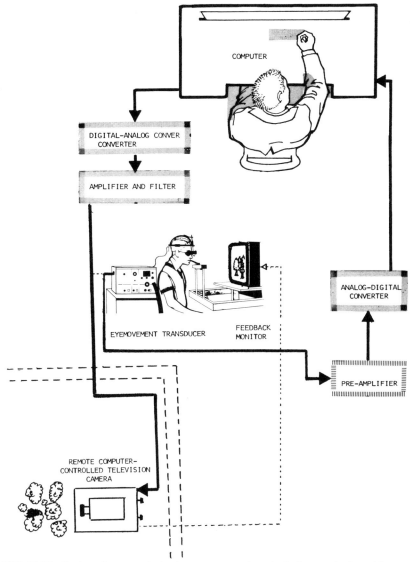

FIG. 12-28. Design of a computerized eye-movement-controlled perceptual machine.

analog of eye movements. The eye-movement signal is (1) amplified, (2) sampled and converted by an analog-digital converter, (3) programmed by a digital computer, (4) deconverted to its analog form by a digital-analog converter, (5) amplified for (6) control of slave motions of a television camera. When the computer system is calibrated to yoke camera motion to eye movements, any change in the movements of the subject's eye will cause the camera to pursue a moving object or to fixate a new visual position. Simultaneously, the camera feeds a televised image back to a monitor which the subject views.

To make an optokinetic machine work accurately, it is necessary to program the computer so that the television camera can track moving objects slowly, but will not overshoot when fast, saccadic movements occur to change fixation. To control this overshooting, the computer is programmed to measure each movement as it is sampled by the system, and to introduce a damping constant into the actuating operations when a high-speed saccadic movement is detected. This damping effect makes it possible to stop the camera accurately when a saccadic movement reaches its termination, and another pursuit movement is started. Such design research on machine cybernetics gives clues about the actual time delays and temporal-control functions which may be involved in guidance of motion systems.

Force Feedback in Anthropomorphous Machines. Anthropomorphous or man-like machines may be designed and built to amplify and extend exactly the force and spatial feedback compliances of arm-hand motion, walking, and body motion in lifting, pushing, digging, and shaping operations (Fig. 12-29). Their scientific significance complements their technologic use because they are the only machines thus far developed to duplicate and transform exactly the space, time, and force compliances of human motion. To develop such machines, it has been necessary to apply previously described cybernetic and systems concepts of human motions of walking, hand-arm action, and posture to design of the feedback circuits and actuator-control, slave, and master components of the machines (General Electric Company, 1969; Mosher, 1964; Smith, 1966b). The success in designing particular manlike machine operations in remote manipulation, machine walking, or exoskeleton operations constitutes one laboratory validation of the concepts of motion and machine cybernetics which have been described.

Several special theories of machine cybernetics have been tested in design studies of the anthropomorphous machines described in figure 12-29. One issue concerned the mechanization of postural control and dealt with the question of whether postural balance could be effected by providing force and position feedback, indicating the relative difference between torso position and standing leg position. Tests conducted by building a large model of a pedipulator confirmed the view that dynamic posture in walking was regulated by force and position feedback factors related to leg and torso action.

A persisting problem of psychomotor behavior and tool-using has been that of the basis of the perceptual attachment of a tool or machine as an extension of the hand or foot of the operator. Studies of design of anthropomorphous devices have indicated that this perceived quality of body attachment of tools and machines depends on space, time, and force feedback

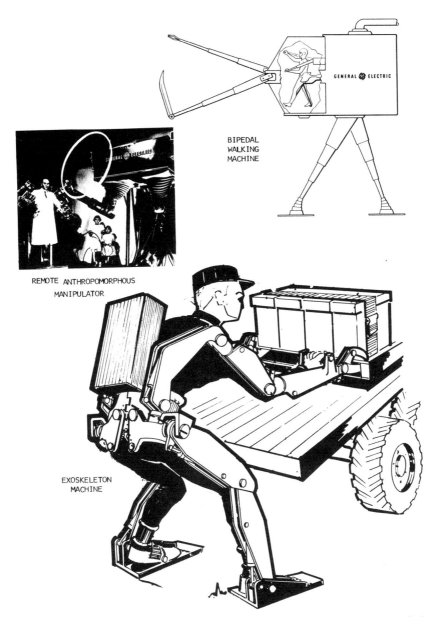

FIG. 12-29. Types of anthropomorphous machines. *Top Left:* Remotely controlled manipulator being used to toss a child's hula hoop. *Top Right:* Pedipulator or bipedal walking machine. *Bottom:* Hardiman or powered exoskeleton (*Courtesy, General Electric Company*).

compliance between instrumental action with both body motion and receptor input. In addition, the feedback effects of different postural, transport, and manipulative movements must be focalized in integrated fashion just as happens in normal unaided motion before the attachment of the body can be experienced. Machines which are designed to have exact feedback compliances with human motion require only the most limited amounts of learning before operators are able to govern them in complex performances with high precision and to sense them as extensions of living motion.

The significance of experimental and developmental design research in machine cybernetics is not limited to industrial, military, and space operations. Manlike optokinetic, head-movement, arm-hand, walking, and exoskeleton machines represent the only significant future scientific solution to adequate design of prosthetic devices which can be made to supplement or replace injured or amputated limbs.

SOCIAL CYBERNETICS AND SOCIAL BEHAVIOR

In a feedback interpretation, social behavior and social learning are controlled by the specialized feedback effects generated in *social tracking* (Smith, 1967). Social tracking involves linking or yoking together the motorsensory systems of two or more persons in reciprocal relationships so that the responses of each one constitute a source of feedback-controlled sensory input for the other (Fig. 12-30). The two people thus react as a unified, self-controlled, closed-loop system in much the same way as a single person controls his responses and sensory inputs by means of closed-loop feedback processes.

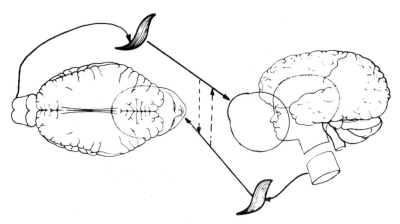

FIG. 12-30. The theory of yoked motorsensory feedback links in social tracking. The motor activities of one individual serve as sources of feedback-controlled sensory input for a second, and vice versa.

Theory of Social Tracking

The concept of social tracking provides a systems approach to the understanding of social learning and organization. All significant forms of social behavior, from intimate sexual union to public group interaction and team play, are organized and specialized in terms of the parameters and conditions of social tracking and feedback control. Research has shown that such tracking can vary in terms of the type of response tracked, the mode of sensory communication used, and the relationship of the feedback-controlled social variables to environmental stimuli and factors. Individuals may be yoked together to complement, compensate, parallel, pursue, oppose, differentiate, or integrate each other's activity. They may be linked together in mutual circuits more or less independently of specific stimuli in the environment, as in sexual behavior, or to control the environment in linked, bridged, parallel, or instrumental relationships. In every case, the effectiveness and patterns of social tracking can be shown to vary systematically as a function of the modes, dimensions, and variables of yoked feedback control.

Research has been carried out on the learning processes involved in social tracking by cross-yoking the motor and sensory systems of two individuals in many different patterns of linked, parallel, and bridged social circuits with both positive and negative feedback relationships and under variable conditions of movement and error control (Smith and Smith, 1969). It was found that learning in social circuits always depended on the occurrence of a systems mode of feedback to the two yoked persons. A systems feedback represented some indication of their joint interaction such as the sum, difference, or an integration of their separate errors. When the feedback that each person received was limited to that from his own motions and gave no indication of the relationships between his movements and that of his partner, there was no learning. In addition, it was found that learning with a systems feedback can be altered in much the same way as individual tracking by delay and displacement of social sensory feedback.

Research on social tracking and learning provides an objective behavioral description of sensitivity training or social-emotional learning, interpersonal adjustment, group coordination, and team play. The various experimental models of social tracking indicate that learning in the social situation is controlled by more than emotionally loaded talk or affiliative rewards and punishments. Social behavior and its learning depend on the development of linked motorsensory skills which involve fleeting dynamic interactions between the movements of two or more persons. Social learning in either intimate interpersonal yokes or in public group situations represents an outstanding expression of human skill in synchronized and organized behavior.

Systems theory and research on learning in social tracking can be used to evaluate the meaning of various techniques of sensitivity training, counseling procedures, and other clinical and social psychologic techniques now being used in industry and business. The results from social feedback research suggest that such methods of training lack relevance and meaning on three main counts—they overemphasize talk, provide no real systems feedback indications of effective response, and lack meaningful theoretic formulation. Evidence indicates that few people learn or change their behavior in counseling and sensitivity training inasmuch as such training, like ordinary social work situations, provides no sustained operational feedbacks of skill factors in various social interactions related to effective performance in the real life situation. To develop effective social training in performance, the critical social tracking patterns in specialized situations must be analyzed in terms of both individual and operational social-tracking factors and training designed in terms of these sources of specialization of behavior. Learning of social sensitivity depends more on recognizing and dealing with these critical systems feedbacks than it does on trying to rationalize individual interactions by talk.

Concepts of and research on social feedback control are fundamental to the development of a human factors science for teaching, instruction, athletics, sports, physical education, communication, and performing arts. The critical elements of educational and teaching science are human factors in dynamically differentiating, integrating, stratifying, grouping, and developing people in relation to work designs, machines, operations, and structural patterns and relationships. Past social science and learning theory have been completely devoid of concepts which can be applied to specification of these social human factors in educational and occupational organization and design. Social tracking theory may be used not only to specify the many parameters, dimensions, and conditions of social and group interaction, but also they may be applied to analysis and specification of the behavioral factors in effective organization. In fact, such theory is the only experimentally meaningful scientific doctrine of social organization thus far developed. The theory therefore fulfills the main requirements of an effective control concept—that is, it can be used to specify the detailed modes and conditions of dynamic control and operations and at the same time define principles of dynamic organization. Effective educational and occupational design depends on clear understanding of these two levels of human social adaptation.

Social Habit Formation

Psychologically, the theory of social feedback control and social tracking defines a systems level of understanding social learning and habit formation. Social habits are distinctive and differ from habits developed in individual patterns of adaptation in that they depend on special modes of yoked mutual feedback control which characterizes interpersonal and group coordination of behavior. It is unlikely that individuals can ever do much about their social habits until they begin to understand the factors of skill needed in social behavior and until they can comprehend the subtle relationships of social tracking between other people and thereby adjust their own social reactions. The theory and facts of learning and performance in social tracking provide the basis for formulating various systems principles of social habit formation.

Two types of social habits may be distinguished—that is, habits of social tracking and socially related individual habits. The latter include such things as individual modes of response such as smoking, fears, etc., which may act to compensate, complement, or interfere with social tracking behavior. Both social tracking habits and socially related habits may be of a general or specialized nature, as described in the section on individual habit formation.

Mutual Feedback Linking of Response Systems in Social Habits. The most fundamental deterministic principles of social habits are that these forms of behavior are the most refined of all modes of human response and that they require mutual feedback linking of the motor and sensory systems of interacting individuals for their development. They not only require training and experience: they demand closed-loop yoking of the receptor and motor systems of social learners if they are to be perfected. Social behavior is not stimulus-determined response, as *S-R* learning theorists have been trying to make out for the past several decades. Rather, it is continuously controlled mutual interaction, not only in the team behavior and interpersonal conduct of adults, but in the imitative behavior of infants and children. To teach children, it is just as important for parents and teachers to track them socially as it is for children to track parents and teachers. Imitation is a mutual process of social habit formation in which each person sacrifices some of his own individuality to become yoked in a closed-loop relationship with the receptor and motor mechanism of other persons. When such mutual interaction does not occur, effective social habits are not learned. It is mutual, crossed- and parallel-yoked motorsensory feedback interactions which are learned as social habits in imitation, parent-child interactions, teaching, sexual behavior, team performance, and the performing arts.

Development of Social Habits. Social habits articulate the maturationally defined built-in modes of social feedback control in the child, such as nursing, visual following of people and moving objects, and tactual social tracking. Active daily experience in early years in tactual social tracking is probably essential for full development of smooth, continuously controlled limb movements and refined bilateral coordination, which serve as the foundation of all skilled individual and social behavior, including sexual behavior. Defects in social habits in adolescents and adults probably reflect disturbances of early development of tactual social tracking.

In developing social habits in children, it is not enough for parents, teachers and others to serve as models: the older person must adjust his behavior to make mutual interaction with the child a reality. Even infants can perform dynamic social tracking of movements of others if these movements are performed at slow speeds. Generally in instilling social habits in children, it is essential to slow down reactions, not only to permit a child to follow critical motions but also to observe and to get effective feedback from the child's movements.

The development of social habit is related with the phasing of critical periods or levels of maturation. The first phases of social learning in infancy and early childhood are limited to acquisition of dynamic mutual imitation, as in speech shadowing and visual and tactual tracking of movements of other people. By five to seven years of age, the child begins to coordinate dynamic social imitation with symbolic and discrete perceptions and educational skills based on recognition of symbolic forms. Such social habits are essential to learn in classroom situations and to organize social habits through verbal and written instructions. At nine to eleven years of age, children begin to learn relative social habits in which they detect the specific private and public relations between other people and react accordingly. During adolescence, these relative social habits encompass sexual behavior in which the perception of the variable relations and emotional expressions between other people are refined and used as a basis for developing a concept of self. In early adulthood, the refined and sophisticated social habits of team behavior can be learned.

Types of Feedback Linking in Social Learning. Social habit formation may occur in different types of interactive arrangements between two or more persons. Basically there are three types of interpersonal linking of people in interpersonal behavior—that is, *one-way imitation, series-linked tracking,* and *parallel-linked tracking.* One-way imitation consists of the acts of one person following another under conditions in which the imitatee pays no attention to or receives no feedback from the imitator to control his response. In mutual imitation, as in all series-linked tracking, the movements of one person act as stimulus input for the second, and vice versa. All complementary behavior, such as use of language and sexual behavior, is based on series-linked social habits. In parallel-linked behavior, each of two or more individuals gets a joint feedback indication of their combined performance and controls his movements in terms of this combined or systems feedback effect. Team behavior, as in orchestral and athletic performance, typically requires sustained parallel-linked tracking.

Opposing and Competitive Social Habits. Competition also is based on social tracking. Competitive and opposing behavior involves negative feedback control in either one-sided or mutual social tracking. Positive competition, as in games or friendly opposition, involves fundamental patterns of mutual positive social coordination on which the rules of the game are based, with various forms of articulated action involving negative feedback-controlled social tracking. Destructive opposition and fighting involve only a limited positive social feedback foundation. Competitive social habits, as learned in games and athletic activity, may represent poor forms of social control if generalized to situations such as sexual interactions, teaching, and work in which articulated positive forms of social coordination are required. Habits of dominance and subordination should not be confused with competitive behavior inasmuch as both series-linked and parallel forms of social tracking induce dominance and subordination of the participating individuals and do not involve equal feedback control over the social situation.

Adaptive Social Habits. In all positive social tracking, as in parent-child relationships, love, sexual behavior, friendship, and team performance, two or more people become a single, organized, self-controlled system. Such a system takes on characteristics of a single organism in that the interacting persons differentiate, specialize, stratify, and integrate their behavior and motorsensory mechanisms to control each other and the environment around them in an organized way. Obviously, such a single social system not only influences the behavior and habits of individuals composing it, but also governs their roles and expressions of personality as individuals in regulating the system and the environment. The most critical variation among the persons is the extent of control that they can level over the social grouping or the surrounding environment. The extent of such feedback control can vary from near zero, as in the case of the completely subordinate wife, to 100 percent. Such variations in adaptive social control define the conditions of dominance and subordination (and so-called conflict habits) within inter-personal and multiperson groups, along with processes of informal and formal leadership and executive action.

Social Design for Social Habit Formation. Social habits are always learned in the context of social designs—that is, the way in which individuals are linked together in series-linked, parallel, or pseudo imitative social tracking circuits. Such habits can be varied by altering the feedback relationships and patterns in such designs, by shifting the degree of feedback control which individuals have over the group and the surrounding environment, and by means of tools, machines, environmental, and institutional designs for social tracking. The principles of effective designs of tools, machines, and environments for social tracking are not the same as those for individual skill, motion, and perception inasmuch as such designs must make provision for the interactive linking of the motorsensory systems of two or more people. Present knowledge of social cybernetics can do much to correct the superficiality of conventional human-engineering approaches to social behavioral design and for the deep ignorance of current social psychology in comprehending the human factors in social interaction.

Learning, Practice, and Social Feedback Design. The rate and degree to which people learn to coordinate their behavior accurately with one another in social situations depends primarily on factors of social feedback and environmental design and not on practice and learning reinforcement factors. Research on different modes of imitation showed that the extent of improvement of such tracking by varying the design of the feedback-control factors was about 50 times the extent of improvement that could be achieved with practice under either poorly designed or well-designed conditions of mutual tracking. In other words, social behavior follows the same general principles of human factors design that have been found to apply to instrumental behavior.

Multiperson Group Habits and Behavior. The social design of three-person groups differs from habits of interpersonal behavior because at least one person of such a group must be able to detect the relative error of social tracking between the other interacting individuals and thus compensate and control this social systems error. We refer to the individual who does such social-tracking error measurement in multiperson groups as a *social monitor.* Basically, parents, teachers, supervisors, coaches, conductors, critics, counselors, managers, executives, and leaders must function as social monitors as well as dominant controllers. Besides detecting accuracy and error in tracking between members of their own group, they also must detect and measure error of the group as a whole in reacting to other groups and to the environment. Habits of teaching, supervision, and leadership are based on such social monitoring and feedback control operations in multiperson groups. Most social institutions for education and work are poorly designed and the habits of supervision and management are poor because teachers, supervisors, and managers generally have no comprehension of the processes of social monitoring and group feedback control. In contrast, coaches and orchestral conductors may represent superior leaders because they not only know how to perform social monitoring operations but how to design practice to detect deficiencies in behavior and design for social tracking among members of a team or group. Bureaucratic design represents the epitome of human folly in both learning and institutional design because its main purpose is to prevent effective social monitoring, not only by leaders and executives, but by the unfortunate persons who supposedly are to be served by it.

Team Habits. Team habits represent a special spectrum of group behaviors in which every person in the group has a specifically defined operational function and skill in social tracking. Effective team habits are based fundamentally not on rigid patterns of specific response learning, but by training all members of a team as a social tracking monitor to detect errors of interaction between other team members and to compensate these coordination errors as they occur. Sophisticated group behavior of any sort requires such social monitoring and compensatory action, not only to correct for mistakes and slips of individual persons, but to maintain the integrity of the group and to soften the emotional effects of social slips on those who produce them. Effective team group habits in athletics and work are based primarily on design of the social-tracking links between team members, the degree of control assigned to persons with required skills, and the techniques used in error monitoring by critical team members.

Feedback Timing in Interpersonal and Group Habits. Most of the learning to be achieved in interpersonal and group habits is not in the matching of movements on a spatial basis, but in proper dynamic timing of social tracking behavior. Such timing is as essential for adequate sexual behavior as it is for symphonic musical production and football team performance. Timing in such social tracking is based on social feedback timing—that is, the time interval between production of movements by one person and the detection and control of sensory effects of these movements by another person. Mutual series-linked modes of social tracking often involve delay of such feedback which acts not only to prevent learning but to degrade social performance. Training and practice in both interpersonal and group skills should be directed toward eliminating such social feedback delays that distort synchronism of movements.

Aid in Social Habit Formation. Willingness to participate or to come halfway in social interaction is another principle of social habit formation. One of the greatest barriers to social learning is restraint and refractory sensitivity about one's own behavior in social situations. Although many individuals want to improve their social skills, they find it difficult to take off the masks of restraint in mutually reacting with others. In adult social relationships, individuals are often afraid to take a chance on being friendly or going halfway with one another because they must take a chance on being rejected. Some individuals persist in turning others off in social situations by irritating behavior simply to avoid the chance of being subordinated by rejection. In order to learn to relate to others, such people must find someone who will do more for them than they will do for themselves or others.

Simulated Social Habit Formation. Social habits may be developed by simulated training, as in sensitivity training, simulated team training, and use of surrogate sex partners to develop adequate sex behavior. The effectiveness of such techniques depends on the extent that they duplicate the actual overt motorsensory interactions demanded in the interpersonal and group situations in which they are to be used. Even with such similarity the artificial training may not be too effective because all social habits are highly specialized in terms of the specific mutual interplay of two or more individuals. The foundations of love, marriage, and team attachments are all based in large part on such mutual feedback specialization in social habits.

Physiologic Components of Social Habits. Past theory of social behavior has been grossly limited because it could give no explanation whatsoever of the connections between physiologic and organic processes and social behavior. Thus the literature of social psychology would have us believe that there are no significant physiologic factors in social behavior except background neural determinants that govern social response as an end product. The theory of social tracking corrects for this vacuum in past social science theory by asserting that social behavior has the same general cellular, neurohormonal, metabolic, organic, and kinesthetic feedback roles in energy production and regulation as individual forms of muscular response. In fact, it is assumed that social behavior has a greater role in metabolism and energy regulation than individual reactions because the former is of greater scope and frequency than purely individual reaction patterns.

Some social habits such as those related to sexual intercourse and nursing behavior are based on mutual processes of physiologic regulation. Other more public social habits of work, athletic behavior, exercise, and social eating and drinking incorporate processes of energy production and metabolism as feedback effects of activity. Changes in social habits may be difficult because of these direct feedback relations with physiologic and emotional states and their accompanying alterations in metabolic and organic control. Generally, the mechanisms of behavioral-physiologic interactions of energy production and metabolic regulation are the bridges between social behavior and physiologic regulation. Habits of drug use, emotional adjustment, eating, sleep, and other motivational habits may be acquired as a part of such social-behavioral-physiologic interactions.

Social tracking activities, much more than any other type of response, determine the daily events of physical conditioning in infants, children, and other young persons. The activity and motivational habits of individuals thus tend to be laid down in relation to the social skills and capabilities of the child and adolescent, and these habits carry with them the fundamental components of metabolic, organic, neurohormonal, and kinesthetic feedback processes of motor activity. We may speculate also that the processes of cortical-cerebellar integration that determine physical conditioning and its learning functions are also specialized through the social feedback mechanisms of the early years of life. It is not uncommon, for example, for adolescents to change their entire pattern of behavior and educational motivation by getting involved in athletic activity, music, or the performing arts, in which the learning of active social tracking habits are required.

SUMMARY

This chapter has summarized the theory, methods, and principles of behavioral cybernetics as applied to the description of the characteristics and determination of psychomotor behavior. The crux of the behavioral cybernetic interpretation is that motor activity is not simply an end product of stimulus, neural and physiologic determination: rather, dynamic response reciprocally regulates environmental stimulation, the sources of environmental stimuli, sensory input, the receptor process, neural activation and integration, energy production in muscle, and various levels of metabolism by reciprocal mechanisms of feedback control of muscular contraction and movement. Therefore, instead of being determined in a linear way by stimulation, perception, learning, and motivation, the action of the motor system self-governs all levels of organized psychophysiologic and environmental adaptation. The following points and principles regarding feedback regulation of psychomotor behavior were pointed out.

1. Behavioral cybernetic theory is a systems approach to psychomotor behavior that defines a new level of experimental study of body motions and psychologic functions in terms of their variable feedback characteristics and determinants.

2. Optical, electronic, electromechanic, closed-circuit television, audio tape, video tape, and real-time computer methods have been developed to conduct experimental systems studies of almost all body motions and their component stimulus, sensory, perceptual learning, integrative, motivational, and physiologic feedback functions.

3. Behavioral feedback theory and methods had their specific origins in military studies of visuomanual tracking behavior in World War II and their more generalized historic background in classic studies of displaced vision and sensory alteration.

4. Lee's studies of delayed auditory feedback of speech were the first to show that guidance and organization of unaided response are based on motorsensory feedback control.

5. Motion systems of the body do not consist of chains of reflexes or discrete responses, but are organized as multidimensional feedback circuits for integration, guidance, timing, and force regulation of posture, dynamic transport movements, and articulated reactions of the limbs and head receptors.

6. Posture consists of interacting motions of the head, torso, and limbs for maintenance of balance, orientation to gravity, and adjustment to acceleration. All aspects of posture are feedback-controlled and involve movement regulation of sensory input of the vestibular, visual, tactual, and kinesthetic systems, each of which operates to determine special characteristics of positional and dynamic stabilization of the body during active motion. The main feedback factors of posture have been studied as stimulus and body tracking mechanisms.

7. Integration and guidance of movements of the two sides of the body in posture and other body motions are based on bilateral neurogeometric detection wherein single central neurons act as feature or difference detectors to register differences in the position and timing of stimulation between matched receptor points on the two sides of the body.

8. Locomotion is feedback-controlled and integrated as self-governed

coordinate motion of the articulated basal action of the foot and striding action of the limbs to control posture while the body moves in space. Various forms of locomotion involve differences in the timing and coordination of basal stepping and striding movements. Locomotion is a form of unaided steering of the body in motion in which movement-controlled vision provides the basis of projected feedforward directional guidance of motion on uninterrupted substrates and vigilant pedal tracking motions on cluttered and uneven substrates.

9. Hand motions consist of variable types of grasping, reaching, throwing, and manipulative movements, all of which are feedback-organized as dynamic motorsensory coordinations of articulated hand reactions, transport movements of the hand and arm, and postural movements. Both manipulative hand reactions and transport arm movements are articulated at several levels of motion, thus making possible a great number of hand motions that can be related to guidance and timing by all different receptor systems.

10. The guidance of the hand in psychomotor activities of cutting, drawing, writing, tracing, forming, piercing, throwing, grasping, etc. depends primarily on sensing the relative space displacement between movement-generated patterns of sensory input.

11. The fields of receptor and perception cybernetics are concerned with the phenomena of response-controlled sensory input and with design and development of responsive display and tracking systems for the analysis and measurement of sensory functions and perception. Responsive displays or body motion-controlled feedback displays represent the behavioral cybernetic foundations of new concepts of perceptual design in education, art, advertising, and rehabilitation.

12. The first experiments on inversion and delay of eye movement-retinal feedback were carried out in terms of experimental plans defined by behavioral cybernetic theory. Findings indicated that, contrary to widely accepted claims of learning and perception theorists, there is no significant adaptation through learning to inversion and delay of the retinal feedback effects of eye movements.

13. A main experimental finding of the past decade which completely changed the theoretic foundations of physiologic motivation of behavior consisted of the proof that muscular contraction and the motor system self-regulate all levels of the biochemical and metabolic operations of energy production for response.

14. The most important application of the facts of muscle contraction, energy production, and metabolic feedback control by the skeletal motor system is in defining feedback theories of physiologic motivation, effects of exercise, the physiologic basis of work performance and learning. The immediate kinesthetic, metabolic, neurohormonal, and organic feedback effects of movement may be considered as the primary physiologic determinants of learning which precede and define the effects of so-called

operant rewards and reinforcements in determining learning and habit formation.

15. New principles of psychomotor habit formation are defined by a feedback systems theory of behavior. Basically, habit is a systems process of self-regulating one's own body functions, behavior, and the environment for the control of learning. Learning is not determined directly by environmental stimuli but by self-governed selection and control of all levels of environmental stimulation and psychophysiologic function, including energy production for response.

16. In psychomotor skills, learning is determined primarily by capabilities of the performer to adapt in a flexible way to variable conditions of space-displaced feedback. The neural basis of learning consists primarily in changing the properties of feature and difference detection of central detector neurons in sensing and reciprocally controlling response-governed displacements of sensory input.

17. The optimal conditions of learning have been proven experimentally to be those in which the individual generates the basic patterns of stimuli to be learned, a fact that generally confirms the systems feedback doctrine of the determination of learning.

18. Feedback principles of habit making and breaking include rules defining: (a) the primary role of the factors of self-determination of learning; (b) the level and degree of capability in self-regulation of behavior as the basis of individual organization of habit; (c) types and patterns of habit formation; (d) the role of feedforward control of response and adjustment; (e) self-discipline in control of activity; (f) role of movement-governed metabolism and energy production; (g) instrumental feedback factors; (h) social framework and integration of habits; (i) integration of movement components; (j) self-governed stimulus selection in perception; (k) temporal feedback factors; and (l) influence of developmental processes and critical periods.

19. Instrumental behavior and learning are determined by specialized feedback factors. Tools and machines transform the space, time, force, and signal feedback properties of movements and sensory input and introduce a specialized parameter of instrumental feedback into behavior that may or may not be compliant with reactive and operational modes of feedback involved in use of implements. The effectiveness of tools and machines in both performance and learning depends on such compliance.

20. Tools and machines are composed technologically of master-control, actuator and slave (or operational) components, the characteristics of which determine the design and operation of the tool or machine. To be effective in learning and behavior, the master-control component must be compliant with the motor factors in behavior, the slave component with sensory processes and receptor action, and the actuator component with properties of integration of particular movement systems and motorsensory mechanisms.

21. Aside from distorted displacements of feedback, motorsensory delays

produced by common machines, including vehicles, are the basis of most of the difficulties in learning to operate implements. Complex machines typically possess actuator designs that violate the natural patterns of coordination of posture, transport, and articulated movements. Similar effects of feedback delay on learning and performance are found in unaided behavior.

22. Social behavior and learning may be described theoretically in terms of doctrines of social feedback control and social tracking. Social tracking consists of the performance of two or more persons in controlling the sensory inputs of each other by mutually interacting movements. In social tracking, movements of one person act to govern the sensory inputs of another and vice versa in a closed feedback-controlled pattern of sustained organized activity.

23. The patterns of social behavior, as in parent-child interactions, sexual behavior, team play, and group activity, vary in terms of the parameters, modes, and conditons of social tracking. The theory of social feedback can be used to describe the determination of both the characteristic patterns of organization and the detailed mechanisms of control of response in commonly occurring types of social adaptation.

24. Individuals learn social responses on the basis of social feedback factors, not by so-called stimulus or affiliative reinforcements. When systems feedback factors are not operative in social situations, persons do not learn socially effective behavior.

25. Social behavior has accompanying feedback-controlled energy-production, metabolic, organic, kinesthetic, and neurohormonal components which with practice and experience tend to become parallel and coherent in interacting individuals. Such interindividual, movement-produced psychophysiologic compliance is the basis of effective and refined behavior in sexual activity, team coordination, work and competitive skills.

26. Of all the skills performed by man, those involving social coordination are probably the most refined and place the greatest demand on individuals. The primary basis of social skill is not in learning, however, but in the modes and conditions of feedback control with which persons track each other and by the ways in which social situations are designed to provide effective systems feedback in mutually yoked behavior.

27. Common forms of social performance such as imitation, mimicking, and communication may vary in terms of the way individuals are linked together in one-sided, mutually-helpful, or opposing feedback relationships. The most effective form of imitation is one in which the imitatee attempts to track and actively aid the imitator in social tracking.

28. Social tracking may involve various types of positive and negative feedback relationships between two or more people. Individuals may be yoked together to complement, compensate, parallel, pursue, oppose,

differentiate, integrate, or transform the sensory effects of each other's activity.

29. Research on social tracking has proved that it is feedback-regulated and varied in effectiveness in terms of the modes, conditions, and factors of closed-loop linking of individuals in social performance.

30. Social habits depend not only on individual capability in learning, but are also governed by the design and feedback control factors in social situations. Principles of social habit formation are based on rules related to (a) the social yoking of individuals into pairs or groups which operate as unified self-controlled systems; (b) types and modes of social feedback control; (c) degree of mutual linking of motorsensory systems of interacting persons; (d) developmental factors determining capability in social tracking; (e) types of feedback linking for social learning; (f) modes of positive negative feedback control of interacting behavior; (g) extent of feedback control of social interactions by component individuals; (h) social cybernetic designs related to tools, communication devices, environmental situations, and architecture; (i) relative roles of practice and effective social cybernetic designs; (j) group patterns and interactions; (k) team factors; (l) social feedback timing and synchronism; (m) training aids and simulation devices; and (n) physiologic components of social behavior.

References

Ansell, S., Waisbrot, A., & Smith, K. U. Hybrid computer analysis of self-regulated heart-rate control. In S. A. Yefskey (ed.), *Proceedings of the First Institute on Law Enforcement Science and Technology*. Vol. 1., New York: Thompson Book Co., 1967, pp. 403–418.

Atkinson, D. E. Biological feedback control at the molecular level. *Science*, 1965, 150, 851–862.

Atkinson, D. E. Regulation of enzyme activity. *Annual Review of Biochemistry*, 1966, 35, 85–124.

Bilodeau, E. (ed.) *Acquisition of skill*. New York: Academic Press, 1966.

Borelli, G. A. *Du motu animalism (Opus Posthumum)*. Rome: A. Bernabo, 1680–1681.

Fitts, P. M. Engineering psychology and equipment design. In S. S. Stevens (ed.), *Handbook of experimental psychology*. New York: John Wiley & Sons, 1951, pp. 1287–1340.

General Electric Company. Hardiman I armtest: Hardiman I prototype project. Schenectady, New York: 1969.

Gould, J., & Smith, K. U. Angular displacement of visual feedback of motion. *Science*, 1962, 137, 619–620.

Helmholtz, H. L. F. *Treatise on physiological optics*. Translated from the *Handbook der physiologischen Optik*. 3rd ed., Rochester, New York: Optical Society of America, 1924–1925.

Hull, C. *Principles of behavior: An introduction to behavior theory*. New York: Appleton-Century, 1943.

Huxley, H. E. The mechanism of muscular contraction. *Science*, 1969, 166, 1356–1366.

James, W. *Principles of psychology*. New York: Holt, 1891.

Keesey, U. T., & Nicholas, D. J. Relation between the on-going electroencephalogram and fluctuations of visibility of a stabilized retinal image. *Journal of Optical Society of America*, 1966, 55, 543.

Lee, B. S. Some effects of side-tone delay. *Journal of the Acoustical Society of America,* 1950, 22, 639–640.

Lee, B. S. Artificial stutter. *Journal of Speech Hearing Disease,* 1951, 16, 53–55.

Miller, N. E. Learning and visceral glandular responses. *Science,* 1969, 163, 434–445.

Mosher, R. Industrial manipulators. *Scientific American,* 1964, 211(4), 88–96.

Mowrer, O. H. *Learning theory and symbolic processes.* New York: John Wiley & Sons, Inc., 1960.

Pavlov, I. P. *Lectures on conditioned reflexes* (Translated from the Russian version by G. V. Aurep). London: Oxford University Press, 1927.

Riggs, L. A., Ratliff, F., Cornsweet, J. C., & Cornsweet, T. N. The disappearance of steadily fixated visual test objects. *Journal of Optical Society of America,* 1953, 43, 495–501.

Skinner, B. F. *Behavior of organisms: An experimental analysis.* New York: Appleton-Century, 1938.

Skinner, B. F. *Science and human behavior.* New York: Macmillan Co., 1953.

Skinner, B. F. *Verbal behavior.* New York: Appleton-Century-Crofts, 1955.

Smith, K. U. Analysis of psychological factors in aircraft gun systems. Special report to the Air Material Command. Project AC-94: NDRC: University of Wisconsin, 1945.

Smith, K. U. Cybernetic theory and analysis of learning. In E. Bilodeau (ed.), *Acquisition of skill.* New York: Academic Press, 1966, pp. 425–482. (a)

Smith, K. U. Review of principles of human factors in design of the exoskeleton and four-legged pedipulator. Unpublished manuscript, Madison, Wisconsin: University of Wisconsin Behavioral Cybernetics Laboratory, 1966. (b)

Smith, K. U. Cybernetic foundations of physical behavior science. *Quest,* 1967, Monograph VIII, 26–89.

Smith, K. U., & Ansell, S. Closed-loop digital computer system for study of the sensory feedback effects of brain rhythms. *American Journal of Physical Medicine,* 1965, 44, 125–137.

Smith, K. U., & Smith, M. F. *Cybernetic principles of learning and educational design.* New York: Holt, Rinehart & Winston, 1966.

Smith, K. U., & Smith, T. J. Systems theory of therapeutic learning with television. *Journal of Nervous and Mental Diseases.* 1969, 148, 386–429.

Smith, K. U., & Smith, W. M. *Perception and motion: An analysis of space structured behavior.* Philadelphia: W. B. Saunders, 1962.

Smith, K. U., & Sussman, H. In E. Bilodeau (ed.), *Principles of skill acquisition.* New York: Academic Press, 1969, pp. 103–138.

Smith, K. U., Luedke, A., & Smith, T. J. Feedback principles of athletic skill and learning. In L. Smith (ed.), *Motor performance and learning.* Chicago: Athletic Institute, 1970.

Stratton, G. M. Some preliminary experiments in vision without inversion of the retinal image. *Psychological Review,* 1896, 3, 611–617.

Stratton, G. M. Vision without inversion of the retinal image. *Psychological Review,* 1897, 4, 341–360.

Stratton, G. M. The spatial harmony of touch and sight. *Mind,* 1899, 8, 463–505.

Thorndike, E. L. *Educational psychology.* Vol. III, New York: Teacher's College, Columbia University, 1913.

Watson, J. B. *Psychology from the standpoint of a behaviorist.* (2nd ed.), Philadelphia: Lippincott, 1924.

Chapter 13

NEUROSCIENCES: MECHANISMS OF MOTOR CONTROL[1]

ROBERT HUTTON
University of Washington

During the past decade, the rapid increase in the number of research journals and professional organizations focusing on problems related to behavior and central nervous system (CNS) function favorably reflects the scientific community's growing concern in this area. Moreover, there has been a greater emphasis on interdisciplinary communication and research, as exemplified by the Neurosciences Research Program (NRP), an international, interuniversity organization founded in 1962 (Quarton et al., 1967; Schmitt, 1970) and the Society for Neurosciences, an organization formed by action of the National Academy of Sciences–National Research Council Committee on Brain Sciences in 1969 (Marshall, 1970). Hence, the term "neurosciences" designates this cooperative interdisciplinary effort and encompasses such fields as neuroanatomy, neurophysiology, neuropsychology, and neurochemistry, to name but a few.

In the study of neurologic processes underlying behavior, perhaps the most basic question to ask is, What factors control motor outflow from the central nervous system? The fundamental importance of motor control to behavior is obvious, but not so apparent is the manner through which large muscle groups can be coordinated by a complex interplay between reflexive and volitionally controlled neural pathways to form smooth and integrated movement patterns. In a recent NRP Bulletin (Evarts et al., 1971), it was noted that three basic aspects of coordinated movement must be fulfilled by the CNS: (1) the appropriate muscle must be selected (spatial control), (2)

[1] The work reported in this chapter has been supported by PHS grant number: 5 TI MH 6415-13.

349

muscle activation or inactivation must occur at the appropriate time (temporal control), and (3) the degree of muscle inactivation must be graded (quantitative control). Neuromotor control theories advanced over the last century to account for the preceding conditions range between two extremes. On the one hand, emphasis has been placed on peripheral input from sensory organs as the prime determinant of motor responses; on the other hand, central patterning of movement is emphasized with peripheral input providing essential but so-called nonspecific sensory information as seen, for example, in experiments (cf: Wilson, 1961; Wilson and Waldron, 1968) in which surgical intervention of peripheral input has been shown to alter frequency or intensity of responding without changing the response pattern. In either case, supportive evidence has been gathered from vertebrate and invertebrate experimentation, and present motor control theories must take both possibilities into consideration.

In this chapter, a brief summary of selected research literature contributing to current neurologic models of motor control is presented. The approach taken is unlike that commonly encountered in the professional journals where the review articles are usually restricted to specific subtopics (frequently neuroanatomically designated) of broad research areas, thus favoring in-depth coverage of the literature at the expense of scope. Since this chapter is written for the reader possessing a limited background in the neurosciences, greater stress has been placed on brief coverage of a number of topics and issues pertinent to current motor control theories. In this manner, the reader may become better acquainted with this type of neurologic research and, hopefully, will be interested enough in one or more of the topics considered to read further. Should the latter be the case, the recent NRP Bulletin edited by Evarts and his associates (1971) represents an excellent beginning point and can be followed by the other references listed (Brisky et al., 1970; Brooks et al., 1970; Brooks and Stoney, 1971; Denny-Brown, 1949; Eccles et al., 1967; Field et al., 1959–1960; Granit, 1966; Granit, 1970; Granit and Kellerth, 1967; Jung and Hassler, 1969; Matthews, 1964; Purpura and Yahr, 1966; Wiesendanger, 1969; Yahr and Purpura, 1967).

HISTORICAL CONSIDERATIONS

Historically the systematic study of CNS function in movement behavior preceded the formal development of subdisciplines we now recognize as neurophysiology, neuropsychology, and the like. Prior to the formulation of the neuron doctrine (1891)[2] and ten years before the successful application

[2] The concept that neurons are morphologically independent cellular units of the CNS and that neuronal interconnections are made by means of protoplasmic bridges (the term *synapse* was introduced later by Sherrington) as opposed to the rival view that neurons form a fused meshlike network, that is, protoplasmic continuum. The German term *Neuron* was introduced by Waldeyer in 1891 although the concept was based largely on the histologic works of Ramon y Cajal, who used the staining techniques developed by Golgi (Barker, 1899).

of electrophysiologic techniques to brain tissue (1870), John Hughlings Jackson, a clinical neurologist, studied central neuromuscular organization through analyses of epileptiform behavior. Jackson proposed that brain tissue, namely the cerebral cortex, was involved in voluntary movement largely on the basis of this clinical evidence. It was believed that epileptic convulsions and palsies represented manifestations of "discharging lesions" and "destroying lesions" in the cerebrum, respectively.[3] In convulsant responses ("fits beginning unilaterally" as he called them), voluntary movements most easily brought under fine control, that is, in the hands, face, tongue, and feet, were first to be affected by lesions localized in cortical tissue found just above the corpus striatum, a subcortical mass of cells. A similar relationship between the site of the lesion and the voluntary movements effected was noted in destroying lesions. To quote Jackson (Taylor, 1931, p. 63):

> The study of cases of hemiplegia shows that from disease of the corpus striatum those external parts suffer most which, psychologically speaking, are most under the command of will and which, physiologically speaking, have the greater number of different movements at the greater number of different intervals. That parts suffer more as they serve in voluntary, and less as they serve in automatic operations is, I believe, the law of destroying lesions of the central nervous centers.

Although Jackson often used the terms *voluntary* and *automatic* in reference to movement, he did not define these as two classes of movement but rather as graded levels of CNS control. Three levels of cerebral organization were postulated which function as a "hierarchy of motor-control in the neural axis ranging upward from most automatic—least voluntary to most voluntary—least automatic" (Walshe, 1943). Muscles were believed to have multiple anatomic representation at each cerebral level, but functionally, they were represented as different orders of *movement.* For example, as a part of convulsant behavior Jackson described "leading movements" and "subordinate movements," which may be performed by the same muscle(s) responding under different levels of cerebral control. Stated simply, the cerebrum was believed to contain "nervous arrangements representing movements."

In 1870, Fritsch and Hitzig introduced an experimental technique which gave rise to modern electrophysiology when they demonstrated that the brain was electrically excitable and, contrary to earlier claims, that cortical function could be localized. These experiments supported Jackson's earlier

---

[3] The neurologic terms *positive* and *negative* symptoms reflect the behavioral effects of these types of lesions. Positive symptoms imply motor behavior arising from the *release* of one neural center's control over another, as is believed to be the case in convulsive or tremor responses. Negative symptoms occur through dysfunction of a neural center, e.g., paralysis. Presently, these terms are used less frequently since they are not easily applicable to neurologic disorders involving complex excitatory and inhibiting neural pathways.

notion of a motor cortex since control of muscular contraction was shown to be localized within certain areas of the cerebral cortex. This was accomplished by electrically stimulating cortical surfaces in dogs and determining which areas evoked muscular contractions. Applying this technique to primates, Ferrier (1888) later corroborated some of Jackson's earlier observations by finding that induced artificial movement often involved muscles most used voluntarily although the responses themselves varied between muscle twitches and gross movements.

With similar electrical techniques, Beevor and Horsley (1887, 1890) designated cortical areas to be predominantly motor or sensory in function. Anatomically, these areas were described as pre-central and post-central gyri, respectively; however, since it has now been well established by more complete mapping techniques (Woolsey, 1958; Woolsey et al., 1952) that there are no *pure* sensory or motor cortical areas, Woolsey and his colleagues have proposed the following nomenclature for a *sensorimotor* system: somatic sensory-motor area I (*Sm I*) for the post-central gyrus (parietal area); somatic sensory-motor area II (*Sm II*) for a "second" sensory cortical area located beneath *Sm I*, somatic motor-sensory area I (*Ms I*) for the pre-central gyrus (frontal area), and somatic motor-sensory area II (*Ms II*) for a supplementary motor area located on the medial surface of each cerebral hemisphere and extending anteriorly from *Ms I*. The term *somatic* implies that within each of these defined cortical areas there exists a complete (although somewhat distorted) figurine of the body surfaces represented by either sensory or motor neurons. The extent of each somatotopic area varies within and across species.

From numerous cortical stimulation studies that followed (Brazier, 1959; Brown and Sherrington, 1912; Leyton and Sherrington, 1917), a somewhat different concept of cortical organization of movement developed. Leyton and Sherrington noted that localized stimulation evoked only fractional or "fragmentary reactions" which usually deviated with repeated stimuli. Since the evoked responses were unlike natural movements, they were interpreted as unitary parts of more complex acts. It was assumed that the motor cortex integrates these parts into a useful whole. That the cortex could perform this integrating function was evident by the lack of stability of the evoked response.

While Jackson theorized that movements are represented in motor cortex, these later investigators proposed that the cortex was a mosaic of unitary parts representing activation points for muscles, that is, "punctate localization." This controversy on the nature of cortico-motor control continued throughout the nineteenth century, as noted by a recent discussion of this issue by Evarts (1967). A further review of this topic, in light of current research, is found under the section entitled Cerebral Cortical Control of Movement.

At the turn of the century, major advances were also made in the area of reflexology. Knowledge concerning sensorimotor integration at the spinal cord level was largely influenced by Sherrington's works on spinal reflexes. It was Sherrington's belief that reflexes reveal fundamental elements found in more complex coordinated responses. Since ventral roots of the spinal cord are motor or largely efferent fibers innervating skeletal muscle tissue and dorsal roots are sensory or afferent fibers arising from sense organs (Bell-Magendie law), reflexive responses and spinal integration of these responses could be systematically studied by controlling ipsilateral or contralateral sensory input from synergistic and antagonistic muscles of the limbs. Supraspinal influences on cord structures could be minimized by making surgical transections at or below the midbrain level, as seen in the so-called decerebrate animal.

As much a behaviorist as he was a neurophysiologist, Sherrington studied reflexive responses and provided plausible functional equivalents to what was then known about neuroanatomic structures. In the latter respect, he relied heavily on the histologic works of Cajal and the neuron concept (Granit, 1967). Sherrington viewed the "integrative action" of neurons to be the ability of these cells to excite or inhibit one another by means of central interneuronal couplings he called synapses (Sherrington, 1947).[4]

From his works arose the concepts of "synaptic connections," "central inhibition," "central excitation," "reciprocal innervation" which is defined as a reflexive inhibitory input from a synergistic muscle to its antagonist during onset of a concentric contraction, and "final common path," defined as the final neural pathway (the motor neuron) from the spinal cord to muscle, thus representing considerable excitatory and inhibitory synaptic convergence within the CNS. According to Granit (1967), the reflexes proving most important for the development of Sherrington's concepts were (1) the ipsilateral flexor reflex—flexion or retraction of the limb to a noxious stimulus; (2) the crossed extensor reflex—extension of the contralateral limb following an ipsilateral flexor response; and (3) the stretch reflex—contractile response to muscle stretch. The stretch reflex or "myotatic reflex" as it is sometimes called was considered to be the basic reflex in standing since extensors, when stretched by the pull of gravity, could prevent the animal from falling. Sherrington recognized a relationship between the neural pathways underlying the stretch reflex and the postural condition of extensor hyperexcitability (decerebrate rigidity), as noted in animals suffering midbrain transections, since the rigidity disappeared when the afferent roots were cut. Granit (1968, p. 69) has summarized this view:

> The decerebrate preparation gave a good stretch reflex from (at the time unknown) muscle receptors. This was described as exaggerated standing. Its basis

[4] These concepts are well elucidated in Sherrington's classic book, *The Integrative Action of the Nervous System,* a composite of his Silliman Lectures given at Yale University in 1904.

> was a "release" of the extensor motoneurons, the alpha motoneurons as we tend to call them today. The stretch reflex disappeared when the afferent nerves were cut and so the basis of postural tone was an autogenetic facilitation of the stretch reflex from muscular afferents. The impulses arose from a muscle and influenced its own motoneurones; hence 'autogenetic.'

Autogenetic facilitation of motor neurons was later shown to involve a monosynaptic reflex arc between muscle spindle afferents and the larger motor neurons (Hoffman, 1922; Lloyd, 1943); however, the manner in which midbrain transections enhanced muscle afferent activity was not yet understood.

Sherrington (1898) had also demonstrated that in decerebrate rigidity if the limb was forcibly moved into flexion, tension rose as expected, but with continued bending the extensors suddenly gave way to flexion. Sherrington interpreted this as evidence for a self-inhibitory (autogenetic inhibition) afferent input from the stretched muscle, a response he called the "lengthening reaction." At that time, autogenetic inhibition and facilitation were only known to depend on intact afferent nerves and further understanding of muscle receptors was needed.

By 1924 Sherrington suggested that muscle spindles and Golgi tendon organs subserve the functions of muscle length detection and muscle tension detection, respectively (Granit, 1967). A few years later, Fulton and Pi-Suñer (1928) presented strong arguments based on histologic and electrophysiologic evidence to support this contention. Basic to their discussion was the histologic evidence that spindles exist parallel muscle fibers and Golgi tendon organs in series with muscle fibers. Given this condition, *passive* muscle stretch could be detected by spindles as a change in muscle length but the problem that during muscle contraction spindle stretch would be unloaded still remained. The functional role of spindles was further complicated by the fact that these organs were also known to encapsulate striated muscle fibers[5] which in turn receive a motor neuronal supply. Further interpretation of spindle activity and motor control depended on the use of more refined techniques developed after Sherrington's time (Granit, 1967).

Although studies on spinal reflexes and cerebro-cortical motor control occupied much of the early experimental literature on CNS involvement in movement, several other neural structures were known to play a prominent role. Prior to the use of stimulation techniques, many investigators employed "ablation" as a surgical method for determining the function of a neural structure by observing the effects of its removal on animal behavior. Using this technique, many observations were reported in the eighteenth century which suggested that the cerebellum was involved in movement behavior.

---

[5] To avoid confusion a distinction is made between striated muscle encapsulated by spindles and the larger mass of striated muscle (e.g., the biceps) surrounding these capsules. The former is referred to as "intrafusal muscle fibers" and the latter as "extrafusal muscle fibers," as originally designated by Sherrington.

Dow (1969) credits Flourens (1842) with developing the concept that the cerebellum exerts regulatory control over motor activity. Flourens had found that although partial cerebellar ablation in Aves resulted in remarkable recovery of function, total removal caused permanent motor deficiencies. Luciani (1969) was noted for cerebellar ablation experiments on primates and subprimates and his detailed descriptions of the symptoms that followed, among which he included motor impairment.

Using stimulation techniques, Lowenthal and Harsely (1897) and also Sherrington (1898) later discovered that decerebrate rigidity could be inhibited by electrical stimulation of the cerebellar anterior lobe, thereby indicating a possible role of the cerebellum in spinal reflexes and spindle-mediated responses. Sherrington (1947) had referred to the cerebellum as the "head ganglion of the proprioceptive system."

It was on the basis of experiments like these that early investigators conceived of a functional relationship between cerebellar input-output and spinal integration of muscle afferents. There was also considerable speculation as to how this related to responses mediated by the cerebral cortex. In 1924, Herrick proposed two possibilities: (1) The cerebellum might regulate movement or posture by facilitating prime movers or inhibiting antagonists of the desired movement from information received from muscle afferents. In this case, long loop reflexes between the cord and cerebellum could be involved in maintaining the appropriate amount of muscle tone for cerebral-controlled responses. (2) Muscle activation by means of the cerebral cortex may involve transmission of simultaneous collateral discharges to the cerebellum, presumably to recruit additional motor neurons by way of cerebellar descending pathways. Several years later, Holmes (1939) proposed the hypothesis that the cerebellum aids in the initiation of motor cortex activity on the basis that initiation of movement is delayed in patients suffering cerebellar lesions. Further elaboration on these points will be discussed in the section entitled Functional Role of the Cerebellum in Movement, where more recent electrophysiologic evidence is considered.

Deep cerebral nuclei, known collectively as the basal ganglia (corpus striatum and globus pallidus), are important supraspinal structures influencing motor output. These structures are often identified in conjunction with cerebral cortical activity as part of the "extrapyramidal system," a purely anatomic designation.[6] According to Jung and Hassler (1969), this system was first described by Starlinger in 1895 and later named by Prus in 1898. Even today, knowledge concerning extrapyramidal functions is poor and exceedingly difficult to interpret. Most of the views on basal ganglionic

---

[6] In the future, the term *pyramidal tract* will be employed to describe that part of the motor-sensory cerebral cortex which anatomically links more directly with motor neurons in the cord (also known as the corticospinal tract). According to Tower (1947), this term was first employed by Türck in 1851.

function in motor control are based on neurologic observations in man since attempts at developing animal models exhibiting similar dysfunctions have largely been unsuccessful.

Lesions of the basal ganglia are characterized by one or more of the following motor disorders: an increase in muscle tone without spastic paresis (muscular rigidity), excess spontaneous and involuntary movements, dissociated synergistic movements, and absence of changes in reflexes (Jung and Hassler, 1969). It should be noted that other supraspinal nuclei not identified as part of this complex may give rise to similar symptoms, e.g., subthalamic nuclei, substantia nigra, and the red nucleus. According to Jung and Hassler, early pathologic studies contributing greatly to this area were conducted by Anton, Vogt and Vogt, Alzheimer, and Wilson, among others.

Brodal (1969) maintains that most basal ganglionic activity influencing motor function is exerted through the cerebral cortex since few descending fibers are known to connect this area with lower spinal areas. Though considerable recent developments have occurred in this area of neurologic research, notably in the field of neuropharmacology and neurochemistry (cf.: Ernest, 1969; O'Malley, 1970; Simpson and Angus, 1970), further discussion of this topic will be limited. Suffice it to say that motor responses mediated by the cerebral cortex in freely moving animals may indirectly reflect activity from these basal ganglionic structures (cf: DeLong and Evarts, 1970). A block diagram of the motor systems previously discussed is shown in figure 13-1. Not shown in the connections of these oversimplified subdivisions are the numerous important interconnections between sensory (unshaded arrows) and nonsensory (shaded arrows) pathways. In the review that follows, greater consideration will be given to spinal,

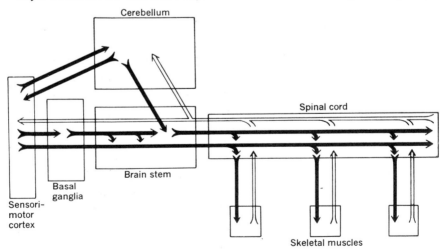

FIG. 13-1. Neural structures of motor control. Explanation in text (*Henneman. In Medical Physiology. V.B. Mountcastle (ed.), 12th ed., St. Louis: C. V. Mosby Co., 1968*).

cerebellar, and sensorimotor cerebro-cortical control of "the final common path" to skeletal muscle tissue.

Since the innovation of the cathode ray oscillograph by Gasser and Erlanger (1922), improved stimulating devices, the development of more precise experimental techniques such as extra- and intracellular electrode recordings, a better though still somewhat fragmented picture of how neurons interact to produce finely coordinated movements is beginning to emerge. It was the purpose of this brief historical introduction to provide the reader with early concepts which have formed the basis for further research on neuromotor function. Admittedly, comprehensive motor control theories have been slow in developing during the latter part of this century, as Houk and Henneman (1967b, p. 433) have pointed out.

> One of the basic difficulties handicapping all research on the motor systems is the lack of a unifying theory of motor function. With good reason it has been felt that the available information is too fragmentary for the formulation of any overall theory and most investigation proceeds without. . . . a comprehensive approach relating all studies on motor function is needed. . . . A closely related problem is that of devising a method of representing the complexities of multiple neural circuits in concise form. To do so requires some means of systematic simplification which does not distort any of the essential features of the system.

In the review which follows, emphasis will be placed on presenting contemporary viewpoints on neuromotor control in simplified theoretic constructs. The degree to which any of the theories considered distorts the available neurologic evidence must ultimately be determined by one's personal assessment of the literature.

SPINAL MOTOR CONTROL

As mentioned previously, muscle spindle activity is known to exert some control over extrafusal muscle by means of a monosynaptic reflex elicited by *passive* stretch. The question remains as to the spindle's role during active contraction since anatomic considerations tell us that spindle stretch would be unloaded, thereby releasing the necessary mechanical stimulus for spindle afferent activity. In order to answer this, a brief discussion of spindle structure and related efferent-afferent neural supply must first be considered.[7]

There are two types of afferent fibers in the spindle—a single group Ia fiber, with primary endings located centrally within the spindle capsule, and one or more group II fibers, with secondary endings located on either side of the spindle (some spindles have no secondary endings). Both types of endings

---

[7] Anatomic terminology for muscle spindles can be quite confusing since many synonyms now exist for the same structures. To avoid this problem, one set of terminology will be adhered to whenever possible throughout this discussion. For a more detailed anatomic analysis the reader is referred to Matthews (1964) or Granit (1970).

terminate on intrafusal muscle fibers which in turn receive a motor neuron. Intrafusal muscle fibers are innervated by so-called fusimotor neurons which are small in size relative to the alpha motor neuron (*AMN*) innervating extrafusal fibers. For our purposes, neuroanatomic considerations need not go beyond this basic discussion.

The stretch reflex is believed to be supported solely by primary endings in spindles usually located in the same or synergistic muscles, while the flexor reflex is due to discharges from group II afferents to flexor motor neurons "whether the secondary endings themselves lie in flexor or in extensor muscles" (Matthews, 1964). In addition, other sensory organs such as cutaneous receptors may contribute to this reflexive response. (The term flexor reflex afferents (*FRA*) has been used to designate this latter group of fibers though Matthews takes exception to this view since it overlooks the possible contribution of secondary endings to length detection. *FRA* include cutaneous afferents, groups II and III muscle afferents and high-threshold joint afferents (Matthews, 1964; Wall, 1970).

Specifically related responses of primary and secondary endings to sudden changes in spindle stretch are defined as "stretch responses" (Matthews, 1964). The primary ending is appreciably more sensitive than secondary endings to dynamic changes in stretch (Harvey and Matthews, 1961). This difference is known to exist despite changes in intrafusal fiber tension due to fusimotor activity, or the type of dynamic stretch employed (Cooper, 1961); however, under static or steady stretch conditions differences in discharge between primary and secondary endings are slight and inconsistent (Matthews, 1964). From this Matthews (1964, p. 245) suggests that "the muscle spindle primary endings signal both the instantaneous length of the muscle and the velocity at which it is being stretched, while the secondary endings signal mainly instantaneous length."

Fusimotor activity can alter the dynamic response of the primary endings or the static response of both primary and secondary endings by presumably changing the mechanical properties of the intrafusal fiber (Bessou et al., 1968). This is commonly referred to as "spindle bias" and it underlies the role of fusimotor activation in determining the final output from spindle afferents. When considering fusimotor control one can conceive of activating a stretch reflex by the following manner: fusimotor activation (motor neuron from spinal cord) $\longrightarrow$ intrafusal contraction (muscle fibers within the spindle) $\longrightarrow$ stimulation of primary endings and the corresponding group Ia fibers leading back to the spinal cord $\longrightarrow$ activation of *AMN* by means of a monosynaptic arc $\longrightarrow$ contraction of extrafusal muscle fibers in the same or synergistic extrafusal muscles. In this way, the spindle can indirectly control muscle contraction without total dependency on stretch stimuli originating externally; perhaps more importantly, the spindle can adjust its own length during active contraction of extrafusal muscles, thereby eliminating or minimizing unloading by resetting intrafusal tension. This indirect pathway for activating extrafusal fibers is commonly referred to as the "gamma loop," the term gamma being a synonym for fusimotor fibers.

Hence, the "final common path" can be activated in two ways—directly by supraspinal or spinal influences on *AMNs* or indirectly by means of supraspinal or spinal influences on the gamma loop. There is evidence to suggest that normal initiation of muscular contraction may involve either route for alpha activation.

On the basis of experiments involving voluntary control over the adductor muscle of the thumb, Merton (1953) hypothesized that voluntary contraction can be initiated by the gamma loop in the manner of a servocontrolled movement. Since alpha activation through the gamma loop would be slower than direct activation, Merton postulated that servocontrolled movement accounted for slower movements and/or postural adjustments. His scheme was presented as follows (Merton, 1953, pp. 251—255):

1) The sensory ending [spindle afferents] detects the difference between the length of the main muscle and the muscular poles of the spindle.
2) The stretch reflex, excited by impulses from the spindle-ending, tends to keep the main muscle at the same length as the spindle.
3) In a steady voluntary or postural effort the length of the muscle is determined by the rate of the "tonic" innervation of the intrafusal fibres, which sets their length.
4) Shortening involves an increased excitation of the intrafusal fibres; as they shorten, the main muscle follows by servo action. Descending pathways mediating voluntary movement would thus end on the small motoneurons [fusimotor fibers].
5) Sudden efforts excite the main motoneurons directly in order to avoid delay due to conduction time to and from the spindle.

In a more recent consideration of spindle control of skeletal muscles, Houk and Henneman (1967) discuss the neurophysiologic evidence in terms of feedback control theory. Here, the spindle is considered to be a transducer which provides continuous flow of information (feedback signal) from the thing controlled (muscle length) to the controlling device (alpha motor neuron). The feedback signal is compared with a control signal which may be considered to be the result of excitatory and inhibitory synaptic convergence on the alphas, and the computed difference (error signal) would alter alpha input to the controlled system to reduce the amount of error. In this manner, a "disturbing force" causing initial stretch to the muscle is counteracted by this feedback system, giving rise to more muscular force. This type of mechanism may underly the recruitment of additional muscular force necessary to overcome a sudden and possibly unexpected load increase placed on a muscle held in a steady state. Fusimotor fibers add an additional dimension to this system by allowing spindle feedback without total reliance on externally (gravity or load changes) induced steady-state changes. Again the speculation is made that alpha inputs are employed where speed is essential and fusimotor input is involved in smooth, continuous control of muscles. Houk and Henneman (1967a,b) also supported earlier views that tendon organs provide continuous feedback which regulates muscle tension and also protects against overload since tendon organ activation results in the inverse of the stretch reflex ("inverse myostatic reflex"), that is, inhibition of motor neurons in the same muscle. This entire system of muscle length and tension control is referred to as the "positional control system." It might be noted that although the terminology has been updated, the concepts advanced by Houk and Henneman are not markedly different from those expressed some 39 years earlier by Fulton and Pi-Suñer (1928).

Functions of group II fibers are noticeably omitted in the aforementioned schemes for spindle control of alpha activity. Since their response may be variable and weak (Lloyd, 1960), Grillner (1969) suggests that secondary endings might play a more important role in mediating proprioceptive information to supraspinal structures. Other considerations of group II function will be discussed later under *FRA* input to cerebellar structures.

Granit (1968) has shown that muscle spindles need some support from fusimotor input to operate a stretch reflex. It is partly on this basis that he proposed a "co-activation theory" for alpha and fusimotor control of motor acts, that is, loop activation brings the alpha fiber closer to the firing threshold needed by a passive stretch. In spite of the functional complications introduced by group II and tendon organ input, Granit (1966) has shown that gamma loop activation of spindle primaries is powerful enough to overcome these autogenetic inhibitory effects and fire the alphas. This leaves us with the questions of how and at what neural levels alpha motor and fusimotor neurons are co-activated (known as "alpha-gamma linkage").

Eldred and his associates demonstrated as early as 1953 that head reflexes generated in the decerebrate cat increased spindle bias by means of fusimotor activity. In such cases, spindle bias was little affected by section of the dorsal roots showing supraspinal control to be independent of afferent input. Although the findings were interpreted more in terms of a servocontrol theory, supraspinal control mechanisms represent one probable level of alpha-gamma linkage. A number of experiments by Corda and associates (1965) and Sears (1964, 1966) have shown that *both* fusimotor and alpha motor neurons supplying external intercostal muscles are driven during the active phase of normal respiration. Presumably the linkage was placed at the spinal level. In a more recent paper by Andersen and Sears (1970), co-activation of the intercostal alpha and fusimotor neurons with reciprocal inhibition of the antagonistic motor neurons was shown at the medullary level of the brain stem.

Linkage may be partially destroyed by acute destruction of the anterior cerebellum (Granit et al., 1955), resulting in a "release" syndrome known as alpha rigidity. In this case, increased alpha discharge is accompanied by decreased fusimotor discharge. Granit and his associates have proposed that the anterior lobe of the cerebellum may be a "switching station" for the two types of motor neuronal control. Linkage by means of cortical control will be dealt with later.

The functional role of fusimotor control over dynamic and static spindle responses must still be analyzed. Phillips (1969) takes up this issue by considering alpha-gamma co-activation in the control of primate finger movements as illustrated in figure 13-2. In this hypothesized scheme, Phillips emphasizes the control of force and velocity of movements rather than stationary postural maintenance. The line *a* to *c* represents a volitional movement of uniform velocity which requires graded recruitment of alpha motor neurons as the movement progresses (displacement).[8]

Considering the movement represented by line *a* to *c* in figure 13-2A, a decrease in spindle feedback due to spindle unloading might be expected but in this case the unloading effect is offset by the fusimotor effect, yielding no net change in spindle feedback, that is, fusimotor fibers are also recruited with displacement, or in other words, "co-activated" along with alpha fibers. At point *b* in figure 13-2A an unexpected resistance reduces the unloading effect (full line) without change in fusimotor activity. Spindle feedback must now increase, as seen in the abrupt change (corresponding to point *b*) in primary endings (*p*) which are driven by both dynamic and static fusimotor activity. The fusimotor-driven secondary endings would respond in a similar manner, but would signal no information relevant to velocity of deviation since they are less sensitive to dynamic changes in muscle length. The net result of both responses is an increase in spindle feedback to compensate for the difference between the intended and actual movement response. The compensated response (not shown) would be indicated by a return of "*b-c*, full line" to the original intended course, "*b-c*, dotted line." The secondaries, while not involved in this case in exciting alpha motor neurons, are thought to provide important information to cerebral and cerebellar levels.

In figure 13-2B an expected reduction is encountered at point *d* as noted by a sudden increase in displacement velocity. Here the spindles are rapidly unloaded, again without a corresponding change in fusimotor output. Note the sudden fall in primary ending discharge (*p*) resulting in a decrease of alpha activation. Had the primary endings been more under the influence of static fusimotor discharge their responses would have resembled that of the secondaries (*S*). Again, the compensated response is not shown in this illustration, but would have been indicated by the sudden unloading effect corresponding to an increase in displacement velocity (*d-c*, full line). If a servocontrol theory had been applied to the preceding example a compen-

[8] The need for alpha recruitment when velocity of movement remains constant might best be understood if "length-tension" relationships in skeletal muscle and the mechanics of the anatomic system employed are considered.

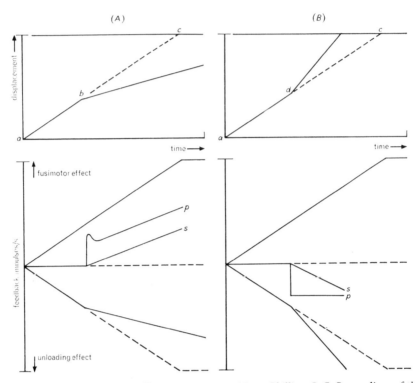

FIG. 13-2. a-γ Coactivation. Explanation in text (*From Phillips, C. G. Proceedings of the Royal Society, B, 1969, 173, pp. 141–174*).

sated response mediated through fusimotor activation or deactivation would have been the result. For such a case to apply, it would have to be assumed that the spindles involved would not have diffuse afferent distributions to motor neurons of other muscles, otherwise the fine coordination seen in finger responses would not be possible. Since this is not always the case (Clough et al., 1968; Phillips, 1969), Phillips employs the alpha-gamma co-activation theory to explain the precise hand movements seen in primates.

Recently Vallbo (1970) and Hagbarth and Vallbo (1968) have studied discharge characteristics of muscular afferents during muscle contraction. Co-activation of *AMNs* and fusimotor neurons was evidenced in recordings from fine electrodes located in human peripheral nerves during voluntary contractions, thus offering further support for simultaneous control of fusimotor and alpha motor neurons during controlled movement (see also Gottlieb et al., 1965).

At present, muscle afferents are not known to influence fusimotor neurons reflexively by length changes although there is some debate on this issue (cf: Granit, 1970). In summary, alpha discharge can be controlled indirectly or co-actively with fusimotor discharge at various levels of the CNS. Much of the evidence favors co-activation versus servocontrolled movement although there is no reason to consider these systems to be mutually exclusive. Fusimotor driving of alphas may also play a significant role in the *conditioning* of motor responses, as shown by Buchwald and her associates (1961, 1964a,b).

Thus far, emphasis has been placed on muscle afferent input as a component of a feedback control system for regulating motor output by means of *AMN* cells. It should be recognized, however, that for the most part any activated population of so-called motor units (*AMN* plus the muscle fibers innervated) cannot be considered a functionally homogeneous mixture even when the motor units comprise the same muscle (cf: Rosenflack and Buchtal, 1970). The individual motor units may differ in size, e.g., number of muscle fibers innervated by a single neuron (Brisky et al., 1970; Henneman et al., 1965; Tokizane and Shimazu, 1964); contractile characteristics, e.g., speed and tension generated (Burke, 1968; Henneman and Olson, 1965; Kugelberg and Edström, 1968); and chemical makeup (Campa and Engel, 1971; Granit, 1970; Kugelberg and Edström, 1968). Functional characteristics of each AMN appear to be closely matched with the functional characteristics of the muscle fibers innervated (Henneman and Olson, 1965; Henneman et al., 1965a). Henneman and his associates (1965b) suggest that the usage of a motor unit is largely an inverse ratio to its size, that is, smaller motor neurons are more readily discharged than larger ones. Furthermore, it seems likely that *AMNs* of small size are used more intensely, innervate muscle fibers which contract more slowly, and are less subject to fatigue that larger *AMNs,* which show more or less the opposite characteristics (Edström and Kugelberg, 1968; Henneman et al, 1965a; Kugelberg and Edström, 1968). This naturally leads to the question of whether some *AMNs* are designed for tonic behavior while others are more structured for quick motor responses, a consideration which, unfortunately, goes beyond the scope of this review. Suffice it to say that motor control involves the activation of three probable types of motor neurons: tonic and phasic *AMNs* and the fusimotor neurons (Granit, 1970; Tokizane and Shimazu, 1964). To this, Kernell (1965), Granit (1966), and Granit and his associates (1966b,c) suggest an additional dimension in *AMN* discharge patterns by reporting that all motor neurons possess a "secondary firing range" in addition to the "primary firing range" normally seen at lower levels of tension. All of these factors point to the important functional consequences of selective *AMN* activation by spinal and supraspinal structures and suggest that much can be learned about CNS input to *AMN* cells by studying the functional profile of the motor unit activated. For further consideration of these factors the interested reader is directed to the following references: (Brisky et al., 1970; Campa and Engel, 1971; Edström and Kugelberg, 1968; Granit, 1970; Granit et al., 1966b; Henneman and Olson, 1965).

FUNCTIONAL ROLE OF THE CEREBELLUM IN MOVEMENT

It has already been pointed out that results of early studies of reflexive behavior led many investigators to believe that the anterior lobe of the cerebellum is richly supplied by muscle afferents and that the cerebellum exerts appreciable control over motor neuronal pathways. Before discussing how this information may be organized, a basic review of cerebellar input-output pathways is necessary since recent theories in cerebellar control of movement are largely formulated on results of functional analyses of neuronal units comprising this structure.

The cerebellum, like the cerebrum, is composed of cells arising from cortical tissue and deeper cells, which we will refer to as deep cerebellar nuclei (*DCN*). The cerebellar cortex receives input from forelimb and hindlimb musculature by means of direct and indirect tracts which carry information from muscle spindles, Golgi tendon organs, certain pressure receptors, touch, and flexor reflex afferents (*FRA*). It should also be recognized that the cerebellum is richly supplied by projections originating from the sensorimotor cortex and vice versa, indicating that among its other numerous functions the cerebellum might be considered an important integrating center for motor events involving both supraspinal and spinal structures.

Anatomically, the cerebellar cortex is supplied by two types of afferent fibers—climbing fiber(s) (*CF*) and mossy fiber(s) (*MF*). Interestingly, the only known pathway out of the cerebellar cortex involves Purkinje cells. The *CF* predominantly synapse on a one-to-one basis with the Purkinje cell, whereupon it exerts strong excitatory activity (however, cf: Murphy and Sabah, 1970). The *MF* input, on the other hand, involves enormous divergence and, through interneuronal cortical connections, may inhibit or excite the Purkinje neuron (Oscarsson, 1967).

The *CF* system is known to originate only from a brain stem structure called the olivary nucleus. Muscle afferents projecting to the cerebellar cortex by means of this indirect pathway carry information from *FRA* and "the convergence of excitatory action is often limited to the nerves of one limb" (Oscarsson, 1967, p. 107). Oscarsson (1967, p. 108) suggests that this indirect pathway "might carry information concerning interneuronal activity involved in segmental motor control" rather than relating directly to peripheral events. This information may serve as feedback concerning the *effectiveness* on interneuronal activity of other descending paths which are in turn influenced by peripheral events (Oscarsson, 1967, 1969).

Muscle afferents from spindles, tendon organs, certain pressure receptors, and touch are carried by means of several direct pathways terminating as *MF* in the cerebellar cortex. Collectively, these tracts carry space- and modality-specific information to the ipsilateral cerebellar cortex which might be utilized in the control of fine movements in individual limbs and in the forwarding of information pertaining to position or stages of movement involving the whole limb (Oscarsson, 1967).

In addition, there is an indirect pathway also involving *MF* input originating from a diffuse brain stem structure known as the reticular nuclei. In this case, the information conveyed is not modality-specific and the cortical receptive fields are large. Oscarsson suggests (1967, p. 108) that this pathway is activated by *FRA* and that it may "carry information from segmental interneurons that integrate descending motor activity and segmental reflex activity."

The direct pathways and the indirect olivary pathway are somatotopically arranged (point to point projection) with the former distributed in transverse zones and the latter distributed in longitudinal zones providing a cross-correlation arrangement. This close relationship between two types of information concerning limb usage may form a functional basis by which the cerebellum integrates information (Oscarsson, 1967; Oscarsson and Uddenberg, 1966). In addition, Oscarsson (1967) notes the convergence characteristics of the pyramidal tract and the ascending indirect cerebellar cortical pathways form spinal structures within the olivary nucleus and suggests that the pyramidal tract and the indirect olivary pathways exhibit various possibilities for interacting at the brain stem level. This close relation between cerebral output and cerebellar input forms the basis for many recently proposed theories to be discussed shortly.

Omitting for a moment the possible mechanisms involved in cerebellar cortical integration, a brief consideration of cortical efferent pathways is in order. Ito (1967) identifies the cerebellar efferent system as having two stages: (1) a Purkinje fiber output to *DCN* (an exception to this is a direct pathway to a nucleus of the vestibular system referred to as Deiters' nucleus), and (2) *DCN* projections to brain stem neurons and the lateral thalamus. On the basis of numerous intracellular recordings, Ito (1967, 1970) and Ito and his associates (1969, 1970) conclude that Purkinje cells are inhibitory and that *DCN* projections are excitatory. The origins of excitatory input to *DCN* appear to be collateral branches from *MF* and *CF* neurons (Ito et al., 1969; Ito et al., 1970).

With reference to Purkinje cell output to *DCN* neurons, Eccles (1969, p. 248) proposes that:

hence there is a background excitation upon which the Purkinje cell inputs exert a sculpturing effect, so producing spatio-temporal forms in the patterns of discharge of these target neurones. Furthermore, it has been shown that this inhibitory depression of neuronal discharge can be handed on from these neurones to neurones next in sequence as a silence or a diminished discharge, which is called disfacilitation, and which can be transmitted indefinitely through the nervous system. Another aspect of this neuronal wiring diagram concerns the inhibitory action of basket cells [an inhibitory intracortical neuron synapsing with Purkinje cells], which can silence the background discharges of Purkinje cells and so can diminish the inhibition of the target neurones, a disinhibition, which is equivalent to an excitatory action, and this in turn can be transmitted along the neuronal pathways from the cerebellum.

As discussed earlier (see the section entitled Historical Considerations) the drastic diminution of decerebrate rigidity by stimulation of the anterior lobe of the cerebellum can now be explained by the widespread inhibitory effects Purkinje fibers have on target cells.

On the basis of these relatively recent neuroanatomic and neurophysiologic findings concerning cerebellar neuronal machinery, a number of theories has been proposed for cerebellar control of movement. A few of these theories will be briefly considered.

Claiming that a more global concept of cerebellar action is needed, Eccles (1967, 1969) has proposed a "dynamic loop hypothesis" for control of movement by the cerebellum. Eccles postulates that stimulation of afferent nerves projecting to the cerebellar cortex evokes diverse *CF* responses of Purkinje cells at various sites of the cortex to form ill-defined to mosaic-like patches of activated cortical tissue. The exact nature of this arrangement differs somewhat from the organization proposed by Oscarsson (1967). *MF*-evoked responses are thought to cause similar mosaic patterns. These evoked responses are described as "subsets of information" where cerebellar integration occurs without significant transfer of information from one small excited cortical zone to another since Purkinje interconnections are weak. It is postulated that control of motor output through these subsets of integration "occur in the total movement process that is evolving under control from the impulses discharged by motoneurones to the muscles" (Eccles, 1967a, p. 338). Off-target movements (error) change cortical receptor activation in the appropriate subsets and in turn cause corrective information to be discharged down descending pathways, thereby changing the evolving movement. Changes in the evolving movement are in turn fed back to the cerebellum. Estimated feedback loop times (in cat) are estimated to be 20 and 30 msec. for forelimb and hindlimb, respectively. Included in this theory are the indirect reciprocal connections between pyramidal tract fibers (from cerebral motor cortex) and Purkinje fibers. Eccles postulates that similar subsets of integration may occur between these systems and that through these connections the cerebrum receives continuous comment from cerebellar output and vice versa.

In a recent publication, Ito (1970) reviews cerebellar control in terms of inhibition, disinhibition (excitation by inhibiting an inhibitor), inhibitory sculpturing, vestibulocerebellar interactions, feedforward control as contrasted to negative feedback (the former allows more flexibility since there is no need for straight forward feedback as seen in the monosynaptic reflex), cerebello-cerebral interaction, and integration of information in the cerebellar cortex. In view of control theory, Ito hypothesizes that cerebello-cerebral interaction may be understood as a "model reference adaptive control system." It is proposed that the initial order for voluntary unskilled movements arises in association cerebral cortex (so-called "quiet" zones that are not primary projection areas for either sensory input or motor output) and is conveyed to spinal motor neurons by means of pyramidal tract fibers. In the early stages the cerebral cortex must be constantly aware of what is being performed by long feedback loops. As voluntary skilled movements are developed with experience, the controlling pathways become more dependent upon cerebellar interventions and control. To elaborate, Ito (1970, pp. 170–171) suggests:

> As the learning process progresses, it is suggested that the large loop through the external world may be effectively replaced by an internal one passing through the cerebellum which would serve as a model of the combination of the spinal motor system, the external world and the sensory pathways. In this view, the original negative feedback system is converted by learning into a feedforward system which needs no straightforward negative feedback loop from the output to input. Adequate performance of this feedforward system is secured only when the model in the neocerebellum is a faithful miniature of the combination of spinal motor system, the external world and the sensory pathways. Various input pathways into the cerebellum in addition to those from the motor area may serve for adjusting characteristics of the internal model from time to time, just as in an adaptive control system.

Marr (1969) has proposed that the cerebellar cortex learns to perform motor skills and maintain posture and balance through learning responses of the Purkinje cell. In this detailed theory a cerebral output related to a movement response also activates Purkinje cells by means of the olivary nucleus. The Purkinje cell learns "the contexts within which their corresponding elemental movements are required, so that the next time such a context occurs the mossy fibre activity stimulates the Purkinje cell which evokes the relevant movement" (Marr, 1969, p. 463). The form of output from the Purkinje cells is in terms of "inhibition sampling." Should the olivary input be driven by receptors (e.g., from spinal structures) rather than the cerebrum, then the cerebellar central may be more related to balance or posture. For this latter scheme a learned conditioned reflex involving environment ——→ receptor ———→ olivary cell ———→ Purkinje cell ———→ effector ———→ environment is viewed as a stabilized negative feedback loop when it is activated by a "learned" mossy fiber. For a detailed analysis of Marr's theory, the interested reader should consult his article as referenced.

In the models proposed by Eccles (1969), Ito (1970), and Marr (1969) as well as others (Evarts and Thach, 1969; Herrick, 1924; Holmes, 1939), there is general agreement that efferent output from the cerebellar cortex plays a strong role in regulating movement although the manner and degree of control emphasized by these investigators differs considerably. However, it should be recognized that the proposed motor functions of the cerebellar circuitry have been based on experimental techniques which render the animal incapable of moving. It is only recently that the responses of cerebellar neurons have been systematically studied and related to freely moving primates.

In a series of studies by Thach (1968, 1970a,b), discharges from Purkinje and *DCN* cells have been recorded and correlated with changes in electromyography (*EMG*) and force output of extrafusal muscles during a lever positioning task. Basically, the task used in all studies required the monkey to perform alternating arm movements while moving a lever horizontally between two stops (cf: Evarts and Thach, 1969). Units recorded were related to wrist flexion and extension or accompanying shoulder movements. Thach modified the training procedure during successive experiments to permit him to look at (1) rapidly alternating movements, (2) reaction time and movement time responses, and (3) holding or "maintained" postural responses.

It was found that Purkinje cells have distinctive discharge patterns: "simple" spikes, presumably caused by *MF* input, and "complex" spikes, often called the *CF* response. Many simple-spike discharges, higher or below resting activity levels, were shown to be temporally related to each successive movement during rapid alternating movements, while complex spikes did not show this consistent temporal relation. *DCN* cells generated only one type of spike and some demonstrated consistent temporal relationships to the movement. In either case, no unit discharges were consistently related to the contralateral limb, and those units that were related to ipsilateral wrist movement or shoulder movement were usually related to each other (Thach, 1968). *DCN* and Purkinje cells were characterized as having high maintained frequencies (e.g., 37 impulses per sec.) even while the animal was motionless. During movement the discharge frequency increased dramatically, with a range between 400 to 500 impulses per sec.

In the situation when the animal was required to perform quick reaction responses while holding two different postures, Thach (1970b, pp. 545–546) summarizes his findings as follows:

> These Purkinje cells and the interposed nuclear cells [*DCN*] . . . to which they project had the following properties in common: 1) changes in frequency at similar times in relation to the onset of movement; 2) for many of them, different patterns of discharge for two different movements; 3) for some of them, different maintained frequencies for two different postures; and 4) the earliest detected change in relation to movement being an increase more commonly than a decrease.

Interestingly, the complex spike was seen to change in relation to quick reaction movements (signal-initiated) but not in the self-paced rapidly alternating movements discussed previously. It is on the basis of these experiments and other observations involving lesion and ablation techniques that Evarts and Thach (1969) have proposed that impulses from the cerebellum may precede and take part in initiating movement by acting on the motor cortex by means of the thalamus (a large subcortical integrating nucleus in the cerebrum). In light of the theoretic considerations of Eccles, Ito, and Marr the preceding evidence offers support for these concepts since in all of these theories, a time-dependent relationship between Purkinje and *DCN* cells and the on-going movement response would be expected. Unfortunately, no information was gained concerning changes in unit discharges while the animal was learning since in all of Thach's experiments unit recordings were made after the animal became highly skilled at the task. It is interesting to note that Evarts (1970) has recently recorded from units in the ventral lateralis (*VL*) of the thalamus (the projection center of cerebellar cortical fibers on the way to the cerebral cortex) while monkeys performed quick reaction responses similar to those in Thach's experiments. Evarts found that increases and decreases of activity in *VL* neurons preceded movement by as much as 100 msec., a lead time which is approximately the same as that of the earliest motor neurons in the motorsensory cortex. In man, similar responses of *VL* neurons during the initiation of movement have been reported in clinical investigations by Jasper (1966) and Hassler (1966). Using microelectrode techniques on patients suffering from Parkinson's disease, these investigators reported units that responded in phase with overt tremor movements and, by stimulating techniques, found some units that would cause the patient to speed up or slow down alternating movements or vocalized phrases. Interestingly, the patients indicated a sense of "initiating" or "willing" the response.

It may seem paradoxical to think initiation of movement might be generated from cerebellar cortical neurons since the only known output is from Purkinje cells and these are inhibitory. Hence, the concept "inhibitory sculpturing" becomes a key factor in this thinking. This brings to mind a speculative statement made some years ago by Eccles (see Kimble, 1967, p. 13) in discussing quantitative neuronal differences at higher CNS levels, compared to cord levels:

> inhibitory phenomena are much more developed in the brain than at lower levels. Inhibitory synapses are much more powerful and much more prolonged in action. I think that memory is, to a considerable extent, inhibitory. This may seem surprising but quite a lot of finely-tuned response can be regarded as due to a chiselling away of random and diffuse output into a more specific output. This would be an inhibitory phenomenon, and certainly, we have an amazing development of inhibition in the brain.

Throughout this discussion, cerebro-cerebellar interrelationships have been emphasized in the initiation of movement responses. Thus far, the role of cerebral motor cortex in controlling movement has only been discussed in a historic sense. Further consideration of selected contemporary literature on this topic follows.

CEREBRO-CORTICAL CONTROL OF MOVEMENT

As discussed earlier, the concept of a "motor cortex" was initially supported by results of electrical stimulation investigations but evidence from more precise "cortical mapping" studies pointed to a large degree of anatomic overlap between sensory and motor cortical neurons. This led subsequent investigators to view these areas as "motorsensory cortex (Ms)" or "sensorimotor cortex (Sm)" from pre-centrally and post-centrally designated tissue, respectively. Although some controversy developed as to the manner in which motor units were cortically represented, most investigators believed that the motorsensory cortex was strongly involved in voluntary movement.

Prior to 1950, stimulation techniques came progressively under disfavor since electrically evoked motor responses were hardly representative of normal movement. It was difficult to localize cortically evoked responses because slight changes in the intensity and frequency of electrical stimulus altered the degree of stimulus spread to adjacent cortical tissue. In reviewing the merits and pitfalls of stimulation techniques, the following statement by Phillips (1966, pp. 397–398) reflects well the growing concern of investigators for more refined techniques:

> In recent years the use of electronic stimulators has provided experiments with what must sometimes seem an embarrassing wealth of parameters (variable pulse duration, amplitude and wave form; variable repetition frequency and train duration). . . . For studies of the evolution of localization in the mammalian series (Woolsey, 1958), it is rational to stick, as Woolsey and colleagues (1952) have done, to a type of stimulation that gives a large range of motor responses; and it is clear that 60 c/s alternating current is ideally suited for this work. But research is also needed to determine the extent to which this particular method maps corticofugal neurons, and the extent to which it maps other cells and axons which play upon their dendrite.

Another source of difficulty was that the evoked response differed according to the initial limb position of the animal. This problem is more readily understood in light of present evidence on "input-output coupling" between motor and sensory information, a topic to be discussed shortly (Asanuma et al., 1968; Brooks et al., 1970; Brooks and Stoney, 1971; Evarts et al., 1971).

A finer control of these parameters was developed by stimulation through (and also recording from) microelectrodes which were precisely positioned with stereotaxic apparatuses (devices for locating electrode tips on the basis of coordinates). Utilizing these techniques, Bernhard and Bohm (1954), Preston and Whitlock (1960, 1961), Phillips (1967, 1969), and others have demonstrated in primates the existence of monosynaptic corticospinal connections between contralateral pyramidal tract neurons (PTNs) of the motorsensory cortex and AMNs located in the spinal cord. Referred to as the corticomotoneuronal (CM) system, these projections were mapped as cortical colonies and believed to be functionally significant fragments of motor unit organization. A functional unit comprising all *PTNs*, which connected monosynaptically with a single *AMN,* was defined as a colony.

By intracellular recording from *AMNs* supplying limb muscles, Phillips and Porter (see Phillips, 1966), Landgren and his associates (1962), and Phillips (1969) have shown that in primates motor neurons of distal muscle groups command greater *CM* excitation but have narrower colonies than proximal muscle groups. Colonies were also found to be intermingled when *CM* activation of *AMNs* from different muscle groups was measured; this was reminiscent of Jackson's early views on "cortical representation of movement." That these cortical effects on *AMNs* are mediated through the pyramidal tract has been verified by Stewart and Preston (1968) and Stewart, Preston, and Whitlock (1968) since cutting this tract in the "pyramidal animal" (basic preparations in which the brain stem is destroyed except for the pyramidal pathway) at the level of the brain stem abolished all initial cortically mediated facilitation or inhibition of *AMNs*.

The existence of a powerful *CM* system in primates must be considered in light of servocontrol of *AMNs* by means of the gamma loop or co-activation theory. If servodriving is to be cortically mediated, independent cortical-fusimotor (*CF*) projections must exist in order to drive spindle afferent either before or during contraction. Koeze and his associates (1968) provide some evidence that a relatively direct as well as indirect *CF* projection system does exist in the baboon's hand. Since no evidence was presented for servodriving by cortical stimulation, it was suggested that independent *CM* and *CF* projections could provide alpha-gamma "co-excitation in the servo-governing of natural movements."

Preston and his colleagues (1967) have studied the facilitative and inhibitory effects of *CM* activation on spindle-mediated monosynaptic reflexes. The relative effectiveness of *CM* activation on *AMNs* has been studied in:

1) cat and primate (rhesus monkey and baboon),
2) distal and proximal hindlimb and forelimb muscles, and
3) extensor and flexor *AMNs*.

It should be noted that in the cat relatively direct cortical projections to *AMNs* always involve one or more spinal interneurons, unlike the mono-synaptic *CM* system (although polysynaptic projections also exist) seen in the primate (cf: Nyberg-Hansen, 1969; Stewart and Preston, 1967).

In the cat, it was generally found that forelimb and hindlimb flexor motor neurons tended to be facilitated and extensor motor neurons inhibited by pre-central cortically evoked volleys upon segmental motor neurons. Inhibition appeared in greater magnitude in slow-contracting extrafusal muscles than in fast-contracting muscle groups. In the baboon, the cortically evoked patterns of *AMN* inhibition and facilitation were more complex as indicated by an early short-lasting facilitation (monosynaptic *CM* activation) followed usually by an inhibitory effect. The early facilitation tended to be greater in fast-muscle extensor and flexor motor neurons than in slow-muscle *AMNs* (Preston and Whitlock, 1961). The period of inhibition was seen to be brief in flexor and "fast" extensor *AMNs* and was often followed by a late facilitative phase. In distal musculature, the initial effect was predominantly facilitation.

In summarizing their findings, Preston and his colleagues (1967, pp. 70–71):

> suggested that the initial inhibitory effect seen in both flexor and extensor motoneuron populations of the primate may serve as a rate-limiting mechanism during cortical driving of motoneurons. The more prolonged period of cortical inhibition seen in baboon and cat motoneurons innervating postural antigravity muscles may function to diminish the control of the common spinal pathway by tonic postural mechanisms during volitional movement behavior. The dominance of cortical facilitation in motoneuron populations innervating distal forelimb musculature of both cat and baboon suggests a correlation between cortical facilitatory control and the variety of skilled movement patterns associated with these muscle groups. In the primate, the direct monosynaptic facilitation is somewhat more pronounced in distal than in proximal muscles of the limbs, and in agreement with Phillips and Porter would seem to relate to the evolving patterns of dexterity and skill seen in the hand and forearm of the primate.

Thus, *CM* and *CF* systems are seen to exist in *MsI*, and *MsI* cortical-evoked volleys tend to produce response patterns in *AMNs* of fast and slow, extensor and flexor, distal and proximal muscle groups which, to some degree, appear functionally correlated with postural and manipulative movement patterns.

Unfortunately, stimulation techniques reveal nothing about cortical involvement in *volitional* motor control. Evarts (1967) has introduced experimental techniques whereby single *PTN* discharges can be correlated with behavioral parameters in freely moving primates. In a series of experiments, Evarts (1966, 1968, 1969) compared the activity of single *PTNs* to measures of force, movement displacement, and electromyography during voluntary movement. Monkeys were trained to perform a displacement task involving wrist flexion and extension against loaded or unloaded resistance. Of the *PTNs* found closely associated to performance of the task, the majority showed discharge frequencies which were related primarily to the magnitude and time derivative of force and secondarily to direction of displacement. No fixed relationships were found between adjacent *PTNs* and only a few showed fixed positive correlations with a movement response as might be expected of two pyramidal neurons driving two motor units of the same muscle. Irrespective of the movement involved, the articular joint was found to be the only common denominator uniting the activity of two adjacent neurons. More notably, all *PTNs* impaled by a single microelectrode penetration demonstrated this same relationship about a single joint, thus suggesting that pyramidal neurons representing muscles acting about a single joint are cortically organized in a columnar array. In relation to this latter finding, Marchiafava (1968) has suggested that this response represents a compromise between the old dispute of Jacksonian versus punctate localization theory, in that both movements and muscles can be represented by neural projections which are localized anatomically about a single joint but are yet able to produce independent and specific movements about the same joint.

The aforementioned temporal relationships between *PTN* discharge and indices of movement responses might suggest that *MsI* areas are involved in voluntary control; however, as Bucy (1968) points out, numerous behavioral studies have shown that "strong, well-coordinated, useful movements are possible in man as well in lower animals without the pyramidal tract" (p. 225).

In a recent study, Beck and Chambers (1970) reported that although unilateral pyramidotomized monkeys exhibited strength deficits (more so in flexors than extensors), these animals had no difficulty in stopping movements quickly and accurately. These findings compare well with Evarts and it would appear that change of force in responding is an important pyramidal tract function. It is generally accepted, however, that there is some loss of fine coordination in bilaterally pyramidotomized animals (Brodal, 1969; Crosby et al., 1969; Jane et al, 1968); however, it is also apparent that motor control of skeletal muscle depends on numerous other descending pathways.

Penfield (1954) contends that there must be a central neural coordinating system capable of producing complicated integration before the appropriate motor impulses are delivered to *MsI* areas. He proposes a "centrencephalic theory" in which considerable emphasis is placed on inputs to descending motor pathways from the diencephalon (neural structures found in the core of the cerebrum), midbrain, and pons as sources of volitional control. In stimulating *MsI* areas, Penfield (see Phillips, 1966) has found no evidence of conscious sensations of volitional intent in his patients. For example, one patient was reported as saying "you made me do that." A few patients have reported a subjective intent when stimulated in *Sm II*. In view of recent concepts concerning, for example, thalamic and cerebellar structures (see the preceding section on Cerebellar Motor Control), Penfield's general theory of a centrencephalic system is beginning to take on more defined neuroanatomic boundaries.

Bearing on Penfield's concept is the work of Vanderwolf (1962, 1969a,b), who in a recent review (Vanderwolf, 1971) summarized and synthesized into a theoretic construct several years of work (mostly on the rat) relating the medial thalamus and hippocampal function (located in the medial temporal lobe of the cerebrum) to behavioral functions. Reaffirming Jackson's original concept of "hierarchial levels of cerebral motor control," Vanderwolf proposes that autonomic behaviors such as emotional expression or shivering are under separate cerebral control from structures mediating more volitional types of responses such as manipulation of an object. He suggests that particular drive states are associated with clusters of automatic responses and that voluntary movements can be temporarily coupled to any one of these clusters. Presumably, the coupling between a drive state and a voluntary movement is found in the forebrain and the triggering mechanism for the overt behavior is believed to be located in the diencephalon.

Since the arguments put forth by Vanderwolf to support this theory are detailed and extensive, the reader is referred to his publications. Vanderwolf's hypothesis on hippocampal function appears as a somewhat radical departure from previously expressed viewpoints. For example, Corkin (1968) studied selected motor skills (rotary pursuit, bimanual tracking, and tapping) in a 40-year-old man suffering *severe amnesia* from a bilateral medial temporal-lobe excision involving the hippocampal structure. This patient's motor performance improved from session to session and normal learning curves were displayed for each task. Interestingly, this improvement occurred despite the patient's not remembering his performance the day before. In view of Vanderwolf's hypothesis, it might be noted that the patient's performance on the tracking tasks was inferior to those of normal persons, although this was attributed to his relatively long reaction times. Starr (1970) has reported a similar case where impairment of recent memory was evident on verbal tasks but not on motor tasks such as maze learning and the playing of new compositions for the piano. In either case, the patients did not show serious motor deficiencies. This finding alone neither refutes Vanderwolf's hypothesis nor does it offer it much support. More evidence is needed from observations on man and primates before any conclusions can be drawn.

There are a number of observations that make the general concept of a centrencephalic integrating system attractive in light of voluntary controlled movement. The previously discussed observations of Thach (1970a,b), Evarts (1967), Jasper (1966), and Hassler (1966) are but a few. In Penfield's scheme, the importance of *MsI* in voluntary motor control has not been denied but rather de-emphasized with respect to earlier held concepts. This would be in keeping with the experimental evidence garnered from ablation, lesion, and microelectrode studies. It is not unexpected to find that the CNS is provided with a number of back-up systems for this kind of motor outflow. However, it might be noted that in intact unanesthetized monkeys, Humphrey and his colleagues (1970) found that by using experimental techniques and a behavioral task similar to that used by Evarts, by recording discharge activity of *PTN*s selected on the basis of their association with one or more movement components, and by using relatively simple quantitative procedures, they could *predict* the time course of various response measurements on the basis of the activity recorded from this small sets of cells. Correlation coefficients between predicted and observed responses (using 5 units) for a number of response measurements were as follows: displacement = .58, velocity = .76, force = .84 and df/dt = .43. The strength of the correlation for force measurements agrees well with the earlier observations of Evarts, although the strength of the correlations for the responses measured may vary depending on the cell-sets quantified. Thus, *MsI* areas seem very much involved in on-going movement activity but it remains to be determined what triggers the appropriate *PTN*s to be activated. Answers to this question must partly depend on a closer look at sensory input and motor output coupling.

Sensory input to *MsI* and *SmI* have been shown to be organized in radially arranged arrays of neurons which receive input from specific contralateral peripheral loci (Asanuma et al., 1968; Brooks et al., 1970; Brooks and Stoney, 1971). Input to neurons in *SmI* columns is generally thought to be modality-specific (Sakata and Miyamoto, 1968; Welt et al., 1967), that is, nearly all the neurons respond to messages from only one adequate stimulus delivered in one specific, local receptive field on the contralateral side (Brooks, 1969), and these columns are known to be sharply demarcated from one another (Thompson et al., 1970). Input to *MsI* columns is polymodal, that is, there is multiple representation of sensory input and considerable overlap among the columns. The nature of the sensory input to these areas has been briefly summarized by Brooks (1969, p. 234):

> The adequate natural stimuli are hairbending, touch, tap, and pressure. About half of all cells in MsI, and three quarters in SI, of the cat are driven by superficial stimuli. Passive movement of joints can excite about one third of the cells in MsI, and these cells are not excited by skin contact, except about one tenth of the total population that can respond to both "somesthetic" and "kinesthetic" messages (Asanuma, et al., 1968; Welt, et al., 1967). These ratios differ somewhat for different investigators (Towe, 1965; Towe, et al., 1968). In the monkey, joint input seems to outweigh that from skin (Albe-Fessard and Liebeskind, 1966). All inputs may, of course, be excitatory or inhibitory. Information about static muscle length appears to reach all brain areas that receive joint and skin inputs (Rosen, 1968, personal communication), while information about changes of muscle length, i.e., velocity of contraction, is channelled to only a narrow strip of MsI at the border of SI (Oscarsson, 1966). Study of the cortical integration of messages from joints and muscles has hardly begun. It will be of the greatest importance, because in voluntary movements many pyramidal tract (PT) cells govern muscles. According to the force of movement exerted or some function of it (Evarts, 1967) . . . or, as Phillips has put it, PT cells discharge according to the resistance that the limb encounters in its movements.

In order to test cortical input-output and relationships or "minimal building blocks" as they have been called (Brooks and Stoney, 1971), some investigators have adopted the technique of relating muscle output to input. For example, Welt and her associates (1967, p. 276) found in the cat that "skin stimulation of the dorsal surface of the paw excites corticofugal neurons that dorsiflex the paw and digits, and, conversely, skin stimulation of the ventral surface excites cells that cause ventroflexion." It is suggested that this may represent one form of a neural substrate for cortical-motor reflex activity to tactile stimulation as seen, for instance, in the "tactile placing reaction." It is assumed that voluntary activity would override this type of cortical reflex.

Combining the technique of intracortical miscrostimulation and unit recording by utilizing the same cortical microelectrode, Asanuma and his colleagues (1968) found afferent inputs to individual efferent zones to be polymodal and stimulated cortico-motor responses to cutaneous input were such as to cause the limb to move toward the stimulus. Sakata and Miyamoto (1968), using similar techniques in unanesthetized cats, found that motor cortical activity could be elicited by physiologic stimulation of the skin and deep tissues, and upon stimulation of the cortical area excited, an aversive direction of movement (away from the stimulus) with respect to the limb area stimulated was often found for zones containing light pressure sensory units. Although the two studies conflict on the nature of the movement with respect to the limb area stimulated, both suggest that "the somatotopically localized sensory projection to the motor cortex provides for a mechanism of finely localized sensory control of cortical motor activity" (Sakata and Miyamoto, 1968, pp. 502–503).

Albe-Fessard and Donaldson (1970) have also used similar techniques to compare "light input-output coupling" between *MsI, SmI,* and posterior parietal cortex (*pp*) in monkeys. In *MsI, SmI,* and in one instance for the *pp* area, many cortical points were found where both cortico-sensory and cortical-evoked movement responses involved the same peripheral area. The extent of topographical interrelationship among these areas is still unknown, but it was suggested that known reciprocal projections between *MsI* and *SmI* might provide a route for the transfer of information concerning the management of the same peripheral area.

Fetz and Baker (1964, p. 223) have recently reported that, in awake monkeys, when cortical cells that had responded to passive movement of a joint in one direction were stimulated, "the muscles of that joint which had the lowest response threshold were those which opposed that movement." Thus, the responses were similar to those seen by Sakata and Miyamoto (1968) when they used pressure stimuli.

Brooks (1969) has suggested that the possible function of these "minimal building blocks," outside of forming the basis for corticofugal reflexes, may be to facilitate or preset movement responses resulting from cortical activation. Not mentioned, however, is the confounding role played by collaterals from *PTN* output which are known to influence somatosensory input at supraspinal levels, thereby altering the size of the excitatory receptive fields of neurons in the somatosensory cortex (Adkins et al., 1966; Evarts et al., 1971). Adkins and associates (1966) have concluded that the *PTN* tract is one route by which the cerebral cortex can modify its own afferent input through internal feedback.

Thus, considerable information processing is seen at all levels of the CNS. Considering the feedback pathways known to exist, the difficulty in formulating precise motor control theories that encompass the data presently available is understandable. Historically, investigators have placed a great deal of reliance on external feedback as a necessary prerequisite for motor responses. Deafferentation (cutting the dorsal roots of the spinal column, thereby depriving the animal of input from somatosensory receptors) studies by Taub and Berman (1968) have indicated that an animal can still use and/or learn to use a deafferented limb even in the absence of vision. Findings such as these may attest to the importance of internal feedback loops or central programming of motor outflow with minimal reliance on feedback systems.

It must be remembered that in evaluating the neurologic research literature, a multitude of variables are brought to bear. These can largely be reduced to two main categories: (1) the experimental techniques vary from one investigator to another as do data analyses, and (2) the animal models utilized invariably differ, ranging from invertebrates to primates. Concerning the latter point with respect to the number of topics discussed in this review, this discussion might best be closed by quoting Towe (Evarts et al., 1971, pp. 44–45):

> Zoologists such as Paul Weiss and James Gray have long recognized that invertebrate nervous mechanisms are organized into hierarchial systems; and even the earliest ethologists, Charles Otis Whitman (1899) and Oskar Heinroth (1910), recognized the existence of innate, genetically determined behaviors. Some behaviors are so specific as to seem reliable taxonomic characters. Meanwhile, we mammalian physiologists focus on the domestic cat and the macaque monkey, with the implicit assumption (in the latter case) that we are studying "little men." We think in terms of either the extreme flexibility of human behavior or the dual-bent character of spinal reflexes, and sometimes attempt to handle the former in terms of the latter. This will forever remain an unsatisfactory approach. When we think of motor behavior, we must include the arena behavior of the Uganda kob, which Helmut Buechner has reported from the Semliki Flats (Buechner, 1963). We must include the sky pointing display of the blue-footed booby and other sulids that Byron Nelson reports from the Galapagos (Nelson, 1968). We must include the strutting dance and flight of the male woodcock, which Aldo Leopold described as commencing on warm spring evenings as soon as the luminance level drops to 0.05 footcandles (Leopold, 1949). We might even try the simple act of walking; much could be learned about motor organization from a careful study of locomotor behavior.

References

Adkins, R. J., Morse, R. W., & Towe, A. L. Control of somatosensory input by cerebral cortex. *Science*, 1966, 153, 1020–1022.

Albe-Fessard, D., & Donaldson, I. M. L. Relation of movements induced by intracortical stimulation to receptive fields of points in the perirolandic and parietal cortex of the monkey. *Journal of Physiology*, 1970, 210, 57–58.

Andersen, P., & Sears, T. A. Medullary activation of intercostal fusimotor and alpha motoneurons. *Journal of Physiology*, 1970, 209, 739–755.

Asanuma, S., Stoney, S. D., Jr., & Abzug, C. Relationship between afferent input and motor outflow in cat motorsensory cortex. *Journal of Neurophysiology*, 1968, 31, 670–681.

Baker, L. F. *The nervous system.* New York: D. Appleton and Company, 1899.

Beck, C. H., & Chambers, W. W. Speed, accuracy, and strength of forelimb movement after unilateral pyramidotomy in rhesus monkeys. *Journal of Comparative and Physiological Psychology,* 1970, Monograph, 70, 1–22.

Beevor, C. E., & Horsley, V. A minute analysis (experimental) of the various movements produced by stimulating in the monkey different regions of cortical centre for the upper limb as defined by Professor Ferrier. *Philosophical Transactions,* 1887, 178, 153.

Beevor, C. E., & Horsley, V. A record of the results obtained by electrical excitation of the so-called motor cortex and internal capsule in the orangutang. *Philosophical Transactions,* 1890, 181, 129.

Bernhard, C. G., & Bohm, E. Cortical representation and functional significance of the corticospinal systems. *Archives of Neurology and Psychiatry,* 1954, 72, 473–502.

Bessou, P., Laporte, Y., & Pagis, B. Frequencygrams of spindle primary endings elicited by stimulation of static and dynamic fusimotor fibres. *Journal of Physiology,* 1968, 196, 47–63.

Brazier, M. A. B. The historical developments of neurophysiology. In J. Field, H. W. Magoun, & V. E. Hall (eds.), *Handbook of physiology, Section 1: neurophysiology.* Vol. 1, Washington, D. C.: American Physiological Society, 1959, pp. 1–74.

Briskey, E. J., Cassens, R. G., & Marsh, B. B. *The physiology and biochemistry of muscle as a food.* Vol. 2. Madison: University of Wisconsin Press, 1970.

Brodal, A. *Neurological anatomy in relation to clinical medicine.* New York: Oxford University Press, 1969.

Brooks, V. B. Information processing in the motorsensory cortex. In K. N. Leibovic (ed.), *Information processing in the nervous system: proceedings.* New York: Springer-Verlag, 1969, pp. 231–243.

Brooks, V. B., & Stoney, S. D. Motor mechanisms: The role of the pyramidal system in motor control. *Annual Review of Physiology,* 1971, 33, 337–392.

Brooks, V. B., Jasper, H. H., Patton, H. D., Purpura, D. P., & Brookhart, J. M. Symposium on cerebral and cerebellar motor control. *Brain Research,* 1970, 17, 539–552.

Brown, G. T., & Sherrington, C. S. On the instability of a cortical point. *Proceedings of the Royal Society, B.,* 1912, 85, 250–277.

Buchwald, J. S., Beatty, D., & Eldred, E. Conditioned responses of gamma and alpha motoneurons in the cat trained to conditioned avoidance. *Experimental Neurology,* 1961, 4, 91–105.

Buchwald, J. S., Standish, M., & Eldred, E. Effect of deafferentation upon acquisition of a conditioned flexion response in the cat. *Experimental Neurology,* 1964, 9, 372–385. (a)

Buchwald, J. S., Standish, M., Eldred, E., & Halas, E. S. Contribution of muscle spindle circuits to learning as suggested by training under Flaxedil. *Electroencephalography and Clinical Neurophysiology,* 1964, 16, 582–594. (b)

Bucy, P. C. Neural mechanisms controlling skeletal muscular activity and its unsolved problems. *Neuroscience Research,* 1968, 1, 251–261.

Buechner, H. K. Territoriality as a behavioral adaption to environment in the Uganda Kob. *Proceedings of XVI International Congress of Zoology,* 1963, 3, 59–62.

Burke, R. E. Firing patterns of gastrocnemius motor units in the decerebrate cat. *Journal of Physiology,* 1968, 196, 631–654.

Campa, J. F., & Engel, W. K. Histochemical and functional correlations in anterior horn neurons of the cat spinal cord. *Science,* 1971, 171, 198–199.

Clough, J. F. M., Kernell, D., & Phillips, C. G. The distribution of monosynaptic excitation from the pyramidal tract and from primary spindle afferents to motoneurones of the baboon's hand and forearm. *Journal of Physiology,* 1968, 198, 145–166.

Cooper, S. The responses of the primary and secondary endings of muscle spindles with intact motor innervation during applied stretch. *Quarterly Journal of Experimental Physiology,* 1961, 46, 389–398.

Corda, M., Eklund, G., & Euler, C. V. External intercostal and phrenic and motor responses to changes in respiratory load. *Acta Physiologica Scandinavica,* 1965, 63, 391–400.

Corkin, S. Acquisition of motor skill after bilateral medial temporal-lobe excision. *Neuropsychologia,* 1968, 6, 255–265.

Crosby, E. C., Taren, A. J., & Davis, R. The anterior lobe and the lingula of the cerebellum in monkeys and man. *Topical Problems in Psychiatry and Neurology,* 1969, 10, 22–39.

DeLong, M., & Evarts, E. V. Somototopic organization of pallidal neurons related to arm movement in the monkey. *Federation Proceedings,* 1970, 29, 1324.

Denny-Brown, D. *The basal ganglia and their relation to disorders of movement.* London: Oxford University Press, 1949.

Dow, R. S. Progress in cerebellar physiology. *Societa Italiana di Biologia Sperimentale,* 38th Assemblea Generale, Alghero Capocaccia, 1969.

Eccles, J. C. Circuits in the cerebellar control of movement. *Proceedings of the National Academy of Science,* 1967, 58, 336–343. (a)

Eccles, J. C. The way in which the cerebellum processes sensory information from muscle. In M. D. Yahr, & D. P. Purpura (eds.), *Neurophysiological basis of normal and abnormal motor activities.* New York: Raven Press, 1967, pp. 379–414. (b)

Eccles, J. C. The dynamic loop hypothesis of movement control. In K. N. Leibovic (ed.), *Information processing in the nervous system: proceedings.* New York: Springer-Verlag, 1969, pp. 245–269.

Eccles, J. C., Ito, M., & Szentagothai, J. *The cerebellum as a neuronal machine.* New York: Springer-Verlag, 1967.

Edström, L., & Kugelberg, E. Histochemical composition, distribution of fibers and fatigability of single motor units, anterior tibial muscle of rat. *Journal of Neurology, Neurosurgery, and Psychiatry,* 1968, 31, 424–433.

Eldred, E., Granit, R., & Merton, P. A. Supraspinal control of the muscle spindles and its significance. *Journal of Physiology,* 1953, 122, 498–523.

Ernest, A. M. The role of biogenic amines in the extrapyramidal system. *Acta Physiologica Pharmacologica,* Netherlands, 1969, 15, 141–154.

Euler, C. V. The control of respiratory movements. In J. B. L. Howell, & E. J. M. Campbell (eds.), *Breathlessness.* Oxford: Blackwell Science Publishing, 1966, pp. 19–32.

Evarts, E. V. Pyramidal tract activity associated with a conditoned hand movement in the monkey. *Journal of Neurophysiology,* 1966, 29, 1011–1027.

Evarts, E. V. Representation of movements and muscles by pyramidal tract neurons of the precentral motor cortex. In M. D. Yahr, & D. P. Purpura, (eds.), *Neurophysiological basis of normal and abnormal motor activities.* New York: Raven Press, 1967, pp. 215–253.

Evarts, E. V. Relation of pyramidal tract activity to force exerted during voluntary movement. *Journal of Neurophysiology,* 1968, 31, 14–27.

Evarts, E. V. Activity of pyramidal tract neurons during postural fixation. *Journal of Neurophysiology,* 1969, 32, 375–385.

Evarts, E. V. Activity of ventralis lateralis neurons prior to movement in the monkey. *Physiologist,* 1970, 13, 191.

Evarts, E. V., & Thach, W. T. Motor mechanisms of the CNS: Cerebrocerebellar interrelations. *Annual Review of Physiology,* 1969, 31, 451–498.

Evarts, E. V., Bizzi, E., Burke, R. E., DeLong, M., & Thach, W. T. Central control of movement. *Neuroscience Research Program Bulletin,* 1971, 9, 1–170.

Ferrier, D. Discussion on cerebral localization. *Transactions of the Congress of American Physicians and Surgeons,* 1888, 1, 337–340.

Fetz, E. E., & Baker, M. A. Response properties of precentral neurons in awake monkeys. *Physiologist,* 1969, 12, 223.

Field, J., Magoun, H. W., & Hall, V. E. (eds.), *Neurophysiology, Section 1: handbook of physiology.* Vols. I, II, III. American Physiological Society, Washington, D. C., 1959–1960.

Fritsch, G., & Hitzig, E. Über die elektrische Erregbarkeit des Grosshirns. *Archiv Anatomie Physiologie,* 1870, 37, 300–332.

Fulton, J. F., & Pi-Suñer, J. A note concerning the probable function of various afferent end organs. *American Journal of Physiology,* 1928, 83, 554–562.

Gasser, H. S., & Erlanger, J. The cathode ray oscillograph as a means of recording nerve action currents and induction shocks. *American Journal of Physiology,* 1922, 59, 473–474.

Gottlieb, G. L., Agarwal, G. C., & Stark, L. Interactions between voluntary and postural mechanisms of the human motor system. *Journal of Neurophysiology,* 1965, 33, 365–381.

Granit, R. (ed.) *Muscular afferents and motor control.* Nobel Symposium I. Stockholm: Almquist and Wiksell, 1966.

Granit, R. *Charles Scott Sherrington–An appraisal.* New York: Doubleday and Company, Inc., 1967.

Granit, R. The functional role of the muscle spindles' primary end organs. *Royal Society of Medicine,* 1968, 61, 69–78.

Granit, R. *The basis of motor control.* New York: Academic Press, 1970.

Granit, R., & Kellerth, J-O. The effects of stretch receptors on motoneurons. In M. D. Yahr & D. P. Purpura (eds.), *Neurophysiological basis of normal and abnormal motor activities.* New York: Raven Press, 1967, pp. 3–28.

Granit, R., Holmgren, B., & Merton, P. A. The two routes for excitation of muscle and their subservience to the cerebellum. *Journal of Physiology,* 1955, 130, 213–224.

Granit, R., Kellerth, J-O., & Szumski, A. J. Intracellular recording from extensor motoneurons activated across the gamma loop. *Journal of Neurophysiology,* 1966, 29, 530–544. (a)

Granit, R., Kernell, D., & Lamarre, Y. Algebraic summation in synaptic activation of motoneurons firing within the "primary range" to injected currents. *Journal of Physiology,* 1966, 187, 379–399. (b)

Granit, R., Kernell, D., & Lamarre, Y. Synaptic stimulation superimposed on motoneurones firing in the "secondary range" to injected currents. *Journal of Physiology,* 1966, 187, 401–415. (c)

Grillner, S. Supraspinal and segmental control of static and dynamic γ–motoneurons in the cat. *Acta Physiologica Scandinavica Supplement,* 1969, 327, 1–34.

Guth, L. "Trophic" influences of nerve on muscle. *Physiological Reviews,* 1968, 48, 645–687.

Hagbarth, K. E., & Vallbo, A. B. Discharge characteristics of human muscle afferents during muscle stretch and contraction. *Experimental Neurology,* 1968, 22, 674–694.

Harvey, R. J., & Matthews, P. B. C. The response of de-efferented muscle spindle endings in the cat's soleus to slow extension of the muscle. *Journal of Physiology,* 1961, 157, 370–392.

Hassler, R. Thalamic regulation of muscle tone and the speed of movements. In D. P. Purpura & M. D. Yahr (eds.), *The thalamus.* New York: Columbia University Press, 1966, pp. 419–436.

Heinroth, O. Beiträge zur Biologie, insbesonders Psychologie und Ethologie der Anatiden, Verh. V. Int. Ornithol. Kongr., 1910.

Henneman, E. Organization of the motor systems–a preview. In V. B. Mountcastle (ed.) *Medical physiology,* Vol. II, St. Louis: C. V. Mosby Company, 1968, pp. 1675–1680.

Henneman, E., & Olson, C. B. Relations between structure and function in the design of skeletal muscles. *Journal of Neurophysiology,* 1965, 28, 581–598.

Henneman, E., Somjen, G., & Carpenter, D. O. Functional significance of cell size in spinal motoneurons. *Journal of Neurophysiology,* 1965, 28, 560–580. (a)

Henneman, E., Somjen, G., & Carpenter, D. O. Excitability and inhibitability of motoneurons of different sizes. *Journal of Neurophysiology,* 1965, 28, 599–620. (b)

Herrick, C. J. Origin and evolution of the cerebellum. *Archives of Neurology and Psychiatry,* 1924, 11, 621–652.

Hoffman, P. Untersuchungen Über die Eigenreflexe (Sehnenreflexe) menschlicher Muskeln. Berlin: Springer, 1922.

Holmes, G. The cerebellum of man. *Brain,* 1939, 62, 1–30.

Houk, J., & Henneman, E. Responses of golgi tendon organs to active contractions of the soleus muscle of the cat. *Journal of Neurophysiology,* 1967, 30, 466–481. (a)

Houk, J., & Henneman, E. Feedback control of skeletal muscle. *Brain Research,* 1967, 5, 433–441. (b)

Humphrey, D. G., Schmidt, E. M., & Thompson, W. D. Predicting measures of motor performance from cortical spike trains. *Science,* 1970, 170, 758–762.

Ito, M. Neuronal circuitry in the cerebellar efferent system. In M. D. Yahr & D. P. Purpura (eds.), *Neurophysiological basis of normal and abnormal motor activities.* New York: Raven Press, 1967, pp. 119–140.

Ito, M. Neurophysiological aspects of the cerebellar motor control system. *International Journal of Neurology,* 1970, 7, 162–176.

Ito, M., Kawai, N., Udo, M., & Mano, N. Axon reflex activation of Dieter's neurons from the cerebellar cortex through collaterals of the cerebellar afferent. *Experimental Brain Research,* 1969, 8, 249–268.

Ito, M., Yoshida, M., Obata, K., Kawai, N., & Udo, M. Inhibitory control of intracerebellar nuclei by the purkinje cell axons. *Experimental Brain Research,* 1970, 10, 64–80.

Jane, J. A., Yashon, D., Becker, D. P., Beatty, R., & Sugar, O. The effect of destruction of the cortico-spinal tract in the human cerebral peduncle upon motor function and involuntary movements. Report of 11 cases. *Journal of Neurosurgery,* 1968, 29, 581–585.

Jasper, H. H., & Bertrand, G. Thalamic units involved in somatic sensation and voluntary and involuntary movements in man. In D. P. Purpura & M. D. Yahr (eds.), *The thalamus.* New York: Columbia University Press, 1966, pp. 365–384.

Jung, R., & Hassler, R. The extrapyramidal motor system. In J. Field, H. W. Magoun, & V. E. Hall (eds.), *Handbook of physiology, Section I: neurophysiology.* Vol. II. Washington, D. C.: American Physiological Society, 1969, pp. 863–927.

Kernell, D. High-frequency repetitive firing of cat lumbosacral motoneurones stimulated by long-lasting injected currents. *Acta Physiologica Scandinavica,* 1965, 65, 74–86.

Kimble, D. P. (ed.) *The anatomy of memory.* Palo Alto: Science and Behavior Books, Inc., 1967.

Koeze, T. H., Phillips, C. G., & Sheridan, J. D. Thresholds of cortical activation of muscle spindles and a motoneurones of the baboon's hand. *Journal of Physiology,* 1968, 195, 419–449.

Kugelberg, E., & Edström, L. Differential histochemical effects on muscle contractions on phosphorylase and glycogen in various types of fibers: Relation to fatigue. *Journal of Neurology, Neurosurgery, and Psychiatry,* 1968, 31, 415–423.

Landgren, S., Phillips, C. G., & Porter, R. Cortical fields of origin of the monosynaptic pyramidal pathways to some alpha motoneurones of the baboon's hand and forearm. *Journal of Physiology,* 1962, 181, 112–125.

Leopold, A. *A sand county almanac and sketches here and there.* New York: Oxford University Press, 1949.

Leyton, A. S. G., & Sherrington, C. S. Observations on the excitable cortex of the chimpanzee, orangutan and gorilla. *Quarterly Journal of Experimental Physiology,* 1917, 11, 135–222.

Lloyd, D. P. C. Conduction and synaptic transmission of reflex response to stretch in spinal cat. *Journal of Neurophysiology,* 1943, 6, 317–326.

Lloyd, D. P. C. Spinal mechanisms involved in somatic activities. In J. Field, H. W. Magoun, & V. F. Hall (eds.), *Handbook of physiology, Section I: neurophysiology.* Vol. II, Washington D. C.: American Physiological Society, 1960, pp. 929–950.

Lowenthal, M., & Harsley, V. On the relations between the cerebellar and other centers (namely cerebral and spinal) with special reference to the action of antagonistic muscles. *Proceedings of the Royal Society of London,* 1897, 61, 20–25.

Marchiafava, P. L. Activities of the central nervous system: Motor. *Annual Review of Physiology,* 1968, 30, 359–400.

Marr, D. A theory of cerebellar cortex. *Journal of Physiology,* 1969, 202, 437–470.

Marshall, L. H. (ed.) Progress report, neuroscience. *Newsletter,* 1970, 1, 1–2.

Matthews, P. B. C. Muscle spindles and their motor control. *Physiological Reviews,* 1964, 44, 219–288.

Merton, P. A. *Speculations on the servo-control of movement.* CIBA Foundation Symposium on the Spinal Cord. London: Churchill, 1953, pp. 247–255.

Murphy, J. T., & Sabah, N. H. The inhibitory effect of climbing fiber activation on cerebellar Purkinje cells. *Brain Research,* 1970, 19, 486–490.

Nelson, B. *Galapagos: islands of birds.* New York: William Morrow and Company, Inc., 1968.

Nyberg-Hansen, R. Do cat spinal motoneurones receive direct supraspinal fibre connections? A supplementary silver study. *Archives Italiennes de Biologie,* 1969, 107, 67–78.

O'Malley, W. E. Pharmacologic and clinical experiences with levodopa: A symposium. *Neurology,* 1970, 20, 1–66.

Oscarsson, O. Functional significance of information channels from the spinal cord to the cerebellum. In M. D. Yahr & D. P. Purpura (eds.), *Neurophysiological basis of normal and abnormal motor activities.* New York: Raven Press, 1967, pp. 93–117.

Oscarsson, O. Termination and functional organization of the ventral spino-olivo-cerebellar path. *Journal of Physiology,* 1968, 196, 453–478.

Oscarsson, O. Termination and functional organization of the dorsal spino-olivocerebellar path. *Journal of Physiology,* 1969, 200, 129–149.

Oscarsson, O., & Rosen, I. Response characteristics of reticulocerebellar neurones activated from spinal afferents. *Experimental Brain Research,* 1966, 1, 320–328.

Oscarsson, O., & Uddenberg, N. Somatotopic termination of spino-olivocerebellar path. *Brain Research,* 1966, 3, 204–207.

Penfield, W. Mechanisms of voluntary movement. *Brain,* 1954, 77, 1–17.

Phillips, C. G. Changing concepts in the precentral motor area. In J. C. Eccles (ed.), *Brain and conscious experience.* New York: Springer-Verlag, 1966, pp. 389–421.

Phillips, C. G. Corticomotoneuronal organization. *Archives of Neurology,* 1967, 17, 188–195.

Phillips, C. G. Motor apparatus of the baboon's hand. *Proceedings of the Royal Society, B.,* 1969, 173, 141–174.

Preston, J. B., & Whitlock, D. G. Precentral facilitation and inhibition of spinal motoneurons. *Journal of Neurophysiology,* 1960, 23, 154–170.

Preston, J. B., & Whitlock, D. G. Intracellular potentials recorded from motoneurons following precentral gyrus stimulation in primate. *Journal of Neurophysiology,* 1961, 24, 91–100.

Preston, J. B., & Whitlock, D. G. A comparison of motor cortex effects on slow and fast muscle innervations in the monkey. *Experimental Neurology,* 1963, 7, 327–341.

Preston, J. B., Shende, M. C., & Uemura, K. The motor cortex-pyramidal system: Patterns of facilitation and inhibition on motoneurons innervating limb musculature of cat and baboon and their possible adaptive significance. In M. D. Yahr & D. P. Purpura (eds.), *Neurophysiological basis of normal and abnormal motor activities.* New York: Raven Press, 1967, pp. 61–74.

Purpura, D. P., & Yahr, M. D. (eds.) *The thalamus.* New York: Columbia University Press, 1966.

Quarton, G. C., Melnechuk, T., & Schmitt, F. O. (eds.) *The neurosciences: a study program.* New York: Rockefeller University Press, 1967.

Rosenflack, P., & Buchtal, F. On the concept of the motor subunit. *International Journal of Neuroscience,* 1970, 1, 27–37.

Sakata, H., & Miyamoto, J. Topographical relationship between the receptive fields of neurons in the motor cortex and the movements elicited by focal stimulation in freely moving cats. *Japanese Journal of Physiology,* 1968, 18, 489–507.

Schmitt, F. O. Promising trends in neuroscience. *Nature,* 1970, 227, 1006–1009.

Sears, T. A. Efferent discharges in alpha and fusimotor fibres of intercostal nerves of the cat. *Journal of Physiology,* 1964, 174, 295–315.

Sears, T. A. The respiratory motoneurone: Integration at spinal segmental level. In J. B. L. Howell & E. J. M. Campbell (eds.), *Breathlessness.* Oxford: Blackwell Science Publishing, 1966, pp. 33–52.

Sherrington, C. S. Decerebrate rigidity and reflex coordinations of movements. *Journal of Physiology,* 1898, 22, 319–332.

Sherrington, C. S. Quantitative management of contraction in lowest-level coordination. *Brain,* 1931, 54, 1–28.

Sherrington, C. S. *The integrative action of the nervous system.* (2nd ed.) New Haven: Yale University Press, 1947.

Simpson, G. M., & Angus, J. W. S. Drug-induced extrapyramidal disorders. *Acta Psychiatrica Scandinavica, Supplement,* 1970, 212, 1–57.

Starr, A. Verbal and motor memory in the amnestic syndrome. *Neuropsychologia,* 1970, 8, 75–88.

Stewart, D. H., & Preston, J. B. Functional coupling between the pyramidal tract and segmental motoneurons in cat and primate. *Journal of Neurophysiology,* 1967, 30, 453–465.

Stewart, D. H., & Preston, J. B. Spinal pathways mediating motor cortex evoked excitability changes in segmental motoneurons in pyramidal primates. *Journal of Neurophysiology,* 1968, 31, 938–946.

Stewart, D. H., Preston, J. B., & Whitlock, D. G. Spinal pathways mediating motor cortex evoked excitability changes in segmental motoneurons in pyramidal cats. *Journal of Neurophysiology,* 1968, 31, 928–937.

Taub, E., & Berman, A. J. Movement and learning in the absence of sensory feedback. In S. J. Freedman (ed.), *The neuropsychology of spatially oriented behavior.* Illinois: Dorsey Press, 1968, pp. 172–192.

Taylor, J. (ed.) *Selected writings of John Hughlings Jackson, Vol. 1: On epilepsy and epileptiform convulsions.* London: Hodder and Stroughton Limited, 1931.

Thach, W. T. Discharge of Purkinje and cerebellar nuclear neurons during rapidly alternating arm movements in the monkey. *Journal of Neurophysiology,* 1968, 31, 785–797.

Thach, W. T. Discharge of cerebellar neurons related to two maintained postures and two prompt movements. I: Nuclear cell output. *Journal of Neurophysiology,* 1970, 33, 527–536. (a)

Thach, W. T. Discharge of cerebellar neurons related to two maintained postures and two prompt movements. II. Purkinje cell output and input. *Journal of Neurophysiology,* 1970, 33, 537–547. (b)

Thompson, W. D., Stoney, S. D., Jr., & Asanuma, H. Characteristics of projections from primary sensory cortex to motorsensory cortex in cats. *Brain Research,* 1970, 22, 15–27.

Tokizane, T., & Shimazu, H. *Functional differentiation of human skeletal muscle.* Tokyo: University of Tokyo Press, 1964.

Tower, S. The pyramidal tract. In P. C. Buxy (ed.), *The precentral cortex.* Urbana: University of Illinois Press, 1947, pp. 151–172.

Vanderwolf, C. H. Medial thalamic functions in voluntary behavior. *Canadian Journal of Psychology,* 1962, 16, 318–330.

Vanderwolf, C. H. Hippocampal electrical activity and voluntary movement in the rat. *Electroencephalography and Clinical Neurophysiology,* 1969, 26, 407–418. (a)

Vanderwolf, C. H. Effects of medial thalamic damage on initiation of movement and learning. *Psychonomic Science,* 1969, 17, 23–25. (b)

Vanderwolf, C. H. Limbic–diencephalic mechanisms of voluntary movement. *Psychological Review,* 1971, 78, 83–113.

Vallbo, A. B. Slowly adapting muscle receptors in man. *Acta Psychiatrica Scandinavica,* 1970, 78, 315–333.

Wall, P. D. Habituation and post-tetanic potentiation in spinal cord. In G. Horn & R. A. Hinde (eds.), *Short-term changes in neural activity and behavior.* Cambridge: Cambridge University Press, 1970, pp. 181–210.

Walshe, F. M. R. On the mode of representation of movements in the motor cortex with special reference to "convulsions beginning unilaterally" (Jackson). *Brain,* 1943, 66, 104–139.

Welt, C., Aschoff, J. C., Kameda, K., & Brooks, V. B. Intracellular organization of cats' motorsensory neurons. In M. D. Yahr & D. P. Purpura (eds.), *Neurophysiological basis of normal and abnormal motor activities.* New York: Raven Press, 1967, pp. 255–293.

Whitman, C. O. Animal behavior. In *Biological Lectures.* Marine Biology Laboratory, Woods Hole. Boston: Ginn and Co., 1899, pp. 285–338.

Wiesendanger, M. The pyramidal tract, recent investigations on its morphology and function. *Ergebnisse der Physiologie,* 1969, 61, 71–136.

Wilson, D. M. The central nervous control of flight in a locust. *Journal of Experimental Biology,* 1961, 38, 471–490.

Wilson, D. M., & Waldron, I. Models for the generation of the motor output pattern in flying locusts. *Proceedings of IEEE,* 1968, 56, 1058–1064.

Woolsey, C. N. Organization of somatic sensory and motor areas of the cerebral cortex. In H. F. Harlow & C. N. Woolsey (eds.), *Biological and biochemical basis of behavior.* Madison: University of Wisconsin Press, 1958, pp. 63–81.

Woolsey, C. N., Settlage, P. H., Meyer, D. R., Spencer, W., Hamuy, T. P., & Travis, A. M. Patterns of localization in precentral and "supplementary" motor areas and their relation to the concept of a premotor area. *Research Publication of the Association for Nervous and Mental Disorders,* 1952, 30, 238–264.

Yahr, M. D., & Purpura, D. P. (eds.) *Neurophysiological basis of normal and abnormal motor activities.* New York: Raven Press, 1967.

Chapter 14

PSYCHOMOTOR TAXONOMIES, CLASSIFICATIONS, AND INSTRUCTIONAL THEORY

M. DAVID MERRILL
Brigham Young University

Human behavior, the elusive phenomenon that it is, is made even more elusive by the relative absence of a common vocabulary system or classification scheme with which to describe it. Behavioral scientists, while working with different types of tasks, tended to communicate as if subdivisions or task categories were unnecessary since the goal was describing and explaining behavior change (learning) and *a theory* of learning seemed more parsimonious than *theories* of learning. In the late 1950's, several investigators working with different types of tasks began to communicate about the relationship among these various types. In early 1962, formal recognition was accorded to categories of human learning by a symposium on the psychology of human learning held at the University of Michigan. Top researchers representing various learning task areas addressed the problem of a taxonomy of human learning. The proceedings of this symposium were subsequently published with Arthur W. Melton as editor (1964). The following year, Robert M. Gagné, a participant at the Michigan symposium, published his classic, *The Conditions of Learning,* which postulated eight types of learning, each of which could be identified by the unique conditions necessary to promote a particular kind of behavior change. The study of psychomotor tasks began much earlier, but recognition of a taxonomy of learning tasks, with psychomotor behavior as a separate category, is relatively recent. Some of the theorists to be discussed in this chapter still prefer to think their work is relative to the whole behavior change continuum rather than to some subcategory of the continuum.

There are few formal taxonomies in the psychomotor domain. The

385

educational world was introduced to the possibility of a taxonomy of psychomotor educational objectives when the cognitive taxonomy produced by Bloom and his co-workers was published (1956). At the time, the authors of the cognitive taxonomy did not feel a taxonomy in the manipulative or motor skill area would be useful. Enthusiasm for the project did not seem improved when the affective domain taxonomy was published (Krathwohl, 1964). As of 1972, a psychomotor taxonomy of educational objectives by these authors seems remote.

Elizabeth J. Simpson (1966, 1970) also recognized that a taxonomy of educational objectives was not likely to be forthcoming from the authors of the cognitive and affective taxonomies so in 1964 she set about the task of defining a similar type of taxonomy of educational objectives. Her taxonomy is designed to classify "educational objectives which emphasize some muscular or motor skill, some manipulation of material and objects, or some act which requires neuromuscular coordination" (Simpson, 1970, p. 3). The organizing concept for her taxonomy is "complexity with attention to the sequence involved in the performance of a motor act" (Simpson, 1970, p. 3).

Physical educators have specified a number of informal classification dimensions which are occasionally used to describe various activities, but as yet a formal classification system has not emerged. The classifications used by practitioners are based primarily on logic and convenience for practice. Some typical dimensions will be described in this paper.

Differential psychologists with their emphasis on identifying independent individual differences in all areas of human performance have been relatively active in the identification of abilities and proficiencies in the psychomotor domain. Guilford made a preliminary attempt to summarize this work and identify interrelationships (1958). By far the most comprehensive work in this area is that done by Fleishman and his co-workers. Fleishman (1964) summarized more than a decade of very active work. The primary research tool was factor analysis, which was applied to very well-conducted interlocking studies. As a result of this work, Fleishman identified eleven ability and nine proficiency factors. While not a formal taxonomy, the resulting classification system is very impressive.

Experimental psychologists have produced an informal classification system based on the tasks they chose for investigation. Prior to his premature death, Fitts and his co-workers began to piece together a formal classification system using as a tool *task analysis* procedures developed during the period in the air force training research laboratories. While not complete, this classification system does provide a start on a largely quantified formal task classification system (Fitts, 1962, 1964; Fitts, Bahrick, Noble and Briggs, 1959).

The nearest approximation to a taxonomy of psychomotor behavior is the category system consisting of eight learning types proposed by Gagné (1970). Two of these eight categories are in the psychomotor domain and do bear a hierarchic relationship to each other. The basis for classification used by Gagné was the existence of unique conditions necessary to promote the given behavior type. Merrill (1971a) extended Gagné's two psychomotor categories by adding a third category. His basis for classification was also the existence of unique behavior promotion and behavior observation conditions. Like Gagné, Merrill's three psychomotor categories bear a hierarchic relationship to one another.

LOGICAL CLASSIFICATIONS BASED ON PRACTICE

Perhaps the most obvious of all classifications is that made by subject matter disciplines. This kind of classification may be trivial to enumerate, but its ingrained fractionated nature is reason enough to hold it up for examination. While variations exist, psychomotor skills can be classed as illustrated in figure 14-1. The basis of classification is traditional and based on the fact that instruction is generally centered in individuals who seldom overlap the categories. Our educational system trains musicians to teach musical instrument playing, coaches to teach sports, vocational educators to teach tool use and machinery operation, etc. To even suggest that we train a psychomotor specialist who could then use his knowledge to teach speech, musical instrument playing, machinery operation, or sports is akin to heresy. The only classification system currently affecting practice is the one illustrated in figure 14-1. Its very visibility tends to make us overlook it as a classification system. Do task characteristics exist which are common across these lines? Do similarities exist which are more useful than the differences in content? If a satisfactory taxonomy of psychomotor behavior with accompanying instructional and evaluational strategies were developed, would a specialist trained in its use have something to contribute across subject matter lines? Would we let him?

Simpson

The taxonomy of psychomotor educational objectives developed by Elizabeth J. Simpson and her students is described in her words in the following paragraphs. Simpson is a home economics educator by training and was motivated to develop this taxonomy by the seeming lack of interest on the part of the authors who produced the taxonomies of cognitive (Bloom et al., 1956) and affective (Krathwohl et al., 1964) systems.

Simpson's taxonomy has seven major levels with appropriate sublevels. The organizing concept is response complexity in very close relation to the steps required in carrying out a psychomotor act. As of this writing, this scheme has not yet appeared in a readily accessible source; hence, Simpson's (1970, section 3, pp. 10–14) description is quoted at length as follows:

> 1.0 *Perception*—This is an essential first step in performing a motor act. It is the process of becoming aware of objects, qualities, or relations by way of the sense organs. It is a necessary but not sufficient condition for motor activity.

Physical Education and
Recreation Skills

*Sports

*Dance

*Exercise

Communication Skills

*Typing

*Handwriting

*Shorthand

Language Skills

*Speech
    native
    foreign

*Facial
    expressions

*Gestures

Who is the
psychomotor
specialist?

Will we ever
cross the walls
of tradition?

Vocational Skills

*Crafts

*Tool use

*Equipment
    operation

*Machine
    operation

Fine Arts Skills

*Instrument
    playing

*Painting,
    drawing

*Dance

*Singing

Why is this the only
classification system
currently in active use?

FIG. 14-1. Representative psychomotor behaviors classified by traditional subject matter categories.

It is basic in the situation—interpretation—action chain leading to motor activity. The category of perception has been divided into three subcategories indicating three different levels of the perception process. This level is a parallel of the first category, receiving or attending, in the affective domain.

1.1 *Sensory stimulation*—Impingement of a stimulus (i) upon one or more of the sense organs.

   1.11 *Auditory*—Hearing or the sense of organs hearing.

   1.12 *Visual*—Concerned with the mental pictures or images obtained through the eyes.

   1.13 *Tactile*—Pertaining to the sense of touch.

   1.14 *Taste*—Determine the relish or flavor of by taking a portion into the mouth.

   1.15 *Smell*—To perceive by excitation of the olfactory nerves.

   1.16 *Kinesthetic*—The muscle sense; pertaining to sensitivity from activation of receptors in muscles, tendons, and joints.

   1.1 *Sensory stimulation*—Illustrative educational objectives. Sensitivity to auditory cues in playing a musical instrument as a member of a group. Awareness of difference in "hand" of various fabrics.
   Sensitivity to flavors in seasoning food.

1.2 *Cue selection*—Deciding to what cues one must respond in order to satisfy the particular requirements of task performance. This involves identification of the cue or cues and associating them with the task to be performed.
It may involve grouping of cues in terms of past experience and knowledge. Cues relevant to the situation are selected as a guide to action; irrelevant cues are ignored or discarded.

   1.2 *Cue selection*—Illustrative educational objectives.
   Recognition of operating difficulties with machinery through the sound of the machine in operation.
   Sensing where the needle should be set in beginning machine stitching.

1.3 *Translation*—Relating of perception to action in performing a motor act. This is the mental process of determining the meaning of the cues received for action. It involves symbolic translation, that is, having an image or being reminded of something, "having an idea," as a result of cues received. It may involve insight which is essential in solving a problem through perceiving the relationships essential to solution. Sensory translation is an aspect of this level. It involves "feedback," that is, knowledge of the effects of the act being performed.

   1.3 *Translation*—Illustrative educational objectives.
   Ability to relate music to dance form.
   Ability to follow a recipe in preparing food.
   Knowledge of the "feel" of operating a sewing machine successfully and use of this knowledge as a guide in stitching.

2.0 *Set*—Set is a preparatory adjustment or readiness for a particular kind of action or experience.
Three aspects of set have been identified: Mental, physical, and emotional.

   2.1 *Mental set*—Readiness, in the mental sense, to perform a certain motor act. This involves, as prerequisite, the level of perception and its subcategories. Discrimination, that is, using judgment in making distinctions, is an aspect of mental set.

      2.1 *Mental set*—Illustrative educational objectives.
      Knowledge of steps in setting the table.
      Knowledge of tools appropriate to performance of various operations.

   2.2 *Physical set*—Readiness in the sense of having made the anatomical adjustments necessary for a motor act to be performed. Readiness, in the physical sense, involves receptor set, that is, sensory attending, or focusing the attention of the needed sensory organs and postural set, or positioning of the body.

2.2 *Physical set*—Illustrative educational objectives. Achievement of bodily stance preparatory to bowling. Positioning of hands preparatory to typing.

2.3 *Emotional set*—Readiness in terms of attitudes favorable to the motor acts taking place. Willingness to respond is implied.

   2.3 *Emotional set*—Illustrative educational objectives. Disposition to perform sewing machine operation to best of ability. Desire to operate a production drill press with skill.

3.0 *Guided response*—This is an early step in the development of skill. Emphasis here is upon the abilities which are components of the more complex skill. Guided response is the overt behavioral act of an individual under the guidance of the instructor or in response to self-evaluation where the student has a model or criteria against which he can judge his performance. Prerequisites to performance of the act are readiness to respond, in terms of set to produce the overt behavioral act and selection of the appropriate response. Selection of response may be defined as deciding what response must be made in order to satisfy the requirements of task performance.

There appear to be two major subcategories, imitation and trial and error.

3.1 *Imitation*—Imitation is the execution of an act as a direct response to the perception of another person performing the act.

   3.1 *Imitation*—Illustrative educational objectives. Imitation of the process of stay-stitching the curved neck edge of bodice.
   Performing a dance step as demonstrated.
   Debeaking a chick in the manner demonstrated.

3.2 *Trial and error*—Trying various responses, usually with some rationale for each response, until an appropriate response is achieved. The appropriate response is one which meets the requirements of task performance, that is, "gets the job done" or does it more efficiently. This level may be defined as multiple-response learning in which the proper response is selected out of varied behavior, possibly through the influence of reward and punishment.

   3.2 *Trial and error*—Illustrative educational objectives.
   Discovering the most efficient method of ironing a blouse through trial and various procedures.
   Determining the sequence for cleaning a room through trial of several patterns.

4.0 *Mechanism*—Learned response has become habitual. At this level, the learner has achieved a certain confidence and degree of proficiency in the performance of the act. The act is a part of his repertoire of possible responses to stimuli and demands of situations where the response is an appropriate one. The response may be more complex than at the preceding level; it may involve some patterning in carrying out the task.

   4.0 *Mechanism*—Illustrative educational objectives.
   Ability to perform a hand-hemming operation.
   Ability to mix ingredients for butter cake.
   Ability to pollinate an oat flower.

5.0 *Complex overt response*—At this level, the individual can perform a motor act that is considered complex because of the movement pattern required. At this level, skill has been attained. The act can be carried out smoothly and efficiently, that is, with minimum expenditure of time and energy. There are two subcategories: resolution of uncertainty and automatic performance.

5.1 *Resolution of uncertainty*—The act is performed without hesitation of the individual to get a mental picture of task sequence. That is, he knows the sequence required and so proceeds with confidence. The act is here defined as complex in nature.

   5.1 *Resolution of uncertainty*—Illustrative educational objectives.
   Skill in operating a milling machine.
   Skill in setting up and operating a production band saw.

5.2 *Automatic performance*–At this level, the individual can perform a finely coordinated motor skill with a great deal of ease and muscle control.

   5.2 *Automatic performance*–Illustrative educational objectives.

      Skill in performing basic steps of national folk dances.

      Skill in tailoring a suit.

      Skill in performing on the violin.

6.0 *Adaptation*–Altering motor activities to meet the demands of new problematic situations requiring a physical response.

   6.0 *Adaptation*–Illustrative educational objectives.

      Developing a modern dance composition through adapting known abilities and skills in dance.

7.0 *Origination*–Creating new motor acts or ways of manipulating materials out of understandings, abilities, and skills developed in the psychomotor area.

   7.0 *Origination*–Illustrative educational objectives.

      Creation of a modern dance.

      Creation of a new game requiring psychomotor response.

Because of the relative inaccessibility of this taxonomy, there has not been very much done in attempting to assess its usefulness. By her own explanation (Simpson, 1970), the scheme that has been developed deals with complex objectives, that is, the behavior required has not only a psychomotor component, but also an affective and cognitive component. The key is that objectives classified by this scheme should have, as a primary focus, some motor performance.

The usefulness of this taxonomy, as listed by Simpson (1970), includes precision in communication and exchange of information, suggesting to teachers additional objectives which could be included in the curriculum, to assist in the specification of objectives. In this writer's opinion, the usefulness of this taxonomy, as the usefulness of taxonomies of cognitive and affective behavior, will depend on the extent to which unique instructional procedures and observational techniques can be developed or defined for each of the various categories. If one kind of psychomotor behavior is not observed or instructed differently than another, then classifying objectives into such a scheme is an academic exercise.

Cratty

A system based on the work of Bryant J. Cratty is illustrated in figure 14-2 (Cratty, 1967). Cratty is a physical educator and author who has written several texts for training physical educators and teachers. His dimensions were chosen because they represent some of the common continua cited by educators in the physical education and vocational skills areas. The classification system is primarily logical and based on practice and experience. In figure 14-2, the values on the dimensions are merely illustrative. Remember that these are continua and imply many subdivisions; the three or four indicated are merely to facilitate communication.

A.

	Wrist Finger (Fine)	Limbs Wrist Fingers	Limbs	Whole Body Trunk Limbs (Gross)
High Force / Low Force				Broad Jump Running Swimming
		Playing Drums	Driving a Golf Ball	Diving Gymnastics
		Driving a Screw	Tennis serve Golf Iron Shot Hammering	Figure Skating
High Accuracy / Low Force	Typing Engraving Lettering	Rifle Shoot Juggling	Golf Putt	Walking Tight Rope

2. FORCE/ACCURACY

1. MUSCLE GROUP

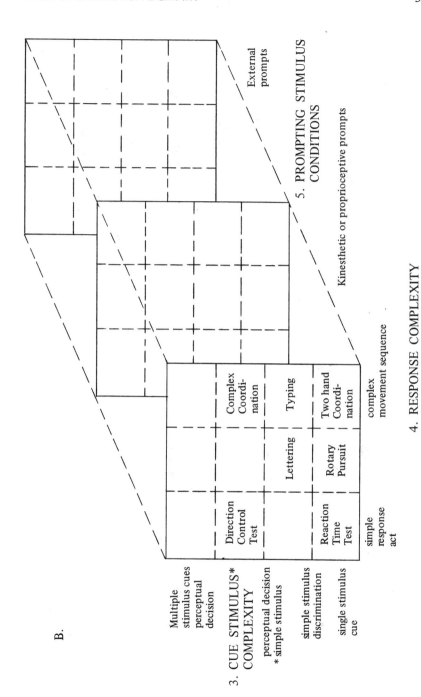

FIG. 14-2. Qualitative continua for classifying movement behavior.

Cratty (1967) cites the following continua:

1. *Fine versus Gross Continuum:* (This continuum is identified in figure 14-2 as muscle group dimension): "Such a classification depends upon the size of the muscle groups involved, the magnitude of space utilized for the movements, and the amount of force necessary to complete the movement" (p. 304). In figure 14-2, the writer tried to simplify Cratty's dimension by limiting it to size of muscle group. The other factors seem to me to be results of combining muscle group size with the force/accuracy continuum.

2. *Force-Accuracy Continuum:* "Quantitatively, motor performance also may be considered as including or requiring varying amounts of force as contrasted to accuracy" (p. 303). Figure 14-2A indicates some representative examples of psychomotor skills which seem to fall into the various categories resulting from combinations of the muscle group and force-accuracy dimensions.

3 & 4. *Simple to Complex Continuum:* This continuum is identified on figure 14-2B as two separate dimensions: (3) cue stimulus complexity, and (4) response complexity. Classification on this continuum "may depend upon the complexity of sensory information that is necessary [cue stimulus complexity], or upon the complexity of the movement pattern required [response complexity]" (pp. 304–305). A stimulus cue can be defined as that stimulus situation which serves as a trigger for the response (Merrill, 1971b). It appeared to me that there were really two dimensions, since a test might require a whole range of stimulus complexity and still require only a single response; while on the other hand, a single stimulus cue can require a whole range of response complexity from simple to complex. Figure 14-2 presents some sample tasks which illustrate this relationship.

5. *Verbal-Motor Continuum:* This continuum is identified in figure 14-2 as prompting stimulus conditions "classified in accordance with the extent to which word cues, either internal or received from an external source, contribute to or support performance" (p. 303). The literature is confusing in its use of the words cues and prompts. The author interpreted Cratty's dimension to refer to what has previously been called prompts (Merrill, 1971b). A prompt is a stimulus situation which reliably evokes some response or response sequence. More than any of the dimensions described thus far, this continuum seems to be the most easily manipulated in the instructional situation. Instruction frequently starts with a large number of external prompts; as practice continues, these prompts are withheld and the learner is required to rely more and more on kinesthetic or proprioceptive prompts. Cratty points out that external prompting is probably more useful with older learners since young children seem to focus more quickly on internal prompts.

6. *Visual-Motor Continuum:* This continuum represents "the classification of a task according to the extent to which visual cues are utilized in its

performance" (p. 303). It seems to be a subpart of the prompting dimension 5. In figure 14-2, Cratty contrasts visual cues with kinesthetic cues and points out their importance early in the instructional sequence, which seems to be a particular kind of prompting rather than a separate dimension.

7. *Personal Equation versus Optimum Effort:* Here, motor performance is "classified as to whether it is dependent upon some combination of an individual's personal equations . . . or whether it is dependent upon ability traits measured under conditions which encourage maximum effort" (p. 304). A "personal equation" relates to how a given person chooses to move when he is not exhorted to demonstrate maximum effort. Since this dimension is a motivation continuum inside the student rather than some characteristic of the task which can be described independently of him, it is not included in figure 14-2.

Cratty listed each continuum separately and made no attempt to claim independence or to point out any relationships between these dimensions. It occurred to the author that it is possible to identify some interdependent relationships among these dimensions. The muscle group and force-accuracy continua (Fig. 14-2A) are closely related but somewhat independent of the other dimensions described (represented in the second diagram in figure 14-2B).

In any category of the diagram (Fig. 14-2A) it is possible to identify tasks which fall into most or all of the categories of the diagram (Fig. 14-2B). For example, lettering is indicated as a high-accuracy, low-force wrist-finger task in diagram A. Analyzing its stimulus properties, it seems to be a matter of simple stimulus discriminations. On the response dimension, it involves moderate response complexity. A second example, reaction time, if measured by pushing a button as soon as a light goes on, is a low-force, high-accuracy (although simple) finger-wrist task which has a single stimulus and a single response act. Similar examples could be identified for almost all possible combinations. The dimensions identified in diagram A are relatively independent of the dimensions indicated in diagram B in figure 14-2.

A second difference between the A dimensions and B dimensions concerns the degree to which the dimension value can be changed to facilitate instruction without seriously changing the nature of the task. The muscle group involved is rather rigid. If the muscle groups used are changed, a different task is really learned. As an obvious example, it would be difficult to learn figure skating by moving a hand over a table to represent various figures. The force-accuracy dimension might be modified slightly without changing the task, but it too is relatively rigid in that a change of much magnitude really changes the task being learned. Hence, A dimensions tend to define the task being performed and are fixed once the task has been selected.

The B dimensions tend to be more easily manipulated. It is possible to simplify a task by reducing the stimulus complexity by focusing on only one part of it at a time. In a like manner, by learning components of a complex performance and then combining these components into more and more complex sequences, the student can simplify response complexity. It is an empirical question as to whether such simplification facilitiates acquisition, retention, or performance.

The prompting dimension is probably the most easily manipulated dimension of all. Perhaps it is impossible to instruct a student in a psychomotor performance without providing some kind of external prompts early in the proceedings. On the other hand, if these prompts continued to be part of the stimulus situation, most observers would seriously question the learner's ability to *really* perform the skill being demonstrated. The manipulation of prompts also needs serious investigation.

Cratty, after identifying the preceding continua, merely points out that these dimensions are important, but leaves some crucial questions unanswered. Assuming that an educator or instructor could reliably classify tasks in the dimensions identified, so what? Does one teach a whole-body high-force task differently than a wrist-finger high-accuracy task? If so, how? Should complex response sequences be broken into components and each component taught prior to combining them into the more complex response pattern? Should external prompts always be introduced early in the sequence? How should these prompts be eliminated? Without a correlated set of instructional conditions, a category system represents a sterile academic exercise.

CLASSIFICATIONS FROM DIFFERENTIAL PSYCHOLOGY

Guilford

Along with all types of mental abilities, investigators, in studying individual differences, have measured a wide variety of psychomotor performances. Most investigators linked relatively independent measures with an array of tests and exercises, many of a high overlap, and frequently identified similar or identical performances by different names.

J. P. Guilford (1958) attempted to order the work to that point by publishing the system which appears in figure 14-3. The two dimensions used by Guilford were the part of the body involved and the type of ability. As with his work on mental abilities, he postulated that there were some types of skills which had not been investigated or measured to that point. The blank spaces in figure 14-3 indicate these areas.

It is interesting to note that Fleishman (1964, see the discussion of this work which follows), subsequent to Guilford's review, separated basic abilities, enduring traits that do not modify a great deal with experience, from proficiency skills, those which are learned as a result of practice and experience. Both of these factors are confounded in Guilford's summary.

Type of Ability

Part of Body Involved	Strength	Impulsion	Speed	Static Precision	Dynamic Precision	Coordination	Flexibility
Gross	General Strength	General Reaction Time		Static Balance	Dynamic Balance	Gross Bodily Coordination	
Trunk	Trunk Strength						Trunk Flexibility
Limbs	Limb Strength	Limb Thrust	Arm Speed	Arm Steadiness	Arm Aiming		Leg Flexibility
Hand		Tapping	Hand Speed		Hand Aiming	Hand Dexterity	
Fingers			Finger Speed			Finger Dexterity	

FIG. 14-3. Matrix of the psychomotor factors with columns for kinds of abilities and rows for the parts of the body involved (*From Guilford, American Journal of Psychology, 1958, 71, p. 164*).

The ability types identified in figure 14-3 include *strength*, which is commonly understood; *impulsion*, "rate at which movements are initiated from stationary positions" (Guilford, 1958, p. 166); *speed*, rate of movements after they are started; *static precision*, accuracy with which bodily positions can be held; *dynamic precision*, precision of directed movements; *coordination*, integrated sensory body movements; and *flexibility*, extent to which a part of the body is free to bend or the scope of movements dependent upon particular joints. In addition to the body parts appearing in figure 14-3, Guilford suggests that a possible additional factor might be the organs involving speech.

Guilford felt that some of the factors investigated prior to his summary were combinations of the factors listed rather than independent factors. These include *muscular endurance* and *circulatory-respiratory endurance*, which he postulates as composites of physiologic characteristics combined with a motivational factor of endurance. *Agility* is thought to be a syndrome of impulsion factors, combined with coordination and speed. *Power* is thought to be a syndrome of speed or impulsion and strength.

Guilford's work was a review, and does not represent a systematic attempt to test the independence of the factors presented. He noted that few tests had been developed, and in some areas, none. He also pointed out that very few attempts to give multiple tests to the same individuals had been undertaken prior to his review.

Fleishman

The most extensive work to date in the study of psychomotor skills and abilities from the orientation of differential psychology is that done by

Fleishman and his co-workers (1962, 1964). Their work included an extensive review of existing tests and previous studies, development of new tests and refinement of existing tests, a series of interlocking correlational studies with factor analysis to isolate ability and proficiency factors, and an extensive national study to establish norms for children in all age groups in the factors identified.

Fleishman differentiates psychomotor ability from psychomotor skill. *Ability* refers to relatively enduring traits of the individual which, unless he is subjected to marked environmental influences, are not likely to change very much once he reaches adulthood. It should be noted that ability traits are not altered by learning or practice, and consequently represent givens rather than objectives for instruction. *Skill,* on the other hand, refers to the level of proficiency obtained on a specific task or limited group of tasks. Skills do vary as a result of practice and learning and, therefore, do represent the objectives of instruction. Fitness refers to the condition of acquiring and maintaining a minimal level of proficiency in a variety of skills.

The procedure used by Fleishman and his co-workers for acquiring data consisted of several phases. In phase one, a comprehensive literature search was conducted to catalogue all previously used tests of psychomotor skills according to the factors they presumably measured and to examine correlations between tests. During phase two, new tests were devised and old tests refined. These instruments were then administered to samples of students, intercorrelations calculated, and factor analysis used to select and devise better instruments to measure the various skill factors identified. In phase three, a comprehensive correlation testing program was undertaken to identify skill factors which could account for fitness. Large numbers of tests were administered to large samples of students. Using factor analysis, the investigators abstracted common factors. Tests which represented more pure measures of each factor were devised or identified and the process repeated until relatively pure measures of each skill factor had been identified.

The result of these experimental efforts, coupled with previous work, allowed Fleishman to identify the following eleven traits: control precision, multilimb coordination, response orientation, reaction time, speed of arm movement, rate control, manual dexterity, finger dexterity, arm-hand steadiness, wrist-finger speed, and aiming.

Fleishman's chapter in this volume discusses these categories in more detail and provides some of the interrelationships of abilities with real-world psychomotor tasks. From the viewpoint of a taxonomy or category system, several items should be noted. First, these categories are not task categories as are the other classification systems discussed in this chapter. Second, these ability traits are thought to be relatively stable and hence cannot be altered very much by instruction. Third, they are relatively independent and do not form any kind of hierarchic or taxonomic relationship with one another.

Fourth, identifying the categories does little to indicate any relationship with instruction. Fleishman's chapter includes some of the relationships of abilities to acquiring or performing various types of psychomotor tasks.

There has been a great deal of recent interest in aptitude treatment interactions (ATI) (see Chronbach and Snow, 1969; Bracht, 1969). Simply stated, it is assumed that persons exhibiting different levels on a given aptitude measure are most appropriately instructed using different treatments. The outcome of a simple treatment by levels experiment should yield a result similar to figure 14-4.

There must be a disordinal interaction, which means that in addition to a significant interaction, the difference between Groups 1 and 3 and the difference between Groups 2 and 4 should also be significant.

One limitation of a factor analytic identification of categories is that the primary determinant of each category is its independence from other categories. The fact that a given category is independent of the other categories does not assure its relationship to anything else. Like most differential psychology studies, the psychomotor abilities identified by Fleishman were not chosen because of their possible relevance to instruction; consequently, it is difficult to identify ATI relationships. Very likely, combinations of aptitudes all weigh to some extent in given instructional situations so that knowing a given learner's ability level does not indicate to a trainer or teacher any information which allows him to adjust instruction to teach the student more adequately. Because a given measured ability is independent of other measured abilities does not mean that it is somehow a truth in the real world. The categories identified are arbitrary ways to look at a slice of behavior. Given a new starting point, it is possible, using the same techniques, to identify a different set of independent categories. It is not my

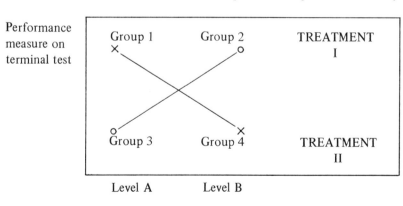

FIG. 14-4. Predicted result of an experiment where an aptitude treatment interaction exists.

intent to belittle the tremendous efforts of Fleishman and his group, but merely to point out that, as with other differential studies, the abilities identified, isolated, and labeled were not chosen with an eye to their instructional relevance. It is possible that an approach, coupling an interest in both categories of abilities with a concern for instructional relevance, may yield a more useful set of ability categories.

The categories identified by Fleishman and his co-workers that are more parallel to the other systems included in this chapter are those classifying skill or proficiency factors. It was concluded that individuals do not possess general physical proficiency or general psychomotor skills; rather, there exists a number of independent proficiencies. A person is fit to the extent that he is proficient in a number of these areas. During the experimental investigations, the categories were examined in many ways, some separated and others combined. When the nationwide proficiency tests were administered, nine factors had been isolated: extent flexibility, dynamic flexibility, explosive strength, static strength, dynamic strength, trunk strength, gross body coordination, gross body equilibrium, and stamina. Details of all of the tests used and instructions for administering them are given in Fleishman's own book (1964).

It is important to note several characteristics of these categories. First, most deal with fitness skills which involve large muscle groups. None of the factors identified measures manipulative skills. It is interesting that most of the ability factors identified in the first set were primarily fine skills or involved wrist-hand manipulation rather than gross body skills. One is led to ask, is the distinction between ability-trait versus proficiency really a valid dimension or is it confounded with the size of the muscle group involved? A set of traits and proficiency skills using the same muscle groups would be more convincing of the trait-proficiency distinction. It must be concluded that the skills identified do not exhaust the domain of psychomotor skills.

A second concern deals with the meaning of the various categories. Here again, the correlational factor analytic methodology concentrates on independence of factors. From an instructional viewpoint, it is interesting to ask whether the training procedures necessary to develop gross body equilibrium differ from procedures for training in dynamic strength, and if so, how? Should each factor be trained for separately?

Because each factor is mostly independent from other factors, these categories are not in a continuum, hierarchy, or taxonomic relationship. This presumes that acquisition of stamina does not require a strength factor or a flexibility factor as a prerequisite.

While the tremendous effort of Fleishman and his colleagues has produced a great deal of normative data, much remains to be done to relate these factors to instruction and training procedures.

CLASSIFICATIONS FROM EXPERIMENTAL PSYCHOLOGY

Fitts

Paul Fitts and his associates (Fitts, Noble, Bahrick, and Briggs, 1959) identified three major classes of independent variables in the analysis of skilled performance. These include (a) organismic, (b) procedural, and (c) task variables. Organismic variables relate primarily to the conditions of the organism such as age, intellectual ability, and other traits. Procedural variables are those non-organic conditions that influence learning such as spaced versus massed practice and reinforcement schedules. Task variables relate to characteristics of various types of psychomotor tasks that determine learning difficulty, instructional procedures, and conditions essential for proficiency attainment. The work of Fitts and his colleagues was primarily devoted to developing a task taxonomy in the hope that it would further the study of individual differences, personality variables, or procedural variables and their relationship to performance.

Most previous task classification systems could be characterized as categories based on static considerations. Figure 14-5 illustrates three dimensions identified by previous investigators. Perhaps the most common

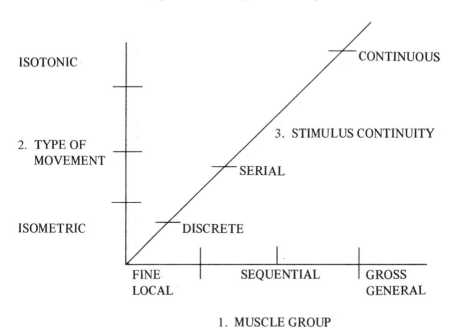

FIG. 14-5. Task variable dimensions of psychomotor skills based on static considerations.

task classification is that based on the muscle system involved. Note that this is a dimension frequently cited by practitioners (Fig. 14-2). Seashore (1951) defined tasks from gross muscle involvement to fine muscle involvement. Fitts and his colleagues (1959) defined this dimension in terms of the muscle groups involved from general to sequential to local.

A second dimension identified by previous investigators is the *type of movement required* by the task. This is frequently called the isometric-isotonic dimension. An isometric movement is one in which the length of the muscle remains constant. The task requires that the organism maintain a given position. An isotonic movement is one in which the muscle shortens under load.

Other investigators have referred to this dimension by various names. Brown and Jenkins (1947) identified three levels of reactions: *static* reactions, in which a body member is held in a fixed position and the requirement of the task is the maintenance of this position; *positioning* reactions, in which a body member is moved from one position of rest to another and the primary requirement of the task is the terminal accuracy of the positioning movement; and *movement* reactions, in which a body member is moved at a given rate and in a given direction along specified pathways, the critical aspect being the achievement of these rates, directions, and pathways.

Hartson (1939) labeled the type of movement dimension with the following categories and subcategories: isometric movements were called *slow tension* movements. This is a state where the opposing muscles are both in a state of relatively high contraction. This category is subdivided into *fixation,* a state in which a limb is stationary, and *moving fixation,* a state in which the limb is in motion. At the isotonic end of the continuum are *ballistic* movements. In ballistic movements one of the opposing muscles is more contracted than the other. This category is subdivided into *stiff ballistic* movement, in which rapid ballistic contraction of one muscle is superimposed on a high level of contraction of the opposing muscle, and *pure ballistic* movement, in which the opposing muscle is under a low tonic contraction.

The third dimension frequently cited for classifying psychomotor tasks is *stimulus response continuity.* Brown and Jenkins (1947) cited three values: *discrete, serial,* and *continuous.* While the dimension could refer to both stimulus and response elements, it is most frequently used to refer to the stimulus characteristics of the task rather than to the response pattern used by the organism. There is considerable evidence that a learner probably responds with discrete response units even to a continuous stimulus situation. A discrete task is one in which the stimulus elements are separated by a considerable interval of time. Fitts and his co-workers suggested that any interval larger than 10 seconds between stimulus events would be viewed by most learners as discrete. Driving a golf ball is an example of a discrete task. When stimulus elements, either identical or different, repeat themselves in a regular pattern at more or less regular intervals, the task is seen as a serial task. The intervals can vary in length from a fraction of a second to a few seconds. Typing is a good example of a serial task. When the intervals between stimulus events are reduced, the task comes to be viewed as a continuous one in which the stimulus pattern is continually changing. Driving a car is a good example of a continuous task.

The unique contribution of Fitts and his colleagues to task classification is their investigation of task dynamics as well as static task conditions. The dynamics of psychomotor tasks were approached from two viewpoints, that of a feedback system, and that of communications or information theory. Three sets of variables have been identified. These are task constancies, some quantitative dynamic characteristics of stimulus continuity, and feedback relationships.

Figure 14-6 illustrates a 2 x 2 representation of *task constancies*. Task constancies are defined by observing the conditions of the environmental objects and the body of the learner during the interval just prior to the initiation of the response or response sequence. Type I response constancy (a self-initiated response sequence following preparation) occurs when the body is at rest and the environmental object to be acted upon is also at rest. The body position is frequently preselected and oriented to relate to the fixed environment. The person usually initiates the response sequence after he

ENVIRONMENTAL OBJECT

	AT REST	IN MOTION
AT REST BODY	TYPE I e.g. Drive golf ball Pick up pencil Thread a needle	TYPE II e.g. Hitting a baseball Aiming gun at duck Following rotary pursuit
IN MOTION	TYPE III e.g. Shooting a layup (basketball) Throw to first base (shortstop)	TYPE IV e.g. Aiming at aircraft from pitching ship Throwing a running pass to moving receiver (football)

FIG. 14-6. Task constancies relating conditions of the body and an environmental object during the interval prior to initiation of response.

prepares or sets himself to respond. Many tasks from everyday experience can be cited as examples: driving a golf ball from a tee, shooting a foul shot in basketball, picking up an object from a surface, and the like.

Type II response constancy (a stimulus-initiated response sequence following preparation) occurs when the environmental object is in motion but the body is at rest. Examples include hitting a baseball, following a rotary pursuit disk, and aiming a gun at a duck or other moving target.

Type III response constancy (a self-initiated response sequence without preparation) occurs when the body is in motion and the environmental object is at rest. Examples include shooting a lay-up in basketball and a shortstop's throwing of the ball to first base while on the run.

Type IV response constancy (a stimulus-initiated response sequence without preparation) occurs when both the body and the environmental object are in motion prior to the initiation of the response. Examples include aiming a gun at an aircraft from the deck of a pitching ship and a quarterback throwing a pass to a running receiver while he himself is running.

Previous investigators have referred to tasks as *self-paced* or *externally paced*. The analysis of task constancies extends this dimension. When the environmental object is at rest the task is self-paced; however, Type I tasks allow time for preparation to respond while Type III tasks do not allow time for preparation. When the environmental object is in motion, tasks are externally paced; however, Type II tasks allow some preparation to respond while Type IV tasks do not allow preparation. It should also be obvious that mastery of Type I tasks is considerably easier than mastery of Type II or Type III tasks and that Type IV tasks are most difficult to master.

When the dynamic characteristics of stimulus continuity are examined, it is possible to be more precise in quantifying values on this dimension. Fitts and his colleagues (1959) cited work by Clark, Fontaine, and Warren (1953) for classifying continuous signals. The following is their modification of the original categories so that this set of values can be applied equally well to continuous and discrete sequences.

Periodic signals are a series of stimulus events that can be specified exactly by a mathematical process and that exhibit periodicity. Examples include signals that can be represented by a square wave form (e.g., a light which goes on and off at regular intervals and to which the subject must make some response when it is on); a sinusoidal wave form (e.g., a tone which increases and decreases in intensity); a sawtooth wave form; and repetitive numerical series. It should be obvious that many discrete stimuli do have these periodic characteristics. Some serial stimuli also are periodic and, if the period is short enough, a periodic signal is considered to be continuous.

Aperiodic signals are a series of stimulus events that can be specified exactly by a mathematical process but which do not exhibit periodicity. Examples include stimulus events which have constant velocity, constant acceleration, or nonperiodic numerical sequences. When a discrete signal does not occur at regular intervals and when the length of the interval is considerable, then it has aperiodic characteristics. Obviously, irregular serial stimulus situations are aperiodic. If the interval length is short enough, then a given continuous signal can be aperiodic.

Random signals are a series of stimulus events which cannot be represented exactly by a mathematical process, but which can be represented by a statistical (probabilistic) function.

Quasi-random signals are a series of stimulus events that cannot be represented in mathematical form or as stationary statical processes. Since it is impossible to replicate such a signal, very little can be done to study such events experimentally.

Categorizing stimulus signals from periodic to quasi-random does not overlap completely with a discrete continuous dimension but it does allow more precision in specifying values for stimulus continuity. Three additional indices have been identified for describing signal sequences and hence stimulus continuity. These are coherence, frequency, and complexity.

Coherence is the degree of specifiable dependence between successive events or values. Two different signals, or two portions of a single signal, are said to be coherent when there is a dependence between their detailed values. The degree of coherence can be specified in several ways. One way is to calculate the percent of redundancy occurring in the signal or between two signals. A second method for quantifying coherence is to determine an autocorrelation function. This function specifies for future intervals of time the average correlation between present and future values of the signal. This index can be calculated for continuous signals or for sequences of discrete events. Procedures for calculating percent redundancy and autocorrelation functions are detailed by Fitts and his colleagues (1959) and in other sources on information theory so they will not be reviewed here.

Frequency refers to the amount of change present in a given signal. It describes the nature of the periodicity. Two signals which are equally coherent may be of greatly different difficulty because of frequency differences. The nature of a given signal's frequency can be determined by specifying a frequency spectrum which gives the number of separate sinusoidal functions required to synthesize the signal and which also specifies the relative power that each function contributes to the resultant wave form. For discrete signals the time interval between events measures frequency and may be constant or have several values.

Complexity of a signal is synonymous with the number of different frequencies required to specify a continuous signal or the number of different time intervals that characterize a discrete signal. Complexity can also refer to the number of different amplitudes present in a given signal.

The third set of dynamic task classifications identified by Fitts and his co-workers is the type of feedback involved. Three main feedback loops have been identified and include internal feedback, environmental feedback, and man-machine feedback.

Internal feedback is stimulus information which is produced by the learner as a result of responding and which is subsequently sensed and monitored by the learner. This type of feedback includes proprioceptive feedback such as seeing oneself move, hearing oneself speak, etc., and/or kinesthetic feedback, the stimulus sensations produced when a muscle moves or stops moving. Investigations (Smith and Smith, 1966) have shown that when this internal feedback loop is disrupted, motor control is difficult or impossible to maintain and response patterns which previously were adaptive become maladaptive.

Environmental feedback is information received by the learner about the effect of his response on the external environment. Other authors (e.g., Merrill, 1971b) have referred to this type of feedback as knowledge of results (KR). While internal feedback occurs as a direct consequence of responding, environmental feedback can be classed into two types: that which occurs as a direct result of having made a particular response, and that which occurs only when provided by some external agent or device. An example of direct environmental feedback is seeing a golf ball rise and arch up the fairway or slice into the rough. An example of indirect environmental feedback is having a coach watching with binoculars where the target is being struck during rifle shooting and reporting this information to the marksman. Even less direct is the report of a forward observer to an artillery gun crew about the location of their hit.

Fitts and his co-workers include a third type of environmental feedback as a separate category. Man-machine feedback occurs when the result of a learner's response is presented to him by means of some mechanical display such as a dial, meter, scope, or other device. Perhaps all indirect environmental feedback really falls into this category. It is not clear on this point from the information available.

Fitts and his colleagues report feedback relationships in much more detail. Figure 14-7 illustrates a signal flow network prepared by Fitts and his group which identifies each of the three types of feedback. The arrow from node 3 to 1 is the internal feedback loop. The environmental feedback loop includes nodes 3 to 4 to 1. The man-machine loop includes nodes 3 to 6 to 7 to 8 to 1.

It can be observed from the diagram that numerous internal feedback loops are indicated. Each of these internal loops also represents some kind of feedback systems which must be considered in describing psychomotor tasks. Among the variables which influence internal feedback and hence the resulting psychomotor responses are the limb dynamics illustrated in figure 14-7 by the response interaction loop at node 3 and the opposing environmental force loop from node 4 back to 3. Internal feedback is also

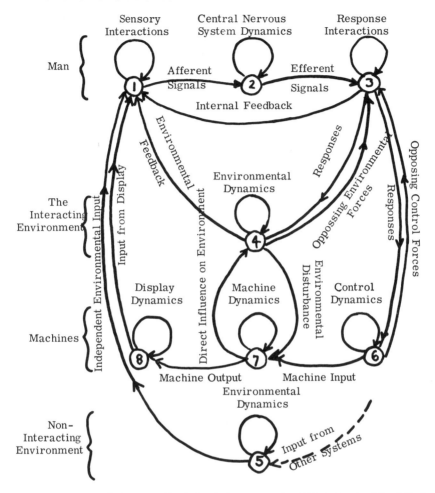

FIG. 14-7. Graph of the generalized signal flow network which is involved in skilled performance. The nodal points represent (1) receptors, (2) central nervous system, (3) effectors, (4) the immediately interacting physical and social environment, including (5) noninteracting environmental information or signal sources, (6) machine controls, (7) machines, and (8) displays.

influenced by sensory interaction (node 1) and the dynamics of the central nervous system (node 2). Interacting forces in the external systems involved are also illustrated in figure 14-7.

The work done by Fitts and his co-workers in providing a taxonomy of task variables in psychomotor learning is the only extensive attempt to date to identify these variables. It is unfortunate that Fitts' early death prevented a continuation of this effort. It is hoped that others working in the field of motor skills instruction might be able to continue the definition of these variables and extend their implications for instruction.

Fitts and his co-workers refer to their classification system as taxonomies of psychomotor task characteristics. The term taxonomy, however, usually refers to an ordered or hierarchic relationship. The categories proposed by Fitts and his associates have not all been specified in a way that infers or specifies an ordered relationship. In fact, some of the proposed category sets are derived from different conceptual bases than other sets.

Gagné/Merrill

Robert Gagné's (1970) classic work on conditions of learning must be cited as the only hierarchically structured taxonomic system for classifying psychomotor skills. Gagné indicated that eight levels or categories of learned behavior could be identified based on the conditions necessary for observing and promoting each category. That is, a separate category was indicated only if a unique set of conditions could be identified for promoting acquisition of that behavior type. Gagné's categories include (1) signal learning (classic conditioning), (2) stimulus response learning (operant conditioning), (3) chaining (motor response sequences), (4) verbal association (serial learning), (5) multiple discriminations (paired associate learning), (6) concept learning (classification), (7) principle learning (rule using), and (8) problem solving (strategies). Gagné's work serves to separate psychomotor learning from other types of behavior and to indicate its relationship to other behavior levels. Two of his categories, stimulus response and chaining, are psychomotor categories. Some instances of these behaviors are thought to be prerequisite to all other behavior types. Stimulus response learning occurs when the learner acquires the ability to make a specific motor response when he is presented with a particular stimulus cue. Chaining occurs when a single stimulus cue triggers an integrated series of responses in which making one of the responses in the series serves to trigger the next response in the sequence and so forth.

Merrill (1971a,b) felt that all psychomotor training was not included in Gagné's two categories and suggested that a category of *complex skill* be inserted following the chaining category. A learner is exhibiting a complex skill when he is able to execute a number of different chains, each corresponding to a particular cue when these cues are presented in varying orders. The presentation of cues are self-paced in some tasks (e.g., golf) but externally paced in others (e.g., tennis). This system suggests three levels of psychomotor skill: (1) acquisition of a single new response act to a specific cue; (2) acquisition of a coordinated series of responses to a given cue; (3) and acquisition of a set of response series, each occurring to a specific cue, when a set of such cues is presented in a self-paced or externally paced sequence.

Because the systems of Fitts and his associates and of Gagné/Merrill are attempts to classify task variables, it is possible to compare the two systems for differences and common elements. The dimension concentrated on by Gagné/Merrill is similar to the stimulus continuity dimension identified by Fitts. However, Fitts concentrates almost entirely on the complex skill category of Merrill, which was omitted from the Gagné system. It should be noted that Fitts' stimulus continuity dimension categories combined stimulus continuity with the type of response. Both the stimulus response and chaining categories of Gagné assume a single stimulus cue. This is a discrete stimulus or a periodic stimulus with a large time interval between stimulus events. The difference between the categories is the type of response emitted by the learner. Merrill (1971a) emphasizes that in the stimulus response category, the response is a new response topography. In the chaining category, the response is a series of integrated response acts. (Note that Cratty identified a response complexity dimension which roughly corresponds to this dimension.) Most of Fitts' categories serve to subdivide Merrill's complex skill category. The periodic-serial-continuous dimension extends the dimension identified by Gagné/Merrill.

The Gagné/Merrill taxonomy assumes that the dimension identified is the one that separates conditions necessary for observing and prompting response acquisition. Consequently, it is assumed that the conditions necessary for learning the topography of a new single response act are the same or similar whether the response involves a manipulative movement of the fingers and wrist or a gross body movement involving the limbs and trunk. The Gagné/Merrill system also assumes similar conditions for both isometric or isotonic type movements. The author is hesitant to press this issue since the empirical evidence is extremely sparse and it might be necessary or desirable to take a multidimensional approach to the specification of instructional principles.

CLASSIFICATION SYSTEMS AND INSTRUCTIONAL THEORY

Classification systems and taxonomic schemes are merely academic exercises unless the categories defined can be related to each other or to other response variables in a way that describes the learning process or provides prescriptive principles which can guide the design of instructional procedures. The categories described in the previous sections of this chapter were all derived by starting with different premises about the purpose of the particular classification attempt. The first system described merely identified the traditional fields of study and/or practice which involve a large component of psychomotor skill. Instruction in each of these areas is characterized primarily by traditional methods and folklore derived by practitioners. This system has the weight of endurance supporting its continuance. However, it assumes that the instructional principles which are, or can be, derived in each of the traditional areas are unique to that type of skill. If this assumption were followed, the result would be an instructional theory for communication skills, a separate instructional theory for vocational skills, one for musical skills, etc.

The Guilford/Fleishman categories started with the assumption of independence of measurement. What observations of psychomotor skill and/or ability can be made that are independent of one another? Having identified such different categories of skill and ability, investigators must determine whether individuals distribute themselves on each of the identified dimensions. An instructional theory based on this system would probably be a set of Aptitude Treatment Interaction rules. That is, different instructional procedures would need to be identified for persons possessing different values of the various aptitudes in such a way that acquisition of the behavior would be maximized for each individual.

The informal dimensions identified by Cratty and the formal systems of Fitts and his co-workers and Gagné/Merrill represent attempts to categorize different types of psychomotor behavior by means of task variables, and also, to identify various task variables that can be manipulated to facilitate acquisition and retention of the various types of psychomotor behavior. In the remaining portion of this chapter, the author will discuss the possible assumptions and dimensions of an instructional theory based on the manipulation of task variables.

The first premise of such an instructional theory is as follows (Merrill, 1971c, p. 7):

Premise 1: It is presumed that there is a limited number of different kinds of behavior and that any instructional outcome is an instance of one or more of these behavior classes.

This assumption would include all types of instructed behavior and would place psychomotor behavior in context with other types of behavior (Merrill, 1971a). Applying the classifications which have been identified this means that according to Cratty's continua, tasks could be categorized on the force-accuracy/muscle group dimensions. According to the systems of Fitts and his associates and/or Gagné/Merrill, tasks could be classified on the stimulus continuity dimension and perhaps subcategorized on the basis of the muscle group and/or type of movement. The first set of experimental investigations necessary to validate this premise would include attempts to verify the independence of the categories included in such continua. That is, can behavioral outcomes be clearly identified as belonging to one category or another? Can it be demonstrated that a student who has acquired behavior in one category has not already acquired behavior in the next higher level of the hierarchy? Do the categories bear a hierarchic relationship, that is, is acquisition of a behavior at a lower level necessary before a learner can acquire behavior at a higher level?

The second premise of such an instructional theory is as follows (Merrill, 1971c, p. 8):

Premise 2: It is presumed that for each behavior class, an optimal information processing strategy can be identified which, if used by a student, provides for optimal attainment of the specified behavior.

If several hierarchic dimensions can be identified which satisfy the first premise, it may be found that even though different categories of behavior can be observed, the strategy required to attain that behavior is the same as the strategy required by another behavior category. The second research effort needed to establish such a theory, both generally and within the psychomotor domain, would be attempts to define and observe the type of information processing strategy used by students in attempting to acquire various types of behaviors. If such strategies can be identified, are they universal? Does every learner acquire a given type of behavior most efficiently and effectively by use of the same strategy as other learners or are some strategies more effective for some students, while others are more effective for others? What are the individual difference measures which enable us to predict the appropriate strategy? It is here, perhaps, that the work of Fleishman and the taxonomies of Fitts and his associates and Cratty/Gagné/ Merrill come together.

The third premise of such an instructional theory is as follows (Merrill, 1971c, p. 9):

Premise 3: It is presumed that by manipulating task variables, it is possible to facilitate the student's use of the appropriate optimal information processing strategy for a given type of behavior.

It is this premise that lies at the heart of an attempt to instruct other learners systematically. Whenever we teach using some artificially contrived environment, including such accepted things as books, demonstrations, and so on, we are manipulating task variables in an attempt to facilitate learning. The third research thrust necessary for establishment of an instructional theory is the identification of task variables which lend themselves to ready manipulation and the specification of prescriptive principles which relate manipulation of these task variables to learner strategy and learner behavior outcomes. In the schemes reviewed, several possible task variables have been identified. It was suggested that in the dimensions identified by Cratty, instructional sequence could be manipulated by moving from simple stimulus situations to more and more complex stimulus cues. It was also suggested that the complexity of the response could be manipulated so that early in the instructional sequence the learner is asked to make simple responses and that the demand for more and more complex response sequences increases as the instruction proceeds. One of the more manipulatable dimensions identified is the prompting dimension. It was suggested that perhaps instruction should move from external prompts to kinesthetic or proprioceptive prompts. Fitts and his colleagues identified several dimensions which could be manipulated. Perhaps instruction on complex skills is facilitated by moving from Type I constancies where both environmental objects and the body are at rest to Type IV constancies where both are in motion. The type, frequency, and amount of feedback can also be manipulated. All of the preceding suggest hypotheses which need much investigation before a prescriptive instructional theory is possible.

It has been suggested that task variables can be roughly classed into three categories. These include: (1) prompting/feedback variables, (2) sequence variables, and (3) stimulus similarity variables (Merrill, 1971c). This categorization might not be complete, but it suggests that the variables identified in the various schemes reviewed in this paper might be studied to separate those variables which define task categories from those variables which define learner strategies and from those task variables which lend themselves to manipulation. Further, beginning with the three categories, variables which have not been identified suggest themselves.

This discussion of the possible form of an instructional theory should not be concluded without indicating that there is an alternative to Premise 3.

Alternate Premise: It is presumed that learners could be taught optimal information processing strategies directly and that the learner can learn to apply these strategies to a wide variety of situations, thus acquiring any behavior that the learner desires without the necessity of structured environment.

The function of instruction would be very different if this premise were to prove to be the more useful. Most current instructional efforts, whether in the psychomotor or cognitive areas, tend to be based on Premise 3 rather than on the alternate premise. Almost all formal education is based on the premise that some manipulation of the environment will facilitate learning. Nevertheless, the alternate premise suggests that perhaps our instructional effort should be concentrated on training learners to apply appropriate strategies and then turn them loose to learn from experience rather than place them in structured situations which attempt to carefully control their learning behaviors.

SUMMARY

In this chapter, several category and/or classification schemes for psychomotor behavior were presented. The most used scheme is one in which psychomotor behavior is divided according to subject areas. A sample of such a scheme was suggested using the categories of: (1) physical education and recreation skills, (2) communication skills, (3) language skills, (4) vocational skills, and (5) fine arts skills. A second system was the taxonomy developed by Elizabeth Simpson. This system consists of the following seven levels together with subdivisions: (1) perception, (2) set, (3) guided response, (4) mechanism, (5) complex overt response, (6) adaptation, and (7) origination. A third system was based on the experience of practice derived from the viewpoint of Bryant Cratty, a physical educator. The five dimensions of the scheme included: (1) muscle group, (2) force/accuracy, (3) cue stimulus complexity, (4) response complexity, and (5) prompting stimulus conditions.

Starting from a differential psychology base, ability categories and skill categories were reviewed from the work of Ed Fleishman and his associates. The ability factors include: (1) control precision, (2) multilimb coordination, (3) response orientation, (4) reaction time, (5) speed of arm movement, (6) rate control, (7) manual dexterity, (8) finger dexterity, (9) arm-hand steadiness, (10) wrist-finger speed, and (11) aiming. The nine skill factors were: (1) extent flexibility, (2) dynamic flexibility, (3) explosive strength, (4) static strength, (5) dynamic strength, (6) trunk strength, (7) gross body coordination, (8) gross body equilibrium, and (9) stamina.

The work of Paul Fitts and his associates was reviewed from the viewpoint of experimental psychology. Dimensions based on static considerations included the (1) muscle group involved, (2) type of movement involved, (3) four types of task constancies, determined by whether just prior to response execution, the body and the environmental object involved were respectively at rest or in motion, (4) other dynamic dimensions such as stimulus continuity, from periodic to continuous, and (5) type of feedback, from internal to man-machine displays.

Gagné's categories of stimulus response learning and chaining were cited as taxonomic categories placing psychomotor behavior in perspective with other types of behavior. Merrill's extension of Gagné's hierarchy was cited as a more complete taxonomy by adding a complex skill category to the two identified by Gagné. The final section of the chapter suggested three premises which might form the foundation of an instructional theory for psychomotor as well as for other types of behavior.

References

Bilodeau, E. A. (ed.) *Acquisition of skill.* New York: Academic Press, 1966.

Bloom, B. S., Engelhart, M. D., Furst, E. J., Hill, W. H., & Krathwohl, D. R. *Taxonomy of educational objectives, Handbook I: cognitive domain.* New York: David McKay, 1956.

Bracht, G. H. The relationship of treatment tasks, personological variables and dependent variables to aptitude-treatment interactions. Unpublished doctoral dissertation, University of Colorado, 1969.

Brown, J. S., & Jenkins, W. D. Analysis of human motor abilities related to the design of equipment and a suggested program of research. In P. M. Fitts (ed.), *Psychological research in equipment design.* Washington D. C.: Government Printing Office, 1947.

Clark, J. R., Fontaine, A. B., & Warren, C. E. The generation of continuous random signals for use of human tracking studies. *USAF HRRC Research Bulletin,* 1953, No. 53-40. (Cited in Fitts et al.), 1959.

Cratty, B. J. *Movement behavior and motor learning.* (2nd ed.). Philadelphia: Lea & Febiger, 1967.

Cronback, L. J., & Snow, R. E. Individual differences in learning ability as a function of instructional variables. Final Report, Contract OEC 4-6-061269-1217, United States Office of Education, Stanford, California: Stanford University, 1969.

Fitts, P. M. Factors in complex skill training. In R. Glaser (ed.), *Training research and education*. Pittsburgh: University of Pittsburgh Press, 1962.

Fitts, P. M. Perceptual motor skill learning. In A. W. Melton (ed.) *Categories of human learning*. New York: Academic Press, 1964.

Fitts, P. M. (ed.) *Human engineering concepts and theory*. Ann Arbor: University of Michigan Press, 1959.

Fitts, P. M., Noble, M. E. Bahrick, H. P., & Briggs, G. E. *Skilled performance*. (Vol. 1 & Vol. 2) Final Report, March, 1959 Contract AF 41(657), United States Air Force, Ohio State University. (NOTE: John Wiley & Sons holds a contract for a book based on this report. Several references to this report cite it as a book in press. As of spring 1972, this report has not been published.)

Fleishman, E. A. The description and prediction of perceptual motor skill learning. In R. Glaser (ed.), *Training research and education*. Pittsburgh: University of Pittsburgh Press, 1962.

Fleishman, E. A. *The structure and measurement of physical fitness*. Englewood Cliffs, N. J.: Prentice Hall, 1964.

Gagné, R. M. *The conditions of learning*. (2nd ed.). New York: Holt, Rinehart, and Winston, 1970.

Guilford, J. P. A system of the psychomotor abilities. *American Journal of Psychology*, 1958, 71, 164–174.

Hartson, L. D. Contrasting approaches to the analysis of skilled movements. *Journal of General Psychology*, 1939, 20, 263–293.

Krathwohl, D. R., Bloom, B. S., & Masia, B. B. *Taxonomy of educational objectives. Handbook II: affective domain*. New York: David McKay, 1964.

Melton, A. W. *Categories of human learning*. New York: Academic Press, 1964.

Merrill, M. D. Necessary psychological conditions for defining instructional outcomes. In M. D. Merrill (ed.), *Instructional design: readings*. Englewood Cliffs, N. J.: Prentice Hall, 1971. (a)

Merrill, M. D. Paradigms for psychomotor instruction. In M. D. Merrill (ed.), *Instructional design: readings*. Englewood Cliffs, N. J.: Prentice Hall, 1971. (b)

Merrill, M. D. *Toward a theory-based approach to instructional development*. Working Paper No. 16. March, 1971. Department of Instructional Research and Development, Brigham Young University. (c)

Seashore, R. H. Work and motor performance. In S. S. Stevens (ed.), *Handbook of experimental psychology*. New York: John Wiley & Sons, Inc., 1951.

Simpson, E. J. *The classification of educational objectives: psychomotor domain*. Urbana: University of Illinois Press, 1966.

Simpson, E. J. The classification of educational objectives in the psychomotor domain. In Floyd Urbach (ed.), *The psychomotor domain of learning*. Papers presented at Teaching Research, Salishan, Oregon; Department of Higher Education, Monmouth, Oregon, July, 1970.

Smith, K. U., & Smith, M. F. *Cybernetic principles of learning and educational design*. New York: Holt, Rinehart & Winston, 1966.

Chapter 15

SYNTHESIS

Robert N. Singer

Florida State University

The preceding chapters help to provide insight into the nature, complexity, and diversity of the psychomotor domain. The material in this book by no means exhausts (a) either the content or the (b) approaches of studying motor behavior. It was intended that the "flavor" of the area be sampled by the reader. Often neglected in research, usually taken for granted in practice, and widely misunderstood, motor skills include a wide variety of behaviors and many approaches are employed to analyze them.

We have seen how the comparative psychologist, military psychologist, individual difference psychologist, physical educator, sports psychologist, experimental psychologist, educational theorist, special educator, neurophysiologist, cybernetician, and engineering psychologist view psychomotor activity. Content and methods of study overlap in some ways; they are uniquely different in other ways.

From the classic work in experimental psychology with it restricted research, concepts, and applications to the applied fields and extended boundaries, the study of psychomotor behaviors has managed to touch many bases. We have noted from the chapter written by Schmidt that experimental psychologists are primarily interested in the usage of refined laboratory tasks and testing situations to study learning phenomena. Of particular concern to Schmidt was the nature of retention, especially the distinction between short-term and long-term retention.

Behavior, in which some consistency is assumed from species to species, can be analyzed not only by observing man. Animals also serve as important subjects since there are many aspects of behavior which are extremely difficult, if not impossible, to study in man. In his chapter, Ratner explained the nature of comparative psychology and offered an example of motor behavior, habituation, that has been extensively researched in subhumans. Conclusions from this research have been found to have direct application for understanding the motor behavior of man.

Psychomotor behavior, demonstrated in the form of skills or generalized movement patterns, cannot be explained or understood without some idea as to the underlying foundation blocks contributing to success: abilities. Fleishman's work, which has extended for two decades, has been concerned with attempting to define those independent psychomotor abilities related to task proficiency. His factor analytic approach has been quite fruitful in providing new dimensions to knowledge of the psychomotor area. Contrasting with the statistical approach but also fruitful in results are Jones' correlational techniques. The nature of the learning process and inter- and intra-individual differences were explained by Jones, who has also been an extensive contributor to the literature.

Many disciplines and occupations have applied the information from the sophisticated laboratory research of such investigators as Schmidt, Ratner, Fleishman, and Jones as well as scholars who have undertaken research uniquely applied to their given area. One example of an area in which much research is going on as well as applied from elsewhere is the military. The very difficult challenge of synthesizing research related to the military was extremely well met by Miller. Various tasks and training methods were discussed. Likewise, Cratty, a very prolific writer, summarized much of his research and that of others and provided insight into the nature of concerns of special educators. The retarded, neurologically impaired, blind, and deaf were analyzed in terms of their motor attributes and motor learning.

More and more educators and parents are turning to perceptual-motor training programs to remedy academic learning problems and disorders. Fleming showed the relationship of the cognitive to the psychomotor and described the nature of the popular perceptual-motor programs in existence. Obviously, there are those who would use certain perceptual-motor (psychomotor) training programs to improve motor skills, and there are others who would advocate particular perceptual-motor programs to improve academic success and self-image.

If any two areas are associated with the physical or the motor, they are physical education and sport. The average person uses the terms physical education and sport interchangeably and the two areas do have many similar concerns. Yet, there exist numerous distinctions, especially related to the type of performer being instructed and the context within which the instruction takes place. Oxendine discussed physical education, pointing out major research applications for those who teach physical activities. Morgan, on the other hand, described the emerging, popular area referred to as sport psychology.

Along with the obvious applied areas, we read chapters in which theory and research were integrated for generalized implications to man and his motor functions. Man was viewed as an information processing agent by Poulton in his analysis of skilled movement. Factors influencing reaction and movement times were emphasized. In Smith's chapter, an extensive overview of years of personal research indicated research directions in behavioral cybernetics. Motor activity and feedback are central to cybernetic theory. With the use of computers, interpretations of research are made for the development of theory and application to psychomotor activity. In the neurosciences, research and theory provide a different perspective, and Hutton presents it admirably. The neurologic bases of movement and response are typically neglected by psychologists. Obviously, any study of psychomotor behavior would be incomplete if information dealing with the neural substrates and mechanisms were withheld.

Finally, Merrill attempted to make order out of the chaotic scene of behavior by offering taxonomies and classifications. Theories and taxonomies help to organize research and provide us with operational guidelines with regard to varied psychomotor activities. Merrill's chapter organizes much of the data already presented in this book as well as research published elsewhere.

My appreciation is extended to these writers for undertaking the very difficult task of synthesizing the research (much of it their own) in their particular areas of concern in the alloted one chapter. The content in any of the chapters could serve as the basis for an entire book, and in some cases, it has. The interested reader and dedicated scholar are referred to the many references at the end of every chapter for supplementary guides to reading matter.

RITTER LIBRARY
BALDWIN-WALLACE COLLEGE